Journal of the Early Book Society
for the study of manuscripts and printing history

Edited by Martha W. Driver
Volume 15, 2012

ISBN: 978-1-935625-11-7
ISSN: 1525-6790

Member

Council of Editors of Learned Journals

™ The paper used in this publication meets the minimum requirements of American National Standard for information Sciences—Permanence of Paper for printed Library Materials,
ANSI Z39.48—1984.

The *Journal of the Early Book Society* is published annually. *JEBS* invites longer articles on manuscripts and/or printed books produced between 1350 and 1550. Special consideration will be given to essays exploring the period of transition from manuscript to print. Authors are asked to follow *The Chicago Manual of Style*. A Works Cited list at the end of the text should include city, publisher, and date. Manuscripts are to be sent, in triplicate, along with an abstract of up to 150 words, to Martha Driver, Early Book Society, Department of English, Pace University, 1 Park Row, New York, New York 10038. Only materials accompanied by a self-addressed, stamped envelope (or international reply coupon) will be returned. Members of the Early Book Society who are recent authors may send review books for consideration to Susan Powell, Reviews Editor, School of English, Sociology, Politics and Contemporary History (ESPaCH), University of Salford, Salford M5 4WT UK. Brief notes on recent discoveries, highlighting little-known or recently uncovered texts and/or images, may be sent to Linne R. Mooney, Centre for Medieval Studies, King's Manor, University of York, York YO1 2EP UK. Subscription information may be obtained from Martha Driver or from Pace University Press.

Those interested in joining the Early Book Society or with editorial inquiries may contact Martha Driver by post or e-mail (MDriver@Pace.edu). Information may also be found at <www.nyu.edu/projects/EBS>. For ordering information, call Pace University Press at 212-346-1405 or visit http://www.pace.edu/press. Institutions and libraries may purchase copies directly from Ingram Library Services (1-800-937-5300).

The editor wishes to thank Gill Kent, Coleman Bentley, Trey Prothro and Mark Hussey, Chair, Editorial Committee, Pace University Press, for their help and advice on this issue.

Journal of the Early Book Society

for the study of manuscripts and printing history

Editor:
Martha W. Driver, *Pace University*

Associate Editors:
Linne R. Mooney, *University of York*
Susan Powell, *University of Salford*

Editorial Board:
Matthew Balensuela, *DePauw University*
Julia Boffey, *Queen Mary, University of London*
Cynthia J. Brown, *University of California, Santa Barbara*
Richard F. M. Byrn, *University of Leeds*
James Carley, *York University*
Joyce Coleman, *University of Oklahoma*
Margaret Connolly, *University of St Andrews*
Susanna Fein, *Kent State University*
Alexandra Gillespie, *University of Toronto*
Vincent Gillespie, *Lady Margaret Hall, Oxford University*
Ann M. Hutchison, *Pontifical Institute of Mediaeval Studies and York University*
Michael Kuczynski, *Tulane University*
William Marx, *University of Wales, Lampeter*
Carol M. Meale, *Bristol University*
Charlotte C. Morse, *Virginia Commonwealth University*
Daniel W. Mosser, *Virginia Polytechnic Institute and State University*
Ann Eljenholm Nichols, *Winona State University*
Judy Oliver, *Colgate University*
Michael Orr, *Lawrence University*
Steven Partridge, *University of British Columbia*
Derek Pearsall, *Harvard University*
Alison Smith, *Wagner College*
Toshiyuki Takamiya, *Keio University*
Andrew Taylor, *University of Ottawa*
John Thompson, *Queen's University, Belfast*
Ronald Waldron, *King's College, University of London*
Edward Wheatley, *Loyola University*
Mary Beth Winn, *SUNY Albany*

Contents

Descriptive Reviews

A Possible Hebraism in *Grisel y Mirabella* and Its Implications: Old Spanish *Cultre* '(Textual) Amulet'

JOSEPH J. GWARA

No scene in *Grisel y Mirabella* (ca. 1475)—the comic romance in which Juan de Flores defends the status and power of women in Isabelline Spain—has generated more scholarly debate than the last, in which the queen of Scotland and her ladies avenge the conviction and suicide of the princess Mirabella by murdering the misogynist defender of men, Torrellas. Promising a night of erotic pleasures, Braçayda (Cressida) lures her erstwhile opponent to a secret chamber where she, the queen, and the women of the court subdue him, bind his hands and feet, strip him naked, gag him, lash him to a stake, tear the flesh from his bones with flaming tongs and with their nails and teeth, malign him during a sumptuous banquet (featuring, by implication, the meat from his own body), force feed him selected delicacies, burn his skeletal remains, and put his ashes in perfume bottles or small coffers to keep as relics. Some women, the narrator adds, choose to wear these capsules around their necks as perpetual reminders of their triumph over their misogynist foe.

Scholars have related the murder of Torrellas variously to the defense of women against their literary detractors,[1] the mythical slaying of Orpheus and Pentheus by the Bacchantes,[2] the Last Supper and Christian martyrdom *in malo*,[3] the unresolved tension between social norms and the human instinct for violence,[4] the carnivalesque subversion of misogyny and patriarchal authority,[5] male anxiety about female aggression and domination,[6] ritual catharsis and the restoration of the patriarchal social order,[7] the struggle for power symbolized by female cannibalism,[8] and the tradition of the monstrous woman.[9] In a recent work, I argue that the misogynist's death is actually a comic inversion of "La muger y la sardina, de rostros en la ceniza" ("Women and sardines, face to the ashes"), an Old Spanish misogynist *refrán* advocating the use of physical and sexual violence to control headstrong women.[10] In effect, Braçayda and the ladies of the court attack the patriarchal antifeminism of Torrellas by skewering him and roasting him alive like a sardine. Serving their archenemy the same bitter meal that he once fed them, they reestablish their superiority in relations between the sexes.

The ritual murder of Torrellas exhibits a number of unusual details, but none is more puzzling than the object to which the narrator compares the ladies' necklace reliquaries. Of the twelve surviving sources of the romance, ten preserve the passage containing the problematic term.[11] The wording varies markedly:

S: El qual, despues que en el no dexaron njnguna carne, los huesos fueron quemados, y de la çenjza dellos guardando cada qual *vna buxeta* por rreliquias de su enemjgo, lo guardauan. Y algunas ovo que, *por non lo olujdar y ver de contino la venga de su enemjgo, como quien trae alguna valerosa cosa, lo trayan consigo,* por que mas a su memoria le fuese presentada la su enemjga vengança por que muy mayor plazer les diese la su cruel muerte. (45.26–31)

T: El qual, despues que en el no dexaron ninguna carne, los huessos fueron quemados, y de su ceniza guardando cada qual *vna buxeta* por reliquias de su enemigo. Y algunas ouo que por *culter* al cuello lo trayan, por que, trayendo mas a su memoria su venganza, mayor plazer les diese. (45.25–28)

V: [lacuna]

I: Y despues que no dexaron ninguna carne en los huessos, fueron quemados, y de su seniza guardando cada qual *vna buxeta* por reliquias de su enemigo. Y algunas houo que por *cultre* en el cuello la traian, por que, trayendo mas a memoria su vengança, mayor plazer houiessen. (45.24–28)

cett.:   Y despues que no dexaron [*G*: le dexaron] ninguna
carne [*EFG*: carne ninguna] en los huessos, fueron
quemados [*G*: se los quemaron], y [*BCDE*: *om.*]
de su ceniza guardando [*G*: guardo] cada qual [*F*:
quanto] *vna buxeta* [*F*: *vna aguxeta*] por reliquias de
su enemigo. E algunas ouo que por *joyel* en el cuello
la trayan, por que, trayendo mas a memoria [*F*: a
la memoria] su vengança, mayor plazer ouiessen.
(45.24–28; lacuna in *H*)[12]

As these excerpts make clear, the ladies put Torrellas's ashes in a "*buxeta*"
(< dim. of Occ. *boissa* 'small box' < VLat. BUXIS 'box'), either a miniature
boxwood chest or, more likely, a pomander or fragrance bottle made of a
precious (or semi-precious) material.[13] Some women, as explained in *I*, wear
this capsule "around their necks as a *cultre*" ("*por cultre en el cuello*"). It is the
word *cultre*—the authorial form, as I intend to show—that caused problems
for many of the scribes and editors of Flores's work. Instead of *cultre*, for example, the sixteenth-century editions (1514–1562) print, without exception,
joyel (< OFr. *joiel* 'jewel' < VLat. *JOCALE* 'jewel' < Lat. JOCUS 'joke, game,
plaything').[14] Since all these editions ultimately derive from *I* (ca. 1495), the
term *cultre* must have been replaced with *joyel* in one of their later common
ancestors, possibly in the suppositious edition of Flores's romance issued by
Jacobo Cromberger around 1510.[15]

Given that a *joyel* was usually a large brooch or badge made of precious
metals and ornamented with pendant gems and/or pearls,[16] I interpret the
new reading as a trivialization, a substitution that turned the narrator's pointed invocation of *cultres* into a conventional value comparison: some ladies
wear their reliquaries like priceless pendant jewels. At least the replacement
word had no impact on the fundamental notion that the women viewed
their *buxetas* as trophies. These ritual objects, as the narrator puts it, gave the
ladies endless pleasure by continually reminding them of their vengeance.

A similar substitution for *cultre* is attested in *S*, the Colombina manuscript (ca. 1490), which is normally the most reliable witness of Flores's
romance. Instead of the expected reading with *cultre*, however, this source
transmits a long descriptive passage lacking any reference to the ladies' necklace reliquaries: "por non lo olujdar y ver de contino la venga de su enemjgo,
como quien trae alguna valerosa cosa, lo trayan consigo" ("so as not to forget
it and to witness continually their vengeance upon their enemy, like someone
who bears a valuable object, they carried it with them"). This clumsy phrasing
does not appear to have a mechanical cause, and I strongly suspect that the
entire passage is a scribal invention, arguably occasioned, once again, by the
word *cultre*. In effect, the scribe of *S* found this word inappropriate—that is,

unintelligible or offensive—and recast the sentence to avoid it, substituting new material based solely on the context. In the process, he made it seem that the ladies carried Torrellas's ashes on their person, perhaps in a *faltriquera* or in another kind of pouch attached to the girdle.[17] As in the case of the post-incunabular editions, however, the scribe retained the notion of perpetual joy in remembrance, emphasizing the fact that the women drew continual pleasure from their trophy reliquaries.

Finally, the reading *culter* in *T*, the Trivulziana manuscript (July 13, 1546), also appears to be a variant, albeit a curiously apt one. This word suggests that the scribe associated authorial *cultre* with Latin *culter* 'knife (*esp.* for killing sacrificial victims or for hunting), razor, plough-coulter,'[18] a word that actually makes some sense in the context of Torrellas's ritual slaughter, at least in its first two acceptations.[19] Certainly, a sacrificial blade would have been an ideal trophy to commemorate the ladies' bloodthirsty victory, and the scribe may have imagined their *buxetas* to be elongated or cultelliform, as might be the case if they had been fashioned from horn, bone, or ivory. This shape, moreover, is highly reminiscent of the phallus, with the implication that the ladies' reliquaries took the form of miniature carved penises. Significantly, two fifteenth-century texts—Enrique de Villena's Castilian translation of the *Aeneid* (1427–1428) and Fray Íñigo de Mendoza's *Coplas de Vita Christi* (1467–1468)—preserve the Spanish derivative *cultro*, described (or depicted) as the flint knife used for ritual circumcision.[20] Perhaps, then, Flores wanted his readers to think that the women had circumcised Torrellas as part of his punishment—a point to which I return below. The reading *culter* is also appealing because Ovid uses the word in the sense of 'sacrificial knife' in the *Metamorphoses*—whose Book III, as observed above, relates the dismemberment of Pentheus, a close analogue for the murder of Torrellas.[21] In keeping with my reading of Torrellas's death as a comic inversion of "La muger y la sardina," the word *culter* may also convey the sense of a small spit or skewer, a fitting symbol of female victory for its gruesome suggestion of anal penetration.

Yet, for all its merits, the reading *culter* is almost certainly a scribal derivation of *cultre*, a copyist's attempt to make sense of an unfamiliar word. In vernacular texts from medieval Spain, *culter* occurs only rarely, in specialized bilingual glossaries and one Latin grammar from the last decades of the fifteenth century (or slightly later).[22] The acceptation of 'spit, skewer,' moreover, is unrecorded, while the usage in the *Metamorphoses* is confined to Books VII and XV, in which the contexts vary markedly from that in Book III.[23] Ovid, in fact, makes no mention of knives in the death of Pentheus, although Agave hurls a *thyrsus*, or pinecone-topped fennel staff, at him.[24] Nevertheless, the form in *T* could acquire some degree of legitimacy if we assumed that Latin CULTER gave rise to Old Spanish *cultre* in an extraliterary context. Indeed, this etymology, as I discuss below, could cast light on one possible interpretation of *cultre* as it relates to the women's suffering at the hands of men.

Modern editors of *Grisel y Mirabella* have made little progress in explaining the origin and meaning of *cultre*. In her critical edition of the work, Maria Grazia Ciccarello di Blasi argues that either *cultre* or *culter* is archetypal, but she dismisses both forms—together with the circumlocution in *S*—as variants of the authorial *culto* 'ornament, necklace' (< Lat. CULTUS 'bodily adornment, dress').[25] She goes on to assert, somewhat contradictorily, that the more common acceptation of 'religious ceremony, belief' for *culto* would actually make better sense in the context.[26] As she sees it, this interpretation dovetails with the notion that Torrellas suffers a ritual execution and that his ashes are put in reliquaries.[27] Fifteen years earlier, I made a similar observation in my London doctoral thesis, suggesting a possible relationship between *cultre* and Latin *cultor* 'worshipper, votary' and/or *colere* 'honor, venerate, respect.'[28] Tentatively glossing *cultre* as 'phylactery,' I interpreted the ritual slaughter of Torrellas as a kind of profeminist martyrdom.[29] At the same time, however, I refrained from treating *cultre* as a mere textual error, since the word is actually found in early modern Spanish, with a critically important pre-1600 attestation reported by Francisco Rodríguez Marín in 1922.[30] His source is Juan de Pineda, *Diálogos familiares de la agricultura cristiana* (Salamanca, 1589), dialogue 20, part 13. I quote the passage in full for its contextualization of the term:

> Leyendo la Suma de Cayetano noté que trata desta materia—y huelgo mucho que se me haya ofrecido a tan buen tiempo—, y que pone siete condiciones, con que se puede descubrir haber tácita invocación del demonio en alguna obra. La primera dice ser cuando se pone alguna condición vana como necesaria para el tal efecto, como que las palabras sanctas sean escritas en pergamino y no en papel, y a tal hora y en tal día, o en tal forma de renglones, como solían algunos eclesiásticos dar cultres escritos de muchos círculos, y sacaban a las bobillas mujercillas buena paga, y aun hombres no muy cuerdos andaban tras ellos; y cierto está ser gran bestialidad creer que por estar las palabras escritas en grandes renglones o pequeños, dentro de círculos o de cuadrados, tengan más virtud.[31]

In conjunction with the adjective *escritos*, the placement of *cultre* under the heading "*Invocación mala*" suggests that the word refers to a written spell or textual amulet intended to help the bearer obtain supernatural favor or protection. Notwithstanding the dramatic references to demonic influence and necromancy, the context is wholly conventional: Pineda denounces the widespread "pagan" belief in the efficacy of textual amulets as irreconcilable with Christian orthodoxy. Fernando Bouza, in fact, quotes this very passage to illustrate the survival of magical writing into the Golden Age, with its concrete manifestations known variously as *cédulas (cedulillas)*, *cartas de toque*, and *nóminas*.[32] Although Bouza does not explain the meaning of the word *cultre*, he places the Pineda reference in the context of superstitious writs that were intended to heal the sick, locate hidden treasure, control others, and ward off evil, among many other functions, including the maleficent.[33]

In an expansive study of textual amulets in the Middle Ages, Don C. Skemer shows that their ritual use was a cultural practice shared by virtually every community in Western Europe. Such objects were a conspicuous part of daily life, springing from a collective belief in the power of the written word and the need for protection from the hazards of a perilous world. Owing to their common origin and function, textual amulets exhibited consistencies in design and manufacture, although individual reactions to them varied. Skemer's broad-based investigation allows us to interpret the two key features of *cultres* as remarked upon by Pineda. First, Pineda's rebuke of clerics who peddled amulets to the ignorant probably reflects the notion that his brethren were complicit idolaters and biblioclasts as well as greedy charlatans. To a large extent, the clerical community itself promoted the belief in the apotropaic power of amulets, partly because of an abiding faith in their spiritual efficacy.[34] This stance persisted despite its condemnation by the Church Fathers and later theologians, for whom this simple expression of faith was a form of pagan worship. Pineda clearly shared the outrage of his learned forebears, and his indignation may have been amplified by an awareness that amuletic texts were often inscribed on parchment excised from sacred books.[35] This practice, which turned countless holy objects into unholy trinkets, would have been a particular affront to a scholar like Pineda.

Second, the *círculos* that Pineda identifies as an intrinsic part of *cultres* clearly refer to the talismanic sigils or magic seals that frequently accompanied the written text. These cartouche-style designs, which often enclosed *characteres* (magical symbols like astrological signs, nonsense words, cryptic letter combinations, etc.), were intended to enhance the apotropaic power of the spell or charm.[36] The circular patterns formed by these sigils are a distinctive visual feature of many decorated amulets that have come down to us, and Pineda's allusion is precise enough to show that the *cultres* he saw bore similar designs.[37] We can be certain, therefore, that Flores's *cultre* was an actual object, not simply a literary invention or an aberrant word accidentally created during the transmission of his romance.

Aside from the references in Flores and Pineda, the only known attestations of the word *cultre* occur in early-sixteenth-century archival sources. In an important monograph exploring the books that once belonged to Isabel la Católica, Elisa Ruiz García exhumes several allusions to *cultres*—with the usual repetitions in parallel documentary sources—from a series of interrelated postmortem inventories dating between December 1504 and late 1505. The relevant account entries are as follows:

> 1. ¶Dos cultres de pergamino syn guarniçión.
> 2. ¶Más dos cultres de pergamino syn guarniçión.
> 3. ¶Un cultre de pergamino con una devoçión estoriada.
> 4. ¶Un cultre de pergamino con una devoçión estoriada.
> 5. ¶Un cultre de pergamino. Apreciose en dos rreales. Conprolo Juan López, guarniçionero, por LXVIII maravedíes.
> 6. ¶Un cultre chequito, de pergamino, de letra muy menuda, de la oraçión de san León.[38]

From these exiguous descriptions—which probably refer to no more than four objects, assuming that items 1–2 and 3–4 (at least) share an identity—Ruiz García deduces that a *cultre* must have been an "objeto de devoción que, a modo de amuleto o escapulario, se solía llevar impuesto o bien se aplicaba sobre una parte del cuerpo en caso de necesidad" ("a devotional object which, like an amulet or scapular, was usually borne devotionally or applied to a given body part in case of need").[39]

Although she comments that *cultres* and other amuletic objects and images reflected "un tipo de religiosidad que estaba vinculado a determinadas plegarias y rezos" ("a form of religiosity linked to certain supplications and prayers"),[40] she otherwise restricts her analysis of the term to a handful of isolated remarks in periodical publications. In a preliminary discussion of item 6, for example, she glosses *cultre* as "una variedad de soporte portátil emparentado morfológicamente con el amuleto" ("a kind of portable medium structurally akin to the amulet"), explaining that the *Oración de san León*—here copied on parchment in a diminutive hand—circulated widely in Spain (and throughout Europe) as a textual amulet until it was banned by the Inquisition in the middle of the sixteenth century.[41] Isabel's personal effects, in fact, included two manuscript *libelli* of this popular amuletic prayer, with elaborately enameled and jeweled gold bindings (or housings), both of which were intended to be worn on a chain around the neck.[42] Such minia-ture books often functioned as self-contained textual amulets, their contents (prayers, litanies, devotional images, etc.) serving as perpetually renewable sources of divine protection and healing. Elsewhere Ruiz García specifically identifies *cultres* as parchment amulets, often in roll form, which were carried or worn on the body, thus allowing the bearer direct and continual contact with their presumed apotropaic power.[43] Throughout the Middle Ages, such objects formed part of everyday devotions despite routine condemnation by the Church hierarchy.

Additional references to *cultres* show up in archival records detailing the personal property of Juana la Loca (d. 1555). Two appear in an inventory of her valuables prepared by her chamberlain Diego de Ribera in 1509, when the mentally unstable queen took up residence in the palace at Tordesillas.[44] The relevant account entries are as follows:

> vn cultre de oro largo esmaltado con vna cadena e vna P de oro con siete diamanticos e vna perla pinjante e vna pomita de oro de quatro verguitas llena de anbar que peso todo junto medio marco e vna ochaba e tomin e medio.[45]

> dos cultres de oro que pesaron quinze castellanos e çinco tomines e ocho granos que diego de ayala entrego a su alteza el año de MDX segun parece por otro libro que hizo el dicho garcia de carreño que esta en la audiencia de la contaduria de quentas donde se presento para comprouacion del cargo desta quenta.[46]

The first entry, as we can see, describes an enameled gold *cultre* and its chain, bearing the letter P (for her husband, Philippe) outlined in tiny dia-monds, to which are attached a pendant pearl and a small gold pomander filled with ambergris. The second entry, less precise, refers to a pair of large gold *cultres* that Diego de Ayala, a goldsmith who frequently worked for the crown, presented to doña Juana in 1510.[47] The context of these entries— the first among Juana's "joyeles e cruces y engastes con piedras e perlas e sin ellas" ("jewels and crosses and settings with or without precious stones and pearls")[48] and the second among her "medallas y enseñas y otras cosas semejantes desta calidad" ("medals and badges and other similar things of this kind")[49]—suggests that although the word *cultre* commonly referred to an amuletic manuscript, it applied equally to the decorative suspension cap-sule that housed it or to the manuscript and capsule in combination. These descriptions, moreover, indicate that *cultres* were somehow distinguishable from other forms of jewelry, presumably because they had an accessible compartment or void that allowed the bearer to insert a holy relic or mystical text. This supposition is confirmed by a more detailed description of the first *cultre*, minus its pomander, which Carlos V presented to his sister Catalina de Austria in 1524:

> otro joyel de una P llena de diamantes con un lomito
> en medio, cada uno que hace talle de P y una perla
> pinjante y en las espaldas una P y una H, y está
> la dicha P asida en un cultre de oro que tiene un
> pergamino dentro con muchos misterios, que pesó
> con una cadenica tres onças y seis ochavas e tres
> tomines y está el dicho cultre esmaltado de unas
> florecicas de trasflor y en lo alto y en lo baxo unos
> tornillos y el cultre es como coluna.[50]

The cylindrical shape of this capsule (*"como coluna"*) indicates that it was intended to house an amulet roll, while the reference to screws (*"unos tornillos"*) suggests that it had a removable panel through which the manuscript was inserted. The description of the amulet itself (*"un pergamino . . . con muchos misterios"*) implies that it contained *characteres* and other mystical symbols, probably copied alongside invocations, prayers, and devotional images. Although, to my knowledge, examples of medieval Spanish *cultres* have not survived, Skemer describes a similar cylindrical enclosure for a St. Margaret roll (dated 1491) almost certainly used by a wealthy French woman as a birth girdle.[51] In the Jewish tradition, amulet cases were also cylindrical or hexagonal in shape.[52]

The etymology of the word *cultre* remains unresolved. One possible etymon, as I have mentioned in my discussion of the Trivulziana reading, is Latin CULTER. Ruiz García, in fact, observes that a popular devotion associated with the Arma Christi—the Instruments of Christ's Passion—begins *"Culter qui circumcidiste sacrosanctam carnem Christi,"* adding that the prayer was perceived to have apotropaic powers.[53] Known through Books of Hours and religious broadsides, this devotion was also used to petition for divine intercession. Ruiz García, however, stops short of declaring that Lat. CULTER gave rise to *cultre* as a generic term for "textual amulet." Certainly, the *cultres* described by Pineda, with their *characteres* and other magical symbols, are strikingly different in design from the usual pictorial representations of the Arma Christi, with the traditional Instruments of the Passion surrounding the crucified Christ.[54] The apparent popularity of the Latin devotion, furthermore, conflicts with the rarity of the word *cultre* in early sources, while the peculiar concentration of citations in archival court documents remains unexplained.

Pending a more thorough analysis of this Latin etymology, therefore, I would suggest a different origin for the word: Rabbinic Hebrew *glturi*, or גלטורי. In an erudite discussion of the origin and meaning of this term, Daniel Sperber argues that it derives from Latin LIGATURAE, citing numerous medieval authorities, including St. Augustine (d. 430) and St. Isidore of Seville (d. 636), who used this plural form (sing. *ligatura*) to refer to the amulets that superstitious Christians wore around their necks or attached to their bodies with straps.[55] Although such amulets often included written spells, they could also contain herbs, bones, and similar objects deemed to have magical potency.[56] In addition to the semantic shift from the cord(s) or strap(s) supporting the amulet to the amulet itself, the word exhibits a consonantal metathesis which, according to Sperber, is consistent with phonological changes seen in other Hebrew borrowings from Latin.[57] If we grant an intuitive phonetic adjustment allowing for a standard pattern of Romance pronunciation—vocalic metathesis, devoicing of initial /g/, and lowering of final /i/—we have in Hebrew *glturi* the source of Old Spanish *cultre*.[58]

Like the majority of Hebraisms in Spanish, this word, with its Talmudic origin, reflects the unique religious and cultural heritage of the Jewish community.[59] Perhaps owing to their traditional use of *mezuzah* (doorpost prayer rolls) and *tefillin* (phylacteries), Jews in the Middle Ages were perceived to be habitual consumers of textual amulets, usually carried on the body as protective charms.[60] In fifteenth-century Spain, in fact, the Inquisition often identified judaizing conversos through their use of amulets and talismans. False converts could be given away by their parchment *nóminas* or by their Hebrew-inscribed medallions and similar apotropaic jewelry.[61] Invariably carried out of sight, these charms constituted prima facie evidence that the bearer was attempting to conceal his or her Jewish faith. Although, as we have seen, Christians also believed in the efficacy of textual amulets, it was the Jews who were most closely associated with them and with their occult powers of protection.[62]

Assuming that my proposed Hebrew etymology is correct, I conjecture that the word *cultre* entered medieval Spanish through the converso community. As de facto intermediaries between Jews and Christians, the conversos served as unofficial interpreters of Jewish culture, exhibiting a special familiarity with Hebrew terminology that reflected traditional Jewish life and thought.[63] The macaronic verse produced by fifteenth-century converso poets proves that notwithstanding the rarity of Hebraisms in Spanish, many Hebrew words were readily understood by informed audiences, including other conversos and Old Christians who had contacts with Jewish commerce, government institutions, and religious customs.[64] Even though Hebrew-derived terms

almost never took root in Spanish, a number of them must have enjoyed
enough currency to establish recognizable points of reference for Jewish
cultural practices—and not necessarily for comic effect. In my view, the
use of the word *cultre* in royal inventories represents the adaptation of the
Hebrew *glturi* by converso functionaries at the Castilian court.

Historians have long known that conversos occupied many high- and
low-level administrative posts in the household of the Catholic Monarchs:
accountants, butlers, chamberlains, secretaries, stewards, treasurers, and
personal servants.[65] This list includes the very individuals who would have
prepared—or supervised the preparation of—the royal inventories refer-
encing *cultres*. To a certain extent, this hypothesis explains the reaction of
the scribes and compositors who encountered *cultre* in the later witnesses
of *Grisel y Mirabella*. Faced with a word that was incomprehensible to an
audience of outsiders, the copyists felt compelled to modify or replace it.

The rarity of *cultre* in early documentation presupposes a certain familiarity with Hebrew terms on Flores's part, perhaps because Flores himself
was a converso or because he was an Old Christian with professional ties
to the Jewish community. Circumstantial evidence supports either of these
propositions, though not without complications. More than twenty years
ago, I suggested that Flores served Fernando and Isabel as a *corregidor* and
pesquisidor after 1477, when he apparently abandoned his literary career.[66]
The *Registro general del sello*, a catalogue of the proceedings of the Castilian
royal chancery, records a series of official transactions between the *corregi-
dor/pesquisidor* Juan (de) Flores and the Jews of Ávila from 1478 to 1480.[67]
Assuming that this royal official and the sentimental author share an identity,
we could establish a link between Flores and the Jewish community within
Ávila that could also explain the writer's knowledge of culturally specific
Hebrew terminology.

Additional evidence indicates that Flores may have served as a liaison
between the Crown and the Inquisition. Between 1491 and 1494, the *Registro
general del sello* refers to a certain Juan Flores as a "*receptor de bienes confiscados
por la Inquisición*" ("receiver of goods confiscated by the Inquisition") in the
city and bishopric of Cuenca.[68] Although we have no proof that this *receptor*
and the writer are the same person, it is tempting to think that Flores had
direct contact with Jewish cultural practices through a professional involvement with the Holy Office. Nevertheless, since all the interactions in Ávila
and Cuenca postdate the composition of *Grisel y Mirabella* (ca. 1475), we
would have to assume that Flores's familiarity with Jewish customs preceded
his royal appointments. Such a familiarity could have earned him his com-
missions as an investigator and Inquisitorial *receptor*.

Equally feasible is the hypothesis that Flores himself was a converso.
Writing in 1986 and 1987, I tacitly assumed that the sentimental author was

an Old Christian with ties to the Castilian nobility, based on documentary sources linking him to the court of Garci Álvarez de Toledo, I Duque de Alba, and to Pedro Álvarez Osorio, I Conde de Lemos.[69] This assumption has been challenged by Dayle Seidenspinner-Núñez, who is unable to reconcile the Osorio family connection with the reference to Flores as the son of "*Ferrando de Flores, vesino de la çibdad de Salamanca*" ("Ferrando de Flores, freeman of the city of Salamanca") in the writer's original appointment as royal chronicler (May 20, 1476). She prefers to identify Flores as the son of a certain Fernand Alfonso de Flores, a Salamanca merchant whose name appears in a real estate contract (May 10, 1469) with the goldsmith García Lopes.[70] As Seidenspinner-Núñez sees it, the merchant's son, with his middle-class upbringing, probable access to a university education, and professional service in the household of the Duke of Alba, best fits the profile of a talented converso administrator who eventually secured a secretarial post at the royal court.[71]

Although this hypothesis accounts for the paternal reference to "Ferrando de Flores," it is ultimately based on a series of coincidences in names, family associations, and places of origin that constitute an insecure foundation for identifying the sentimental writer as a middle-class converso.[72] In fact, an affiliation with the Álvarez de Toledo and Osorio families offers equally compelling circumstantial evidence of Flores's converso roots. As Roth intimates, the ducal court of Alba was a haven for converso intellectuals and entertainers, including the poet/composer Juan del Encina and the author/physician Francisco López de Villalobos.[73] Roth also points out that Lope de Barrientos, writing about 1450, named the Osorios as one of the prominent Christian noble families with converso members—arguably an allusion to their marital alliances with the Enríquez and Quiñones families.[74] In terms of Flores's literary activity, moreover, it is important to recall that conversos commonly occupied the post of royal chronicler (e.g., Alvar García de Santa María, Juan de Mena, Alfonso de Palencia, Fernando de Pulgar, Diego de Valera) and that Flores's own chronicle exhibits all the hallmarks of late-fifteenth-century converso political thought as summarized by Seidenspinner-Núñez: unconditional support for absolutist and antifeudal monarchy, a messianic view of the Catholic Monarchs, and a perception that Castilian hegemony was providential.[75]

At the same time, scholars like Seidenspinner-Núñez are beginning to interpret *Grisel y Mirabella* as a converso work, specifically as an exposé of the abuses that flow from an irrational and morally blind absolutism.[76] Given the date of approximately 1475 that I have proposed for Flores's romance, *Grisel y Mirabella* could be read as a pre-Inquisitorial object lesson in the dangers of unrestrained political power.[77] In this cultural and literary context, then, Flores's possible connection to a well-known converso family like the Osorios should not be rejected out of hand. As Linda Martz observes, affluent conversos often sought to assimilate into the dominant Christian society by marrying into upper-class families.[78] Did Juan de Flores or his father Ferrando follow the same path by marrying into a branch of the Osorio family? Could the term "*sobrino*" ("nephew") conceal a collateral relationship by marriage? No less an authority than Alonso López de Haro, writing in the seventeenth century, refers to a certain Juan Flores as the husband of Beatriz de Quiñones, a descendant of Alvaro Pérez Osorio, lord (*señor*) of Villalobos and Castroverde, on her mother's side.[79] Pending a more thorough investigation of the genealogical sources, therefore, I defer judgment on Seidenspinner-Núñez's proposed biography of Flores while accepting that a converso ancestry could explain his familiarity with a Hebraism like *cultre*, whether he was the son of a converso merchant and/or the in-law of a nobleman with Jewish roots. At the very least, his use of the term suggests that he belonged to a linguistically sophisticated and bicultural "in crowd" at court, not unlike the audience that must have enjoyed the converso satire in the *Cancionero de Baena* a generation before.

The recovery of the meaning '(textual) amulet' for *cultre* allows me to advance an alternative explanation for the variant readings in the different witnesses of *Grisel y Mirabella*. As explained above, the passage containing *cultre* in the Colombina manuscript (45.26–31) was recast, ostensibly because the scribe found the word incomprehensible. In view of the origin and meaning of *cultre*, however, it is possible that the alteration had a different trigger: Flores's celebratory invocation of a ritual object that smacked of superstition at best and crypto-Judaism at worst. Arguably offended by the reference to an idolatrous practice, the scribe of S may have censored the word by substituting a circumlocution. Such pious emendations are rife in medieval manuscripts, and S transmits many other examples. Perhaps the most striking appears in the opening sentence of Braçayda's third speech in the debate with Torrellas:

S: ¡O, quan enemjgo y lastimero os mostrays, Torrellas, pareçe que para maldecir de nosotras naçistes! (19.2–3)

T: Ya os veo tan lastimero y enemigo, Torrellas, que paresce que, para maldezir de nosotras, sy en el altar fallascedes de que os aprouechar, sin hazer dello conziencia, de allí lo tomariades. (19.2–4)

cett.:   Yo os veo tan lastimero, Tor[r]ellas, y mas enemigo
que parece que, para maldezir de nosotras, si en
el altar fallassedes malicias de que os podiessedes
aprouechar, sin fazer dello [*F:* della] consciencia, de
alli las [*GH:* lo] tomariades. (19.2–4)[80]

In this excerpt, the textual variation between *S* and the other sources does
not have an obvious mechanical explanation. To me, in fact, the comparative
brevity and wrenched syntax of the sentence in *S* suggest that it is an ad hoc
substitution. Considering Braçayda's profane allegation that Torrellas would
twist holy words before the altar of God if it helped his antifeminist cause, I
conjecture that the scribe recast Flores's original (as preserved by *T* and the
printed editions) in order to eliminate the blasphemous image. This copyist, we can imagine, would have been no less discomfited by the heterodox
implications of the word *cultre*, causing him to rewrite the passage in *S* as an
impromptu act of censorship. By the same token, the substitution "*joyel*" in
the sixteenth-century editions could represent the work of a censor. Logically, any published reference to a superstitious or idolatrous practice after
around 1480 would have drawn the scrutiny of Inquisitorial authorities, and
a savvy printer would have saved himself considerable trouble by eliminating
the word. He may even have done so at the direction of an official corrector.
The evidence suggests, then, that the readings in *S* and the post-incunabular
editions stem from the social and religious realities of early modern Spain.

In light of the term *cultre*, the ritual murder of Torrellas—the climactic
moment in *Grisel y Mirabella*—takes on new levels of meaning. Associated
with supernatural power, both protective and aggressive, amulets heal the
wounded and ward off enemies. Like Christian crosses, they are usually
worn over the heart—"the gateway to the soul," in Skemer's words,[81] not to
mention the locus of love—as magical remedies for the ailments of body
and soul. Following the death of Mirabella and the misogynist's slanderous
attacks, the ladies have an urgent need for such supernatural medicine. Their
trophy capsules, perpetual reminders of their victory, offer solace as much
as pleasure. If we accept the derivation of the term from Latin CULTER and
the association with the Passion, then the reference to *cultres* would suggest that some women likened their suffering to that of Christ on the cross,
taking comfort from His pain and ultimate sacrifice. In a sense, Flores's new
disciples of feminism derive their inner strength from torment endured
through faith, just as the Christian community drew inspiration from the
prototypical martyrdom of Jesus. The women's pain at the hands of men and
their second-class status are tolerable because they know their cause is just
and their ultimate triumph assured.

In keeping with the possible derivation of *cultre* from Hebrew *glturi*, however, the ladies' *buxetas* also have more menacing connotations. Traditionally,
the bearers of amulets enjoyed continued protection from their enemies,
seen or unseen. By means of their *buxetas*, strategically placed over the heart,
the ladies ward off their foes in love: those men who would brand them as
seductresses, exploit their emotional weaknesses, and deny them standing
in society. Like holy relics, these amulets repulse would-be attackers with an
unseen magic. In this case, though, the relics are unholy: the misogynist's
body, reduced to ashes, channels the power of female righteousness in the
face of male persecution.

In addition, amulets could inflict real harm on one's enemies, radiating an
aggressive force against evildoers. As we see above, the ladies' proto-feminism
is fundamentally violent, as befits their revolutionary claim to authority.
The dominant theme of female empowerment and its corollary, emasculation, lead me to speculate that Flores's audience would have understood
the ladies' *buxetas*—surrogate *cultres*, in the narrator's words—as having a
phallic design. As we saw in the case of an elaborate *cultre* owned by Juana la
Loca, amulet capsules were often tube-shaped to accommodate prayer rolls.
Occasionally, medieval apotropaic jewelry also took the form of the male
genitals, as illustrated by the *higa*, an amulet traditionally believed to repulse
the evil eye.[82] Carved like a miniature fist with the thumb inserted between
the index and middle fingers, the *higa* simulates the penis and testicles.[83] As
such, the object threatens anal penetration.

A phallic shape for the ladies' capsules would also harmonize with
Flores's use of the Old Spanish proverb "La muger y la sardina, de rostros
en la ceniza," which implies that women are no less capable than men of
"sticking it to their enemies."[84] Staking a claim to virility, the women emas-
culate their counterparts, perhaps using their amulets to cast a binding spell
of impotence. As indicated by *T*, moreover, the phonetic similarity of *cultre*
and Latin *culter* could have given rise to a popular etymology or, at minimum,
a subconscious verbal association that conjured up the image of circumcision, routinely derided as a form of emasculation. With its suggestion of a
stereotypical Jewish ritual, then, the word *cultre* may well have had a special
resonance with the conversos in Flores's audience, concealing an inside joke
about the background of specific individuals.

In *Grisel y Mirabella*, Flores crafted a tale of female empowerment that
exploits a lexical code rich with ironic innuendo and double entendres. A
critical part of this code is Old Spanish *cultre* 'textual amulet.' The narrator's
pointed remark that some women of the Scottish court wear the misogynist's
ashes "as *cultres*" reveals an underlying belief system in which ritual objects
were held to have the power to heal, protect, and/or inflict harm. The tubular

shape of *cultres* and their likely association with ritual circumcision suggest that women acquire power through emasculation, an example of Flores's brutal sexual humor. Nevertheless, the ladies' amulets would likely have provoked positive reactions among many members of Flores's original audience. Despite condemnation by the Church and connotations of idolatry, *cultres* were mainstream devotional objects, found even among the possessions of Isabel la Católica and Juana la Loca. In this context, therefore, Flores would seem to say that women are empowered by the relics of an old masculinist order. Protected by this spiritual energy earned through the suffering endured at the hands of their enemies, the women constitute a new alliance—one headed by Isabel herself—which is poised to assume both sexual and political authority in a transitional age.

United States Naval Academy

Acknowledgments
I thank Nancy F. Marino and E. Michael Gerli for their helpful comments on an earlier version of this paper.

APPENDIX: THE SOURCES OF *GRISEL Y MIRABELLA*

Manuscripts
V: Biblioteca Apostolica Vaticana, Vatican City, Vat. Lat. 6966, fols. 68r–76v.

S: Biblioteca Colombina, Seville, MS 5-3-20, fols. 69r–86r.

T: Biblioteca Trivulziana, Milan, MS 940, fols. 1r–76v.

Early Printed Editions
I: *Tractado compuesto por Iohan de Flores a su amiga*. Lérida, Spain: Henrique Botel, ca. 1495. Copies: Biblioteca Nacional, Madrid, I-2181; Huntington Library, San Marino, California, 87232.

A: Juan de Flores, *La hystoria de Grisel y Mirabella, con la disputa de Torrellas y Braçayda*. Seville, Spain: Juan Varela de Salamanca, August 28, 1514. Copy: Biblioteca de Catalunya, Barcelona, Espona 80 8°.

B: Juan de Flores, *La historia de Grisel y Mirabella, con la disputa de Torrellas y Braçayda*. Seville, Spain: Jacobo Cromberger, 1524. Copy: The British Library, London, C.63.h.20.

C: Juan de Flores, *La hystoria de Grisel y Mirabella, con la disputa de Torrellas & Braçayda*. Toledo, Spain: [Miguel de Eguía], December 17, 1526. Copy: Bibliothèque Nationale, Paris, Rés. Y²820.

D: Juan de Flores, *La historia de Grisel y Mirabella, con la disputa de Torrellas y Braçayda*. Seville, Spain: Juan Cromberger, 1529. Copy: Biblioteca

Nacional, Madrid, Col. Cerv. Sedó 8.630.

E: Juan de Flores, *La historia de Grisel & Mirabella, con la disputa de Torrellas y Braçayda*. Seville, Spain: Juan Cromberger, 1533. Copy: Bibliothèque de la Sorbonne, Paris, Rés. XVI 879 8°.

F: Juan de Flores, *La historia de Grisel y Mirabella, con la disputa de Torrellas y Braçayda*. Cuenca, Spain: Juan de Canova, March 16, 1561. Copy: Biblioteca Pública e Arquivo Distrital de Évora, Séc. XVI-2725.

G: Juan de Flores, *La historia de Grisel y Mirabella, con la disputa de Torrellas y Braçayda*. Burgos, Spain: Philippe de Junta, 1562. Copy: Biblioteca Nacional, Madrid, R-31364 no. 3.

H: Juan de Flores, *La historia de Grisel y Mirabella, con la disputa de Torrellas y Braçayda*. Burgos, Spain: Philippe de Junta, 1562. Copy: Hispanic Society of America, New York. (Note: A different setting of type.)

NOTES

1. Barbara Matulka, *The Novels of Juan de Flores and Their European Diffusion: A Study in Comparative Literature* (New York: Institute of French Studies, 1931; repr. Geneva: Slatkine, 1974), 158–166.
2. Alan D. Deyermond, "El hombre salvaje en la novela sentimental," *Filología* 10 (1964 [1966]): 97–111, 106–108; Patricia Crespo Martín, "Violencia mitológica en *Grisel y Mirabella*," *La corónica* 29.1 (2000): 75–87.
3. Marina S. Brownlee, "Language and Incest in *Grisel y Mirabella*," *Romanic Review* 79 (1988): 107–128, 123–125; Brownlee, *The Severed Word: Ovid's "Heroides" and the "Novela Sentimental"* (Princeton, NJ: Princeton University Press, 1990), 206–207; Brownlee, "Verbal and Physical Violence in the *Historie of Aurelio and Isabell*," in *Vengeance in the Middle Ages: Emotion, Religion and Feud*, ed. Susanna A. Throop and Paul R. Hyams (Farnham, UK: Ashgate, 2010), 137–150, 144–146.
4. Jorge Checa, "*Grisel y Mirabella* de Juan de Flores: Rebeldía y violencia como síntomas de crisis," *Revista Canadiense de Estudios Hispánicos* 12 (1987–1988): 369–382, 369, 376–378.
5. Barbara F. Weissberger, "Role-Reversal and Festivity in the Romances of Juan de Flores," *Journal of Hispanic Philology* 13 (1988–1989): 197–213, 201–205; Weissberger, *Isabel Rules: Constructing Queenship, Wielding Power* (Minneapolis: University of Minnesota Press, 2004), 182–183.
6. Lillian von der Walde Moheno, "El episodio final de *Grisel y Mirabella*," *La corónica* 20.2 (1992): 18–31, 27–28; Walde Moheno, *Amor e ilegalidad: "Grisel y Mirabella," de Juan de Flores*, Publicaciones de Medievalia 12, Estudios de Lingüística y Literatura 34 (Mexico City: Universidad Nacional

Autónoma de México and El Colegio de México, 1996), 242–244.

7. John T. Cull, "Irony, Romance Conventions, and Misogyny in *Grisel y Mirabella* by Juan de Flores," *Revista Canadiense de Estudios Hispánicos* 22 (1997–1998): 415–430, 419–420, 424, 427–428.

8. Alberto Prieto-Calixto, "Mujeres y caníbales: Rituales violentos en *Grisel y Mirabella* de Juan de Flores," *Cincinnati Romance Review* 21 (2002): 77–90, 78, 84–88.

9. Antonia Petro, "La tradición de la mujer monstruo en *Grisel y Mirabella*," *Crítica Hispánica* 29.1–2 (2007): 213–233, 214–215, 223, 229–231.

10. Joseph J. Gwara, "'La muger y la sardina, de rostros en la ceniza': An Old Spanish Proverb in *Grisel y Mirabella*," in *Juan de Flores: Four Studies*, ed. Joseph J. Gwara, Papers of the Medieval Hispanic Research Seminar 49 (London: Department of Hispanic Studies, Queen Mary, University of London, 2005), 49–73.

11. For the complete list of witnesses, plus the *sigla* used to identify them, see the Appendix. I cite from the page proofs of my own edition of *Grisel y Mirabella*. With the exception of <R>, which I transcribe as <rr>, I have respected the orthography of the original sources; however, I have modernized capitalization, punctuation, and word-spacing. Abbreviations have been silently expanded.

12. Here and elsewhere my translations reflect scribal and/or authorial anacoluthon: *S*: "Who, after they left no flesh on him, his bones were incinerated, and each keeping a phial with ashes from them as a relic of their enemy, they kept it. There were some who, so as not to forget it and to witness continually their vengeance upon their enemy, like someone who bears a valuable object, they carried it with them, so that they would remember their harsh vengeance and so that his cruel death would give them even greater pleasure." *I*: "And after they left no flesh on his bones, they were incinerated, and each keeping a phial of ashes as relics of her enemy. And there were some who wore it around their necks as a *cultre*, so that, by calling to mind their vengeance, they might have even greater pleasure."

13. On the meaning of "*buxeta*," see Martín Alonso, *Diccionario medieval español: Desde las Glosas emilianenses y silenses (s. X) hasta el siglo XV*, 2 vols. (Salamanca, Spain: Universidad Pontificia de Salamanca, 1986), 1:544, *s.v. boxeta* ('*bujeta, cajita*'), and 558, *s.v. bujeta* (repeating, for the most part, the definitions in the *Diccionario histórico de la lengua española*, vol. 2, *B–Cevilla* [Madrid: Academia Española, 1936], *q.v.*); Julio Cejador y Frauca, *Vocabulario medieval castellano* (Madrid: Hernando, 1929; repr. New York: Las Americas, 1968), 81, *s.vv. bujeta, buxeta* ('*cajita*'); Juan Corominas and José A. Pascual, *Diccionario crítico etimológico castellano e hispánico*, Biblioteca Románica Hispánica, V (Diccionarios) 7, 6 vols. (Madrid: Gredos, 1980–1991), 1:693–694, *s.v. bujeta* ('*diminutivo del lat. vg.* BŪXIS, -ĬDIS,' dismissing

as a probable *"vana preocupación etimológica"* the assertions of Antonio de Nebrija and Alfonso de Palencia that the vessel was necessarily made of box-wood); Sebastián de Covarrubias Horozco, *Tesoro de la lengua castellana o española*, ed. Ignacio Arellano and Rafael Zafra, Biblioteca Áurea Hispánica 21 (Pamplona, Spain: Universidad de Navarra; Madrid: Iberoamericana; Frankfurt am Main, Germany: Vervuert, 2006), 368, *s.vv. bujeta/bugeta* (*'cierto género de vaso pequeño y pulido en que se echan olores'*); and *Diccionario histórico*, 394, *s.v. bujeta* (*'cajita o pequeña vasija'; 'pomo, o cajita de perfumes'*). I have been unable to verify the etymology proposed by the Real Academia Española dictionary (< Prov. *boiseta*), although it may derive from Friedrich Diez, *Etymologisches Wörterbuch der romanischen Sprachen*, 5th ed. (Bonn: Adolph Marcus, 1887), 61, *s.v. bosso*. Examples from the Corpus Diacrónico del Español (CORDE) of the Real Academia Española, available at http://corpus.rae.es/cordenet.html, show that a *buxeta* could be made from various materials, including alabaster, bamboo, boxwood, ebony, glass or rock crystal (*"cristal"*), gold, horn, iron, ivory, precious stones, and silver. They contained such objects and substances as consecrated hosts, cosmetics (quicksilver, rouge, white lead), electuaries, herbs and spices, jewelry, locks of hair, medicinal oils and unguents, perfumes and fragrant resins (ambergris, balsam, civet, mastic, musk, myrrh), poison, stones, tar (pitch), victuals, and water; in figurative terms, they could also house anguish, evils, and memories. In *F*, the reading *"aguxeta"* ('lacet') is a further corruption or substitution; on this word, which refers to an ornamental ribbon or braided cord commonly used to secure a man's hose to his doublet or to close up the openings of a lady's sleeves, see Carmen Bernis, *Trajes y modas en la España de los Reyes Católicos*, vol. 1, *Las mujeres*; vol. 2, *Los hombres* (Madrid: Instituto Diego Velázquez, Consejo Superior de Investigaciones Científicas, 1978–1979), 2:53; Vicente García de Diego, *Diccionario etimológico español e hispánico* 2nd rev. ed., ed. Carmen García de Diego (Madrid: Espasa-Calpe, 1985), 12, *s.v. agujeta*, and 438, *s.v. acúcŭla*; Bodo Müller, *Diccionario del español medieval*, 2 vols. and fascicles 21–26 of vol. 3, Sammlung Romanischer Elementar- und Handbücher, Dritte Reihe: Wörterbücher 12 (Heidelberg, Germany: C. Winter, 1987–), 2:531, *s.v. agujeta*; and Margarita Tejeda Fernández, *Glosario de términos de la indumentaria regia y cortesana en España: Siglos XVII y XVIII* (Málaga, Spain: Universidad de Málaga; Real Academia de Bellas Artes de San Telmo, 2006), 31–32. The reading *"aguxeta"* clearly arose from the perception that the ladies used a decorative ribbon to suspend Torrellas's ashes from their necks.

14. I accept the etymology proposed by Corominas and Pascual, *Diccionario crítico etimológico*, 3:530–531, *s.v. joya*, in which Old French *joie* ('jewel') is considered a back-formation of *joiel*, popularly mistaken for a diminutive form, with both words eventually borrowed into Old Spanish. The same position,

supported by different evidence, is taken in Joan Coromines, Joseph Gulsoy, and Max Cahner, *Diccionari etimològic i complementari de la llengua catalana*, 9 vols. (Barcelona: Curial Edicions Catalanes; Caixa de Pensions "La Caixa," 1980–1991), 4:899–901, *s.v. joiell*. Presumably following the Real Academia Española dictionary, Alonso, *Diccionario medieval español* (2:1274–1275, *s.vv. joya, joyel*) persists in treating *joyel* as a Spanish diminutive of *joya*. Writing in 1943, Juan Terlingen, *Los italianismos en español desde la formación del idioma hasta principios del siglo XVII* (Amsterdam: N.V. Noord-Hollandsche Uitgevers Maatschappij, 1943), 336, classified *joyel* as an Italianism, but his view has been thoroughly discredited; see John Corominas, "Review of J. H. Terlingen, *Los italianismos en español desde la formación del idioma hasta principios del siglo XVII*," *Symposium* 2 (1948): 106–119, 110–111, 113.

15. As I demonstrate in my Ph.D. thesis (Joseph J. Gwara, "A Study of the Works of Juan de Flores, with a Critical Edition of *La historia de Grisel y Mirabella*," 2 vols., Ph.D. thesis, University of London, Westfield College, 1988, 1:289–325), all the sixteenth-century editions descend from an ancestor after *I* (ca. 1495) but prior to *A* (1514). Assuming a regular cycle of reprints, I conjectured that Jacobo Cromberger issued an edition of *Grisel y Mirabella*, now lost, around 1510 (ibid., 427 n. 20).

16. Tejeda Fernández, *Glosario de términos*, 295–296, *q.v.*; see also Priscilla E. Muller, *Jewels in Spain, 1500–1800* (New York: Hispanic Society of America, 1972), 17 and 20, where she glosses *joyel* as "important jewel" and "independent jewel," respectively.

17. On the *faltriquera*, a woman's "pocket" or pouch meant to be worn underneath the outer garment, see Tejeda Fernández, *Glosario de términos*, 247; and for the etymology, Federico Corriente, "Reflejos iberorromances del andalusí {ḫṭr}," *Al-Andalus–Magreb* 1 (1993): 77–87; repr. in Túa Blesa and María Antonia Martín Zorraquino, eds., *Homenaje a Félix Monge: Estudios de lingüística hispánica* (Madrid: Gredos, 1995), 135–141. Corominas and Pascual, *Diccionario crítico etimológico*, 2:842–843, *s.v. faltriquera*, offer copious dialectal observations without proposing an etymology. The most celebrated Old Spanish reference to a *faltriquera*, found in Act III of *Celestina*, suggests that this accessory could be quite capacious; Fernando de Rojas, *La Celestina: Comedia o tragicomedia de Calisto y Melibea*, ed. Peter E. Russell, 3rd rev. ed., Clásicos Castalia 191 (Madrid: Castalia, 2007), 304.

18. P. G. W. Glare, ed., *Oxford Latin Dictionary* (Oxford: Clarendon Press, 1982), 466; see also *Thesaurus linguae latinae*, vol. 4, *con–cyulus* (Leipzig, Germany: Teubner, 1906–1909), cols. 1316–1317, *q.v.*

19. As far as I can tell, "*culter*" retained its ritual connotation in medieval Latin, although the word was used more consistently in the generic sense of 'knife' or 'coulter'; see, e.g., R. E. Latham et al., *Dictionary of Medieval Latin from British Sources*, vol. 1, *A–L* (London: Oxford University Press for The

British Academy, 1975–1997), 1:530, *s.v. culter*; J. F. Niermeyer and C. van de Kieft, *Mediae latinitatis lexicon minus: Lexique latin médiéval—Medieval Latin Dictionary—Mittellateinisches Wörterbuch*, rev. ed., ed. J. W. J. Burgers, 2 vols. (Leiden, Holland: Brill, 2002), 1:374, *q.v.*; R. E. Latham, *Revised Medieval Latin Word-List from British and Irish Sources* (London: Oxford University Press for The British Academy, 1965), 124, *q.v.*; and Walther von Wartburg, *Französisches etymologisches Wörterbuch: Eine Darstellung des galloromanischen Sprachschatzes*, vol. 2.2, *coinquinare–cytisus* (Basel, Germany: Helbing & Lichtenhahn, 1946), 1502–1503, *q.v.* Numerous diminutive forms carried the sense of 'knife, blade,' though not obviously for sacrificial purposes. In Charles du Fresne du Cange, *Glossarium mediæ et infimæ latinitatis*, ed. Léopold Favre, 10 vols. (Niort, France: L. Favre, 1883–1887; repr. in 11 vols., Bologna, Italy: Forni, 1981–1982), 2:650–651, the word is listed under its diminutive forms, with the sense of 'small knife, coulter.' The word is not recorded in Alexander Souter, *A Glossary of Later Latin to 600 A.D.* (Oxford: Clarendon Press, 1949).

20. Enrique de Villena, *Obras completas*, ed. Pedro M. Cátedra, 3 vols. (Madrid: Turner, 1994–2000), 2:314–315; Julio Rodríguez-Puértolas, *Fray Íñigo de Mendoza y sus "Coplas de Vita Christi,"* Biblioteca Románica Hispánica 4, Textos 5 (Madrid: Gredos, 1968), 393–395. In a supplement to his *Tesoro*, originally published in 1611, Sebastián de Covarrubias likewise defines "*cultro*" as "*el cuchillo del sacrificio*"; Sebastián de Covarrubias Horozco, *Tesoro de la lengua castellana o española*, ed. Ignacio Arellano and Rafael Zafra, Biblioteca Áurea Hispánica 21 (Pamplona, Spain: Universidad de Navarra; Madrid: Iberoamericana; Frankfurt am Main, Germany: Vervuert, 2006), 651, *s.v. cuitral*. For additional information, see Alonso, *Diccionario medieval español*, 1:837, *s.v. cultro*; and García de Diego, *Diccionario etimológico*, 18, *s.vv. cuitral, cultral*, and 613, *s.vv. cŭltĕllus, cŭlter, cŭltrālis*. The early sense of 'circumcision scalpel' for *culter* is also recorded in the *Thesaurus linguae latinae*, col. 1316.

21. Ovid, *Metamorphoses*, ed. G. P. Goold, trans. Frank Justus Miller, Loeb Classical Library 42–43 (Cambridge, MA: Harvard University Press; London: Heinemann, 1977–1984), 1:3.511–733.

22. See Antonio de Nebrija, *Introductiones latinae* [Salamanca, Spain, January 16, 1481], ed. Antonio Cortijo and Ángel Gómez Moreno, in *ADMYTE: Archivo digital de manuscritos y textos españoles*, vol. 1 (Madrid: Micronet; Ministerio de Cultura, Biblioteca Nacional, 1992), CD-ROM disc 1, item 7, fol. 52v (*s.v. Nouacula*); Nebrija, *Vocabulario de romance en latín: Transcripción crítica de la edición revisada por el autor (Sevilla, 1516)*, ed. Gerald J. MacDonald (Madrid: Castalia, 1973), 60 (*s.v. cuchillo*), 129 (*s.v. mangorrero cuchillo*), and 187 (*s.v. tiseras*), reprinting the lemmata and glosses from Nebrija, *Vocabulario español-latino (Salamanca ¿1495?)*, facsimile ed.

(Madrid: Real Academia Española, 1951), sigs. d6v, i2r, n1r; Antonio de Nebrija and Gabriel Busa, *Diccionario latín-catalán y catalán-latín (Barcelona, Carles Amorós, 1507)*, ed. Germán Colón and Amadeu-J. Soberanas, Biblioteca Hispánica Puvill, Literatura, Diccionarios 2 (Barcelona: Puvill, 1987), 50 [sig. d1v] (*s.v. culter*) and 183 [sig. B4r] (*s.v. coltell*); Alfonso de Palencia, *Universal vocabulario en latín y en romance: Reproducción facsimilar de la edición de Sevilla, 1490*, 2 vols. (Madrid: Comisión Permanente de la Asociación de Academias de la Lengua Española, 1967), 1: fol. 81v [sig. l1v] (*s.v. clunadum*), fol. 153r [sig. v1r] (*s.v. faliscis*), fol. 165v [sig. x5v] (*s.v. forca*), fol. 218r [sig. 2e2r] (*s.v. instrumentum*), fol. 258r [sig. 2k2r] (*s.v. machera*); 2: fol. 442r [sig. I8r] (*s.v. secespita*). Most of these examples come from the CORDE of the Real Academia Española.

23. In Book VII, a *culter* is used to spill blood in a pair of rejuvenation spells and in a vain sacrifice to Jove to lift the plague in Aegina (Ovid, *Metamorphoses*, 1:7.244, 314, 599). In Book XV, Pythagoras references the *culter* in condemning the ritual slaughter of bulls, while the same weapon is used in sacrifices celebrating the arrival of the serpent-shaped Aesculapius to Tiber Island (ibid., 2:15.134, 735).

24. Ibid., 1:3.712.

25. Juan de Flores, *Grisel y Mirabella*, ed. Maria Grazia Ciccarello di Blasi, Dipartimento di Studi Romanzi, Università di Roma "La Sapienza," Testi, Studi e Manuali 18 (Rome: Bagatto, 2003), 187–188.

26. Ibid., 188.

27. Ibid., 186–187.

28. Gwara, "Study of the Works," 2:1110–1112, note to 45.38–41.

29. Ibid., 2:1112.

30. Francisco Rodríguez Marín, *Dos mil quinientas voces castizas y bien autorizadas que piden lugar en nuestro léxico* (Madrid: privately published, 1922), 101.

31. Juan de Pineda, *Diálogos familiares de la agricultura cristiana*, ed. Juan Meseguer Fernández, Biblioteca de Autores Españoles 161–163, 169–170, 5 vols. (Madrid: Atlas, 1963–1964), 3:340; emphasis added. "In reading Cajetan's *Summa*, I noticed that he addresses this matter—and I am delighted that it has come to my attention in such a timely fashion—and he sets out seven conditions by which to determine whether the devil has been tacitly invoked in any undertaking. The first, he says, is when some vain condition is deemed necessary for a certain outcome, as when holy words are written on parchment and not paper, and at such and such a time and on such and such a day, or in lines of such and such a shape, just as some clerics would offer *cultres* written inside many circles, and made a good living off of foolish women, and even dim-witted men would seek them out; and certainly it is the height of animal stupidity to think that because words are written in a large

or small script, within circles or squares, they are somehow more powerful." Pineda's source is Cajetan's commentary on the *Summa theologiæ* of Aquinas, part II.2, Q. 96 ("De superstitionibus observantiarum"), Art. 4 ("Utrum suspendere divina verba ad collum sit illicitum"). I have consulted the 1588 Venice edition; see Thomas Aquinas, *Summa totius theologiæ S. Thomæ de Aquino doctoris angelici ordinis prædicatorum, cum commentariis et opusculis R. D. D. Thomæ de Vio Caietani Cardinalis S. Xisti*, 3 parts in 5 vols. (Venice, Italy: Apud Iuntas [Giunta], 1588), 2.2: fols. 240v–242v. Cajetan does not reference *cultres* in his remarks (fol. 242r).

32. Fernando Bouza, *Corre manuscrito: Una historia cultural del Siglo de Oro* (Madrid: Marcial Pons, Ediciones de Historia, 2001), 93–108. For more on the postmedieval use of *nóminas* in Spain, chiefly as a means of preventing or curing illness, see Sebastián Cirac Estopañán, *Los procesos de hechicerías en la Inquisición de Castilla la Nueva (tribunales de Toledo y Cuenca)* (Madrid: Consejo Superior de Investigaciones Científicas, Instituto Jerónimo Zurita, 1942), 88–104; Heliodoro Cordente Martínez, *Brujería y hechicería en el obispado de Cuenca*, Divulgación Cultural 2 (Cuenca, Spain: Diputación Provincial de Cuenca, 1990), 105–127; and Tejeda Fernández, *Glosario de términos*, 51–53, *s.v. amuleto*. Pedro Ciruelo, *Reprouacion de las supersticiones y hechizerias*, ed. Alva V. Ebersole (Valencia, Spain: Albatrós, 1978), 77–78, 85–93, provides an invaluable account of textual amulets in the sixteenth century.

33. Bouza, *Corre manuscrito*, 95–96.

34. Don C. Skemer, *Binding Words: Textual Amulets in the Middle Ages* (University Park: Pennsylvania State University Press, 2006), 21–22, 47–58.

35. Ibid., 128–130.

36. Ibid., 17–18.

37. For images of textual amulets with talismanic sigils (Pineda's "*círculos*"), see Skemer, *Binding Words*, 200–201, figs. 5 and 6, reproducing Canterbury Cathedral Library, Add. MS 23, and 215, fig. 7, reproducing British Library, Add. MS 15505, fol. 22r; and especially Cordente Martínez, *Brujería y hechicería*, 106–114. Examples of amuletic texts with such sigils could be multiplied; see, e.g., the German scroll (ca. 1600) sold at Sotheby's on December 7, 2010 (London, Western Manuscripts and Miniatures, sale no. L10241, lot 34).

38. Elisa Ruiz García, *Los libros de Isabel la Católica: Arqueología de un patrimonio escrito* (Salamanca, Spain: Instituto de Historia del Libro y de la Lectura, 2004), 578–579. "1. ¶Two parchment *cultres* without housing. 2. ¶Two more parchment *cultres* without housing. 3. ¶A parchment *cultre* with a devotional image. 4. ¶A parchment *cultre* with a devotional image. 5. ¶A parchment *cultre*. Appraised at two *reales*. Purchased by Juan López, jewelry maker, for sixty-eight *maravedíes*. 6. ¶A miniature *cultre*, on parchment, in

a tiny hand, of Pope Leo's prayer." A marginal note in an inventory from 1505 indicates that Pedro Sarabia took possession of three *cultres*, together with several other manuscripts, on July 10 of that year (ibid., 44 n. 26). The surviving evidence indicates that none of these *cultres* was inherited from Enrique IV; Miguel-Ángel Ladero Quesada, "Capilla, joyas y armas, tapices y libros de Enrique IV de Castilla," *Acta historica et archaeologica mediaevalia* 26 (2005): 851–873.

39. Ruiz García, *Los libros*, 587, *q.v.*

40. Ibid., 182; see also ibid., 252–253.

41. Elisa Ruiz García, "Los *Libros de Horas* en los inventarios de Isabel la Católica," in *De libros, librerías, imprentas y lectores*, ed. Pablo Andrés Escapa, El Libro Antiguo Español 6 (Salamanca, Spain: Universidad de Salamanca, Seminario de Estudios Medievales y Renacentistas, 2002), 389–419, 416–418; see also Ruiz García, *El imaginario de una reina: Páginas selectas del patrimonio escrito de Isabel la Católica* (Madrid: A y N, 2007), 90–92. Ruiz García and Isabel García-Monge, "Una muestra de religiosidad popular: La *Oración de san León*," *Memoria Ecclesiae* 20 (2002): 581–596, place the *Oración de san León* in a wider context, recognizing it as an expression of popular devotion bordering on ritual magic. At the same time, however, they fail to recognize the text as yet another variant of the so-called *prière de Charlemagne*. According to the most common version of the legend, Christ sent this powerful apotropaic prayer to Charlemagne in a Heavenly Letter delivered by Pope Leo III. For details, see Skemer, *Binding Words*, 96–105; and Joseph J. Gwara and Mary Morse, "A Birth Girdle Printed by Wynkyn de Worde," *The Library: Transactions of the Bibliographical Society*, 7th series, 13.1 (2012): 33–62, 40. The diffusion of the prayer in the Iberian Peninsula is studied in Arthur L.-F. Askins, "Notes on Three Prayers in Late 15th Century Portuguese (the *Oração da Empardeada*, the *Oração de S. Leão, Papa*, and the *Justo Juiz*): Text History and Inquisitorial Interdictions," *Península: Revista de Estudios Ibéricos* 4 (2007): 235–266, 249–251; and Víctor Infantes, "El gran hallazgo de un pequeño libro que una vez fue incunable: La *Oración de las ordenanzas de la Iglesia* del Papa León III Magno," *Gutenberg-Jahrbuch* 70 (1995): 93–101.

42. Ruiz García, "Los *Libros de Horas*," 417; see also Ruiz García, *El imaginario*, 90–92; Ruiz García, *Los libros*, 181; and Ruiz García, "Los libros de Isabel la Católica: Una encrucijada de intereses," in *Libro y lectura en la Península Ibérica y América (siglos XIII a XVIII)*, ed. Antonio Castillo Gómez, La Imprenta, Libros y Libreros 11 (Salamanca, Spain: Junta de Castilla y León, Consejería de Cultura y Turismo, 2003), 53–77, 61–62. Although Ruiz García does not mention it, the "*cultre chequito de pergamino*" (item 6) appears to have been the very manuscript removed from one of the two *libelli* (cf. Ruiz García, "Los *Libros de Horas*," 416: "Que pesó dicho librillo, sin el

dicho pergamino *que se le quitó*"—emphasis added). Perhaps one of these *libelli* ended up in the hands of Catalina de Austria, who received in 1519, by order of Carlos V, "un colgante en forma de libro de oro y esmalte" from the treasury of her mother, Juana la Loca. Annemarie Jordan-Gschwend, "Juana de Castilla y Catalina de Austria: La formación de la colección de la reina en Tordesillas y Lisboa," in *Juana I de Castilla, 1504–1555: De su reclusión en Tordesillas al olvido de la historia: I Simposio Internacional sobre la Reina Juana I de Castilla, Tordesillas (Valladolid), 23 y 24 de noviembre de 2005*, ed. Miguel Ángel Zalama (Tordesillas, Spain: Ayuntamiento de Tordesillas, 2006), 143–171, 150 n. 40.

43. Elisa Ruiz García, "La devoción o la búsqueda de la felicidad (1400–1545)," *Litterae: Cuadernos sobre Cultura Escrita* 2 (2002): 41–57, 47–48; Ruiz García, "Proceso de ritualización de algunas devociones privadas," in *Ritos y ceremonias en el mundo hispano durante la edad moderna*, ed. David González Cruz, Collectanea 60 (Huelva, Spain: Universidad de Huelva, 2002), 317–329, 318–319.

44. The surviving inventory is a later copy made by Alonso de Ribera, who assumed his father's office in 1523. The document was edited by Ferrandis, who misdated it to 1545 and failed to record the final disposition of the itemized property. See Miguel Ángel Zamala, *Juana I: Arte, poder y cultura en torno a una reina que no gobernó* (Madrid: Centro de Estudios Europa Hispánica, Dirección General del Libro [Ministerio de Cultura], Sociedad Estatal de Conmemoraciones Culturales, Diputación de Valladolid, 2010), 300–304; Zamala, "El tescro de la reina Juana I en Tordesillas: Relación de su expolio," in *Carlos V y las artes: Promoción artística y familia imperial*, ed. M. J. Redondo Cantera and M. A. Zalama (Valladolid, Spain: Junta de Castilla y León, Consejería de Educación y Cultura; Universidad de Valladolid, 2000), 45–66, 45–46; and Zalama, *Vida cotidiana y arte en el palacio de la reina Juana I en Tordesillas*, Estudios y Documentos 58 (Valladolid, Spain: Universidad de Valladolid, 2000), 379–382.

45. José Ferrandis, ed., *Datos documentales para la historia del arte español*, vol. 3, *Inventarios reales (Juan II a Juana la Loca)* (Madrid: Consejo Superior de Investigaciones Científicas, Instituto Diego Velázquez, 1943), 178. "An enameled *cultre* of pure gold with a chain and a gold P with seven small diamonds and a pendant pearl and a gold pomander filled with ambergris which all together weighed half a mark, one *ochava*, and one-and-a-half *tomines*."

46. Ibid., 197–198. "Two gold *cultres* which weighed fifteen *castellanos* and five *tomines* and eight grains which Diego de Ayala gave her majesty in 1510, according to what appears in another book kept by the aforesaid García de Carreño, which is in the chamber of the *Contaduría de Cuentas*, where it was produced to satisfy the requirements of this accounting."

47. Ruiz García, *Los libros*, 37.

48. Ferrandis, 175.
49. Ibid., 195.
50. Zalama, "El tesoro," 50; Zalama, *Vida cotidiana*, 387. "Another piece of jewelry in the form of a P covered in diamonds with a small seam down the middle, each half of which forms a P, and a pendant pearl, and on the shoulders a P and an H, and said P is attached to a gold *cultre* which has a parchment inside with great mysteries, which weighed, with a small chain, three ounces and six *ochavas* and three *tomines*, and said *cultre* is enameled with inlaid flower enameling with screws above and below, and the *cultre* is shaped like a column." The other part of this *cultre* passed to Juana de Austria upon the death of Juana la Loca; see Zalama, *Vida cotidiana*, 385. Zalama speculates that in 1510 Fernando el Católico plundered Diego de Ayala's two gold *cultres*, which together weighed more than three kilograms, for their melt value. Zalama, "El tesoro," 57; Zalama, *Vida cotidiana*, 405. Both, however, may have passed to don Luis de Rojas, Marqués de Denia, who selected from doña Juana's estate "dos libricos o cultres esmaltados de rosicler y blanco que son para tener reliquias" to satisfy part of an outstanding debt for his services to the queen. Zalama, "El tesoro," 59; Zalama, *Vida cotidiana*, 407.
51. Skemer, *Binding Words*, 158–159, 245–246; New York, Pierpont Morgan Library, M1092.
52. T. Schrire, *Hebrew Magic Amulets: Their Decipherment and Interpretation* (London: Routledge & K. Paul, 1966; repr. New York: Behrman House, 1982), 76. Muller, *Jewels in Spain*, discusses several jewels and jeweled cases which are similar in use and/or design to *cultres*, including a hollow (?) tubular cross described in 1503 (18), a Hispano-Moresque cassolette (23), a reliquary pendant "with two small half-doors" probably from the collection of Juana la Loca (51; cf. the crystal reliquary pendant in fig. 102), a gold articulated *axorca* "enclosing the Mysteries of the Passion" (58), jeweled *libelli* and reliquary crosses, often with pendant pomanders (61–64), and various amuletic lockets (72–74). None of these objects, however, is called a *cultre*. For additional examples of European jewels and enclosures with the same features, many of which are Hispanic, see Jill Hollis, ed., *Princely Magnificence: Court Jewels of the Renaissance, 1500–1630: 15th October 1980–1st February 1981* [exhibition catalogue] (London: Debrett's Peerage for the Victoria and Albert Museum, 1980), 47–48 (no. 8, a prophylactic pendant), 48–50 (no. 11, a girdle prayer book), 51 (no. 13, a *memento mori* pendant), 53 (no. 19, a pectoral cross), 65–66 (nos. 55–56, IHS pendants), 66–67 (no. 58, a talismanic locket), 68–69 (no. 66, a locket), 78–79 (nos. 90–91, lockets), 79 (no. 94, a reliquary cross), 80 (no. 96, a reliquary pendant), 81–84 (nos. 98–111, various pendants, including scent bottles), 89–90 (no. 121, a *memento mori* pendant), and 103–104 (no. P11, a portrait of a Spanish prince wearing an amulet). Of these items, no. 108 (pictured on 81) may be the closest to a

cultre as discussed here, although the pendant is not cylindrical.

53. Ruiz García, "La devoción," 47.

54. See, for example, the image in ibid., 55.

55. Daniel Sperber, *Magic and Folklore in Rabbinic Literature*, Bar-Ilan Studies in Near Eastern Languages and Culture (Ramat-Gan, Israel: Bar-Ilan University Press, 1994), 76–79. For additional examples of *ligaturae* as referenced by the Latin fathers, see Skemer, *Binding Words*, 30–47. For the medieval period, see also Henry Charles Lea, *Materials toward a History of Witchcraft*, ed. Arthur C. Howland, intro. George Lincoln Burr, 3 vols. (Philadelphia: University of Pennsylvania Press, 1939; repr. New York: Thomas Yoseloff, 1957), 1:133, 142, 167, 186, 205, 400; 2:935. In general, Lea speaks of ligatures as binding spells between men and women, mainly husbands and wives, which caused impotence if the man strayed; he does not refer to *cultres*. Carmen Caballero Navas, "Magia: Experiencia femenina y práctica de la relación," in *De dos en dos: Las prácticas de creación y recreación de la vida y la convivencia humana*, ed. Montserrat Cabré i Pairet, et al., Cuadernos Inacabados 38 (Madrid: Horas y Horas, 2000), 33–54, 47–48, specifically relates *glturi* to the binding spells that women were believed to cast in order to secure the love of a man. The meaning of *glturi* as 'amulet' is widely known in the Hebrew exegetical tradition; Sperber, *Magic and Folklore*, 74–75.

56. William Smith and Samuel Cheetham, eds., *A Dictionary of Christian Antiquities*, 2 vols. (London: John Murray, 1875–1880), 2:990–992, *s.v. ligaturae*.

57. Sperber, *Magic and Folklore*, 76.

58. The devoicing of initial /g/ is a rare phenomenon in Spanish but not linguistically implausible: the opposite process, the voicing of initial /k/, is well established in the language (e.g., Lat. CATTUS > Sp. *gato* 'cat'). The initial /k/ in OSp. *cultre* may have something to do with the perception of Hebrew pronunciation in early modern Spain, or it may represent an instinctive realignment with *cult–*, given that *gult–* is an unnatural sound combination in Spanish.

59. Ibid., 71–73. Only a handful of Hebrew words entered Spanish directly instead of through Greek and Latin; many proposed etymologies in fact have been challenged. If we omit technical borrowings (mostly religious), the standard short list of Spanish Hebraisms includes *desmazalado* 'miserable, weak, unfortunate'; see David M. Bunis, *A Lexicon of the Hebrew and Aramaic Elements in Modern Judezmo* (Jerusalem: Magnes Press, Hebrew University of Jerusalem; Misgav Yerushalayim, Institute for Research on the Sephardi and Oriental Jewish Heritage, 1993), 19; Corominas and Pascual, *Diccionario crítico etimológico*, 2:469–470, *q.v.*; Yakov Malkiel, "A Latin-Hebrew Blend: Hispanic *desmazalado*," *Hispanic Review* 15 (1947): 272–301; Paul Wexler, *Three Heirs to a Judeo-Latin Legacy: Judeo-Ibero-Romance,*

Yiddish and Rotwelsch, Mediterranean Language and Culture Monograph Series 3 (Wiesbaden, Germany: Otto Harrassowitz, 1988), 74 n. 397; *malsín,* 'slanderer, informer'; see Salustio Alvarado, "Hebraísmos en español y búlgaro," *Boletín de la Real Academia Española* 71 (1991): 133–156, 139; Bunis, *A Lexicon,* 19; Corominas and Pascual, *Diccionario crítico etimológico,* 3:787, *q.v.;* Norman Roth, "La lengua hebrea entre los cristianos españoles medievales: Voces hebreas en español," *Revista de Filología Española* 71 (1991): 137–143, 141; Wexler, *Three Heirs,* 68, 72; *máncer* 'bastard'; see Alvarado, "Hebraísmos," 139; Bunis, *A Lexicon,* 19; Corominas and Pascual, *Diccionario crítico etimológico,* 3:795–96, *q.v.; tacaño* 'miserly, cheap'; see Alvarado, "Hebraísmos," 143; Corominas and Pascual, *Diccionario crítico etimológico,* 5:363–67, *q.v.;* Yakov Malkiel, "Dubious, Pseudo-, Hybrid, and Mock-Orientalisms in Romance," in *Semitic Studies in Honor of Wolf Leslau on the Occasion of his Eighty-Fifth Birthday, November 14th, 1991,* ed. Alan S. Kaye, 2 vols. (Wiesbaden, Germany: Otto Harrassowitz, 1991), 2:991–1003, 996–998; Wexler, *Three Heirs,* 72 n. 378; and *trefa/trefe* 'not kosher, unfit for consumption by Jews'; see Alvarado, "Hebraísmos," 144; Corominas and Pascual, *Diccionario crítico etimológico,* 5:616–618, *s.v. trefe;* Roth, "La lengua hebrea," 142. Lists of unincorporated Spanish Hebraisms, culled from administrative records and a few literary sources, can be found in Roth, "La lengua hebrea," 140–142; Paul Wexler, "Marrano Ibero-Romance: Classification and Research Tasks," *Zeitschrift für Romanische Philologie* 98 (1982): 59–108, 76–78; and Wexler, *Three Heirs,* 64–75 (§1.5). I am indebted to Steven Dworkin for his expert advice on Old Spanish Hebraisms and especially for sharing with me his unpublished material on the subject.
60. Overviews of the Jewish amuletic tradition and Christian perceptions of it can be found in Schrire, *Hebrew Magic Amulets,* 69–73; and Skemer, *Binding Words,* 33–37, 112–115. See also Juan Blázquez Miguel, *Huete y su tierra: Un enclave inquisitorial conquense* (Huete, Spain: Ayuntamiento de Huete; Madrid: Librería Anticuaria Jerez, 1987), 58–59; Bouza, *Corre manuscrito,* 95; and for an illustration of a Hebrew amulet with *characteres,* Cordente Martínez, *Brujería y hechicería,* 115. David M. Gitlitz, *Secrecy and Deceit: The Religion of the Crypto-Jews* (Philadelphia: Jewish Publication Society, 1996), 194 n. 10, reports that the Sephardic museum in Toledo owns a fifteenth-century Hebrew amulet.
61. Gitlitz, *Secrecy and Deceit,* 186–187, 437 n. 13. For sample documentation and trial testimony, see Yitzhak Baer, *A History of the Jews in Christian Spain,* 2nd ed., trans. Louis Schoffman, 2 vols. (Philadelphia: Jewish Publication Society, 1992), 2:338, 352, 360; and Haim Beinart, ed., *Records of the Trials of the Spanish Inquisition in Ciudad Real,* 4 vols. (Jerusalem: Israel National Academy of Sciences and Humanities, 1974–1985), 1:xxxii, 58, 275, 277, 367, 369, 372, 389–390, 393, 420; 4:413. Skemer, *Binding Words,* 231 has

general remarks on amulets discovered by the Spanish Inquisition.

62. Gitlitz, *Secrecy and Deceit*, 184.

63. David M. Bunis, "Distinctive Characteristics of Jewish Ibero-Romance, circa 1492," *Hispania Judaica Bulletin* 4 (2004): 105–137, 136–137.

64. For general information on converso poetry, especially the incorporation of Hebrew words, I have consulted Cristina Arbós, "Los cancioneros castellanos del siglo XV como fuente para la historia de los judíos españoles," in *Jews and Conversos: Studies in Society and the Inquisition: Proceedings of the Eighth World Congress of Jewish Studies held at the Hebrew University of Jerusalem, August 16–21, 1981*, ed. Yosef Kaplan (Jerusalem: World Union of Jewish Studies; Magnes Press, Hebrew University of Jerusalem, 1985), 74–82, 79–80; Francisco Cantera Burgos, "El *Cancionero de Baena*: Judíos y conversos en él," *Sefarad* 27 (1967): 71–111; Gitlitz, *Secrecy and Deceit*, 475–479; Gregory B. Kaplan, *The Evolution of "Converso" Literature: The Writings of the Converted Jews of Medieval Spain* (Gainesville: University Press of Florida, 2002); Francisco Márquez Villanueva, "Jewish 'Fools' of the Spanish Fifteenth Century," *Hispanic Review* 50 (1982): 385–409; and Josep M. Sola-Solé and Stanley E. Rose, "Judíos y conversos en la poesía cortesana del siglo XV: El estilo políglota de Fray Diego de Valencia," *Hispanic Review* 44 (1976): 371–385.

65. Francisco Márquez Villanueva, "Conversos y cargos concejiles en el siglo XV," *Revista de Archivos, Bibliotecas y Museos* 63 (1957): 503–540; María del Pilar Rábade Obradó, *Una élite de poder en la corte de los Reyes Católicos: Los judeoconversos* (Madrid: Sigilo, 1993), 25–31; Norman Roth, *Conversos, Inquisition, and the Expulsion of the Jews from Spain*, rev. ed. (Madison: University of Wisconsin Press, 2002), 126–133; Julio Valdeón Baruque, "Motivaciones socioeconómicas de las fricciones entre viejocristianos, judíos y conversos," in *Judíos, sefarditas, conversos: La expulsión de 1492 y sus consecuencias*, ed. Ángel Alcalá (Valladolid, Spain: Ámbito, 1995), 69–88, 81.

66. Joseph J. Gwara, "The Identity of Juan de Flores: The Evidence of the *Crónica Incompleta de los Reyes Católicos*," *Journal of Hispanic Philology* 11 (1986–1987): 103–130, 205–222, 214–218.

67. *Registro general del sello*, 16 vols. (Valladolid, Spain: Consejo Superior de Investigaciones Científicas, 1950–1992), 2:23 no. 165, 37 no. 275, 290 no. 2064, 358 no. 2528, 377 no. 1972; 3:32 no. 230, with many additional entries that probably refer to the same dispute.

68. Ibid., 8:30 no. 213, 495 no. 3369, 499 no. 3394; 9:239 no. 1531, 310 no. 1990, plus other related entries; 10:487 no. 2621, 228 no. 1193; 11:223 no. 1492, 315 no. 2075. The Receiver of Goods was a royal official who safeguarded the interests of the Crown while serving on the Inquisitorial Court; Haim Beinart, "Two Documents Concerning Confiscated Converso

Property," *Sefarad* 17 (1957): 280–313, 281. For more detailed information, see Henry Charles Lea, *A History of the Inquisition of Spain*, 4 vols. (New York and London: Macmillan, 1906–1907), 2:315–387.

69. Gwara, "The Identity," 116–119, 221–222; on the Osorio connection, see also Joseph J. Gwara, "A New Epithalamial Allegory by Juan de Flores: *La coronación de la señora Gracisla* (1475)," *Revista de Estudios Hispánicos* (St. Louis) 30 (1996): 227–257, 252 n. 3.

70. Dayle Seidenspinner-Núñez, "Conversion and Subversion: Converso Texts in Fifteenth-Century Spain," in *Christians, Muslims, and Jews in Medieval and Early Modern Spain: Interaction and Cultural Change*, ed. Mark D. Meyerson and Edward D. English, Notre Dame Conferences in Medieval Studies 8 (Notre Dame, IN: University of Notre Dame Press, 1999), 241–261, 259–260 n. 25; the contract is discussed in Carmen Parrilla, "Un cronista olvidado: Juan de Flores, autor de la *Crónica incompleta de los Reyes Católicos*," in *The Age of the Catholic Monarchs, 1476–1516: Literary Studies in Memory of Keith Whinnom*, ed. Alan Deyermond and Ian Macpherson, *Bulletin of Hispanic Studies*, Special Issue (Liverpool, UK: Liverpool University Press, 1989), 123–133, 126–127, 131.

71. Seidenspinner-Núñez, "Conversion," 259–260 n. 25. For analogous cases of middle-class conversos in Toledo, see Linda Martz, "Converso Families in Fifteenth- and Sixteenth-Century Toledo: The Significance of Lineage," *Sefarad* 48 (1988): 117–196, 162–166. The entries in the *Registro general del sello* identify the *corregidor/pesquisidor* Juan de Flores as a *"vecino de Toledo,"* but the name Flores does not appear in any of the Inquisitorial records analyzed by Martz nor in Roth's list of common converso surnames in Toledo; Roth, *Conversos*, 378.

72. By way of comparison, no fewer than five conversos named Diego Sánchez de San Pedro lived in late fifteenth- and early sixteenth-century Toledo. Even the Inquisition had difficulty telling them apart. Martz, "Converso Families," 126, 141–142.

73. Roth, *Conversos*, 177–178, 181.

74. Ibid., 93.

75. Seidenspinner-Núñez, "Conversion," 247.

76. Ibid., 250–253.

77. For further information on converso leanings in sentimental romances, see Francisco Márquez Villanueva, "*Cárcel de amor*, novela política," *Revista de occidente* 14 (1966): 185–200; Márquez Villanueva, "Historia cultural e historia literaria: El caso de *Cárcel de amor*," in *The Analysis of Hispanic Texts: Current Trends in Methodology*, ed. Lisa E. Davis and Isabel C. Tarán, Second York College Colloquium (New York: Bilingual Press, 1976), 144–157; and Regula Rohland de Langbehn, "El problema de los conversos y la novela sentimental," in *The Age of the Catholic Monarchs, 1476–1516:*

Literary Studies in Memory of Keith Whinnom, ed. Alan Deyermond and Ian Macpherson, *Bulletin of Hispanic Studies*, Special Issue (Liverpool, UK: Liverpool University Press, 1989), 134–143. Considerably more has been written on the legal and political aspects of Flores's works, especially the theme of repression under absolute monarchy; see, e.g., E. Michael Gerli, "Gender Trouble: Juan de Flores's *Triunfo de Amor*, Isabel la Católica, and the Economies of Power at Court," *Journal of Spanish Cultural Studies* 4 (2003): 169–184; Álvaro R. González, "La figura del poder en *Grisel y Mirabella*," *Romance Languages Annual* 11 (2000): 465–469; and Helen Cathleen Tarp, "Legal Fictions: Literature and Law in *Grisel y Mirabella*," *eHumanista* 7 (2006): 95–114, available at http://www.ehumanista.ucsb.edu/volumes/ volume_07/index.shtml. Antonio Cortijo Ocaña postulates a personal connection linking Flores, Pere Torroella, and the Lucena family as a part of his case for a proto-Celestinesque genre emanating from the University of Salamanca, where Luis de Lucena, author of the *Repetición de amores*, may have known Fernando de Rojas; Antonio Cortijo Ocaña, *La evolución genérica de la ficción sentimental de los siglos XV y XVI: Género literario y contexto social*, Colección Támesis, Serie A: Monografías 184 (London: Tamesis, 2001), 192–211; and Cortijo Ocaña, "An Inane Hypothesis: Torroella, Flores, Lucena, and *Celestina*?" in *Multicultural Iberia: Language, Literature, and Music*, ed. Dru Dougherty and Milton A. Azevedo, Research Series 103 (Berkeley: University of California at Berkeley, 1999), 40–56, available at http://escholarship.org/uc/item/53p1j36j. To his list of commonalities we should now add, crucially, the writers' converso origins and/or sympathies.
78. Martz, "Converso Families," 165–166.
79. Alonso López de Haro, *Nobiliario genealógico de los reyes y títulos de España*, 2 vols. (Madrid: Luis Sánchez, 1622; facsimile repr. Ollobarren, Navarre, Spain: Wilsen, 1996), 1:430, 434.
80. S: "Oh, how hostile and wretched you show yourself to be, Torrellas, it seems that you were born to malign us!"; TI: "I now perceive you to be so wretched and hostile, Torrellas, that it appears that if you found anything useful at the altar to curse us with, you would take it from there without conscience!"
81. Skemer, *Binding Words*, 135.
82. Writing in 1420–1425, Enrique de Villena described the use of a "*manezuela*" against the evil eye, listing many other popular protections against the same threat, including sacred *libelli* and textual amulets; Enrique de Villena, *Obras completas*, ed. Pedro M. Cátedra, 3 vols. (Madrid: Turner, 1994–2000) 1:332–333. He does not mention *cultres*. See also Muller, *Jewels in Spain*, 23–24, pls. 29 and 30, documenting the use of *higas* to protect royalty as late as 1602 and 1607.
83. Rafael Salillas, *La fascinación en España: Brujas, brujerías, amuletos*

(Madrid: ptd. Eduardo Arias, 1905; repr. Barcelona: MRA, 2000), 77–80; for images, see Muller, *Jewels in Spain*, 69, fig. 94; and G. J. de Osma, *Catálogo de azabaches compostelanos precedido de apuntes sobre los amuletos contra el aojo, las imágenes del Apóstol-Romero y la Cofradía de los Azabacheros de Santiago* (Madrid: n.p., 1916), 1–28, 181–182, 209–210, 221–222, 224–227, 233–234.
84. Gwara, "La muger y la sardina," 66–67.

WORKS CITED

Alonso, Martín. *Diccionario medieval español: Desde las Glosas emilianenses y silenses (s. X) hasta el siglo XV*. 2 vols. Salamanca, Spain: Universidad Pontificia de Salamanca, 1986.

Alvarado, Salustio. "Hebraísmos en español y búlgaro." *Boletín de la Real Academia Española* 71 (1991): 133–156.

Aquinas, Thomas. *Summa totius theologiæ S. Thomæ de Aquino doctoris angelici ordinis prædicatorum, cum commentariis et opusculis R. D. D. Thomæ de Vio Caietani Cardinalis S. Xisti*. 3 parts in 5 vols. Venice, Italy: Apud Iuntas [Giunta], 1588.

Arbós, Cristina. "Los cancioneros castellanos del siglo XV como fuente para la historia de los judíos españoles." In *Jews and Conversos: Studies in Society and the Inquisition: Proceedings of the Eighth World Congress of Jewish Studies held at the Hebrew University of Jerusalem, August 16–21, 1981*, ed. Yosef Kaplan. Jerusalem: World Union of Jewish Studies; Magnes Press, Hebrew University of Jerusalem, 1985, 74–82.

Askins, Arthur L.-F. "Notes on Three Prayers in Late 15th Century Portuguese (the *Oração da Empardeada*, the *Oração de S. Leão, Papa*, and the *Justo Juiz*): Text History and Inquisitorial Interdictions." *Península: Revista de Estudios Ibéricos* 4 (2007): 235–266.

Baer, Yitzhak. *A History of the Jews in Christian Spain*. 2nd ed. Translated by Louis Schoffman. 2 vols. Philadelphia: Jewish Publication Society, 1992.

Beinart, Haim, ed. *Records of the Trials of the Spanish Inquisition in Ciudad Real*. 4 vols. Jerusalem: Israel National Academy of Sciences and Humanities, 1974–1985.

——. "Two Documents Concerning Confiscated Converso Property." *Sefarad* 17 (1957): 280–313.

Bernis, Carmen. *Trajes y modas en la España de los Reyes Católicos*, vol. 1, *Las mujeres*; vol. 2, *Los hombres*. 2 vols. Madrid: Instituto Diego Velázquez, Consejo Superior de Investigaciones Científicas, 1978–1979.

Blázquez Miguel, Juan. *Huete y su tierra: Un enclave inquisitorial conquense*. Huete, Spain: Ayuntamiento de Huete; Madrid: Librería Anticuaria Jerez, 1987.

Bouza, Fernando. *Corre manuscrito: Una historia cultural del Siglo de Oro.* Madrid: Marcial Pons, Ediciones de Historia, 2001.

Brownlee, Marina S. "Language and Incest in *Grisel y Mirabella.*" *Romanic Review* 79 (1988): 107–128.

———. *The Severed Word: Ovid's "Heroides" and the "Novela Sentimental."* Princeton, NJ: Princeton University Press, 1990.

———. "Verbal and Physical Violence in the *Historie of Aurelio and Isabell.*" In *Vengeance in the Middle Ages: Emotion, Religion and Feud*, ed. Susanna A. Throop and Paul R. Hyams. Farnham, UK: Ashgate, 2010, 137–150.

Bunis, David M. "Distinctive Characteristics of Jewish Ibero-Romance, circa 1492." *Hispania Judaica Bulletin* 4 (2004): 105–137.

———. *A Lexicon of the Hebrew and Aramaic Elements in Modern Judezmo.* Jerusalem: Magnes Press, Hebrew University of Jerusalem; Misgav Yerushalayim, Institute for Research on the Sephardi and Oriental Jewish Heritage, 1993.

Caballero Navas, Carmen. "Magia: Experiencia femenina y práctica de la relación." In *De dos en dos: Las prácticas de creación y recreación de la vida y la convivencia humana*, ed. Montserrat Cabré i Pairet, et al. Cuadernos Inacabados 38. Madrid: Horas y Horas, 2000, 33–54.

Cantera Burgos, Francisco. "El *Cancionero de Baena*: Judíos y conversos en él." *Sefarad* 27 (1967): 71–111.

Cejador y Frauca, Julio. *Vocabulario medieval castellano.* Madrid: Hernando, 1929; repr. New York: Las Americas, 1968.

Checa, Jorge. "*Grisel y Mirabella* de Juan de Flores: Rebeldía y violencia como síntomas de crisis." *Revista Canadiense de Estudios Hispánicos* 12 (1987–1988): 369–382.

Cirac Estopañán, Sebastián. *Los procesos de hechicerías en la Inquisición de Castilla la Nueva (tribunales de Toledo y Cuenca).* Madrid: Consejo Superior de Investigaciones Científicas, Instituto Jerónimo Zurita, 1942.

Ciruelo, Pedro. *Reprouacion de las supersticiones y hechizerias.* Edited by Alva V. Ebersole. Valencia, Spain: Albatrós, 1978.

Cordente Martínez, Heliodoro. *Brujería y hechicería en el obispado de Cuenca.* Divulgación Cultural 2. Cuenca, Spain: Diputación Provincial de Cuenca, 1990.

Corominas, John. Review of J. H. Terlingen, *Los italianismos en español desde la formación del idioma hasta principios del siglo XVII. Symposium* 2 (1948): 106–119.

Corominas, Juan, and José A. Pascual. *Diccionario crítico etimológico castellano e hispánico.* Biblioteca Románica Hispánica, V (Diccionarios) 7. 6 vols. Madrid: Gredos, 1980–1991.

Coromines, Joan, Joseph Gulsoy, and Max Cahner. *Diccionari etimològic i complementari de la llengua catalana*. 9 vols. Barcelona: Curial Edicions Catalanes; Caixa de Pensions "La Caixa," 1980–1991.

Corriente, Federico. "Reflejos iberorromances del andalusí {ḥṭr}." *Al-Andalus–Magreb* 1 (1993): 77–87; repr. in Túa Blesa and María Antonia Martín Zorraquino, eds., *Homenaje a Félix Monge: Estudios de lingüística hispánica*. Madrid: Gredos, 1995, 135–141.

Cortijo Ocaña, Antonio. *La evolución genérica de la ficción sentimental de los siglos XV y XVI: Género literario y contexto social*. Colección Támesis, Serie A: Monografías 184. London: Tamesis, 2001.

——. "An Inane Hypothesis: Torroella, Flores, Lucena, and *Celestina*?" In *Multicultural Iberia: Language, Literature, and Music*, ed. Dru Dougherty and Milton A. Azevedo. Research Series 103. Berkeley: University of California at Berkeley, 1999, 40–56. Available at http://escholarship. org/uc/item/53p1j36j.

Covarrubias Horozco, Sebastián de. *Tesoro de la lengua castellana o española*. Edited by Ignacio Arellano and Rafael Zafra. Biblioteca Áurea Hispánica 21. Pamplona, Spain: Universidad de Navarra; Madrid: Iberoamericana; Frankfurt am Main, Germany: Vervuert, 2006.

Crespo Martín, Patricia. "Violencia mitológica en *Grisel y Mirabella*." *La corónica* 29.1 (2000): 75–87.

Cull, John T. "Irony, Romance Conventions, and Misogyny in *Grisel y Mirabella* by Juan de Flores." *Revista Canadiense de Estudios Hispánicos* 22 (1997–1998): 415–430.

Deyermond, Alan D. "El hombre salvaje en la novela sentimental." *Filología* 10 (1964 [1966]): 97–111; repr. with additions in Alan D. Deyermond, *Tradiciones y puntos de vista en la ficción sentimental*. Publicaciones de Medievalia 5. Mexico City: Universidad Nacional Autónoma de México, 1993, 17–42.

Diccionario histórico de la lengua española, vol. 2, *B–Cevilla*. Madrid: Academia Española, 1936.

Diez, Friedrich. *Etymologisches Wörterbuch der romanischen Sprachen*. 5th ed. Bonn: Adolph Marcus, 1887.

Du Cange, Charles du Fresne. *Glossarium mediæ et infimæ latinitatis*. Edited by Léopold Favre. 10 vols. Niort, France: L. Favre, 1883–1887; repr. in 11 vols. Bologna, Italy: Forni, 1981–1982.

Ferrandis, José, ed. *Datos documentales para la historia del arte español*, vol. 3, *Inventarios reales (Juan II a Juana la Loca)*. Madrid: Consejo Superior de Investigaciones Científicas, Instituto Diego Velázquez, 1943.

Flores, Juan de. *Grisel y Mirabella*. Edited by Maria Grazia Ciccarello di Blasi. Dipartimento di Studi Romanzi, Università di Roma "La Sapienza," Testi, Studi e Manuali 18. Rome: Bagatto, 2003.

———. *La historia de Grisel y Mirabella*. Edited by Joseph J. Gwara.

García de Diego, Vicente. *Diccionario etimológico español e hispánico*. 2nd rev. ed. Edited by Carmen García de Diego. Madrid: Espasa-Calpe, 1955.

Gerli, E. Michael. "Gender Trouble: Juan de Flores's *Triunfo de Amor*, Isabel la Católica, and the Economies of Power at Court." *Journal of Spanish Cultural Studies* 4 (2003): 169–184.

Gitlitz, David M. *Secrecy and Deceit: The Religion of the Crypto-Jews*. Philadelphia: Jewish Publication Society, 1996.

Glare, P. G. W., ed. *Oxford Latin Dictionary*. Oxford: Clarendon Press, 1982.

González, Álvaro R. "La figura del poder en *Grisel y Mirabella*." *Romance Languages Annual* 11 (2000): 465–469.

Gwara, Joseph J. "The Identity of Juan de Flores: The Evidence of the *Crónica Incompleta de los Reyes Católicos*." *Journal of Hispanic Philology* 11 (1986–1987): 103–130, 205–222.

———. "'La muger y la sardina, de rostros en la ceniza': An Old Spanish Proverb in *Grisel y Mirabella*." In *Juan de Flores: Four Studies*, ed. Joseph J. Gwara. Papers of the Medieval Hispanic Research Seminar 49. London: Department of Hispanic Studies, Queen Mary, University of London, 2005, 49–73.

———. "A New Epithalamial Allegory by Juan de Flores: *La coronación de la señora Gracisla* (1475)." *Revista de Estudios Hispánicos* (St. Louis) 30 (1996): 227–257.

———. "A Study of the Works of Juan de Flores, with a Critical Edition of *La historia de Grisel y Mirabella*." 2 vols. Ph.D. thesis, University of London (Westfield College), 1988.

Gwara, Joseph J., and Mary Morse. "A Birth Girdle Printed by Wynkyn de Worde," *The Library: Transactions of the Bibliographical Society*, 7th series 13.1 (2012): 33-62.

Hollis, Jill, ed. *Princely Magnificence: Court Jewels of the Renaissance, 1500–1630: 15th October 1980–1st February 1981* [exhibition catalogue]. London: Debrett's Peerage for the Victoria and Albert Museum, 1980.

Infantes, Víctor. "El gran hallazgo de un pequeño libro que una vez fue incunable: La *Oración de las ordenanzas de la Iglesia* del Papa León III Magno." *Gutenberg-Jahrbuch* 70 (1995): 93–101.

Jordan-Gschwend, Annemarie. "Juana de Castilla y Catalina de Austria: La formación de la colección de la reina en Tordesillas y Lisboa." In *Juana I de Castilla, 1504–1555: De su reclusión en Tordesillas al olvido de la historia: I Simposio Internacional sobre la Reina Juana I de Castilla, Tordesillas (Valladolid), 23 y 24 de noviembre de 2005*, ed. Miguel Ángel Zalama. Tordesillas, Spain: Ayuntamiento de Tordesillas, 2006, 143–171.

Kaplan, Gregory B. *The Evolution of "Converso" Literature: The Writings of the Converted Jews of Medieval Spain*. Gainesville: University Press of Florida, 2002.

Ladero Quesada, Miguel-Ángel. "Capilla, joyas y armas, tapices y libros de Enrique IV de Castilla." *Acta historica et archaeologica mediaevalia* 26 (2005): 851–873.

Latham, R. E. *Revised Medieval Latin Word-List from British and Irish Sources*. London: Oxford University Press for The British Academy, 1965.

Latham, R. E., et al. *Dictionary of Medieval Latin from British Sources*, vol. 1, *A–L*. London: Oxford University Press for The British Academy, 1975–1997.

Lea, Henry Charles. *A History of the Inquisition of Spain*. 4 vols. New York and London: Macmillan, 1906–1907.

———. *Materials toward a History of Witchcraft*. Edited by Arthur C. Howland. Introduction by George Lincoln Burr. 3 vols. Philadelphia: University of Pennsylvania Press, 1939; repr. New York: Thomas Yoseloff, 1957.

López de Haro, Alonso. *Nobiliario genealógico de los reyes y títulos de España*. 2 vols. Madrid: Luis Sánchez, 1622; facsimile repr. Ollobarren, Navarre, Spain: Wilsen, 1996.

Malkiel, Yakov. "Dubious, Pseudo-, Hybrid, and Mock-Orientalisms in Romance." In *Semitic Studies in Honor of Wolf Leslau on the Occasion of his Eighty-Fifth Birthday, November 14th, 1991*, ed. Alan S. Kaye. 2 vols. Wiesbaden, Germany: Otto Harrassowitz, 1991, 2:991–1003.

———. "A Latin-Hebrew Blend: Hispanic *desmazalado*." *Hispanic Review* 15 (1947): 272–301.

Márquez Villanueva, Francisco. "*Cárcel de amor*, novela política." *Revista de occidente* 14 (1966): 185–200.

———. "Conversos y cargos concejiles en el siglo XV." *Revista de Archivos, Bibliotecas y Museos* 63 (1957): 503–540.

———. "Historia cultural e historia literaria: El caso de *Cárcel de amor*." In *The Analysis of Hispanic Texts: Current Trends in Methodology*, ed. Lisa E. Davis and Isabel C. Tarán. Second York College Colloquium. New York: Bilingual Press, 1976, 144–157.

———. "Jewish 'Fools' of the Spanish Fifteenth Century." *Hispanic Review* 50 (1982): 385–409.

Martz, Linda. "Converso Families in Fifteenth- and Sixteenth-Century Toledo: The Significance of Lineage." *Sefarad* 48 (1988): 117–196.

Matulka, Barbara. *The Novels of Juan de Flores and Their European Diffusion: A Study in Comparative Literature*. New York: Institute of French Studies, 1931; repr. Geneva: Slatkine, 1974.

Müller, Bodo. *Diccionario del español medieval*. 2 vols. and fascicles 21–26 of vol. 3. Sammlung Romanischer Elementar- und Handbücher, Dritte Reihe: Wörterbücher 12. Heidelberg, Germany: C. Winter, 1987–.

Muller, Priscilla E. *Jewels in Spain, 1500–1800*. New York: Hispanic Society of America, 1972.

Nebrija, Antonio de. *Introductiones latinae* [Salamanca, Spain, January 16, 1481]. Edited by Antonio Cortijo and Ángel Gómez Moreno. In *ADMYTE: Archivo digital de manuscritos y textos españoles*. Vol. 1. Madrid: Micronet; Ministerio de Cultura, Biblioteca Nacional, 1992.

——. *Vocabulario de romance en latín: Transcripción crítica de la edición revisada por el autor (Sevilla, 1516)*. Edited by Gerald J. MacDonald. Madrid: Castalia, 1973.

——. *Vocabulario español-latino (Salamanca ¿1495?)*. Facsimile ed. Madrid: Real Academia Española, 1951.

Nebrija, Antonio de, and Gabriel Busa. *Diccionario latín-catalán y catalán-latín (Barcelona, Carles Amorós, 1507)*. Edited by Germán Colón and Amadeu-J. Soberanas. Biblioteca Hispánica Puvill, Literatura, Diccionarios 2. Barcelona: Puvill, 1987.

Niermeyer, J. F., and C. van de Kieft. *Mediae latinitatis lexicon minus: Lexique latin médiéval—Medieval Latin Dictionary—Mittellateinisches Wörterbuch*. Rev. ed., ed. J. W. J. Burgers. 2 vols. Leiden, Holland: Brill, 2002.

Osma, G. J. de. *Catálogo de azabaches compostelanos precedido de apuntes sobre los amuletos contra el aojo, las imágenes del Apóstol-Romero y la Cofradía de los Azabacheros de Santiago*. Madrid: n.p., 1916.

Ovid. *Metamorphoses*. Edited by G. P. Goold. Translated by Frank Justus Miller. Loeb Classical Library 42–43. Cambridge, MA: Harvard University Press; London: Heinemann, 1977–1984.

Palencia, Alfonso de. *Universal vocabulario en latín y en romance: Reproducción facsimilar de la edición de Sevilla, 1490*. 2 vols. Madrid: Comisión Permanente de la Asociación de Academias de la Lengua Española, 1967.

Parrilla, Carmen. "Un cronista olvidado: Juan de Flores, autor de la *Crónica incompleta de los Reyes Católicos*." In *The Age of the Catholic Monarchs, 1476–1516: Literary Studies in Memory of Keith Whinnom*, ed. Alan Deyermond and Ian Macpherson. *Bulletin of Hispanic Studies*, Special Issue. Liverpool, UK: Liverpool University Press, 1989, 123–133.

Petro, Antonia. "La tradición de la mujer monstruo en *Grisel y Mirabella*." *Crítica Hispánica* 29.1–2 (2007): 213–233.

Pineda, Juan de. *Diálogos familiares de la agricultura cristiana*. Edited by Juan Meseguer Fernández. Biblioteca de Autores Españoles 161–163, 169–170. 5 vols. Madrid: Atlas, 1963–1964.

Prieto-Calixto, Alberto. "Mujeres y caníbales: Rituales violentos en *Grisel y Mirabella* de Juan de Flores." *Cincinnati Romance Review* 21 (2002): 77–90.

Rábade Obradó, María del Pilar. *Una élite de poder en la corte de los Reyes Católicos: Los judeoconversos.* Madrid: Sigilo, 1993.

Registro general del sello. 16 vols. Valladolid, Spain: Consejo Superior de Investigaciones Científicas, 1950–1992.

Rodríguez Marín, Francisco. *Dos mil quinientas voces castizas y bien autorizadas que piden lugar en nuestro léxico.* Madrid: privately published, 1922.

Rodríguez-Puértolas, Julio. *Fray Íñigo de Mendoza y sus "Coplas de Vita Christi."* Biblioteca Románica Hispánica 4Textos 5. Madrid: Gredos, 1968.

Rohland de Langbehn, Regula. "El problema de los conversos y la novela sentimental." In *The Age of the Catholic Monarchs, 1476–1516: Literary Studies in Memory of Keith Whinnom,* ed. Alan Deyermond and Ian Macpherson. *Bulletin of Hispanic Studies,* Special Issue. Liverpool, UK: Liverpool University Press, 1989, 134–143.

Rojas, Fernando de. *La Celestina: Comedia o tragicomedia de Calisto y Melibea.* Edited by Peter E. Russell. 3rd rev. ed. Clásicos Castalia 191. Madrid: Castalia, 2007.

Roth, Norman. *Conversos, Inquisition, and the Expulsion of the Jews from Spain.* Rev. ed. Madison: University of Wisconsin Press, 2002.

———. "La lengua hebrea entre los cristianos españoles medievales: Voces hebreas en español." *Revista de Filología Española* 71 (1991): 137–143.

Ruiz García, Elisa. "La devoción o la búsqueda de la felicidad (1400–1545)." *Litterae: Cuadernos sobre Cultura Escrita* 2 (2002): 41–57.

———. *El imaginario de una reina: Páginas selectas del patrimonio escrito de Isabel la Católica.* Madrid: A y N, 2007.

———. "Los *Libros de Horas* en los inventarios de Isabel la Católica." In *De libros, librerías, imprentas y lectores,* ed. Pablo Andrés Escapa. El Libro Antiguo Español 6. Salamanca, Spain: Universidad de Salamanca, Seminario de Estudios Medievales y Renacentistas, 2002, 389–419.

———. *Los libros de Isabel la Católica: Arqueología de un patrimonio escrito.* Salamanca, Spain: Instituto de Historia del Libro y de la Lectura, 2004.

———. "Los libros de Isabel la Católica: Una encrucijada de intereses." In *Libro y lectura en la Península Ibérica y América (siglos XIII a XVIII),* ed. Antonio Castillo Gómez. La Imprenta, Libros y Libreros 11. Salamanca, Spain: Junta de Castilla y León, Consejería de Cultura y Turismo, 2003, 53–77.

———. "Proceso de ritualización de algunas devociones privadas." In *Ritos y ceremonias en el mundo hispano durante la edad moderna,* ed. David González Cruz. Collectanea 60. Huelva, Spain: Universidad de Huelva, 2002, 317–329.

Ruiz García, Elisa, and Isabel García-Monge. "Una muestra de religiosidad popular: La *Oración de san León.*" *Memoria Ecclesiae* 20 (2002): 581–596

Salillas, Rafael. *La fascinación en España: Brujas, brujerías, amuletos.* Madrid: ptd. Eduardo Arias, 1905; repr. Barcelona: MRA, 2000.

Schrire, T. *Hebrew Magic Amulets: Their Decipherment and Interpretation.* London: Routledge & K. Paul, 1966; repr. New York: Behrman House, 1982.

Seidenspinner-Núñez, Dayle. "Conversion and Subversion: Converso Texts in Fifteenth-Century Spain." In *Christians, Muslims, and Jews in Medieval and Early Modern Spain: Interaction and Cultural Change,* ed. Mark D. Meyerson and Edward D. English. Notre Dame Conferences in Medieval Studies 8. Notre Dame, IN: University of Notre Dame Press, 1999 241–261.

Skemer, Don C. *Binding Words: Textual Amulets in the Middle Ages.* University Park: Pennsylvania State University Press, 2006.

Smith, William, and Samuel Cheetham, eds. *A Dictionary of Christian Antiquities.* 2 vols. London: John Murray, 1875–1880.

Sola-Solé, Josep M., and Stanley E. Rose. "Judíos y conversos en la poesía cortesana del siglo XV: El estilo polígloto de Fray Diego de Valencia." *Hispanic Review* 44 (1976): 371–385.

Souter, Alexander. *A Glossary of Later Latin to 600 A.D.* Oxford: Clarendon Press, 1949.

Sperber, Daniel. *Magic and Folklore in Rabbinic Literature.* Bar-Ilan Studies in Near Eastern Languages and Culture. Ramat-Gan, Israel: Bar-Ilan University Press, 1994.

Tarp, Helen Cathleen. "Legal Fictions: Literature and Law in *Grisel y Mirabella.*" *eHumanista* 7 (2006): 95–114. Available at http://www.ehumanista.ucsb.edu/volumes/volume_07/index.shtml.

Tejeda Fernández, Margarita. *Glosario de términos de la indumentaria regia y cortesana en España: Siglos XVII y XVIII.* Málaga, Spain: Universidad de Málaga; Real Academia de Bellas Artes de San Telmo, 2006.

Terlingen, Juan. *Los italianismos en español desde la formación del idioma hasta principios del siglo XVII.* Amsterdam: N.V. Noord-Hollandsche Uitgevers Maatschappij, 1943.

Thesaurus linguae latinae, vol. 4, *con–cyulus.* Leipzig, Germany: Teubner, 1906–1909.

Valdeón Baruque, Julio. "Motivaciones socioeconómicas de las fricciones entre viejocristianos, judíos y conversos." In *Judíos, sefarditas, conversos: La expulsión de 1492 y sus consecuencias,* ed. Ángel Alcalá. Valladolid, Spain: Ámbito, 1995, 69–88.

Villena, Enrique de. *Obras completas.* Edited by Pedro M. Cátedra. 3 vols. Madrid: Turner, 1994–2000.

Walde Moheno, Lillian von der. *Amor e ilegalidad: "Grisel y Mirabella,"* de *Juan de Flores*. Publicaciones de Medievalia 12, Estudios de Lingüística y Literatura 34. Mexico City: Universidad Nacional Autónoma de México and El Colegio de México, 1996.

——. "El episodio final de *Grisel y Mirabella*." *La corónica* 20.2 (1992): 18–31.

Wartburg, Walther von. *Französisches etymologisches Wörterbuch: Eine Darstellung des galloromanischen Sprachschatzes*, vol. 2.2, *coinquinare– cytisus*. Basel, Germany: Helbing & Lichtenhahn, 1946.

Weissberger, Barbara F. *Isabel Rules: Constructing Queenship, Wielding Power*. Minneapolis: University of Minnesota Press, 2004.

——. "Role-Reversal and Festivity in the Romances of Juan de Flores." *Journal of Hispanic Philology* 13 (1988–1989): 197–213.

Wexler, Paul. "Marrano Ibero-Romance: Classification and Research Tasks." *Zeitschrift für Romanische Philologie* 98 (1982): 59–108.

——. *Three Heirs to a Judeo-Latin Legacy: Judeo-Ibero-Romance, Yiddish and Rotwelsch*. Mediterranean Language and Culture Monograph Series 3. Wiesbaden, Germany: Otto Harrassowitz, 1988.

Zalama, Miguel Ángel. *Juana I: Arte, poder y cultura en torno a una reina que no gobernó*. Madrid: Centro de Estudios Europa Hispánica, Dirección General del Libro (Ministerio de Cultura), Sociedad Estatal de Conmemoraciones Culturales, Diputación de Valladolid, 2010.

——. "El tesoro de la reina Juana I en Tordesillas: Relación de su expolio." In *Carlos V y las artes: Promoción artística y familia imperial*, ed. M. J. Redondo Cantera and M. A. Zalama. Valladolid, Spain: Junta de Castilla y León, Consejería de Educación y Cultura; Universidad de Valladolid, 2000, 45–66.

——. *Vida cotidiana y arte en el palacio de la reina Juana I en Tordesillas*. Estudios y Documentos 58. Valladolid, Spain: Universidad de Valladolid, 2000.

Importing Books to London in the Late Fifteenth and Early Sixteenth Centuries: Evidence from the London Overseas Customs Accounts

YVONNE RODE

This paper expands on research on the importing of books into England in the late fifteenth and early sixteenth centuries by utilizing a valuable but underused resource: the overseas customs accounts. The customs accounts can improve our knowledge about the early book trade by analyzing the importation of books into England, a lucrative business, given the inability of printers in England to meet a rising demand for books at this time, which led to a subsequent dependence on printed texts from overseas.[1] This import trade in books can be tracked in the overseas customs accounts enrolled with the Exchequer, which contain quantitative data on the value, volume, and description of books imported through the Port of London. Further information on the importers, many of whom were printers and publishers, shows that the trade developed from a craft to an international business within a few decades of the development of movable type and the printing press.

With mass production of texts made possible by the handpress, printers needed to develop larger distribution areas, as local markets were unable to consume a press's entire output. Paris, Antwerp, Cologne, Venice, and Lyon became centers of book production because as cities on well-established trade routes, they already had the warehousing, distribution, and financing infrastructure.[2] Mass production also made books more affordable and thus promoted greater demand. Demand also increased as literacy rose, and merchants, tradesmen, and craftsmen saw the need to keep accounts of transactions, submit bills, and keep gild records.[3] Due to the domination of Latin as the main language of texts, where a book was printed did not matter, as long as it could be economically delivered to its customers.[4]

Previous Research on the Importation of Books to England

The development of early book history as a discipline has encouraged research into the origins of books imported into England. Most of that research has been bibliographic studies focused on determining the place of production by examining extant collections and analyzing date and origin of imprints (e.g., by Lotte Hellinga, Nicholas Barker, and Margaret Lane Ford). Ford's survey of institutional catalogues shows that 85 percent of the late fifteenth-century books available in England came from just eight different cities; Hellinga and Barker both find that Italy and Germany accounted for a high proportion of early sixteenth-century books, or at least those in university and monastic libraries.[5]

The downside of this research method is that it can only attest to a particular tome having made its way to England at some point, because we do not know if the book was purchased abroad by an individual or imported to be sold locally. The institutional libraries that this method concentrates on had very particular needs, notably specific texts for the education and training of their communities. Thomas Bodley, for example, considered pamphlets and popular works unworthy of inclusion in the library he founded at Oxford in 1603.[6] These types of publications seem, moreover, to have been valued less than religious, scientific and legal works and would thus not have been given the care necessary to survive to the present day, a bias that skews studies of the type done by these three scholars in favor of expensive editions.[7] Analyzing fifteenth-century bookseller's advertisements in Germany, Curt Bühler finds that few of the 176 books exist today, as the copies were "literally read to pieces."[8] This point is important, as areas producing deluxe works may appear to have dominated the trade, when this might not have been the case.

Subject specialization also often developed in a given city or region. Nicholas Barker shows that imprints from Venice accounted for 45 percent of pre-1500 printed books at Oxford University.[9] Venice was a center of the printing of humanist and legal texts, the type of books one would expect to find at a university.[10] In contrast, of the 395 books with identifiable origins at Syon Abbey, only 34 (8.7 percent) were printed in Venice.[11] This small number is understandable, as a monastery would have less need for works of humanism or law. Lotte Hellinga uses the incunable catalogues of several

Scottish and English universities to determine the places of origin cf the texts in their collections.[12] Her survey of 1,000 books shows that the Low Countries and Germany were the main suppliers of printed books before 1490, but their influence waned as the Latin textbooks that these countries were supplying began to be printed in England. On the other hand, imports from Italy and France increased up through 1500, as Italy provided humanist works and France supplied liturgical books.[13]

Other scholars have examined wills and inventories for similar information discerned from title lists.[14] Carol Meale shows that often a medieval woman would list only her most expensive book in her will.[15] Although these sources list specific texts of their owners or institutions, they cannot tell us when or how these texts arrived in England.

The Customs System

We can gain a more precise idea of the scope, organization, and value of the import trade in books by turning to the overseas customs accounts that record merchandise imported and exported plus the duty imposed, which depended on the type and value of the merchandise and status of the importer.[16] Duties collected from customs were a significant source of royal revenue in the fourteenth and fifteenth centuries—amounting to more than 50 percent of crown revenue in the late fourteenth century.[17] The summary accounts that record the total customs survive in a nearly continuous series for five hundred years to the eighteenth century.[18]

The detailed accounts, which would itemize merchandise such as books, are called the particular accounts and were used as the basis for the summary accounts. The survival of particular accounts is somewhat spotty, but they provide far more details than the summary accounts, including the date the ship entered the port, information on its shipmaster (and occasionally the ship name and home port), its cargo and merchants, and customs valuations. There are two types of particular accounts: those kept by the collectors of customs tend to be fuller than the audited accounts compiled by the controller.[19] Both the collector's and the controller's accounts would be sent to the Exchequer, where they would be compared against each other.[20] There were different accounts depending on the specific type of customs duty assessed. Some duties targeted only alien (foreign) merchants, not denizens (English merchants, or those who had been named denizens and had rights similar to natives). Other duties were applied only to certain goods, such as wine (called tunnage), wool, hides, or cloth.[21] Separate accounts were kept for the wool customs, petty customs, and cloth customs and tunnage and poundage.[22]

The most important particular customs accounts for the study of book imports were poundage accounts and petty accounts. Both poundage and petty duties were applied to a large range of goods and based on an *ad valorem* tax. Petty customs were paid by denizens, aliens, and Hanseatic merchants, although certain individuals, groups (primarily Hanse merchants), or entire towns could be exempt or be given special privileges.[23] Alien merchants paid petty and poundage duties on all merchandise, while poundage duties, plus customs on cloth, wool, woolfells, and hides, plus a subsidy on wine were also paid by all other merchants regardless of status.[24] Individual particular accounts could record several types of customs, not only petty customs and poundage but also tunnage, or subsidies on cloth exports, or ancient customs on wool and hides. Both petty and poundage accounts for London are incomplete for the fifteenth and sixteenth centuries.[25]

Several changes occurred during the fifteenth and sixteenth centuries in how books and other merchandise were assessed for customs charges. The valuations given to book imports when they first appeared in the fifteenth century were part of a system that began in 1303, in which customs duties were charged on a particular group of imports and exports as an *ad valorem* rate, usually 3d. per £1 of value.[2] Although this implies that the rate represents the true value of the commodity, N. S. B. Gras and other scholars argue that these customs valuations were often below real market price and denoted the lowest value the merchant knew the customs official would accept.[27]

Over time, these low evaluations became fairly standardized, particularly for the most frequently traded commodities. In 1507 a *Book of Rates* was created, which Gras believed was compiled from previous agreements between London customs officials and the Merchant Adventurers of London; it is likely that the *Book of Rates* merely recorded valuations that had been employed for a long time, although the *Book* had no official status when it was compiled.[28] Cobb's comparison of the 1507 rates with customs account entries from 1502/3 and 1506, for instance, finds few differences between the recorded values and those listed in the 1507 rates book.[29] Cobb suggests that the 1507 rates represent a first attempt officially to fix customs duties for London, although for the most part these rates were already in place.[30]

Complaints about widely fluctuating rates at different ports led Henry VIII in 1532 to put a new national customs system in place; this development consisted in part of applying the 1507 *Book of Rates* to the entire country.[31] Books do not appear among the 1507 rates, but primers are listed at 20d per dozen.[32] In 1545 a new rate book, *The Rate of the Custome House both Inwarde and Outwarde*, was issued, containing more than twice as many commodities as the previous version, with many of the old commodity values remaining unchanged.[33] Books finally appeared in the rate book of 1545, rated at £4 per basket or maund of unbound books and 40s per half-maund of unbound books.[34]

The consistency of the data in the customs accounts makes them an ideal economic source for analyzing the business side of the book trade. A typical customs account entry from 1537 reads: "Item: In the ship of William Johnson, entered on the 16th day of November . . . Frances Brykman, alien, for one basket containing *bokes unbounde* price 4 pounds."[35] The entries give us a limited amount of information to work with: the name of the importer, whom we may or may not be able to identify, plus his or her status; a vague description of the type of book; the container it was shipped in (for a rough idea of quantity); and the duty collected. This is still enough information to establish an image of the book trade when we examine accounts over several decades.

This type of data allows us to address several questions: Did any particular person or group of persons dominate the book trade for any length of time? Is it possible to establish where these books came from? What was the value of those books? More specifically, was a trend developing of merchants who specialized in importing books or were books just one of many commodities that could be imported to turn a profit?[36]

Previous Use of the Customs Accounts by Book Historians

The customs accounts have been used previously to research book importation into London in the late Middle Ages. The earliest study is a number of short surveys by Henry Plomer in the 1920s focused on a few well-known printers and publishers who appeared in the accounts (e.g., Francis Birckman and Wynkyn de Worde).[37] Julian Roberts, C. Paul Christianson, and N. J. M. Kerling also examine customs accounts while researching the early book trade.[38] Julian Roberts uses the London customs accounts and port books as sources while researching the book collection of Oxford University, but seems to be interested only in the importers involved and does not discuss any other data found in the accounts.[39] Similarly, Christianson's research on the book trade in London led him to use the customs accounts as one of many sources for investigating the stationers and printers of that time.

Although Nelly Kerling examined all extant London customs accounts from 1460 to 1492 and sometimes goes into great detail, she gives only a few specific examples of particular importers.[40] Paul Needham shows how customs accounts can be used when researching the early book trade but focuses on the workings of the customs system and type of information in the accounts.[41] Despite their thorough examination of some accounts, these scholars do not present their findings statistically, making it difficult to establish any patterns.[42]

These earlier studies of book imports using the overseas customs accounts tend to provide only a snapshot of the book trade for a very specific time or place or focus on particular individuals, and there is currently no large-scale overview. More information about book imports through the Port of London from 1450 to 1540 can be found by examining a larger collection of customs accounts. For my research I created an Access database to analyze information culled from the accounts and identify large patterns, such as changes in how values were assessed and the total customs levies on imported books per year; other sources provided information on the people involved and their roles in the trade.

London was medieval England's largest port; around 1480, London controlled almost 61 percent of the country's overseas trade by value.[43] Through the first decade of the sixteenth century, it accounted for more than 50 percent of overseas customs income, reaching 58 percent in 1506/7.[44] From around 1400 to 1540, approximately 80 percent of goods by value went through the Port of London.[45] London was also the center of political, cultural, and social life in England, along with nearby Winchester.[46] Consumer demand for goods such as spices, jewels, and books was also higher in London than in provincial towns.[47] Those living outside London would frequently purchase luxury goods there, either in person or via an agent.[48] In addition, London handled a large proportion of trade by aliens, who were leading participators in the early book trade.[49] This prominence was partly due to favorable regulations initially governing aliens involved in the book trade when England was still dependent on the Continent for books.[50]

This study focuses on the London customs accounts because London was clearly the center of the British book trade in the late Middle Ages. An examination of the customs accounts in print for other ports finds few book imports outside of London. Several accounts have been published for Southampton covering the fifteenth and early sixteenth centuries.[51] The cargoes of books were very small; for example, one in 1480 was for seven cases of printed books on paper and another, in 1509, was for five dozen service books and psalters.[52]

For this paper I examined eleven overseas customs accounts enrolled at the National Archives, chosen for their coverage of a full year of data and spread as evenly as possible over the period studied.[53] Of the accounts I examined, nine were petty customs accounts and two were tunnage and poundage accounts, with eight petty accounts and one tunnage and poundage account containing book imports.[54]

The two earliest accounts (1457/8 and 1471/2) I examined contained no imports of books.[55] This agrees with Kerling's findings that there were no imports of books through the Port of London before 1477.[56] Kate Harris believes evidence of the printing of books in English on the Continent in the 1450s shows that commercial importing of books began much earlier.[57] As I have no data from my two earliest customs accounts, this article focuses on book imports to London between 1480 and 1540.[58]

Estimating Customs Values

The nine accounts examined for this study allow us to get a rough idea of the values of book cargoes over time. Problems arise, however, with books imported along with other items, as a single valuation is given for a whole cargo, not the individual books. There are several different ways to estimate a value for the books alone. For example, in 1480/1 Henry Franckenbergk twice imported a hogshead containing books, both valued at £14. One contained only books, while the second hogshead included books and three pieces of Holland linen cloth eighty ells in length.[59] The total customs duties paid for book-only cargoes for the customs year 1480/1 was £150 10s, but this does not include Franckenbergk's hogshead containing books and linen nor five other book imports, also part of mixed cargoes, for which separate values for the books in each shipment are not provided. To include these book imports in our totals, we need to find a way to estimate the value of the books. If we look elsewhere in the account, we can find an entry for Holland cloth alone and extrapolate its average price to subtract from the total for the books and cloth, for a customs value of 13s 2d per piece.[60] We can then subtract the value of the cloth from the total value of the cargo in order to determine what part of the valuation can be attributed to book imports (£11 1s 6d). The method is not perfect, but it does allow us to get a better idea of the total value of book imports over time.

Unfortunately, establishing a value this way is not always possible, depending on the number and type of items included in the cargo. On June 2, 1481, for instance, Lewis Aufan, an alien, imported a large mixed cargo in a barrel containing, among other things, "two small books."[61] Although these two books may only amount to a few shillings or pence in value, there are also some large quantities of books in other cargoes each year with valuations that need to be estimated in order not to skew our totals. In these cases, we can calculate an average price from books in other entries, which range anywhere from a shilling per book to 6s 4d, with an average of 2s 6d. But these values are all for cargoes described as "diverse histories," whereas we are also applying them to cargoes of "*libris*," "*parvus libris*," and "*prentyd bokes*."[62] Without further research we cannot be sure of the difference between these categories.

When considering the totals, therefore, it needs to be kept in mind that values were estimated for a number of cargoes. Sometimes an estimate is not possible, as, for example, with two mixed cargoes in 1507/8 that record *libris impressus* and *alys* (other); we do not know what else was in the container.[63] It is also important to remember that the early valuations were for declared value (*ad valorem*), but this changed to a fixed rate (discussed further below), so we need to be careful comparing fluctuations in the values of book imports from year to year.

Even given these difficulties in calculating values, the accounts do provide good information about the duties collected on book imports (Table 1).[64] The import of books fluctuated greatly, increasing and decreasing substantially within a few years, and value decreased by £30 6s (about 20 percent) between 1480/1 and 1490/1. This reduction may be explained by the appointment by Henry VII of Peter Actors as royal stationer for life in December 1485. This position exempted him from paying customs duties on books "printed and not printed" imported into any port in England.[65] Actors was responsible for more than half the recorded imports by value (£58 worth) in 1480/1, and his freedom from paying duties could account for the significant decrease in the number of recorded imports.[66]

Import totals rose again in 1502/3 by almost £16) but then decreased by more than one third by 1507/8 and another fifth by 1512/3 (from £136 0s 4d to £89 to £71 13s 4d). Another substantial drop of nearly 56 percent occurred in just two years (to £40 by1514/5). Some of the decrease could be attributed to England's war with France, which may have affected imports from overseas.[67] Not only might merchants fear for the safety of their goods, but the impressment of merchant ships for naval service during wartime was not uncommon and would cause further disruptions in trade.[68] According to the economist Richard Britnell, these disruptions were especially strong in 1512/3, 1522 to 1524, and 1528, and we see this reflected in the steep decline in imports in the totals from the 1510s.[69] Trade in Europe was also impeded by civil unrest on the Continent at this time. On several occasions in the first decade of the sixteenth century, Anton Koberger wrote to the Basel printer-publisher Johann Amerbach that trade had come to a standstill: "We are beset with terrible war and costs to us grow greater every day. There is absolutely no trade at all, and nobody can do any business because of the war."[70]

From 1514/5 to 1520/1, imports rose more than fourfold, to £181 13s 4d, the highest total for the period surveyed. 1520/1 is the one year a poundage account instead of a petty account was used, which means it contains not only alien importers but also native and denizens. Although we find the greatest number of importers and highest total of books imported by value, this is not due to the number of nonalien imports, as they amount to only £4 of the total customs collected, with an additional portion of a mixed cargo totaling another £4. This £8 makes up slightly more than 4 percent of the yearly value.[7] Unfortunately there is large gap in surviving accounts through the 1520s, and the next full year's account available is for 1534/5, when we see a 23 percent drop to £140 (1534/5).

In 1534 the importing of bound books, along with the privilege of selling such books retail, was revoked by Henry VIII.[72] An Acte for Prynters and Bynders of Bokes required books to be imported unbound because English binders were "destitute of worke and lyke to be undon, except somme reformacion here in be hade."[73] The total of imports for 1537/8, after this ruling went into effect, dropped 45 percent to £78. One prominent importer in 1534/5 who does not appear in the 1537/8 account is the French printer François Regnault. Regnault complained to Thomas Cromwell about the act concerning imported bound books because he was unable to sell bound books he had previously brought over.[74] His specialty, primers in English, was also affected by another proclamation forbidding the translation of Scripture into English, and by 1538 Regnault had stopped printing primers for the English market.[75]

Fluctuations in yearly import totals over the decades were due to various reasons, such as war affecting trade and regulations that may have limited or frustrated would-be importers. What is clear is that the numbers of small importers, who brought in single cargoes and were never seen again, can be seen as making up the bulk of the yearly differences. One or two importers dominated each year's trade and made up the majority of the year's total by value, with the most prominent reaching 30 percent to 40 percent and even up to 60 percent. Studies of other commodities and additional accounts could show whether there was an overall decline in trade in the early sixteenth century (for example, due to unrest making trade difficult) or whether there was a slump specifically in the demand for books from overseas. In addition, a survey of more poundage accounts could show if aliens truly dominated the trade, as appears from the small number of native importers in 1520/1.

The method of assessing customs duties for books changed over the fifteenth and sixteenth centuries and needs to be taken into account when comparing totals over time. There is the possibility that standard customs rates on books (although unofficial until 1545) were already being applied as early as 1490, as 72 percent of cargoes from 1490/1 were given rounded values (e.g., 40s, 60s, and 100s), while less than half (46 percent) of the books-only cargoes from 1480/1 were given rounded values. This is assuming that a rounded value would be a sign of a move toward a standard rate, while a nonrounded value (e.g., £10 3s 4d for a chest of 67 volumes) would reflect an *ad valorem* value. Rounded values rise to 100 percent for all book-only consignments from 1507/8 on. With *ad valorem* rates, each book in a cargo should have been valued separately, and the values then added up to determine the duty to be charged. Rounded values imply that factors and customs collectors were not examining each book but giving an approximate value to either each book or the entire cargo. I believe this is evidence that books were becoming a common enough commodity that the customs collectors knew the general value of books and no longer saw a need for a detailed review of the contents of a shipment of books. In addition, by 1507, when the first rate book was issued, baskets of books were already conforming to the future 1545 rate of £4 per basket and £2 per half-basket. In 1507/8, five of eight baskets were assessed at £4. In 1512/3 and 1537/8, all the baskets were rated for £4, with all half-baskets for £2, and in 1534/5, eighteen of twenty basket and half-basket shipments were at the future rate. Although books did not appear in the customs rates book until 1545, it seems that they had already become a common enough commodity to be given a standard, if not official, rate decades earlier.[7] It is possible that books were inadvertently left out of the 1507 rate book, since it seems the rate of baskets of books was already standardized and being applied by this time.

International Connections of the Printer-Publishers

The customs accounts also illustrate the multinational scope of the early book trade. It is important to remember, however, that the origin of the book importer or of his ship was not an indication of where the books originated or were printed.[77] On July 8, 1502, one Frederick Vanegmond imported a basket of *libris impressus* and paid 40s in customs.[78] This Vanegmond was in fact Frederick Egmondt, who was a stationer in London and Paris.[79] He was having books printed for him in Venice by Johannes Hertzog[80] and seemed to be importing them on Dutch ships, if the names of their shipmasters are any clue,[81] which could also explain how his name became "Vanegmond" in the rolls.[82] Here is an example of a Flemish merchant in Paris and London who was importing Venetian books on Dutch ships. This is just a single case where we have evidence of all the parties involved. Another complicating factor was that merchant ships often visited more than one port before arriving at their final destination.[83]

We can account for where some of these imported books were printed, particularly in the later years, by focusing on merchants who not only specialized in importing books but also had them printed on commission specifically for the market in England. Many of these imprints can be identified through the *English Short Title Catalogue* (STC), although more publishers can be identified in the later decades than in the fifteenth century.[84] There was no equivalent to a printer's mark in earlier manuscript books, although on occasion a text is found with a scribe's signature.[85] A study of German incunables from the 1470s through the 1490s shows that the number of books that included the name of the printer rose from 42.6 percent in the 1470s to 54.7 percent in the 1490s.[86] By 1500, about 70 percent of French incunables included the name of the printer.[87] Once the appearance of the printer's name became more common, the names of publishers also begin to appear. It therefore becomes possible to match the names of importers who were also publishers by using the STC to identify imprints where their names occurred.[88] It was not until 1542 that England began requiring the name of the printer, author, and date of publication to be included in any books to be sold in the country; many earlier texts may have only a title or title and date and no publisher information.[89]

Another invaluable resource is E. Gordon Duff's *Century of the English Book Trade*, which provides background information on merchants and others involved with the book trade in England.[90] He compiled this information from various sources, including the letters of denization and act of naturalization, returns of aliens, and marriage licenses. Less useful are records of the Stationers' Company, which do not start until 1554. The company had existed informally from 1403 as a guild of textwriters, limners, and stationers (in various combinations), but was not incorporated until 1557.[91]

The numbers of merchants who were associated with at least one imprint generally increased over time (Table 3). In 1480/1, only one book importer is known to have been involved with the printing of a book: John van Acon, who was responsible for 6.2 percent of the total value of books imported in that time.[92] By the 1530s, printer-publishers were responsible for more than 80 percent of the totals by value, accounting for 88.5 percent for 1534/5 and 82 percent for 1537/8, an almost fourteen-fold increase from 1480/1.[93]

The growing participation of professional printers and publishers in the importation of books is also evident in the family connections between importers, printers, and publishers. Francis Birckman, who imported 19.2 percent of the 1534/5 total by value, was the son of another Francis, who was responsible for 4.5 percent of 1502/3's imports. The elder Birckman was from Cologne and in partnership with the Antwerp printer Gerard Cluen, a relative of his wife, Gertrude van Amersfoordt.[94] In the colophon of a book of English canon law printed for him in 1525 in Antwerp by Christopher Ruremond,[95] he is identified as "*honesti mercatoris.*"[96] Five years later, a Sarum Use missal was printed for him in Paris by Nicholas Prevost.[97] This extended Birckman family had shops all over Europe, and members were known to attend the Frankfurt fair in search of books.[98] Both John and Arnold Birckman worked as agents for many booksellers in London.[99]

In addition to the Birckmans, other family connections within the book trade included the brothers Andrew and John Rewe, who were importing from the 1480s into the 1500s.[100] Andrew Rewe imported books printed by Basel printer Johann Amerbach in the 1490s. Rewe also asked Amerbach to send specific authors and titles, along with general requests for works in areas like moral philosophy and law.[101] One letter asks "if there are new books anywhere, don't hesitate to notify me," implying that Amerbach would send not only his own books but also books by other printers.[102] Amerbach, along with fellow Basel printers Johann Petri and Johann Froben, worked closely with Anton Koberger of Nuremberg, whose business acumen made him the biggest printer in Germany until he turned to focusing his energies on publishing.[103]

The employment of numerous printers by publishers in many different cities was quite common at this time.[104] Like Francis Birckman, the London stationer and bookbinder John Reynes also employed the printing services of both Prevost and van Ruremond. In 1527 a Sarum *Graduale* was printed for him by Prevost, and eighteen years later, a Sarum *Processionale* was printed for him by van Ruremond.[105] Along with Reynes, two other bookbinders, Godfrey Bac and Nicholas Spiernick, also imported books into London. Godfrey Bac appears only once in the customs accounts: for £1-worth of printed books in May 1503.[106] Bac is mentioned as a bookbinder in the Register of the Guild of St. Luke in 1492 and later married the widow of the Antwerp printer Mathias van der Goes.[107] He was one of the overseers of the will of the London bookseller John Boeidens, who was the godfather of Bac's daughter Elizabeth.[108] Boeidens imported £3-worth of books in 1490/1 and £9-worth in 1502/3.[109] There are no specific titles linked to Bac in the STC before 1510, but it is not unreasonable to think he might have been supplying Boeidens with the Latin grammars he specialized in printing.[110] Nicholas Spiernick, who imported books in 1507/8, was a stationer and bookbinder in Cambridge descended from a family of bookbinders in the Low Countries.[111]

Some importers, many of whom were printers themselves, even collaborated to have texts published. The colophon of a 1519 edition of a Book of Hours printed in Paris by Nicholas Higman shows it was made on behalf of Francis Birckman and François Regnault.[112] An edition of Terence was printed in Paris in 1504 with the title page ending "*venundantur londinie in edibus optimorum bibliopolarum winandi de worda, Michaelis Morini & Iohannis Brachij*."[113] De Worde and Morin both appear in the accounts as importing books in 1502/3, and *Iohannis Brachij*, or John Bray, was a binder from Oxford.[114] De Worde produced an edition of Sarum Hours in 1497 with Julian Notary and later published a liturgical book in 1509 with Jacob Ferrebouc; both of these were printed in Paris.[115]

These multinational connections show that it is not possible to determine where a particular cargo of books could have been printed using just the customs accounts alone. But the customs accounts in conjunction with other sources show the book trade as an increasingly large-scale international commercial venture that drew on family networks that crossed national borders.

A Growing Specialization in the Book Trade

A small group of people had begun to dominate the market at an early date. The two biggest importers in each year were responsible for nearly 40 percent or more of the trade, with the exception of 1502/3 at 29.4 percent (Table 1). Along with these prominent importers were merchants importing books with other types of goods. One third of the shipments in 1480/1 included other goods, and that includes those from the two biggest book importers, Peter Actors and Henry Franckenbergk.[116] In contrast, in later years other goods were imported along with books on only a few occasions, a sign that the book trade had moved out of the hands of the general merchant completely.[117] Two of the fourteen other mixed cargoes included consignments of paper for printers Julian Notary and William Faques in 1502/3.[118] On the same ship as William Faques, John Syton imported two fattes (containers similar to vats) of books plus a barrel of pouch-rings and other goods.[119]

There was a single mixed-cargo consignment in 1490/1 that included 1,200 primers for Nicholas le Pelletre.[120] Primers appear in accounts from two other years (Table 2). In 1512/3, there were three cargoes totaling 19 gross and 8 dozen for Cornelius van Kessel and another cargo of 8 gross for Anthony Vivaldi.[121] There were four consignments of primers in 1520/1. William Fever imported two cargoes of primers totaling 15 gross and 2 dozen, including 3 gross described as "borded primers."[122] Thomas Thorne and Stephen Litler imported smaller quantities of 4 gross and half a gross respectively during the same period.[123] These must have been the type of primers that Paul Needham mentions were imported by the dozen or gross outside the purview of the Stationers and were imported and sold with other cheap goods,[124] because these primer cargoes included items such as spectacles, combs, caps, and beads. There was only one other mixed shipment for 1512/3, and that was for George Chastelain, who also imported thirty-three rolls of latten plate.

Shipments with cargoes listed as "*libris impressus*" and "other" ("*alys*"), making it impossible to estimate the book values, occur twice in 1507/8 for Wynkyn de Worde and Nicholas Gerall and in 1520/1 for the London printer-publisher and stationer Henry Pepwell.[125]

Although the number of mixed cargoes fluctuated, many included only other printing-related items such as paper and boards, which were probably for binding. Of eleven mixed shipments for 1520/1, one was a shipment of books and paper and three consisted of books and "bordes" or "bordes for books," presumably for binding.[126] Primers accounted for four of the remaining mixed cargoes.[127] Finally, on September 4, 1536, Lambert Johnson imported half a basket of books and—perhaps to keep them safe—one basket of thirteen dozen locks for cupboards, the only mixed shipment found in that account.[128] There were no mixed shipments for 1537/8.

While some merchants were clearly specializing in importing books as early as 1480/1, others were bringing over a few with other goods to see if they, too, could turn a profit from books. As early as the 1490s, specialization was developing, but we also see a doubling in the number of people involved in importing books within ten years. While Actors and Franckenbergk dominated the trade in 1480/1, accounting for 83.1 percent of imported books between them, they seemed to be just merchants who bought and sold books. Later importers, in contrast, were involved in many different aspects of the trade, including printing, publishing, and binding.

In 1480/1 and 1490/1, only one of the book importers was known to be otherwise involved in the book trade. In 1502/3 the number of importers had almost doubled to eighteen, with eleven known to be involved specifically in the book trade (Tables 1 and 3). They accounted for 62.4 percent of the total value of imported books for that year (£83 0s 8d), although not all of the books they were importing were specifically printed or published for them. Five of these importers were printers: Michael Morin, Wynkyn de Worde, William Faques, George Mittelhus, and Julian Notary, while two were binders: Henry Cony and Godfrey Bac. Each of these men accounted for one shipment each, and Faques and Notary were also importing paper.

One printer who was importing as early as 1502 was Wynkyn de Worde, who took over Caxton's press after Caxton's death in 1491.[129] De Worde imported £10-worth of books on March 14, 1503.[130] In 1507/8, de Worde imported five cargoes totaling £22 and a sixth cargo also containing "other" (*alys*) goods whose value could not be estimated; his cargoes accounted for at least 25 percent of that year's total.[131] De Worde and his fellow printer-publisher Francis Birckman were responsible for eleven of seventeen cargoes that year, with the six remaining individuals importing goods on one occasion each. Two stationers also appeared, each importing books valued at £4: the London stationer and bookbinder John Richards, and the Cambridge stationer Nicholas Spierinck.[132] The accounts for 1512/3 and 1514/5 were dominated by the London stationer Arnold Harrison, who accounted for 40 percent and 60 percent of the total, respectively.[133] If we discount the primers imported by Cornelius van Kessel and Anthony Vivaldi, Harrison was responsible for 63 percent of the total in 1512/3. Besides Francis Birckman, the only other importer for 1512/3 who had known connections to the book trade as a printer or publisher was George Chastelain. Birckman and Chastelain imported only £14-worth, or less than 20 percent of the total consignments.[134] Chastelain was a stationer in London and Oxford and had several works printed for him by Richard Pynson.[135] If the primers are excluded (as chapmen's ware, which was not handled by the Stationers), the number of shipments that include nonbook merchandise decreased each year except for 1520/1.

Although 1520/1 saw an increase in the number of people importing books, the trade was dominated by just a few people: Spierinck, Thomas

Bottall, Birckman, Harrison, and William Fever were responsible for 80 percent of consignments by value.[136] Nicholas Spierinck accounted for more than 28 percent of all imports. Twelve other merchants appear only once each, with a few, such as Wynkyn de Worde and John Reynes, bringing in multiple shipments of small cargoes. The number of book importers declined to ten in 1534/5, but six were directly involved in the book trade in other capacities. They accounted for £120 of the total value of all book imports, or 85.7 percent. This includes the Parisian printers François Regnault and Jean Petit, the stationer-publishers John Reynes and Reginald Wolff, and the Antwerp printer Godfried van Haeghen. The sixth was the son and namesake of Francis Birckman, taking over from his father, who died around 1529.[137] Birckman, Reginald Wolff, and the stationer-publisher John Cockes were three of the five importers in 1537/8 who were known to be directly involved in printing and publishing.[138] Their imports totaled £64 or 83 percent of books by value for that period.

All but one of the accounts that recorded evidence of book imports were for petty customs, which was paid only by aliens. The account for 1520/1 was for tunnage and poundage, a duty also paid by natives and denizated aliens. Only three importers were identified as *indigena* in this account: two natives, the author Henry Pepwell and London stationer John Gough, plus an as-yet unidentified Thomas Thorne.[139] They imported £4-worth of books and a mixed cargo worth another £4.[140] The total for imports was over £181, showing that nonaliens made up an insignificant part of the trade for this year. Obviously a single account does not provide enough evidence to draw firm conclusions, and more tunnage and poundage accounts will have to be examined to determine if aliens truly dominated the import business.

Conclusion

A systematic analysis of a wide range of overseas customs accounts helps to illuminate and extend our understanding of the early trade in books in England. The first entry for the import of books in extant London customs accounts was in December 1477, and by 1480/1 there was already a lively book trade, with several merchants specializing in importing books. Since Peter Actors was named Stationer to the King within several years of his first appearance in the accounts, there is a good chance that he and several others had already been involved in the book trade when they first surfaced in the customs accounts. Although the customs accounts do not provide title lists or exact numbers, we can make general estimates, using duties paid, about the most prominent importers and their role in the trade.

The increase in the number of book importers who were also involved in printing or publishing texts shows that within thirty years of the first shipment of books appearing in the customs accounts, the importing of books moved out of the hands of general merchants—those who were involved in importing non book-related goods—and into the hands of specialists, a sign of the development of a formal book industry. By the beginning of the sixteenth century, books were being imported by people involved in printing, publishing, and binding books (Table 3). It is possible that a higher percentage of earlier importers were involved in the book trade, but there are difficulties involved in identifying those importers who were involved in publishing due to nonstandardized spelling of names and the fact that a smaller proportion of incunables identified their printer or publisher. Without the examination of additional poundage accounts, we cannot be sure if aliens truly dominated the import trade, but natives made up an insignificant proportion of the one poundage account included. Difficulties arise in filling out the data due to the number of surviving full-year accounts for either petty or poundage accounts, sometimes forcing large gaps between years examined.

While economic historians have used customs accounts for the study of luxury and nonluxury commodities, so far the study of the movement of books has been overlooked. Changes in the customs duties applied to books over the period studied show them moving from a luxury object, deserving of special individual examination and evaluation, to a common commodity with a fixed price within a few decades of the explosion of printing presses throughout the Continent and England. Economic data has in general been overlooked by book historians, who have tended to rely on title lists and bibliographic surveys when trying to establish the movement of books across countries. This study helps fill out that data with quantitative information provided by the customs accounts which give a good idea of printed texts coming through the Port of London to fill the needs of readers in that country.

Westchester Community College

Table 1. Total Value and Percent of Book Imports into the Port of London by Merchant

Year	Merchant	No. of Shipments	Total value	Percent
1480/1	Peter Actors[a]	7	£72 9s 4d	48.6
	Henry Franckenbergk[b]	5	£48 8s 4d	32.5
	Andrew Rewe	1	£13	8.7
	John van Acon*	1	£9 6s 8d	6.2
	Bernard van Utrecht	1	£2 6s 8d	1.6
	John de Barde	1	£1	0.7
	Paul van Malder[c]	1	£1	0.7
	Lewis Aufan[c]	1	15s	0.5
	Peter Wallkyn[c]	1	12s 6d	0.4
	Francis Mathew[c]	1	2s 6d	0.1
	Totals		£149 1s	100.0
1490/1	Gerard Millar	1	£60	50.0
	Nicholas Beneland	2	£18 8s	15.5
	John Rewe	3	£17 6s	14.5
	Peter Actors	1	£10	8.3
	Herman Anngell	1	£10	8.3
	John Boetdens[d]	1	£3	2.5

	Name	Count	Amount	%
	Elizabeth van Acon	1	£1 10s	0.9
	Nicholas Pelletre[d]	1	?	?
	Totals		£120 4s	100.0
1502/3	John Anthoe	1	£20	14.7
n	John Coleynse	2	£20	14.7
	Frederick Egmondt*	5	£15	11.0
	Jacob Hansett	3	£13	10.5
	Michael Morain*	1	£10	7.3
	Wynkyn de Worde*	1	£10	7.3
	John Boeidens*	3	£9	6.6
	John Sytonf	1	£8	5.9
	Francis Birckman*	3	£8	5.9
	William Faques[g]*	1	£4	2.9
	George Mittelhus*	1	£3 6s 8d	2.4
	John Bars	1	£3	2.2
	John Bonase	1	£3	2.2
	Julian Notary[g]*	1	£3	2.2
	Henry Cony	1	£2	1.5
	Andrew Rewe	1	£2	1.5
	Godfrey Bac*	1	£1	0.7
	Cornelius Johnson	1	13s 8d	0.5

		Totals	£136 0s 4d	100.0
1507/8	Francis Birckman*	5	£25	28
	Wynkyn de Worde[h]*	6	£22	25
	John van Ceffryn	1	£20	22.5
	John Coleynse	1	£10	11
	Adrian Cornell	1	£4	4.5
	Jean Richard*	1	£4	4.5
	Nicholas Spierinck*	1	£4	4.5
	Nicholas Gerall[h]	1	?	?
		Totals	£89	100.0
1512/3	Arnold Harrison[i]	4	£28	40
	Cornelius van Kessel[j]	3	£19 13s 4d	27
	Francis Birckman*	1	£8	11
	Anthony Vivaldi	1	£8	11
	George Chastelain[k]*	1	£6	8
	George Bart[l]	1	£2	3
		Totals	£71 13s 4d	100.0
1514/5	Arnold Harrison	4	£24	60
	John Reynes*	2	£12	30
	Wynkyn de Worde*	1	£4	10
	Edward Nicholson	1	?	?
		Totals	£40	100.0

1520/1				
	Nicholas Spierinck*	3	£52	28.6
	Thomas Bottall	7	£24	13.2
	Francis Birckman*	3	£20	11.0
	Arnold Harrison	5	£20	11.0
	William Fever	2	£15 3s 4d	8.3
	Ambrose Geron	1	£8	4.4
	John Reynes*	2	£8	4.4
	Wynkyn de Worde*	3	£6	3.3
	Roland Franke	2	£4	2.2
	Bernard Gauton	1	£4	2.2
	Cornelius Hermann	1	£4	2.2
	John Raymt	1	£4	2.2
	John Thorn	1	£4	2.2
	Ambrose de Viro	1	£4	2.2
	Thomas Thorne	1	£3	1.7
	John Gough*	1	£1	0.5
	Stephen Litler	1	10s	0.3
	Godfrey van Howe[m]	1	?	0.0
	Henry Pepwell[m]*	1	?	0.0
	Curt [ ]son[m]	1	?	0.0
	Reginald Oliver[m]*	1	?	0.0
	Totals		£181 13s 4d	

1534/5			
François Regnault*	3	£47	33.6
Francis Birckman II*	7	£27	19.2
Godfried van Haeghen*	7	£26	18.6
Jean Petit*	1	£12	8.6
Nicholas Gilles*	1	£6	4.3
Lambert Johnson	3	£6	4.3
John van Hare	1	£4	2.8
James Nicholson*	1	£4	2.8
John Reynes*	1	£4	2.8
Reginald Wolff*	1	£4	2.8
	Totals	£140	100.0
1537/8			
Francis Birckman II*	8	£28	34.1
John Cockes*	8	£28	34.1
Reginald Wolff*	3	£12	14.6
Henry van Armann	3	£10	12.2
Herman Evans	1	£4	4.9
	Totals	£82	100.0

Sources: Public Record Office (PRO), E122/194/25 (1480/1); PRO, E122/78/9 (1490/1); PRO, E122/80/3 (1502/3); PRO, E122/80/5 (1507/8); PRO, E122/82/9 (1512/3); PRO, E122/82/3 (1514/5); PRO, E122/81/8 (1520/1); PRO, E122/82/8 (1534/5); PRO, E122/81/18 (1537/8).

Notes: These customs valuations are far below actual retail value. In general, forenames are anglicized, and surnames preferred by Duff in Century of the English Book Trade are used. Several cargoes included other goods, and several methods were used to estimate the value of books in these shipments, see explanation in text.

*Printer-publishers (see Table 3).

ᵃPrice of one chest of books estimated to be £9 11s averaged from prices of chest of books found in other entries in this account.

ᵇPrice of 80 ells of Holland linen cloth estimated to be 39s 6d based on 554 ells at £13 13s 4d found in same accounts and deducted from one shipment.

ᶜTotals are estimated as 2s 6d per book based on the average price in other entries (range of 1s to 6s 4d). The prices found in the entries were all for "diverse histories" but are here being applied to "books," "printed books," and "small books."

ᵈThis merchant imported 1,200 primers (normally imported by the dozen or gross). This is their only occurrence in this account and there is nothing to compare them to for an estimate of price.

ᵉI treat Hans Conelyns, Hans Conelanyns, and Hans Coxelens as the same person and associate him with the London mercer and self-professed bibliophile John Coleyns. See Christianson, "London's Book-Trade," 142.

ᶠSyton imported two fattes (a container similar to a vat) of libris along with other goods. There is only one other entry for libris in this account, imported in a basket, which was equivalent in cost to a basket of libris impressus. Since those were equivalent in value, I use an equivalent value of two fattes of libris impressus for the fattes of libris.

ᵍTo find the value for books, I deduct 2s 4s per ream of paper from the total. This is based on the average price of a ream of paper found in other entries in this account.

ʰPrice for mixed baskets of libris impressus including "other" cannot be estimated.

ⁱOne cargo cut off after lib. Estimated to be cargo of libris impressus, like his three other cargoes.

ʲValue of 1512/4 primers (20d per dozen) is taken from the 1507 Book of Rates, see Gras, Early English Customs System, Appendix C.

ᵏ6s deducted from cargo for 33 rolls of latten plate. Based on rate of 20s per 100 rolls of black latten in the 1507 Book of Rates.

ˡSmall (parvus) basket interpreted as half-basket and estimated at £2 based on the average rate per basket.

ᵐFour mixed cargoes of libris impressus and other goods for which no estimations could be made, totaling £13 16s 8d.

Table 2. Value of Books Imported into the Port of London by Type of Book and Year

Descriptions	1480/1a	1490/1	1502/3	1507/8	1512/3	1514/5	1520/1	1534/5	1537/8	Totals
Bokes			£12 13s 8d	£9						£21 13s 8d
Prentyd Bokes	12s 6d			£4						£4 12s 6d
Unbound Bokes								£44	£12	£56
Diverse Histories	£145 11s									£145 11s
Libris, Parvus Libris	£2 15s		£11	£11		£32	?[f]	£10		£66 15s
Libris Depictus	2s 6d						?[g]			2s 6d
Libris Impressus		£85 10s	£112 6s 8d	£65[c]	£44[d]	£8[e]	£163[h]	£70		£547 16s 8d
Diverse Libris Impressus		£34 14s					?[i]			£34 14s
Libris Unbound									£20	£20
Libris Impressus Unbound								£10	£46	£56
Libris Impressus Bound & Unbound								£6		£6
Libris Impressus Unbound and Bokes									£4[j]	£4
Primers[b]		?			£27 13s 4d	£40	£18 13s 4d			£46 6s 8d
Totals	£149 1s	£120 4s	£136 0s 4d	£89	£71 13s 4d	£40	£181 13s 4d	£140	£82	£1009 11s

Sources: See Table 1.

Notes: These customs duties are based on valuations far below actual retail value.

[a]The values for the various types of books were determined by averaging the prices of ship
ments of diverse histories, so these values cannot be used for comparison. The prices
of two chests of books included in cargoes containing other goods were also determined
by averaging the price of other chests. See explanation in text.

[b]Only one shipment of primers appears in 1490/1, making it impossible to value. Price f
or primers (20d per dozen) from 1507 on is taken from the 1507 *Book of Rates*, see
Gras, Early English Customs System, Appendix C. 1520/1 includes one shipment of t
hree gross "borded primers."

[c]Values for mixed cargoes containing *libris impressus* cannot be estimated as remaining goods
are described as "other" ("*alys*").

[d]Three entries for baskets of *libris impressus* were used to estimate other values: One small
(*parvus*) basket is interpreted as half-basket, estimated at £2. Entries for 2 baskets with
prices cut off are valued at £4. One entry cut off after "lib" entered as *libris impressus*
and valued at £4, as importer had three other shipments, all *libris impressus*. One small
chest containing *libris impressus* and 33 rolls of latten plate valued at £6 6s, estimated
to be £6. Based on 1507 *Book of Rates* for 100 rolls of black latten at 20s (rates for latten
plate given by 100 weight).

[e]One mixed cargo totaling £8 6s 8d includes a basket of *libris impressus* and "other" ("*alys*")
that cannot be estimated.

[f]One cargo of *libris* and "bordes" that cannot be estimated, total value 33s 4d.

[g]Four mixed cargoes of *libris impressus* and other items that cannot be estimated, totaling
£21 6s 8d.

[h]Two mixed cargoes; the first contains *libris impressus*, "cardes" and "other"; the second
contains 20 reams of paper and *libris depictus* that cannot be estimated. Although paper
is listed in the 1507 *Book of Rates*, there is no value given. See Gras, Early English Cus
toms System, Appendix C. Total value of shipment is 86s 8d.

[i]One maund of diverse *libris impressus* and various other items that cannot be estimated.
Total value £5. One mixed cargo of one barrel of bokes and a half-basket of *libris impressus* unbound for £4.

Table 3. Value of Books Imported into the Port of London by Publisher or Printers by Year

Year	No. of Importers	No. of Publishers or Printers	Total Value Imported by Publishers or Printers
1480/1	10	1	£9 6s 8d (6.2%)
1490/1	8	1	£3 (4.8%)
1502/3	18	9	£63 6s 8d (46.5%)
1507/8	8	4	£55[b] (62%)
1512/3	6	2	£10[c] (14%)
1514/5	4	2	£16 (40%)
1520/1	21	8	£77[d] (42.4%)
1534/5	10	8	£130 (92.8%)
1537/8	5	3	£64 (83%)
Totals[a]	90	38	£428 1s 4d (42.3%)

Sources: See Table 1. Duff, *Century*; E. Gordon Duff, *The Stationers, Printers and Bookbinders of Westminster and London from 1476 to 1535* (Cambridge: Cambridge University Press, 1906); C. Paul Christianson, *A Directory of London Stationers and Book Artisans, 1300, 1500* (New York: Bibliographical Society of America, 1990); STC.

Notes: Printer-publishers marked with an * in Table 1. This does not mean that all of the books imported by these merchants were printed on commission for them. Many importers were difficult to identify.

[a]Several importers appear in multiple accounts; the total number of individual importers is 75, and the number of individual printer-publishers is 30.

[b]Two cargoes containing "other" goods could not be estimated. Total value £11 14s 4d.

[c]Average for known printer-publishers is 31 percent (£14 of £44) when imports of primers are excluded.

[d]One cargo containing "other" goods could not be estimated. Total value £4.

APPENDIX A: THE SOURCES

This study draws on eleven fairly complete and legible overseas accounts of petty customs or poundage for the port of London from 1457 to 1535. The accounts were chosen largely on the basis of which were likely to contain information on book imports and which could be most easily filmed in the Public Record Office (PRO). Only one of the accounts is in print: that for 1480/1, edited by H.S. Cobb.

Using the National Archives database, a list was created of accounts that could possible contain cargoes of books (petty customs and tunnage and poundage accounts). All accounts of five membranes or fewer were eliminated, as they were unlikely to cover a full year. Accounts were selected at intervals of five to ten years, although there are no extant accounts between 1523 and 1533.

E122/203/4. 36 Hen. VI. Covers 12 months. The first legible date is November 12, 1457, on fol. 2; the last legible date is August 4, 1458, on fol. 29r. Bound in book form containing 36 folios, all of them recording imports. Tunnage and poundage.

E122/194/19. 11–12 Edw. IV. Covers 10½ months from September 29, 1471, to August 4, 1472. Consists of 18 membranes; imports cover membranes 1–17d. Petty customs, particulars of account.

E122/194/25. 20–21 Edw. IV. Covers 12 months from September 29, 1480, to September 29, 1481. Consists of 27 membranes; imports cover membranes 1–11d. Petty customs, controllment of account. Although I worked mainly from Cobb's edition of this account, I checked several entries in the original account to see how he translates the different terms for books.

E122/78/9. 6–7 Hen. VII. Covers 12 months from September 29, 1490, to September 29, 1491. Consists of 18 membranes; imports cover membranes 1–6d. Petty customs, controllment of account.

E122/80/3. 18–19 Hen. VII. Covers 12 months from September 29, 1502, to September 29, 1503. Consists of 29 membranes; imports cover membranes 1–13d. Petty customs, controllment of account.

E122/80/5. 23–24 Hen. VII. Covers 12 months from September 29, 1507, to September 29, 1508. Consists of 32 membranes; imports cover membranes 1–15d. Petty customs, particulars of account.

E122/82/9. 4–5 Hen. VIII. The first legible date for 1512/3 is October 4 in the middle of membrane 1, while the last legible date is September 5 on membrane 29d, with membranes 30 and 30d also containing exports, so it seems to have a full year. Consists of 46 membranes; imports cover membranes 1–30d. Petty customs, controllment of account.

E122/82/3. 5–6 Hen. VIII. Probably covers 12 months. First legible date on membrane 3 is November 6, 1514, to September 25, 1515. Consists of 36 membranes; imports cover membranes 1–14d. Petty customs, described as view/controllment of account.

E122/81/8. 11–12 Hen. VIII. Covers 11 months from October 3, 1520, to August 22, 1521. Consists of 44 membranes; imports cover membranes 1–43d. Nearly half of membranes 11–15 are missing. Tunnage and poundage, particulars of account. Account is not catalogued as tunnage and poundage but includes imports by *indigena*, so it cannot be petty customs.

E122/82/8. 26–27 Hen. VIII. Covers 12 months from September 29, 1534, to September 29 1535. Consists of 48 membranes; imports cover membranes 1–22d. Petty customs, controllment of account.

E122/81/18. 28–29 Hen. VIII. Covers 11½ months from October 6, 1537, to September 26, 1538. Consists of 17 membranes; imports cover membranes 1–16d. Petty customs.

NOTES

1. Dennis Rhodes, "Don Fernando Colón and His London Book Purchases, June 1552," in *Studies in Early European Printing and Book Collecting* (London: Pindar Press, 1983), 163–180. Ninety percent of the 80 surviving texts were printed outside England, and the "English" texts were all printed by foreign printers. David Rundle notes that the purchase was for more than 200 books. See David Rundle, "English Books and the Continent," in *The Production of Books in England 1350–1500*, ed. Alexandra Gillespie and Daniel Wakelin (New York: Cambridge University Press, 2011), 176–178.

2. Andrew Pettegree, "Centre and Periphery in the European Book World," *Transactions of the Royal Historical Society*, 18 (2008): 104–105.

3. Marjorie Plant, *The English Book Trade: An Economic History of the Making and Sale of Books* (London: George Allen and Unwin Ltd., 1974), 36. Malcolm Parkes refers to this group as "pragmatic readers," those who needed to read for business. They joined the "professional readers," scholars associated

with the universities and the church. Another group was "cultivated readers," who read for pleasure. See Malcolm Parkes, "The Literacy of the Laity,"
in *The Medieval World*, ed. David Daiches and Anthony Thorlby, Literature
and Western Civilization 2 (London: Aldus Books, 1973), 555, 558–559;
J. B. Trapp, "Literacy, Books and Readers," in *The Cambridge History of the
Book in Britain III, 1400–1557*, ed. Lotte Hellinga and J. B. Trapp (New York:
Cambridge University Press, 1999), 32–33.
4. Rundle, "English Books," 280. In addition, French was also prominent at
this time, but losing favor.
5. Lotte Hellinga, "Importation of Books Printed on the Continent into
England and Scotland before *c*1520," in *Printing the Written Word: The Social
History of Books circa 1450–1520*, ed. Sandra Hindman (Ithaca, NY: Cornell
University Press, 1991), 205–224; Nicholas Barker, "The Importation of
Books into England, 1460–1526," in *Beiträge zur Geschichte des Buchwesens
im Konfesionellen Zeitalter*, ed. Herbert G. Göpfert (Wiesbaden, Germany:
In Kommission bei O. Harrassowitz, 1985), 251–266; and Margaret Lane
Ford, "Importation of Printed Books into England and Scotland," in *The
Cambridge History of the Book in Britain III, 1400–1557*, ed. Lotte Hellinga
and J. B. Trapp (New York: Cambridge University Press, 1999),179–201.
6. Alexandra Halasz, *The Marketplace of Print: Pamphlets and the Public Sphere
in Early Modern England* (New York: Cambridge University Press, 1997), 1.
7. Kate Harris, "Patrons, Buyers and Owners: The Evidence for Ownership
and the Rôle of Book Owners in Book Production and the Book Trade," in
Book Production and Publishing in Britain, 1375–1475, ed. Jeremy Griffiths
and Derek Pearsall (New York: Cambridge University Press, 1989), 166.
8. Curt F. Bühler, *The Fifteenth-Century Book: The Scribes, the Printers, the
Decorators* (Philadelphia: University of Pennsylvania Press, 1960), 59–60.
George Winship notes that of the 1,300 fifteenth-century imprints of Cologne, two thirds could be described as "assigned readings" for the university
and were only six to twelve leaves each. See George Parker Winship, *Printing in the Fifteenth-Century* (Philadelphia: University of Pennsylvania Press,
1940), 57–58.
9. Barker, "Importation of Books," 263. Venetian imprints were 600 of 1,328
books.
10. One reason Venice became the center of humanist printing is that there
was little chance of humanist texts being suppressed in the republic. Elizabeth Eisenstein estimates that Venice accounted for half of Italy's output in
the fifteenth century. Elizabeth L. Eisenstein, *The Printing Press as an Agent
of Change: Communications and Cultural Transformations in Early-Modern
Europe* (New York: Cambridge University Press, 1979), 389–389. See also
Horatio F. Brown, *The Venetian Printing Press, 1469–1800: An Historical Study*

Based upon Documents for the Most Part Hitherto Unpublished (Amsterdam: Gérard Th. Van Heusden, 1969), 40.

11. Barker, "Importation of Books," 266.

12. Hellinga, "Importation of Books," esp. 209–210. Universities include Cambridge, St. Andrews, Oxford, and Aberdeen. She also examined books at the National Library of Scotland.

13. Hellinga, "Importation of Books," esp. 218–222.

14. For example, Alan Piper and Meryl Foster, "Evidence of the Oxford Book Trade, about 1300," *Viator* 20 (1989): 155–160; and Barker, "Importation of Books," 251–266.

15. Carol Meale, "'Alle the Bokes that I Have of Latyn, Englisch, and Frensch': Laywomen and their Books in Late Medieval England," in *Women and Literature in Britain: 1150–1500,* ed. Carol Meale (Cambridge, UK: Cambridge University Press, 1996), 128–158. Meale was discussing fifteenth-century women; the books for the latter half of the century could possibly be printed. See also Margaret Spufford, "Libraries of the 'Common Sort,'" in *The Cambridge History of Libraries in Britain and Ireland, Vol. 1: to 1640,* ed. Elisabeth Leedham-Green and Teresa Webber (New York: Cambridge University Press, 2006), 520–521. Discussing sixteenth- and seventeenth-century collectors, Spufford notes that cheap books would show up in probate inventories if the owner had a collection worth more than a pound.

16. N. S. B. Gras, *The Early English Customs System: A Documentary Study of the Institutional and Economic History of the Customs from the Thirteenth to the Sixteenth Century* (Cambridge, MA: Harvard University Press, 1918), 59–77; see also Henry Cobb, "Local Port Customs Accounts Prior to 1550," *Journal of the Society of Archivists* 1 (1959): 213–224.

17. Henry Cobb, "'Books of Rates' and the London Customs, 1507–1558," *Guildhall Miscellany* 4 (1971): 1.

18. The national system was in place as early as the thirteenth century, with local customs existing possibly as far back as the eighth century; see Gras, *Early English Customs,* 14; Cobb, "Local Port Customs," 214. The summary accounts are in The National Archives, UK, PRO E356 class.

19. Gras, *Early English Customs,* 96; 142; H.S. Cobb, *The Overseas Trade of London Exchequer Customs Accounts, 1480–1,* London Record Society Publications 27 (London: London Record Society, 1990), xxii–xxvi. Gras refers to the controller's account as a "poor duplicate" of the collector's account, although the controller's account can be used if the collector's account does not survive. After 1478 there were accounts compiled by a surveyor in a similar manner to the controller. See Cobb, *Overseas Trade,* xxvi.

20. Gras, *Early English Customs,* 96.

21. Ibid., 94–99; 130; Cobb, "Local Port Customs," 214.

22. Cobb, *Overseas Trade*, xiii.

23. See Cobb, "Books of Rates," 2; Cobb, "Local Port Customs," 222–223; also Paul Needham, "The Customs Rolls as Documents for the Printed-Book Trade in England," in *The Cambridge History of the Book in Britain III, 1400–1557*, ed. Lotte Hellinga and J. B. Trapp (New York: Cambridge University Press, 1999), 154. Henry II declared the merchants of Gotland (who later formed the core of the Hanse) free of customs duties and tolls on imports and exports in 1237, although the Hanse needed to reestablish its privileges on a regular basis, often with limited success. The Hanse was charged the 1303 duty but was exempt from the cloth duty of 1347 as well as a temporary subsidy on wine and wool that year. This exemption did not prevent some customs officials from attempting to collect these duties anyway. In 1471, Edward IV confirmed Hanse privileges, but continuation of privileges depended on an annual renewal. See T. H. Lloyd, *England and the German Hanse, 1157–1611: A Study of Their Trade and Commercial Diplomacy* (New York: Cambridge University Press, 1991), esp. 17, 34, 57, 61–62, 204.

24. Cobb, "Books of Rates," 1; Cobb, *Overseas Trade*, xii.

25. For a complete picture of the London overseas trade, all of these accounts (wool customs; petty customs and cloth customs, and tunnage and poundage) would be needed for a given year, but not all the accounts survive. Paul Needham estimates that only 30 percent of petty customs (which would include book imports) between the years 1475 and 1554 survive, while Henry Cobb establishes that there is no single year from 1461 to 1509 where all three accounts survive See Needham, "Customs Rolls," 155–156; Cobb, *Overseas Trade*, xiii–xiv.

26. Gras, *Early English Customs*, 121.

27. Ibid., 122. See also H. S. Cobb, "Introduction," in *The Overseas Trade of London Exchequer Customs Accounts, 1480–1*, London Record Society Publications 27 (London: London Record Society, 1990), xxv; Peter Ramsey, "Overseas Trade in the Reign of Henry VII: The Evidence of Customs Accounts," *Economic History Review* 6 (1953): 178.

28. Gras, *Early English Customs*, 123. Ramsey, "Overseas Trade," 178; Henry Cobb, "The Medieval Royal Customs and Their Records," *Journal of the Society of Archivists* 6 (1979): 229.

29. Cobb, "Books of Rates," 5; PRO, E122/80/2 and E122/79/12. Changes were for woad, salt, and pewter.

30. Cobb, "Books of Rates," 6.

31. Ibid., 8. Gras, *Early English Customs*, 124. In an earlier article, Gras says that the local customs "by no stretch of the imagination or misinterpretation of facts" expanded into national customs. See N. S. B. Gras, "The Origin of the National Customs-Revenue of England," *Quarterly Journal of Economics* 27 (1912): 128.

32. Gras, *Early English Customs*, Appendix C, 694–706. Additions and corrections in Cobb, "Books of Rates," Appendix.
33. Cobb, "Books of Rates," 11. The 1507 book contained 300 items, while 790 were listed in the 1545 book.
34. Needham, "Customs Rolls,"159–160.
35. PRO, E 122/81/18, membrane 1d.
36. For example, if they were importing only books or book-related goods such as paper, or a wide range of merchandise. Needham discusses cheap books (e.g., primers) sold outside the regular book trade and belonging to the realm of "chapmen's ware," which included playing cards, knives, spectacles, and other small items. These books were imported by the dozen or gross and are considered under a different category here. See Needham, "Customs Rolls," 159.
37. Henry Robert Plomer, "The Importation of Books into England in the Fifteenth and Sixteenth Centuries: An Examination of Some Customs Rolls," *The Library* 4 (1923): 146–150; expanded upon in Henry Robert Plomer, "The Importation of Low Country and French Books into England, 1480 and 1502–3," *The Library* s.4, 9 (1928/9): 165–168. Plomer examined PRO, E122/194/24 (1480/1), E122/78/9 (1490/1), E122/79/5 (1494/5), and E122/80/2 (1502/3). Plomer writes that he abandoned his research due to the "monotony" of seeing the same names over and over again.
38. Julian Roberts, "Importing Books for Oxford, 1500–1640," in *Books and Collectors, 1200–1700: Essays Presented to Andrew Watson*, ed. James Carley and Colin G. C. Tite (London: British Library, 1997), 317–333; C. Paul Christianson, "The Rise of London's Book-Trade," in *The Cambridge History of the Book in Britain III, 1400–1557*, ed. Lotte Hellinga and J. B. Trapp (New York: Cambridge University Press, 1999), 128–147; and N. J. M Kerling, "Caxton and the Trade in Printed Books," *Book Collector* 4 (1955): 190–199.
39. Roberts, "Importing Books for Oxford," 322–324. Roberts examined PRO, E122/81/9 (1520/1), E122/80/2 (1502/4), E122/86/6 (1534/5), and E122/86/8 (1556/7).
40. Kerling, "Caxton and the Trade," 193.
41. Needham, "Customs Rolls," 148–163. His article has been an invaluable guide.
42. Needham himself complains of this more than once in his own article. See Needham, "Customs Rolls," 149, 153.
43. Maryanne Kowaleski, "Port Towns: England and Wales 1300–1540," in *The Cambridge Urban History of Britain*, vol. 1, ed. Peter Carter (New York: Cambridge University Press, 2000), 477–478 and table 19.1.
44. Ramsey, "Overseas Trade," 179–181; and Cobb, "Books of Rates," 2. Accounts not cited.

45. Caroline Barron examined petty customs, and customs on wool, cloth, and wine. See Caroline M. Barron, *London in the Later Middle Ages: Government and People 1200–1500* (New York: Oxford University Press, 2004), 84–117 and figs. 5.2, 5.10, and 5.12. See also Howard W. Winger, "Regulations Relating to the Book Trade in London from 1337 to 1586," *Library Quarterly* 26 (1965): 158.

46. James Raven, *The Business of Books: Booksellers and the English Book Trade* (New Haven, CT: Yale University Press, 2007), 9, 54.

47. Barron, *London in the Later Middle Ages*, 46, 69.

48. Christopher Dyer, "The Consumer and the Market in the Later Middle Ages," *Economic History Review* 42 (1989): 308–309, 320, 325. Dyer examined household accounts dated between 1280 and 1500.

49. Kowaleski, "Port Towns," 481–483. London handled 65.4 percent of alien trade from 1478 to 1482, although this accounted for only 37.1 percent of total London overseas trade at that time. See also Ramsey, "Overseas Trade," 180; Olive Coleman, "The Collectors of Customs in London under Richard II," in *Studies in London History Presented to Philip Edmund Jones*, ed. A. E. J. Hollaender and William Kellaway (London: Hodder & Stoughton, 1969), 185.

50. Raven, *Business of Books*, 30–31. For a discussion of the regulations affecting aliens and trade, see Winger, "Regulations"; and A. W. Reed, "The Regulation of the Book Trade before the Proclamation of 1538," *Transactions of the Bibliographical Society* 15 (1917): 157–184.

51. Covering 1439–1440; 1443–1444; 1469–1467, 1477–1481 and 1509–1510.

52. *Liber Alienigenus* (Southampton local customs account), vol. II, fol. 6 (Dec. 22, 1480) and account fol. 23r (Dec. 23, 1509) in D. B. Quinn, *The Port Books or Local Customs Accounts of Southampton for the Reign of Edward IV, Vol. II, 1477–1481*, Publications of the Southampton Record Society 38 (Southampton, UK: Cox and Sharland, Ltd., 1938), 247; and Thomas B. James, ed., *The Port Book of Southampton, Vol. I (Weeks 1–26)*, Southampton Record Society 32 (Southampton, UK: University of Southampton, 1990.) See also D. B. Quinn, *The Port Books or Local Customs Accounts of Southampton for the Reign of Edward IV, Vol. I, 1469–1471*, Publications of the Southampton Record Society 37 (Southampton, UK: Cox and Sharland, Ltd., 1938); Thomas B. James, ed. *The Port Book of Southampton, Vol. II (Weeks 27–52)*, Southampton Record Society 33 (Southampton, UK: University of Southampton, 1990); Henry Cobb, *The Local Port Book of Southampton for 1439–40*, Southampton Record Series 5 (Southampton, UK: University of Southampton, 1961); Olive Coleman, *The Brokerage Book of Southampton, 1443–4*, Southampton Record Series 4 (Southampton, UK: University of Southampton, 1961). Coleman notes that much of the luxury

goods entering Southampton were immediately brought to London, with Italians accounting for over 80 percent of goods sent to London. See Olive Coleman, "Trade and Prosperity in the Fifteenth Century: Some Aspects of the Trade of Southampton," *Economic History Review* 16 (1963): 12. C. Paul Christianson has found imports of books through Southampton in 1494/5 (6 cargoes), 1502, and 1504. See C. Paul Christianson, "The Rise of London's Book-Trade," in *The Cambridge History of the Book in Britain III, 1400–1557*, ed. Lotte Hellinga and J. B. Trapp (New York: Cambridge University Press, 1999), 141–142. Christianson lists accounts for only 1502/5, E122/209/2 (15–17 Henry VIII). The only additional information he provides is the names of two of the importers. I did not examine printed accounts that fall outside the time period of this paper. Stuart Jenks is currently working on transcribing all extant customs accounts for London.

53. I transcribed all cargoes from digital photographs of the originals. Dr. Maryanne Kowaleski photographed the import section of seven accounts (1457/8, 1471/2, 1490/1, 1502/3, 1507/8, 1512/3, and 1534/5); I photographed the accounts for 1514/5, 1520/1, and 1537/8. To this group I added the print account for 1480/1 in Cobb, *Overseas Trade*. For a full description of the accounts, see Appendix A. I would like to thank Dr. Maryanne Kowaleski for allowing me to use her photographs for this project, Dr. Heather Wolfe at the Folger Institute for help in transcribing some difficult entries, and Dr. Mary Erler for her helpful comments on an earlier version of this paper. The fiscal year for collecting customs ran from Michaelmas (Sept 29) to Michaelmas, and I am abbreviating the 12-month period as 1514/5, e.g., to represent Sept. 29, 1514, through Sept. 28, 1515.

54. Eight of the petty accounts and one of the poundage accounts contained book imports. The tunnage and poundage account is E122/81/8 (1520/1).

55. PRO, E122/203/4 (1457/8); and PRO, E122/194/19 (1471/2).

56. Kerling, "Caxton and the Trade," 191. She examined London accounts from 1460 to 1492.

57. Harris, "Patrons, Buyers and Owners," 182.

58. The 1457/8 and 1520/1 accounts are for tunnage and poundage; all the remaining accounts examined are petty customs, which only aliens were liable to pay. See Needham, "Customs Rolls," 154.

59. Cobb, *Overseas Trade*, nn.23 and 30; 7-8; 11-12.

60. Cobb, *Overseas Trade*, n.181; 62-63. Although the two entries vary slightly in number of ells per piece, there are only a few entries that contain only Holland cloth, and this one was the closest in size per piece, so it is the best available figure there is. Based on the value given for Holland cloth for July 21 1481, (13 13s 4d for 20 pieces), it averages out to 13s 2d per piece. The only difference is that the entry is for 20 pieces at 554 ells, or an average of 27.7 ells per piece, while our entry is 3 pieces at 80 ells, or 26.6 ells per piece.

61. For example, on June 2, 1481, on the *Valentyn* of London, Lewis Aufan, alien, imported 1 barrel with 17 mirrors; 4 pounds of thread; 2 small books; 2,000 bone beads; 1 small box; 1 old feather-bed; 2 images; and 12 pounds of pineapple kernels, worth 33s 4d combined. Cobb, *Overseas Trade*, n.139. Cobb identifies pineapple kernels as "the edible seeds of the pine cone." Perhaps pine nuts? Cobb, *Overseas Trade*, Glossary, 184.

62. Cobb, *Overseas Trade*, n.1, 139 (*parvus libris*), n.156 (*libris*), n.144 (prentyd bokes). I discuss the various descriptions of books and shipping units in a forthcoming paper, Yvonne Rode, "Sixty-Three Gallons of Books: Shipping Books to London in the Late Middle Ages," in *Manuscripts and Printed Books in Europe 1350–1550: Packaging, Presentation and Consumption*, ed. Susan Powell and Emma Cayley (Exeter, UK: University of Exeter Press, 2012).

63. PRO, E 122/80/5, membranes 8 and 13.

64. The "values" are the customs duties collected, not the actual values of the books.

65. William Campbell, ed., *Materials for a History of the Reign of Henry VII, from Original Documents Preserved in the Public Record Office* (London: Longman, 1873), 211; see also Kerling, "Caxton and the Trade", 193; Winger, "Regulations," 164; and E. Gordon Duff, "Actors (Peter)," in *A Century of the English Book Trade* (London: Bibliographical Society, 1948), 1.

66. Kerling, "Caxton and the Trade," 195. Nelly Kerling believes that Henry Franckenbergk, the second largest importer in 1480/1, may have also taken advantage of Actors' privileges and imported books under his name to avoid paying. Kerling does not elaborate on why she believes this but states that it may explain why "hardly any" imports of books by aliens are recorded around this time.

67. Lloyd, *England and the German Hanse*, 204.

68. Clifford S. L. Davies, "Henry VIII and Henry V: The Wars in France," in *The End of the Middle Ages? England in the 15th and 16th Centuries*, ed. John L. Watts (Thrupp, UK: Sutton Publishing Ltd., 1998), 245; and Richard Britnell, "The English Economy and the Government 1450–1550," in *The End of the Middle Ages? England in the 15th and 16th Centuries*, ed. John L. Watts (Thrupp, UK: Sutton Publishing Ltd., 1998), 103.

69. Britnell, "English Economy," 103.

70. Barbara C. Halporn, ed., *The Correspondence of Johann Amerbach: Early Printing in Its Social Context* (Ann Arbor: University of Michigan Press, 2000), n. 174; also nn. 175–180.

71. *Indigena* importers were Henry Pepwell, John Gough, and Thomas Thorne. The mixed cargo totaling £4 was not figured into the total so no estimate could be made for the proportion of books to other goods (see Table 4 for explanation).

72. Both bound and unbound books are listed in this account.

73. 25 Henry VIII, c15. (15 Jan. 1534) in James Gardiner, ed., *Letters and Papers, Foreign and Domestic, Henry VIII, Vol. 7,* (London: Longman, Green, Longman and Roberts, 1883), 23–24, Medieval and Early Modern Sources Online, http://tannerritchie.com/memso.php; *The Cambridge History of the Book in Britain III, 1400–1557,* ed. Lotte Hellinga and J. B. Trapp (New York: Cambridge University Press, 1999), Appendix, 609–10. Howard Winger believes this regulation has more to do with keeping an eye on incoming texts than to benefit local book artisans, as the unbound sheets would be sent in bulk to wholesalers instead of being dispersed to numerous retailers, making them easier to control. See Winger, "Regulations," 169.

74. Winger, "Regulations," 176. Regnault is not listed as importing bound books in 1534/5.

75. Mary C. Erler, "*The Maner to Lyue Well* and the Coming of English in François Regnault's Primers of the 1520s and 1530s," *The Library* (1984): 239–240; and Erler, "Devotional Literature," in *The Cambridge History of the Book in Britain III, 1400–1557,* ed. Lotte Hellinga and J. B. Trapp (New York: Cambridge University Press, 1999), 503–504. For examples of his primers, see STC 15984, 16208, 15394, 16148, and 16204. It was one of Regnault's Books of Hours that Sir Thomas More took with him to the Tower of London before he was executed. See also Eamon Duffy, *Marking the Hours: English People and Their Prayers 1240–1570* (New Haven, CT: Yale University Press, 2006), 136–137.

76. Needham, "Customs Rolls," 160.

77. Cobb, *Overseas Trade*, xxxviii.

78. PRO, E 122/80/3 membrane 11.

79. Egmondt himself was Flemish. See Erler, "Devotional Literature," 501–502.

80. E.g., STC 16167, 15874, 15801.5, and 16168. Hertzog specialized in liturgical books in red and black. See Barker, "Importation of Books," 256.

81. Wigar Johnson, Walter van Delfe, and Jacob Van Larre.

82. Vanessa Harding states that we can "safely assume" that surnames with "van" indicate a Dutch origin. See Vanessa Harding, "Cross-Channel Trade and Cultural Contacts: London and the Low Countries in the Later Fourteenth Century," in *England and the Low Countries in the Late Middle Ages,* ed. Caroline Barron and Nigel Saul (New York: St. Martin's Press, 1995), 162.

83. Ibid., 157.

84. The *English Short-Title Catalogue* lists pre-1642 books printed by or for the English market. Available online at http://estc.bl.uk (accessed March 28, 2008).

85. Rudolf Hirsch, *Printing, Selling and Reading 1450–1550* (Wiesbaden, Germany: Otto Harrassowitz, 1974), 25–26.

86. Ibid., 25–26.

87. Margaret M. Smith, *The Title-Page: Its Early Development 1460–1510* (New Castle, DE: Oak Knoll Press, 2000), 95.

88. Nonstandardized spelling of names can make it difficult to identify printer-publishers; e.g., "G. Back" (STC 18873.7), "Govaert Bac" (STC 13606.3), and "Godfry Back" (STC 23155).

89. 33 Henry VIII, c177 (17 March 1542), in James Gardiner, ed., *Letters and Papers*, 78–79. See also Raven, *Business of Books*, 55–56.

90. E. Gordon Duff, *A Century of the English Book Trade* (London: Bibliographical Society, 1948). The *Oxford Dictionary of National Biography*, however, includes only two of the importers discussed in this paper (Wynkyn de Worde and Julian Notary) and concentrates on their lives and activities within England. See *Oxford Dictionary of National Biography* (Oxford: Oxford University Press, 2004–2011), http://oxforddnb.com.

91. Peter W. M. Blayney, *The Stationers' Company before the Charter, 1403–1557* (Cambridge: Worshipful Company of Stationers and Newspaper Makers, 2003), 15, 18; Duff, *Century*, xv–xvii; Graham Pollard, "The Company of Stationers before 1557," *The Library* 18 (1937): 9, 11. Only members of the Stationers were permitted to sell books retail in London. To join the guild, it was necessary to become a citizen. See Christianson, "Rise of London's Book Trade," 145.

92. Plomer, "Importation of Low Country," 165.

93. There is no way to know what proportion of texts in a given consignment make up books printed or published by their importer.

94. Duff, "Birckman (Francis)" and "Birckman (Francis), II," in *Century*, 14.

95. P. J. A. Franssen, "Jan van Doesborch (?–1536), Printer of English Texts," *Quaerendo* 16 (1986): 262; Duff, "Ruremond, Rémonde, or Endhoven (Christopher van)," in *Century*, 140–141.

96. STC 1711; he also printed Sarum missals for Birckman, e.g., STC 15822 and 16207. See also Duff, "Ruremond," in *Century*, 140–141.

97. STC 16240. Marjorie Plant surveyed 105 pre-1540 Sarum Missals in the British Museum and found that only 24 of them were printed in England. The majority (67) are French. See Plant, *English Book Trade*, 25.

98. Christianson, "Rise of London's Book Trade," 140. About the Frankfort fair, see Hirsch, *Printing*, 63–64.

99. E. Gordon Duff, *The Printers, Stationers, and Bookbinders of Westminster and London from 1476 to 1535* (Cambridge: Cambridge University Press, 1906): 219.

100. Duff, "Ruwe or Rue (Andrew)" and "Ruwe or Rue (John)," in *Century*, 142.

101. Halporn, *Correspondence,* nn. 43–44. Rewe signed letter 43 (8 Aug. 1495) as "Andreas Ruwe, German bookdealer" but letter 44 (8 Feb. 1496) as "Andreas Ruwe, Bookdealer in London."
102. Ibid., n. 44.
103. *Ibid.,* 207–211; see also n.65.
104. Hirsch, *Printing,* 56–57.
105. Duff, "Reynes (John)," in *Century,* 135–136; e.g., STC 15863. Ruremond's printing activities were to come to an end in 1531, when he died in prison in Westminster for selling English-language New Testaments. His illicit activities had been known to Cardinal Wolsey as early as 1526, but Ruremond avoided arrest by staying out of England until 1530. See Duff, "Ruremond," in *Century,* 140–141.
106. PRO, E 122/80/3, membrane 9d.
107. Plomer, "Importation of Low Country," 166.
108. Ibid.
109. PRO, E 122/78/9, membrane 3d, and E 122/80/3, membranes 5d, 9d, and 11 (1490/1 and 1502/3 respectively).
110. These were printed especially for the English market, e.g., STC 18873.7, 23155, 231641, and 13606.3. See also Franssen, "Doesborch," 263.
111. Duff, "Speryng (Nicholas)," in *Century,* 151.
112. STC 15924.
113. STC 23885.3.
114. Duff, "Bray (John)," in *Century,* 17.
115. STC 15884 and STC 16160.
116. Cobb, *Overseas Trade,* n.1, 30. Franckenbergk is the first importer of books recorded in the customs accounts, for £6-worth in December 1477 (PRO, E 122/194/22). See Kerling, "Caxton and the Trade," 192.
117. Pollard, "The English Market for Printed Books, *The Sandars Lectures,* 1959" *Publishing History* 4 (1978): 19–20. He also credits the decrease in the number of general merchants involved in the book trade to the registration of copyright, although nonmembers of the Stationers' Company were able to purchase publishing rights.
118. PRO, E122/80/8, membranes 13 and 6; Faques became Royal Stationer upon Actors' death *ca.* 1504, restyling himself Printer to the King. See Duff, "Actors (Peter)" and "Faques (William)," in *Century,* 1, 45; and Winger, "Regulations," 164.
119. PRO, E 122/80/8, membrane 6.
120. PRO, E 122/78/9, membrane 6.
121. PRO, E 122/82/5, membranes 17, 19, 22, and 29d.
122. PRO, E 122/81/8, membranes 21 and 26d.
123. PRO, E 122/81/8, membranes 43 and 23.

124. Needham, "Custom Rolls," 159.
125. PRO, E 122/80/5, membranes 8 and 13, and PRO, E 122/82/8, membrane 9. See Duff, "Pepwell (Henry)," in *Century*, 119–120; Frederic Avis, "England's Use of Antwerp Printers 1500–1540," *Gutenberg-Jahrbuch* 48 (1973): 234–235.
126. PRO, E 122/81/8, membranes 30d (paper), 21 (two entries), and 23d ("bordes" and "bordes for bokes"). Excluding primers and printing-related items, there were only two mixed cargoes for this year (7%).
127. PRO, E 122/81/8, membranes 21, 23, 26d, and 43.
128. PRO, E 122/82/8, membrane 21.
129. Duff, "Worde (Wynkyn de)," in *Century*, 173.
130. PRO, E 122/80/8, membrane 6d. Duff says he was granted denization in 1496. If so, he should not have paid customs in 1503 or 1508. See Duff, "Worde (Wynkyn de)," in *Century*, 173–174.
131. PRO, E122/80/5, membranes 6d (2 cargoes), 9, 9d, and 13 (2 cargoes). One of the cargoes on membrane 13 included "other" ("*alys*") goods and could not be estimated.
132. PRO, E122/80/5, membranes 14 and 15. See also Duff, "Speryng (Nicholas)," in *Century*, 151. Speryng/Spierinck was from a family of bookbinders in the Low Countries. Richardson is also from the Low Countries. See Christianson, "Rise of London's Book–Trade," 138, 145.
133. Christianson, "Rise of London's Book–Trade," 141. Christianson notes that Harrison was not a Stationer and could only sell books wholesale.
134. Duff, "Birckman (Francis)," and "Birckman (Francis) II," in *Century*, 14.
135. Duff, "Chastelain (George)," in *Century*, 26.
136. I have been unable to identify Thomas Bottall.
137. Duff, "Birckman (Francis)" and "Birckman (Francis) II," in *Century*, 14.
138. Duff, "Cockes (John)," in *Century*, 29.
139. Duff, "Gowghe, Gouge, or Gough (John)," and "Pepwell (Henry)," in *Century*, 58–59, 119–120.
140. PRO, E122/81/8, membranes 9 and 43 (two entries).

WORKS CITED

Primary Sources
National Archives, Public Record Office. London. Exchequer, K.R. Customs Accounts, E122/78/9; E122/80/3; E122/80/5; E122/81/8; E122/81/18; E122/82/3; E122/82/8; E122/82/9; E122/194/19; E122/194/25; E122/203/4.
Acts of Court of the Mercer's Company 1453–1527. With an introduction by Lætitia Lyell. Cambridge, UK: Cambridge University Press, 1936.

Campbell, William, ed. *Materials for a History of the Reign of Henry VII, from Original Documents Preserved in the Public Record Office.* London: Longman, 1873.

Cobb, H. S., ed. *The Local Port Book of Southampton for 1439–40.* Southampton Record Series 5. Southampton, UK: University of Southampton, 1961.

———. *The Overseas Trade of London Exchequer Customs Accounts, 1480–1.* London Record Society Publications 27. London: London Record Society, 1990.

Coleman, Olive, ed. *The Brokerage Book of Southampton, 1443–4.* Southampton Record Series 4. Southampton, UK: University of Southampton, 1961.

Early English Books Online. http://eebo.chadwyck.com.

Gardiner, James, ed. *Letters and Papers, Foreign and Domestic, Henry VIII.* Vol. 7. London: Longman, Green, Longman and Roberts, 1883. Medieval and Early Modern Sources Online. http://tannerritchie.com/memso.php

Given-Wilson, Chris, ed. *The Parliament Rolls of Medieval England, 1275–1504.* Leicester, UK: Scholarly Digital Editions and the National Archives, 2005. http://www.sd-editions.com/PROME/home.html. Halporn, Barbara C., ed. *The Correspondence of Johann Amerbach: Early Printing in Its Social Context.* Ann Arbor: University of Michigan Press, 2000.

James, Thomas B., ed. *The Port Book of Southampton, Vol. I (Weeks 1–26).* Southampton Record Society 32. Southampton, UK: University of Southampton, 1990.

———, ed. *The Port Book of Southampton, Vol. II (Weeks 27–52).* Southampton Record Society 33. Southampton, UK: University of Southampton, 1990.

Quinn, D. B., ed. *The Port Books or Local Customs Accounts of Southampton for the Reign of Edward IV, Vol. I, 1469–1471.* Publications of the Southampton Record Society 37. Southampton, UK: Cox and Sharland, Ltd., 1938.

———. *The Port Books or Local Customs Accounts of Southampton for the Reign of Edward IV, Vol. II, 1477–1481.* Publications of the Southampton Record Society 38. Southampton, UK: Cox and Sharland, Ltd., 1938.

Secondary Sources

Armstrong, Elizabeth. "English Purchases of Printed Books from the Continent, 1465–1526." *English Historical Review* 94 (1979): 268–290.

Avis, Frederick. "England's Use of Antwerp Printers 1500–1540." *Gutenberg-Jahrbuch* 48 (1973): 234–240.

Barker, Nicholas. "The Importation of Books into England, 1460–1526." In *Beiträge zur Geschichte des Buchwesens im Konfesionellen Zeitalter,* ed. Herbert G. Göpfert. Wiesbaden, Germany: In Kommission bei O. Harrassowitz, 1985, 251–266.

Barron, Caroline M. *London in the Later Middle Ages: Government and People 1200–1500.* New York: Oxford University Press, 2004.

Blayney, Peter W. M. *The Stationers' Company before the Charter, 1403–1557.* Cambridge, UK: Worshipful Company of Stationers and Newspaper Makers, 2003.

Britnell, Richard. "The English Economy and the Government, 1450–1550." In *The End of the Middle Ages? England in the 15th and 16th Centuries,* ed. John L. Watts. Thrupp, UK: Sutton Publishing Ltd., 1998, 89–116.

Brown, Horatio F. *The Venetian Printing Press, 1469–1800: An Historical Study Based upon Documents for the Most Part Hitherto Unpublished.* Amsterdam: Gérard Th. Van Heusden, 1969.

Bühler, Curt F. *The Fifteenth-Century Book: The Scribes, the Printers, the Decorators.* Philadelphia: University of Pennsylvania Press, 1960.

Campbell, William A., ed. *Materials for a History of the Reign of Henry VII from Original Documents Preserved in the Public Record Office.* London: Longman and Co., 1873.

Cheney, C. R., ed. *Handbook of Dates for Students of English History.* Rev. ed. Royal Historical Society Guides and Handbooks 4. New York: Cambridge University Press, 2000.

Christianson, C. Paul. *Directory of London Stationers and Book Artisans, 1300–1500.* New York: Bibliographical Society of America, 1990.

———. "The Rise of London's Book-Trade." In *The Cambridge History of the Book in Britain III, 1400–1557,* ed. Lotte Hellinga and J. B. Trapp. New York: Cambridge University Press, 1999, 128–147.

Cobb, Henry. "'Books of Rates' and the London Customs, 1507–1558." *Guildhall Miscellany* 4 (1971): 1–13.

———. "Local Port Customs Accounts Prior to 1550." *Journal of the Society of Archivists* 1 (1959): 213–224.

———. "The Medieval Royal Customs and Their Records." *Journal of the Society of Archivists* 6 (1979): 227–229.

Coleman, Olive. "The Collectors of Customs in London under Richard II." In *Studies in London History Presented to Philip Edmund Jones,* ed. A. E. J. Hollaender and William Kellaway. London: Hodder & Stoughton, 1969, 181–194.

———. "Trade and Prosperity in the Fifteenth Century: Some Aspects of the Trade of Southampton." *Economic History Review* 16 (1963): 9–22.

Davies, Clifford S. L. "Henry VIII and Henry V: The Wars in France." In *The End of the Middle Ages? England in the 15th and 16th Centuries,* ed. John L. Watts. Thrupp, UK: Sutton Publishing Ltd., 1998, 235–252.

Driver, Martha W. *The Image in Print: Book Illustration in Late Medieval England and Its Sources*. London: British Library, 2004.

Duff, E. Gordon. *A Century of the English Book Trade*. London: Bibliographical Society, 1948.

——. "Frederick Egmondt, an English Fifteenth Century Stationer." *The Library* 2 (1890): 210–216.

——. *The Printers, Stationers, and Bookbinders of Westminster and London from 1476 to 1535*. Cambridge, UK: Cambridge University Press, 1906.

Duffy, Eamon. *Marking the Hours: English People and Their Prayers 1240–1570*. New Haven, CT: Yale University Press, 2006.

Dyer, Christopher. "The Consumer and the Market in the Later Middle Ages." *Economic History Review* 42 (1989): 305–327.

Eisenstein, Elizabeth L. *The Printing Press as an Agent of Change: Communications and Cultural Transformations in Early-Modern Europe*. New York: Cambridge University Press, 1979.

The English Short-Title Catalogue. http://estc.bl.uk.

Erler, Mary C. "Devotional Literature." In *The Cambridge History of the Book in Britain III, 1400–1557*, ed. Lotte Hellinga and J. B. Trapp. New York: Cambridge University Press, 1999, 495–525.

——. "*The Maner to Lyue Well* and the Coming of English in François Regnault's Primers of the 1520s and 1530s." *The Library* (1984): 229–243.

Febvre, Lucien, and Henri-Jean Martin. *The Coming of the Book: The Impact of Printing 1450–1800*. Translated by David Gerard. New York: Verso, 1997.

Foot-Romme, Mirjam M. "Influences from the Netherlands on Bookbinding in England during the Late Fifteenth and Early Sixteenth Centuries." In *Communications: The Eleventh International Congress of Bibliophiles, Brussels, September 21–27, 1979*, ed. P. Culot and E. Rouir. Brussels: Association Internationale de Bibliophile, 1981, 39–64.

Ford, Margaret Lane. "Importation of Printed Books into England and Scotland." In *The Cambridge History of the Book in Britain III, 1400–1557*, ed. Lotte Hellinga and J. B. Trapp. New York: Cambridge University Press, 1999, 179–201.

Franssen, P. J. A. "Jan van Doesborch (?–1536), Printer of English Texts." *Quaerendo* 16 (1986): 259–280.

Gras, N. S. B. *The Early English Customs System: A Documentary Study of the Institutional and Economic History of the Customs from the Thirteenth to the Sixteenth Century*. Cambridge, MA: Harvard University Press, 1918.

——. "The Origin of the National Customs-Revenue of England." *Quarterly Journal of Economics* 27 (1912): 107–149.

Halasz, Alexandra. *The Marketplace of Print: Pamphlets and the Public Sphere in Early Modern England*. New York: Cambridge University Press, 1997.

Harding, Vanessa. "Cross-Channel Trade and Cultural Contacts: London and the Low Countries in the Later Fourteenth Century." In *England and the Low Countries in the Late Middle Ages*, ed. Caroline Barron and Nigel Saul. New York: St. Martin's Press, 1995, 153–168.

Harris, Kate. "Patrons, Buyers and Owners: The Evidence for Ownership and the Rôle of Book Owners in Book Production and the Book Trade." In *Book Production and Publishing in Britain, 1375–1475*, ed. Jeremy Griffiths and Derek Pearsall. Cambridge Studies in Publishing and Printing History. New York: Cambridge University Press, 1989, 163–199.

Hellinga, Lotte. "Importation of Books Printed on the Continent into England and Scotland before c1520." In *Printing the Written Word: The Social History of Books circa 1450–1520*, ed. Sandra Hindman. Ithaca, NY: Cornell University Press, 1991, 205–224.

Hirsch, Rudolf. *Printing, Selling and Reading 1450–1550*. Wiesbaden, Germany: Otto Harrassowitz, 1974.

Kerling, N. J. M. "Caxton and the Trade in Printed Books." *Book Collector* 4 (1955): 190–199.

Kowaleski, Maryanne. "Port Towns: England and Wales 1300–1540." In *The Cambridge Urban History of Britain*, vol. 1, ed. Peter Carter. New York: Cambridge University Press, 2000, 467–494.

———. "Warfare, Shipping and Crown Patronage: The Impact of the Hundred Years War on the Port Towns of England." In *Money, Markets and Trade in Late Medieval Europe: Essays in Honour of John H. A. Munro*, ed. Lawrin Armstron, Ivana Elbl, and Martin M. Elbl. Boston: Brill, 2007, 233–254.

Lloyd, T. H. *England and the German Hanse, 1157–1611: A Study of Their Trade and Commercial Diplomacy*. New York: Cambridge University Press, 1991.

Meale, Carol. "'Alle the Bokes that I Have of Latyn, Englisch, and Frensch': Laywomen and Their Books in Late Medieval England." In *Women and Literature in Britain: 1150–1500*, ed. Carol Meale. Cambridge, UK: Cambridge University Press, 1996, 128–158.

Needham, Paul. "The Customs Rolls as Documents for the Printed-Book Trade in England." In *The Cambridge History of the Book in Britain III, 1400–1557*, ed. Lotte Hellinga and J. B. Trapp. New York: Cambridge University Press, 1999, 148–163.

———. "Haec Sancta Ars: Gutenberg's Invention as Divine Gift." *Gazette of the Grolier Club* 42 (1990): 101–120.

Oxford Dictionary of National Biography. Oxford: Oxford University Press, 2004–2011. http://oxforddnb.com.Parkes, Malcolm. "The Literacy of the Laity." In *The Medieval World*, ed. David Daiches and Anthony

Thorlby. Literature and Western Civilization 2. London: Aldus Books, 1973, 555–577.

Pettegree, Andrew. "Centre and Periphery in the European Book World." *Transactions of the Royal Historical Society* 18 (2008): 101–128.

Piper, Alan, and Meryl Foster. "Evidence of the Oxford Book Trade, about 1300." *Viator* 20 (1989): 155–160.

Plant, Marjorie. *The English Book Trade: An Economic History of the Making and Sale of Books.* London: George Allen and Unwin Ltd., 1974.

Plomer, Henry Robert. "The Importation of Books into England in the Fifteenth and Sixteenth Centuries: An Examination of Some Customs Rolls." *The Library* ser. 4, 4 (1923): 146–150.

———. "The Importation of Low Country and French Books into England, 1480 and 1502–3." *The Library* ser. 4, 9 (1928/9): 165–168.

Pollard, Graham. "The Company of Stationers Before 1557." *The Library* 18 (1937): 1-38.

———. "The English Market for Printed Books *The Sandars Lectures, 1959.*" *Publishing History* 4 (1978): 7-48.

Ramsey, Peter. "Oversees Trade in the Reign of Henry VII: The Evidence of Customs Accounts." *Economic History Review* 6 (1953): 173–182.

Raven, James. *The Business of Books: Booksellers and the English Book Trade.* New Haven, CT: Yale University Press, 2007.

Reed, A. W. "The Regulation of the Book Trade before the Proclamation of 1538." *Transactions of the Bibliographical Society* 15 (1917): 157–184.

Rhodes, Dennis E. "Don Fernando Colón and His London Book Purchases, June 1552." In *Studies in Early European Printing and Book Collecting.* London: Pindar Press, 1983, 163–180.

Roberts, Julian. "Importing Books for Oxford, 1500–1640." In *Books and Collectors, 1200–1700: Essays Presented to Andrew Watson,* ed. James Carley and Colin G. C. Tite. London: British Library, 1997, 317–323.

Rode, Yvonne. "Sixty-Three Gallons of Books: Shipping Books to London in the Late Middle Ages." In *Manuscripts and Printed Books in Europe 1350–1550: Packaging, Presentation and Consumption,* ed. Susan Powell and Emma Cayley. Exeter, UK: University of Exeter Press, forthcoming, 2012.

Rundle, David. "English Books and the Continent." In *The Production of Books in England 1350–1500,* ed. Alexandra Gillespie and Daniel Wakelin. New York: Cambridge University Press, 2011, 276–291.

Smith, Margaret M. *The Title-Page: Its Early Development, 1460–1510.* New Castle, DE: Oak Knoll Press, 2000.

Spufford, Margaret. "Libraries of the 'Common Sort.'" In *The Cambridge History of Libraries in Britain and Ireland, Vol. 1: to 1640,* ed. Elisabeth

Leedham-Green and Teresa Webber. New York: Cambridge University Press, 2006, 520–526.

Sutton, Anne F. *The Mercery of London: Trade, Goods and People, 1130–1578.* Burlington, VT: Ashgate, 2005.

Thompson, James Westfall. *The Frankfort Book Fair: The Francofordiense Emporium of Henri Estienne.* Burt Franklin Bibliography and Reference Series 145. New York: Burt Franklin, 1968.

Trapp, J. B. "Literacy, Books and Readers." In *The Cambridge History of the Book in Britain III, 1400–1557,* ed. Lotte Hellinga and J. B. Trapp. New York: Cambridge University Press, 1999, 31–43.

Winger, Howard W. "Regulations Relating to the Book Trade in London from 1337 to 1586." *Library Quarterly* 26 (1965): 157–195.

Winship, George Parker. *Printing in the Fifteenth Century.* Philadelphia: University of Pennsylvania Press, 1940.

Two Leicestershire Romance Codices: Cambridge, University Library MS Ff.2.38 and Oxford, Bodleian Library MS Ashmole 61

MICHAEL JOHNSTON

In analyzing the history of Middle English books, it is rare to find extensive connections between surviving manuscripts, and thus, when we alight on such connections, they can be quite telling. For example, scholars have recently drawn attention to the host of scribes active in London during the late fourteenth and early fifteenth centuries, many of whom copied multiple manuscripts of Middle English literature. From such analyses, a picture of loosely affiliated freelance copyists has emerged as the model dominating London book production in the century before Caxton.[1] Ralph Hanna also depicts Yorkshire scribes active in copying out multiple manuscripts, signaling an active literary culture far from the capital.[2] And the region of Bury St. Edmunds is known to have produced a series of high-end Lydgate manuscripts, providing us with a picture of yet another provincial book-producing locale—this one apparently specializing in the literature of their local luminary.[3] Yet individual manuscripts of Middle English romance— which was demonstrably a popular genre, with more than a hundred extant manuscripts—survive as almost completely discrete entities, with few identifiable connections to other manuscripts or to wider patterns of scribal dissemination.[4]

I wish here to draw attention to previously overlooked connections between two of the most important compilations of Middle English romance: Cambridge, University Library MS Ff.2.38 (hereafter CUL) and Oxford, Bodleian Library MS Ashmole 61 (hereafter Ashmole). As I argue below, both manuscripts share a paper stock, and both were copied out by a scribe from Leicestershire. Thus, both of these codices were almost certainly provincial productions for a provincial readership, made around the same time in the same locale for a similar sort of reader. But as I also argue, both manuscripts evince different production models—CUL being more organized and bearing the signs of production by a provincial professional, Ashmole being comparatively miscellaneous and amateur. Examining the connections between these manuscripts shows that romance was often produced by remarkably ad hoc procedures, making its production quite different from the more organized and cooperative ventures of London scribes.[5]

Containing nine romances, CUL represents one of the genre's most important compilations: in terms of the number of its romances, it is second only to the Auchinleck Manuscript (Edinburgh, National Library of Scotland MS Advocates 19.2.1) and equal to the Lincoln Thornton Manuscript (Lincoln, Cathedral Library MS 91).[6] It is entirely in a single hand (a mixture of Anglicana and Secretary), which can be conservatively dated to the late fifteenth–early sixteenth century; however, given the many features it shares with Ashmole and the consistent dates offered by its four paper stocks, we should almost certainly locate CUL on the earlier end of this date range, roughly the last quarter of the fifteenth century.[7] It is entirely on paper and divides its texts into two roughly homogeneous sections: religious and didactic texts (fols. 3r–63r) and romances (fols. 63r–261v). Its didactic texts include *Pety Job,* "The Long Charter of Christ," "How the Good Man Taught His Son," and *vitae* of Margaret, Mary Magdalene, Thomas Becket, and Katherine. Its romances include the popular *Robert of Sicily, Guy of Warwick* (the unique fifteenth-century version), Northern *Octavian,* and *Sir Eglamour of Artois.*

Ashmole is best known for its unusual format—tall and narrow—which led many earlier scholars to presume this was a minstrel's holster book.[8] Ashmole bears many broad similarities to CUL: this manuscript, like CUL, is copied entirely by a single scribe and is datable to roughly the second half of the fifteenth century.[9] Like CUL, Ashmole is entirely on paper.[10] Also like CUL, Ashmole contains numerous examples of didactic and religious literature, as well as romances; unlike CUL, however, Ashmole does not divide its romances and its didactic literature into separate sections. Instead, the texts are scattered throughout in seemingly random fashion, likely following whatever exemplars were at hand for the scribe. The didactic/religious texts in Ashmole include *The Northern Passion,* Lydgate's *Dietary,* Maidstone's *Seven Penitential Psalms,* and *The Stations of Jerusalem.* The romances include *Sir Isumbras, The Earl of Tolous, Sir Cleges,* and *Sir Orfeo.*

Both watermark and linguistic evidence point to a common origin—both time and place—for these two manuscripts. CUL contains four stocks of paper, while Ashmole has three, but most important to the present purposes, my analysis of the paper indicates that they both share a stock. That is, the fourth stock present in CUL and the third stock present in Ashmole are identical to one another, and both are quite close to Briquet 11194, a hand surmounted by a flower (Savoy, 1485).[11] Analysis of the marks is much easier in CUL, which is a folio manuscript and thus has its marks in the center of the leaf; Ashmole, by contrast, is a quarto, and the gutters thus obscure the marks. However, my measurements of the marks show that they are identical in size: from the bottom of the hand to the top of the flower, measuring right along the chain line, the mark is 77 millimeters tall, while the widest part of the mark (*viz.*, between the outer edge of the hand's thumb and pinky) measures 24 millimeters. (Beta-radiographs of the watermarks in Ashmole, made when the manuscript was disbound, are kept in a file with the manuscript, and analysis of these allows measurements of the width of these marks, otherwise impossible due to the manuscript's binding.)[12]

It should be noted that there are two slight variations in Ashmole's version of this mark: in one, the flower on top of the hand is symmetrical, with three leaves on each side of a center spike, while on the other a leaf emerges vertically from the center spike, leaving two leaves on the left of the spike and three on the right. This slight variation is no doubt due to the twinning of watermarks in paper mills of the period.[13] In a 1985 essay Friedrich Hülsmann first tentatively noted the commonality between CUL's and Ashmole's paper stocks, arguing that "both scribes used similar sorts of paper," which my own work with the manuscripts confirms.[14] However, given the common linguistic evidence uniting both manuscripts, and given the identical size of the mark in both manuscripts, I think it more than justified to identify these paper stocks as identical, not just "similar"—imported, that is, from the same mill, and, as I argue below, likely acquired from the same paper-seller in Leicester.

Although watermarks must be treated cautiously when used as evidence for dating, the stocks in both manuscripts point to a date in the last quarter of the fifteenth century, one that is consistent with the script employed by both scribes. My own analysis of the stocks in both manuscripts confirms Hülsmann's watermark identification on all points.[15] Since each watermark can be dated to the last quarter of the fifteenth century, we can consider such evidence as a reliable guide to the dating of both codices—a case strengthened by the appearance of one of the watermarks in both codices, while the association of the two manuscripts is further strengthened by the evidence, which I now address, that they are from the same region.

A Linguistic Atlas of Late Mediaeval English (LALME) reveals that the scribe of CUL hailed from Leicestershire, just west of the city of Leicester.[16] Of course, the Linguistic Profiles in LALME are merely a best fit for the data and are not meant to be taken as exact locations. Moreover, these data indicate only where the scribe learned to write, not where he copied out the manuscript itself—scribal mobility, that is, must always be kept in mind.[17] For the present purposes, the key point to note is that LALME also locates the scribe of Ashmole in Leicestershire, just to the northeast of the city of Leicester—that is, from the same region as the scribe of CUL.[18] Internal evidence from Ashmole further supports a connection between this manuscript and the city of Leicester: the scribe copied into his manuscript a uniquely surviving verse legend on the founding of the Feast of All Saints and All Souls. As it happens, Leicester's Corpus Christi Guild marked All Saints' Day as one of its three principal festivals.[19] Moreover, the scribe of Ashmole signed his name, Rate, on nineteen different occasions throughout the manuscript, a name that shows up in Leicestershire wills and among the freemen of the city in the Leicester archives.[20] Thus, it is almost certain that Ashmole was produced in Leicester for a Leicester readership. The facts that CUL's scribe has a similar linguistic profile and used paper from the same source urge us to examine these two codices side by side.

The linguistic and watermark evidence uniting these two manuscripts strongly suggests that both scribes purchased their paper in Leicester, which would form the most proximate and only nearby commercial center, one that could serve the scribes of two such books. There is, in fact, evidence of book production in Leicester during this period, so importation and distribution of paper to service such a market should not be a surprise.[21] The Abbey of St. Mary de Pratis, an Augustinian house located just outside the city walls, was one of the primary educational sites for the children of city elites; in the period when CUL and Ashmole were produced, the abbey held more than 1,100 manuscripts. The abbey definitely had a scriptorium, though evidence of vernacular literary production there is quite limited. John Manly and Edith Rickert do, however, make the case that London, British Library MS Harley 7333, a compendium containing a host of Middle English texts, including *The Canterbury Tales*, was likely produced at St. Mary de Pratis.[22] Moreover, the abbey's collection of books did contain a smattering of "romances and other texts in Anglo-Norman."[23]

Given that the abbey's 1492 catalogue lists books that the precentor, William Charyte, "*scribi fecit,*" we can be confident that around the time of CUL's and Ashmole's production, its scriptorium was active—though this catalogue mentions no Middle English texts. There was also book production within the city: parchment makers are attested as early as the end of the twelfth century, while a street in Leicester came to be known as Parchment

Lane. The late fourteenth century provides evidence of scribal activity in the city, as well. In 1389, Archbishop Courtenay visited Leicester in an attempt to crack down on Lollardy, and while there he questioned two men, Michael Scrivener and William Parchmentmaker, both with trade names pointing unambiguously to book production.

Beyond sharing a common paper stock and a scribe from the same region, there is no indication that the scribes of these two manuscripts were connected in any way. Thus, after likely acquiring their paper from the same place, both scribes went about their separate copying endeavors. There are six texts common to CUL and Ashmole, though in none of the cases are both manuscripts' copies derived from the same exemplar: first, the so-called *Stimulus consciencie minor*;[24] second, the religious lyric, "With Sharp Thorns That Beth Keen";[25] third, "How the Wise Man Taught His Son";[26] fourth, "The Lament of Mary";[27] fifth, "The Adulterous Falmouth Squire";[28] and sixth, the romance known as *The Earl of Tolous*.[29]

So in both CUL and Ashmole, we meet scribes working in the same vicinity at the same time and acquiring at least one stock of paper from the same source. But from there, both scribes took different routes to creating their compilations: the scribe of CUL crafted a relatively well-organized volume with evidence of a good deal of forethought invested in the manuscript's layout and appearance—the signs of a professional book producer. As Felicity Riddy comments about CUL, "The most obvious assumption is that the manuscript was commissioned for urban domestic use from a local professional."[30] I think Riddy is correct that this manuscript was produced on commission—though the evidence affords us only speculation on this point. The CUL-scribe divides the codex into two main thematic sections: the opening series comprises religious texts and moral exempla (fols. 3r–63r), while the subsequent series contains exclusively romances (fols. 63r–end).[31] Even within these larger units, the scribe manages to create sub-units: the manuscript opens with a series of moral-didactic texts (fols. 3r–35v), followed by a series of hagiographies (fols. 35v–47v). After a few more didactic texts, the scribe places two texts about adultery (fols. 56r–59r). And then there is a large span of romances at the end of the volume. Moreover, he employs a uniform mise-en-page throughout, using a double-column format and leaving several inches of blank space between each text, which he usually fills in with an *explicit* or a title for the following text.[32] He also compiles his manuscript into twenty-leaf quires: such a regular collation would fit with a scribe who sat down to copy out a series of texts which he had before him from the start, or at least a scribe who could count on reliable access to texts.

The CUL-scribe also regularly employs catchwords and quire signatures. Of the manuscript's thirteen surviving quires, only one—the second—has multiple stocks of paper. One would expect this state were the scribe to have been a professional, with access to a large supply of paper from the beginning of his copying. A scribe working in such conditions would be able to sit down and produce the manuscript as a single unit, working with large batches of homogeneous paper.

By contrast, Ashmole 61 is remarkably haphazard. To begin with, the manuscript is tall and narrow, the paper folded vertically rather than horizontally, measuring 415 millimeters by 137 millimeters, which left space for only one column. Beyond the idiosyncratic format of the book, we can also find evidence for peculiar production patterns in the scribe's repeated inscription of his name. On nineteen different occasions he signs "Rate," "Amen quod Rate," or some variation on this phrase, as mentioned above. Moreover, this Rate has drawn, at seemingly random intervals, a series of fish and roses at the conclusion of texts throughout the manuscript.[33] Beyond their usual occurrence at the end of texts, there is no discernible pattern to these drawings, meaning they were likely added according to Rate's whimsy. A professional scribe producing a book would hardly have signed his own name repeatedly or drawn a series of what are presumably esoteric illustrations in a volume meant for someone else, suggesting that Rate probably made this for his own household's consumption. Finally, unlike CUL, there is no generic organizational pattern to the manuscript.

Our knowledge of book production in late medieval England is in general quite limited, but within this limited field of knowledge, the lion's share of scholarly attention, as well as the most fruitful speculation, has gone to books produced in London by commercial *scriptores*. With late medieval vernacular books, it is only those produced in London about which we can construct a narrative of production tying manuscripts together into a book-making industry, with cooperation between scribes and thus connections between individual manuscripts—however decentered and germinal such production efforts were. But one suspects—and such a study has never been undertaken, though it is clearly a desideratum—that most books of Middle English in the late fourteenth and fifteenth centuries were not produced by someone with experience in producing multiple codices: more like Rate, less like Adam Pynkhurst, that is.

As Curt F. Bühler writes about the fifteenth-century book, "The professional production of manuscripts was dwarfed, I am convinced, by the quantity of books produced by the enterprise which, for want of a better term, one may call the 'every man his own scribe' movement. There was nothing, of course, to prevent anyone from writing his own manuscripts."[34] The vast majority of England's literate middle class and minor aristocracy lived far from London, and thus it would have been most natural for such consumers to look to local scribes to copy out books for them. Such is likely the case with CUL. And if Ashmole were indeed made by Rate for use in his own household, this would afford us yet another production model lying outside of the circuit of London production: the homemade miscellany. As Michael Sargent comments, "[W]e need to know much more about the non-centralized production of non-canonized books."[35]

Connections between books produced by such "non-centralized" procedures tend to be elusive—such products were not invested with the cultural capital that came with book production in the capital, and thus they were more susceptible to the ravages of time. But in recovering the literary and cultural significance of Middle English romance, we need to be attentive to the connections between surviving manuscripts, however scant. The more such connections emerge, the sharper our picture will be. My intuition is that by the fifteenth century, romance had been pushed to the margins, relegated to an inferior cultural position compared to Chaucer, Gower, and Langland, whose works occupied London copyists in the century before Caxton. As the canon took shape in the city, romance remained in the provinces. But until scholars take up further connections between romance manuscripts of the period, such must remain only an intuition.

Purdue University

Acknowledgments

I wish to thank the Huntington Library and the British Academy for their Fellowship for Study in Great Britain, and the Bibliographical Society (London) and Bibliographical Society of America for their Fredson Bowers Award, which underwrote the costs for much of this research. I also wish to thank Ralph Hanna and Robyn Malo for their comments on drafts of this essay.

NOTES

1. See, e.g., A. I. Doyle and M. B. Parkes. "The Production of Copies of the *Canterbury Tales* and the *Confessio Amantis* in the Early Fifteenth Century," in *Medieval Scribes, Manuscripts, and Libraries: Essays Presented to N. R. Ker*, ed. M. B. Parkes and A. G. Watson (London: Scolar Press, 1978), 163–210; Linne R. Mooney, "Chaucer's Scribe," *Speculum* 81 (2006): 97–138; Mooney, "Locating Scribal Activity in Late-Medieval London," in *Design and Distribution of Late Medieval Manuscripts in England*, ed. Margaret Connolly and Linne R. Mooney (Woodbridge, UK: York Medieval Press, 2008), 183–204; and Simon Horobin, "Adam Pinkhurst and the Copying of British Library, MS Additional 35287 of the B Version of *Piers Plowman*," *Yearbook of Langland Studies* 23 (2009): 61–83. See also Linne Mooney, Simon Horobin, and Estelle Stubbs, Late Medieval English Scribes, Centre for Medieval Studies,

University of York, 2011, http://www.medievalscribes.com, who catalogue the scribes active in copying multiple codices of Chaucer, Gower, Langland, Trevisa, and Hoccleve.

2. Ralph Hanna, "Yorkshire Writers," *Proceedings of the British Academy* 121 (2003): 91–109.

3. Kathleen Scott, "Lydgate's Lives of Sts. Edmund and Fremund: A Newly-Located Manuscript in Arundel Castle," *Viator* 13 (1982): 335–366; and Simon Horobin, "The Edmund-Fremund Scribe Copying Chaucer," *Journal of the Early Book Society* 12 (2009): 191–201.

4. A few exceptions should be noted. We know, for example, that both Lincoln, Cathedral Library MS 91 and London, British Library MS Additional 31042 were copied out and owned by Robert Thornton, an esquire from the North Riding of Yorkshire. We also know that the Findern family of Derbyshire, who owned Cambridge, University Library MS Ff.1.6, also owned other manuscripts. On Thornton and his manuscripts, see George R. Keiser, "Lincoln Cathedral Library MS. 91: Life and Milieu of the Scribe," *Studies in Bibliography* 32 (1979): 158–179; Keiser, "More Light on the Life and Milieu of Robert Thornton," *Studies in Bibliography* 36 (1983): 111–119; John J. Thompson, *Robert Thornton and the London Thornton Manuscript: British Library MS Additional 31042*, Manuscript Studies 2 (Cambridge, UK: D. S. Brewer, 1987); and Michael Johnston, "A New Document Relating to the Life of Robert Thornton," *The Library* 7th ser. 8.3 (2007): 304–313. On the Finderns and their manuscripts, see Rossell Hope Robbins, "The Findern Anthology," *PMLA* 69.3 (1954): 610–642; Keiser, "MS. Rawlinson A. 393: Another Findern Manuscript," *Transactions of the Cambridge Bibliographical Society* 7 (1980): 445–448; and Kate Harris, "The Origins and Make-up of Cambridge University Library MS Ff.1.6," *Transactions of the Cambridge Bibliographical Society* 8 (1983): 299–333.

5. For more on the connections between Middle English romance and provincial gentry households, see Michael Johnston, *Romance and the Gentry in Late Medieval England* (forthcoming).

6. For descriptions of the manuscript, see Gisela Guddat-Figge, *Catalogue of Manuscripts Containing Middle English Romances* (Munich, Germany: Wilhelm Fink, 1976), 94–99; and Frances McSparran and P. R. Robinson, "Introduction," in *Cambridge University Library MS Ff.2.38* (London: Scolar Press, 1979), vii–xxv.

7. Guddat-Figge, *Catalogue of Manuscripts*, 94, suggests the middle of the fifteenth century, while P. R. Robinson, "Palaeographical Description and Commentary," in *Cambridge University Library MS Ff.2.38*, xii, suggests the late fifteenth–early sixteenth century.

8. For this debate, and a resounding refutation of the minstrel connections of such manuscripts, see Andrew Taylor, "The Myth of the Minstrel

Manuscript," *Speculum* 66.1 (1991): 43–73. For a valuable reframing of this debate, see George Shuffelton, "Is There a Minstrel in the House?: Domestic Entertainment in Late Medieval England," *Philological Quarterly* 87.1–2 (2008): 51–76.

9. George Shuffelton, ed., *Codex Ashmole 61: A Compilation of Popular Middle English Verse* (Kalamazoo, MI: Medieval Institute, 2008), 3–5, suggests a rough date of 1500 for this manuscript, noting, however, that the scribe's hand is closer in appearance to the script of the mid-fifteenth century. Likewise, Guddat-Figge, *Catalogue of Manuscripts*, 249, dates the manuscript to the late fifteenth–early sixteenth century.

10. The most thorough work on Ashmole is Lynne S. Blanchfield, "'An Idiosyncratic Scribe': A Study of the Practice and Purpose of Rate, the Scribe of Bodleian Library MS Ashmole 61," PhD diss., University College of Wales, Aberystwyth, 1991. See also Blanchfield, "The Romances in MS Ashmole 61: An Idiosyncratic Scribe," in *Romance in Medieval England*, ed. Maldwyn Mills, Jennifer Fellows, and Carol Meale (Cambridge, UK: D. S. Brewer, 1991), 65–87; and Blanchfield, "Rate Revisited: The Compilation of the Narrative Works in MS Ashmole 61," in *Romance Reading on the Book: Essays on Medieval Narrative Presented to Maldwyn Mills*, ed. Jennifer Fellows et al. (Cardiff: University of Wales Press, 1996), 208–220. For an edition of the entire manuscript and further discussion of its make-up, see Shuffelton, *Codex Ashmole*.

11. In all aspects, this mark matches Briquet 11194, except that Briquet's version has an –R on the palm of the hand, something lacking in this mark as it appears in CUL and in Ashmole.

12. Oxford, Bodleian Library Refs. LXXIV.27.

13. Allan H. Stevenson, "Watermarks Are Twins," *Studies in Bibliography* 4 (1951–52): 57–93.

14. Friedrich Hülsmann, "The Watermarks of Four Late Medieval Manuscripts Containing *The Erle of Tolous*," *Notes and Queries* 230 (1985): 12.

15. Ibid., 11–12. The watermarks in CUL are, in the order in which they appear within the manuscript, good matches with Briquet 14237 (Namur, 1474), 22 (Soleure, 1478), 11323 (Palermo, 1479–84), and 11194 (Savoy, 1485). The watermarks in Ashmole, in the order in which they appear within the manuscript, are good matches with Briquet 694 (Palermo, 1479), 11194 (Savoy, 1485), and 10116 (Deville, 1488). P. R. Robinson, "Palaeographical Description and Commentary," in *Cambridge University Library MS Ff.2.38*, xii, notes only three watermarks in CUL. For another identification of the watermarks in Ashmole, see Bruce Barker-Benfield's unpublished notes at Oxford, Bodleian Library Refs. LXXIV.27. Barker-Benfield's analysis modifies that of A. J. Bliss, ed., *Sir Orfeo*, 2nd. ed. (Oxford: Clarendon Press, 1966). Coincidentally, Phillipa Hardman, "Introduction," in *The Heege Manuscript:*

A Facsimile of National Library of Scotland MS Advocates 19.3.1, Leeds Texts and Monographs n.s. 16 (Leeds, UK: Leeds Studies in English, 2000), 4, notes that one of the watermarks in Advocates 19.3.1 is "identical to Briquet's pattern 22," a mark also found in Ashmole 61. No one has yet followed up on the potential connections between these two manuscripts. Angus McIntosh, M. L. Samuels, and Michael Benskin, eds., *A Linguistic Atlas of Late Mediaeval English* (Aberdeen: University of Aberdeen Press, 1986), 3:608–609, analyze the dialect of the main scribe of the Advocates Manuscript as LP 29, located to Grid 400 412, in the far southwest corner of the West Riding of Yorkshire, just over the border with Lancashire and just north of the border with Derbyshire.

16. McIntosh, Samuels, and Benskin, eds., *A Linguistic Atlas*, 3:244–45 analyze the dialect as LP 531, located to Grid 445 305.

17. Richard Beadle, "Prolegomena to a Literary Geography of Later Medieval Norfolk," in *Regionalism in Late Medieval Manuscripts and Texts: Essay Celebrating the Publication of A* Linguistic Atlas of Late Mediaeval English, ed. Felicity Riddy (Cambridge, UK: D. S. Brewer, 1991), 90–91, expresses what I think is a healthy skepticism about positing too much scribal mobility. On the usefulness and limitations of LALME, see Simon Horobin, "Mapping the Words," in *The Production of Books in England, 1350–1500*, ed. Alexandra Gillespie and Daniel Wakelin (Cambridge, UK: Cambridge University Press, 2011), 59–78.

18. McIntosh, Samuels, and Benskin, eds., *A Linguistic Atlas*, 3:233–34 analyze the dialect as LP 71, located to Grid 478 318. See also Shuffelton, ed., *Codex Ashmole*, 4.

19. Julia Boffey and A. S. G. Edwards, eds., *New Index of Middle English Verse* (London: British Library, 2005), #1685. Shuffelton, ed., *Codex Ashmole*, 198–211; fols. 73r–78v. This connection is noted in Blanchfield, "Romances in MS Ashmole," 85.

20. Henry Hartopp, ed., *Calendar of Wills and Administrations Relating to the County of Leicester, Proved in the Archdeaconry Court of Leicester, 1495–1649, and in the Peculiars of St. Margaret Leicester, Rothley, Groby, Evingston, and the Unproved Wills, etc., Previous to 1801: All Now Preserved in the Probate Registry at Leicester*, British Record Society 27 (London: British Record Society, 1902), 10, 32. A William Ratt also shows up in an arbitration involving the city of Leicester from 1493. See Mary Bateson, ed., *Records of the Borough of Leicester, Being a Series of Extracts from the Archives of the Corporation of Leicester, 1327–1509*, rev'd. W. H. Stevenson and J. E. Stocks, vol. 2 (London: J. C. Clay and Son, 1901), 441. See also Henry Hartopp, ed., *Register of the Freemen of Leicester, 1196–1700: Including the Apprentices Sworn before*

Successive Mayors for Certain Periods, 1646–1700, ([Leicester, UK]: Edgar Backus, 1927), 54, 61. For a thorough discussion of this scribe's identity, see Blanchfield, "Idiosyncratic Scribe," 146–69. The variations in spelling of the scribe's name should not be surprising, for he even spells his own name variously within the manuscript. He usually records "Amen quod Rate," but on fol. 107r, he writes "Amen quod Rathe."

21. In what follows, I draw from the excellent discussion found in John Hinks, "The Beginnings of the Book Trade in Leicester," in *The Moving Market: Continuity and Change in the Book Trade*, ed. P. Isaac and B. McKay (New Castle, DE: Oak Knoll Press, 2001), 27–38. See also Teresa Webber, "Latin Devotional Texts and the Books of the Augustinian Canons of Thurgarton Priory and Leicester Abbey in the Late Middle Ages," in *Books and Collectors, 1200–1700: Essays Presented to Andrew Watson*, ed. James P. Carley and Colin G. C. Tite (London: British Library, 1997), 27–41; and Webber, "The Books of Leicester Abbey," in *Leicester Abbey: Medieval History, Archaeology and Manuscript Studies*, ed. Joanna Story, Jill Bourne, and Richard Buckley (Leicester, UK: Leicester Archaeological and Historical Society, 2006), 127–146. For a further attestation of manuscript production in Leicester, see Michael Gullick and Teresa Webber, "Summary Catalogue of Surviving Manuscripts from Leicester Abbey," in *Leicester Abbey: Medieval History, Archaeology and Manuscript Studies*, 189-192.

22. John M. Manly and Edith Rickert, eds., *The Text of* The Canterbury Tales: *Studied on the Basis of All Known Manuscripts*, 8 vols. (Chicago: University of Chicago Press, 1940), 1:214–218. Cf. Gullick and Webber, "Summary Catalogue," 189, who suggest that Harley 7333 was produced locally, but not in the abbey itself.

23. Webber, "Books of Leicester Abbey," 129.

24. Boffey and Edwards, eds., *New Index of Middle English Verse*, #244; fols. 14va–19rb (in CUL); fols. 120r–128r (in Ashmole). See Shuffelton, ed., *Codex Ashmole*, 310–330. This moral-didactic verse treatise survives in seven total manuscripts, though no critical edition of the text exists that accounts for all of the manuscripts. A full collation of the texts lies beyond the scope of the present essay, but a simple comparison of the two versions demonstrates that these could not have come from the same exemplar—the frequent changes in phrases alone suggest different textual traditions, not scribal substitutions or emendations. The poem is in Karl Horstmann, ed., *Yorkshire Writers: Richard Rolle of Hampole and His Followers*, 2 vols. (London: Sonnenschein, 1895–1896), 2:36–45, presenting an edition from London, British Library Royal MS 17.B.xvii, for which Horstmann also consulted readings in London, British Library Additional MS 10053.

25. Boffey and Edwards, eds., *New Index of Middle English Verse*, #4200; fol. 33ra (in CUL); fol. 150v (in Ashmole). See Shuffelton, ed., *Codex Ashmole*, 385–386. In this case, the stanzas are in a completely different order in each version.

26. Boffey and Edwards, eds., *New Index of Middle English Verse*, #1877 and 1985; fols. 53ra–54rb (in CUL); fol. 6r–v (in Ashmole). See Shuffelton, ed., *Codex Ashmole*, 32–34.

27. Boffey and Edwards, eds., *New Index of Middle English Verse*, #2619 and 1447; fols. 55vb–56rb (in CUL); fols. 106r–107r (in Ashmole). See Shuffelton, ed., *Codex Ashmole*, 274–77. The version in CUL lacks what are the first three stanzas of the version in Ashmole, and there are numerous textual variants between them.

28. Boffey and Edwards, eds., *New Index of Middle English Verse*, #2052; fols. 56rb–57va (in CUL); fols. 136v–138v (in Ashmole). See Shuffelton, ed., *Codex Ashmole*, 351–356.

29. See Gustav Lüdtke, ed., *The Erl of Tolous and the Emperes of Almayn: Eine englische Romanze aus dem Anfange des 15. Jahrhunderts* (Berlin: Weidmannsche Buchhandlung, 1881), 1–23, whose collation of the extant manuscripts shows that Ashmole lacks a number of verses present in the three other surviving manuscripts of this romance. As Lüdtke demonstrates, Ashmole and Lincoln, Cathedral Library MS 91 compose a textual family that is discrete from CUL. In particular, Lüdtke shows that manuscripts "A und B [i.e. CUL and Oxford, Bodleian Library MS Ashmole 45, respectively] einerseits und C und D [i.e. Lincoln, Cathedral MS 91 and Ashmole, respectively] anderseits stehen sich als gesonderte gruppen gegenüber AB = x, CD = y" [A and B, on the one hand, and C and D, on the other hand, stand as separate groups where AB = x, CD = y]; ibid., 5.

30. Felicity Riddy, "Temporal Virginity and the Everyday Body: *Le Bone Florence of Rome* and Bourgeois Self-Making," in *Pulp Fictions of Medieval England: Essays in Popular Romance*, ed. Nicola McDonald (Manchester, UK: Manchester University Press, 2004), 199.

31. The only possible exception to this division is the appearance of *The Seven Sages of Rome* in the second section. This is a text that while not, strictly speaking, a romance, narrates the importance of counsel to secular lordship, which is certainly a central romance motif. Thus, it fits relatively comfortably within the second section of this manuscript, provided we maintain a flexible understanding of genre.

32. On rare occasions he employs a single-column format, comprising only nine leaves of the whole manuscript.

33. For a reproduction of one such drawing, see Shuffelton, ed., *Codex Ashmole*, 18.

34. Curt F. Bühler, *The Fifteenth-Century Book: The Scribes, the Printers, the Decorators* (Philadelphia: University of Pennsylvania Press, 1960), 22–23.
35. Michael Sargent, "What Do the Numbers Mean? A Textual Critic's Observations on Some Patterns of Middle English Manuscript Transmission," in *Design and Distribution of Late Medieval Manuscripts in England*, ed. Margaret Connolly and Linne R. Mooney (Woodbridge, UK: York Medieval Press, 2008), 244.

WORKS CITED

Bateson, Mary, ed. *Records of the Borough of Leicester, Being a Series of Extracts from the Archives of the Corporation of Leicester, 1327–1509*. Vol. 2. Revised by W. H. Stevenson and J. E. Stocks. London: J. C. Clay and Son, 1901.

Beadle, Richard. "Prolegomena to a Literary Geography of Later Medieval Norfolk." In *Regionalism in Late Medieval Manuscripts and Texts: Essays Celebrating the Publication of A Linguistic Atlas of Late Mediaeval English*, ed. Felicity Riddy. Cambridge, UK: D. S. Brewer, 1991, 89–108.

Blanchfield, Lynne S. "'An Idiosyncratic Scribe': A Study of the Practice and Purpose of Rate, the Scribe of Bodleian Library MS Ashmole 61." PhD diss., University College of Wales, Aberystwyth, 1991.

———. "Rate Revisited: The Compilation of the Narrative Works in MS Ashmole 61." In *Romance Reading on the Book: Essays on Medieval Narrative Presented to Maldwyn Mills*, ed. Jennifer Fellows et al. Cardiff: University of Wales Press, 1996, 208–220.

———. "The Romances in MS Ashmole 61: An Idiosyncratic Scribe" In *Romance in Medieval England*, ed. Maldwyn Mills, Jennifer Fellows, and Carol Meale. Cambridge, UK: D. S. Brewer, 1991, 65–87.

Bliss, A. J., ed. *Sir Orfeo*. 2nd. ed. Oxford: Clarendon Press, 1966.

Bühler, Curt F. *The Fifteenth-Century Book: The Scribes, the Printers, the Decorators*. Philadelphia: University of Pennsylvania Press, 1960.

Doyle, A. I., and M. B. Parkes. "The Production of Copies of the *Canterbury Tales* and the *Confessio Amantis* in the Early Fifteenth Century." In *Medieval Scribes, Manuscripts, and Libraries: Essays Presented to N. R. Ker*, ed. M. B. Parkes and A. G. Watson. London: Scolar Press, 1978, 163–210.

Guddat-Figge, Gisela. *Catalogue of Manuscripts Containing Middle English Romances*. Munich, Germany: Wilhelm Fink, 1976.

Gullick, Michael, and Teresa Webber. "Summary Catalogue of Surviving Manuscripts from Leicester Abbey." In *Leicester Abbey: Medieval History, Archaeology and Manuscript Studies*, ed. Joanna Story, Jill Bourne, and Richard Buckley. Leicester, UK: Leicester Archaeological and Historical Society, 2006, 173–192.

Hanna, Ralph. "Yorkshire Writers." *Proceedings of the British Academy* 121 (2003): 91–109.

Harris, Kate. "The Origins and Make-up of Cambridge University Library MS Ff.1.6." *Transactions of the Cambridge Bibliographical Society* 8 (1983): 299–333.

Hartopp, Henry, ed. *Calendar of Wills and Administrations Relating to the County of Leicester, Proved in the Archdeaconry Court of Leicester, 1495–1649, and in the Peculiars of St. Margaret Leicester, Rothley, Groby, Evingston, and the Unproved Wills, etc., Previous to 1801: All Now Preserved in the Probate Registry at Leicester.* British Record Society 27. London: British Record Society, 1902.

———. *Register of the Freemen of Leicester, 1196–1700: Including the Apprentices Sworn before Successive Mayors for Certain Periods, 1646–1700.* [Leicester, UK]: Edgar Backus, 1927.

The Heege Manuscript: A Facsimile of National Library of Scotland MS Advocates 19.3.1. Introduction by Phillipa Hardman. Leeds Texts and Monographs n.s. 16. Leeds, UK: Leeds Studies in English, 2000.

Hinks, John. "The Beginnings of the Book Trade in Leicester." In *The Moving Market: Continuity and Change in the Book Trade,* ed. P. Isaac and B. McKay. New Castle, DE: Oak Knoll Press, 2001, 27–38.

Horobin, Simon. "Adam Pinkhurst and the Copying of British Library, MS Additional 35287 of the B Version of Piers Plowman." *Yearbook of Langland Studies* 23 (2009): 61–83.

———. "The Edmund-Fremund Scribe Copying Chaucer." *Journal of the Early Book Society* 12 (2009): 191–201.

———. "Mapping the Words." In *The Production of Books in England, 1350–1500,* ed. Alexandra Gillespie and Daniel Wakelin. Cambridge, UK: Cambridge University Press, 2011, 59–78.

Horstmann, Karl, ed. *Yorkshire Writers: Richard Rolle of Hampole and His Followers.* 2 vols. London: Sonnenschein, 1895–1896.

Hülsmann, Friedrich. "The Watermarks of Four Late Medieval Manuscripts Containing *The Erle of Tolous.*" *Notes and Queries* n.s. 230.1 (1985): 11–12.

Johnston, Michael. "A New Document Relating to the Life of Robert Thornton." *The Library* 7th ser. 8.3 (2007): 304–313.

———. *Romance and the Gentry in Late Medieval England.* Forthcoming.

Keiser, George R. "Lincoln Cathedral Library MS. 91: Life and Milieu of the Scribe." *Studies in Bibliography* 32 (1979): 158–179.

———. "More Light on the Life and Milieu of Robert Thornton." *Studies in Bibliography* 36 (1983): 111–119.

———. "MS. Rawlinson A. 393: Another Findern Manuscript." *Transactions of the Cambridge Bibliographical Society* 7 (1980): 445–448.

Lüdtke, Gustav, ed. *The Erl of Tolous and the Emperes of Almayn: Eine englische Romanze aus dem Anfange des 15. Jahrhunderts.* Berlin: Weidmannsche Buchhandlung, 1881.

Manly, John M., and Edith Rickert, eds. *The Text of* The Canterbury Tales: *Studied on the Basis of All Known Manuscripts.* 8 vols. Chicago: University of Chicago Press, 1940.

McSparran, Frances, and P. R. Robinson. "Introduction." In *Cambridge University Library MS Ff.2.38.* London: Scolar Press, 1979.

Mooney, Linne R. "Chaucer's Scribe." *Speculum* 81.1 (2006): 97–138.

———. "Locating Scribal Activity in Late-Medieval London." In *Design and Distribution of Late Medieval Manuscripts in England*, ed. Margaret Connolly and Linne R. Mooney. Woodbridge, UK: York Medieval Press, 2008, 183–204.

Mooney, Linne, Simon Horobin, and Estelle Stubbs. Late Medieval English Scribes. Centre for Medieval Studies, University of York, 2011. http://www.medievalscribes.com.

Riddy, Felicity. "Temporal Virginity and the Everyday Body: *Le Bone Florence of Rome* and Bourgeois Self-Making." In *Pulp Fictions of Medieval England: Essays in Popular Romance*, ed. Nicola McDonald. Manchester, UK: Manchester University Press, 2004, 197–216.

Robbins, Rossell Hope. "The Findern Anthology." *PMLA* 69.3 (1954): 610–642.

Sargent, Michael. "What Do the Numbers Mean? A Textual Critic's Observations on Some Patterns of Middle English Manuscript Transmission." In *Design and Distribution of Late Medieval Manuscripts in England*, ed. Margaret Connolly and Linne R. Mooney. Woodbridge, UK: York Medieval Press, 2008, 205–244.

Scott, Kathleen. "Lydgate's Lives of Sts Edmund and Fremund: A Newly-Located Manuscript in Arundel Castle." *Viator* 13 (1982): 335–366.

Shuffelton, George, ed. *Codex Ashmole 61: A Compilation of Popular Middle English Verse.* Kalamazoo, MI: Medieval Institute, 2008.

———. "Is There a Minstrel in the House?: Domestic Entertainment in Late Medieval England." *Philological Quarterly* 87.1–2 (2008): 51–76.

Stevenson, Allan H. "Watermarks Are Twins." *Studies in Bibliography* 4 (1951–1952): 57–93.

Taylor, Andrew. "The Myth of the Minstrel Manuscript." *Speculum* 66.1 (1991): 43–73.

Thompson, John J. *Robert Thornton and the London Thornton Manuscript: British Library MS Additional 31042*. Manuscript Studies 2. Cambridge, UK: D. S. Brewer, 1987.

Webber, Teresa. "The Books of Leicester Abbey." In *Leicester Abbey: Medieval History, Archaeology and Manuscript Studies*, ed. Joanna Story, Jill Bourne, and Richard Buckley. Leicester, UK: Leicester Archaeological and Historical Society, 2006, 127–146.

——. "Latin Devotional Texts and the Books of the Augustinian Canons of Thurgarton Priory and Leicester Abbey in the Late Middle Ages." In *Books and Collectors, 1200–1700: Essays Presented to Andrew Watson*, ed. James P. Carley and Colin G. C. Tite. London: British Library, 1997, 27–41.

Love Stories on Paper in Middle English Verse Love Epistles

MARTHA RUST

In Chaucer's version of the story of Troilus and Criseyde, epistles fuel and document every stage of the lovers' affair; indeed, as Sarah Stanbury remarks, the poem is "so full of letters we might almost call it an epistolary romance."[1] Extrapolating from a remark in Criseyde's final letter to Troilus, I would suggest that it is a romance on paper as well. Responding to Troilus's epistolary cries of distress, Criseyde writes in that final missive, "Youre lettres ful, the papir al ypleynted / Conceyved hath myn hertes pietee."[2] Though it fails as a depiction of letter-writing in ancient Troy—where lovers, had they sent each other letters, would have used clay tablets—this reference to paper letters provides valuable evidence of the use of paper for letter-writing in England during the time of Chaucer's composition of this verse epistle, sometime in the mid-1380s.[3] The sixteen surviving manuscripts of *Troilus and Criseyde*, whose production dates span the fifteenth century, reflect increases during that period in the use of paper for a different purpose: that is, for transmitting works of literature in books (see table).[4] While paper was used very rarely for books at the beginning of the century, it is estimated that about 20 percent of books were made of paper by mid-century, and 50 percent or more by the end, and *Troilus and Criseyde* manuscripts neatly follow this trend.[5] By the end of the fifteenth century, then, fictional literary letters were just as likely to be set down on paper as real ones.

While surviving *Troilus and Criseyde* manuscripts thus provide a small-scale reflection of an important change in the technology of book production during the fifteenth century, they also mark the inception and flowering of a peculiarly fifteenth-century literary phenomenon: the popularity of verse love epistles. The earliest extant manuscript of *Troilus and Criseyde*, Cambridge University Library MS Gg.4.27, preserves several early specimens of this genre, while the flyleaves of the latest, Bodleian Library MS Arch. Selden B.24, preserve one of their lovesick offspring.[6] As seems fitting for a genre of popular literature whose evolution coincides with the growing acceptance of paper for literary compositions, most of the manuscripts that preserve Middle English verse love epistles are themselves composed of paper. Indeed, among the twenty manuscripts produced during the fifteenth century that contain these poems, only four are made entirely of parchment.[7]

Manuscripts of "Troilus and Criseyde"

Date	MS	Parchment	Paper
1400-1424	Cp (1398)	Parchment	
	Cl	Parchment	
	H1	Parchment	
	Gg	Parchment	
	H2	Parchment	
	R		Paper
1425-1450	A	Parchment	
	D	Parchment	
	J	Parchment	
	S2		Paper and parchment
	Ph		Paper and parchment
	H4		Paper
1451-1475	H5	Parchment	
	H3	Parchment	
	Dg		Paper
1476-1500	S1		Paper
Dates and Sigla from M. C. Seymour, "The Manuscripts of Chaucer's *Troilus*," *Scriptorium* 46 (1992): 107-21.			

But the link between paper and verse love letters is not only codicological but ontological as well. Like paper, these literary epistles recycle material originally meant for other things: verse love epistles borrow epistolary *formulae* meant originally for formal, often institutional communiqués, while medieval paper was constructed out of fibers that had their first use as clothing. And like the paper on which they are most often preserved, these verse fabrications also exist within a larger context of cultural disapprobation, a disapproval, moreover, that turns upon a perception in them of somewhat similar foibles: paper is held suspect because of its presumed fragility and heterogeneous composition, love letters for their association with improper, covert affections fed by an unseemly array of libidinous acts.

In the opening section of this article, I demonstrate these correspondences first by examining the physical properties and social history of paper—considering parchment at key points for comparison—and then by surveying texts that refer to the moral perils of sending and receiving letters. This overview makes way, in turn, for an exploration of two manuscripts that preserves a verse love letter on paper. As I show, the ontological parallels between verse love epistles and paper intersect in that manuscript to form the ideal matrix for a tale of love and literature in a world of paper.

I

Historians of late-medieval English book production stress that it was the relatively low price of paper compared to parchment that was the major factor determining paper supplanting parchment over the course of the fifteenth century.[8] Given the substantial economic advantage of paper over parchment, it is somewhat surprising that the use of paper for books did not grow even more quickly than it did. The delay in the acceptance of paper in England—exemplified, as just noted, in manuscript copies of *Troilus and Criseyde*—was the effect of a stubborn skepticism about the material in both Europe and England that stemmed from perceptions running the gamut from the practical to the faintly paranoid: from an early and relatively well-founded concern about its fragility, to Christian intolerance for anything associated with Muslims or Jews, to a more vaguely expressed distaste for its ambiguous and heterogeneous composition.

The story of paper begins in China, but I begin my account of the sources of European ambivalence toward it with a look at its physical properties in contrast to those of parchment, for even in their differing biological and chemical codes, parchment and paper suggest two opposing narrative structures: parchment has to do with diachronic lines of transmission, paper with synchronic circulation—a fitting structure, as I show later in this article, within which to build an epistolary love affair.

Lines of Transmission and Networks of Circulation in Paper and Parchment

Silvie Turner opens her book on fine paper by observing, "How easy it is to take paper for granted. A substance composed simply of the interlacing of fibres into a compact web."[9] On a molecular level, the fibers that make up that compact, ever-so serviceable web are long chains of cellulose molecules. A complex carbohydrate, cellulose is the primary component of plant cell walls and the chemical compound that gives a cell "wall" the strength worthy its name. Cellulose also has the important property of being exceedingly hygroscopic, and it is this affinity for water—or on a chemical level, a readiness to form hydrogen bonds—that gives paper its strength and flexibility.[10] During the papermaking process, the raw materials for paper—all of which derive ultimately from plants, be they linen rags, hemp ropes, or wood chips—first undergo a process of maceration by beating, pounding, or bruising, which reduces them to a mass of cellulose fibers. As preeminent paper historian Dard Hunter explains, the fibers are then "intermixed with water, and by the use of a sieve-like screen ... lifted from the water in the form of a thin stratum ... leaving a sheet of matted fibre upon the screen's surface. This thin layer of intertwined fibre is paper."[11]

In contrast, parchment is a product of the middle—dermis—layer of animal skins, in medieval England primarily calf- and sheepskins.[12] Two further layers make up the dermis; the larger of these is called the fiber-network layer, which is made up almost completely of collagen in the form of connective tissue fibers. Unlike cellulose, which is a carbohydrate, collagen is a protein; putting this difference another way, cellulose deteriorates into glucose, collagen into gelatin. In living skin, the collagen fibers of the dermis spread out in what R. Reed calls "a complex and random manner to form a network" with "fibres running in all directions."[13]

In the course of being refined to form parchment, the dermis layer of the animal skin is first bathed in lime to remove all vestiges of hair, and then stretched on a frame to dry. This second step—drying the skin while simultaneously stretching it—has the effect of radically reorganizing the collagen fibers so that they now form layers that run parallel to the parchment surfaces; in its state as finished parchment, in other words, the dermis manifests a much more orderly structure than the random network it encompassed in living skin. While paper also consists of layers of fibers, cellulose fiber may traverse only a fraction of a sheet's total depth, so the network of fibers within layers maintains a high degree of randomness.[14] As paper scientists M. Deng and C. T. J. Dodson put it, "our primary reference structure for paper is a random array of fibres in two dimensions, a *2-dimensional random network*."[15] In fact, Deng and Dodson go so far as to declare in the title of their book—*Paper: An Engineered Stochastic Structure*—

that paper's randomly determined—that is, "stochastic"—structure is its defining feature. Because of this characteristic, the precise structure of a given sheet of paper is impossible to predict; as Deng and Dodson explain, "[p]aper . . . has the peculiar property that it is definitely inhomogeneous but in a theoretically unknown way."[16]

On a microscopic level, then, both paper and parchment comprise fiber networks, but the network that constitutes paper is the less orderly and predictable of the two. The same could be said of the macroscopic networks in which parchment and paper were produced, procured, and put to use in late-medieval England. Parchment was a domestic product, both in the sense that it was made in England—and by the fifteenth century, had been for centuries—and in the sense that it came from domesticated animals, homegrown in native pastures. As such, it came into being and inhered within a set of systems whose orbits were relatively predictable and circumscribed: the temperate British climate; the seasonal cycles of farming and animal husbandry; a time-honored and "low-tech" set of tools and methods for flaying, liming, stretching, and drying; and indigenous routes of transportation and centers of commerce.[17]

Moreover, throughout its use as a surface for the written language of humans, parchment retains various marks of its ties to the land and more generally to the kingdom of nature: the "hair" and "flesh" sides of a leaf of parchment are easily distinguishable by their hues, spotted animals yield spotted parchment, parchment texture varies with an animal's diet and according to the body part it once covered, and various pathological conditions—from rheumatism to invasion by mites—leave their traces on parchment surfaces.[18] In turn, those parchment surfaces lend the books in which they are bound an honorary place in the medieval bestiary, or so Layamon—author of the early thirteenth-century *Brut Chronicle*—would have a reader imagine, for in a memorable kenning at the beginning of his *Chronicle* he refers to pages, which in the England of his day could only have been parchment, as "boc-felle," or "book skin."[19] And where today's codicologist may be uncertain of the precise mammalian origins of a given sample of "boc-felle," a new species of expert, the paleogeneticist, may be able to settle the matter by analyzing its DNA.[20]

Given the memories it keeps of its own homeland and past, if parchment were a subgenre of literature, it would be an epic. Parchment holds onto alphabetical characters tenaciously too, and for this reason it has been the writing material par excellence for securing cultural memories—from Holy Scripture, to literary epics, to legal charters.[21] As M. T. Clanchy puts it in his comments on medieval writing materials, "to write on parchment was . . . to make a lasting memorial."[22] In contrast, if paper were a literary subgenre, it would belong with works whose value accrues from their currency—as goods in circulation—rather than from their monumentality: pieces along the lines of the "tydynges" "Geffrey" seeks in the whirling House of Rumor in Chaucer's *House of Fame*, or the "[t]idynges of sondry regnes" the merchants in "The Man of Law's Tale" bring back from their travels.[23] Like those merchants' tidings, paper in medieval England always came from "sondry regnes" beyond its shores—from Italy, France, Germany, Castile, and the Low Countries—and bore the proprietary marks of the craftspeople who made it rather than the natural marks parchment preserves.[24]

Moreover, since paper was a commodity bought and sold on an international market, its importation into England both depended upon and furthered the country's money economy. The earliest paper documents in England are perfect examples of the intimate relationship between the circulations of paper and money: the sheets of paper thought to be the oldest in England's Public Record Office preserve letters sent from Italy between 1296 and 1303 to Edward I's bankers, a society of Italian merchant-bankers known as the Riccardi of Lucca; and the first documents produced on paper in England were the registers of two seaport towns: King's Lynn, beginning in 1307, and Lyme Regis in 1309.[25] Records on paper from another coastal town—Southampton—document the continued flow of paper into England from foreign ports during the fifteenth century.[26]

According to those records, four bales of paper were included in the cargo of a carrack from Genoa that entered the port of Southampton on March 27, 1430. Packed in with the paper were two sacks of cotton, six packets of grain of paradise, twenty-three tuns of oil, a bundle of "brazil"—a wood for making red dye—seven jars and one barrel of green ginger, three bales of nut-gall, seventy-six bales of woad—the raw material for a blue dye—and twelve "bales de cendres."[27] Next to the list of dyes and spices in this cargo, those four bales of Genovese paper look rather mundane to an early twenty-first-century reader, but for one Laurens Markysan, who purchased them, they may yet have had a touch of the exotic. For like the fame of the Christian beauty named Custance that the merchants of "The Man of Law's Tale" carried with them from Rome, paper, as I show below, embodied an unsettling reminder of the "diversitee" of other cultures.[28] And like the tidings that circulate in the House of Rumor, barely distinguishable from gossip, rumors, and outright lies, paper was also shadowed by persistent rumors of its own unreliability.[29] A look at some episodes from the history of paper in Europe reveals that its reputation rests in large part on its ambiguous relationship to the natural world or, more specifically, to its status as a social construction.

Feeble Paper and Faulty Texts

The craft of papermaking got its first foothold in the west on the Iberian Peninsula. Two books made out of paper survive from twelfth-century Spain, and evidence suggests that the paper for them was made in Toledo rather than having been imported from the East.[30] The earliest eyewitness report to come down to us of paper being made in Spain was written by the twelfth-century geographer Muhammad al-Idrisi, who marvels at the paper produced in the town of Xátiva in his book *Nuzhat al-Mushtaq*. He reports, "[p]aper is manufactured there such as is found nowhere else in the world."[31] Although Spanish papermakers counted both Muslims and Christians in their ranks, another eyewitness account of paper manufacture in twelfth-century Spain records at least one Christian's distaste for it on the basis of his prejudice against the Jews who sold it and whose scriptures were written upon it.

Recounting a pilgrimage to Saint James of Compostella in Spain in his *Noni tractatis adversis Judaeorum inveteratam duritiem* (1143–1144), Peter the Venerable speaks of seeing books made of paper containing writings sacred to the Jewish faith. His comments appear in Chapter 5, entitled *De ridiculis atque stultissimis fabulis Judaeorum* ["On the ridiculous and most stupid fables of the Jews"], where he sees in the bizarre composition of paper a fitting materialization of the preposterous fables of the Talmud:

> Legit, inquit, Deus in coelis librum Talmuth. Sed cujusmodi librum? Si talem quales quotidie in usu legendi habemus, utique ex pellibus arietum, hircorum, vel vitulorum, sive ex biblis vel juncis orientalium paludum, aut ex rasuris veterum pannorum, seu ex qualibet alia forte viliore materia compactos, et pennis avium vel calamis palustrium locorum, qualibet tinctura infectis descriptos.

> [God, it says, reads the book of Talmud in Heaven. But what kind of a book? Is it the kind we have in daily use, made from the skins of rams, goats, or calves? Or, is it made from reeds and rushes out of Eastern swamps, or from old rags, or from some other more vile material, and written upon with birds' quills or reed pens from swamps dipped in any kind of ink?][32]

As Peter would have it, the peculiarity of the Talmud as a material object is in itself enough to prove the ludicrousness of its claims. In addition, as he aligns Christian books made on parchment with the quotidian familiarity of domesticated rams, goats, and sheep and opposes them with Jewish books made out of reeds and rushes from *eastern* swamps—in spite of the fact that if paper were made in Spain at this time, it would have been fabricated from reeds and rushes from swamps that were actually quite Western—he wishfully places swamps, Jews, and their ridiculous books and paper outside the borders of Western civilization. Finally, as Peter describes the composition of paper in terms of progressively messier categories of refuse—from the stagnant muck of swamps to the shredded remains of cast-off clothing and, last, to the noxious and open-ended category *qualibet alia forte viliore materia* [some other more vile material]—he equates the heterogeneous and often unknowable composition of paper with processes of corruption; in doing so, Peter's description of paper conveys the implication that the material might degrade even sensible Christian texts, should they be inscribed on it.

If Peter the Venerable, writing in the twelfth century, implicitly links the perceived moral integrity of Christian writings to the material fact of their preservation on parchment, Emperor Frederick II of Germany, writing nearly a century later, makes an analogous connection overtly, linking parchment to the inviolable durability of imperial authority. In the Constitutions of Melfi, issued in 1231, he expresses a hope that the mandates recorded in public instruments should persist for many future times, and so that they not succumb to age, he stipulates that hereafter all such instruments should be committed to parchment only: "Volumus etiam et sancimus ut predicta instrumenta publica et alie similes cautiones nonnisi in pergamenis in posterum conscribantur" [We also affirm that the aforementioned public documents and other similar securities shall in the future be enrolled on parchment only]. Moreover, he declares, documents written on paper have no authority at all: "Ex instrumentis in chartis papiri scriptis ... nulla omnino probatio assumatur" [From instruments written on paper ... no evidence whatsoever is taken].[33]

In spite of the sometimes skeptical, even hostile response in some quarters to paper's debut in Europe, the papermaking industry took hold and continued to grow on the Continent from the late thirteenth century onward.[34] Although the industry was not permanently established in England until the late seventeenth century, the English also found more and more uses for paper.[35] L. C. Hector notes that by the end of the fourteenth century, "paper is almost as likely as parchment to be the material chosen for household accounts"; moreover, as the fifteenth century got underway, "the comparative cheapness of paper ensured its being preferred for less formal documents (in which there was an ever-increasing preponderance of correspondence and memoranda of all kinds) and for the newer purposes generally."[36] Still, as Erik Kwakkel points out, "it was a long time before paper was used for making books with a non-documentary content, such as copies of literary texts," and rumors of its unreliability and a vague air of indecency hampered paper's progress and persisted into the fifteenth century.[37] Perhaps the most famous among late-medieval critics of paper was Johannes Trithemius, abbot of the Benedictine monastery at Spohnheim. In his *De laude scriptorum* (1492) he wrote:

> Quis nescit quanta sit inter scripturam et impressuram distantia? Scriptura enim, si membranis imponitur, ad mille annos poterit perdurare, impressura autem, cum res papirea sit, quamdiu subsistet? Si in volumine papireo ad ducentos annos perdurare potuerit, magnum est; quamquam multi sunt qui propria materia impressuram arbitrentur consumendam. Hoc posteritas iudicabit.

> [All of you know the difference between a manuscript and a printed book. The word written on parchment will last a thousand years. The printed word is on paper. How long will it last? The most you can expect a book of paper to survive is two hundred years. Yet, there are many who think they can entrust their works to paper. Only time will tell.][38]

Trithemius's denunciation of paper is restrained compared to Peter the Venerable's, but it bears a certain resemblance to it nevertheless: his doubting *quamdiu subsistet?* a reverberation of Peter's more deprecating *sed cujusmodi librum?*; his skepticism about the judgment of those who find paper a satisfactory medium for their work a faint echo of Peter the Venerable's association of paper with the foolishness of the Jews.

While I know of no late-medieval English writer who spoke in such overt terms against paper, several sources suggest that Trithemius might have found kindred spirits in England. A Cambridge University statute dated 1480 stipulates that a keeper of the university treasury who accepted any books written or printed on paper [*libros aliquos, in papiro scriptos vel impressos* as a pledge for a loan would receive a demerit.[39] As H. E. Bell asserts, this statute is an indication of "how considerable a diminution in value" resulted from the use of paper for a book.[40] A literary reflection of the low esteem in which paper was held shows up in a dialogue between Faith and Understanding on the topic of government in the English translation of Alain Chartier's *Le traité de l'esperance* (s. XV²). There Faith advises Understanding to look for the cause of social problems in the king's actions, not God's: "Seeke wele in thi feble papir and examyn the compte of their offices where the diffaulte is, and seeke not the diffaulte in the perfite bounte where no faute may be."[41]

Whereas in the Cambridge University statute, fiduciary prudence mandates the rejection of paper, here the feebleness of paper seems both to produce and to reflect the faulty accounts it keeps.

The counsel of prudence would also advise against a certain kind of conspicuous consumption associated with paper in late-medieval England. Enumerating the species of the sin of pride, Chaucer's Parson singles out the practice of decorating food with paper castles as an example of "Pride of the table"; that is, the habit of consuming "excesse of diverse metes and drynkes, and namely swich manere bake-metes and dissh-metes, brennynge of wilde fir and peynted and castelled with papir, and semblable wast, so that it is abusioun for to thynke."[42] The primary sense of the Parson's "and semblable wast" here is most likely "and similar kinds of profligate consumption," but the phrase also registers a reminder that paper is itself a kind of waste—in the sense of refuse or trash—in that it is composed of cast-off materials. In this second sense, then, a paper castle decorating food exemplifies the underlying essence of the sinful pride with which the Parson finds fault: it is the characteristic heterogeneity of garbage, of paper, and of the proscribed "*diverse* metes and drynkes" that make all these "semblable" conglomerations an "abusioun for to thynke."

Although these examples of the ignominy of paper in late-medieval England may seem lightweight—"paper-thin," even—in themselves, when they are considered in the light of late-medieval metaphors and idioms involving parchment, an opposition between paper and parchment on the basis of standards of ethics and morality becomes more apparent. As the passage quoted above from Chartier's *Le traité de l'esperance* implies, paper was associated with faulty writing; parchment, on the other hand, was a guarantee not only of the durability of a written thing but also of its truth. In this way, as if to assure the infallibility of King David's prophecy that the Messiah would spring from his line, the author of the *Cursor mundi* stresses that the prophesy was written on parchment: "Als written es in parchemin, þat it com vte o þat pepin þat þat wreche adam fel fra."[43] Similarly, in *Sir Gowther*, a short romance surviving in two fifteenth-century English manuscripts—one made of paper, the other of parchment—the author implies that the value of his tale inheres in the parchment on which it has been preserved: "Þis is wreton in parchemyn, / A story boþe gud and fyn."[44]

These literary references to parchment as the very integument of a text deemed "good and fine" reflect a continued preference for parchment for formal documents in England throughout the fifteenth century and beyond. Just one example of that preference is visible in the correspondence of John Shillingford, mid-fifteenth-century Mayor of Exeter. [45] Writing to his deputies in London in the spring of 1448, he refers to some documents he had requested from the Chancellor, noting with some indignation that they had been sent to him not only late but also on paper and only afterwards, and at his request, on parchment: "the articulis were delyvered us but a Thursday a fore Palme Sonday, and that full sympelly yn paper, and afterwarde, at cure prayer and request, yn parchement, but noght endented, as covenant was."[46]

In addition to its function as a mark of truth and reliability, parchment also appears in several contexts as a symbol of spiritual purity. In *Cleanress*, for instance, the author asserts that the process of confession renders a person as clean and bright as parchment that is ready to be written upon: "polysed als playn as parchmen schauen."[47] Since the sinner is figured as someone "tomarred in myre" in the short passage preceding this line, the procedures for preparing an animal skin for writing—washing, polishing, and shaving—work well as metaphors for the absolution given by confession.[48] Similarly, a Latin sermon that survives in two manuscripts, one from the early twelfth century, the other from the mid-thirteenth, refers to the preparation of parchment for writing as part of an extended description of the process by which Christians may become *"scriptores Dei"* [scribes of the Lord]:

> ... qualiter Dei scriptores efficiamur videamus. Pergamena igitur in qua Deo scribimus pura conscientia est, ubi omnia bona opera nostra notas perennis memorie sumunt et Deo nos commendabiles faciunt. Cultellus quo raditur timor Dei est. . . . Pumex quo planificatur disciplina est desiderii celestis. . . . Creta cuius minutiis dealbatur assiduam sanctarum cogitationum curam designat, que conscientiam splendidam reddit.

> [let us consider how we may become scribes of the Lord. The parchment on which we write for him is a pure conscience, where all our good works are everlastingly recorded to make us acceptable to God. The knife with which it is scraped is the fear of God. . . . The pumice with which it is made smooth is the discipline of heavenly desire. . . . The chalk with whose fine particles it is whitened signifies an unbroken meditation of holy thoughts, which makes our conscience resplendent.][49]

In sharp contrast to these cleansing operations that parchment-making entails, paper manufacture involves *making* a mire—essentially by letting a pile of sodden rags rot—and thus, if it were to be put to use in a metaphor for any psychological process, papermaking might serve better in one depicting moral decay than in one figuring regeneration.[50]

These differences in the figurative uses and representations of paper and parchment point back to the physical differences between the two discussed earlier in this article; putting it another way now, parchment is produced through a refinement of a natural product, while paper is made out of the degradation of a mass of things that, borrowing from the Parson once more, are an "abusioun for to thynke." Medieval paper historian C. M. Briquet captures this distinctiveness of paper well:

> ce qui distingue essentiellement le papier du parchemin et du papyrus, ses congénères à savoir d'être, non une production naturelle, préparée ou travaillée d'une manière spéciale, mais une matière fabriquée, obtenue par la transformation d'autres produits.

> [that which distinguishes paper from parchment and papyrus, its relations, is that it is not a natural product, prepared or worked with in a special manner, but an artificial material, obtained through the transformation of other things].[51]

Though deemed unsuitable for many purposes—among them, for texts meant to last many centuries, as Trithemius asserts—such an artificial fabrication comprises an apt environment for more ad hoc texts—in particular, for epistolary expressions of amorous desire. As the love stories I recount in the next section of this essay show, paper as a medium *"obtenue par la transformation d'autre produits"* enables like transformations in characters who commit their writing to it in the cause of love.

Paper and Love Tokens

Lucien Febvre and Henri-Jean Martin note that even when paper was considered an inappropriate material for books and documents, it was acceptable for more ephemeral written things such as letters and rough drafts of documents.[52] Precisely because of their ephemeral nature—with respect as much to their linguistic content as to their material support—few of these papers survive. We may surmise, however, that paper was in common use for letters in England in the second half of the fourteenth century from literary references to paper letters such as the one cited above in *Troilus and Criseyde*.[53] But if evidence of the use of paper for letters in fourteenth-century England is scant and circumstantial, its use for the same purpose in the fifteenth century is abundantly obvious in the form of several families' letter collections. Most well-known among these are the Paston letters, which date from 1425 and are all written on paper.[54]

Given this testimony, we may be sure that fifteenth-century love letters were also written on paper, and indeed, the Paston collection preserves several specimens of the genre.[55] With this evidence of paper love letters in mind, a survey of representations of amorous epistolary acts—of reading, writing, sending, or disposing of love letters—in fifteenth-century treatises on conduct for women, in Chaucer's "The Merchant's Tale," and in *Troilus and Criseyde* reveals an intriguing parallel between perceptions of love letters and perceptions of the material to which they were entrusted in late-medieval England: that both were cheap and probably nasty.

In a passage that interestingly rearranges the terms used by the Parson to depict "pride at table," the English translation of the *Book of the Knight of La Tour-Landry* (1483) advises its young female readers to follow the example of those chaste women who "kepith hem suerly withoute delycious metes, for the flesshe is tempted by delicious metes and drinkes, the whiche bene leteres and kindelers of the brondes of lecherye."[56] Using lust-provoking food as a figurative representation of love letters, the author of the *Book of the Knight* depicts the danger of an inner blaze of erotic appetite that the consumption of delicious love letters by naïve and nubile young women might fuel. At the same time, by associating epistles with kindling, this author implicitly refers to letters written on paper—a material that in burning more quickly would be superior to parchment for lighting the "brondes of lecherye"—and in so doing, he suggests that the danger that letters pose inheres in their customary medium: that is, in paper.[57]

The fifteenth-century treatise for religious women entitled *Disce mori* proscribes the exchange of love letters in similar terms:

> The V[the] tokene of flesshly love is þat þat oon lover
> sendeth to þat oþer lettres of love, tokenes and
> yiftes, which be worshipped, kissed, used and kept
> as reliques; and maken either to oþer diners, sopers
> and feestes, and þere either kerveth and leieth to
> oþer þe swettest morsels, and eithre trede prively
> on oþers foote undre þe table, and many an oþer
> amourous looke þei ween þei stele oon of þat oþer
> and suche oþer observances, to longe to write here,
> þei use. Þei suppose unaspied to kyndel with more
> and more þe fire of þeire seide flesshly love.[58]

Again we find love letters and lavish cuisine working together to speed lovers' immoderate metabolisms, but what is most interesting to me in this passage is the impression of disorder that emerges from its extremely additive structure. Here the exchange of "lettres of love" operates within a covert and proliferative commerce in which objects and acts meant properly for something else are recycled and combined in an indecent catachresis of texts, feet, morsels, looks, and tokens that has value for the lovers alone. Even as the writer attempts to define this commerce, its manifestations get away from him—lovers exchange "tokenes *and* yiftes," "diners, sopers *and* feestes," and "*many* an oþer amourous looke"—so that ultimately the writer's enumerative abilities are exhausted. Just as Peter the Venerable left off describing the composition of paper with a sweeping "*qualibet alia forte viliore materia*," here the list of lovers' practices breaks off with the open-ended category "suche oþer observances, to longe to write here."

   While *The Book of the Knight of La Tour-Landry* and *Disce mori* are both addressed to unmarried women, a conduct manual addressed to a married woman, *Le ménagier de Paris* (ca. 1394), shows that even epistles from a woman's husband retain a certain risqué quality. In that work, a Parisian householder instructs his wife to read and respond to his letters in private and to read and reply to all others in public.[59] The householder's advice on epistolary decorum suggests an implicit continuum between epistolary and carnal intercourse; given this tacit correlation, the ritual of conducting all other epistolary exchanges in public becomes a symbolic performance of the wife's faithfulness even as it acknowledges the seductive threat that letters pose. In view of the specific choreography of letter-reading recommended in *Le ménagier*, Criseyde's public display of horror at the sight of Troilus's first letter is that of a woman well tutored in the fine points of epistolary etiquette insofar as it relates to her marital status. As she scolds Pandarus, she points to her "estat"—that is, to her widowhood—as that which he offends in publicly offering her a letter from a suitor: "To myn estat have more reward, I preye, / Than to his lust!"[60] By specifying that Criseyde both reads and replies to Troilus's letter in private, though, the narrator also signals that Criseyde already considers Troilus a possible lover.

   The services of Pandarus and the generic decorum of the romance genre afford the epistolary exchange in *Troilus and Criseyde* the dignity that befits its legendary subjects, but in "The Merchant's Tale," a sitcom about middle-class life, we witness the lovers' epistolary flirtations in piquant detail. Here, the love letters May and Damyan exchange act in conjunction with bodily gestures just as they do in the description of the "V^the tokene of flesshly love" in the *Disce mori*: as the Merchant recounts, "by writyng to and fro / And privee signes wiste he what she mente / And she knew eek the fyn of his entente."[61] Sarah Stanbury notes that the love letters in this tale "never move far from the body or its functions," and indeed, at the moment in the narrative when these lines occur, "privee signes" makes a punning reference to the first letter May received from Damyan, which she read in the privy.[62] In that earlier scene, the unchaste alliance between love letters and bodily functions reaches a low point as May, having read the letter, "rente it al to cloutes atte laste, / And in the pryvee softely it caste."[63] Here the letter, which a fifteenth-century reader would picture as a paper one, gets mixed up with certainly much more vile material—*viliore materia*—than that from which it was made.

As shown, characterizations of paper and of flirtatious epistolary exchanges display a peculiar resonance: both are associated with excess and with tawdry fragmentations and rearrangements of materials and practices meant properly for other things. In addition, since the depictions of love letters that I touch upon above make little mention of the discursive content of these letters, they imply that the letters' seductive power resides more with their status as objects—-as "tokens" of affection—than with that whatever "sweet nothings" they have to say. As literary representations of paper love letters, verse love epistles operate at a remove from the network of negative characterizations surrounding both paper and love letters; as fictional epistles bound into books, they were never put into circulation in the heated economy of gestures and body parts depicted in *Disce mori*, nor were they necessarily written on paper, as I argue that actual late-medieval love letters were. Nevertheless, since verse love epistles are specimens of a poetic genre that refers to a nexus of signification in which the material aspect of a written thing carries somewhat more weight than its propositional content, the writing surfaces on which they are conveyed comprise an important component of the dramatic scenes these letters stage. In the next section of this article, I explore two paper manuscripts and relate the stories of two letter writers who make use of the properties of paper as a means of furthering their otherwise impossible love affairs.

II

As Martin Camargo explains, Middle English verse love epistles spring from a matrix of both literary and diplomatic influences: from French fixed-form lyrics, on the one hand, and from the medieval *ars dictaminis*, coupled with an increased use of English in public and private documents, on the other. Even though Middle English verse love epistles show a likeness to diplomatic epistles preserved from this period, Camargo argues that their closest predecessor is literary: specifically, the "Litera Troili" in Chaucer's *Troilus and Criseyde*.[64] In fact, while John Taylor identifies the letters in *Troilus and Criseyde* as the earliest extant letters written in English, Camargo attributes the vogue that verse love epistles enjoyed in fifteenth-century England in large part to the renown of that same work.[65]

In the verse love epistle genre, then, material and intellectual practices from diverse social spheres are knit together: from the rules governing Latin prose composition—and the pedagogical and clerkly spheres in which those rules were learned and practiced—to the fashions that influenced Middle English lyric forms—and the courtly realms in which those forms proliferated. Moreover, as specimens of a highly derivative genre characterized by tactical reuses of various social rituals, verse love epistles bear an ontological resemblance to paper, which is also a product of recycled social ritual, though from a material rather than discursive domain. Indeed, given the synchronicity of the fashion for verse love epistles and increases in the use of paper in England, it seems prudent to conclude that the availability of paper contributed to the verse love epistle fad just as surely as did the popularity of Chaucer's *Troilus and Criseyde*.

The narratives I turn to next suggest that in addition to its availability, paper's properties also contribute to and even enable the affairs enacted in fifteenth-century verse love epistles. In addition, the letter writers featured here advance in their amorous pursuits by bending the ontological parallels between epistles and paper toward points of convergence. In turn, those tales teach the advantages of investing one's romantic desires in the medium of paper, for as they show, a paper letter remedies—by "re-mediating"—the shortcomings of speech and all the perils and impossibilities of physical presence that speech entails. In effecting this remediation, the fictional letter-writing personae of verse love epistles call attention in one way or another to the medium of paper even as they employ that medium to enhance a sense of erotic immediacy.[66] In the first epistolary performance, a tongue-tied lover demonstrates the intimacy with one's beloved that a paper letter may afford; in the second performance, the environment of paper helps a lover enact an affection that dare not "speak" its name.

Looking Good in Paper

The device that opens a window onto my first "love story in paper" is accomplished by the fictional writer of a Middle English verse love epistle to which I refer briefly above, *La compleyn*, which is appended in two manuscripts to Lydgate's *Temple of Glas* and preserved in a third as an independent piece.[67] Reaching the end of a lengthy and detailed "dytee" (l. 595) on the rejection he has suffered from his beloved lady, the lovesick letter writer in this poem raises the possibility that his beloved might be moved to reject his letter as well as his person:

> If my worde amysse be spoke,
> And or þat ye þer-on be wroke,
> To casten fully in þe fyr,
> I prey you first to maken cler
> With a goode looke, and with no more.
> And if hit shal be al to-tore,
> With-outen mercy, and to-rent,
> I prey yowe with my best entent,
> þat with youre owen handes sofft
> þat ye reende and brek it offt:
>
> For youre touche, I dare wel seyne,
> Wel þe lasse shal ben his peyne. (ll. 605–616)

Strategic references to the surface of the very letter the poet is in the process of writing are frequent in Middle English verse love epistles and often function, as this one does, to create a metonymic link between the writer and his letter. Several of these references take the form—common in other genres of medieval literature as well—of authorial addresses to the composition as a material object, along the lines of "go, litil bill, and say thoue were with me," thus inviting a vision of the "body" of the letter as a living and speaking creature.[68] This writer takes that tactic further, however, in two ways: first by attributing to the letter the capacity for feeling touch and even pain, he realizes in an arrestingly tangible way the pragmatic implications of the clichéd 'go, litil bill" address. Second, a curious slippage in pronominal references to the writer's "worde"—from "my worde," to "hit," to "his"—mark in this passage the successive stages of a hypothetical, fantastical re-mediation of the writer's desires by which he is able to present himself to his beloved rather more persuasively than he has been able to do in her presence. In the course of this progressive shift in the form of his mediation, the writer first figures his "worde"—already a mediation of his amorous feelings—as spoken, then as an object—"hit"—and finally as a gendered, creaturely "worde"—a message who has a sense of touch and looks a lot like paper, given "his" vulnerability to being shredded and burned.

In the process of narrating this hypothetical metamorphosis, the writer draws a contrast between the relative allure of spoken words versus words on paper when it comes to winning over a reluctant lady. Here a spoken word would seem always already likely to have gone "amysse," and indeed, the writer takes up a good portion of the letter that precedes this passage with embarrassed recollections of his inability to speak in his beloved's presence. Moreover, in those recollected memories the writer's incoherence as a speaker coincides with a certain bodily incoherence as well. Of a recent parting from his beloved, the writer recalls:

> How I of ʒow myn leue tok,
> And in euery member quok;
> For verry wo & dystresse
> Ne myghte [I] not a word expresse
> Of al myn wo, allas the whyle!
> For al myn olde peyntede style
> Was clene a-gon & out of mynde. (ll. 33–39; Schick's emendation)

By contrast, a written word—as the writer envisions his here—gets what "he" wants even in the process of being torn to bits: the immediacy of his lady's touch. As the writer envisions the relief his letter would feel were his lady to "reende and brek" "him" with her "owen handes sofft," he activates the materiality of his message and specifically the properties of paper, which would make his letter conducive to rending and breaking by feminine hands. In doing so, the writer not only transforms a potential act of disdain into an act of mercy but also presses his beloved to notice that even as she reads, she has been caught, for in granting the letter her touch, she is touched in turn by his vulnerable yet forcibly present and tangible "worde." In addition, since the friability of paper is its key mechanism, this ingenious love trap marks an intersection between the two separate threads of late-medieval culture that I trace above: imputations of paper's fragility, on the one hand, and warnings of the dangers of love letters, on the other. In this way, the letter writer demonstrates that courting one's beloved in the guise of paper may kindle a responsive flame more effectively than any speeches one might deliver in an "olde peyntede style"; in other words, this letter writer's performance shows that paper commands a "rhetoric" of its own, in this case, the *pathos* of its fragility.

In my reading of this poem, I am so far passing over in silence the fact that while the writer refers to the materiality of his epistle, he does not specify that it is a letter on paper, a matter that would seem somewhat fatal to my argument. In addressing this embarrassment, I would first concede that the author is not explicitly thematizing paper in this poem. On the other hand, I would contend that a medieval reader of the poem would visualize a paper letter, first, because the range of evidence discussed above suggests that paper was the medium for personal letters by the early fifteenth century, at the time this literary personal letter was composed; and second, because although I have not tried it myself, authorities I trust tell me that parchment is not conducive to shredding the way paper is. Thus the writer's suggestion that his lady "reende" the letter "and brek it offt" would lend support to a reader's assumption that the threatened letter was on paper rather than parchment. Finally, our author does not have his letter-writing persona refer to his missive as one on paper simply because it could not have been written on anything else, for the letter is not only an expression *on* paper but also an expression *of* paper; that is, its persona is a paper character, a fabrication, a social construction, a go-between or medium between two more parchment-like characters—that is, creatures enveloped in skin.

In his essay "Sensations of the Page," Michael Camille points out that medieval readers had "an intensely somatic experience of the page," and indeed, the lover in this epistolary situation would seem to anticipate the multisensorial quality of his beloved's reading experience in inventing the ploy I am discussing.[69] The letter writer's evocation of his lady's handling of his page might arouse the sense of touch in a reader handling this verse love epistle in a book as well, especially if its pages were like the pages of a letter: that is, if it were a book with paper pages. As it happens, although this poem is preserved in three manuscripts, this particular passage comes down to us in only one, London, British Library Additional MS 16165, an early fifteenth-century volume made of paper.[70] Additional 16165 is probably best known for its reputation as the first literary anthology produced by John Shirley (ca. 1366–1456), one of the fifteenth century's best-known scribes.[71] Except for two leaves of parchment at the beginning and one at the end, the tome is made wholly of paper.[72] On the evidence of its watermarks, Lyall concludes that the anthology was begun in the 1420s and probably completed by around 1425, giving it a claim to being among the earliest literary collections to have been written on paper in England.[73]

As an early literary compilation on paper, Additional 16165 makes an especially interesting candidate for a consideration of the possibility the verse love epistle it preserves raises; that is, that once noticed and thus activated, the character of paper might redefine the "sensation" of a literary work. While the fictional letter writer in the poem examined above makes a persuasive show of the fragile aspect of his letter, a consideration of the paper stocks, textual content, and intended audience of this anthology makes way for a recognition of paper's networked, circulatory quality—its instantiation in and facilitation of circulatory networks, be they of the recycling of clothing as rags, the circulation of water in water-powered mills, the travels of merchants and the exchange of money, or the circulation of texts—as the perfect articulation of the literary ambience of Additional 16165. In this way, paper may be understood as the essence of Additional 16165, both as a literary anthology and as a material book.

Additional 16165 is one of two anthologies that Shirley supplied with a versified table of contents; toward the beginning of the one in Additional

16165 (*IMEV* 1426), he avers that he has obtained his texts in many locales—that he "sought þe copie / in many a place"—a declaration that, though he may have been unaware of it, he could have made regarding his paper as well.[74] The volume binds together a total of eleven different paper stocks; taken together, they offer a striking picture of the "sondry regnes" from which paper traveled to arrive in the shops of the grocers, mercers, and haberdashers of early fifteenth-century London where Shirley might have bought his. Here are the *Cross and Mounts* watermarks of Treviso and Savoy, a *Cherries* mark from Frankfurt, the *Crown of Harlem*, the *Bull of Bourges*, the *Bow and Three Circles* of Palermo, the *Bull's Head with Septfoil* of Vicenza, and a *Tower* mark that could have come from as far away as Palermo or as close as Antwerp.[75]

Reflecting this variety of paper stocks, the texts Shirley gathers in this volume also represent a heterogeneous mix of sources and traditions; they include several lengthy prose translations—Chaucer's translation of Boethius's *Consolation of Philosophy*, John Trevisa's of *The Gospel of Nicodemus*, and Edward, the second Duke of York's translation of Gaston Phébus's *Livre de chasse*, entitled *The Master of Game*—together with lyric poetry on devotional and secular topics and two long poems by Lydgate, *The Complaint of the Black Knight* and *The Temple of Glas*.[76] Shirley brings a degree of unity to these disparate works through the consistency of his own voice in the headings and colophons he supplies for them. Combining the resonance of a headline with the seductive appeal of gossip, that voice makes connections between the world of literature and the wide world of the "news" or "tydynges." For instance, *The Master of Game* gets the heading "The booke of huntyng, the whiche is cleped the Maystre of the game, contreved and made by my lord of York, that dyed at Achincourt, the day of the batayle, in his soverain lordes service," and *The Temple of Glas* is presented as "Une soynge moult plesaunt, fait à la request d'un amoreux, par Lidegate, le Moygne de Bury."[77]

Taking into account the likelihood that Shirley acquired his exemplars for many of these texts through his associations with courtly circles— what Ralph Hanna has termed Shirley's "insider connections"—we may envision Additional MS 16165 as a volume that comes into being through an extensive "matrix" of inter-connected systems, and we may recognize in the relationships among those many systems the character of paper: paper's heterogeneous composition and its production in a variety of interdependent systems.[78]

And if Additional MS 16165 comes into being through a matrix of systems, its audience involves networks as well. Judging from the amateurish quality of the execution of this and other Shirleian anthologies, Julia Boffey and John Thompson surmise that Shirley produced these volumes as "sample books": books to be lent to his friends or associates to help them in choosing works for more deluxe volumes of their own.[79] This understanding of Shirley's anthologies accords with the request with which he concludes Additional 16165's verse table of contents:

> And whane ye haue þis book ouerlooked /
> Þe right lynes / with þe crooked /
> And þe sentence / vnderstonden /
> With Inne youre mynde hit fast ebounden
> Thankeþe þauctoures þat þeos storyes
> Renoueld haue / to youre memoryes /
> And þe wryter / for his distresse
> Whiche besechiþe / youre gentylnesse
> Þat ye sende þis booke ageyne
> Hoome to *Shirley* / þat is right feyne
> If hit haþe beon / to yowe plesaunce.[80]

Once again, we may recognize in this passage and in the very notion of a "sample book" the character of paper: moving through and so producing a complex association of friends and potential clients, this book is a paper book not only in the sense that is made of paper but also in the sense that it articulates the qualities of paper. Commenting on these lines from Additional 16165's table of contents, Ralph Hanna observes, "[t]he book belongs within a social situation, one in which, like in the game of love, life is thoroughly imbued with literary activity."[81] In view of its papery content, Additional 16165 also brings into view a "literary activity" that, like the game of love played out in its verse love epistle, partakes most intimately of the quality of paper.

Like almost all Middle English verse love epistles, the specimen in Additional 16165 includes no reply; paradoxically, then, most poems in this genre have an aura of disconnected melancholy that is not quite in tune with the rustle of the busy world of paper, a world that includes the commerce of letters.[82] The absence of any accompanying reply for these letters invites readers to imagine addressees for them in the real world outside the book, or to invent a story in which the poet's ardor is either doused or requited in a more carnal way than the exchange of letters allows. Indeed, in the epistolary "love trap" discussed above, once the lady yields to her lover by destroying his missive—or by not destroying it—the need for letter-writing as a mode of lovemaking will have passed, and the letter may just as well be shredded and "casten fully in þe fyr" (l. 607). In the pair of verse love epistles I examine next—two satiric epistles in Oxford, Bodleian Library MS Rawlinson Poet. 36—the second is a response to the first.[83] This pair of letters is an exception that proves the rule, however, for the "love story in paper" it narrates helps to explain why most verse love epistles do not come in pairs even as it provides another view of paper as an environment for self-mediation.

An Odd Couple

I begin to unfold this second romance by examining some of the facets of these two letters' peculiarities: first the appearance of their pairing on the pages of Bodleian Library MS Rawlinson Poet. 36 and then their satiric content. Before that, however, a brief description of the manuscript is in order. Rawlinson Poet. 36 is a slim "volume" of just nine paper leaves dating to the second half of the fifteenth century. Structurally the manuscript consists of two gatherings, each of a different paper stock: folios 1–5 are *Raisin* (similar to Briquet 13,008; ca. 1452, Darmstadt), and folios 6–9 are *Monts* (similar to Briquet 11,704; 1443, Verona).[84] The change in paper stock corresponds with a change of hand beginning at folio 6 recto: folios 6–9 verso are written in an anglicana book hand typical of the late fifteenth century, distinguishable in part by the specific shapes of its two-compartment G and A.[85] Although the script of the first five leaves might also be classed an anglicana book hand, it is much more current and displays more irregularities in its letter forms.[86]

The texts in the manuscript's first gathering include a Valentine's Day poem by Lydgate (*IMEV* 3065), a poem with the refrain "service is non eritage" (*IMEV* 1446), another with the refrain "gode rule ys out of remembrans" (*IMEV* 1982), the two satiric verse love epistles that concern me here (*IMEV* 3832 and 2437), two "stand-alone" verse love epistles (*IMEV* 1334 and 1510), and an eight-line stanza on old age (*IMEV* 1652). The second gathering is wholly occupied by a short treatise on the virtues of the Mass (*IMEV* 333). The manuscript's two gatherings—the one devoted to secular, the other to devotional material—thus constitute a framing pair for the pair of satiric epistles preserved in the first gathering, a point to which I return below.

Unlike the other verse love letters in this manuscript, each missive in this unique pair has the look of a real letter, for each is preceded on the page by a superscription: that part of a letter that functions, much as the address on an envelope does today, to direct the letter to its addressee. Here these superscriptions also give a first impression of the sharp satire to follow: the first one reads, "To my trew loue and able / As the wedyr cok he is stable / Thys letter to hym be deliueryd"; the address for the second reads, "To you, dere herte, variant and mutable / Lyke to Carybdis whych is vnstable." Each superscription forms a block of indented text, set above and slightly apart from the rest of the epistle in the same manner in which addresses are arranged in surviving personal letters from this period.[87] While the verse love epistle in Additional 16165 conjured an image in a reader's mind's eye of a single epistle with certain corporeal attributes—an ability to feel pain, for instance—the page layout of these poems, together with their directive texts, gives the impression to a reader's physical eye of two bodies of text in circulation, one answering the other. And in the paper space of Rawlinson Poet. 36, these epistolary bodies articulate not only the currency of paper but also its artifice: its unnaturalness—borrowing from Briquet—or, putting it another way, its status as a social construction. A look at what those textual bodies have to transmit adumbrates a pedagogical situation as the backdrop for their play with the social constructions of gender.

Written as an exchange of letters between a man and woman, these two letters—for lack of a manuscript title, I shall refer to them as the Rawlinson epistles—skillfully invert late Middle English verse love epistle conventions; for instance, the first line of the woman's letter, "Vnto you most froward þis lettre I write," counters the deferential, flattering tone with which most verse love epistles begin. Similarly, the man's letter begins with a variation on the popular salutation in which the beloved is addressed as a flower—"Right fresshe flour, who I ben have and shal" is how Troilus rendered it—only to compare the aroma of this precious flower to the noxious-smelling bloom of the feverfew plant: "Fragrant as fedyrfoy to mannys inspeccion" (1–2).[88] These poems toy with other poetic formulae, too, for the bulk of each missive itemizes the ugly physical features of the addressee, in this way satirizing the conventions of poetic catalogues of beauty as well. But in addition to their witty play within the generic confines of verse love epistles and catalogues of beauty, these poems also depart in crucial ways from both genres. A consideration of these departures suggests that the Rawlinson epistles satirize the discourse and customs of polite, heterosexual society in order to give voice to the pedagogical world of late-medieval students and teachers: a homosocial realm in which play with epistles and self-representations is part of the curriculum. As we see below, the artificial surfaces of paper make a fitting support for this project.

We may approach this analysis by turning first to the Rawlinson epistles' transgressions—as opposed to simple inversions—of verse love epistle conventions. To begin, most Middle English verse love epistles, as I remark above, are not written as pairs. The opposite is true, however, of medieval collections of epistolary formulae: in those collections, which were often used for teaching purposes, model letters and replies are presented together.[89] In fact, the only other paired set of Middle English verse love epistles, the early fifteenth-century macaronic "De amico ad amicam" and its "Responsio," bears a certain resemblance to the paired letters in one such collection of model letters, the anonymous early fifteenth-century allegorical treatise on letter-writing called *Regina sedens rhetorica*. In that work, the headings for letters initiating a correspondence resemble the heading for the poem "De *amico ad amicam,*" for each clearly specifies the sample letter's author and recipient—"*Littera de milite ad militem,*" "*Littera de filio ad patrem,*" "*Littera de sorore ad sororem,*" and so on. Similarly, each letter's reply bears the label "*Responsio.*"[90]

The fact that one of the two manuscript witnesses to "*De amico ad amicam*" and "*Responsio*" is a collection of pedagogical material—a "scrappy student notebook," as Boffey puts it—further emphasizes the tie between works teaching Latin prose composition and this particular set of love poems.[91] The codicological and rhetorical relations of "*De amico ad amicam*" suggest, in turn, that there may be a connection between pedagogical practices and the only other surviving Middle English epistolary twosome—the satiric pair under consideration here.

A second anomalous feature of these satiric missives with respect to the verse love epistle genre is their inclusion of catalogues of beauty—or, in this case, of ugliness. Although as a rule, verse love epistles do compliment the beloved on her beauty, they do not anatomize it, concentrating, instead, on the writer's suffering and on his eagerness to serve his lady's every whim. Indeed, Rossell Hope Robbins opines that the author of the Rawlinson epistles "deserves due credit for his innovations in these two [poems], namely, the catalogue of charms in combination with the love letter."[92] In contrast, head-to-toe depictions of feminine beauty were standard classroom fare; speaking of Latin instruction in the twelfth century, F. J. E. Raby remarks, "[e]very schoolboy learned how to describe a woman's beauty, and how to write an 'invective' against women."[93]

Influential models for these inventories were Matthew of Vendôme's description of Helen of Troy in his *Ars versificatoria* and Geoffrey of Vinsauf's discussion of stylistic ornament in the *Poetria nova*.[94] These Latin verse models were also incorporated into English dictaminal treatises; for instance, the *Libellus de arte dictandi rhetorice* (ca. s. xii[3/4]) attributed to Peter of Blois recommends personal description as a means to embellish an epistle and offers as an example a catalogue of feminine beauty.[95] Thomas Merke's *Formula moderni et usitati dictaminis* (s. xiv[med]) also recommends the inclusion of descriptions in letters, noting that many models for such descriptions may be found in *De bello troiano*.[96] The inclusion of exhaustive personal descriptions in the Rawlinson epistles, then, suggests the influence of Latin models of composition.[97]

While catalogues of loveliness are rare in Middle English verse love epistles, the catalogues in these particular missives are especially so and not simply because they invert the genre by enumerating flaws instead of charms. Satiric catalogues of feminine beauty appear in England as early as the twelfth century, and by the fifteenth, both Hoccleve and Lydgate had contributed to the genre. So, Lydgate's satire begins, "My fayr lady, so fressh of hewe" and then—with characteristic Lydgatean prolixity—proceeds to describe her "Fro the heed to the novyl, and so forth down," along the way noting "Here greet shulderys, square and brood," "hire bely so large / . . . [thar] / She is no bot, she is a barge," "Hire buttokys / . . . brood as is a Spaynych stede"—and "so forth down."[98] In Hoccleve's "Humorous Praise of His Lady," the "beloved" is similarly favored: with "bowgy cheekes," which are "softe as clay," a nose so large "þat it ne shal / Reyne in hir mowth / though shee vp-rightes lay," a large mouth "with lippes gray," a chin that can barely be seen, and a "comly body / shape as a foot-bal."[99]

The catalogues in these two letters, then, are not strange because they are satiric; instead, two more subtle particulars make them unique. First, ironic catalogues of a man's handsomeness are virtually unknown; as Jan Ziolkowski notes, the catalogue in the first letter in this epistolary duo is the only satiric catalogue of a man's handsomeness found in Middle English lyric poetry.[100] There are inventories of masculine *ugliness* in Middle English lyrics—the description of the giant in the alliterative *Morte Arthure*, for instance—but no other ironic portraits.[101] Nor does the secular Latin poetic tradition offer examples of such descriptions; again, there are portraits of hideously ugly men but no blatantly ironic catalogues of a man's charms that I know of.[102] Second, satiric catalogues of feminine beauty typically suggest that the subject of the description is possessed of a ravenous sexual appetite. For instance, Lydgate's lampoon notes that his lady likes good bowmen, "specially, / Hym that can shote bothe styffe and lowe."[103] In the satiric descriptions in the Rawlinson epistles, however, it is the man who is accused of being salacious. For instance, the first letter compares him to a hare, "Your forehed, mouth, and nose so flatte, / In short conclusyon best lykened to an hare" (9); the further observation "So vngoodly youre helys ye lyfte" (27) may be another allusion to this notoriously cupidinous member of the medieval bestiary. The woman described in the second letter is ugly, to be sure, but there is nothing in the catalogue to suggest that an insatiable or promiscuous sexuality lurks beneath her "nyce aray" (46). While it may be argued that this is just another one of the poems' several generic inversions, the two catalogues deviate from the gender stereotypes, with all the sexual innuendoes devoted to the man and none to the woman.

Assuming, as it is surely prudent to do, that both of these letters were actually written by a man, the uncharacteristic and dissymmetrical attention given to the man's sexual appetite hints at the possibility of a homoerotically charged subtext in these poems that is just submerged beneath a layer of heterosexual farce. For as the poet insinuates in the voice of a woman that his male correspondent is sexually voracious, we may discern a whispered avowal that our author knows something about being an object of such an appetite. That is, in assuming the voice of a woman—someone who would "naturally" be in a position to have intimate knowledge about such a proclivity in a man—the poet may let on that he has his own "unnatural" fund of experiences upon which to draw in making this accusation.

If we keep in mind these poems' pedagogical affiliations, the attention they give to matters of rhetoric and composition affords a clue regarding the players in this hypothetical homosocial subtext. The first writer's remark "The Goodlynesse of your persone is esye to endyte" (3) may be read not only as a potshot at the recipient's relative lack of "goodlynesse," which is therefore easy to describe, but also as a slight against the vacuous and boring *descriptio pulchritudinis* exercise itself. When this insinuation is considered together with the second writer's immediate critique of the first's composition—"The Ynglysch of Chaucere was nat in youre mynd" (8), he notes—then the exchange begins to look like one between a schoolmaster and a student. In this scenario, the woman's satiric love letter would be a stand-in for a letter from a quite "literally" feminized student who is commenting on his master's very active libido. The lover's reply would act as a cover story—or cover letter—for the schoolmaster, who shrugs off the student's impudence by invoking the source of his institutionalized power in the situation: his expertise with grammar and rhetoric.

Evidence from numerous sources suggests that along with learning from model letters like those presented in treatises such as *Regina sedens rhetorica*, students also practiced the delicate art of adjusting prose style to suit the relative social positions of letter writer and addressee by assuming various fictional voices in their own compositions—voices of women as well as of men. In her study of practices of declamation based on texts featuring rape scenes, Marjorie Curry Woods argues that the role play such exercises required also had the effect of aiding boys in their negotiation of the middle territory of adolescence, "a site of anxiety about control in two directions: those who control the boy and those whom he might be able to control."[104] Since assuming the voice of the one in control in these texts, as Woods goes on to point out, was to assume the voice of a man inflicting some form of sexual violence on either a woman or a weaker man, these declamatory exercises taught rape, rhetoric, and manliness-as-dominance all in one neat pedagogical package.[105] For a boy—or a teacher remembering his boyhood—to write a sexually insulting letter to a teacher in the voice of a woman and to answer it in the voice of a man would thus be very much in keeping with his classroom experience.

While these declamatory practices did not explicitly stage scenes of sexual relations between male students and teachers, literary treatments of the topic are not without precedent. Commenting on Dante's inclusion of Priscian among the sodomites in the *Inferno*, Boccaccio writes:

> I judge [Dante] put him here to represent those
> who teach his doctrine, since the majority of them
> are believed to be tainted with that evil. For most
> of their students are young; and being young,
> are timorous and obey both the proper and the
> improper demands of their teachers. And because
> the students are so accessible, it is believed that the
> teachers often fall into this sin.[106]

A large collection of model letters included in a late-twelfth- or early thirteenth-century French dictaminal treatise contains a pair of model letters that dramatize a man's attempt to seduce a boy and the boy's corresponding resistance to his advances. Although the two letter writers are not specifically depicted as teacher and student, the poems' inclusion in a dictaminal treatise situates the fictional relationship within a pedagogical environment.[107] The gist of the first letter is well summarized by its title, "*Quidam hortatur puerum ad spurcitiam*" [A Man Encourages a Boy to Indecency]; in the second, "*Responsio pueri*" [The Boy's Reply], the boy responds to the man's advances by, among other things, saying that he is warned by the fall of Sodom and Gomorrah and will not descend to "this filthy vice which displeases God" [*vicium inquinatum . . . quod Deo displicet*].[108]

If we agreed that the Rawlinson epistles dramatize a student-teacher relationship, we might still ask the question: In what affective register is it performed? Should these letters' derisiveness be taken at face value or, given the artifice already noted in the letters, should they be read as affectionate instead—that is, as a kind of lovingly jesting parody within a parody? Picking up on a suggestion in Carolyn Dinshaw's discussion of the reputed quarrel between Chaucer and Gower, I would first observe that an imputation of hostility can function as a handy way to deny homosocial affection.[109] At a certain point it does not matter whether these epistles are actually less vituperative and more affectionate than they seem; it is enough to observe that the verse love epistle genre—supported by the artificial "character" of paper—affords a setting for such an expression of the gendered politics and homosocial energy of the classroom.

Moreover, a number of Middle English poems give witness to men's use of the verse epistle as a means to address both their beloved enemies and friends. So, John Paston III writes a letter in verse to the Earl of Oxford, which begins "My ryght good lord, most knyghtly gentyll knyght" and continues with a detailed account of his suffering during their separation.[110] John Pympe writes to John Paston complaining that while traveling in France, his friend has not answered his letters: "Fresh amorouse sihtys of cuntreys ferre *and* straunge / Have all fordoone yowr old affeccioun. / In plesurys new yo*wr* hert dooth soore *and* raunge" (*IMEV* 866); and Lord Grey de Ruthyn writes a verse epistle to his archenemy with the gleeful lines:

> But we hoope we shalle do the a pryve thyng;
> A roope a ladder, and a ring,
> Heigh on gallowes for to henge,
> And thus shalle be your endyng. (*IMEV* 557)[111]

Considering these uses of verse love epistle conventions in letters written by men to men, together with the traces of the pedagogical scene that I identify in the Rawlinson epistles, it seems just possible that this paired composition conveys a student's affection for his teacher—and for the heady delight of trying on new voices and bodies on paper. Indeed, as a writing surface constituted by the canny reuse of clothing, paper affords not only a fitting physical surface for these activities but also an answering conceptual *materia*. The concluding line in a short poem on the topic of "an exemplary schoolboy's day" in a fifteenth-century collection of grammatical texts, Bodleian Library MS Rawlinson D.328, succinctly depicts the affective classroom environment—a mixture of fear, affection, and respect—from which this pair of verse love epistles might have been written, for the poem concludes with the admonition, "*Timor et amor et honor Magistri*" [Fear, love, and honor teachers].[112]

Before leaving these letters and the world of paper, I return to a consideration of their pairing. As argued above, the singularity of the "normal" verse love epistle tends to gesture past its bookish confines toward the consummation of the desire it expresses in the world outside the text. My investigation of the Rawlinson epistles suggests, in contrast, that a *pair* of verse love letters portrays an amorous intercourse that remains forever textual and, more specifically, forever papery, manifest in tweaked and repurposed rhetorical turns and figures. The Rawlinson epistles hint, then, that there is no place for whatever affections they convey and no place for the hybrid personae who voice them in the world outside the text unless, just possibly, it is in the world of paper, whether on paper pages or in the clerkly, pedagogical realm that dealt in texts and text-making, texts that by the time this pair of epistles was written, were increasingly produced on paper.[113] Finally, the misfit quality of these two literary epistles and of the sentiments they convey is reflected in the pairing of the gathering that preserves them with a much less flamboyant book-mate, the "Virtues of the Mass."

New York University

NOTES

1. Sarah Stanbury, "Women's Letters and Private Space in Chaucer," *Exemplaria* 6.2 (1994): 271–285, 280.
2. Geoffrey Chaucer, *Troilus and Criseyde*, in *The Riverside Chaucer*, ed. Larry D. Benson. 3rd edn. (Boston: Houghton, 1989), V.1597–1598.
3. Gower commits a similarly revealing anachronism around the same time in his "Tale of Ulysses and Penelope" in the *Confessio amantis*; there Penelope admonishes Ulysses in a letter that he "non other paper waste" in writing her back but "come himself in alle haste." John Gower, *Confessio amantis*, in *The English Works of John Gower*, ed. G. C. Macaulay, 2 vols. (London: Oxford UP, 1900-1901), IV.198, 197. Judging from the Paston letters, paper was definitely the accepted medium for personal letters by the early fifteenth century, for Davis notes that all of them are on paper, the earliest dated 1425. Norman Davis, *Paston Letters and Papers of the Fifteenth Century* (Oxford: Clarendon Press, 1971), xxxiii. Another early use of paper in England was for keeping town records. R. J. Lyall, "Materials: The Paper Revolution," in *Book Production and Publishing in Britain: 1375-1475*, ed. Jeremy Griffiths and Derek Pearsall (Cambridge: Cambridge UP, 1989), 11-29, 13.
4. The manuscripts that are made of both paper and parchment employ parchment for the inner and outermost bifolia of each quire, a common method of strengthening quires in early paper books; on which, see Michelle P. Brown, *Understanding Illuminated Manuscripts: A Guide to Technical Terms* (Malibu, CA: J. Paul Getty Museum in association with the British Library, 1994), s.v. "paper."
5. Lyall, "Materials," 12. For a statistical analysis of paper manuscripts produced on the Continent, see Erik Kwakkel, "A New Type of Book for a New Type of Reader: The Emergence of Paper in Vernacular Book Production," *The Library* 7th ser., 4 (2003): 219–248.
6. The poems in Gg.4.27 are *"De amico ad amicam"* and its *" Responsio"* (*IMEVs* 16 and 19) and *"La compleyn"* (*IMEV* 147), which concludes Lydgate's *Temple of Glas* in this and one other manuscript. In his discussion of the precursors to the verse love epistle genre in English, Martin Camargo sees the macaronic *"De amico ad amicam"* and *" Responsio"* as marking the end point of the genre's prehistory; he puts *"La compleyn,"* on the other hand, near the genre's beginning. He dubs the poem a "boundary case" because it does not employ standard epistolary formulae, but he includes it under the verse love epistle rubric because of its allusions to numerous aspects of the epistolary situation. Martin Camargo, *The Middle English Verse Love Epistle* (Tübingen, Germany: Niemeyer, 1991), 45, 172. I discuss *"La compleyn"* and its other manuscript witness, London, British Library Additional MS 16165, in further detail below. The verse love epistle in Oxford, Bodleian

Library MS Arch. Selden B.24 is *IMEV* 2478; Rossell Hope Robbins, ed., "O Lady, I schall me dress with besy cure," in *Secular Lyrics of the XIVth and XVth Centuries*, 2nd ed. (Oxford: Clarendon Press, 1955), 197–198. Three *Troilus and Criseyde* manuscripts also contain Hoccleve's *Letter of Cupid*: Oxford, Bodleian Library MS Digby 181; Oxford, Bodleian Library MS Arch. Selden. B.24; and Cambridge, Trinity College MS R.3.20. Though technically not a verse love epistle, Hoccleve's *Letter* is, nevertheless, an epistle on the topic of love. M. C. Seymour dates Gg.4.27 to ca. 1398 and Selden B.24 to ca. 1490. M. C. Seymour, "The Manuscripts of Chaucer's *Troilus*," *Scriptorium* 46 (1992): 107–121, 111, 120.

7. Four of the remaining sixteen manuscripts do include some parchment leaves: Aberystwyth, National Library of Wales Brogyntyn MS ii.1 (olim Porkington 10)contains twenty-four parchment leaves (out of 212), but Brogyntyn's verse love epistle (*IMEV* 1241) is itself on paper. Auvo Kuriven, "MS Porkington 10: Description with Extracts," *Neuphilologische Mitteilungen* 54 (1953): 33–67, 34. Similarly, London, British Library Additional MS 16165 includes four parchment leaves out of 258; Ralph Hanna, "John Shirley and British Library, MS Additional 16165," *Studies in Bibliography* 49 (1996): 95–105, 96; with the verse love epistle (*IMEV* 147) on paper; Oxford, Bodleian Library MS Lat. 98 C.66 (olim Capesthorne) "includes a few parchment additions"; Deborah Youngs, "Vision in a Trance: A Fifteenth-Century Vision of Purgatory," *Medium Aevum* 67 (1998): 212–226, 212; and finally, British Library Sloane MS 1212 contains six parchment leaves with the verse love epistle appearing on one of them; Julia Boffey, *Manuscripts of English Courtly Love Lyrics in the Later Middle Ages* (Woodbridge, UK: D. S. Brewer, 1985), 14. For a complete list and brief descriptions of manuscripts containing Middle English verse love epistles, see Camargo, *Middle English Verse*, 171–183, app. 1.

8. As Lyall points out, paper was already much cheaper than parchment at the close of the fourteenth century—a quire of paper cost the same as a skin of parchment but provided eight times as many leaves—and as paper production increased steadily in Europe during the fifteenth century, its price fell even more: at mid-century it was half what it was at the beginning, and half again by the end; Lyall, "Materials," 10–11. For further discussions of the cost of paper, see André Blum, *On the Origin of Paper*, trans. Harry Miller Lydenberg (New York: Bowker, 1934), 35; Allan Stevenson, *The Problem of the Missale Speciale* (London: Bibliographic Society, 1967), 49; and Lucien Paul Victor. Febvre and Henri-Jean Martin, *The Coming of the Book: The Impact of Printing 1450–1800*, trans. David Gerard (London: NLB, 1976), 17–18.

9. Silvie Turner, *The Book of Fine Paper* (New York: Thames and Hudson, 1998), 13.

10. As M. Deng and C. T. J. Dodson explain, paper is held together by hydrogen bonds both within and between cellulose fibers: "the fibrous material in paper is held together by hydrogen bonds between hydroxyl groups of cellulose molecules on the surfaces of adjacent fibres. The same type of bonds hold the cellulose molecules in the fibrils and the fibrils in the fibres." M. Deng and C. T. J. Dodson, *Paper: An Engineered Stochastic Structure* (Atlanta, GA: TAPPI, 1994), 25. Much of Deng and Dodson's work deals with paper from the perspective of theoretical math and physics; for a somewhat more accessible introduction to the science of paper, see William E. Scott and James C. Abbott, *Properties of Paper: An Introduction*, 2nd rev. ed. (Atlanta, GA: TAPPI, 1995); and for a brief discussion of paper chemistry for nonspecialists, see Jules Heller, *Papermaking* (New York: Watson-Guptill, 1978), 23–24.

11. Dard Hunter, *Papermaking: The History and Technique of an Ancient Craft* (New York: Dover, 1978), 5. The most complete account of the history of papermaking is Hunter's; see also Turner, *Book of Fine Paper*, 13–25. For a vivid account of contemporary papermaker Timothy Barrett's engagement with the history of papermaking in developing his craft, see Mark Levine, "Can a Papermaker Help to Save Civilization?," *New York Times* 17 Feb. 2012 Http://www.nytimes.com/2012/02/19/magazine/timothy-barret. Accessed 15 July 2012.

12. The layers above and below the dermis are the epidermis and hypodermis respectively. For a detailed explanation of the anatomy of animal skins used in "skin products"—leather and parchment—together with discussions of the microscopic properties of these products and the methods of their production, see R. Reed, *Ancient Skins, Parchments and Leathers* (London: Seminar Press, 1972), 13–45.

13. Ibid., 29 and 120.

14. I draw here from the introductory remarks on paper structure in Deng and Dodson, *Paper*, 1–3.

15. Ibid., 2 (emphasis in original).

16. Ibid., 27.

17. For an analysis of the supply of parchment in the thirteenth century in the areas of Wiltshire and Suffolk, based on tax returns, see M. T. Clanchy, *From Memory to Written Record: England 1066–1307*, 2nd ed. (Oxford: Blackwell, 1993), 122–123. Commenting on improvements in the quality of parchment between the thirteenth and fourteenth centuries, R. F. Hunnisett speculates that a surge in demand for writing material stemming from the growth in legal record-keeping during this period "must have given rise to larger scale and more efficient production and supply." R. F. Hunnisett, "What Is a Plea Roll?" *Journal of the Society of Archivists* 9 (1988): 109–114, 110. While sources of parchment—in the form of sheep and calves—may

have been quite local for many communities, records also survive of its importation: in the twelfth century from within the British Isles by monasteries—on which, see Christopher de Hamel, *A History of Illuminated Manuscripts* (London: Phaidon, 1994), 86–87; and Clanchy, *From Memory*, 120–121—and in the fifteenth century by merchants from as far away as Italy, on which, see Alwyn A. Ruddock, *Italian Merchants and Shipping in Southampton 1270–1600* (Southampton, UK: Southampton University College, 1951), 75. The growth of a sturdy cluster of parchment makers in London from the mid-fourteenth century through the fifteenth suggests that the use of imported parchment for books was far from the norm, however. On London parchmeners and the parchment business there, see C. Paul Christianson, "Early London Bookbinders and Parchmeners," *Book Collector* 34 (1985): 41–54, 41–47; Christianson, *A Directory of London Stationers and Book Artisans 1300–1500* (New York: Bibliographical Society of America, 1990), passim; and Christianson, *Memorials of the Book Trade in Medieval London* (Woodbridge, UK: D. S. Brewer, 1987), 6, 24. Records pertaining to investigations of Lollardy preserve the names of parchment makers in towns outside London; on these, see Anne Hudson, "Lollard Book Production," in *Book Production and Publishing in Britain, 1375–1475*, ed. Jeremy Griffiths and Derek Pearsall (Cambridge: Cambridge University Press, 1989), 129. An artisanal craft such as parchment making would most likely have been learned by following the master's example rather than written instructions; nevertheless, a handful of such instructions have been gleaned from sources of English provenance. For examples, see Reed, *Ancient Skins*, 151–152; and G. S. Ivy, "The Bibliography of the Manuscript Book," in *The English Library before 1700*, ed. Francis Wormald and C. E. Wright (London: Athlone, 1958), 35.

18. The "hair" side of parchment is the side adjacent to the epidermis, the "flesh" side to the hypodermis. The hair side is also called the grain side; see Reed, *Ancient Skins*, fig. 2. The pattern of hair follicles on this surface varies across animal species and is called the "grain pattern"; ibid., 25. For examples of the color contrast between hair and flesh sides, see the images of Berkeley, University of California, Bancroft Library MS 132 and Berkeley, University of California, Robbins Collection MS 4 in *Digital Scriptorium*, University of California at Berkeley, http://bancroft.berkeley.edu/digitalscriptorium/; for examples of parchment made from spotted animals, see Berkeley, University of California, Robbins Collection MS 79, fols. 85v–86r; and New York, Columbia University Rare Books and Manuscripts Library, Plimpton 29, fol. 70v, also in *Digital Scriptorium*. Reed discusses the effects of disease, environmental factors, and diet on parchment texture as well as the texture differences among parchment from various body parts; Reed, *Ancient Skins*, 35–37. On the latter, see also J. P. Gumbert, "Skins, Sheets and Quires," in

New Directions in Later Medieval Manuscript Studies, ed. Derek Pearsall (York UK: York Medieval Press, 2000), 82.

19. *Layamon: Brut Edited from British Museum MS Cotton Caligula A. IX and British Museum MS Cotton Otho C. XIII*, ed. G. L. Brook and R. F. Leslie, EETS o.s. 250 (London: Oxford University Press, 1963–1978), 26.

20. See Joachim Burger, "Palaeogenetics of Parchment," in *Microanalysis of Parchment*, ed. René Larsen (London: Archetype, 2002), 159–161.

21. I borrow here from Abbot Adam of Eynsham, who explains in the prologue of his *Vita* of Saint Hugh of Lincoln that he has been asked to produce a lasting memorial of the saint, not by speaking plain words that pass away quickly, *on nudis loquendo uerbis perfunctorie transeuntibus*], but rather in tenacious written letters [*tenacibus scribendo litteris*]; Adam of Eynsham, *Magna Vita Sancti Hugonis: The Life of St. Hugh of Lincoln*, ed. Decima L. Douie and David Hugh Farmer, 2 vols. (Oxford: Clarendon Press, 1985), 1:1. (Translations mine unless otherwise noted.) For a discussion of this passage in the context of medieval attitudes to writing as an archival practice, see M. T. Clanchy, "'Tenacious Letters': Archives and Memory in the Middle Ages," *Archivaria* 11 (Winter 1980–1981): 115–125. Clanchy also mentions the passage briefly in Clanchy, *From Memory*, 144.

22. Clanchy, *From Memory*, 144.

23. Geoffrey Chaucer, *House of Fame*, in *Riverside Chaucer*, l. 729; Chaucer, *The Canterbury Tales*, in *Riverside Chaucer*, II:181. As C. David Benson points out, "tydyngs" are linked in the poem with the present: with "news from the real world rather than from books"; C. David Benson, "The 'Love-Tydynges' in Chaucer's *House of Fame*," in *Chaucer's Dream Visions and Shorter Poems*, ed. William A. Quinn (New York: Garland, 1999), 221-41, 222. Here, too, "tydyngs" are associated with travel and faraway lands, for the House of Rumor—where "Geffrey" finally hears some "tydyngs"—is "in alle tymes" full of peripatetic characters: shipmen, pilgrims, pardoners, curriers, and messengers (ll. 2121–2128, *Riverside*).

24. For a detailed account of paper imports from these areas, see David John Duncan, "The Paper Trade and Industry in Medieval England," MA thesis, University of Virginia 1995, 4–11. For histories of the origins of watermarks, see Hunter, *Papermaking*, and Augusto Zonghi, "Watermarks in Paper, Their Origin and Importance," in *Zonghi's Watermarks*, ed. E. J. Labarre (Hilversum, Holland: Paper Publications Society, 1953), 50–62.

25. Clanchy, *From Memory*, 120. For a discussion and bibliography of the Riccardi letters, see Richard W. Kaeuper, *Bankers to the Crown: The Riccardi of Lucca and Edward I* (Princeton, NJ: Princeton University Press, 1973), 71–73; for further details on the registers of King's Lynn and Lyme Regis, see Ivy, "Bibliography of the Manuscript," 36.

26. Portions of Southampton's medieval "port books," which record the customs collected on ships' cargoes unloaded there, are edited in five volumes: the earliest, edited by Paul Studer, covers the records kept in Anglo-French by water-bailiff Robert Florys from 1427 to 1430; two later volumes, edited by D. B. Quinn, cover the periods of 1469–1471 and 1477–1481; two final volumes, edited by Thomas Beaumont James, cover 1509-1510. Among the edited records for the fifteenth century, only Studer specifies that they are written on paper. Paul Studer, ed., *The Port Books of Southampton, or (Anglo-French) Accounts of Robert Florys, Water-Bailiff and Receiver of Petty-Customs, A.D. 1427–1430* (Southampton, UK: Southampton Record Society, 1913), v. While these records provide a glimpse of the import side of the paper trade, the archives of the London Grocers Company offer a look at the retailer's side; for an edition of a portion of this material, see John Abernathy Kingdon, ed., *A Facsimile of the First Volume of Manuscript Archives of the Worshipful Company of Grocers of the City of London, A. D. 1345–1463* (London: Grocers Company, 1883–1886); for numerous references to grocers' and mercers' stock in paper, see Pamela Nightingale, *A Medieval Mercantile Community: The Grocers' Company and the Politics and Trade of London 1000–1485* (New Haven, CT: Yale University Press, 1995). Haberdashers also sold paper; for an inventory of a haberdasher's stock recorded in 1378 that includes paper, see Edith Rickert, *Chaucer's World*, ed. Clair C. Olson and Martin M. Crow (New York: Columbia University Press, 1948), 28–30. From the archives of the Old London Bridge, Christianson cites purchases of paper from both haberdashers and grocers beginning in the fifteenth century; Christianson, *Memorials of the Book Trade*, 26.

27. Studer, *Port Books,* 112. The text is in Anglo-French; my list makes use of the translations Studer provides in his footnotes, and I have further translated *balet*—in *balet de Graine de paradis*—as "packet" (from *balle, gros paquet de merchandises* [*Grand Larousse* s.v. "balle"]) and *fardel*—in *fardel de brasil*—as "bundle" (*OED* s.v. "fardel"). Studer translates *cendres* as "cinders"; given the other dyestuffs in this cargo, however, the term should probably be taken as a reference to the raw materials for *cendre bleu,* which *Grand Larousse* defines as a blue color obtained from pulverized azurite or oxidized copper (*belle couleur bleue qu'on obtient par la pulversiation de l'azurite, ou cuivre carbonaté*). The term has this sense in a seventeenth-century treatise on painting: Pierre Lebrun, *Original Treatises on the Arts of Painting,* ed. and trans. Mary P. Merrifield, with new intro by S. M. Alexander (New York: Dover, 1967), 761, 772, 786, and 816. For additional notices of paper in the Southampton port books, see Studer, *Port Books,* 78; and D. B. Quinn, *The Port Books or Local Customs Accounts of Southampton for the Reign of Edward IV,* Publications of the Southampton Record Society 37 and 38 (Southampton, UK: Cox and Sharland, Ltd., 1937–1938), 2: 147, 163, and 194.

28. Chaucer, *Canterbury Tales*, in *Riverside Chaucer*, II.220.
29. Registering a link between tidings and unreliable forms of discourse, Chaucer's narrator remarks that the House of Rumor is "ful of tydynges / . . . / And over alle the houses angles / Ys ful of rounynges and of janges"; Chaucer, *House of Fame*, in *Riverside Chaucer*, ll. 1957–1960. Later he reports seeing shipmen and pilgrims carrying bags with "scrippes bret-ful of lesinges, / Entremedled with tydynges"; ibid., ll. 2123–2124.
30. The books are the "Mozarabic Missal" and the "Latin Glossary of Silos"; for descriptions and illustrative plates of both, see Oriol Valls I Subirà, trans. Sarah Nicholson, *The History of Paper in Spain X–XIV Centuries* (Madrid: Empresa Nacional de Celulosas, 1978),102–103 and 122–126. For discussion of documentary evidence of papermaking even earlier in Spain, see ibid., 86–100.
31. Quoted in ibid., 133. Muhammad al-Idrisi, *Nuzhat al-Mushtaq* (*The Delight of Him Who Desires to Journey through the Climates*) was written in 1154.
32. Petri Venerabilis, *Noni tractatis adversis Judaeorum inveteratam duritiem*, ed. J. P, Migne, *Patrologia Latina* 189:606, accessed February 3, 2012 in *Patrologia Latina Database* (Proquest: 1996-2012), cols. 507–650. Translation from Blum, *On the Origin*, 57. For further discussion of this chapter, see Dominique Iogna-Prat, *Ordonner et exclure: Cluny et la société chrétienne face à l'hérésie, au judaïsme et à l'Islam 1000–1150* (Paris: Aubier, 1998), 300–304.
33. Frederick II, *Historia diplomatica Friderici Secundi*, ed. J. L. A. Huillard Bréholles (Parisiis, excudebant Plon fratres, 1854), vol. 4. Pt 1, 56–57.
34. The Italian city of Fabriano lays claim to the earliest paper mill in Europe outside Spain; documentary sources date its founding to sometime before 1264. On its date, see Jonathan M. Bloom, *Paper before Print: The History and Impact of Paper in the Islamic World* (New Haven, CT: Yale University Press, 2001), 211; Zonghi, "Watermarks in Paper," 50; and Hunter, *Papermaking*, 474. It seems that paper was also made for a short time in Genoa, for a document from the year 1235 records that in Genoa on June 24 an Englishman named Walter contracted himself to work for a year making paper, "*causa faciendi papirum*"; quoted in R. Lopez, "The English and the Manufacture of Writing Materials in Genoa," *Economic History Review* 10 (1940): 132–137, 133. There are records referring to mills in France dating from 1348, in Germany from 1390, and in Flanders from 1405; Blum, *On the Origin*, 32–33.
35. England's first mill was established by John Tate sometime in the mid-1490s on one of the tributaries of the River Lee near Hertford; for a complete discussion of Tate's paper, together with an account of the rise and fall of his mill, see Richard L. Hills, *Papermaking in Britain, 1488–1988: A Short History*

(London: Athlone, 1988), 5–12; see also Hunter, *Papermaking*, 116. For the story of the many false starts of paper manufacture in England following Tate's first attempt, see Hills, *Papermaking*, 45–56.

36. L. C. Hector, *Handwriting of English Documents* (London: Edward Arnold, 1958), 17. For a detailed inventory of royal, aristocratic, clerical, and mercantile uses of paper in England beginning in the fourteenth century, see Duncan, "Paper Trade," 25–31. For studies of the price of paper, see above, n. 8.

37. Kwakkel, "New Type," 222.

38. Johannes Trithemius, *In Praise of Scribes: De Laude Scriptorum*, ed. Klaus Arnold and trans. Roland Behrendt (Lawrence, KS: Coronado Press, 1974), 62–63. The abbot's equation of printed books with paper books is noteworthy in itself. As Febvre and Martin point out, it was the flourishing of the papermaking industry that assured the success of the printing press; Febvre and Martin, *Coming of the Book*, 30. James J. O'Donnell points out that by 1515 Trithemius appears to have changed his mind, for by then he makes reference to "that wondrous and previously unheard-of art of printing books"; James J. O'Donnell, *Avatars of the Word: From Papyrus to Cyberspace* (Cambridge, MA: Harvard University Press, 1998), 79. Interestingly, in a section of their preface to *Origins of Cyberspace* subtitled "Why This Book Was Printed on Paper," Diana H. Hook and Jeremy M. Norman defend in similar terms their decision to publish their work in print rather than as electronic text (though it would seem from our perspective that Hook and Norman have more realistic cause for concern than Trithemius did!): "In 2001 there was no clear solution to how digital information would be preserved on the Internet for more than a few years.... Though the storage of digital information was a rapidly growing industry, it was focused on relatively short-term storage—months, a few years, perhaps decades at the most." Diana H. Hook and Jeremy M. Norman, *Origins of Cyberspace: A Library on the History of Computing, Networking, and Telecommunications* (Novato, CA: historyofscience.com, 2002), 60.

39. Cambridge University Commission, *Documents Relating to the University and Colleges of Cambridge* (London: G. E. Eyre and W. Spottiswoode, for Her Majesty's Stationery Office, 1852), 1:409. On this topic the statute reads:

> nullus custos alicujus cistae in praedicta universitate fundatae vel deinceps fundandae, libros aliquos, in papiro scriptos vel impressos, pro cautione sive parte cautionis quovis modo deinceps recipiat sub pœna unius marcae universitati applicandae; et ad hoc statutum

> volumus singulos custodes in suis admissionibus
> corporale praebere juramentum.
> [no keeper of any money box into which money
> goes in or out in the aforementioned university
> shall receive any books written or printed on paper
> as a pledge or as part of a pledge in any manner
> under penalty of one demerit and to this statute we
> wish all guardians of the treasury to offer a bodily
> oath.]

40. H. E. Bell, "The Price of Books in Medieval England," *The Library* 4th ser., 17 (1936): 312–332, 321.
41. Alain Chartier, *Le traité de l'esperance*, in *Fifteenth-Century English Translations of Alain Chartier's* Le traité de l'esperance *and* Le quadrilogue invectif, ed. Margaret S. Blayney, EETS o.s. 270 and 281, vol. 1 (London: Oxford University Press, 1974–1980), 30, ll. 19–21. The French original reads "cerche en ton foible papier, et examine le compte de leur office ou est le deffault, et ne quier point la faulte en la parfaicte bonté qui raemple lez autrez deffaulx"; Alain Chartier, *Le livre de l'espérance*, ed. François Rouy (Paris: Librairie Honoré Champion, 1989), pr. VI.154–156. Chartier composed *Le livre de l'espérance* in 1428.
42. Chaucer, *Canterbury Tales*, in *Riverside Chaucer*, X. 444-445. In their explanatory notes to *Sir Gawain and the Green Knight*, Malcolm Andrew and Robert Waldron suggest that the author of the poem alludes to this custom in describing the fantastical intricacy of Lord Bercilak's castle: "So mony pynakle payntet watz poudred aywquere / . . . / Þat pared out of papure purely hit semed"; Malcolm Andrew and Ronald Waldron, eds., *The Poems of the Pearl Manuscript: Pearl, Cleanness, Patience, Sir Gawain and the Green Knight* (Exeter, UK: Exeter University Press, 1987), ll. 800-802 and note.
43. Richard Morris, ed., *Cursor mundi*, EETS o.s. 57, 59, 62, 66, 68, 99, and 101 (London, Trübner 1874–1893), ll. 8503-8505.
44. Karl Breul, ed., *Sir Gowther: Eine englische Romanze aus dem XV Jahrhundert* (Opele, Poland: E. Franck, 1886), ll. 751-752.
45. Stuart A. Moore, ed., *The Letters and Papers of John Shillingford Mayor of Exeter 1447–50*, Camden Society New Series 2, vol. 2 (Westminster, 1871). Shillingford's correspondence concerns his attempts to solve a long-standing dispute between the secular and ecclesiastic arms of government in the city of Exeter. Ian Maxted notes that the letters themselves are all written on paper; Ian Maxted, "Education and literacy in medieval Devon," in *Exeter Working Papers in British Book Trade History* 12, http://bookhistory.blogspot.com/2007/01/devon-book-26.html. Hector notes that the English

Chancery used parchment for many of its documents "until the 19th century and later"; Hector, *Handwriting*, 16. Clanchy argues that the continued use of parchment for the most important documents even centuries after the introduction of paper is a consequence of English documentary culture having taken root during the twelfth and thirteenth centuries, when paper was virtually unknown in England; Clanchy, *From Memory*, 120. According to Clanchy, then, parchment was an integral component of documentary discourse.

46. Moore, *Letters and Papers of John Shillingford*, 55.

47. *Cleannness*, in Andrew and Waldron, *Poems of the Pearl Manuscript*, I.1134. In their note to this line, Andrew and Waldron quote the use of the same metaphor in a twelfth-century sermon directed at manuscript illuminators.

48. Ibid., I.1114.

49. Mary A. Rouse and Richard H. Rouse, ed. and trans., "From Flax to Parchment: A Monastic Sermon from Twelfth-Century Durham," in *New Science out of Old Books: Studies in Manuscripts and Early Printed Books in Honour of A. I. Doyle*, ed. Richard Beadle and A. J. Piper (Aldershot, UK: Scolar Press, 1995), 7 and 9. The sermon comes down to us in Durham, Durham Cathedral MS B.IV.12 and in Cambridge, Gonville and Caius College MS 351/568. Ivy prints a translation of an extract from this sermon in "Bibliography of the Manuscript," 33–34.

50. Hunter explains that the first step in turning linen rags into paper was to press them into water-soaked balls and then to pile the balls together, keeping them wet for six weeks to two months; this combination of prolonged moisture and pressure would cause the rags to ferment and then to disintegrate. This mass of broken-down rags was then ready for the stamping mill, which would reduce it to a pulp of cellulose fibers. Hunter, *Papermaking*, 153.

51. C. M. Briquet, *Les filigranes* (Paris: A. Picard, 1907), 1:1.

52. Febvre and Martin, *Coming of the Book*, 30.

53. John Taylor asserts that the letters in *Troilus and Criseyde* also hold claim to being the earliest surviving letters to have been written in English, "although not actually dispatched through the post." John Taylor, "Letters and Letter Collections in England, 1300–1420," *Nottingham Medieval Studies* 24 (1980): 57–70, 67.

54. Davis, *Paston Letters*, 1:xxxiii. Other fifteenth-century letter collections include the Stonor letters, the Plumpton letters, correspondence by Shillingford, the Cely letters, and the Marchall letters. For helpful introductions to these collections and bibliography of print editions, see Laetitia Lyell, *A Mediaeval Post-Bag* (London: Jonathan Cape, 1934). For a briefer but more recent overview of this material, see Taylor, "Letters and Letter Collections," and for a study of a small collection of letters written

by one Elizabeth, Lady Zouche—all of which are written on paper—see Edith Rickert, "Some English Personal Letters of 1402," *Review of English Studies* 8 (1932): 257–263. Julia Boffey discusses the general character of the content of these letters; Julia Boffey, "Middle English Lives," in *The Cambridge History of Medieval English Literature*, ed. David Wallace (Cambridge, UK: Cambridge University Press, 1999), 610–634, 612–615.

55. One is a letter from Margery Brews to John Paston III (Davis, *Paston Letters*, no. 415); another is a letter from John Paston possibly to the Earl of Oxford (ibid., no. 351), which I discuss in further detail below.

56. Geoffroy de la Tour Landry, *The Book of the Knight of La Tour-Landry*, ed. Thomas Wright, EETS o.s. 33 (London: N. Trübner, 1868), 54.

57. In his *De proprietatibus rerum*, Bartholomaeus Anglicus evokes an image of burning parchment to describe a cramped muscle, which suggests that parchment burns in a relatively drawn-out manner—perhaps not the best material for kindling. Here is the passage in John Trevisa's translation: "þe senewe schrinkeþ and riueleþ as parchemyne iput in þe fure, and þerfore þe weye of spritis in þe synewes is istopped and þe vertue of lif and of reuling is ilette." Bartholomaeus Anglicus, *On the Properties of Things: John Trevisa's Translation of Bartholomaeus Anglicus De proprietatibus rerum: A Critical Text*, gen. ed. M. C. Seymour, 3 vols. (Oxford: Clarendon Press, 1975–1988), 1:357, ll. 31–33.

58. Quoted in Lee W. Patterson, "Ambiguity and Interpretation: A Fifteenth-Century Reading of *Troilus and Criseyde*," *Speculum* 54 (1979): 297–330, 305-306.

59. "Si vous conseille que lettres amoureuses et secretes de vostre mary vous les recevez en grant joye et reverence, et secretement tout seule les lisez tout apart vous, et toute seule lui rescripvez de vostre main . . . et nulles autres lettres ne recevez ne lisiez, ne ne rescripvez a autre personne, fors par estrange main, et devant chascun et en publique les faittes lire." Georgine E. Brereton and Janet M. Ferrier, eds., *Le ménagier de Paris* (Oxford: Clarendon Press, 1981), 56. "And I counsel you that you receive with great joy and reverence the loving and private letters of your husband, and secretly and all alone read them unto yourself, and all alone write again unto him with your own hand . . . and receive not nor read any other letters, nor write unto no other person, save by another's hand and in another's presence, and cause them to be read in public." Eileen Power, trans., *The Goodman of Paris (Le Ménagier de Paris):A Treatise on Moral and Domestic Economy by a Citizen of Paris (c. 1393)* (London: Routledge, 1928), 106. For a discussion of the politics of domestic space in this passage, see Sarah Stanbury, "Women's Letters and Private Space in Chaucer": 282–285, 271–272.

60. Chaucer, *Troilus and Criseyde*, in *Riverside Chaucer*, II.1133–1134.

61. Chaucer, *Canterbury Tales*, in *Riverside Chaucer*, IV.2104–2106

62. Stanbury, "Women's Letters," 283.

63. Chaucer, *Canterbury Tales,* in *Riverside Chaucer,* IV.1953–1954.

64. Camargo, *Middle English Verse,* 89–91.

65. Ibid., 123; for Taylor's assertion, see above, n. 53.

66. In suggesting that paper letters "re-mediate" speech, I draw from the use of the term in Jay David Bolter and Richard Grusin, *Remediation: Understanding the New Media* (Cambridge, MA: MIT Press, 1999). There they define the "double logic" of remediation as an activity that satisfies our culture's "contradictory imperatives for immediacy and hypermediacy" (5), where the logic of "hypermediacy" "acknowledges multiple acts of representation and makes them visible" as such (33–34). As we see below, the lovers in these verse epistles finds immediacy in hypermediacy and in this way demonstrates the "double logic" of remediation.

67. *Index of Middle English Verse (IMEV)* 147, in John Lydgate, *Lydgate's Temple of Glas,* ed. J. Schick, EETS e.s. 60 (Milwood, NY: Kraus Reprints, 1987), 59–67. I quote parenthetically from this edition throughout this section.

68. *IMEV* 2247, l. 21, in Frederick J. Furnivall, ed., *Political, Religious, and Love Poems,* EETS o.s. 15 (London: Kegan Paul, 1903), 68. Other verse love epistles that develop such metonymic associations between the lover and his letter include *IMEV* nos. 2182, 3291, 1789, and 2510. For a list of Middle English works outside the verse love epistle genre that employ the "go little . . . " envoy, see Schick's notes in Lydgate, *Lydgate's Temple,* 122–123.

69. Michael Camille, "Sensations of the Page: Imaging Technologies and Medieval Illuminated Manuscripts," in *The Iconic Page in Manuscript, Print, and Digital Culture,* ed. George Bornstein and Theresa Tinkle (Ann Arbor: University of Michigan Press, 1998), 33–53, 38.

70. The earliest witness to the poem is in a parchment manuscript, Cambridge University Library MS Gg.4.27 (ca. 1398), but as Schick explains, the leaf on which the wooing device of the torn letter would have appeared—which was also the manuscript's last leaf—has been lost. See Schick, *Lydgate's Temple of Glas,* xxii. Fragments of this verse love epistle also appear in another parchment manuscript, London, British Library MS Sloane 1212 (ca. 1420), which does not include these lines.

71. The most complete account of Shirley's career is in Margaret Connolly, *John Shirley: Book Production and the Noble Household in Fifteenth-Century England* (Aldershot, UK: Ashgate, 1998).

72. Julia Boffey and John J. Thompson note that most of Shirley's extant writing is on paper and that he appears to have employed parchment as a means to strengthen his books. Julia Boffey and John J. Thompson, "Anthologies and Miscellanies: Production and Choice of Texts," in *Book Production and Publishing in Britain, 1375–1475,* ed. Jeremy Griffiths and

Derek Pearsall (New York: Cambridge University Press, 1989), 279–315, 306. Additional 16165 measures 11 5/8 inches by 8 ½ inches and consists of 258 leaves. Eleanor P. Hammond, "Omissions from the Editions of Chaucer," *Modern Language Notes* 19 (1904): 35–38, 37.

73. Lyall, "Materials," 19-20. See also Hanna, "John Shirley," 99-100.

74. London, British Library MS Additional 29729 is the other Shirley production graced with a verse table of contents (*IMEV* 2598); Hammond publishes both of them in Eleanor P. Hammond, *English Verse between Chaucer and Surrey* (New York: Octagon, 1965), 194–197.

75. Lyall provides watermark information for ten of the paper stocks; the paper in the manuscript's first quire has not been identified; Lyall, "Materials," 16–19. For details on these marks' origins beyond those offered by Lyall, I consulted Hanna, "John Shirley," 99–100; and Briquet, *Les filigranes*.

76. For a detailed list of the manuscript's texts and descriptions of each of them, see Connolly, *John Shirley*, 27–51. Commenting on the heterogeneity of all of Shirley's productions, Boffey and Thompson remark, "the distinctions between the works of different authors, between religious and secular material, between different literary forms, are generally unobserved." Boffey and Thompson, "Anthologies," 286.

77. Quoted from the manuscript description in British Library's online *Manuscripts Catalogue*, http://www.bl.uk/catalogues/manuscripts/INDEX. asp.

78. Hanna, "John Shirley," 101.

79. Boffey and Thompson, "Anthologies," 284. Hanna views Shirley's motives in producing Additional 16165 slightly differently, suggesting that "He envisions borrowing of his book for private and unsupervised use, perhaps even recopying, with eventual return to him." Hanna, "John Shirley," 103.

80. *IMEV* 1426, ll. 88–89, Hammond, *English Verse*, 196.

81. Hanna, "John Shirley," 103.

82. The only other paired set of Middle English verse love epistles is the early fifteenth-century macaronic "*De amico ad amicam*" and its "*Responsio*" (*IMEV* nos. 16 and 19); upon which I remark briefly below.

83. This pair of letters survives uniquely in Rawlinson Poet. 36; for descriptions of the manuscript, see Rose Cords, "Fünf me. Gedichte aus den Hss. Rawlinson Poetry 36 und Rawlinson C. 86," *Archiv für das Studium der neueren Sprachen und Literaturen* 135 (1916): 292–302, 292; and Rossell Hope Robbins, "Two Middle English Satiric Love Epistles," *Modern Language Review*, 37 (1942): 415–421, 415. The epistles are printed in Robbins, "Two Middle English," 416–417, from which I quote parenthetically throughout this section; and also in Rossell Hope Robbins, *Secular Lyrics of the XIVth and XVth Centuries*, 2nd ed. (Oxford: Oxford University Press, 1955), 219–222; and Cords, "Fünf me.," 296–298.

84. Briquet, *Les filigranes*.

85. For a description and illustration of this script (though not from this manuscript), see M. B. Parkes, *English Cursive Book Hands* (Berkeley: University of California Press, 1980), xxii and pl. 3.ii.

86. Despite these differences in script, it is possible that both quires were written by the same person; Parkes illustrates a very similar deterioration in one scribe's hand across a single manuscript in *English Cursive Book Hands*, pl. 21.i–iii.

87. See, e.g., Davis, *Paston Letters*, pl. 3.

88. Chaucer, *Troilus and Criseyde*, in *Riverside Chaucer*, V.1317. *IMEV* nos. 868, 2311, and 2823 all begin with some variation of the "Right fresshe flour" salutation.

89. See Michael Camargo, ed., *Medieval Rhetorics of Prose Composition: Five English Artes Dictandi and Their Tradition* (Binghamton, NY: Medieval and Renaissance Texts and Studies, 1995), for examples of model letters and replies. In his study of twenty-five manuscripts that he judged to reflect the teaching of Latin in fourteenth- and fifteenth-century England, Brother Bonaventure found that one third contained treatises on the art of letter-writing; Brother Bonaventure, "The Teaching of Latin in Later Medieval England," *Medieval Studies* 23 (1961): 1–20, 5. A review of Camargo's descriptions of the manuscripts preserving medieval English dictaminal treatises reveals that these treatises frequently accompany other works on Latin prose and verse composition as well as short Latin-English glossaries and *proverbia*, associations that suggest that many of these volumes—along with the letter-writing treatises and model letters they include—might have been used for pedagogical purposes; Camargo, *Medieval Rhetorics*, passim.

90. *IMEV* nos. 16 and 19 are published in E. K. Chambers and F. Sidgwick, eds., *Early English Lyrics: Amorous, Divine, Moral and Trivial* (London: A. H. Bullen, 1907), 15–19. Camargo also notes a general resemblance between the Latin titles of *IMEV* nos. 16 and 19 and those in Latin letter collections; Camargo, *Middle English Verse*, 46. *Regina sedens rhetorica* is edited in Camargo, *Medieval Rhetorics*, 169–219. Another paired set of Middle English verse epistles—but not of verse *love* epistles—appears on the flyleaf of Cambridge, St. John's College MS G.28: one is an attack on the friars (*IMEV* 3697); the other is a friar's defense (*IMEV* 161).

91. Boffey, *Manuscripts*, 89. The manuscript is British Library MS Harley 3362, a paper manuscript. Boffey characterizes it as a "Pedagogical anthology of English, Latin and French verse and prose." Ibid., 192. As noted above, the other manuscript that preserves "*De amico ad amicam*" and "*Responsio*" is Cambridge University Library Gg 4.27, an ornate late-fourteenth-century anthology of Chaucer's works. Taken together, the two codicological contexts

of these poems represent the two extremes of the pedagogical/courtly continuum from which Middle English verse love epistles arise.

92. Robbins, "Two Middle English," 421.

93. F. J. E. Raby, *A History of Secular Latin Poetry in the Middle Ages*, 2 vols. (Oxford: Clarendon Press, 1934), 2:45.

94. Edmond Faral, ed., *Ars versificatoria*, in *Les arts poétiques du XIIe et du XIIIe siècle* (Paris: Honoré Champion, 1958), 129–130; Faral, *Poetria nova*, in *Les arts poétiques*, 221–222.

95. Carmago, *Medieval Rhetorics*, 72.

96. Ibid., 134.

97. Only one other Middle English verse love epistle includes such a catalogue, and in that poem (*IMEV* 2478.5), references to Virgil, Horace, Lucan, Statius, and Ovid (21–22) hint at the same kind of link to the classroom that I am arguing for in the case of the Rawlinson epistles.

98. John Lydgate, "A Satirical Description of His Lady," in *A Selection from the Minor Poems of Dan John Lydgate*, ed. James Orchard Halliwell-Phillipps (London: Percy Society, 1840), 2:199–205.

99. Thomas Hoccleve, "Hoccleve's Humorous Praise of His Lady," in *Hoccleve's Works*, ed. Frederick J. Furnivall and I. Gollancz, vol. 2, EETS e.s. 73 (London: Oxford University Press, 1925), 37–38.

100. Jan Ziolkowski, "Avatars of Ugliness in Medieval Literature," *Modern Language Review* 79 (1984): 1–20, 13.

101. *Morte Arthure*, ll. 1098–1101, quoted in Ziolkowski, "Avatars," 9.

102. A catalogue of a man's ugliness is preserved in a thirteenth-century "rhetorical anthology" (Glasgow, Hunterian V.8.14, fols. 100v–101r), which, according to its editor Bruce Harbert, "may have been put together for a group of students of rhetoric." Bruce Harbert, ed., *A Thirteenth-Century Anthology of Rhetorical Poems: Glasgow MS Hunterian V.8.14* (Toronto: Pontifical Institute of Mediaeval Studies, 1975),

4. Raby notes that Matthew of Vendôme's description of Davus in the *Ars versificatoria* (ll.125–128) "might" be considered a satire; Raby, *History*, 2:45.

103. Lydgate, "Satirical Description," 202.

104. Marjorie Curry Woods, "Rape and the Pedagogical Rhetoric of Sexual Violence," in *Criticism and Dissent in the Middle Ages*, ed. Rita Copeland (Cambridge, UK: Cambridge University Press, 1996), 56–86, 69.

105. Ibid., 73.

106. Charles S. Singleton, ed. and trans., *The Divine Comedy* (Princeton, NJ: Princeton University Press, 1970), 2:270.

107. In Thomas Stehling, ed. and trans., *Medieval Latin Poems of Male Love and Friendship* (New York: Garland Press, 1984), 90–93. I am grateful to Marjorie Curry Woods for informing me about these letters. Stehling notes

that a few other letters in the collection also touch on homosexuality: "in one a bishop tells an abbot to discipline his homosexual monks . . . and in another canons complain they had been seduced by the chapter's head when they entered the chapter as young boys." The manuscript that originally contained this treatise no longer exists, having been destroyed sometime after a transcription of it was made in the eighteenth century; ibid., 157.
108. Ibid., 93.
109. Carolyn Dinshaw, "Rivalry, Rape, and Manhood: Gower and Chaucer," in *Chaucer and Gower: Difference, Mutuality, Exchange*, ed. R. F. Yeager (Victoria, B.C.: University of Victoria Press, 1991), 130–152, 134.
110. *IMEV* 2267.5, Davis, *Paston Letters*, no. 351. Davis argues that this letter may have been written by John Paston to the Earl of Oxford, but James Gairdner's edition of the letters reassuringly entitles the poem "Verses Written by a Lady in the Reign of Henry VI of Edward IV. to an absent Lord with whom she was in love." James Gairdner, ed., *The Paston Letters, A.D. 1422–1509* (New York: AMS, 1965), 6:67.
111. *IMEV* 866, Davis, *Paston Letters*, no. 776; *IMEV* 557, F. C. Hingeston, ed., *Royal and Historical Letters during the Reign of Henry the Fourth*, Rerum Britannicarum medii aevi scriptores 18 (London: Longman, 1860), xxiii and 38.
112. David Thomson, *A Descriptive Catalogue of Middle English Grammatical Texts*. New York: Garland, 1979), 292.
113. In his study of paper manuscripts from the Low Countries, Erik Kwakkel argues that clerks had the lion's share of the paper book market; Kwakkel, "New Type," 245.

WORKS CITED

Primary Sources

Adam of Eynsham. *Magna Vita Sancti Hugonis: The Life of St Hugh of Lincoln*. Ed. Decima L. Douie and David Hugh Farmer. Oxford: Clarendon, 1985. 2 vols.

Andrew, Malcolm, and Ronald Waldron, eds. *Sir Gawain and the Green Knight. The Poems of the Pearl Manuscript: Pearl, Cleanness, Patience*, Rev. ed. Exeter: Exeter University Press, 1987.

Anglicus, Bartholomæus. *De Proprietatibus Rerum*. Trans. John Trevisa. Gen. Ed. M. C. Seymour. Oxford: Oxford University Press, 1975-1988. 3 vols.

The Book of the Knight of La Tour-Landry. Ed. Thomas Wright. EETSOS 33. London, 1868.

Camargo, Martin, ed. *Medieval Rhetorics of Prose Composition: Five English Artes Dictandi and Their Tradition*. Binghamton: Medieval and Renaissance Texts and Studies, 1995.

Cambridge University Commission, *Documents Relating to the University and Colleges of Cambridge*. London: G. E. Eyre and W. Spottiswoode, for Her Majesty's Stationery Office, 1852.

Chartier, Alain. *Le Livre de l'espérance*. Ed. Francois Rouy. Paris: Librairie Honoré Champion, 1989.

——. trans. anon. *"Fifteenth-century English Translations of Alain Chartier's Le traite de l'esperance and Le quadrilogue invectif."* Ed. Margaret S. Blayney. EETSOS 270 and 281. London: Oxford University Press, 1974-1980.

Chaucer, Geoffrey. *The Riverside Chaucer*. Gen. Ed. Larry D. Benson. 3rd ed. New York: Houghton, 1987.

Cursor Mundi. Ed. Richard Morris. EETSOS 57, 59, 66, 68, 99, and 101. London, 1874-1893.

Dante Alighieri. *The Divine Comedy*. Ed. and Trans. Charles S. Singleton. Princeton: Princeton University Press, 1970. 6 vols.

Davis, Norman. *Paston Letters and Papers of the Fourteenth Century*. Oxford: Clarendon P, 1971. 2 vols.

Faral, Edmond ed., *Les arts poétiques du XIIe et du XIIIe siècle*. Paris: Honore Champion, 1958.

Frederick II. *Historia Diplomatica Friderici Secundi*. Ed. J. L. A. Huillard Breholles. Torino: Bottega D'erasmo, 1963.

Furnivall, Frederick J., ed. *Political, Religious, and Love Poems*. EETSOS 15. 2nd ed. London: Kegan Paul, 1903.

Gairdner, James. *The Paston Letters, A.D. 1422-1509*. New Complete Library Ed. New York: AMS, 1965.

Gower, John. *Confessio amantis. The English Works of John Gower.* Ed. G. C. Macaulay. EETSES 81 and 82. London: Oxford University Press, 1900-1901. 2 vols.

Higden, Ranulph. *Polychronicon.* Trans. John Trevisa. Ed. Churchill Babington. *Rerum Britannicarum Medii Ævi Scriptores* 41. London: Longman, 1865-1886. 8 vols.

Hoccleve, Thomas. "Hoccleve's Humorous Praise of his Lady." *Hoccleve's Works.* Vol. 2. EETSES 73. Ed. Frederick J. Furnivall and I. Gollancz. London: Oxford University Press, 1925. 37-38.

Kingdon, John Abernathy. *A Facsimile of the First Volume of Manuscript Archives of the Worshipful Company of Grocers of the City of London, A. D. 1345-1463.* London: Grocers Company, 1883-1886. 2 vols.

Le Menagier de Paris. Ed. Georgine E. Brereton and Janet M. Ferrier. Oxford: Clarendon, 1981.

———. trans. Eileen Power. *The Goodman of Paris: A Treatise on Moral and Domestic Economy by a Citizen of Paris.* London: Routledge, 1928.

Layamon. *Layamon: Brut Edited from British Museum ms. Cotton Caligula A. IX and British*

Museum ms. Cotton Otho C. XIII. Ed. G. L. Brook and R. F. Leslie. EETSOS 250. London: Oxford University Press, 1963-1978. 2 vols.

Lydgate, John. "A Satirical Description of His Lady." *A Selection from the Minor Poems of Dan John Lydgate.* Ed. J. O. Halliwell. Vol 2. London: Percy Society, 1840. 199-205.

———. *Lydgate's Temple of Glas.* Ed. J. Schick. EETSES 60. 1891. New York, Kraus Reprints, 1987.

Moore, Stuart. A. *The Letters and Papers of John Shillingford Mayor of Exeter 1447-50.* Camden Society New Series 2. Westminster, 1871.

Peter the Venerable. *Noni Tractatis adversis Judæorum inveteratam duritiem. Patrologia Latina.* Ed. J. P. Migne. *Patrologia Latina. Patrologia Latina Database.* Proquest,1996-2012. 189.507-650.

Quinn, D. B. *The Port Books or Local Customs Accounts of Southampton for the Reign of Edward IV.* Southampton: Southampton Record Society, 1937-38. 2 vols.

Sir Gowther: Eine englische romanze aus dem XV jahrhundert. Ed. Karl Breul. Oppeln: E. Franck, 1886.

Studer, Paul. *The Port Books of Southampton, or (Anglo-French) Accounts of Robert Florys, Water-Bailiff and Receiver of Petty-Customs, A.D. 1427-1430.* Southampton: Southampton Record Society, 1913.

Trithemius, Johannes. *In Praise of Scribes: De Laude Scriptorium.* Ed. Klaus Arnold. Trans. Roland Behrendt. Lawrence: Coronado, 1974.

Secondary Sources

Bell, H. E. "The Price of Books in Medieval England." *The Library* Series 4 17 (1937): 312-32.

Benson, C. David. "The 'Love-Tydynges' in Chaucer's *House of Fame*." *Chaucer's Dream Visions and Shorter Poems*. Ed. William A. Quinn. New York: Garland, 1999. 221-41.

Bloom, Jonathan. *Paper Before Print: The History and Impact of Paper in the Islamic World*. New Haven: Yale University Press, 2001.

Blum, André. *On the Origin of Paper*. Trans. Harry Miller Lydenberg. New York: Bowker, 1934.

Boffey, Julia. *Manuscripts of English Courtly Love Lyrics in the Later Middle Ages*.Woodbridge: D. S. Brewer, 1985.

———. "Middle English lives." *The Cambridge History of Medieval English Literature*. Ed. David Wallace. Cambridge: Cambridge University Press, 1999. 610-34.

———. "Some London Women Readers and a Text of *The Three Kings of Cologne*." *The Ricardian* 9 (1996): 387-96.

Boffey, Julia, and John J. Thompson. "Anthologies and Miscellanies: Production and Choice of Texts." *Book Production and Publishing in Britain 1375-1475*. Ed. Jeremy Griffiths and Derek Pearsall. Cambridge: Cambridge University Press, 1989. 279-315.

Bolter, Jay David, and Richard Grusin. *Remediation: Understanding New Media*. Cambridge, MA: MIT 1999.

Bonaventure, Brother. "The Teaching of Latin in Later Medieval England." *Medieval Studies* 23 (1961): 1-20.

Briquet, C. M. *Les filigranes*. Paris: A. Picard, 1907. 4 vols.

Brown, Michelle. *Understanding Illuminated Manuscripts: A Guide to Technical Terms*. Malibu: J. Paul Getty Museum, 1994.

British Library. *Manuscripts Catalogue*. 12 Jun. 2005. http://www.bl.uk/catalogues/manuscripts/.

Burger, Joachim. "Palaeogenetics of Parchment." *Microanalysis of Parchment*. Ed. René Larsen. London: Archetype, 2002. 159-61.

Camargo, Martin, ed. *Medieval Rhetorics of Prose Composition: Five English Artes Dictandi and Their Tradition*. Binghamton: Medieval and Renaissance Texts and Studies, 1995.

———. *The Middle English Verse Love Epistle*. Tubingen: Niemeyer, 1991.

Camille, Michael. "Sensations of the Page: Imaging Technologies and Medieval Illuminated Manuscripts." *The Iconic Page in Manuscript, Print, and Digital Culture*. Ed. George Bornstein and Theresa Tinkle. Ann Arbor: University of Michigan Press, 1998. 33-53.

Christianson, C. Paul. *A Directory of London Stationers and Book Artisans, 1300-1500*. New York: Bibliographical Society of America, 1990.

———. "Early London Bookbinders and Parchmeners." *Book Collector* 34 (1985): 41-54.

———. *Memorials of the Book Trade in Medieval London: The Archives of Old London Bridge*. Woodbridge: D. S. Brewer, 1987.

Clanchy, M. T. *From Memory to Written Record: England 1066-1307*. 2nd. ed. Oxford: Blackwell, 1993.

———. "'Tenacious Letters': Archives and Memory in the Middle Ages." *Archivaria* 11 (Winter 1980–1981): 115–125.

Connolly, Margaret. *John Shirley: Book Production and the Noble Household in Fifteenth- Century England*. Aldershot: Ashgate, 1998.

Constable, Giles, ed. *The Letters of Peter the Venerable*. 2 vols. Cambridge: Harvard University Press, 1967.

Cords, Rose. "Fünf me. Gedichte aus den Hss. Rawlinson Poetry 36 und Rawlinson C. 86." *Archiv für das studium der neueren sprachen und literaturen* 135 (1916): 293-302.

De Hamel, Christopher. *A History of Illuminated Manuscripts*. London: Phaidon, 1994.

Deng, M., and C. T. J. Dodson. *Paper: An Engineered Stochastic Structure*. Atlanta: TAPPI, 1994.

Dinshaw, Carolyn. "Rivalry, Rape, and Manhood: Gower and Chaucer." *Chaucer and Gower: Difference, Mutuality, Exchange*. Ed. R. F. Yeager. Victoria: University of Victoria Press. 130-52.

Duncan, David John. "The Paper Trade and Industry in Medieval England." MA Thesis. University of Virginia. 1995.

Febvre, Lucien, and Henri Martin. *The Coming of the Book: The Impact of Printing 1450-1800*. Trans. David Gerard. London: NLB, 1976.

Gumbert, J. P. "Skins, Sheets and Quires." *New Directions in Later Medieval Manuscript Studies*. Ed. Derek Pearsall. York: York Medieval Press, 2000. 81-92.

Hammond, Eleanor P. *English Verse between Chaucer and Surrey*. New York: Octagon, 1965.

———. "Omissions from the Editions of Chaucer." *Modern Language Notes* 19.2 (1904): 35-38.

Hanna, Ralph. "John Shirley and British Library, MS Additional 16165." *Studies in Bibliography* 49 (1996): 95-105.

Harbert, Bruce, ed. *A Thirteenth-Century anthology of Rhetorical Poems: Glasgow MS Hunterian V.8.14*. Toronto: Pontifical Institute of Mediaeval Studies, 1975.

Hector, L. C. *Handwriting of English Documents*. London: Edward Arnold, 1958.

Heller, Jules. *Papermaking*. New York: Watson-Guptill, 1978.

Hills, Richard L. *Papermaking in Britain 1488-1988: A Short History*. London: Athlone, 1988.

Hook, Diana H., and Jeremy M. Norman (with contributions by Michael R. Williams). *Origins of Cyberspace: A Library on the History of Computing, Networking, and Telecommunications*. Novato: historyofscience.com, 2001.

Hudson, Anne. "Lollard Book Production." *Book Production and Publishing in Britain: 1375-1475*. Ed. Jeremy Griffiths and Derek Pearsall. Cambridge: Cambridge University Press, 1989. 125-42.

Hunnisett, R. F. "What is a plea roll?" *Journal of the Society of Archivists* 9 (1988): 109-14.

Hunter, Dard. *Papermaking: The History and Technique of an Ancient Craft*. 1947. New York: Dover, 1978.

Iogna-Prat, Dominique. *Ordonner et exclure: Cluny et la société chrétienne face à l'hérésie, au judaïsme et à l'islam 1000-1150*. Paris: Aubier, 1998.

Ivy, G. S. "The Bibliography of the Manuscript Book." *The English Library before 1700*. Ed. Francis Wormald and C. E. Wright. London: Athlone, 1958. 32-65.

Kaeuper, Richard W. *Bankers to the Crown: The Riccardi of Lucca and Edward I*. Princeton: Princeton University Press, 1973.

Kurvinen, Auvo. "MS Porkington 10: Description with Extract." *Neuphilologische Mitteilungen* 54 (1953): 33-67.

Kwakkel, Erik. "A New Type of Book for a New type of Reader: The Emergence of Paper in Vernacular Book Production." *The Library* 7th series. 4 (2003): 219-248.

Lebrun, Pierre. *Original Treatises on the Arts of Painting*. Ed. and Trans. Mary P. Merrifield. New York: Dover, 1967.

Lopez, R. "The English and the Manufacture of Writing Materials in Genoa." *Economic History Review*. 10 (1940): 132-37.

Lyall, R. J. "Materials: The Paper Revolution." *Book Production and Publishing in Britain: 1375-1475*. Ed. Jeremy Griffiths and Derek Pearsall. Cambridge: Cambridge University Press, 1989. 11-29.

Lyell, Lætitia. *A Mediaeval Post-Bag*. London: Jonathan Cape, 1934.

Maxted, Ian. "Education and literacy in medieval Devon" *Exeter Working Papers in British Book Trade History* 12. http://bookhistory.blogspot.com/2007/01/devon-book-26.html.

Nightingale, Pamela. *A Medieval Mercantile Community: The Grocers' Company and the Politics and Trade of London 1000-1485*. New Haven: Yale University Press, 1995.

O'Donnell, James J. *Avatars of the Word: From Papyrus to Cyberspace*. Cambridge: Harvard University Press, 1998.

Parkes, M. B. *English Cursive Book Hands 1250-1500*. 1969. repr. Berkeley: University of California Press, 1980.

Patterson, Lee W. "Ambiguity and Interpretation: A Fifteenth-Century Reading of *Troilus and Criseyde*." *Speculum* 54 (1979): 297-330.

Raby, F. J. E. *A History of Secular Latin Poetry in the Middle Ages*. Oxford: Clarendon Press, 1934. 2 vols.

Reed, R. *Ancient Skins Parchments and Leathers*. London: Seminar Press, 1972.

Reynolds, R. L. "Some English Settlers in Genoa in the Late Twelfth Century." *Economic History Review* 4 (1933): 317-23.

Rickert, Edith. *Chaucer's World*. Ed. Clair C. Olson and Martin M. Crow. New York: Columbia University Press, 1948.

——. "Some English Personal Letters of 1402." *Review of English Studies* 8 (1932): 257-63.

Robbins, Rossell Hope, ed. *Secular Lyrics of the XIVth and XVth Centuries*. 2nd ed. Oxford:Oxford University Press, 1955.

Robbins, Rossell Hope. "Two Middle English Satiric Love Epistles." *Modern Language Review* 37 (1942): 415-21.

Rouse, Mary A. and Richard H Rouse. "From flax to parchment: a monastic sermon from twelfth-century Durham." *New Science Out of Old Books: Studies in Manuscripts and Early Printed Books in Honour of A. I. Doyle*. Ed. Richard Beadle and A. J. Piper. Hants: Scolar Press, 1995. 1-13.

Ruddock, Alwyn A. *Italian Merchants and Shipping in Southampton 1270-1600*. Southampton: University College, 1951.

Scott, William E., and James C. Abbott (in collaboration with Stanley Trosset). *Properties of Paper: An Introduction*. 2nd Rev. ed. Atlanta: TAPPI, 1995.

Seymour, M. C. "The Manuscripts of Chaucer's *Troilus*." *Scriptorium* 46 (1992): 107-21.

Stanbury, Sarah. "Women's Letters and Private Space in Chaucer." *Exemplaria* 6.2 (1994): 282-285.

Steiner, Emily. *Documentary Culture and the Making of Medieval English Literature*. Cambridge: Cambridge University Press, 2003.

Stevenson, Allan. *The Problem of the Missale Speciale*. London: Bibliographic Society, 1967.

Stehling, Thomas. ed. and trans. *Medieval Latin Poems of Male Love and Friendship*. New York: Garland, 1984.

Subirà, Oriol Valls I. *The History of Paper in Spain X-XIV Centuries*. Madrid: Empressa Nacional de Celulosas, 1978.

Taylor, John. "Letters and Letter Collections in England, 1300-1420." *Nottingham Medieval Studies* 24 (1980): 57-70.

Thomson, David. *A Descriptive Catalogue of Middle English Grammatical Texts*. New York: Garland, 1979, 282.

Turner, Silvie. *The Book of Fine Paper*. New York: Thames and Hudson, 1998.

Woods, Marjorie Curry. "Rape and the pedagogical rhetoric of sexual violence." *Criticism and Dissent in the Middle Ages*. Ed. Rita Copeland. Cambridge: Cambridge University Press, 1996. 56-86.

Youngs, Deborah. "Vision in a Trance: A Fifteenth-Century Vision of Purgatory." *Medium Ævum*. 67 (1998): 212-34.

Ziolkowski, Jan. "Avatars of Ugliness in Medieval Literature." *Modern Language Review* 79 (1984): 1-20.

Zonghi, Augusto. "Watermarks in Paper, their Origin and Importance." From the Italian, 1911.

Zonghi's Watermarks. Ed. E. J. Labarre. Hilversum: Paper Publications Society, 1953. 50-61.

Female Readers, Passion Devotion, and the History of MS Royal 17 A. xxvii

DOROTHY KIM

Introduction: Diachronic History

James Simpson's article "Diachronic History and the Shortcomings of Medieval Studies" articulates a possibility that cuts against the grain of medieval intellectual tradition: a way to push back on what he sees as the nostalgic, melancholic posture of philology. Philology, he claims, "characteristically treats its objects as definitively entombed and dead." The scholar's work is set: the task of recovering "the pristine wholeness of segments of the past."[1] Within this argument's scope, the agendas of periodization—particularly the break between the medieval and early modern—represent the rhetoric of revolutions. Revolution engenders ruptures; philology requires rupture "in order to legitimate and justify its own project of restoration."[2] The upshot of his argument places a high value on what he terms "diachronic historicism"—one in which scholars articulate a consciousness of how "the medieval" cannot be divorced from Classicism and Protestantism, "the powerful counters by which it was aggressively formed."[3] This article—at leagues and in conversation with these imperatives—performs a version of diachronic historicism centered on an object: a manuscript in the Royal collection at the British Library.

In critical parlance, my article evaluates the history of one manuscript from its inception to its potential and speculative use and meaning upon its seventeenth-century entrance into the Royal Library at St. James's Palace. I am tangling with new—albeit really old—ideas about how objects function through time. At its core, my work is enmeshed with often-imagined, traditional subjects: bibliography, philology, and material culture. These traditional disciplines and their aim—material analysis and contextual history—also intersect concomitantly with new theoretical discussion in the critical arena of object-oriented ontology—the philosophical study of existence centered on things.[4] Although object-oriented ontology developed from critical work in philosophy by Graham Harman on speculative realism and what he terms object-oriented philosophy or guerilla metaphysics, medievalists Eileen Joy and Jeffrey Jerome Cohen have taken object-oriented ontology into the field of medieval studies. In medieval studies, object-oriented ontology has taken a different direction to focus on what Cohen and Joy term "speculative medievalisms" to think about the deep history of objects.[5] In effect, these discussions have reasserted what history-of-the-book scholars and material-culture specialists have been addressing: the breakdown of periodicity, the evaluation of material objects and their effects on readers and producers, and the effects of readers and producers on the material book.

But wading into philology also unearths the theoretical double specter of origins and nostalgia. In 1990, Stephen Nichols refashioned manuscript studies as a new critical mode in a special edition of *Speculum* on "The New Philology."[6] In "New Philology," manuscript studies take center stage and are posited as a "postmodern return to the origins of medieval studies" that ruptures the early modern centering of history through "humanism, the Reformation, and the invention of the printing press."[7] The manuscript matrix and its detailed analysis encourage an interdisciplinary and diverse approach that mirrors the conditions and situation of the manuscripts studied. Thus manuscript studies, the "new philology," reveals how "medieval culture did not simply live with diversity, it cultivated it."[8] Although the manuscript matrix is a site of radical contingencies, "of chronology, of anachronism, of conflicting subjects, of representation," the pitfall in moving backward to pure origins rests on an inescapable obstacle—the past can never be pristinely recreated.[9] Daniel Leech-Wilkinson, while discussing the modern invention of medieval music, exposes this fantasy with the unattainable hope of a "faithful" recreation of the original medieval performance.[10] Instead, our historical excavations will always be mediated through a slightly skewed lens of nostalgia; the modern world will always participate in shaping the past's narrative.

Additionally, philology itself has its own shadowed theoretical past in which the study of origins became the method of distinguishing racial superiority.[11] Geoffrey Harpham points to the recent interest by a wide range of contemporary critics—including Edward Said and Paul de Man—who have invoked a return to philology as a way to pure critical spaces where methodology and narrow detail will open new theoretical vistas. He warns us not to see scholarly virtuousness in smallness, nor to jettison methodology or the quest for comprehensive knowledge; rather, Harpham argues, we should use philology as a "revealing mirror" that exposes scholarship's "highest aspirations and darkest fears."[12] Our duty lies in distinguishing them.

The backward-glancing and genealogical mode of philology has hampered critical discussions of philology's potential utility. Instead of returning to the originary moment, object-oriented ontology moves in the other direction—forward and into the future. Object-oriented ontology can also displace the genealogical stemma and diagram to introduce a system of interlinked spheres in which objects touch and affect each other in relational rather than directly linked ways.

Levi Bryant's recent post and comment on Eileen Joy's Swedish Twitter University lecture crystallizes how object-oriented ontology revisits the scholarly arenas of bibliography, philology, and material culture:[13] "Object-oriented criticism for its part . . . begins from the premise not of the *meaningfulness* of the text, but of the *materiality* of the text. *The text is something*."[14] He highlights a text's circulation in the world and how "texts have the capacity to *affect other bodies*."[15] His thesis posits that "criticism is a production based on the affectivity of the text . . . the question is no longer the question of what the text *means* with the aim of *closing* the text, but rather is the question of what the text *builds*."[16] The forward rather than backward motion of object-oriented ontology permits the unloosening of tight and narrow philological and genealogical lines and opens a rupture into historical scholarship that allows a more capacious and relational view focused on living, dynamic objects.

This article charts a diachronic history of an unassuming devotional manuscript in the British Library through five centuries of circulation. I consider how textual materiality builds, transforms, and travels through the hands of scribes, readers, book owners, and others who have affected the book's production, accretion, and use. Ultimately, the question I am answering is how this object—this composite manuscript—circulates, builds, and negotiates meaning in three distinct historical moments: its early thirteenth-century production, its fifteenth-century repackaging and additions, and its seventeenth-century purchase and employment. How does female devotion to Christ's Passion surface and transform in speculative female hands through five centuries?

MS Royal 17 A. xxvii: The Object

Two scholarly communities—one interested in the thirteenth-century early Middle English Katherine Group and Wooing Group texts,[17] the other centered on its fifteenth-century illuminated *Arma Christi* and the multiple lyric Passion verses in the manuscript's second section—have cultivated interest in London, British Library, MS Royal 17 A. xxvii. Both groups, part of a growing constellation of critics, have centered scholarly attention on anchoritic texts, early women's literary history, and religious literature. Between the manuscript's covers, readers discover the indescribable horrors of hell, the naked and vicious torture of young virgins, the mass conversion of pagans, the knife of Christ's circumcision and the whip of Christ's scourging, and a textual amulet that promotes safe births. The interpretive options for this book are myriad and require separate study. Instead, this article will concentrate on the object itself and its multilayered journey to the British Library's Royal collection.

The British Library catalogue description of MS Royal 17 A. xxvii very tentatively suggests, with a question mark,[18] that the manuscript's two parts were bound together after the Middle Ages—perhaps during the seventeenth century.[19] This article reevaluates the physical, historical, and internal evidence in these two manuscript sections to consider how and why they may have been bound together in the late Middle Ages and how these devotional pieces—separated by two centuries—could become a cohesive devotional text. Rather than being a haphazardly bound volume, MS Royal 17 A. xxvii had a late-medieval readership that could have potentially utilized this manuscript, with its thirteenth- and fifteenth-century parts, as a comprehensible devotional text centered on Christ's Passion. In addition, this article tackles another set of probable readers in the seventeenth-century world of Charles II's court: How could this manuscript, as an identifiable object of female Catholic devotion, be employed by or imagined for Catherine of Braganza, Charles II's barren wife?

Part I. The Material Book: Manuscript Contents and Physical Description

MS Royal 17 A. xxvii, well known to Middle English scholars interested in the thirteenth-century Katherine Group, stands as one of a handful of manuscripts that includes the sermon *Sawles Warde*; the *vitae* of St. Katherine, St. Margaret, and St. Juliana; and a Wooing Group text, *Þe Oreisun of Seinte Marie* (also known as *On Lofsong of Ure Lefdi*). Three hands copied these thirteenth-century pieces on folios 1 to 70v. Hand A copied folios 1r to 8v and 11r to the end of the first paragraph on folio 45v; Hand B worked on folios 9r to 10v and 58v to 70v; and Hand C penned the beginning of paragraph 2 on folio 45v to the end of 58r.[20] An early fifteenth-century hand emerges as the candidate behind the fifteenth-century Latin and Middle English sections.[21]

Ann Savage and Nicholas Watson conjecture that at least the Wooing Group texts in general, and possibly the Royal manuscript's *Þe Oreisun of Seinte*

Marie, would have been circulating on their own on single leaves or in small booklets.[22] Savage and Watson propose that the Royal manuscript originally contained the entirety of *Þe Oreisun of Seinte Marie*. This text currently fits on two sides of one leaf and stops abruptly near the end of a sentence, at " sunfule willeliche," about halfway through the piece.[23] Catherine Innes-Parker further refines Savage and Watson's point by writing that "Unlike *Ancrene Wisse* and the texts of the Katherine Group, the *Wohunge*, and the prayers which together form the Wooing Group likely originally circulated on scrolls or individual leaves."[24] In a recent volume devoted to the Wooing Group, Nicholas Watson speaks of the "portmanteau" qualities of the Wooing Group texts in content and argues for their inherent portability.[25]

I take the idea of portability further by using MS Royal 17 A. xxvii as an example of a category of manuscript portability in which units of texts comprise "booklets" that can be gathered together to form a composite volume. The idea of booklet compilation is not unusual, but MS Royal 17 A. xxvii may attest to a practice of circulating booklets of material separately before intentionally assembling them together to form a bound manuscript. Pamela Robinson explains the property of the booklet when she defines three different units in a manuscript: quire (the basic physical unit), pecia (mainly in universities), and the booklet. The booklet is a "self-contained unit" that "originated as a small but structurally independent production containing a single work or a number of short works."[26] She cautions us not to imagine that booklets would be made up of only a quire (a small unit); rather they could include several quires. In the case of MS Royal 17 A. xxvii's first segment, a number of the criteria that she delineates to identify booklets precisely matches this manuscript's physical shape.

In MS Royal 17 A. xxvii's first section, dated between ca. 1220 and 1230, several scholars have speculated that the lack of *Hali Meiðhad* indicates that this book is a very early manuscript of the Katherine and Wooing groups.[27] Thus it is probable that *Hali Meiðhad* was produced later or possibly may have been made contemporaneously but did not circulate in concert with these other materials.[28] One piece of evidence bolsters the theory about the chronological order in which these Wooing and Katherine Group texts were composed: another Wooing Group text, *On Lofsong of Ure Louerde*, is almost certainly a source text for a piece of *Hali Meiðhad*.[29]

Meg Laing dates the manuscript to ca. 1220 to 1230 and locates the language in the West Midlands. She believes it is similar but not identical to the language of Oxford, Bodleian Library MS Bodley 34 (the early Katherine Group manuscript) and the early manuscript of *Ancrene Wisse*, Cambridge, Corpus Christi College MS 402.[30] In her catalogue of early Middle English manuscripts, she does not mention the presence of the fifteenth-century material on folios 71 to 95. This section contains several devotional pieces, including a Latin form of confession; *Arma Christi* verses with color images and an indulgence; two hymns to the Virgin; a vision of St. Thomas of Canterbury concerning the Seven Joys; a hymn on the eight verses from the Psalter that will save one from damnation if one says them daily, as revealed by the Devil to St. Bernard; the *Fifteen Oes* in Latin, with a long rubric that tells of a *"femina quedam solitaria et reclusa"* to whom the number of Christ's wounds was revealed; and a prayer with a 6,000-year indulgence granted by Pope John.[31]

The fifteenth-century material is linguistically located by *A Linguistic Atlas of Late Medieval English* in the northwest Midlands,[32] and the dialect of "the prose introduction to a poem in this section (ff. 86v-88v)" is thought to be that of Staffordshire.[33] The volume—whether bound together in the late Middle Ages or in the seventeenth century—is regionally associated with the West Midlands. Although two centuries apart, the manuscript's two sections are from the same geographic location (see Map 1).[34]

The geographical connections between Gloucestershire, Worcestershire, Staffordshire, and Shropshire (see Map 1) place the activities surrounding MS Royal 17 A. xxvii within a specific area of the West Midlands region. As shown in the following table of the manuscript's contents, the thirteenth-century portion is primarily in English, while the fifteenth-century part is a mixed English and Latin compilation.

1. Contents of MS Royal 17 A. xxvii

Sawles Warde	1r–10v	13th century
St. Katherine	11r–36v	13th century
St. Margaret	37r–56r	13th century
St. Juliana	56r–70r	13th century
Oreisun of Seinte Marie	70r–70v	13th century
Form of Confession (Latin)	71r–72r	15th century
Arma Christi	72v–81r	15th century
Two Hymns to the Virgin	81r–83v	15th century
Vision of St. Thomas of Canterbury about the Seven Joys (Latin)	83v–86v	15th century
Hymn about St. Bernard and the Devil	86v–88v	15th century
The Fifteen Oes (Latin)	88v–95r	15th century
Indulgence Prayer (Latin)	95r–97r	15th century

I have examined one of the last pages of this manuscript (fol. 97r) under ultraviolet light. Unfortunately, due to former chemical treatments on the manuscript after 1921, it was impossible to see what the 1921 catalogue refers to as "an erased chronological note referring to 1403."[35] This date gives a threshold point for picturing when the fifteenth-century Passion materials, including the *Arma Christi*, would have been generated and began independent circulation. However, by examining the manuscript's physical shape and its parts, I believe I can discern how MS Royal 17 A. xxvii may have been used and compiled by its readers in stages through a system of booklets.

Quires

All of MS Royal 17 A. xxvii's leaves measure around 160 mm to 163 mm in length. Quires from both the thirteenth-century and the fifteenth-century sections also show pricking marks at the edge of their outer vertical leaves, while all the gatherings are approximately the same size and shape. This similarity may indicate that the vellum was shaped as standard eight-leaf quires or that it was cut at the same time, but the fifteenth-century content was not added until later.[36] Although both sections probably circulated separately before they were bound together as a manuscript, the quires create a composite system of booklets that would make it easy in the fifteenth century to add another section to an already portable book.

Robinson has identified several features that indicate when a manuscript was assembled as a collection of booklets. A number of the features, she explains, are quite obvious, but several other booklet features cannot be discerned from regular catalogue descriptions or without a collation of the book.[37] For MS Royal 17 A. xxvii, the following features are present in the manuscript: catchwords within a booklet; its own series of quire signatures; soiled outer leaves that suggest independent circulation before being bound together; the number of leaves in a quire is not uniform throughout; and a modified quire structure that adds or subtracts extra leaves.[38] Her criteria do not suggest that a manuscript with only one or even two of these features would definitely be recognized as a booklet compilation. Rather, the presence of several of these criteria—she identifies ten—would dramatically increase the probability of a manuscript's being a booklet compilation.

Ralph Hanna has revised Robinson's booklet hypothesis by adding three more potential criteria: variation in material (shifts between paper and vellum and quality of vellum); variation of sources that the manuscript copies; and variation in subject matter in different parts of the manuscript.[39] He also refines Robinson's criteria by ranking the most important features that indicate a booklet system. He places "independent systems of signatures in different parts of a manuscript" as primarily important; after this criterion, the variation in size of final quires, whether longer or shortened by cutting, is ranked second in significance.[40]

Hanna's refinement of Robinson's original work also attempts to separate the owners/vendors and producers of books[41] by taking into account the more commercial production that had become standard in the late Middle Ages. Hanna's refinements operate very well with a number of fourteenth- and fifteenth-century examples that he evaluates. However, for MS Royal 17 A. xxvii, his enhancements do not necessarily fit.

Early Katherine Group and Wooing Group manuscript production information is quite sparse. The volumes,[42] including MS Royal 17 A. xxvii (fols. 1–70v), were produced locally, probably by religious scribes near their patrons. They were not products of commercial ateliers in book-producing centers in either university towns (Oxford) or London. The contextual background of the early *Ancrene Wisse* manuscripts is the clearest example. We do know that one of the early readerships for *Ancrene Wisse* was a group of three female anchoresses, and the production of this guide seems to have been through the request of its early readers.[43] As for the texts in the Bodley 34 manuscript (Katherine Group), there is no absolute consensus on their readership other than that they were women—whether religious, anchoritic, or lay. Their dates are fixed by language as between approximately 1200 and 1250.[44] The texts are dated after the Fourth Lateran Council (1215) but before around 1250 on both paleographic and linguistic grounds.[45]

The early manuscripts of *Ancrene Wisse*,[46] the Katherine Group, and the Wooing Group are part of a matrix of vernacular religious material produced in the West Midlands between 1200 and 1250 originally for female readers. I also believe that these manuscripts, including MS Royal 17 A. xxvii, are products of a book production model in which readers/patrons and scribes had a close, hands-on book-producing relationship.[47] These works were also in their early production (i.e., original composition and compilation moments), so the identification of exemplar sources (one of Hanna's criteria for booklet production) is quite difficult.

Thus the producers and the readers/owners of the codex and the booklets would have had an enmeshed production relationship. The female readers may have requested specific booklets for use at different times but also wanted an entire book of booklets bound together. Ralph Hanna discusses what he terms the "bespoke" model of production that he sees as having occurred with the Auchinleck Manuscript (Edinburgh, National Library of Scotland Advocates, MS 19.2.1). In his speculation about this incredibly large manuscript's production, he imagines that once it became "bespoke" (a client's special request), there was probably a series of requests for specific items—this week I ask for a *Beves*; two weeks from now I want a *Sir Orfeo*. He believes it possible that at several points during the Auchinleck Manuscript's production, book sections may have been given to the patron for use and then returned.[48] This kind of production relationship for the Auchinleck Manuscript is how I see production working in MS Royal 17 A. xxvii.

Both physical and textual portability would have been the key for this system to work. The manuscripts are all on the smallish size.[49] If the Wooing Group texts were originally imagined by the patron as circulated pieces on scrolls or leaves, it would also mean that these little units of vernacular religious material would have been used immediately after production for reading and—as the form of scroll or leaf production suggests—for oral recitation. Gathering the booklets together into a codex and binding them as a volume may have been the last stage of a flexible cycle of booklet use and selection. This proposed scenario suggests the close direction and intimacy of reader/patron with the scribal book producer. Thus reader and scribe would have had ongoing contact—from requesting a booklet (for instance, a Wooing Group text) to establishing the manuscript's textual order and commissioning the binding of the entire booklet group.

MS Royal 17 A. xxvii has five of the features Robinson discusses as hallmarks of a booklet compilation structure. It also contains the top three criteria that Hanna distinguishes as the most important to define a booklet compilation: "independent systems of signatures in different parts of a manuscript," "variation in size of possible final quires," and "blank leaves at the end of quires, often cut away."[50]

Quire Structure

The 1921 Gilson and Warner catalogue description suggests the following for quire structure: "Gatherings of 8 leaves, (ii², ix, x⁶), the numeration beginning with iii (art. 2). Artt. 6-12 are in an early 15th cent. hand. Gatherings of 8 leaves (last³)."[51] I have reassessed and reordered the quire structure.

Thirteenth-Century Section
Quire 1: quire (4 sheets folded) + a bifolium / 2 single leaves[52]
Quire 2: quire (4 sheets folded), 11r
Quire 3: quire (4 sheets folded), 19r
Quire 4: quire (4 sheets folded), 27r
Quire 5: quire (4 sheets folded), 35r
Quire 6: quire (4 sheets folded), 43r
Quire 7: quire (4 sheets folded), 51r
Quire 8: quire (3 sheets folded), 59r
Quire 9: quire (3 sheets folded), 65r

Fifteenth-Century Section
Quire 10: quire (4 sheets folded), 71r
Quire 11: quire (4 sheets folded), 79r
Quire 12: quire (3 sheets folded + 1
leaf +1 bifolium), 88r

Most of the quire structure in MS Royal 17 A. xxvii consists of eight-leaf quires, with a few exceptions. In the thirteenth-century section, the beginning quire contains ten leaves and the section ends with two six-leaf quires. Likewise, the end of the manuscript's fifteenth-century part has an unusual nine-leaf quire. The compilation of the quire information, the contents, and the scribal hands together reveal a more solid picture of how this manuscript could have been produced in booklets and circulated as smaller devotional texts before being bound together.

British Library, MS Royal 17 A. xxvii

Item/Contents	Folios	Quires	Hands (A, B, C, D)
Sawles Warde	1r–10v	1	A: 1r–8v; B: 9r–10v
St. Katherine	11r–36v	2, 3, 4, 5	B: 11r–36v
St. Margaret	37r–56r	5, 6, 7	B: 37r–45v (end of paragraph 1); C: 45v (beg. of paragraph 2)–56r
St. Juliana	56r–70r	7, 8, 9	C: 56r–58r; B: 58v–70r
Oreisun of St. Marie	70r–70v	9	B: 70v
Form of Confession (Latin)	71r–72r	10	D (15th-c. hand)
Arma Christi	72v–81r	10 and 11	D
Two Hymns to the Virgin	81r–83v	11	D
Vision of St. Thomas of Canterbury about the Seven Joys (Latin)	83v–86v	11	D
Hymn about St. Bernard and the Devil	86v–88v	11 and 12	D
The Fifteen Oes (Latin)	88v–95r	11 and 12	D
Indulgence Prayer (Latin)	95r–97r	12	D

If we examine the thirteenth-century section of this chart and its textual collations, the most unusual quire is the first one. Quire 1 is a ten-leaf quire that contains all of *Sawles Warde*. It also has a scribal inscription at the end of *Sawles Warde* after a large "AMEN" on folio 10v. In it, the scribe identifies himself by name as John and writes:

> Par seinte charite biddeð a pater noster for iohann þet þeos boc *prat*
> Hpa se þis prit haveð ired. Ant crist him haveð spa
> isped. Ich bidde þar seinte charite. þet ȝe bidden ofte
> For me. Aa p*ater* no*ster*. Ant ave marie. Þet ich mote þ*et* lif her
> drehen. Ant ure lauerd þel i cpemen. I mi ȝuheðe
> ꝺ in min elde. Þet ich mote ih*esu* crist in saple ȝelden.
> AMEN:[53]

> [For St. Charity requires that whosoever this writ
> (legal document) has read, must say a Pater Noster
> for John that this book wrote. And Christ has made
> him so prosperous. I say a prayer for St. Charity. That
> you pray often for me. Continually a Pater Noster.
> And an Ave Maria. That I may this life endure here.
> And our Lord well please (serve). In my youth and
> in my old age. So that I may yield my soul to Jesus
> Christ. Amen.][54]

This scribal note is written by Hand B (whom I now call Scribe B), who completed the text on two extra leaves at the end of the first booklet. He is also the scribe of the last folio in the manuscript's thirteenth-century portion. I believe that *Sawles Warde* and quire 1/booklet 1 were written after *St. Katherine, St. Margaret,* and *St. Juliana* partly because of the evidence of this note. The other famous scribal note in the Katherine Group material occurs in Bodley 34. At the end of *St. Juliana* in Bodley 34, the life finishes with the following verse purportedly written by the *vita*'s translator:

> Hwen drihtin o domes dei windweð his hweate. Ant
> [weopð] þet dusti chef to hellene heate. He mote
> beon a corn i godes guldene edene. Þe turnde þis of
> latin to engliSche ledene. Ant he þet her least. On
> wrat swa as he cuðe. AMeN.[55]

> [When the Judge at Doomsday winnows his wheat,
> And drives dusty chaff into hell's heat,
> Make him a seed in God's golden Eden,
> Who translated to English this story from Latin.

And also the one who last wrote this as well as he
could Amen.][56]

These scribal notes—asking for God's and Christ's prayer—separate
potential units in the manuscript. In the case of Bodley 34, it appears that
readers should see *St. Katherine, St. Margaret,* and *St. Juliana* as one cohesive
unit. Similarly, in MS Royal 17 A. xxvii, *Sawles Warde* should be imagined as
a separate unit because the scribe ends it here with a personal prayer—rather
than at the conclusion of either *St. Juliana* or *Þe Oreisun of Seinte Marie.* The
existence of this separate unit also makes it plausible that *Sawles Warde* could
have circulated separately from the Katherine Group *vitae.* But the quire
evidence suggests that the *Sawles Warde* booklet may have been requested
when the volume was bound, because the scribal note is included at the end
of this quire.

Scribe B (as the chart above shows) has his hand in all the thirteenth-
century quires. It would make logical sense for him to put this note at the
end of the final quire that he finishes. In addition, the added two-leaf section
(either two separate leaves or a bifolium) allows him to complete this odd
first quire.[57] The first quire fits into Robinson's discussion of booklet feature
8: "A scribe may have had difficulty in fitting a text into the quire structure of
a 'booklet' and, consequently, have modified that structure ... the gathering
may have an extra leaf (or leaves) in order to accommodate the conclusion
of the text."[58] These extra leaves, and the fact that a different scribe finishes
them strongly with a personal note, implies that this was the last booklet to
be composed in MS Royal 17 A. xxvii's thirteenth-century section. It also
bolsters the theory that Scribe B was probably the volume's main scribal
contact and organizer for the female reader.

Further structural evidence demonstrates that readers (and definitely
the scribes) saw quire 1 and *Sawles Warde* as separate from the Katherine
Group *vitae.*[59] Quire 2 begins with the *Life of St. Katherine* and at the top of
folio 11r is a note, "auit p.u.m." At the bottom of quire 3 is the quire signature
"ii" on folio 19r. These quire signatures continue with "iii" at the bottom of
folio 27r (quire 4); "iiii" at the bottom of 35r (quire 5); "v" at the base of
folio 43r (quire 6); and "vi" at the base margin of folio 51r (quire 7). These
quire markings vigorously support the hypothesis that the Katherine Group
saints' lives were imagined as separate from *Sawles Warde* and were probably
the manuscript's first booklet.

I believe that the entirety of the Katherine Group *vitae,* from *St. Katherine*
through *St. Juliana,* was imagined as one reading unit—one booklet. There
is no quire signature for *Sawles Warde* (quire 1). These quire signatures stop
when the quires become six-leaf rather than eight-leaf quires. However, the
base of folio 58v has the catchword "del" (with a slash across), that corresponds

to the first word of the new quire on folio 59r, "deles." The evidence of a catchword here may reveal that the organizing scribe miscalculated how many quires were necessary to finish this booklet. Nonetheless, Scribe B continued finishing the rest of *St. Juliana* and used a catchword to link the last two six-leaf quires to what appears to be a planned unit that included all three saints' lives.

Nevertheless, Scribe B's estimate of what it would take to finish the Katherine Group in all probability had him remove a bifolium from each of the two eight-leaf quires. But he overestimated what he actually needed—or possibly underestimated. If he overestimated, the addition of the first half of *Þe Oreisun of Seinte Marie* becomes the filler for the blank page at the end of this booklet. If he underestimated, then *Þe Oreisun of Seinte Marie* was an integral part of the booklet unit. Either way, the choice of this text corresponds with the reading interests of the female readers as seen in other Wooing Group manuscripts—including *Ancrene Wisse* and the Katherine Group materials. If *Þe Oreisun of Seinte Marie* was a later addition, then it was left incomplete because the booklet was already formed and there was no more room. However, this latter scenario does make much more likely Savage and Watson's suggestion that the intention was for this manuscript to include all of *Þe Oreisun of Seinte Marie*. But unlike what seems quite standard for many of the other Wooing Group texts—the circulation first as separate scrolls and on individual leaves—I believe that *Þe Oreisun* was conceived, although probably after the completion of the three *vitae*, to be part of this booklet unit. As I discuss later in this article, *Þe Oreisun* can be read as a comment on the Katherine Group *Lives* and especially on the end of *St. Juliana*.

Thus the manuscript and textual evidence in MS Royal 17 A. xxvii indicates that the manuscript was probably planned with a booklet structure in which the Katherine Group saints' lives (plus *Þe Oreisun of Seinte Marie*) were one separately circulated booklet. The other booklet, produced later, would be quire 1, containing *Sawles Warde*. The scribal note at the end of the quire suggests that this was the last piece finished and that it was by Scribe B—the organizing scribe. However, I do not think this indicates that the booklets have been sewn out of order. Instead, the odd quire structures in the thirteenth-century portion's last two quires demonstrate that when the thirteenth-century part of MS Royal 17 A. xxvii was bound together (both booklets), the position of *Sawles Warde*—as the first text—was a choice on the part of the reader(s) who probably commissioned this section.

The practice of gathering portable booklets into a single volume is not an unusual phenomenon. Rather, as Robinson writes, "medieval readers frequently assembled together a number of 'booklets' to form a composite volume. Many manuscripts demonstrate that the practice of forming such a collection was current in the middle ages."[60] Robinson also affirms that the prevalence of booklet compilations could also explain the use of the term "*quarterno/quarternus*" and "*libellus*" in medieval library catalogues. She argues that the use of these terms in "inventories and in titles . . . must indicate a 'booklet' (though in other contexts they may have had a different sense)."[61] She gives an example of this from the catalogue of the Lanthony Priory library, which lists the volume as *Psalterium Ivonis, parvus quaternus,* corresponding to London, Lambeth Palace Library, MS 540.[62]

With the larger thirteenth-century portion of the manuscript functioning as portable booklets, it is not a far stretch to imagine that the fifteenth-century section would have fit in appropriately as another booklet added to this volume. The first page is darker and more faded than the previous thirteenth-century verso. The vellum of the fifteenth-century section is also darker, rougher, and appears to be of a different quality from the leaves of the earlier sections, although of approximately the same size. None of the texts or groups of text in this section makes up several booklets, but rather the entire fifteenth-century portion is itself a separate booklet. The quire structure shows that no single quire ends a text except for the last quire. Undoubtedly, from the last quire's odd nine-leaf structure, the extra leaf and bifolium were supplemented to finish the booklet volume with an indulgence—the last item in the manuscript. The fifteenth-century booklet probably circulated separately in the fifteenth century, but its parts were clearly imagined as a structural unit. I discuss below the textual and internal evidence supporting this argument that the manuscript's last section was a separate anthology of devotional texts.

The last pieces of physical evidence that we may evaluate for potential clues to this manuscript's life are the sewing holes. Unfortunately, the history of the binding is very uncertain. The British Library records that the manuscript's last binding was completed April 19, 1956. No information or notes about this binding exist. But because of the manuscript's portable and composite nature, it is difficult to say with absolute certainty if the sewing holes would help identify the volume's pre-seventeenth-century binding. Yet the note mentioning 1403 on the manuscript's last leaf suggests a tantalizing time frame for speculation about this manuscript and its readers.[63]

Manuscript Provenance and Manuscript History

Other than the geographical locations vis-à-vis linguistic analysis, our information about this manuscript really begins after the Reformation, with a Gloucestershire family in the seventeenth century. The Royal Library catalogue places the thirteenth-century section of the manuscript in John Theyer's library; it also positions the fifteenth-century material as possibly being in the same library. However, the catalogue questions whether it was already bound together or extant as separate manuscripts when the Theyer collection entered King Charles II's Library at St. James's Palace in 1673.[64]

John Theyer (1598–1673) was a lawyer whose family was from Brockworth, Gloucestershire.[65] Anthony Wood, his contemporary, records this information in his *Athenae Oxonienses*:

> John Theyer was born of genteel parents at Cowpers-hill in the parish of Brockworth, near to, and in the county of, Glocester, began to be conversant with the muses in Magdalen college an. 1613, aged 16 years or thereabouts, where continuing about three years, partly under the tuition of John Harmar, retired to an inn of chancery in London called New Inn, where spending as many years in obtaining knowledge in the common law,[66] he receded to his patrimony, and, as years grew on, gave himself up mostly to the study of venerable antiquity, and to the obtaining of the ancient monuments thereof (manuscripts) in which he did so much abound, that no private gentleman of his rank and quality did ever, I think, exceed him. He was a bookish and studious man, a lover of learning and the adorers thereof, a zealous royallist, and one that had suffer'd much (in the rebellion that began 1642) for the king's and church's cause. ... In the same year (1643) our author Theyer was adorned with the degree of master of arts... About which time he the said Theyer being discovered to be a man of parts, was persuaded to embrace the Roman-catholic religion by father "Franc." Philips a Scot, confessor to Henrietta Maria the queen consort. He hath also written, *A friendly Debate between the Protestants and the Papists*—MS. But before it was quite fitted for the press the author died, and what became of it afterwards, I know not. His death hapned at Cowpers-hill on the 25th of Aug. in sixteen hundred seventy and three, and two days after was buried among his ancestors in the church-yard at Brockworth before-mention'd, particularly near to the grave of his grandfather—Theyer who had married the sister of one Hart the last prior of Langthony near Glocester. He then left behind him a library of ancient manuscripts consisting of the number of about 800, which he himself had for the most part collected. The foundation of it was laid by his grandfather who had them from prior Hart, and he from the library of Langthony when it was dissolved, besides houshold stuff belonging to that priory.

Afterwards Charles Theyer (grandson to our author John Theyer who in his last will had bequeathed them to him) did offer to sell them to the university of Oxon, but the price being too great, they were sold to Robert Scot of London bookseller, who soon after sold them to his majesty king Ch. II. to be reposed in his library at S. James's, he having first, as I have been informed, cull'd them.[67]

Theyer was known to have an extensive and valuable library of manuscripts, a family collection. A large portion of this collection purportedly came from his grandmother's brother, Richard Hart (or Hempstead), the last prior of Lanthony Secunda (1534–1539)—a house patronized by the de Lacys and the Bohuns. Lanthony Secunda was an Augustinian house just outside Gloucester (established 1136).[68] Lanthony Prima was founded by Hugh de Lacy in 1108 in Monmouthshire, and both houses were dedicated to the Virgin. By the time of the Dissolution, Lanthony Secunda had become the main priory, and their possessions in 1535 included manors and rental income in Brockworth and Hempstead. Richard Hempstead (Hart), the last prior, signed the priory over to the Crown and received a pension of £100 a year, with pensions from £4 to £8 a year for the other twenty-four canons.[69]

Upon John Theyer's death, his collection went to his grandson Charles Theyer, who originally tried to sell it to the University of Oxford. Edward Bernard evaluated the collection in 1673. He made an inventory—a list that has been preserved in the Bodleian Library—in which he briefly describes 312 manuscripts and "adds a note that there were some others of less value."[70] The suggested sale price was too steep, and the collection then went to a London bookseller, Robert Scott, who valued the collection at £841 and 12 shillings. A Mr. Beveridge, rector of St. Peters Cornhill, and a Mr. Will Jane, canon of Christ Church, Oxford, reassessed the collection for the amount of £572, 3 shillings, and 6 pence. It was the last large collection to be folded into the King's Library at St. James's Palace; the King's Library eventually became one of the main British Library collections.[71]

It is tantalizing to suppose that the manuscript's two separate sections were at Lanthony Secunda, because that definitively would localize these devotional texts to a house in the West Midlands. However, the Theyer collection's history is not as straightforward as it appears. We have received the bulk of our contemporary seventeenth-century information from Anthony Wood's description in the *Athenae Oxonienses*, quoted above, in which he gives us the information that "He [Charles Theyer] then left behind him a Library of ancient Manuscripts consisting of the number of about 800." Wood also supplies us with the tantalizing tidbit that this collection was "cull'd" by Charles II before 312 manuscripts entered into his library.

M. R. James addresses these inconsistencies in number and the questions of the collection's provenance and circulation, not to mention where the other approximately 488 manuscripts might have gone, in *The Manuscripts in the Library at Lambeth Palace*, published by the Cambridge Antiquarian Society in 1900.[72] In regards to a timeline, apparently by 1673 the Theyer collection contained 334 manuscripts.[73] They had been acquired from around "twenty different monastic houses, particularly from the west of England," including manuscripts from Gloucestershire (Minchinhampton, Painswick, Meysey Hampton), Worcester, Hereford, and London.[74] Reginald Foole believes that Anthony Wood's number of 800 is completely inaccurate.[75] But Woods' family appears to have had more personal ties with the Theyers.[76] Evidence from the collecting habits of early modern antiquarians, such as Theyer's contemporary, Henry Savile, shows that large antiquarian collections were often broken up and sold.[77] One wonders if these phantom missing manuscripts may have been part of the collection before 1673 but were dispersed or sold to another large library.

James refers to Edward Bernard's *Catalogi librorum manuscriptorum Angliae et Hiberniae in unum collecti* (CMA; 1697) and its list of 312 manuscripts belonging to Charles Theyer of Gloucestershire.[78] The list conforms, with a few exceptions, to David Casley's *Catalogue of the Manuscripts of the King's Library*,[79] now in the British Library. But James points out that the Theyer collection as catalogued in the CMA in 1697 is not consistent with what we know of the library at Lanthony Secunda. We have a handlist of the library from 1380 in Harley MS 460. Henri Omont printed this list in 1892.[80] He writes:

> Catalogue des manuscrits du prieuré de Lanthony (glocestersire). (xive siècle.)
>
> Le Prieuré de Lanthony, de l'ordre de S. Augustin, fut fondé, en 1136, par Milon, comte de Hereford, à Hyde, près de Glocester.[81] C'était une colonie du prieuré de Lanthony (Monmouthshire), établi quelques années auparavant, en 1108,[82] et qui lui donna son nom.
>
> La bibliothèque du prieuré de Lanthony, beaucoup plus importante que les précédents, comptait près de 500 volumes au début du XIVe siècle, quand l'inventaire en fut dressé, non plus à la fin d'un volume, mais sur un cahier séparé, qui est maintenant conservé sous le no 460 du fonds de Harley, au Musée Britannique.[83]

[The manuscript catalogue of Lanthony priory (Gloucestershire). (14th century.)

The Lanthony Priory, of the order of St. Augustine, was
founded in 1136 by Milon, Count of Hereford,
in Hyde, near Gloucester. It was a colony of Lanthony Priory (Monmouthshire), which was established some years beforehand in 1108, and from
whom the former was given its name.

The library of Lanthony Priory, which is very much more
important than its predecessors, consisted of nearly 500 volumes at the beginning of the fourteenth
century, when the inventory was drawn up, not at
the end of a volume but in a separate notebook,
which is now preserved within MS Harley 460, at
the British Museum.][84]

The list enumerates nearly 500 volumes, but Omont lists only 486 items.[85] James's own examination of the Theyer manuscripts led him to place only a handful at Lanthony Secunda. What he discovers instead is that quite a number of Lambeth Palace Library's manuscripts were from Lanthony Secunda.[86] The bulk of the British Library's Theyer collection, then, was probably manuscripts collected by the Theyer family from their location in Gloucestershire. But if the Lanthony Secunda library was at one point part of the Theyer family collection, a number of the manuscripts seem to have entered Lambeth Palace Library. James cannot identify the date in which these manuscripts became part of Lambeth Palace Library after the Dissolution. However, the lack of Lanthony Secunda manuscripts indicates that John Theyer's collection probably consisted of his own and his family's personal library together with an active collection from the areas in and around Gloucestershire.

In this way, John Theyer's and his family's post-Dissolution collection may parallel that of another early seventeenth-century collector, Henry Savile of Banke. Henry Savile and his family were based in Yorkshire, and he was known for his collection of manuscripts.[87] Savile's collection, like Theyer's, was a multigenerational family affair—he appears to have inherited some of the collection from his father and grandfather. He augmented this family collection with his own acquisitions, particularly the collection of John Nettleton, another Yorkshire collector, who seems to have acquired thirty-one manuscripts with the hope of a return to Catholicism.[88] The Savile collection drew heavily on the dissolved monastic collections of northern England, including the libraries at Fountains, Rievaulx, and Byland.[89] Vickie

Larsen points out that although Savile's collection held an inordinately large number of English religious manuscripts—including the works of St. Brigit, St. Catherine, Richard Rolle, and Walter Hilton—Savile himself was an antiquarian collector rather than a religious reader.[90] With the parallel example of Savile in mind, John Theyer's collection of manuscripts may have also exhibited similar tendencies: drawing from local sources in Gloucestershire and Worcestershire but also collecting anew on the private market.

A perusal of the CMA along with the Royal manuscript catalogue and the Theyer sale catalogue reveals that several manuscripts hail from this region and from several cathedral libraries. For example, MS Royal 4 C. II, a twelfth-century commentary on Jerome, belonged to Worcester Cathedral library, as did MS Royal 6 C. vii, a twelfth-century collection of Gregory's epistles.[91] James also points out that many of them are Gloucester and Worcester manuscripts. The geographical connections between Gloucestershire, Worcestershire, Staffordshire, and Shropshire place the activities surrounding MS Royal 17 A. xxvii within a specific area of the West Midlands region.

In addition, several manuscripts in the collection also contain notes that show Theyer's book-buying habits in the mid-seventeenth century, including prices for purchasing books from specific individuals. For example, MS Royal 7 B. VII contains a note by John Theyer on folio 2: "Fer this and 9 MS. more marked onely with this [Theyer monogram], in all ten in number, to pay seaven poundes at Michaelmas terme 1650."[92] Theyer acquired volumes from the collections of several famous early book collectors, such as John Lumley,[93] Henry Savile, and even Matthew Parker's library at Cambridge. MS Royal 7 B. XI and 7 B. XII contain the collected works of Thomas Cranmer, Archbishop of Canterbury, from Matthew Parker's library; by September 4, 1659, John Theyer owned both Cranmer volumes.[94]

Although it would be fantastic to trace MS Royal 17 A. xxvii's direct provenance, it is currently impossible to connect this manuscript to the library at Lanthony Secunda. But we can place the manuscript in the local environs of the Theyer family in Gloucestershire and with the family's book connections in Worcestershire. And I believe we can trace the family's collecting interests back to the Dissolution, at the very least, if not earlier.

As for the question of when the thirteenth- and fifteenth-century sections of the Royal manuscript were bound together, I would direct our attention back to the CMA to evaluate the evidence we have from Bernard's catalogue. The Royal manuscript catalogue description of MS Royal 17 A. xxvii asserts the likelihood that they were bound together after the Theyer collection became part of the King's library. The catalogue tentatively states (with a "?") that MS Royal 17 A. xxvii probably corresponds to two potential entries in the CMA: catalogue nos. 6435 and 6662. In other words, the Royal catalogue has connected these two CMA entries as the most likely matches to MS Royal 17 A. xxvii:

> 6435.199: "An English Exposition on the Gospel"[95]

> 6662.292: "Verses on several texts of Holy scripture"[96]

> On folio 22r of the Theyer sale catalogue, MS Royal app. 70, is the following entry:

> 243 "A booke of ye passion of Jesus Xt in English verse wh Pictures"

The catalogue description of this item states that "Another list of the same collection (omitting 24 unimportant items) is in Harley MS 695, f. 313, and is printed, with some corruptions, in Bernard's *Catal. MSS. Angliae.*"[97] Item 243 is not in Bernard's catalogue but is clearly identifiable as MS Royal 17 A. xxvii because the description directly corresponds with the manuscript's fifteenth-century *Arma Christi*. Theyer's monogram is visible on an opening flyleaf and on folio 70b—the latter being at the top of the last leaf that contains *Þe Oreisun of Seinte Marie*. Thus the thirteenth-century portion of the Royal manuscript is also certainly a part of Theyer's collection. However, the description of item 243 in the sale catalogue is most apt: this volume does contain Passion verses and meditations in English with pictures.

I do not believe that CMA items 6435 and 6662 actually refer to this manuscript. Almost every other CMA description that is connected to a Theyer sale-catalogue item has a much closer catalogue entry correlation than the example of MS Royal 17 A. xxvii. If not, the CMA description mirrors the Theyer sale-catalogue entry. For example, MS Royal 10 B. XI corresponds to the CMA entry 6559 "Gubernatio regni secundum justitiam as Ed. III. Reg." The Theyer sale-catalogue entry for this item is "67 Gubernatio Regni Secundum Iustitiam, ad Edwardū ʒtium."[98] The close correspondence between the CMA entries and the Theyer sale catalogue is standard throughout.[99] Therefore, if one examines both the Royal manuscript catalogue's identified CMA entries with the identifiable Theyer sale-catalogue item, there is no means to connect them to each other. Several entries in the Theyer sale catalogue do not occur in Bernard's CMA—this is undoubtedly another example.

The mark of Theyer's monogram on the thirteenth-century portion of the manuscript with this clear description from the sale catalogue of the fifteenth-century portion —243 "A booke of ye passion of Jesus Xt in English verse wh

Pictures"—strongly supports the theory that the two sections were bound together before the volume came into the King's Library at St. James's Palace. In addition, they were probably bound together, at the very least, when in the hands of the Theyer family, after the Dissolution. Beyond the manuscript's physical evidence and its possible provenance, the internal evidence of the texts in MS Royal 17 A. xxvii—the way in which this portable, devotional volume functions—constitutes the strongest evidence for the likelihood that the volume may have also been brought together earlier in the late Middle Ages, possibly in the fifteenth century.

Part II. Late-Medieval Women Reading the Passion

The evidence within the manuscript that suggests the two portions were bound before the seventeenth century comes in both its physical makeup and its internal contents and cues. Beyond the bibliographic and physical evidence in MS Royal 17 A. xxvii, the strongest case for the circulation of the two sections as one manuscript in the sixteenth century and possibly the late fifteenth century comes from the correlations evident in the manuscript contents. The Theyer sale-catalogue entry describes this manuscript as a book on the Passion of Christ; all of the pieces in the shorter fifteenth-century portion fit this description, but several of the thirteenth-century items do as well.

For a devotional readership, the manuscript functions seamlessly as a devotional object. Scholars have imagined the devotional readership for the thirteenth-century as religious women; in the fifteenth century, the readers were probably lay and/or religious women. The pieces form a linking— although flexible and composite—devotional program that focuses on Christ's Passion.

For example, the most prominent visual signature in the first half is the opening of *St. Margaret*. The colorful rubrication and elaborate penwork highlight the importance of St. Margaret. The first line after the distinct rubrication is: "Efter ure lauerdes pine. ant his passiun. ant his deð on rode" (After our Lord's pain. And his passion. And his death on the cross) [100] This line links specifically with the central passages of Þe Oreisun of Seinte Marie: the meditation on the Passion and Christ's body and a discussion of bodily pain. Until the publication of a recent volume on the Wooing Group, devotion to the Passion and an interest in meditation on the pain, suffering, and dismembered parts of Christ's Passion, had been discussed only as a late-medieval focus. However, Catherine Innes-Parker rewrites this history of affective devotion to Christ's Passion. She recognizes that the Wooing Group materials, especially Þe Oreisun of Seinte Marie, make up perhaps the earliest "stand-alone' Passion meditation in Middle English, and thus the first of a genre which would come to dominate the vernacular theology of the fourteenth and fifteenth centuries."[101]

In the full text of *Þe Oreisun of Seinte Marie*, the prayer begins by invoking Mary through the Passion:

> Swete lefdi seinte marie meiden ouer meidnes þu bere þat blissful bern. þe arerde mon cun þat wes adun ifallet þurh adames sunnen. ant þurh his hali passiun weorp þen deouel adun ant herehede helle.[102]

> [O sweet Lady, holy Mary, maiden beyond all other maidens, who bore that joyous child, who raised up all humanity which had fallen down through Adam's sin, and who through his holy passion threw the devil down and harrowed hell.][103]

The invocation of the Lady and the Holy Passion is just a small example of how the Passion becomes a large, focused object of devotion in the poem's second half. As Innes-Parker points out, this is the first stand-alone Passion meditation but also one that is similar to "those that accompany the later Arma Christi images."[104]

In the poem's second half, the text breaks down the Passion into identifiable body parts and tactile objects:

> bi þe herde hurtes *and* þe unwurðe wowes ðet he for us sunfule willeliche þolede. bi his deaðfule grure. *and* bi his blodie swote. bi his eadi beoden in hulles him one. bi his nimunge. *and* bindunge. bi his ledunge forð. bi al *þet* me him demde. bi his cloðes wrixlunge. Nu red. nu hwit. him on hokerunge. bi his scornunge. *and* bi his spotlunge. *and* bufettunge. *and* his heliunge. bi þe þornene crununge. bi ðe kineȝerde of rode. him of scornunge. bi his owune rode. on his softe schuldres. so herde druggunge. bi þe dulte neiles. bi þe sore wunden:* bi þe holie rode. bi his side openunge. bi his blodi Rune þet ron inne monie studen. in umbe keoruunge. in his blod

---

* *punctus elevatus*

swetunge. in his pine þornene crunu*n*ge. erest in his
one hond *and* seoððen in his oðer. olast in his side
þurlunge wið-ute sore wund*e*.[105]

[by the hard injuries (hurts) and by the unworthy
wrongs that he willingly suffered for us sinful
creatures; by his mortal agony, and by his bloody
sweat; by his blessed prayers in the hills by himself;
by his capture and binding; by his leading forth; by
all that he was doomed to; by his change of raiment,
now red, now white, (put) on him in mockery; by
his scorning, and by his spitting and buffeting, and
by his blinding; by the crown of thorns; by the
scepter of reed given him in scorn; by his own cross,
so hard dragging on his soft shoulders; by the blunt
nails; by the sore wounds; by the holy rood; by the
opening in his side; by his bloody stream that ran
in many places, in his circumcision, in his blood-
sweating, in his pain through the crown of thorns;
(through the nails) first in his one hand and then
in his other; lastly in the piercing of his side, beside
(other) sore wounds.][106]

The litany of the Instruments of the Passion in MS Royal 17 A. xxvii's
Arma Christi (within the second fifteenth-century part) is prefigured in
Þe Oreisun of Seinte Marie. The "cloðes wrixlunge. Nu red. Nu hwit" (his
change of raiment, now red, now white) identifies the "*Tunica inconsutilis
et vestis purpuria*" (indiscreet coat and purple garments) on folio 75r of the
Arma Christi.[107] The three items, "his scornunge. and bi his spotlunge. and
bufettunge" (his scorning, and by his spitting and buffeting), correlate with
several sections of the *Arma Christi*. These comprise the "*Manus depillans et
alapans* / The hond, lord, þat tare of þyn here" (Slapping and pushing hand
/ the hand, Lord, that tears out your ear) on folio 74v; the "*Virge et flagella*"
(rods and whips), the "ȝerdes" (clubs/sticks), and the "scourges" (whips)
used to scourge Christ on folio 75r; and the "*Iudeus spuens in facie Christi* /
þe iewe þat spit in goddus face" (The Jews spitting in Christ's face / the Jew
that spit in God's face) on folio 78r.[108]
    Further correspondences include the "heliunge" (blindfolding) with
"*Velamen ante oculos* / þe clothe be-fore þin ine to" (the covering before
the eyes / the cloth before your two eyes) on folio 74v;[109] the "þornene
crununge" (the crown of thorns) with "*corona spinea*" (crown of thorns) on

folio 75v;[110] the "kineȝerde of rode" (scepter of reed) and "Him of scornunge. bi his owune rode. on his softe schuldres" (given him in scorn; by his own cross, on his soft shoulders)[111] with *"Arundines* / Crist had a stroke with a rede" (The Reeds / Christ had a blow with a reed)[112] on folio 74v; the "dulte neiles" (blunt nails) with *"Clavi* / þe nayles þorow fet and handus to" (Nails / the nails through two feet and hands) on folio 76v;[113] the "holie rode" (holy rood / cross) with *"Christus portas crucem in humero* / þe cros be-hind his bakbon" (Christus at the gates with the cross on [his] shoulder / the cross behind his backbone) on folio 78r;[114] and the "umbe keoruunge" (circumcision) with *"Cultellus circumsicionis.* / þis knif be-tokeneþ circumsicion" (the little knife of circumcision / this knife that signifies circumcision) on folio 73r.[115]

The poetic imagery of *Þe Oreisun of Seinte Marie* is a precise enumeration and itemization of Christ's Passion, pain, and Instruments. It acts as a bridge between the thirteenth-century materials and the fifteenth-century texts in MS Royal 17 A. xxvii. Additionally, the Passion devotion in both the thirteenth- and fifteenth-century texts is funneled through objects (reed, nails, whips, clubs, circumcision knives) that allow the layering and building up of religious meaning two centuries apart. The manuscript allows Passion objects to multiply and in the *Arma Christi* visualizes them with colored images of each Passion item. Thus, the manuscript's Passion devotion— its affective program for its female readers—occupies the true center of discursive concerns concretized in material practice. Although Innes-Parker notes the correlation between the Wooing Group Passion meditations and the *Arma Christi*, she does not make the direct correlation between these two texts in MS Royal 17 A. xxvii.[116]

The *Arma Christi* Booklet

The Passion of Christ, and especially the litany of his Arms, Wounds, and material and verbal/visual objects becomes the focal point of the fifteenth-century booklet in the Royal manuscript. The fifteenth-century section begins with a Latin text on confession, which in function mirrors the first portion of the *Þe Oreisun of Seinte Marie*. It continues to a full *Arma Christi* text with detailed colored images of each Instrument of the Passion—concluding with an indulgence. The final texts, Marian lyrics, also center on Christ's Passion and the utility of prayer to resist Hell. In these lyrics, Christ's Passion is invoked:

> ffor his woundes fyue: þat Ronnen alle on blood,
> ffor þe loue of swete Ihesu: þat dyede on þe Rod,
> Get me heuene blisse: Ladi feir and god.[117]

[For his wounds five: that run all with blood,
for the love of sweet Jesus: that died on the cross,
Get me heaven's bliss: lady fair and good.][118]

Visually, the reference to the five wounds has an iconographic history linked to the *Arma Christi*: its earliest expression was accompanied by the Instruments of the Passion. Flora Lewis highlights this connection and describes how both traditions "epitomize the desire to encompass and anatomize the Passion" through the consistent fragmenting and reassembling of Christ's body.[119] Lewis also discusses how the Passion meditation invites readers to imagine themselves in the scene of the Passion[120] and to take up the arms of Christ as a way to help their own fight against the Devil.[121] In the Royal manuscript's fifteenth-century portion, the link between Hell's horrors and the Devil's temptations, on the one hand, and the objects and symbols of Christ's Passion, on the other, becomes a repeated body of salvation discourse—but grounded as an object-oriented or materialist discourse.

The vision of St. Thomas of Canterbury also focuses on Christ's Wounds, and the hymn about St. Bernard and the Devil centers once more on help to repudiate Hell and damnation. The second hymn to the Virgin and the hymn about St. Bernard and the Devil employ similar language to solicit aid against the Devil and Hell. In the second hymn to the Virgin, the reader is asked to pray to the virgin to:

schilde us from helle pyne.
Shilde me lady fro(m) worldes schame.
And fro alle wicked fame.
Schilde me lady from villani.
And from wicked companye. (fol. 83r)

[shield us from Hell's pain.
Shield me, Lady, from the world's shame.
And from all wicked fame.
Shield me, Lady, from villainy.
And from wicked company.][122]

The verse emphasizes the term "schilde" as the verb "to protect/save," but the verb also means to provide with a shield or arms.[124] In this way, the term forges a link between the *Arma Christi* text and the iconographic tradition of envisioning the *Arma Christi* and also the Wounds of Christ as Christ's heraldic shield.[124] It carries the reader into a courtly and military milieu of vernacular devotion and builds the devotional focus on another object.

In the hymn about St. Bernard and the Devil, a similar image is recalled:

> I[long green letter]llumina oculos meos ne
> umq(uam) obdormia(m)
> ȝyf liȝt unto myn eȝe siȝt
> þat I nouȝt slepe whan I schal dye
> lat nouȝt my fo in gostly siȝt
> seyn I haue ou hym þe maystrie
> but shilde me fro þat foule wiȝt. (fol. 86v)[125]

> [Give light to my eyes, lest I never sleep
> Give light unto my eyesight
> That I shall not sleep when I shall die
> Let not my foe in ghostly sight
> I have seen him alas the power
> But shield me from that foul creature.][126]

The St. Bernard text again divulges a lexical and textual layering that shifts from direct Passion narrative to explications of how the Passion items can be used to help "schilde" readers from the foulness of Hell, the Devil, and damnation. The verse's emphasis on seeing also links ocularly to the *Arma Christi* item of the blindfolded Christ (fol. 74v) and to the first item in the *Arma Christi*—the "vernicle," the cloth that held an impression of Christ's face after St. Veronica used it to wipe Christ's face on the way to Calvary.

The verse about Veronica's cloth functions as a mini–*Arma Christi*. The poetic section breaks up Christ's face into different objects visualized on the vernicle: "His moth, his nose, his ine to, / His berd, his here did al so" (his mouth, his nose, his two eyes, / his beard, his ear did also).[127] The devotional poem then petitions Christ, through the object of Veronica's veil, to "schilde" the reader from all her or his life's sins with the "wittes fiue."[128] The poem asks for forgiveness of the sins of the devout through looking at the "syht" of Christ's likeness on Veronica's veil. Thus the veil performs as a heraldic relic—an unfurled cloth rather than a vellum roll—that grants an indulgence: forgiveness of sins for all who gaze upon this image (see Figure 1). An illustration on folio 72v depicts two angels who have unfurled the vernicle's image for the reader's visual consumption. In this manner, the devotional texts in MS Royal 17 A. xxvii builds female affective devotion onto material objects, transforming the nonpresent object—the mimetic visual image of Veronica's cloth—into a material object with power that can affect the reader.

One of the last items in the Royal manuscript, the popular fifteenth-century text the *Fifteen Oes*, is "devotional prayers memorializing Jesus's Passion," usually containing fifteen sections that begin with "O," followed by an accompanying verse.[129] Similar to the *Arma Christi*, the *Fifteen Oes* required not only recitation of the Passion meditation, but also looking at and reading the physical text.[130] The *Fifteen Oes* concentrate explicitly and graphically on Christ's physical suffering and torment. For example, the second "O" discusses how the Jews "fastened your [Christ's] blessed hands to the cross with blunt nails" and then pierced Christ's feet, stretched his body, and dislocated and broke his bones.[131] Each of the *Fifteen Oes* encourages the reader to visualize the Crucifixion, with Christ's wounds, blood, and suffering, in graphic detail. An indulgence prayer follows the *Fifteen Oes*. The text was also a popular late-medieval indulgence prayer that would often offer salvation for multiple family members. In this way, the *Fifteen Oes* is another set of popular female religious devotion that transforms the text into an object "carrying talismanic significant" that could promise salvation, miracles, and defense against Hell.[132]

All the pieces in the second section of MS Royal 17 A. xxvii correspond to Kathleen Kamerick's discussion of the *Arma Christi* image, text, and popular use in late-medieval devotional culture in *Popular Piety and Art in the Late Middle Ages*.[133] In particular, she emphasizes the links between the texts devoted to the Passion, the *Arma Christi*, intercessions, and prayers against Hell and the hour of death with the occurrence of indulgences. These indulgences banked time away from Hell and Purgatory by the very looking at or reciting of the *Arma Christi* and these other texts. Significantly, the Royal manuscript has three sets of indulgences: two in the *Arma Christi* and another at the manuscript's end.

The *Arma Christi* indulgence, the first, promises aid from St. Peter and Pope Innocent. It pledges to give whoever sees it every day for a year an indulgence of "Haþ vi. M. vii C. v. and fifti ʒere/ And half ʒere and daʒes þre" (fol. 81r) (Have six thousand seven hundred five and fifty year/and half a year and days three)."[134] Within the *Arma Christi*, there is a separate indulgence, the second, just for gazing at the vernicle: "And ich bischop sayd to-for-hand / For syʒt of þe vernacul hath graunt / xl dayus to pardon" (And I, the bishop who said earlier/ for the sight of the vernacle shall grant/ 40 days to pardon).[135] The last item, the third indulgence, granted by Pope John, promises a separate 6,000-year indulgence.

These multiple indulgences transform the manuscript from a series of texts that stand as a remembrance of Christ's Crucifixion and suffering to an object of power. The Instruments of the Passion are used in the poems as the reader's shield against the battle with the Devil and the fires of Hell. And finally, as the indulgences attest, the manuscript itself has become an object—a talisman, a textual amulet, a physical shield protecting the reader from Hell and the Devil.[136] The indulgence from the Royal manuscript's *Arma Christi* speaks to its female readers as a gendered talisman: "to wymen hit is meke and mild / When þey trauelne of her chi[l]d" (to women who are meek and mild / when they travail [labor] of their child) (fol. 80v).[137] Hence the book became a charm against dangerous childbirth.[138] The manuscript layers multiple smaller objects within the composite cupboard of devotional texts for potential female readers and transforms itself into a material object that affects female devotion: it is a reliquary holding smaller material relics that can be deployed for the benefit of its female audience. The qualities of its materiality—the ability to see and touch—have now become the conduits in which it exercises its material force.

The "Scourgen"

Up to this point, I have endeavored to bring into relief a larger picture of the manuscript. I am shifting my gaze now to take one item from the *Arma Christi* and one detail in the *Life of St. Juliana* to consider how an object permits a late-medieval female reader to contextualize both the book's thirteenth- and fifteenth-century devotion. How could she adapt these materials into a composite devotional practice? There are other connections and narrative strands from the two parts of this manuscript: an interest in charity, lexical interest in the term "bon/ban," and an emphasis on the Jews. But I would like to concentrate on one detail in the *Life of St. Juliana* and its connection to the *Þe Oreisun of Seinte Marie* and the *Arma Christi*. This link demonstrates how materials two centuries apart can present a visual, meditative, and object-oriented exercise for late-medieval and even early modern readers.

The early Middle English *Life of St. Juliana* is known for its violence—especially in its detailed description of the virgin saint's torture of the Devil. Both the Latin *vita* in Bodley 285 and the early Middle English *Life* in MS Royal 17 A. xxvii explain that Juliana uses her chains—her bonds—to punish the Devil. There is only one set of images that take the cues of the early Middle English Katherine Group *Lives* (*St. Katherine, St. Margaret*, and *St. Juliana*) and visualize these vernacular lives: illustrations in Cambridge, Fitzwilliam Museum MS 370. Unlike St. Katherine and St. Margaret, who have quite an extensive iconographic tradition in thirteenth-century English manuscripts, Juliana's image in this manuscript is unique because it is the only one—the only identified visual evidence—that has survived from thirteenth-century England.

Fitzwilliam 370, a manuscript containing eighteen full-page miniatures with accompanying notes in Lombardic capitals at the top of each page,[139] is a "picture book" with only nine surviving folios. Four separate descriptions were made of this book over the last century: Lucy Sandler's entry in *Later Gothic Manuscripts* (1986), Wormald and Giles's description in the *Fitzwilliam Illuminated Catalogue* (1982),[140] M. R. James's article in the *Walpole Society* (1937), and Paul Binski and Stella Panayotova's commentary for the recent *Cambridge Illuminations* catalogue (2005).[141]

In the last image of Fitzwilliam 370, St. Juliana is using a knotted whip—a "scourgen," with a solid handle—not her chains (see Figure 2). This whip is not only the type of weaponry used in *St. Katherine*, the previous *vita*, to flagellate the virgin saint, but is also a visual marker of the weapons used by those who tortured Christ: one of the Instruments of the Passion. By switching the torture weapons, Fitzwilliam 370 disturbingly transforms this difficult moment in the English *St. Juliana* into a scene where Juliana becomes a persecutor of Christ. Does it allow the possibility for a reader during this two-century period to understand her positionality within the semiotics of Jewishness?

Fitzwilliam 370's iconography of St. Juliana is also exceptional because it does not seem to continue in other later manuscripts. In an illuminated manuscript of the *Legenda aurea*, San Marino, Huntington Library MS HM 3027, the iconography of St. Juliana is shown in two scenes in a single decorated section (fol. 34). This manuscript, a Parisian product of the late thirteenth century, was in England by the last quarter of the fourteenth century.[142] On the left side, St. Juliana is binding the Devil with her bonds inside her prison cell; on the right side, she kneels and waits for her executioner to behead her.[143] The executioner's pose is eerily reminiscent of St. Juliana's stance in Fitzwilliam 370—he holds his female victim with his left hand while he raises his sword with his right.[144] This image does not follow the iconographic cues in Fitzwilliam 370, which indicates that the visual program in Huntington Library MS HM 3027 must be following the text of the *Legenda aurea* rather than a vernacular version.

The inclusion of one of the *Arma Christi* in this unique St. Juliana picture is not done *ex nihilo*. In Fitzwilliam 370's fourth image (fol. 2v), we have the scene of the Judgment, which includes several interesting details: four angels hold Instruments of the Passion (top left, green cross; top right, lance; lower left, three nails; lower right, crown of thorns). Christ sits in judgment in the center of a mandorla wearing only a piece of blue cloth. We can see his wounds on his side and on his feet.[145] This early visual expression of the cult of the five Wounds and the Instruments of the Passion becomes, in the later Middle Ages, part of Christ's heraldic shield. The "scourge" is not in this image but has been "lent" to St. Juliana.

This late-thirteenth-century manuscript, Fitzwilliam 370, becomes the linchpin that links the thirteenth-century *St. Juliana* with the fifteenth-century *Arma Christi* in MS Royal 17 A. xxvii. Given that the Royal manuscript's thirteenth-century portion includes Katherine, Margaret, and Juliana, and finishes off with one of the Wooing Group texts—focused on Christ's scourging and buffeting—bringing in an *Arma Christi* text fits an interpretive devotional logic. Instead of ending with images of Juliana gleefully torturing the Devil, the *Arma Christi* tradition allows the readers to revise this ending and reimagine Juliana as a warrior who has taken the Instruments of the Passion to fight the Devil and the demons. She has been rehabilitated from torturer to soldier of Christ.

In MS Royal 17 A. xxvii, the *Arma Christi* text is accompanied by visual images of the instruments. The visual iconography's purpose is to be a meditative visual template. For the "scourgen," this visual meditation encompasses a descriptive poem and image of the "scourgen" (fol. 75r), now shown as a cat-o'-nine-tails or knotted whip. The reader is urged to ruminate on the following verse:

> *Virge et flagelle.*
> With ȝerdes grete þow were to-dachud,
> With scourges smert al to-lachud,
>   Þat peine me soker of sinnus,
>   Of slouth and of idelnes.[146]

> [*Rods and Whips.*
> With great rods you were to be beaten,
> With scourges sharp all to be lashed,
>   That pain my succor of sins,
>   Of sloth and of idleness.][147]

Jeffrey Hamburger's work on the *Rothschild Canticles* and Flora Lewis's work on devotional images explain the prominence and function of the *Arma Christi* tradition in text and iconography.[148] Widely popular among female religious readers and especially nuns, the *Arma Christi* (although often in codex form, in roll for specific use) could allow women—as exemplified occasionally by the Virgin Mary—to take up the weapons of Christ to help fight demons and the Devil. Thus female readers could become Christ's warriors and were depicted as such. However, almost all the depictions show a passive, defensive fighting female figure using these arms, these Instruments of the Passion. Juliana rewrites this role and stands as an active pursuer of Christ's enemies; the active stance corresponds to a model of active devotion encouraged by the mendicant orders (Dominican and Franciscan).

As a thirteenth-century devotional unit, the Katherine Group *Lives* and *Þe Oreisun of Seinte Marie*—combined with the background of the only visual tradition in existence of St. Juliana—become a holistic devotional unit. One can see how a female religious reader would have been able to extract a unique devotional reading about Christ's Passion and the role of saints and women in fighting the Devil. This combination of both the thirteenth-century and the fifteenth-century booklets permits MS Royal 17 A. xxvii to become a full exploration of Passion meditation and reach its devotional apogee as a literary, visual, and tactile object of devotion.

By reading the two parts together, the Royal manuscript allows its female readers a way to revise the end of the *vitae* in the Katherine Group: to transform Juliana from a violent torturer to a soldier taking up the weapons of Christ (scourge) to fight the Devil. She is still an oddity, even in the *Arma Christi* tradition, because she is aggressively active. But for our manuscript's late-medieval and early modern readers—particularly the women—the inclusion of the *Arma Christi* usually signaled a pastoral, public viewing, with importance placed on the power of visual meditation. In most *Arma Christi* manuscripts (especially in rolls), the point is that the daily looking at the *Arma Christi* (manuscript, scroll, images) will gain an indulgence against sin.[149] This would permit the focus of devotion to incorporate the earlier works but shift the prominence onto this visual and oral relic. And thus our "scourgen" demonstrates how religious texts two centuries apart can be rewritten, reread, reused, and reconceived by later devotional readers.

The Boundaries of a Female Audience

The audience for the thirteenth-century material has always been imagined as female religious readers. The fifteenth-century section has texts corresponding to another manuscript, British Library, MS Additional 37787, a Worcestershire miscellany produced in the late fourteenth century by John Northwood, a monk at Bordesley.[150] Although produced in a monastic setting, MS Additional 37787 has several signs of female lay ownership in the fifteenth and sixteenth centuries. Goditha Peyto, wife of Sir Edward Peyto, owned the manuscript in the fifteenth century; she subsequently passed it on to another woman. Manuscript notes also show female ownership in the sixteenth century.[151]

Nita Baugh suggests a connection between this Worcestershire miscellany, MS Royal 17 A. xxvii, and the Vernon manuscript (Oxford, Bodleian Library MS Eng. Poet a. 1). The overlap of materials and what she perceives as similarities in hand and mise-en-page indicate to Baugh that all three may have been produced at Bordesley. I do not see quite the same hand in these two manuscripts—the Worcestershire miscellany and the Royal manuscript—and several of the pieces are differently laid out and are occasionally in different languages. Nonetheless, they are neighboring manuscripts with textual overlap and a geographical proximity; they may speak to different ways in which female readers may have read and used these texts—in a cloister or out in the world.

In the case of MS Royal 17 A. xxvii, although our information about its earlier pre-1600 circulation is tentative, looking at connected and related local manuscripts from the same period can help fill out a picture of circulation and readership. The devotion to the Passion of the late-medieval female readers of this manuscript allowed for a flexible and portable reading and religious practice. One can imagine a late-medieval reader of MS Royal 17 A. xxvii meditating on the horrors of Hell and damnation as described in both the first text, *Sawles Warde*, and the fifteenth-century hymn about St. Bernard and the Devil. She could trace the reenactment of the passion through the *Life of St. Juliana*, *Þe Oreisun of Seinte Marie*, and the *Arma Christi*. She had myriad ways to use the book: as a reader, as a meditative reciter and practitioner, and finally as a believer in its effectiveness as a devotional talisman. Our female reader was the ultimate composite reader for a composite and mutable book.

Part III. Reading MS Royal 17 A. xxvii in the King's Library at St. James's Palace

If MS Royal 17 A. xxvii, as a book itself, is an object that signals a materialist, female, and affective devotional practice, its material status also marks it as a thoroughly Catholic one, particularly after the Reformation. I would like now to turn to the third section of this diachronic history: the manuscript's possible affective use and its material signs as it enters the King's library (Old Royal Library) at St. James's Palace in 1678. In this section, I plan to reexamine Charles II's interest as a book collector, his religious status, and his wife's status as an English symbol of royal Catholicism—particularly against the backdrop of the 1678 Popish plot.

Anthony Wood's account in the *Athenae Oxonienses* testifies that Charles II "cull'd" the Theyer collection to pull the more than 300 volumes into the Royal manuscript collection. But if we are to imagine Charles II as a potential Restoration reader of MS Royal 17 A. xxvii, then how does this volume of virgin *passiones*, Passion lyric, and an *Arma Christi* text fit into what we know about Charles II as a reader and man of letters? Charles II's library has been called "that of a private gentleman—a gentleman virtuoso, a patron of the Royal Society—in other words, a gentleman who happened to be a king."[152] From T. A. Birrell's work on the bindings of Charles II's library, we get a small glimpse into how he fashioned his library as a cosmopolitan gentleman scholar.

In 1662, Charles bought the library of John Morris, "the master of the London Bridge waterworks," which was "an excellent, well-balanced, virtuoso's library of a gentleman scholar—he was a gentleman because he never published anything." This contained more than 1,400 volumes of mainly

French, Italian, and Spanish books with a humanistic and historical bent and
"a considerable interest in *belles lettres*."[153] Charles II's own personal library
at Whitehall contained more than a thousand volumes, with almost half of
the books from the sixteenth century. He also purchased from Robert Scott,
London bookseller, the library of Pierre de Montmaur, a professor of Greek
at the Collège Royal in Paris, whose collections seems to have consisted of a
number of French historical materials.[154] His second purchase from Robert
Scott was the Theyer collection of manuscripts—"the last significant group
of illuminated and other medieval manuscripts" to become part of the Old
Royal Library.[155]

Kathleen Doyle's recent discussion of the Royal Library collection
highlights how "the popular view of Charles II as a monarch who does not
'rank highly' either as a patron or a collection must be revised, at least in
relation to the manuscript portion of the library."[156] She argues, in fact, that
Charles II may have been attempting to reestablish, reassemble, and collect an
appropriate royal library for a magnificent kingly court. Therefore, although
we have information about Charles II as a bibliophile who may have disliked
reading or had bad Latin, we also possess other, contradictory evidence that
reveals his keen interest in books, especially manuscripts, in the St. James's
Palace Library.[157]

After he acquired the Theyer collection in 1681—a collection built up
by a known Royalist and converted Catholic—Charles II wrote to Henri
Justel, Louis XIV's former secretary, to appoint him his chief manuscript
inspector and curator.[158] He invited Justel to organize his library at St. James's
in "such method and indexes as shall be most convenient to render them
useful towards the advancement of learning."[159] He also gave Justel the power
to evaluate the manuscripts belonging to the Bishop of London and others in
order to decide if they might enhance the King's Library at St. James's. Justel
had a mandate to gain the assistance of all the keepers of libraries in order to
organize, reassemble, and supplement the King's Library at St. James's. Doyle
discusses a substantial number of inventories and catalogues pertaining to
the various sections of the King's Library that have survived from the second
half of the sixteenth century—all of which is documentary evidence of an
interest in organizing and cataloguing the library during Charles II's reign.[160]

Charles also cared enough about the King's Library at St. James's Palace
to have appointed a bookbinder immediately upon his accession to the throne
in June 1660. Samuel Mearne would bind close to a thousand volumes in
Charles II's royal collection, with design supervision possibly by the king
himself.[161] By May 1675, Samuel Mearne and his son Charles began to hold
the newly created office of "Bookbinder, Bookseller, and Stationer to the
King for their life and the life of the survivor."[162] At this point, with Mearne's
and his son's expected long tenure as the official royal stationers, Charles

II appears to have imagined his royal library as a permanent and ongoing project for future posterity.

Charles II's private library at Whitehall also included several manuscripts—including at least three or four breviaries with extensive and beautifully done illuminations—and, by all appearances, this was his personal collection.[163] One manuscript in the Whitehall private collection has been tentatively identified as the *Queen Mary Psalter*.[164] I believe his two different libraries may have served different visions: the personal library at Whitehall was for his own private use, where many of the volumes were personal gifts, while the Royal Library was envisioned as a formal monarchial collection. Nonetheless, the manuscripts in the Whitehall library indicate that Charles II himself may have had a personal interest in perusing these early volumes. They were beautifully illuminated and would have been compatible with Charles II's reputation as an art collector. Although the Theyer collection contains a number of beautifully illuminated manuscripts, the majority—more than 240—are not decorated.[165] Along with Charles II and his manuscript curator, Justel, the royal collection at St. James's Palace may have been open to other family members, including the queen, Catherine of Braganza.

Catherine of Braganza: Catholic Queen, Catholic Reader

Catherine of Braganza lived at St. James's Palace before she moved her chapel, priests, and monks permanently to Somerset House in 1671 after the death of Charles II's mother, Queen Henrietta Maria, in 1669. St James's was the site where Charles had originally rebuilt the Catholic chapel for her personal use. It seems logical that Catherine would have availed herself of the library at St. James's, since she also built a religious house next to the St. James's chapel that was completed and occupied by January 1667.[166] Furthermore, Charles II was known to have ordered devotional items for her as gifts. He asked his sister for devotional art to put in Catherine's breviary. Accounts suggest she welcomed this personalized supplement to her devotions gladly, since the images were beautifully executed and unique.[167]

Historians have described Catherine of Braganza's influence on the English court as small because of her inability to produce an heir to the throne. However, as a Catholic queen in a country progressively more hostile to suspected covert Catholic conspiracies, she, like her mother-in-law, Queen Henrietta Maria, had a symbolic function as the public face of Catholic dissent in England.[168] Several scholars discuss the controversies and unease of fashioning female Catholic identity in the seventeenth century because of the legal, religious, and gender expectations at work. Megan Matchinske details a change in the interior subjectivity of women, which had earlier been associated with "the spiritual, with conversation between priests and penitents."[169]

Later Tudor and Stuart female interiority included the home, the domestic sphere, and especially, in the case of female Catholics, the hidden closet. However, issues surrounding public, civic discourse and also a woman's legal status reshaped female subjectivity with the pressure of the state and the public sphere. For Catholic women, this meant that they became "covert" agents of religious and political dissent. The private interior lives of Catholic married women were considered highly suspect in the seventeenth century for numerous reasons. Because Catholicism had to be practiced in the private sphere, a Catholic mother and housewife was "crucial to her faith community." She facilitated the practice of Catholicism at home and educated her children.[170]

Moreover, female Catholic recusants were hard to prosecute because as married women, they were "*femmes covertes*" and under the jurisdiction of their husbands. Because the state was reluctant to intrude on the domestic household, punishing Catholic women was difficult. Their ambiguous public and legal identity permitted Catholic women during the seventeenth century to establish their domestic spaces as sites of religious and political resistance.[171] Resistance came in multiple forms: hiding priests in priest's holes, preaching and trying to convert neighbors, keeping Mass vestments and materials, and bringing "Popish books" into the house. In this manner, Queen Catherine and her mother-in-law, Queen Henrietta Maria, also functioned as "*femmes covertes*." But their private spaces of resistance—their private chapels at St. James's and Somerset House—became public symbols of Catholic England. Because of their royal status, their private devotions and religious beliefs were constantly under public surveillance.

Catherine of Braganza, the Popish Plot, and Catholic Books

By 1678, Catherine of Braganza had been accused of conspiracy, and her fate appeared sealed with the rise of two events: William Bedloe's accusation that her servants had murdered Sir Edmund Berry Godfrey at Somerset House; and the formal calumny of Titus Oates and his accusation of attempted regicide. She was charged with high treason, and Bedloe's and Oates's depositions against her in Parliament would be the first in a series of clearly false testimony. She proclaimed her innocence, and Charles II was her staunchest supporter. However, the supposed Popish Plot provided an opportunity for Parliament to propose acts against her directly—including one for her banishment from Whitehall, and even a divorce bill introduced in the House of Lords on November 17, 1680.[172]

During the Popish Plot (revealed in 1678), the anti-Catholic public began insulting Catherine on the way to chapel at Somerset House. This led her to return to worship at the chapel at St. James's Palace in January 1680 because it was not as accessible to the public.[173] Although the accusations leveled at Catherine during the Popish Plot were false, she did break laws regarding the procurement and circulation of Catholic books. The records reveal that both Henrietta Maria and Catherine obtained and purchased Catholic devotional texts in England. In November 1662, the customs officer "deliver[ed] a packet of books for the Queen Mother, containing 300 copies of Cardinal Richelieu's Instruction, 20 of Avila's Spiritual epistles, and five or six Rhenish Testaments."[174] The inclusion of Teresa of Avila's work demonstrates Henrietta Maria's interest in mystical spirituality. The dowager Queen, near the end of her life, also read daily from the *De imitatione Christi*.[175]

We know from courtiers' personal letters that Catherine was a devout religious reader. In March 1681, Catherine was seen to be seeking solitude, "being retired most part of the day at her devotions and reading."[176] The Popish Plot and its aftermath appear to have caused her to withdraw from active court pursuits to a contemplative existence. We also have evidence that Catherine of Braganza acquired Catholic printed books domestically. In 1669, the Stationers' Company reported the printer John Winter to the authorities because he had printed a "Popish book" in Theodore Sadler's bookshop. Catherine of Braganza came to testify for John Winter that she had "given and Granted Lycense and Authority to John Winter Printer in this Citty of London, to print [the book] for her Majesty's vse; a Pious book, intituled, 'A Lyturgicall discourse of the holy Sacrafice of the Masse.'"[177] The evidence reveals that she was purchasing Catholic books domestically for her own use.

Printing became more dangerous after the Popish Plot. In November 1678, the House of Lords drafted an "Act for the better discovery and more speedy conviction of Popish Recusants"; Clause 3 concerns "cutlers and armourers, booksellers and printers, who are papists."[178] Printers, including James Thompson, were questioned and imprisoned. The authorities had been tipped off that "Thompson, a printer in Fetter Lane, against whom information had been given that he had printed several Popish Books."[179] They had found "near 30,000 catechisms and other books." The records from the Lords Committee for Examinations note that James Thompson was "a papist living in Eagle court near Somerset House."[180] His seized books were publicly burned at the Old Exchange. Arrests continued with James Thompson's printer, Nathaniel Thompson, and his binder, William Vere.[181] Nathaniel Thompson confessed to having printed thousands of Popish books. The apparent conspiracy of booksellers and printers widened as Thompson's associate Thomas Child was arrested. Titus Oates would charge another bookseller, Moore, as "a Seller of Popish Books," and accused him of supplying £500 pounds of books to Somerset House.[182] Moore had been suspected before because in 1676, "there were divers Popish and unlicensed books belonging to Moor, Turner and Dod lodged in three warehouses over the stables in Somerset House."[183] In these sundry accusations, Somerset House, the private residence of the queen, featured prominently.

Many of the charges and accusations early in the Popish Plot toward booksellers, printers, and binders were also connected geographically to Somerset House. Clearly, Somerset House and its purported overflowing collection of Catholic books were considered dangers to the state. The historical accounts suggested that Catherine was covertly, and against the King's law, keeping contraband items at her private chapel.

Although it is clear she had no involvement in any regicidal plot, Catherine did remain a staunch Catholic and cultivated a public image as a Catholic monarch. We can see her shape her Catholic public persona through her royal portraits. In her earlier royal portraits, Sir Peter Lely, a Protestant, highlighted her youth; in contrast, Jacob Huysmans, a Catholic, painted her later portraits and represented her "as a mature and sensuous beauty." In 1664, Huysmans painted her as St. Catherine of Alexandria, the prolific converter of pagans to Christianity, who was "cruelly mistreated by the Roman Emperor (as Catherine had been by the King)."[184] W. Sherwin and R. Thompson engraved a widely-circulated copy of this portrait.[185] It is worth noting here that the Katherine Group materials in MS Royal 17 A. xxvii include a life of St. Katherine of Alexandria that highlights Katherine's particular efficacious role as a converter of pagans.

Within her private household, Catherine also had Catholic allies who may have urged her to take the mantle of England's Catholic queen. Serenus Cressy (Hugh Paulinus Cressy), one of Catherine of Braganza's chaplains from the time of her 1662 arrival in England, was a converted English Catholic monk who edited Walter Hilton's *Scale of Perfection* in 1659[186] and also produced the first edition of Julian of Norwich's *XVI Revelations of Divine Love* (1670).[187] He lived primarily at Somerset House, the symbolic space and center of Catholicism in London during the reigns of both Queen Henrietta Maria and Queen Catherine.[188] Cressy was a follower of Augustine Baker, who was in charge a generation earlier of the Benedictine nunnery in northern France at Cambrai, which was filled with young English Catholic women—including one of the daughters of Thomas More.[189] Baker himself wrote to Sir Robert Cotton asking to borrow works of medieval devotion for the nuns, including copies of works by Richard Rolle and Walter Hilton, as well as *The Cloud of Unknowing*.[190] He also possessed a copy of the works of Julian of Norwich. Larsen points out that although Baker revived "medieval English mystical writers within counter-Reformation Catholicism," he was acting as a dissident within mainstream Catholic culture.[191] But it is Baker's example that Cressy draws upon in England to appeal to his queen and also to the English Catholic female reader.

As Catherine of Braganza's chaplain, Cressy dedicated to her an ecclesiastical history, *The Church History of Brittany*.[192] In it, he encourages the queen to visualize herself as part of an illustrious constellation of Catholic monarchs. He presents:

> A great well-ordered Army of such glorious Saints of your own Sexe will the following History discover to YOUR MAJESTY, and this of all States, Wives, Widdowes and Virgins, and which was wonderfull, some of them all these, both Wives, Widows and yet Virgins. So that here YOU may sest before your eyes a numerous Variety of Heavenly Patterns of Your own rank.[193]

Larsen explains how Cressy wished to cast Catherine of Braganza in the role of England's Catholic mother. He urged her to model herself on many of the queens in his English religious history: the queens who converted the people to the true religion and protected the church.[194] I consider these small pieces of evidence to be indicative of Catherine of Braganza's connection to an English Catholic subculture—one that entailed the reading of mystical devotional texts that signaled an entwined English national and medieval Catholic past.

But a final piece of material evidence, I believe, exposes Catherine's willingness to cast herself in the role of England's Catholic queen—a queen who genealogically positioned herself as participating in a revised history of Catholic queens that protected the true English Church. When Catherine returned to Portugal in 1693, she brought a relic of Thomas Becket, which she eventually placed at her private chapel at Bemposto Palace.[195] The relic was a processional cross that containing "um fragmento do báculo de S. Tomás Becket, Arcebispo de Cantuária" (a fragment of the staff of Saint Thomas Becket, Archbishop of Canterbury).[196] The cross included an inscription identifying it as a pastoral cross and relic of St. Thomas Becket for Queen Catherine (1664),[197] and was inscribed with a monogram of two C's for Catherine and Charles, with an English crown.[198] Pinto conjectures, although there is no concrete evidence, that Charles II may have offered the cross to Catherine in 1664.[199]

On November 6, 1538, Henry VIII had denounced Thomas Becket as a traitor to the Crown for rebelling against Henry II and had him excised from the English martyrology. The Canterbury relics were dispersed and destroyed; Pinto speculates that the remaining relics—like the processional cross—may have passed into royal possession during Henry VIII's reign. As one of the most potent symbols of an English medieval Catholic past—and a political rebel against the king to boot—Thomas Becket and his story would have resonated with seventeenth-century Catholics. By bringing the cross to Portugal, Catherine allied herself with one of the most important pre-Reformation English saints and relics. She fashioned her Catholic royal identity in alignment with Cressy's British history—as an English Catholic queen, ready to defend the true church and convert the English people back to the true religion.

Within this contextual background, I would like to examine several items of the Theyer collection that match the reading tastes of the female English recusant—as imagined and fostered by both Augustine Baker abroad and Serenus Cressy in England. Charles II or another royal family member appears to have been an avid reader of Middle English Passion texts. From the collection that he "cull'd" he also pulled "32. The Mirror of the Life of Jesus Christ,"[200] several Wycliffite pieces (Bible and sermons: items 4, 40, 62, 117), "85. Reginald Peacockes book cald ye flower to the devote,"[201] and "103. The Divinio Cloud of unknowing. Devout + fruitfull doctrines out of the Life of Katharine of Siena."[202] These items do not quite fit with what we know of Charles II's interest in *belles lettres*, but if one brings together the texts in MS Royal 17 A. xxvii, Nicholas Love's *The Mirror of the Blessed Life of Jesus Christ*, *The Cloud of Unknowing*, and *The Orchard of Syon*, we have assembled a small library of vernacular contemplative and devotional literature perfectly appropriate for recusant female readers.[203]

The manuscripts I enumerate and their Middle English antiquity would have only further cemented a revised religious history—one in which a female reader could trace the genealogy of female Catholic ancestors through texts like *The Orchard of Syon* and the *vita* of Catherine of Siena. Cressy's edition of Julian of Norwich's works was published in its original Middle English, which would have funneled into Cressy's nationalist Catholic aims of imagining Middle English as "literally the voice of the mother tongue."[204]

If not for himself, the likely imagined Catholic reader for the volumes Charles had been "culling" was his devout wife, Catherine of Braganza.[205] In these manuscripts from the Theyer collection, one can discern a philological, nostalgic, but decidedly revisionist interest in a Catholic past deliberately shaped by seventeenth-century agendas. In this historical instance, these manuscripts have become objects that signal potential Catholic dissent and a revised English religious history.

As a manuscript entering the King's Library at St. James's Palace, MS Royal 17 A. xxvii would have fit the reading program of a controversial Catholic subculture. It would have corresponded with Catherine of Braganza's own fashioning of her image as a Catholic queen. The texts, especially the fifteenth-century portions, would have been comprehensible to her because several of them were in Latin, and she may have had some familiarity with

Middle English from Serenus Cressy. Catherine also would have identified the familiar visual vocabulary depicted in the *Arma Christi* of Christ's Passion.

As an object, MS Royal 17 A. xxvii would have represented a link to the pre-Reformation Catholic past. Moreover, the manuscript as a material artefact would have also addressed Catherine more personally with the identifiable *Life of St. Katherine* and would have spoken to her specific dynastic situation. As a text that includes a protection for women in childbirth, it may have held for her a poignant private resonance with her own lack of children, particularly during a period of intense anti-Catholic sentiment toward the queen and controversy over the succession. Charles II made a deathbed conversion to Catholicism, and although it is unclear whether Catherine may have had a hand in this, it was her priest, Father Huddlestone, who administered the last rites to the king.[206]

Conclusion

MS Royal 17 A. xxvii is both a modest and an extraordinary manuscript. Complex and rich, paradoxical and unassuming, this small object of female devotion illuminates, however opaquely, the mysteries of female Catholic devotion. To my mind, it indicates a hidden history: the story of a voice triply repressed—that of a female, a Catholic, a foreigner—as she seeks agency through moments of bricolage that are not isolated but rather manifest now as almost invisible traces. As a material object, MS Royal 17 A. xxvii reveals its diverse paths of usage: as an intimate object of creation and conversation between male scribe and female reader; as an interwoven and composite devotional text that speaks to a range of female readers; and as an object with a dual significance—as a potential public symbol of recusant Catholicism and as a private comfort to a barren Queen.

Vassar College

Acknowledgments

My thanks must go to Vickie Larsen, who originally directed me to Serenus Cressy and Catherine of Braganza; Karen Robertson, who generously opened up the world of seventeenth-century Catholic recusant women; Khanh Ho, Andrea Jones, Julie Park, Hiram Perez, Kathleen Doyle, and Sara Torres for suggestions, encouragement, and editing help; the outside readers who made great suggestions; and to Martha Driver, for her patience in helping me get this large article under control.

NOTES

1. James Simpson, "Diachronic History and the Shortcomings of Medieval Studies," in *Reading the Medieval in Early Modern England*, ed. David Matthews and Gordon McMullan (Cambridge, UK: Cambridge University Press, 2007), 27.
2. Ibid., 23.
3. Ibid., 19.
4. The best definition is still Ian Bogost's definition posted on his blog: "What Is Object-Oriented Ontology? A Definition for Ordinary Folk." Ian Bogost—Videogame Theory, Criticism, Design, http://www.bogost.com/blog/what_is_objectoriented_ontolog.shtml. He writes: "Ontology is the philosophical study of existence. Object-oriented ontology ("OOO" for short) puts *things* at the center of this study. Its proponents contend that nothing has special status, but that everything exists equally—plumbers, cotton, bonobos, DVD players, and sandstone, for example. In contemporary thought, things are usually taken either as the aggregation of ever smaller bits (scientific naturalism) or as constructions of human behavior and society (social relativism). OOO steers a path between the two, drawing attention to things at all scales (from atoms to alpacas, bits to blinis), and pondering their nature and relations with one another as much with ourselves."
5. Graham Harman, *The Quadruple Object* (Alresford, UK: Zero Books, 2010), 119. He writes: "By contrast, object-oriented ontology holds that the human world relation has no privilege at all. Thanks to Whitehead, who posited the single category of 'prehension' as a primitive form of relation from which all others are build, Kant's human-world duopoly is faced with a serious rival…. The question is whether this obvious difference between humans and non-humans deserves to be made into a basic ontological rift. For we are merely biased if we assume that humans are a decisive rupture in the world. The difference between people and minerals is vast indeed, but so is that between stars and black holes, or hunter-gatherers and string theorists. The point is to avoid the Taxonomic Fallacy of assuming that basic ontological divides can be identified with specific kinds of entities." ibid. See also, Graham Harman, *Guerilla Metaphysics: Phenomonology and the Carpentry of Things* (Peru, Illinois: Open Court Press, 2005), 1. He writes: "This book calls for what might be termed an object-oriented philosophy, and in this way rejects both the analytic and continental traditions. The ongoing dispute between these traditions, including the sort of 'bridge building' that starts by conceding the existence of the dispute, misses a prejudice shared by both: their primary interest lies not in objects, but in human *access* to them. The so-called linguistic turn is still the dominant model for the philosophy

of access, but there are plenty of others—phenomenology, hermeneutics, deconstruction, philosophy of mind, pragmatism. None of these philosophical schools tells us much of anything about objects themselves; indeed, they pride themselves on avoiding all naïve contact with nonhuman entities. By contrast, object-oriented philosophy holds that the relation of humans to pollen, oxygen, eagles, or windmills is no different in kind from the interaction of these objects with each other. For this reason, the philosophy of objects is sometimes lazily viewed as a form of scientific naturalism, avoiding any prior technical critique of the workings of human knowledge. But quite unlike naturalism, object-oriented philosophy adopts a bluntly *metaphysical* approach to the relations between objects rather than a familiar physical one. In fact, another term that might be employed for object-oriented philosophy is *guerilla metaphysics*—a name meant to signify that the numerous present-day objections to metaphysics are not unknown to me, but also that I do not find them especially compelling." Ibid. For the medieval reframing of object-oriented ontology and speculative medievalisms, see Eileen Joy, "Don't Mess with the Yohan or the Flower Girls: More AVMEO Audiofiles," In the Middle, http://www.inthemedievalmiddle.com/2011_03_01_archive.html. She writes: "Those interested in the possible (im)possibilities of writing object histories (which also means writing the history of how objects move through and are translated within multiple locations and temporalities) when the object itself is never really stable or coherent to begin with will find Carla's talk extremely provocative and useful." See also Jeffrey Jerome Cohen, "Sublunary," In the Middle, http://www.inthemedievalmiddle.com/2011/09/sublunary.html. In this post, he frames a lecture he delivered: "I introduced my talk at Speculative Medievalisms as a textual laboratory, an experimental mixing of worlds that do not often touch through modern and medieval texts (a philosophical essay, a work of historiography, a Breton lay) that are about how unlike worlds touch and what happens in the aftermath of that encounter. My aim was to take Object Oriented Ontology seriously: not as a critical mode to be applied, but as an articulation of concept/tools that might reconfigure how we think about the workings of some narratives... as well as how these narratives in their workings potentially transform these concepts when they enter their worlds."

6. Stephen Nichols, "Introduction: Philology in a Manuscript Culture," *Speculum* 65.1 (January 1990): 1–10.

7. Ibid., 7.

8. Ibid., 8.

9. Ibid.

10. Daniel Leech-Wilkinson, *The Modern Invention of Medieval Music: Scholarship, Ideology, Performance* (Cambridge, UK: Cambridge University Press, 2002), 1–12.

11. The history of philology's difficult racially-charged past is outlined in Geoffrey Harpham, "Roots, Race, and the Return to Philology," *Representations* 106.1 (Spring 2009): 34–62, esp. 54–56.

12. Ibid.

13. Eileen Joy, "Notes toward a Speculative Realist Literary Criticism #STU09," *Svenska Twitteruniversitetet*, http://svtwuni.wordpress.com/2011/12/21/eileen-a-joy-stu09/. See also Levi R. Bryant, "Speculative Realist Literary Criticism," Larval Subjects, http://larvalsubjects.wordpress.com/2011/12/23/speculative-realist-literary-criticism/.

14. Bryant, "Speculative."

15. Ibid.

16. Ibid.

17. Bella Millett describes the Katherine Group: "This title is now generally used to cover the five works found in Bodley 34: the lives and passions of three virgin martyrs, Seinte Katerine (SK), Seinte Margarete (SM) and Seinte Iuliene (SJ); a work on virginity, called by the Bodley 34 scribe Epistel of Meidenhad… and a treatise on the custody of the soul, Sawles Warde (SW)" (5). She explain the term the Wooing Group: "The 'Wooing Group' is the term used by W. Meredith Thompson, 213 (1958), to group together four lyrical meditations on Christ and the Virgin Mary…" (5). See Bella Millett with George B. Jack and Yoko Wada, *Annotated Bibliographies of Middle English Literature: II. Ancrene Wisse, the Katherine Group, and the Wooing Group* (Cambridge, UK: D.S. Brewer, 1996), 5.

18. The British Library Catalogue description of MS Royal 17 A. xxvii has been digitized; British Library, "MS Royal 17 A. xxvii," *British Library Manuscripts Catalogue*, http://www.bl.uk/catalogues/manuscripts/HITS0001.ASP?VPath=html/39426.htm&Search=17+A.+xxvii&Highlight=F. This catalogue description of MS Royal 17 A. xxvii a copy of G. F. Warner and J. P. Gilson, *Catalogue of Western Manuscripts in the Old Royal and King's Collections*, 4 vols. (London, 1921), with index in vol. 3 and plates in vol. 4. The description is in Warner and Gilson, *Catalogue*, 2:220–221. E-mail correspondence with the British Library indicates that a new catalogue description should be available for this shelfmark by October, 2011. The new catalogue description of MS Royal 17 A. xxvii is in the *Catalogue of Illuminated Manuscripts*: http://www.bl.uk/catalogues/illuminatedmanuscripts/results.asp.

19. British Library, "MS Royal 17 A. xxvii," *British Library Manuscript Catalogue* states, "the first part of the MS. is certainly (ff. I, 70 b), the second probably, from the Theyer library, but perhaps as distinct MSS. Theyer sale-cat. No. 243 (?); CMA. 6435 and 6662."

20. Margaret Laing, *Catalogue of Sources for a Linguistic Atlas of Early Medieval English* (Rochester, NY, and Suffolk, UK: D. S. Brewer), 105.

21. British Library, "MS Royal 17 A. xxvii," *British Library Manuscript Catalogue.*

22. Anne Savage and Nicholas Watson, trans. and intro., *Anchoritic Spirituality: Ancrene Wisse and Associated Works* (New York: Paulist Press, 1991), 28–29.

23. See W. Meredith Thompson, *Þe Wohunge of Ure Lauerd*, EETS os. 241 (Oxford: Oxford University Press, 1958), 19; Richard Morris, ed., intro., and trans., *Old English Homilies and Homiletic Treatises of the Thirteenth Centuries*, EETS os. 29 (Oxford: Oxford University Press, 1868), 204–207.

24. Catherine Innes-Parker, "*The Wohunge of Ure Lauerd* and the Tradition of Affective Devotion: Rethinking Text and Audience," in *The Milieu and Context of the Wooing Group*, ed. Susannah Mary Chewning (Cardiff: University of Wales Press, 2009), 97.

25. Nicholas Watson, "Afterward: 'On Eise,'" in *The Milieu and Context of the Wooing Group*, ed. Susannah Mary Chewning (Cardiff: University of Wales Press, 2009), 195–196. Watson uses a bit of Bella Millett's work on Continental sermons to discuss topical portability. See Bella Millett, "The Pastoral context of the Trinity and Lambeth Homilies," in *Essays in Manuscript Geography: Vernacular Manuscripts of the English West Midlands from the Conquest to the Sixteenth Century*, ed. Wendy Scase (Turnhout, Belgium: Brepols, 2007), 43-64.

26. Pamela Robinson, "The 'Booklet': A Self-Contained Unit in Composite Manuscripts," *Codicologica* 3 (1980): 46–69, 46.

27. Laing, *Catalogue of Sources*, 105.

28. Innes-Parker, "*Wohunge*," 97.

29. The Wooing Group includes seven works in five manuscripts. The thirteenth-century corpus includes *On Ureisun of Ure Louerde, On wel Swuðe God Ureisun of God Almihti, On Lofson of Ure Louerde, On Lofsong of Ure Lefdi, Þe Oreisun of Seinte Marie*, and *Þe Wohunge of Ure Lauerd*. Recently, scholars have also begun to include the fourteenth-century *A Talkying of the Loue of God*, which is based on the Wooing Group material. See Susannah Mary Chewning, "Introduction," in *The Milieu and Context of the Wooing Group*, ed. Susannah Mary Chewning (Cardiff: University of Wales Press, 2009), 3. See also her note clarifying possible confusion about *On Lofsong of Ure Lefdi* and *Þe Oreisun of Seinte Marie*. She writes: "There is some confusion about the two texts titled by Thompson as *On Lofsong of Ure Lefdi* and *Þe Oreisun of Seinte Marie*. The *Lofsong* appears in two manuscripts, Nero and Royal, and the *Oreisun* appears as a fragment in Royal. Morris gave the *Lofsong* its title, while the *Oreisun* has a title in the Royal manuscript. *Þe Oreisun of Seinte Marie* is a fragment of thirty-one lines and appears to be a transcription of the first forty-four lines of *On Lofsong of Ure Lefdi*." Ibid., 20. See also Thompson, *Wohunge*; Morris, *Old English Homilies*. See also Innes-Parker, "*Wohunge*," 97.

30. Laing, *Catalogue of Sources*, 105.

31. British Library, "MS Royal 17 A. xxvii," *British Library Manuscript Catalogue*.

32. Angus McIntosh, M. L. Samuels, and Michael Benskin, *A Linguistic Atlas of Late Medieval English*, 4 vols. (Aberdeen, Scotland: Aberdeen University Press, 1986), 1:115.

33. Bella Millett with George B. Jack and Yoko Wada, *Annotated Bibliographies*, 55.

34. Margaret Laing informs me that she has located the dialect of Cambridge, Corpus Christi College 402 and Oxford, Bodleian Library MS Bodley 34 on the southern Shropshire/northern Worcestershire border. Staffordshire borders Shropshire and Worcestershire.

35. See British Library, "MS Royal 17 A. xxvii," *British Library Manuscript Catalogue*.

36. This was suggested by Derek Pearsall at the Early Book Society dinner at the University of York in July 2011.

37. Robinson, "Booklet," 52.

38. Ibid., 47–48.

39. Ralph Hanna III, "Booklets in Medieval Manuscripts: Further Considerations," *Studies in Bibliography* 39 (1986): 108.

40. Ibid., 111. Hanna discards several of Robinson's features as not useful as a litmus test for booklet structures but rather a useful sign of production issues. See ibid., 107–110.

41. Ibid., 101.

42. These include, for the Katherine Group, Oxford, Bodleian Library MS Bodley 34, and London, British Library MS Cotton Titus D. xviii. Both were produced before ca. 1225. The early Wooing Group manuscripts include London, British Library MS Cotton Titus D. xviii; London, British Library MS Cotton Nero A. xvi (ca. 1225–1250); and London, Lambeth Palace Library MS 487 (ca. 1200). Laing locates Lambeth MS 487 on the Shropshire/Herefordshire border (Laing, *Catalogue of Sources*, 111); the BL MS Cotton Titus D. xviii contains several different dialectal specificities within the W. Midlands (South Chester, Shropshire, Worcestershire); ibid., 81–82; and BL MS Cotton Nero A. xvi is from south Worcestershire, not far from the Gloucestershire border (ibid., 78).

43. Laing, *Catalogue of Sources*, 15.

44. Ibid., 24, 124. Laing suggests a date of ca. 1225–1250 for Corpus Christi College 402 and puts Bodley 34 earlier, at between 1200–1225.

45. Bella Millett, ed., *Ancrene Wisse: A Corrected Edition of the Text in Cambridge, Corpus Christi College, MS 402, with Variants from Other Manuscripts*, 2 vols., EETS os. 325 (Oxford: Oxford University Press, 2005–2006), I: 12–13.

46. The two most important ones are Cambridge, Corpus Christi College MS 402 and London, British Library MS Cotton Cleopatra C. vi.

47. See Innes-Parker, *"Wohunge,"* 96–122, for a discussion of what kind of female reader would be behind the production of Wooing Group manuscripts. See also Anne Savage, "The Communal Authorship of *Ancrene Wisse,"* in *A Companion to Ancrene Wisse,* ed. Yoko Wada (Cambridge, UK: D. S. Brewer, 2003), 45–56.

48. Ralph Hanna, *London Literature 1300–1380* (Cambridge, UK: Cambridge University Press, 2005), 76–77.

49. Savage and Watson make the comment about these early *Ancrene Wisse,* Katherine Group, and Wooing Group manuscripts: "They all look somewhat alike. They are small, between five and nine inches high, and compact enough to be held easily in the hand. They are written neatly and clearly, in handwriting of no great size, on good parchment (sometimes with small holes in it) which is still exceptionally clean"; Savage and Watson, *Anchoritic Spirituality,* 7.

50. Hanna, "Booklets," 107–111.

51. British Library, "MS Royal 17 A. xxvii," *British Library Manuscript Catalogue.*

52. Ibid. See also Warner and Gilson, *Catalogue,* II:221. The *British Library Manuscript Catalogue* lists the two leaves/bifolium (though it looks more like a bifolium) as quire 2. I include it as an extension of quire 1 because it makes a booklet unit.

53. My transcription of the piece on fol. 10v; all red letters appear here in bold. This is a diplomatic edition of the text. Abbreviations are expanded, but winums, thorns, and yoghs are not normalized. See also R. M. Wilson, *Sawles Warde, an Early Middle English Homily* (Leeds, UK: Leeds School of English, 1938), 42. This is the only manuscript that includes this scribal note at the end of *Sawles Warde.*

54. My translation.

55. S.R.T.O. d'Ardenne, ed., *Þe Liflade ant te Passiun of Seinte Iuliene.* EETS os. 248 (London, New York, Toronto: Oxford University Press, 1961), 71.

56. Savage and Watson, *Anchoritic Spirituality,* 321.

57. The last binding of the manuscript was in 1956, according to an e-mail from the curators at the British Library on August 18, 2011. They have noted it in the new manuscript description in the *Catalogue of Illuminated Manuscripts.*

58. Robinson, "Booklet," 48.

59. In my book project, *Medieval Women and English Exoticism,* I consider the importance of reading Bodley 34 in order from Katherine, Margaret, and Juliana through to *Hali Meiðhad* and *Sawles Warde.* The placement of *Sawles*

Warde first in MS Royal 17 A. xxvii completely changes the reading frame of this devotional volume. I believe that it would direct a different kind of devotional regimen of reading to its female reader that would begin with an interest in moderation before moving into the extreme violence of the Katherine Group lives and the Wooing Group Passion narrative. Unpacking this reading practice and the importance of order in MS Royal 17 A. xxvii requires another article.

60. Robinson, "Booklet," 54.

61. Ibid., 53.

62. Ibid., 53.

63. The suggestion to examine the sewing holes was made by audience members at the Early Book Society conference at the University of York in 2011, where I first delivered this paper.

64. The *British Library Manuscript Catalogue* states: "The first part of the MS. is certainly (ff. I, 70b), the second probably, from the Theyer library, but perhaps as distinct MSS. Theyer sale-cat. No. 243 (?); CMA. 6435 and 6662."

65. John Theyer's dates and biographical information are in Charlotte Fell-Smith and Robert J. Haines, "John Theyer," in *Oxford Dictionary of National Biography*, http://www.oxforddnb.com/view/article/27178.

66. "It was to this John Theyer that Wood's mother, at one period, thought of sending our author, in order to his being brought up as an attorney"; Anthony Wood, *Athenae Oxonienses. An Exact History of all the Writers and Bishops Who Have Had Their Education in the University of Oxford*, 4 vols., 3rd ed. (London: printed for F.C. and J. Rivington, 1813-1817), 3:996 footnote no. 6.

67. Wood, *Athenae Oxonienses*, 3:996-998

68. Information about Lanthony Secunda, the priors, and the noble families associated with it is in William Page, ed., "Houses of Augustinian Canons: The Priory of Lanthony by Gloucester," in *Victoria County History: A History of the County of Gloucester*, vol. 2 (London: Archibald Constable and Co., 1907), 87–91, available online at British History Online, http://www.british-history.ac.uk/report.aspx?compid=40276.

69. Ibid.

70. Reginald Poole, "Review of British Museum. *Catalogue of Western Manuscripts in the Old Royal and King's Collection* by George F. Warner and Julius P. Gilson," *English Historical Review* 37.147 (July 1922): 452.

71. This is from MS Royal appendix, no. 70, p. 46: "A thin volume in folio 32 being a catalogue of the manuscripts [numbered from 1 to 336] formerly in the possession of John Theyer."

72. M. R. James, *The Manuscripts in the Library at Lambeth Palace*, Cambridge Antiquarian Society 33 (London: George and Bell and Sons, 1900). See also Edward Bernard, *Catalogi librorum manuscriptorum Angliae et Hibernicae in*

unum collecti cum indice alphabetico (Oxford: University Press, 1697); here-inafter, the CMA.

73. Kathleen Doyle, "Old Royal Library: 'A Greate Many Noble Manuscripts yet Remaining,'" in *Royal Manuscripts: The Genius of Illumination*, ed. Scot McKendrick, John Lowden, and Kathleen Doyle with Joanna Frónska and Deidre Jackson (London: British Library, 2011), 81.

74. Ibid., 81; see also Poole, "Review," 452.

75. Ibid.

76. As mentioned in note 67, the family's ties were strong enough that at one point Anthony Wood's mother considered sending him to Theyer to be trained as a lawyer.

77. F.J. Levy, "Henry Savile," in *Oxford Dictionary of National Biography*, http://www.oxforddnb.com/view/article/68220?docPos=4.

78. James, *Manuscripts*, 2; CMA, 2:198–203.

79. David Casley, *A Catalogue of the Manuscripts of the King's Library* (London, 1734).

80. Henri Omont, "Anciens catalogues de bibliothèques anglaises (XIIe–XIVe siècle)," in *Zentralblatt für Bibliothekswesen*, 9 (May 1892): 207–222.

81. For a history of Lanthony, see William Dugdale, *Monasticon Anglicanum: A History of the Abbies and Other Monasteries, Hospitals, Frieries, and Cathedral and Collegiate Churches, with Their Dependencies, in England and Wales*, 6 volumes in 8 parts (London: Longman, Hurst, Rees, Orme and Brown, 1817–1830), II: 58–73. British Library, MS Cotton. Jul. D. X contains a history of the priory of Lanthony.

82. Ibid., 2:60.

83. Omont writes: "Cahier in folio, de 11 feuillets en parchemin, mesurant 300 millim. Sur 202. Le texte du catalogue occupe les fol. 3–11vo. Les additions au catalogue sont de deux mains différentes; la plus récente, notée addition postérieure, semble dater du récolement de 1380. Entre chaque rayon, le rédacteur du catalogue a toujours reservé trois lignes pour les accroissements futurs de la bibliothèque." Omont, "Anciens catalogues," 209.

84. My translation.

85. Omont, "Anciens catalogues," 207–222.

86. See James, *Manuscripts*, 2–3.

87. F. J. Levy, "Savile, Henry, of Bank."

88. Ibid.

89. Andrew G. Watson, *The Manuscripts of Henry Savile of Banke* (London: Bibliographic Society, 1969), 2 and 9. See also Vickie Jeanne Larsen, "The Pious Fringe: Julian of Norwich's Readers and Their Books, 1413–1843," PhD diss., University of Iowa, 2009, 116–117. My thanks to Vickie Larsen, who first suggested Catherine of Braganza as a potential reader and pointed out the connection to Serenus Cressy.

90. Larsen, "Pious Fringe," 117.

91. See British Library, "MS Royal 4 C. ii," *British Library Manuscripts Catalogue*, http://www.bl.uk/catalogues/manuscripts/HITS0001. ASP?VPath=html/38242.htm&Search=4+C.+ii&Highlight=F. See also British Library, "MS Royal 6 C. vii," *British Library Manuscripts Catalogue*, http:// www.bl.uk/catalogues/manuscripts/HITS0001.ASP?VPath=html/38398. htm&Search=6+c.vii&Highlight=F.

92. See British Library, "MS Royal 7 B. vii," *British Library Manuscripts Catalogue*, http://www.bl.uk/catalogues/manuscripts/HITS0C01. ASP?VPath=html/38439.htm&Search=7+B.+vii&Highlight=F.

93. Kathryn Barron, "John Lumley," in *Oxford Dictionary of National Biography*, http://www.oxforddnb.com/view/article/17179?docPos=8.

94. See British Library, "MS Royal 7 B. xi and 7 B. xii," *British Library Menuscripts Catalogue*, http://www.bl.uk/catalogues/manuscripts/HITS0C01. ASP?VPath=html/38443.htm&Search=7+B.+xi&Highlight=F.

95. CMA, 199.

96. CMA, 202.

97. British Library, "MS Royal App. 70," *British Library Manuscripts Catalogue*, http://www.bl.uk/catalogues/manuscripts/HITS0001. ASP?VPath=html/39883.htm&Search=John+Theyer&Highlight=T.

98. Folio 6r.

99. I have collated all of the CMA, the Theyer sale catalogue (Royal App. 70), and the Royal catalogue descriptions. Reading through the file, which is more than 400 pages in 10-point type, I was amazed to see how so many items are expressed identically in the CMA and the Theyer sale catalogue.

100. Frances M. Mack, *Seinte Marherete þe Meiden ant Martyr*, EETS os. 193 (London: Oxford University Press, 1934), 3. My translations.

101. Innes-Parker, "*Wohunge*," 96.

102. Morris, *Old English Homilies*, 305. See also Thompson, *Wohunge*, 19.

103. Savage and Watson, *Anchoritic Spirituality*, 329.

104. Innes-Parker, "*Wohunge*," 107.

105. Morris, *Old English Homilies*, 207. See Thompson, *Wohunge*, 17–18, for a diplomatic edition. The section is cut off in Royal 17 A. xxvii: "bi þe harde hurtes. Ant te unwurðe wohes þat he for us sunfule willeliche..." (Morris, *Old English Homilies*, 305).

106. Morris, *Old English Homilies*, 204–206. See also the translation in Savage and Watson, *Anchoritic Spirituality*, 329–330.

107. Richard Morris, ed., intro., and trans, *Legends of the Holy Rood: Symbols of the Passion and Cross-Poems*, EETS (OS) 46 (London: N. Trübner & Co., 1871), 178. This has an edition of the *Arma Christi* with penned images of the Royal 17 A. xxvii *Arma Christi* and the British Library, MS Add. 22029 *Arma Christi*.

108. Ibid., 188.
109. Ibid., 178.
110. Ibid., 180.
111. Ibid., 176.
112. Ibid.
113. Ibid., 184.
114. Ibid., 190.
115. Ibid., 172.
116. Innes-Parker, "*Wohunge*," 107.
117. Carl Horstmann, *Minor Poems from the Vernon Manuscript* (London: K. Paul, Trench, Trübner & Co., 1892), 31–32.
118. My translation.
119. Flora Lewis, "The Wound in Christ's Side and the Instruments of the Passion: Gendered Experience and Response," in *Women and the Book: Assessing the Visual Evidence*, ed. Lesley Smith and Jane Taylor (London: British Library, 1997), 204.
120. Ibid., 209.
121. Ibid., 222.
122. My translation.
123. See "schēlden" in *Middle English Dictionary*, http://quod.lib.umich.edu/cgi/m/mec/med-idx?type=byte&byte=176742559&egdisplay=compact&egs=176766491.
124. See Kathryn Smith, *Art, Identity, and Devotion in Fourteenth-Century England* (London: British Library, 2003), 175.
125. My transcription; endings of abbreviated words and description of the first letter are in parentheses.
126. My translation.
127. Morris, *Legends*, 170.
128. Ibid.
129. Rebecca Krug, trans. and intro., "The Fifteen Oes," in *Cultures of Piety: Medieval English Devotional Literature in Translation*, eds. Anne Clark Bartlett and Thomas H. Bestul (Ithaca, NY, and London: Cornell University Press), 107.
130. Ibid., 111.
131. Ibid., 113.
132. Jennifer Summit, *Lost Property: The Woman Writer and English Literary History, 1380–1589* (Chicago and London: University of Chicago Press, 2000), 115. Summit discusses the status of the *Fifteen Oes* as a representative Catholic (i.e., ritualistic, visual, and object-oriented) pre-Reformation text and how the Protestant Reformation attempted to rehabilitate and reform this text; it stands as an example of how cultural material can adapt rather

than be part of a historical project that posits either continuity or change; ibid., 122.

133. Kathleen Kamerick, *Popular Piety and Art in the Late Middle Ages: Image Worship and Idolatry in England, 1350–1500* (New York: Palgrave MacMillan, 2002).

134. Morris, *Legends*, 196. Translations are my own.

135. Ibid., 196. See also Rossell Hope Robbins, "The 'Arma Christi' Rolls," *Modern Language Review* 34.3 (July 1939), 415–421, who discusses many of the different indulgences attached to *Arma Christi* texts. The translation is my own.

136. See Don C. Skemer, *Binding Words: Textual Amulets in the Middle Ages* (University Park: Pennsylvania State University Press, 2006), 235–278

137. The translation is my own.

138. Morris, *Legends*, 196.

139. Lucy Freeman Sandler, *Gothic Manuscripts 1285–1385*, 2 vols. in *A Survey of Manuscripts Illuminated in the British Isles*, gen. ed. J. J. G. Alexander (London: Harvey Miller, 1986), 1:27. The manuscript measures 183 mm by 135 mm.

140. Francis Wormald and Phyllis M. Giles, *A Descriptive Catalogue of the Additional Manuscripts in the Fitzwilliam Museum Acquired between 1895 and 1979 (Excluding the McClean Collection)*, 2 vols. (Cambridge, UK: Cambridge University Press, 1982).

141. M. R. James, "An English Picture-Book of the Late Thirteenth Century," *Walpole Society* 25 (1937): 23–32 and plates IX–XVII; Paul Binski and Stella Panayotova, eds., *The Cambridge Illuminations: Ten Centuries of Book Production in the Medieval West* (Turnhout, Belgium, and London: Harvey Miller, 2005), 183.

142. See "Jacobus de Voragine, *Legenda aurea*," in *Guide to Medieval and Renaissance Manuscripts in the Huntington Library* (San Marino, CA: Huntington Library Press, 1989), available online at http://sunsite.berkeley.edu/hehweb/HM3027.html. See C. W. Dutschke with R. H. Rouse, et al., *Guide to Medieval and Renaissance Manuscripts in the Huntington Library* (San Marino, CA: Huntington Library Press, 1989).

143. The image is available online at Digital Scriptorium Huntington Catalog Database, http://dpg.lib.berkeley.edu/webdb/dsheh/heh_brf?CallNumber=HM+3027&Description=&page=2.

144. This image of St. Juliana is reproduced in Karen A. Winstead, trans. and intro., *Chaste Passions: Medieval English Virgin Martyr Legends* (Ithaca, NY: Cornell University Press, 2000), 11.

145. See James, "English Picture-Book," plate XII.

146. Morris, *Legends*, 180.

147. My translation.

148. Jeffrey Hamburger, *The Visual and the Visionary* (New York: Zone Books, 1998), 304–308; Lewis, "Wound in Christ's Side," 221.

149. There are nineteen *Arma Christi* verse texts in codex or roll (and occasionally in the stubs) in medieval manuscripts. There is also a small tradition of copies in print. See Anthony Bale, *The Jew in the Medieval Book* (Cambridge, UK: Cambridge University Press, 2006), 175–176.

150. See John Northwood, *A Worcestershire Miscellany*, ed. Nita Baugh (Bryn Mawr, PA: Bryn Mawr College, 1956), 15–16.

151. Ibid.

152. T. A. Birrell, *English Monarchs and Their Books* (London: British Library, 1987), 77.

153. Ibid., 56–58.

154. Doyle, "Old Royal Library," 81. Doyle refers to Oxford, Bodleian Library, MS Tanner 314, folio 94, a letter to William Sancroft from Robert Scott.

155. Doyle, "Old Royal Library," 81.

156. Ibid., 85.

157. Ibid., 82. Doyle cites several examples from various contemporary accounts, including comments from Gilbert Burnet, Bishop of Salisbury; George Savile, 1st Marquess of Halifax; and John Mordaunt, Viscount Mordaunt of Avalon.

158. Doyle, "Old Royal Library," 81. Letter to Henri Justel, December 3, 1681, in F. H. Blackburne Daniell, ed. *Calendar of State Papers, Domestic. Charles II. 1680-Dec. 31, 1681.* (London: Her Majesty's Stationery Office, 1921), 601.

159. Doyle, "Old Royal Library," 82. Letter to Justel, in Daniell, *Calendar*, 601.

160. Doyle, "Old Royal Library," 82.

161. Ibid., 83. See also Birrell, *English Monarchs*, 54–58.

162. Miriam Foote, "Samuel Mearne," in *Oxford Dictionary of National Biography*, http://www.oxforddnb.com/view/article/52143.

163. Ibid.

164. Gilson, Julius P. "Introduction," in George F. Warner and Julius P. Gilson, *Catalogue of Western Manuscripts in the Old Royal and King's Collections*, 4 vols (London: British Museum, 1921), I: xxv, n. 11.

165. Doyle, "Old Royal Library," 83.

166. S. M. Wynne, "Catherine of Braganza," in *Oxford Dictionary of National Biography*, http://www.oxforddnb.com/view/article/4894?docPos=1 .

167. Ibid.

168. Frances E. Dolan, *Whores of Babylon: Catholicism, Gender, and Seventeenth-Century Print Culture* (Ithaca, NY, and London: Cornell University Press, 1999). See also Dolan, "The Command of Mary: Marian Devotion, Henrietta

Maria's Intercessions, and Catholic Motherhood," in *Whores of Babylon*, 95–156; and Dolan, "'The Wretched Subject the Whole Town Talks Of': Elizabeth Cellier, Popish Plots, and Print," in *Whores of Babylon*, 157–210.

169. Megan Matchinske, *Writing, Gender, and State in Early Modern England: Identity Formation and the Female Subject* (Cambridge, UK: Cambridge University Press, 1998), 4.

170. Edith Snook, *Women, Reading, and the Cultural Politics of Early Modern England* (Aldershot, UK: Ashgate, 2005), 86–87.

171. Ibid., 87. See Marie B. Rowlands, "Recusant Women 1560–1640," in *Women in English Society 1500–1800*, ed. Mary Prior (London: Methuen, 1985), 158–159.

172. Wynne, "Catherine of Braganza."

173. Ibid.

174. D. F. McKenzie and Maureen Bell, *A Chronology and Calendar of Documents Relating to the London Book Trade, 1641–1700*, vol. 1 (Oxford: Oxford University Press, 2005), 493.

175. Caroline Hibbard, "Henrietta Maria," in *Oxford Dictionary of National Biography*, http://www.oxforddnb.com/view/article/12947?docPos=1.

176. Ibid. See also Lady Tuke to Mary Evelyn, March 20, 1681[–2], British Library, Evelyn MS ME6.

177. Larsen, "Pious Fringe," 166. See McKenzie and Bell, *Chronology and Calendar*, 1:613–618.

178. McKenzie and Bell, *Chronology and Calendar*, 2: 213.

179. ibid., 2:206–207.

180. Ibid., 206.

181. Ibid., 207.

182. Ibid., 209.

183. Ibid., 116.

184. Edward Corp, "Catherine of Braganza and Cultural Politics," in *Queenship in Britain 1660–1837: Royal Patronage, Court Culture and Dynastic Politics*, ed. Clarissa Campbell Orr (Manchester, UK, and New York: Manchester University Press, 2002), 62.

185. Ibid., 71.

186. Walter Hilton, *Scale of Perfection*, ed. S. Cressy (London, 1659).

187. Patricia C. Brückmann, "Hugh Paulinus Cressy," in *Oxford Dictionary of National Biography*, http://www.oxforddnb.com/view/article/6676. See also Julian of Norwich, *XVI Revelations of Divine Love* (London: R. F. S. Cressy, 1670).

188. See a discussion of Henrietta Maria's use of Somerset House and its chapel and environs as a Catholic center of worship in Dolan, *Whores of Babylon*, 95–156.

189. David Daniel Rees, "David Baker (Augustine)," in *Oxford Dictionary of National Biography*, http://www.oxforddnb.com/view/article/1110?docPos=1.
190. Larsen, "Pious Fringe," 117. For a facsimile of the original letter see Augustine Baker, "Letter CCLXVI: Mr. Augustine Baker to Sir Robert Cotton, entreating for a present of Books for the English Monastery at Cambray," in *Original Letters, Illustrative of English History; Including Numerous Royal Letters: From Autographs in the British Museum, and One or Two Other Collections*. Ed. Sir Henry Ellis. 2nd series, vol. 3 of 4 volumes (London: Harding and Lepard, Pall-Mall East, 1827), 256-258. The letter is in MS Cotton Julius C. III, folio 187 in the British Library.
191. Larsen, "The Pious Fringe," 148.
192. Serenus Cressy, *The Church History of Brittany from the Beginning of Christianity to the Norman Conquest* (London, 1668).
193. Serenus Cressy, "To the Queen," in *The Church History of Brittany*, n.p.
194. Larsen, "Pious Fringe," 171.
195. Augusto Cardosa Pinto, *A cruz processional de capela de D. Catarina de Bragança, rainha de Inglaterra* (Lisboa: Fundacão de Casa de Bragança, 1956).
196. Ibid., 8. All translations from the Portuguese are my own.
197. Ibid., 12. Pinto transcribes: "CRUX/PASTORALIS/SANCTI/THOMAE/ARCHI.EPISCOPI/CANTUARIENSIS/A.REGINA/CATHARINA/IN. AMPLIOREM/FORMAM/REDUCTAM/ANNO/16.64"; ibid., 12.
198. Ibid., 8.
199. Ibid., 23.
200. This is Nicholas Love's *The Mirror of the Blessed Life of Jesus Christ* in MS Royal 18 C. x. See Nicholas Love, *The Mirror of the Blessed Life of Jesus Christ*, ed. Michael G. Sargent (Exeter, UK: University of Exeter Press, 2005).
201. This is MS Royal 17 D. IX. See Reginald Pecock, *Þe folewer to Þe Donet*, ed. E. V. Hitchcock EETS os. 164 (Oxford: Oxford University Press, 1924, repr. 1971).
202. This does not have a corresponding manuscript in the Royal collection but it seems to be a manuscript containing the *Cloud of Unknowing* and probably a copy of *The Orchard of Syon*—a Middle English version of Bridget of Sweden's book of divine doctrine.
203. See Michael Sargent, "What Kind of Writing Is *A Talkying of Þe Love of God?*," in *The Milieu and Context of the Wooing Group*, ed. Susannah M. Chewning (Cardiff: University of Wales Press, 2009), 179.
204. Larsen, "Pious Fringe," 175.
205. This idea was suggested by Vickie Larsen after I delivered my paper at the Early Book Society conference in York in 2011.
206. Corp, "Catherine of Braganza," 65.

WORKS CITED

d'Ardenne, S. R. T. O., ed. *Þe Liflade ant te Passiun of Seinte Iuliene*. EETS os. 248. London, New York, Toronto: Oxford University Press, 1961.

Bale, Anthony. *The Jew in the Medieval Book*. Cambridge, UK: Cambridge University Press, 2006.

Baker, Augustine. "Letter CCLXVI: Mr. Augustine Baker to Sir Robert Cotton, entreating for a present of Books for the English Monastery at Cambray." in *Original Letters, Illustrative of English History; Including Numerous Royal Letters: From Autographs in the British Museum, and One or Two Other Collections*, edited by Sir Henry Ellis. 2nd series, 4 vols. London: Harding and Lepard, Pall-Mall East, 1827.

Barron, Kathryn. "John Lumley." In *Oxford Dictionary of National Biography*. http://www.oxforddnb.com/view/article/17179?docPos=8.

Bernard, Edward. *Catalogi librorum manuscriptorum Angliae et Hiberniae in unum collecti cum indice alphabetico*. Oxford: Oxford University Press, 1697.

Binski, Paul, and Stella Panayotova, eds. *The Cambridge Illuminations: Ten Centuries of Book Production in the Medieval West*. Turnhout, Belgium, and London: Harvey Miller, 2005.

Birrell, T. A. *English Monarchs and Their Books*. London: British Library, 1987.

Bogost, Ian. "What Is Object-Oriented Ontology? A Definition for Ordinary Folk." Ian Bogost—Videogame Theory, Criticism, Design. http://www.bogost.com/blog/what_is_objectoriented_ontolog.shtml.

British Library. "MS Royal 4. C. ii." *British Library Manuscripts Catalogue*. http://www.bl.uk/catalogues/manuscripts/HITS0001.ASP?VPath=html/38242.htm&Search=4+C.+ii&Highlight=F.

——."MS Royal 6 C. vii." *British Library Manuscripts Catalogue*. http://www.bl.uk/catalogues/manuscripts/HITS0001.ASP?VPath=html/38398.htm&Search=6+c.vii&Highlight=F.

——. "MS Royal 7 B. vii." *British Library Manuscripts Catalogue*. http://www.bl.uk/catalogues/manuscripts/HITS0001.ASP?VPath=html/38439.htm&Search=7+B.+vii&Highlight=F.

——. "MS Royal 7 B. xi and Royal 7 B. xii." *British Library Manuscripts Catalogue*. http://www.bl.uk/catalogues/manuscripts/HITS0001.ASP?VPath=html/38443.htm&Search=7+B.+xi&Highlight=F.

——. "MS Royal 17 A. xxvii." *British Library Manuscripts Catalogue*. http://www.bl.uk/catalogues/illuminatedmanuscripts/record.asp?MSID=8521&CollID=16&NStart=170507.

———. "MS Royal 17 A. xxvii." *Catalogue of Illuminated Manuscripts*. http://www.bl.uk/catalogues/illuminatedmanuscripts/results.asp.

———. "MS Royal App. 70." *British Library Manuscripts Catalogue*. http://www.bl.uk/catalogues/manuscripts/HITS0001.ASP?VPath=html/39883.htm&Search=John+Theyer&Highlight=T.

Brückmann, Patricia C. "Hugh Paulinus Cressy." In *Oxford Dictionary of National Biography*. http://www.oxforddnb.com/view/article/6676.

Bryant, Levi R. "Speculative Realist Literary Criticism." Larval Subjects. http://larvalsubjects.wordpress.com/2011/12/23/speculative-realist-literary-criticism/.

Casley, David. *A Catalogue of the Manuscripts of the King's Library*. London, 1734.

Chewning, Susannah Mary. "Introduction." In *The Milieu and Context of the Wooing Group*, ed. Susannah Mary Chewning, 1-25. Cardiff: University of Wales Press, 2009.

Cohen, Jeffrey Jerome. "Sublunary." In the Middle. http://www.inthemedievalmiddle.com/2011/09/sublunary.html.

Corp, Edward. "Catherine of Braganza and Cultural Politics." In *Queenship in Britain 1660–1837: Royal Patronage, Court Culture and Dynastic Politics*, ed. Clarissa Campbell Orr, 53-73. Manchester, UK, and New York: Manchester University Press, 2002.

Cressy, Serenus. *The Church History of Brittany from the Beginning of Christianity to the Norman Conquest*. London, 1668.

Daniell, F.H. Blackburne, ed. *Calendar of State Papers, Domestic. Of the Reign of Charles II. 1680-Dec. 31, 1681*. London: Her Majesty's Stationery Office, 1921.

Dolan, Frances E. *Whores of Babylon: Catholicism, Gender, and Seventeenth-Century Print Culture*. Ithaca, NY, and London: Cornell University Press, 1999.

Doyle, Kathleen. "Old Royal Library: 'A Greate Many Noble Manuscripts yet Remaining.'" In *Royal Manuscripts: The Genius of Illumination*, ed. Scot McKendrick, John Lowden, and Kathleen Doyle with Joanna Frónska and Deidre Jackson, 66-93. London: British Library, 2011.

Dugdale, William. *Monasticon anglicanum: A History of the Abbies and Other Monasteries, Hospitals, Frieries, and Cathedral and Collegiate Churches, with Their Dependencies, in England and Wales*. 6 vols. in 8 parts. London: Longman, Hurst, Rees, Orme and Brown, 1817–1830.

Dutschke, C. W., with R. H. Rouse, et al. *Guide to Medieval and Renaissance Manuscripts in the Huntington Library*. San Marino, CA: Huntington Library Press, 1989.

Fell-Smith, Charlotte, and Robert J. Haines. "John Theyer." In *Oxford*

Dictionary of National Biography. http://www.oxforddnb.com/view/article/27178.

Foote, Miriam. "Samuel Mearne." In *Oxford Dictionary of National Biography*. http://www.oxforddnb.com/view/article/52143.

Gilson, Julius P. "Introduction." In *Catalogue of Western Manuscripts in the Old Royal and King's Collections*, George F. Warner and Julius P. Gilson, 4 vols. , I: xi-xxxii. London: British Museum, 1921.

Hamburger, Jeffrey. *The Visual and the Visionary*. New York: Zone Books, 1998.

Hanna, Ralph III. "Booklets in Medieval Manuscripts: Further Considerations." *Studies in Bibliography* 39 (1986).

———. *London Literature 1300-1380*. Cambridge, UK: Cambridge University Press, 2005.

Harman, Graham. *Guerilla Metaphysics: Phenomonology and the Carpentry of Things*. Peru, Illinois: Open Court Press, 2005.

———. *The Quadruple Object*. Alresford, UK: Zero Books, 2010.

Harpham, Geoffrey Galt. "Roots, Races and the Return to Philology." *Representations* 106.1 (Spring 2009): 34–62.

Hibbard, Caroline. "Henrietta Maria." *Oxford Dictionary of National Biography*. http://www.oxforddnb.com/view/article/12947?docPos=1.

Hilton, Walter. *Scale of Perfection*. Edited by S. Cressy. London, 1659.

Horstmann, Carl. *Minor Poems from the Vernon Manuscript*. London: K. Paul, Trench, Trübner & Co., 1892.

Innes-Parker, Catherine. "*The Wohunge of Ure Lauerd* and the Tradition of Affective Devotion: Rethinking Text and Audience." In *The Milieu and Context of the Wooing Group*, ed. Susannah Mary Chewning, 96-122. Cardiff: University of Wales Press, 2009.

"Jacobus de Voragine, *Legenda aurea*." In *Guide to Medieval and Renaissance Manuscripts in the Huntington Library*. San Marino, CA: Huntington Library Press, 1989. Available online at http://sunsite.berkeley.edu/hehweb/HM3027.html.

James, M. R. *The Manuscripts in the Library at Lambeth Palace*. Cambridge Antiquarian Society 33. London: George and Bell and Sons, 1900.

———. "An English Picture-Book of the Late Thirteenth Century." *Walpole Society* 25 (1937): 23–32.

Joy, Eileen A. ""Don't Mess with the Yohan or the Flower Girls: More AVMEO Audiofiles." In the Middle. http://www.inthemedievalmiddle.com/2011_03_01_archive.html.

———. "Notes toward a Speculative Realist Literary Criticism #STU09." *Svenska Twitteruniversitetet*. http://svtwuni.wordpress.com/2011/12/21/eileen-a-joy-stu09/.

Julian of Norwich. *XVI Revelations of Divine Love*. London: R. F. S. Cressy, 1670.

Kamerick, Kathleen. *Popular Piety and Art in the Late Middle Ages: Image Worship and Idolatry in England, 1350–1500*. New York: Palgrave MacMillan, 2002.

Krug, Rebecca, trans. and intro. "The Fifteen Oes." In *Cultures of Piety: Medieval English Devotional Literature in Translation*, eds. Anne Clark Bartlett and Thomas H. Bestul, 107-117. Ithaca, NY, and London: Cornell University Press.

Laing, Margaret. *Catalogue of Sources for a Linguistic Atlas of Early Medieval English*. Rochester, NY, and Suffolk, UK: D. S. Brewer.

Larsen, Vickie Jeanne. "The Pious Fringe: Julian of Norwich's Readers and Their Books, 1413–1843." PhD diss., University of Iowa, 2009.

Leech-Wilkinson, Daniel. *The Modern Invention of Medieval Music: Scholarship, Ideology, Performance*. Cambridge, UK: Cambridge University Press, 2002.

Levy, F. J. "Savile, Henry, of Banke." In *Oxford Dictionary of National Biography*. http://www.oxforddnb.com/view/article/68220?docPos=4.

Lewis, Flora. "The Wound in Christ's Side and the Instruments of the Passion: Gendered Experience and Response." In *Women and the Book: Assessing the Visual Evidence*, ed. Lesley Smith and Jane Taylor, 204-229. London: British Library, 1997.

Love, Nicholas. *The Mirror of the Blessed Life of Jesus Christ*. Edited by Michael G. Sargent. Exeter, UK: University of Exeter Press, 2005.

Mack, Frances. M. *Seinte Marherete Þe Meiden ant Martyr*. EETS os. 193. London: Oxford University Press, 1934.

"Map of the Historic Counties of England." *Pictures of England*. http://www.picturesofengland.com/mapofengland/historic-uk-counties.html.

Matchinske, Megan. *Writing, Gender, and State in Early Modern England: Identity Formation and the Female Subject*. Cambridge, UK: Cambridge University Press, 1998.

McIntosh, Angus, M. L. Samuels, Michael Benskin. *A Linguistic Atlas of Late Medieval English*. 4 vols. Aberdeen, Scotland: Aberdeen University Press, 1986, 1:115.

McKenzie, D. F., and Maureen Bell. *A Chronology and Calendar of Documents Relating to the London Book Trade, 1641–1700*. 2 vols. Oxford: Oxford University Press, 2005.

Millett, Bella, ed. *Ancrene Wisse: A Corrected Edition of the Text in Cambridge, Corpus Christi College, MS 402, with Variants from Other Manuscripts*. 2 vols. EETS os. 325. Oxford: Oxford University Press, 2005-2006.

———. "The Pastoral context of the Trinity and Lambeth Homilies." in *Essays in Manuscript Geography: Vernacular Manuscripts of the English West*

Midlands from the Conquest to the Sixteenth Century. ed. Wendy Scase, 43-64. Turnhout, Belgium: Brepols, 2007.

Millett, Bella, with George B. Jack and Yoko Wada. *Annotated Bibliographies of Middle English Literature: II. Ancrene Wisse, the Katherine Group, and the Wooing Group*. Cambridge, UK: D.S. Brewer, 1996.

Morris, Richard,. ed., introd., and transl., *Old English Homilies and Homiletic Treatises of the Thirteenth Centuries*. EETS os. 29. (Oxford: Oxford University Press, 1868).

——, ed., intro., and trans. *Legends of the Holy Rood: Symbols of the Passion and Cross-Poems*. EETS os. 46. London: N. Trübner & Co., 1871.

Nichols, Stephen. "Introduction: Philology in a Manuscript Culture." *Speculum* 65:1 (January, 1990).

Northwood, John. *A Worcestershire Miscellany*. Edited by Nita Baugh. Bryn Mawr, PA: Bryn Mawr College, 1956.

Omont, Henri. "Anciens catalogues de bibliotheques anglaises (XIIe–XIVe siècle)." *Zentralblatt für Bibliothekswesen* 9 (May 1892): 207–222.

Page, William, ed. "Houses of Augustinian Canons: The Priory of Lanthony by Gloucester." In *A History of the County of Gloucester*, vol. 2. British History Online. http://www.british-history.ac.uk/report.aspx?compid=40276.

Pecock, Reginald. *Þe folewer to Þe Donet*. Edited by E. V. Hitchcock. EETS os. 164. Oxford: Oxford University Press, 1924, reprinted 1971.

Pinto, Augusto Cardosa. *A cruz processional de capela de D. Catarina de Bragança, rainha de Inglaterra*. Lisboa: Fundacão de Casa de Bragança, 1956.

Poole, Reginald. "Review of British Museum. *Catalogue of Western Manuscripts in the Old Royal and King's Collections* by George F. Warner, Julius P. Gilson." *English Historical Review* 37:147 (July 1922): 450-458.

Rees, David Daniel. "David Baker (Augustine)." In *Oxford Dictionary of National Biography*. http://www.oxforddnb.com/view/article/1110?docPos=1 .

Robbins, Rossell Hope. "The 'Arma Christi' Rolls." *Modern Language Review* 34:3 (July 1939): 415–421.

Robinson, Pamela. "The 'Booklet': A Self-Contained Unit in Composite Manuscripts." *Codicologica* 3 (1980): 46–69.

Rowlands, Marie B. "Recusant Women 1560–1640." In *Women in English Society 1500–1800*, ed. Mary Prior, 149–180. London: Methuen, 1985.

Sandler, Lucy Freeman. *Gothic Manuscripts 1285–1385*. 2 vols. *A Survey of Manuscripts Illuminated in the British Isles*, gen. ed. J. J. G. Alexander. London: Harvey Miller, 1986.

Sargent, Michael. "What Kind of Writing Is *A Talkying of Þe Love of God?*' In

The Milieu and Context of the Wooing Group, ed. Susannah M. Chewning, 178-193. Cardiff: University of Wales Press, 2009.

Savage, Anne. "The Communal Authorship of *Ancrene Wisse.*" In *A Companion to* Ancrene Wisse, ed. Yoko Wada, 45-56. Cambridge, UK: D. S. Brewer, 2003.

Savage, Anne, and Nicholas Watson, trans. and intro. *Anchoritic Spirituality:* Ancrene Wisse *and Associated Works*. New York: Paulist Press, 1991.

"Schēlden." *Middle English Dictionary*. http://quod.lib.umich.edu/cgi/m/mec/med-idx?type=byte&byte=176742559&egdisplay=compact&egs=176766491.

Simpson, James. "Diachronic History and the Shortcomings of Medieval Studies." In *Reading the Medieval in Early Modern England*, ed. David Matthews and Gordon McMullan, 17-30. Cambridge, UK: Cambridge University Press, 2007.

Skemer, Don C. *Binding Words: Textual Amulets in the Middle Ages*. University Park: Pennsylvania State University Press, 2006.

Smith, Kathryn. *Art, Identity, and Devotion in Fourteenth-Century England*. London: British Library, 2003.

Snook, Edith. *Women, Reading, and the Cultural Politics of Early Modern England*. Aldershot, UK: Ashgate, 2005.

Summit, Jennifer. *Lost Property: The Woman Writer and English Literary History, 1380–1589*. Chicago and London: University of Chicago Press, 2000.

Thompson, W. Meredith. *Þe Wohunge of Ure Lauerd*. EETS os. 241. Oxford: Oxford University Press, 1958.

Tuke, Lady, to Mary Evelyn. March 20, 1681[–2]. British Library, Evelyn MS ME6.

Warner, George F., and Julius P. Gilson. *Catalogue of Western Manuscripts in the Old Royal and the King's Collections*. 4 vols. London: British Museum, 1921.

Watson, Andrew G. *The Manuscripts of Henry Savile of Banke*. London: Bibliographic Society, 1969.

Watson, Nicholas. "Afterward: 'On Eise.'" In *The Milieu and Context of the Wooing Group*, ed. Susannah Mary Chewning, 194-210. Cardiff: University of Wales Press, 2009.

Watson, Nicholas, and Anne Savage. *Anchoritic Spirituality*. New York: Paulist Press, 1991.

Wilson, R. M. *Sawles Warde, an Early Middle English Homily*. Leeds, UK: Leeds School of English, 1938.

Winstead, Karen A., trans. and intro. *Chaste Passions: Medieval English Virgin Martyr Legends.* Ithaca, NY: Cornell University Press, 2000.

Wood, Anthony. *Athenae Oxonienses. An Exact History of all the Writers and Bishops Who Have Had Their Education in the University of Oxford.* 4 vols. London: Printed for F.C. and J Rivington, 1813-1817, 3rd ed.

Wormald, Francis, and Phyllis M. Giles. *A Descriptive Catalogue of the Additional Manuscripts in the Fitzwilliam Museum Acquired between 1895 and 1979 (Excluding the McClean Collection).* 2 vols. Cambridge, UK: Cambridge University Press, 1982.

Wynne, S. M. "Catherine of Braganza." In *Oxford Dictionary of National Biography.* http://www.oxforddnb.com/view/article/4894?docPos=1.

Map 1: The Historic Counties of England.
(From http://www.picturesofengland.com/mapofengland/historic-uk-counties.html)

How Francis Thynne Read His Chaucer

MEGAN COOK

The ambitions of Francis Thynne (c.1545–1608), antiquarian and herald, far outstripped his accomplishments. What we know of his personal life, marred by persistent financial problems, an unhappy marriage, and "that cruel tyrant the unmerciful gout," suggests it was not a pleasant one. In his professional life he was marginally more successful, but despite the zeal with which he pursued his studies in the fields of alchemy, arms, and British antiquities, he produced no major works of his own, and it would be possible to write a history of any of these fields in early-modern England without special reference to his contributions. Nevertheless, if not an innovator like his friends William Camden and Sir Robert Cotton, Thynne was a solid, contributing citizen of his milieu, whom an admiring Frederick Furnivall described as "at least high in the second rank of antiquaries of his day."[1] He was a member of the Elizabethan Society of Antiquaries, contributed work on Scotland to the revised edition of Holinshed's *Chronicles*, and in 1602 was created Lancaster Herald, achieving his long-standing goal of admission to the College of Arms.

Like his better-known contemporary Camden, he counted William Cecil, Lord Burghley, among his patrons; he also found favor with luminaries such as William Brooke, Lord Cobham; Thomas Egerton, Lord Chancellor; and Henry Howard, Earl of Northampton. Also like Camden, who became Clarenceaux King at Arms in 1597, Thynne's antiquarian studies complemented and at times overlapped with his duties as herald. At his death in late 1608, Thynne left writings in manuscript on historical, genealogical, and alchemical topics, in addition to his contributions to various printed volumes. Many of Thynne's manuscripts found their way into Cotton's famous library, and today more than fifty survive.[2] These manuscripts suggest a scholar whose interests, though diverse, centered around an ardent desire to understand the past in all its dimensions. In the words of Thynne's bibliographer, David Carlson:

> no single contemporary figure better than Francis Thynne, both by the nature of his various interests and by the ways in which he combined the kinds of knowledge he acquired, confirms that all the forms of Elizabethan science, in the broad sense of the term, embodied a single, unified way of thinking about things.[3]

In important ways, Francis charted his own path in Tudor society, but he was also the son of William Thynne, chief clerk in the kitchens of Henry VIII. In 1532, the elder Thynne, working in conjunction with Brian Tuke, another courtier-cum-antiquarian, produced the first single-volume edition of Chaucer's *Works*. In a letter dedicating the volume to Henry, Thynne explains that as "divers imprints" came into his hands, he "easily and without great study might and have deprehended in them many errours, falsities, and depravation."[4] With "cost and pain," he writes, he obtained for his edition "very true" copies of those works of Chaucer's that had already been printed, as well as those that were "never till now imprinted, but [were] remaining almost unknowne, and in oblivion."[5] With additions and some alterations, the 1532 text remained the basis for all printings of Chaucer's *Works* until the eighteenth century.[6]

Although William Thynne died in 1546, when Francis was just a year or two old, Francis claimed to have inherited from his father a singularly impressive collection of Chaucer manuscripts, including one bearing numerous inscriptions reading "examinatur Chaucer."[7] Unfortunately, Francis was unable to hold onto this remarkable collection, selling some manuscripts in the 1570s during a period of acute financial distress that culminated in two years' imprisonment in the White Lion in Southwark. The remaining manuscripts, he says, were later stolen from his house in Poplar.

Despite the loss of this collection, Thynne apparently planned his own edition of Chaucer, one that would "set out Chaucer with a Coment in our tongue, as the Italians haue Petrarke and others in their language."[8] An edition of Chaucer modeled on the popular annotated editions of Italian poets would, no doubt, have served to bolster the reputation of both poet and commentator.[9] There is no evidence that, prior to 1598, Thynne had actually taken any practical steps toward such an edition. Nevertheless, he took exception to the appearance of Thomas Speght's edition of the *Works*, published that same year. While the text of Speght's edition is based on the 1561 edition of John Stow, who is in turn relying on the work of William Thynne,

Speght's edition adds two new poems ("The Flower and the Leaf" and the "Assembly of Ladies") and, more important from Thynne's perspective, a host of interpretive devices. As described on the *Works'* frontispiece, these include an account of Chaucer's progeny, a biographical sketch, arguments to "every book," a glossary of more than two thousand "hard words," a list of authors cited, and various "difficulties opened." While Speght's engagement with the text is limited, the paratextual apparatus as a whole testifies to a new level of editorial self-consciousness.

Thynne responded to this new edition with an open letter addressed to Speght, bearing the prolix title *Animadversions uppon the Annotations and Corrections of some imperfections of impressions of Chaucers workes (sett downe before tyme, and nowe) reprinted in the yere of oure lord 1598*. In it, Thynne praises his father's edition and accuses Speght of depriving him of his rightful patrimony as a Chaucerian editor. (Though Thynne was in his late fifties in 1598, his spirited defense of his father's work suggests that his interest in recovering "Father Chaucer" has something to do with his own absent father.)[10] The letter describes, often in great detail, more than fifty errors that Thynne finds in Speght's edition. These are mostly not in the text of the poems themselves but in the biographical sketch, genealogical diagrams, and hard-word lists that accompany them—the places where Thynne's expertise as a scholar overlaps with Speght's most visible presence as an editor. Speght seems to have received Thynne's corrections graciously but not unreservedly, and incorporates many (but not all) of them in the revised edition of the *Works* published in 1602.

This, then, is one way in which Francis Thynne read his Chaucer, specifically Speght's 1598 Chaucer: as an edited collection that could be critiqued on the basis of the conventions of sixteenth-century antiquarian scholarship. This in itself marks an important shift in the history of Chaucerian reading: Thynne, like Speght, approaches the text not only as an aesthetic object, but as a site for historical inquiry, no longer simply for a general readership but also fit for study as part of the collective heritage of something recognizable, through geographical, political, and (increasingly) linguistic unity, as England.

Thynne's querulous letter would have likely been forgotten entirely had he not presented a copy to his patron Sir Thomas Egerton, Lord Ellesmere, in December 1599.[11] The manuscript survives, and in 1875 Frederick Furnivall edited it for the Early English Text Society, thus making it accessible to generations of Middle English scholars. Their assessments, by and large, have not been kind. The *Animadversions* is often dismissed as the work of a hack jealous for his father's reputation. To be fair, Thynne is not a particularly accurate or insightful scholar. In the words of Derek Pearsall, "his judgment is poor, his understanding of context unsound, and he lacks all sense of the difference between important and trivial matters. He is, in fact, the perfect pattern of the pedant."[12] Yet the very things that make the *Animadversions* so objectionable to contemporary scholars afford a better understanding of the place of Chaucer and his works in scholarly discourse at the end of the sixteenth century. For Francis Thynne, Chaucer's poems clearly did not dwell in a separate literary realm but were a part of the native historical inheritance that he sought to document, study, and popularize throughout his career.

The form and content of Thynne's notes on Chaucer are consistent with his other antiquarian writings, especially the papers he delivered to the Society of Antiquaries in the 1590s and the first decade of the seventeenth century. These short treatises would have been delivered orally to the Society, which met regularly in the quarters of William Dethick, Garter King of Arms, to discuss a preset topics ranging from the history of sterling money to the origin of the shire as a division of land and the historical role of the Earl Marshall in the English court. Although it is impossible to say how many papers Thynne wrote and delivered in the years the Society was active (roughly 1590 to 1607), his work features prominently in the collection of materials related to the Society of Antiquaries compiled by the eighteenth-century antiquarian Thomas Hearne.[13] Like the *Animadversions*, these were papers prepared for an audience of peers by professionals working within a commonly understood framework of scholarly practice. We know Thynne revised his work because in several cases we have in manuscript an early draft of papers that Hearne printed in a revised state.

Thynne engaged in a similar practice when it came to his comments on Chaucer. Thynne's copy of the 1598 edition of Speght's *Works*, preserved today by the Houghton Library at Harvard University, shows evidence of a sustained scholarly engagement with the poet's work.[14] The book has been trimmed and rebound and is now a sophisticated copy incorporating leaves from at least one other codex. While some of Thynne's annotations may be lost entirely as a result, in many places it is possible to reconstruct the content, if not the exact wording, of notes surviving in partial form. The sheer volume of notes, all written in Thynne's distinctive script, indicates that he was a much more engaged reader of the *Works* than has previously been assumed and that he may even have made significant progress toward the commentated version of Chaucer that he speaks about in the *Animadversions*.

Broadly speaking, these notes can be grouped into two categories: those concerned with the historical context of Chaucer's life and works and those concerned with the particulars of Chaucer's language, either within the context of the poems themselves or as discussed in the supplementary materials found at the back of the *Works*. Both categories make it clear that Thynne was just as interested in Speght's work as an editor as in the poems themselves and that he approached both Chaucer's writing and Speght's commentary from the intellectual perspective of an early-modern antiquarian rather than as poet or literary critic. In margins and on blank leaves, Thynne offers hundreds of additions, revisions, and amplifications to Speght's own biographic, linguistic, and historical commentary. His comments in effect insert Chaucer into a growing body of knowledge about the English past— especially but by no means solely its great and powerful characters—being produced through the activities of chronicle historians such as Holinshed, antiquarians such as William Camden, and the more prosaic scholarship of the Society of Antiquaries.

Copies of sixteenth-century editions of Chaucer's *Works* are not infrequently annotated,[15] but the notes in the Thynne copy are of considerable interest because they can be identified as the work of a single specific reader. Moreover, they can be dated to the decade between 1598, the year of publication, and Thynne's death, which probably occurred in late 1608. Some of Thynne's annotations to the volume must predate 1602 because they include the rough draft of the two prefatory poems he contributed to the revised edition of the *Works* that appeared in that year. His use of the volume continued after the appearance of the revised *Works* until at least 1605, as indicated by a note on "the Dreame of Chaucer" (the "Book of the Duchess") which makes reference to the edition of John Stow's *Annals* published that year.[16] Many of the criticisms that Thynne voices in the *Animadversions* are recognizable; for example, he writes on folio 10r that Katherine Swynford's children by John of Gaunt were born prior to their marriage, and on 14v he supplements Speght's note about "Iohn Cuthenbergus, knight" with alternative accounts of the invention of printing taken from the work of the German theologian David Chytraeus and from Matthew Parker's life of Tomas Burchier.[17] Although it is not possible to determine whether the annotations were made before or after Thynne wrote his letter to Speght, both comments are also found in the *Animadversions*.

As these examples indicate, while Thynne's notation is scattered throughout the volume, he focuses most closely on the paratextual material added by Speght. I would suggest two reasons for this emphasis: first, it provides the best opportunity for Thynne to engage with the *Works* in a scholarly capacity; and second, its presence marks the clearest difference between the 1598 edition and his father's. Within this paratextual realm, Thynne devotes the most attention to Speght's historical and lexicographical commentary, passing over Speght's discussion of aesthetic and scholarly issues with little comment.[18]

The notes to Speght's "Arguments to Every Tale and Book," which follow the "Life of Chaucer," provide the first indication that Thynne has done more than track down Speght's errors. The arguments are short summaries of each of the *Canterbury Tales* and most of Chaucer's longer poems, with an occasional comment on source or genre; Derek Pearsall characterizes them as "short, pithy, and accurate for the most part."[19] Thynne does not dispute Speght's characterization of the form or content of the poems. Instead, he focuses on Chaucer's sources and analogues, topics generally left unexamined by Speght. Although in the context of the *Works* Thynne's comments appear as literary, the concerns behind them are analogous to the preoccupations with source and influence that mark his genealogical and heraldic work and Tudor antiquarian scholarship more generally. The papers presented at the Society's meetings focus by and large on the history of institutions and concepts whose importance is readily recognized in the present; Chaucer's reputation as a national poet makes the history of his works a kind of literary analogue to a study of the development of currency in Britain or the pedigree of a noble family.

Thynne identifies sources or analogues for thirteen of the *Canterbury Tales* in total, relying in many cases on his knowledge of Gower and Boccaccio. He writes that the Knight's Tale is "oute of the theseidee [sic] of Bocas but not wholy," and discounts the Franklin's Tale's self-identification as a Breton lay, writing instead that "[this?] is Taken oute of Fi]lo-copo of Bocas."[20] Thynne also demonstrates thorough knowledge of Gower's *Confessio Amantis*. Perhaps influenced by Leland and Bale's identification of Gower as a poetic mentor for Chaucer, Thynne finds correspondences between a number of the Tales and Gower's poem, including the Man of Law's Tale, the Wife of Bath's Tale, the Canon's Yeoman's Tale, the Physician's Tale, and the Maniciple's Tale. Here, too, are the first of Thynne's many notes pertaining to the *Roman de la Rose*, which he appears to have known primarily through Jean Molinet's early sixteenth-century prose moralization.[21] While Speght writes of Chaucer's *Romaunt* that "this booke was made in French by John Clopinell, *alias* John Moon," Thynne adds that it was begun by "Guilliam Loris" and only finished by Jean de Meune. In a related comment at the top of the page, Thynne also notes the existence of Jean Gerson's rebuttal of the *Roman de la Rose*, and offers a capsule summary of the ensuing *querelle*.

Thynne is also interested in Chaucer's use of works without a named author. He writes of the Second Nun's Tale that "this tale of St. Cecyle haue I in written hande compiled in verses whiche Chaucer hathe holy fowlowed in the matter but not in the forme of the verse." In an unusual (for Thynne) comment on versification, he clarifies further that, in the Second Nun's Tale, "chaucer hathe formened into one other staffe & he must adde somethynge more: therefore to make the verse the fuller," one of several early-modern comments indicating struggle to recover the rules of Middle English versification. This interest in source material carries through to marginal notes on the text itself, as at the incipit of "Anelida and Arcite," where Thynne quotes

"Frausus [Fransus?]," author of a work "de insignibus," on Corinna's supposed victory over Pindar.[22]

Thynne's annotations bring to mind the activities of a more widely celebrated annotator of early-modern books, the humanist, scholar, and friend of Spenser, Gabriel Harvey. Like Thynne, Harvey owned and annotated a copy of the 1598 edition of the *Works*, and while early copies of Chaucer are not infrequently marked by readers, Harvey's and Thynne's books constitute two rare occasions where marginalia can be attributed to a specific annotator and situated within the broader record of that annotator's intellectual engagement. In the case of Harvey, more than one hundred annotated books survive out of the perhaps 3,500 volumes that constituted his library.[23] In the case of Thynne, his notes to Chaucer can be compared both with the more polished text of the *Animadversions* and with his antiquarian writings more generally.

Though the paths of the two men probably did not cross, they were members of the same generation: Harvey was born in 1550, just a few years after Thynne. Both pursued scholarly and courtly vocations with limited success and both experienced significant professional frustrations and setbacks. Only Harvey had the benefit of university training, an important distinction, since while both men read widely and deeply, Thynne cannot be called a "humanistically trained reader" in the same sense as Harvey.[24] Harvey was a prodigious collector of books despite financial setbacks, while Thynne, perpetually in penury, seems to have owned far fewer volumes. Conversely, as a professional researcher Thynne probably spent much more time with older archival materials, including the records of the Exchequer and Parliament rolls from which he cites in the *Animadversions*.

Harvey's annotations have been widely studied, most notably by intellectual historians Anthony Grafton and Lisa Jardine. In an influential 1990 essay, "'Studied for Action': How Gabriel Harvey Read His Livy," Jardine and Grafton describe Harvey's characteristically humanistic mode of reading and annotating as one that is "intended to *give rise to something else*"[25] This practice "characteristically envisaged some other outcome of reading beyond accumulation of information," whether that outcome was action in the political, legal, religious, or cultural sphere. Examining annotations in Harvey's copy of Livy, which represent a series of discrete readings over the course of several decades, Grafton and Jardine consider Harvey's engagement with Livy in a variety of personal and professional contexts and trace the ways in which the exigencies of a particular occasion for reading shape Harvey's annotations.

Like Thynne, Harvey owned and annotated a copy of the 1598 edition of Chaucer's *Works*.[26] Though Harvey lived until 1630, it is one of the latest of his surviving books in terms of date of publication. It was probably read and annotated by Harvey during his embittered retirement in his ancestral home at Saffron Walden in Essex, to which Harvey had retreated in the aftermath of his pamphlet war with university wit Thomas Nashe, which had culminated in 1596 with Nashe's *Have with You to Saffron-Walden*.[27] While Harvey, withdrawn from public life, cannot be said to have studied his Chaucer "for action" in the same way he had read his Livy decades earlier, the substantial annotations nevertheless show a sustained interest in the relationship between the Middle English poet's world and the literary and intellectual world of early-modern England.

There are several possible ways of aggregating Harvey's annotations to his Chaucer and comparing them to Thynne's: their nature, their density, their position within the text, and their content. In their reading of Harvey's Livy, Grafton and Jardine stress that Harvey, like other humanistic readers, did not read or annotate books in isolation, instead working with several volumes systematically. Although Harvey copied few passages directly from other volumes into his Chaucer, his comments nevertheless show that he thought through Chaucer in conjunction with other texts both classical and contemporary.

Like the Thynne copy, Harvey's Chaucer, now held at the British Library, shows evidence of a reader interested in both the text itself and in Speght's commentary upon it.[28] The differences in the ensuing commentary are illustrative of the differences between a materialist-antiquarian and philosophic-humanistic reading paradigm. First, Harvey, much more than Thynne, is interested in questions of poetic excellence. While references to Chaucer in marginalia found in other books owned by Harvey indicate a special regard for Chaucer's scientific acumen, especially as demonstrated in the *Treatise on the Astrolabe*, Harvey considers him here first and foremost as the paradigmatic English-language poet.[29] Second, Harvey is primarily concerned with the writers and writing that come after Chaucer. By commenting on later poets, he populates the span of literary history between Chaucer's compositions and his own reading of them with notables such as Skelton, Hawes, Spenser, Sidney, Shakespeare, and Ascham. Thynne, by contrast, looks backward from Chaucer as he considers the historical and literary factors that informed his writing. Although elsewhere in his writing he displays a particular fondness for the works of Edmund Spenser, in his notes to the *Works*, everything he describes or references happened before or, at the latest, during Chaucer's lifetime.

These differences play out in the notes that both men make to the "Arguments" section of their respective copies of the *Works*. Unlike Thynne, who takes them as prompts to consider sources for the poems, Harvey uses the space around Speght's arguments to the *Canterbury Tales* to provide his own brief characterizations of plot and genre. Harvey observes, for example, that the Knight's Tale contains "historical pageants," while in the same space in his own copy Thynne writes, "this tale is take oute of the theseidee of Bocas but not wholy for Chaucer begynnethe not . . . muche about a quarter of the booke be ended." The printed account of the Shipman's Tale leads Harvey to remark on "The Smithes tale, in the new Canterburie Tales," but as Speght has already identified the source of the tale ("Bochas in his Nouels") Thynne makes no further comment. Such annotations might be intended to aid in extracting quotations from the Tales themselves or to assist in comparison with other works of similar theme or genre.[30]

Perhaps most tellingly, in addition to the interest in Chaucer's influence displayed in his list of later writers, Harvey's reading of Chaucer is highly sensitive to the implications and applications of the poems. Throughout the volume, passages are marked for entry into a commonplace book or summarized in a way that highlights their topical relevance outside the text. Thynne's annotations, by contrast, show only a passing interest in the moral content of the poems. Instead, they record Thynne's efforts to understand the text better by illuminating its historical circumstances and lexical particularities. Notably, the hard-word list is among the most heavily annotated sections in Thynne's copy of the *Works* but is left completely untouched by Harvey. Conversely, while the section of Speght's biographical sketch of Chaucer entitled "His Books" prompts Harvey's litany of later writers, is left totally unannotated by Thynne.

Most notably, Harvey's marginalia is full of musings on the later history of English literature, including, famously, the earliest mention of Shakespeare's *Hamlet*. Harvey's discussions primarily concern the literary merit of post-Chaucerian English writers. Although he discusses some classical and continental authors, these tend to be the sixteenth-century writers. In other words, one way of understanding Harvey's notes is as an overview of Chaucerian influence, cataloging the accomplishments in English literature either enabled or anticipated by Chaucer. To adopt this position, of course, one must embrace the early-modern view that Chaucer really was the singular "well of English undefiled" who, by his poetic and linguistic invention, made his native vernacular fit for serious literary work. One must also approach Chaucer primarily as a literary figure rather than viewing him, as Thynne does, as a historical personage interesting in part because of his connections with other well-placed individuals.

While we are left to speculate as to what application, if any, Gabriel Harvey may have had in mind when annotating his Chaucer, Thynne's notes trace a "purposeful reading in process" like that found by Grafton and Jardine in Harvey's Livy. Thynne's remarks in the *Animadversions* and Speght's comments concerning Thynne's contributions to the revised 1602 edition of Chaucer tell us that Francis Thynne had hoped to produce an annotated edition of the *Works*; his reading is thus dedicated to producing the kind of commentary that would both reflect the erudition of its author and guide other readers, perhaps readers like Harvey, in their own engagement with the text. Though this work was never completed, the *Animadversions* give us some sense of what commentary by Thynne might have looked like: heavy on the historical details and factual assertions. Though Thomas Speght writes, in the revised address to the reader in 1602, that Francis Thynne had "had a purpose . . . to set out Chaucer with a Coment in our tonge, as the Italians haue *Petrarke* and others in their language," his commentary, as well as Speght's, is more strongly reminiscent of English antiquarian scholarship.[31]

Thynne displays a concern with accuracy and rectitude that begins in his notes to the biographical sketch of Chaucer and carries over into his engagement with the poems themselves. Discrete passages throughout the volume (but especially in the earlier sections) are heavily annotated by Thynne, who emends line readings, identifies allusions, and cross-references difficult words with entries in Speght's glossary. In the *Canterbury Tales*, parts of the General Prologue, the Knight's Tale, and the Squire's Tale receive line-by-line attention, as do passages from the *Romaunt of the Rose*, which Thynne compares closely with Jean Molinet's prose moralization. In many places, however, Thynne is just as concerned with proper contextual understanding as with textual accuracy. Sprinkled throughout the *Works* are marginal references to historical writers like Thomas of Walsingham and Matthew of Paris, whom Thynne uses to explain difficult allusions and references to historical events and persons. In total, he cites more than forty outside sources. The appearance of these secondary references suggests a liminal position for the *Works* in Thynne's intellectual landscape, at once literary and historical: on the one hand, he turns to familiar historical works in order to establish dates and confirm names within Chaucer's text; on the other, Thynne draws on Molinet to better understand the literary context of Chaucer's translation of the *Roman de la Rose* and his comments to the Arguments indicate that he knew some medieval texts, such as Gower's *Confessio Amantis*, very well.

Like Stow's edition of 1561, the 1598 edition of the *Works* makes use of a woodcut frame from the 1550 edition of Edward Hall's chronicle *The Union of the Two Noble and Illustre Famelies of Lancastre and York*. Here the woodcut serves as an internal title page for both the *Canterbury Tales* and the *Romaunt of the Rose*, as well as for Lydgate's *Siege of Thebes*, added at the end of the volume just before the supplementary material. These pages are blank on the verso, and for the two Chaucer poems, Thynne has filled them with related historical notes. In the case of the *Canterbury Tales*, Thynne uses this space primarily for notes on locations mentioned in the General Prologue's description of the Knight.[32] While Thynne's marginal notes are mostly written in English, these notes are generally taken from secondary sources and written in Latin.

Thynne will not be the last scholar to attempt to identify the Knight as a historical personage, but he may be the first. In the margin opposite the beginning of the description of the Knight in the General Prologue, Thynne writes that the knight "semeth to me to be" Sir Matthew Gournay, a professional soldier of some renown who served John of Gaunt and died about 1406. As evidence he cites Gournay's epitaph, quoted in Camden's *Remains*.[33] Thynne draws heavily upon his antiquarian background in order to corroborate the Knight's itinerary: in the description of the Knight, he cites Holinshed, Walsingham, Hakluyt (who cites the General Prologue's portrait of the Knight in his famous *Navigations*), and Sebastian Munster (whom he refers to again in the description of the Monk and possibly the Pardoner), as well as "Pancirolus," either the elder or the younger of a father/ son pair of legal scholars. The careful cross-referencing no doubt reflects the zeal with which Thynne began the project, but it also hints at what the stakes of an identification might be for an antiquarian such as Thynne: if the knight can be shown to be an historical personage, can the other pilgrims, though more anonymous, be read as equally anchored in a particular time and place? By reading Chaucer's Knight in the context of the same sources that are the bread and butter of his antiquarian research, Thynne is practicing a kind of literary historicism *avant la lettre*.

Subsequent descriptions are less heavily annotated, but in the General Prologue, Thynne also begins his practice of correcting the text, which will carry on throughout the Tales and into the rest of the Works. Thynne clearly had strong ideas about how the text should read (largely based on his understanding of meter and Middle English pronunciation), but it is not always possible to reconstruct what motivates his changes. While many of his comments in the *Animadversions* concern cases in which Speght's reading differs from William Thynne's second edition of 1542, which Francis Thynne regarded as the fullest expression of his father's editorial practice, Thynne does not appear to have undertaken any sort of collation between the two. He lets many of Speght's changes stand (though in 1598 these are comparatively few, so slight that Derek Pearsall suggests they are as likely to derive from compositional error) and in many cases proposes emendations that contradict both the 1542 and the 1598 editions.[34]

Where do these changes come from? It is possible that Thynne had recourse to some manuscripts while working with the 1598 Works, which might explain why certain texts in which Thynne does not otherwise declare an interest, such as the Squire's Tale, are heavily corrected, while the text of other works in which Thynne might have taken an interest (*Troilus and Criseyde*, for one) are not. One particularly extended example of Thynne's corrective activities can be found on folios 27v to 28v, corresponding to modern fragment IV, lines 1257 to 1511. In this passage, encompassing roughly the first half of the Merchant's Tale, Thynne makes more than fifty changes to the text. These are idiosyncratic and not derived wholesale from any early printed edition, including the 1542 *Works*. A larger number of Thynne's emendations do correspond to readings found in Caxton's second edition of the *Canterbury Tales* (1483). It seems likely that Thynne had access to a copy of this edition, since he refers to it in the *Animadversions* and in a note to the Tale of Sir Thopas.

Whatever Thynne's sources and rationale may have been, in many cases his ambitions as a corrector clearly outstrip his abilities as a reader of Middle English. His emendation of "loue" to "leue" in the description of the Pardoner, "full loud song he, come hider loue soone," is just one case in which his suggested change further confuses the sense of a difficult line. In other instances, however, such his emendation of Speght's "whom to Athenes" to "hom to Athenes" at line 2701 of the Knight's Tale, his changes correct earlier missteps and improve the sense of the line.[35] Often, such corrections are a matter of good luck and patient reading, but his emendation of "Mereturicke" to "Mercenricke" in the Nun's Priest's Tale depends upon his knowledge of the ancient British kingdom of Mercia, knowledge more the purview of a specialist like Thynne than the apparent generalist Speght. This is an extreme example, but in Thynne's explicatory notes, one can easily grasp the utility of his historical approach.

When these corrections have a practical function for Thynne (a corrupted name or word cannot be researched or defined), their affinity with papers delivered at the Society of Antiquaries is readily apparent. The papers by Thynne and others, collected in Thomas Hearne's *Curious Discourses* (1721/1777), typically begin with an etymological analysis of the key terms under discussion; this method is influentially promoted in Jean Bodin's *Method for the Easy Comprehension of History*.[36] Thynne proceeds in a similar fashion in his note to the Monk's Prologue (80v), which suggests that the English word "dann" should be pronounced like the Spanish word "Don." He explains that the Spanish have a practice of "calling the same to euery greate estate or gentleman as Don ferdinando, don Alvarez," and suggests that both "dann" and "Don" have a common origin in the Latin *dominus*. Their divergence is a historical process: words "Such like" dann and Don "[are] contrac[te]d and in corruptone of dominis for so in tymes past was dominus writen and p[ro]nounced. . . . From dominus yt came to Domnis, from thence to Don and so to Dan emongst the English." In form and content, this note both mimics the etymological scholarship of early-modern antiquarians and anticipates the philologically and linguistically oriented work of eighteenth- and nineteenth-century Chaucerians.

As with the verso of the *Canterbury Tales* title page, Thynne uses the verso of the *Romaunt* title page as a sort of interior index or commonplace leaf on which to record relevant passages from other works. Typically and tellingly, Thynne uses it to reflect not on the poem itself or its reception but on its sources and relationship to other works by Chaucer. Thynne collects a number of references to romance as a genre in Chaucer's other works, including the Tale of Sir Thopas and *Troilus and Criseyde,* and transcribes from the *Legend of Good Women* the God of Love's judgment against Chaucer for translating the *Roman de la Rose.* He also copies two passages from the "olde french written Romaunt in vers" and compares them with the equivalent sections of Molinet's moralization, perhaps as part of an attempt to establish the accuracy and reliability of his preferred proxy for the Old French original. Unusually, Thynne also uses this space to make some notes on Chaucer's versification, writing that "in this Romaunt of the rose Chaucer varieth in the forme of his verse for he hathe in the same some of v. fete most of fowre fett and manye but of thre feete. some of 3 and a halfe & some of iiij and a halfe"; he then provides examples of each sort of line. Thynne's desire to situate Chaucer's *Works* in a network of texts and sources is also evident here: in his annotations to Chaucer's *Romaunt* he refers to the *Historia Britanniae* of Richard White, an Anglo-Catholic antiquary and jurist who lived and wrote abroad, and the French writer Bartholomeus Cassanaeus.

Mindful of the *Romaunt* as a translation, Thynne reads it with an according degree of distance. At folio 116r, for example, next to the line "within my twenty yere of age," he warns that "this must not be entended of chaucers age. for they are the wordes of the frenche moralizatoure. & of the olde written verse as I have noted in the page before jetting [jotting] downe the wordes of both those bookes," a reference to his notes on the title page. Perhaps because Thynne is most concerned with the relationships of the *Romaunt* to Molinet's *Roman de la Rose Moralisé* and through the Molinet to the Old French original, corrections are less dense in the *Romaunt* than in the most heavily annotated passages of the *Canterbury Tales,* though they do appear throughout. These alterations seem to be primarily for the sake of sense and meter, perhaps made using the guide that Thynne wrote out for himself on the verso of the title page.

Thynne also takes pains to note correspondences between the French source and Chaucer's text, and this care extends down to the level of individual words. Thynne effectively glosses certain words in the text, underlining them and jotting a synonym in the margin. The presence of the word in the margin is unusual; when Thynne encounters a hard word found in Speght's list, his usual practice is to underline it in the text and note the folio number opposite the entry for the word in the glossary. While other early-modern annotators add synonyms or short definitions in the margin opposite difficult words, Thynne's marginalia in the *Romaunt* do not seem to be evidence of his difficulty in comprehending Chaucer's language; rather,

Thynne is comparing Chaucer's words with those found in French sources. At folio 122r, for example, the word "nutmegges" is underlined and "nois mugades" is written in the margin, while on the same folio "arbres domeshes" is inscribed opposite Chaucer's "homely trees." This attention to Chaucer's French sources and their influence on Chaucer's lexicon anticipates the interests and even the methods of Joseph Mersand's influential work, *Chaucer's Romance Vocabulary.*[37]

Unfortunately, while Thynne leaves several substantive notes in the *Romaunt*, the layout of these pages leaves narrower margins than those found in the *Canterbury Tales*, and a greater portion of the material has been lost to trimming as a result. Those notes still legible suggest that in addition to language, Thynne was concerned with the overall structure of the work and recognized that it was only a partial translation of the French original. He first notes this at 129v, when he observes Chaucer omitting material corresponding to the fifteenth chapter of the prose romance, and at folio 142v he observes with some concern that "here do chaucer leave oute all that is in the Romant of the rouse in the proose moralized from the middle of the 25 chapter untille the 51 chapter with whiche he begynneth here agayne."

The specificity of these comments indicates that Thynne must have read the *Romaunt* with a copy of Molinet's text close to hand, either in manuscript or in one of several early sixteenth-century printed editions. In addition, Thynne's notes on the verso of the title page indicate that he had access to at least parts of the *Roman de la Rose* in the original Old French. It is not clear from his notes whether his preference for Molinet derives from the fact that it was easier for him to understand than the de Meun/Lorris text, or simply that he had more regular access to a copy of it. Thynne probably had at least some familiarity with French works in manuscript, since in the *Animadversions* he describes seeing a copy of the *Romance of the Rose* that is "the oldest written copye that eyer was (to be founde in Englande, yf my coniecture fayle me not) by the age of the french woordes," and his work as a genealogist and antiquary would have required him to handle Anglo-Norman documents.[38]

The *Canterbury Tales* and the *Romaunt of the Rose*, the first two texts in the *Works*, receive more of Thynne's comments than the rest of Chaucer's poetry combined. Thynne's annotations to the next work in the sequence, *Troilus and Criseyde*, are very light and concentrated on a four-folio section between 170v and 174r. This sharp drop-off might be a register of Thynne's declining interest in the project as a whole or lack of enthusiasm for the particular text, or it may simply reflect an absence of suitable exemplars or source material with which to compare the work (like other early-modern commentators, Thynne does not seem to recognize *Il Filostrato* as a source, despite his familiarity with Chaucer's use of Boccaccio in the *Canterbury Tales*). His most sustained comment is not on the text of *Troilus and Criseyde* at all, but on Robert Henryson's "Testament of Cressid," which is appended to it. Thynne underlines the references to Chaucer in the text and writes, "this testament of c[reseide] semeth by many p[laces?] here in not to be made [by Chay]cer for that he often men[tions?] Chaucers discourses of Troyl[us &] Cressed."[39] The "Testament" had been printed with Chaucer's *Works* since his father's first edition of 1532, and most early readers, including Shakespeare, seem to have taken it as a part of Chaucer's *Troilus*. Thynne is the first reader whose responses are preserved for us who attended carefully enough to the "Testament" to note the logical inconsistency of its ascription to Chaucer.

The same cannot be said of his treatment of Thomas Usk's *Testament of Love*, attributed here to Chaucer. Probably influenced by Speght's use of the work in his biographical sketch of Chaucer, Thynne writes in the margins of the autobiographical passages notes such as "Chaucer in disgrace of the Kinge," and "Chaucer restored to the Kinges favor." He is on firmer ground with the "Letter of Cupid" when he notes that "In the editione of 1542 yt is only intituled as the print is here / this is not Chaucers but oclyve (fol. 326)" and writes, next to the poet's reference to Chaucer's death, that "this pleynlye shews yt was none of chaucers . . . after his deathe for ch[aucer] dyed 25. October. 1400."[40]

Notably absent from Thynne's commentary is any more than a passing discussion of Chaucer's classical sources. When Thynne does observe classical references that are not already signaled by mention of the authority within the text, they are extraordinarily straightforward: he notes on folio 352, for example, on Chaucer's line "I woll now sing if that I can / The armes, and also the man" that the source is "Virgil l. primus eneados." This is not to say that Thynne is not well versed in classical imagery and mythology; he clearly is, as evidenced by a lengthy note on Athena/Minerva at folio 291, which breezily summarizes her role in the founding of Athens without citing a source. It seems likely, though, whether by preference or necessity, that Thynne's knowledge of such material came through medieval and early-modern sources rather than through direct engagement with the classical text. Rather than referring to Ovid directly, for example, he takes his summary of the Philomela story from Girolamo Cardano's *De consolatione* (Venice, 1541) in a note on the "Cuckow and the Nightengale."

As with many readers, it appears Thynne's attention to Chaucer's minor works was somewhat selective, although he provides several substantial explicatory comments to several pieces. His interest in heraldry helps explain his knowing observation, on the line "wearing of gilt spurres maketh no knight" that in the past knights were invested with a pair of gold spurs as part of their promotion from squire to knight, and that this accounts for the fact that "esquires" are called "spurrs" in certain parts of England (fol. 305v). Similarly, though no source is cited, the study of sepulchral arms probably accounts for Thynne's familiarity with a reference to St. Barbara in the church of St. Dominic in Naples, referred to in the margin of folio 344/343. An annotation to the "Parliament of Fowles," a poem Thynne gives only passing attention, bears special attention. In his comments on the line "and eke the hardie Asshe," Thynne makes a tantalizing reference to "the notes before in paper bound with this booke" (f. 249r). The only reference to the "Parliament of Fowles" in the printed prefatory materials is in the Arguments section, and this includes no material related to the ash. Nor is this line discussed in the *Animadversions*. The note would seem to indicate, then, that Thynne prepared further materials on Chaucer, at one time bound with the *Works*, which do not survive or have not been traced.

The most heavily annotated section of the *Works* is not the text at all but the material added by Speght at the back of the volume, especially the glossary, Speght's list of "the old and obscure words of Chaucer, explained." Thynne apparently made good use of this list, underlining some words and supplying folio references for many. In most cases where he adds a folio reference, he underlines the word in question both in the glossary and in the text. Thynne also makes his own additions to the list. Significantly, he does not provide explanations or definitions, suggesting that for Thynne the list functions as an index of lexical difference but not necessarily as a register of actual linguistic difficulty. Although lexical commentary is a major component of the *Animadversions*, space considerations mean he can add only the briefest of notes to Speght's definitions, as when he writes that "hasard," defined by Speght as "dicing," is "an especiall play at dice." Like the glossary itself, Thynne's additions are representatively distributed across the letters of the alphabet, suggesting that the list was compiled in the course of reading the *Works* rather than written in alphabetical order.[41]

Thynne also makes additions to Speght's list of "the French in Chaucer, translated" and adds more than thirty names to the list of "Most of the Authors cited by G. Chaucer in his works." These additions are not recounted in the *Animadversions* (although Thynne does criticize Speght for overlooking numerous authors); however, about a dozen appear in the revised list in Speght's 1602 edition. An addition to the entry on Geoffrey of Vinsauf in 1602 closely echoes the wording of Thynne's marginal note in his copy of the *Works*, raising the possibility that Speght saw Thynne's copy or that the two men had additional communication about the list.[42] Thynne also sets his hand to "Corrections of some faults, and Annotations vpon some places." In many cases he simply adds references to sources not cited by Speght, drawing upon authorities cited elsewhere in his notes, including Molinet, Natalis Comes, Matthew of Paris (especially on Hugh of Lincoln), John Gower, Thomas Walsingham, and William Caxton. Clearly, Thynne sees himself here engaged in a common project with Speght: both the list itself and the corrections to it are predicated on the notion that such a list is useful to have and a worthy part of the editor's project.

To modern readers, Thynne's notes can seem jarringly trivial or pedantic. Thynne often seems insensible to the poetic concerns that motivate modern literary study of Chaucer's poetry, and he refrains from positioning himself as a poetic successor to Chaucer, as do many fifteenth- and early sixteenth-century poets.[43] He is not a medieval reader of Chaucer, nor is he a modern scholar. Yet Thynne's concerns with lexicography, orthography, and historical context should not be unfamiliar to contemporary readers; this kind of commentary continues to form the bedrock of other sorts of aesthetic criticism. More important, Thynne's would not have been unfamiliar to his own contemporaries, the heralds, historians, and would-be collectors who moved in the circles around his patrons, Burghley and Howard, who admired luminaries like Cotton and Camden, and who participated with him in the activities of the Society of Antiquaries.

If Harvey's annotations to his Livy preserve for us the polysemous nature of humanistic reading practice, Thynne's notes to his Chaucer exemplify a related but substantively different way of reading, one that I would like to call antiquarian reading. While this mode of reading may address itself to a literary text, it privileges the production of knowledge about the text over interpretation of it. Concomitantly, it considers primarily the past's relationship to itself (as evident in Thynne's interest in Chaucer's sources) rather than (as in the case of Harvey's reading) its relationship or applicability to the present. In both cases, Chaucer, for both Thynne and Harvey a figure with a singular relationship to English poetry, lies at the center of the reading.

As shown above, Thynne and Harvey made recourse to a number of outside references, works, and historical materials, as well as to other literary texts they found to be related to Chaucer's work (see appendix). The contrast between the texts mentioned by each annotator is illustrative of the differences in their perspective. Harvey tends to look forward in his annotations, using Chaucer as a starting point for a broader consideration (both temporally and generically) of English literary traditions. Thynne, by contrast, tends to work backward from Chaucer, considering not influence on future writers but literary and historical sources. While Harvey moves forward and outward from Chaucer's text, Thynne moves backward and inward.

Thynne's work, marginal both bibliographically and to what we think of today as the history of reading, suggests we broaden our concept of the cultural and literary discourses in which Chaucer signified at the end of the sixteenth century and consider more seriously the role that scholarly readers played in shaping Chaucer's reception. Thynne does not appear to be one of those "congenial souls" that Dryden imagines treasuring Chaucer and loving his lines throughout the ages, and yet our studies of Chaucer's reception still focus primarily on those readers whose affective relationship to the text mirrors our own. Thynne represents a different part of the story but one that, as his careful notes, his influence on Speght, and the two dozen manuscripts that passed through his hands might suggest, nevertheless consists of some of the closest, most detailed, and best-informed encounters with the text.

Bowdoin College

APPENDIX

1. Authors and Texts Referred to by Gabriel Harvey in His Annotations to the 1598 Edition of Chaucer's Works

(Names and titles marked with an * are cited multiple times. Titles in brackets are inferred from Harvey's references to the text.)

Author (if given)	Work (if given)
Ludovico Ariosto	*Orlando Furioso*, trans. Sir John Harrington (1591)
Axiophilus (Harvey?)	
Guillaume de Salluste Du Bartas	Translations by Joshua Sylvester
Boethius	*Consolation of Philosophy*
–	*Cobler of Canterbury*
George Chapman	Translations of Homer
Chrysotechnus (Harvey?)	
Henry Constable	*Diana* (1594)
Samuel Daniel*	
Thomas Deloney	*The Gentle Craft (In Praise of Shoemakers)*
Thomas Drant	*Horace his Arte of Poetrie, Pistles and Satyrs*
Sir Edward Dyer	*Amaryllis*
Eunapius	*Lives of the Sophists*
Euripides	[Untraced translation]
Abraham Fraunce	*Countesse of Pembrokes Yuychurch* (1591)
William Gager	
George Gascoinge	*Posies* (1575)
Arthur Golding	*The Fifteen Books of Ovid's Metamorphoses* (1575)
John Gower*	
Roger Hakluyt	[*Principle Navigations*]
Hierocles of Alexandria	Commentary on the Golden Verses of Pythagoras

John Heywood*	Epigrams
Thomas Hoccleve	
Henry Howard, Earl of Surrey	
James VI, King of Scotland	
John Lydgate*	*Siege of Thebes*
Sir Thomas More*	*Works* (individual texts also cited)
–	*Mirror for Magistrates*
Stephanus Niger	*Commentarioli S. Nigri in aurea carmina Pythagorae*
Thomas John Owen	*Latin epigrammata*
Palingenius	*Zodiacus vitae*
Francisco Petrarch	*Translations of sonnets by Wyatt and others*
Thomas Phaer*	*The Seven First Bookes of the Eneidos of Virgil*
Flavius Philostratus	*Lives of the Sophists*
–	*The Pleasant History of John Winchcom*
Angelo Polizano	[untraced]
Sir Walter Raleigh	*Cynthia*
Seneca the Younger	*[Dialogues]*
William Shakespeare	*Venus and Adonis, Lucrece, Hamlet*
Sir Philip Sidney	*Astrophil and Stella, The Countess of Pembroke's Arcadia*
Edmund Spenser*	*Faerie Queene*
John Studley, Thomas Nuce, and Jasper Heywood	*Seneca his tenne Tragedies translated into English* (1581)
Thomas Newton	
Tarquino Tasso	*Gerusalemme Liberata*, trans. Richard Carew (1594)
Thomas Watson	
William Warner	*Albion's England*

2. *Authors and Texts Referred to by Francis Thynne in His Annotations to the 1598 Edition of Chaucer's Works*

(Names and titles marked with an * are cited multiple times)

Author (if given)	Work (if given)
A. Primary Sources	
–	Manuscript life of St. Cecilia
–	Rolls of Parliament*
–	Patent Rolls*
B. Literary Texts	
Giovanni Boccaccio	*Filostrato, Tesedia*
Gerolamo Cardano Geoffrey	*De Consolatione*
Chaucer	*Canterbury Tales* (Westminster, 1483, Caxton's 2nd ed.) *Works* (London, 1542; 2nd printing, William Thynne's ed.)
John Gower	*Confessio Amantis**
Horace	[*Ars Poetica*]
John Molinet	*Roman de la Rose Moralisé** (many references; Thynne appears to have undertaken a sustained comparison between Molinet's prose translation and Chaucer's own translation)
Ovid	*Metamorphoses*
Francesco Petrarch	*Trionfi* (an annotated edition)
Geoffrey of Vinsauf	[*Poetria Nova*]
Virgil	*Aeneid*
C. Historical Works	
William Camden	*Remaines of a Greater Worke, Concerning Britaine* (London, 1605)
Nicholas Gill	"his French history" (untraced)
Unidentified history of Ireland (poss. Holinshed?)	
Matthew of Paris	*Chronica Maiora* (London, 1571; ed. Matthew Parker)
–	"Notes of Hollingshedd" (Thynne's notes for rev'd 1587 ed. of the *Chronicle*)
Matthew Parker	*Life of Thomas Burchier, Archbishop of Canterbury*
John Stow	*Annales* (London, 1605)
[Jacques de Vitry]	*Historia Orientalis*

Thomas Walsingham	[*Historia Anglicana*]* (probably Matthew Parker's 1574 abridgement, *Historia Anglicana brevis*)
Richard White	"his[tory of] Br[i]ta[i]n" (untraced)
William of Malmesbury	*Libellus de regibus Saxonicus*

D. Reference Works: Legal, Cartographic, Lexicographic and Other

Guillelmus de Sancto Amore	[*Opera*]
Bartholomeus Anglicus	*De proprietatibus rerum*
Bartholomaeus Cassaneus	*Catalogus gloriae mundi*
David Chytraeus	
Natalis Comes	[*Mythologiae*]*
Mathaeus Dresser	*Isagoges historicae* (Leipzig, 1594)
Francesco Filelfo	
Robert Gaguin	*Les gestes romaines*
Galfridus Grammaticus	*Proptarum parvulorum sive clericorum*
"Hipomanus" (untraced; hagiographer?)	
John of Salisbury	*Policraticus*
Philip Melanchthon	
Sebastian Münster	*Cosmographia universalis*
Guido Panciroli	
Thomas Norton	*Ordinal of Alchemy*
Pliny the Elder	*Naturalis historia*
Ptolomey	[*Quadripartitum*]
Johannes Ravisius Texsor	*Officinae epitome*
Elias Reusner	*Basilicon, opus genealogicum catholicum* (Frankfurt, 1592)
Adriano Romano	*Parvum teatrum urbium** (Frankfurt, 1595)
Bonifacius Simoneta	*Persecutionum Christianorum historia*
Laurentius Surius	*De probatis sanctorum historiis* (Cologne, 1570–1577)
Symeon Metaphrastes	
Nicholas Upton	*The Armory of Honor*
Jean de Vigney	*Le jeu de éches moralisé*

NOTES

1. Francis Thynne, *Animadversions vppon the Annotacions and Corrections of Some Imperfections of Impressiones of Chaucers Workes... Reprinted in the Yere of Oure Lorde 1598*, ed. Frederick Furnivall, EETS o.s. 9 (London: Oxford University Press, 1876, rpt. 1965), xlv.

2. See David Carlson, "The Writings and Manuscript Collections of the Elizabethan Alchemist, Antiquary, and Herald Francis Thynne," *Huntington Library Quarterly* 52.2 (1989): 203–272.

3. Ibid., 203.

4. Geoffrey Chaucer, *The Works of Geffray Chaucer Newly Printed, with Dyuers Workes Whiche Were Neuer in Print Before* (London: Thomas Godfray, 1532), a.iiv (STC 5068).

5. Greg Walker and others have observed how Thynne's edition, with its dedication to Henry VIII, participates in Tudor policies of centralization and standardization, though Walker also argues that the inclusion of several didactic poems with the *Works'* prefatories constitutes a kind of critique of the increasingly autocratic monarch. See Greg Walker, *Writing under Tyranny: English Literature and the Henrician Reformation* (Oxford: Oxford University Press, 2005), 29–72.

6. These include reprints of Thynne's edition in 1542 and ca. 1550, an expanded edition in 1561 (with new texts supplied by the antiquarian John Stow), and Thomas Speght's edition of 1598 (revised and reprinted in 1602 and reprinted again in 1687). John Urry's edition of Chaucer's *Works*, eventually published in 1721, was the first to attempt a wholesale recollation from manuscripts. Thomas Tyrwhitt used a copy of the 1687 reprint as the basis of his 1775–1777 edition of the *Canterbury Tales*. On these editions, see William L. Alderson, "John Urry (1666–1715)," in *Editing Chaucer: the Great Tradition*, ed. Paul G. Ruggiers (Norman, OK: Pilgrim Books, 1984); see B. A. Windeatt, "Thomas Tyrwhitt (1730–1786)," in the same.

7. According to Thynne, his father had "commsione to serche all the liberaries of Englande for Chaucers Workes so that oute of all the Abbies of this Realme ... he was fully furnished the multitude of Bookes. emongest whiche, one coppye of some part of his wookres came to his handes subscribed in diuers places withe 'examinatur Chaucer'" (Thynne, *Animadversions*, 6). Since the *Works* were first published in 1532, such a quest could have been undertaken in that year at the very latest, a year before John Leland received his own commission to search the monastic libraries. No evidence of such a commission survives, if it ever existed. Simon Horobin suggests that the

manuscript referred to here may be British Library MS Egerton 2726, a copy of the *Canterbury Tales* later in the possession of Stephan Bateman (this corresponds with Thynne's claims in the *Animadversions* that a portion of his manuscripts were given or sold to Bateman). Egerton 2726 bears in several places the corrector's mark "ex.," but no mention is made of Chaucer. I am grateful to Professor Horobin for sharing with me this work, originally presented at the 2010 meeting of the New Chaucer Society.

8. Geoffrey Chaucer, *The Workes of our Antient and Learned English Poet, Geffrey Chaucer*, ed. Thomas Speght (London, Adam Islip, 1602), a.iv.

9. There are strong parallels between the prefatory materials in the Speght *Works* and fifteenth- and sixteenth-century editions of the *opera* of Dante and especially Petrarch, which include *vitae* of the poets and lists of their more difficult words, as well as substantial marginal explication, despite their comparatively small size. Some of the most widely printed Petrarchan commentaries were those of Alessandro Vellutello (also known for his commentary on Dante's *Commedia*) and Giovanni Andrea Gesualdo. The significant differences in the ways that these and other commentaries present Petrarch's life and works are explored in William J. Kennedy, "Versions of a Career: Petrarch and His Renaissance Commentators," in *European Literary Careers: The Author from Antiquity to the Renaissance*, ed. Patrick Cheney and Frederick A. de Armas (Toronto, ON: University of Toronto Press, 2002), 146–154.

10. In her introduction to *Refiguring Chaucer in the Renaissance*, Theresa Krier draws on Lacan and Klein to argue that in the *Animadversions*, Chaucer stands in for Thynne's own absent father, William, and that Chaucer's ability to fulfill this role for Francis is an expression of the "inexhaustibility" of Chaucer for Renaissance readers. See Theresa M. Krier, ed., *Refiguring Chaucer in the Renaissance* (Gainesville, FL: University Press of Florida, 1998), 7–9.

11. The *Animadversions* manuscript was purchased by Henry Huntington with the rest of the Bridgewater library in 1917 and is now San Marino, Huntington Library EL.34.B.11. The Ellesmere *Canterbury Tales*, now also held at the Huntington, was already in the possession of the Egerton family at the time Thynne wrote.

12. Derek Pearsall, "Thomas Speght," in *Editing Chaucer: The Great Tradition*, ed. Paul Ruggiers (Norman, OK: Pilgrim Press, 1984), 84.

13. Thomas Hearne, ed. *A collection of curious discourses written by eminent antiquaries upon several heads in our English antiquities*. 2nd ed. (London: W. and J. Richardson, 1771).

14. Cambridge, Harvard University, Houghton Library fMS 1221.

15. See, e.g., the copy in the Beinecke Library at Yale University described in Antonina Harbus, "A Renaissance Reader's English Annotations to Thynne's 1535 Edition of Chaucer's *Works*," *Review of English Studies* 59.240 (2008): 342–355. While the copy examined by Harbus is, like Thynne's, extensively

annotated by a single reader from the mid-sixteenth century, the anonymity of that reader makes it difficult to situate his or her notations within a broader intellectual context. See also Alison Wiggins, "What Did Renaissance Readers Write in Their Printed Copies of Chaucer?" *The Library: The Transactions of the Bibliographical Society* 9.1 (2008): 3–36, and Robert C. Evans, "Ben Jonson's Chaucer," *English Literary Renaissance* 19.3 (1989): 325-345.

16. Thynne quotes the following passage, taken from page 16 of the *Annals*, giving Stow as its source: "John de Vigney, in his Booke named The Moralization of the Chesse, sayeth that the same game of the Chesse, was deui[sed] by Xerxes the philosopher otherwise named philometor to reprove and correct the euill mynde of a famou[s Ty]rant called evill meridoch. kinge of Babilon as is supposed about the yere before Christes birthd 614."

17. On Swynford, see Thynne, *Animadversions*, 23. On the history of printing, see ibid., 27. Although there is no record of a Society of Antiquaries meeting to discuss the history of printing, Thynne might have known these sources through research for his 1587 letter to Burghley on the history of written communication, preserved in London, British Library MS Lansdowne 27, fols. 70-75v.

18. While Thynne comments extensively on Speght's "Life of Chaucer" in the *Animadversions*, no analogous notes are found in his copy of the *Works*. It seems likely that Thynne made notes elsewhere, as the Houghton copy does contain underlining in a number of passages in the "Life" touching on topics (the possibility that the Chaucers were merchants of the staple, the assertion that Gower and Chaucer both studied at the Inns of Court) taken up at greater length in the *Animadversions*.

19. Pearsall, "Thomas Speght," 76.

20. I use square brackets to indicate letters lost to trimming which I have supplied by conjecture.

21. Molinet's translation was printed at least three times in the early sixteenth century, by Guillaume Balsarin (Lyon, 1503), Anthoine Verard (Paris, 1511), and Michel Le Noir (Paris, 1521).

22. I have been unable to identify the text referred to here.

23. Harvey's library is described in Virginia F. Stern, *Gabriel Harvey: His Life, Marginalia and Library* (Oxford: Clarendon, 1979).

24. See Lisa Jardine and Anthony Grafton, "'Studied for Action': How Gabriel Harvey Read His Livy," *Past and Present* 129 (1990): 30.

25. Ibid.

26. Now London, British Library MS Additional 42518.

27. See Stern, *Gabriel Harvey*.

28. The prefatory materials have underlining for emphasis as well as bracketing and open commas in the margins.

29. A portion of Harvey's marginalia is printed in G. C. Moore Smith, ed., *Gabriel Harvey's Marginalia* (Stratford-upon-Avon, UK: Shakespeare Head, 1918). In his copy of Dionysius Periegetes, *Surueye of the World* (1572), 159, Harvey records some of the "Notable Astronomical descriptions in Chawcer, & Lidgate; fine artists in manie kinds, & much better learned then owre moderne poets." He begins with "Chawcers conclusions of the Astrolabie, still excellent, vnempeachable: especially for the Horizon of Oxford," and goes on to record a number of references to astrological and seasonal phenomena drawn from Chaucer's works and Lydgate's *Siege of Thebes*. Other references to Chaucer's *Astrolabe* can be found in Harvey's copy of John Blagrave, *The Mathematical Iewel* (London, 1585).

30. Harvey's commonplace book, to which he made additions until the early seventeenth century, is now London, British Library MS Additional 32494. Portions of it are published in Moore Smith, *Gabriel Harvey's Marginalia*. On humanistic note-taking and organizational practices, see Ann Blair, "Reading Strategies for Coping with Information Overload ca. 1550–1700," *Journal of the History of Ideas* 64.1 (2003): 11–28; and William H. Sherman, *Used Books: Marking Readers in Renaissance England* (Philadelphia: University of Pennsylvania Press, 2008).

31. Thomas Speght, "To the Reader," in Chaucer, *Works* (1602). Neither of Speght's editions comes close to providing the kind of detailed, dense marginal commentary found in sixteenth-century Italian editions of Petrarch, such as *Petrarcha con doi commenti sopra li sonetti et canzone. El primo del ingeniosissimo Misser F. Philelpho. L'altro del sapientissimo Misser A. da Tempo novamente addito. Ac etiam com lo commento del eximio Misser N. Peranzcne, overo Riccio Marchesiano sopra li Triumphi, con infinite nove acute & excellente expositione* (1522). Indeed, the margins of all the Tudor Chaucers are strikingly bare, with the exception of manicules in the margins of some sections of the 1602 edition of Speght's Chaucer (see Claire Kinney, "Thomas Speght's Renaissance Chaucer and the Solaas of Sentance in *Troilus and Criseyde*," in *Refiguring Chaucer in the Renaissance*, ed. Theresa M. Krier [Gainesville, FL: University Press of Florida, 1998], 66–84) and misinterpreted printers' marks in a 1550 edition (on this, see Joseph A. Dane, "Fists and Filiations in Early Chaucer Folios, 1532–1602," *Studies in Bibliography: Papers of the Bibliographical Society of the University of Virginia* 51 [1998]: 48–62). Moreover, unlike the Italian Trecento poets, once collected into a single volume, Chaucer's works are always published in their entirety and in large, monumental folios.

32. The transcript of the Harvard copy suggests these notes may be an attempt to identify the knight with Sir Miles de Stapleton, although Thynne's annotations to the description of the Knight in the General Prologue also offer Sir Matthew Gournay as a possible model. In his introduction to *The*

Anonimalle Chronicle 1333 to 1381, from a ms. Written at S. Mary's Abbey, York, and now in the Possession of Lieut.-Col. Sir William Ingilby, Bart., V.H. Galbraith (Manchester, UK: Manchester University Press, 1927), discusses Thynne's use of the manuscript and its connection to de Stapleton.

33. William Camden, *Remianes of a greater worke, concerning Britaine . . .* ([London]: G[eorge] E[ld] for Simon Waterson, 1605), 45.

34. Pearsall, "Thomas Speght," 79.

35. Line numbers are taken from the *Riverside Chaucer*.

36. See Jean Bodin, *Method for the Easy Comprehension of History*, trans. Beatrice Reynolds (New York: Columbia University Press, 1945).

37. See Joseph E. Mersand, *Chaucer's Romance Vocabulary* (New York: Comet Press, 1937). Mersand's role in consolidating a more contemporary conflation of Chaucer with the development of English is discussed in Christopher Canon, *The Making of Chaucer's English* (Cambridge, UK: Cambridge University Press, 1998).

38. Thynne, *Animadversions*, 74.

39. Chaucer, *Workes,* ed. Speght, fol. 194r.

40. Ibid., fol. 329r; the date of death is that given by Speght.

41. On the composition of Speght's glossary, see especially Johan Kerling, *Chaucer in Early English Dictionaries* (Leiden, The Netherlands: Leiden University Press, 1979), 15.

42. Thynne's note, largely trimmed, also seems to reference "his book entituled" and a "rhetorical figure." In addition, he strikes through Speght's claim that Richard's death occurred while hunting, substituting "at the siege of a castle" instead. In 1602, Speght revises this entry accordingly, writing that, "he did write in his book entituled *de artificio loue[n]di*, by way of example of mourning, vnder the Rethorical figure of Apostrophe, a complaint for the death of *Richard* the first, who was slaine with an arrow at the siege of the castle of Chalne in Normandie."

43. See Seth Lerer, *Chaucer and His Readers: Imagining the Author in Late-Medieval England* (Princeton, NJ: Princeton University Press, 1993).

WORKS CITED

Alderson, William L. "John Urry," in *Editing Chaucer: The Great Tradition*, edited by Paul G. Ruggiers, 93-117. Norman, OK: Pilgrim Books, 1984.

The Anonimalle Chronicle 1333 to 1381, from a ms. Written at S. Mary's Abbey, York, and now in the Possession of Lieut.-Col. Sir William Ingilby, Bart, edited by V.H. Galbraith. Manchester, UK: Manchester University Press, 1927.

Blair, Ann. "Reading Strategies for Coping with Information Overload ca. 1550–1700," *Journal of the History of Ideas* 64.1 (2003): 11–28.

Bodin, Jean. *Method for the Easy Comprehension of History*, trans. Beatrice Reynolds. New York: Columbia University Press, 1945.

Camden, William. *Remanes of a greater worke, concerning Britaine . . .* [London]: G[eorge] E[ld] for Simon Waterson, 1605.

Canon, Christopher. *The Making of Chaucer's English*. Cambridge, UK: Cambridge University Press, 1998.

Carlson, David. "The Writings and Manuscript Collections of the Elizabethan Alchemist, Antiquary, and Herald Francis Thynne." *Huntington Library Quarterly* 52.2 (1989): 203–272.

Chaucer, Geoffrey. [*The Canterbury Tales*.] [Westminster: W. Caxton, 1483.]

———. *The Works of Geffray Chaucer Newly Printed, with Dyuers Workes Whiche Were Neuer in Print Before*. London: Thomas Godfray, 1532.

———. *The woorkes of Geffrey Chaucer, newly printed, with diuers addicions, whiche were neuer in printe before*. London: John Kingston for John Wright, 1561.

———. *The Workes of our Antient and Learned English Poet, Geffrey Chaucer*. London: Adam Islip, 1598 and 1602.

Dane, Joseph A. "Fists and Filiations in Early Chaucer Folios, 1532–1602," *Studies in Bibliography: Papers of the Bibliographical Society of the University of Virginia* 51 (1998): 48–62.

Evans, Robert C. "Ben Jonson's Chaucer." *English Literary Renaissance* 19.3 (1989): 325-345.

Harbus, Antonia. "A Renaissance Reader's English Annotations to Thynne's 1535 Edition of Chaucer's *Works*." *Review of English Studies* 59.240 (2008): 342–355.

Hearne, Thomas, ed. *A collection of curious discourses written by eminent antiquaries upon several heads in our English antiquities*. 2nd edition. London: W. and J. Richardson, 1771.

Jardine, Lisa and Anthony Grafton. "'Studied for Action': How Gabriel Harvey Read His Livy," *Past and Present* 129 (1990): 30-78.

Kennedy, William J. "Versions of a Career: Petrarch and His Renaissance Commentators." In *European Literary Careers: The Author from Antiquity* to the Renaissance, edited by Patrick Cheney and Frederick A. de Armas. 146-164. Toronto, ON: University of Toronto Press, 2002.

Kerling, Johan. Chaucer in Early English Dictionaries. Leiden, Holland: Leiden University Press, 1979.

Kinney, Claire. "Thomas Speght's Renaissance Chaucer and the Solaas of Sentance in Troilus and Criseyde." In Refiguring Chaucer in the Renaissance. Edited by Theresa M. Krier. 66-84. Gainesville, FL: University Press of Florida, 1998.

Krier, Theresa M. ed., Refiguring Chaucer in the Renaissance. Gainesville, FL: University Press of Florida, 1998.

Lerer, Seth. Chaucer and His Readers: Imagining the Author in Late-Medieval England. Princeton, NJ: Princeton University Press, 1993.

Mersand, Joseph E. Chaucer's Romance Vocabulary. New York: Comet Press, 1937.

Pearsall, Derek. "Thomas Speght." In Editing Chaucer: The Great Tradition, edited by Paul G. Ruggiers, 71-92. Norman, OK: Pilgrim Books, 1984.

Sherman, William. Used Books: Marking Readers in Renaissance England. Philadelphia: University of Pennsylvania Press, 2008.

Smith, G.C. Moore, ed., Gabriel Harvey's Marginalia. Stratford-upon-Avon, UK: Shakespeare Head, 1918.

Stern, Virginia F. Gabriel Harvey: His Life, Marginalia and Library. Oxford: Clarendon, 1979.

Stow, John. The Annales of England. London: George Bishop and Thomas Adams, [1605].

Thynne, Francis. Animadversions vppon the Annotacions and Corrections of Some Imperfections of Impressiones of Chaucers Workes . . . Reprinted in the Yere of Oure Lorde 1598. Edited by Frederick Furnivall. EETS o.s. 9. London: Oxford University Press, 1876, rpt. 1965.

Walker, Greg. Writing under Tyranny: English Literature and the Henrician Reformation. Oxford: Oxford University Press, 2005.

Wiggins, Alison. "What Did Renaissance Readers Write in Their Printed Copies of Chaucer?" Library: The Transactions of the Bibliographical Society 9.1 (2008): 3–36.

Windeatt, B.A. "Thomas Tyrwhitt (1730–1786)," in Editing Chaucer: the Great Tradition. Edited by Paul G. Ruggiers. 117-143. Norman, OK: Pilgrim Books, 1984.

Manuscripts and Annotated Books

Thynne, Franics. Letter to Lord Burghley. London, British Library MS Lansdowne 27, fols. 70-75v.

———. Annotations to Chaucer's *Works* (1598). Cambridge, Harvard University, Houghton Library fMS 1221.
———. *Animadversions*. San Marino, Huntington Library EL.34.B.11.
Harvey, Gabriel. Commonplace book. London, British Library MS Additional 32494.
———. Annotations to Chaucer's *Works* (1598). London, British Library MS Additional 42518.

A Petition Written by Ricardus Franciscus

HOLLY JAMES-MADDOCKS AND DEBORAH THORPE

Kew, The National Archives, C 49/30/19 (hereafter TNA C 49/30/19), a petition seeking the exoneration of the late Duke Humphrey of Gloucester (d. 1447), is distinctive among such supplicatory writing for the unusual extent of its ornamentation. Its "flamboyant, spiky script"[1] supports elaborate ascenders and descenders featuring many novelties: ballooning hearts; a scroll (illusionistically entwined around the ascender of the h in Humphrey) citing the duke's personal motto; and bright blue and red ink that colors the extensive strapwork emerging from his name. Such calligraphic virtuosity is instantly recognizable as the effusive "trademark décor" of the well-known scribe Ricardus Franciscus.[2]

Although the petition is undated, unenrolled, and finds no cross-reference in the parliament rolls, it was almost certainly written for the opening session of parliament in November 1450.[3] According to Bale's Chronicle, on the 8th November 1450, shortly after the opening of parliament, the commons "presented unto the king a bill desiring the seid duke of gloucestre might be proclaime a trewe knight."[4] Of pertinence to the parliamentary concerns of 1450 is a reference to Gloucester's keeping of "the Kinges livelode unto his owne [i.e., Henry's] use and prouffit," which coincides with the arguments for resumption put forward during this assembly.[5] The most tantalizing evidence concerning the context of this petition, however, is a letter from Hans Winter written in London on November 15, 1450, to the Grandmaster of the Teutonic Order, Ludwig von Erlingshausen. He writes that parliament began with a schedule entered "by the commons of England *and the servants of the noble prince of York* and also by the servants and faithful of the noble prince of Gloucester desiring justice for the traitors who killed him so shamefully and were of counsel therto"; he adds, "this has now been delayed until the noble prince of York comes."[6] This is the only contemporary remark to link York's servants, and by extension, York himself, to the instigation of this petition. This paper aims to analyze the potential circumstances surrounding Franciscus's writing of such an unusually ornamented petition for what John Watts has termed "the Yorkist interlude" of November and December 1450.[7] We hope the outcome will shed more light upon one of those men whom Gwilym Dodd has termed "the clerks and scribes whose role in the writing of petitions is as obscure as it is important."[8]

The outbreak of Cade's rebellion brought the previous parliament to an abrupt close and the November 1450 assembly was hastily convened as a measure intended to restore control in the wake of popular uprising after the loss of Normandy in 1449.[9] In particular, the defeated lieutenant-general of France, Edmund Beaufort, Duke of Somerset, came under direct attack, and it is the commonly-held view that Richard, duke of York, himself recently returned from his lieutenancy in Ireland, provided a figurehead around whom Somerset's critics could rally.[10] York's famous bill calling for justice upon the traitors, and presented to the king at the end of September 1450, is tantalizingly ambiguous in its refusal to directly implicate Somerset and allows us only to guess at his true motives in ordering Somerset's arrest on December 1st.[11] A second bill, presented by York to the king sometime between the end of September and the start of parliament on November 6, is addressed in particular to the "trewe lords of the kings counsele" and used the same words as Cade's rebels in calling for the punishment of "traitors" "ibroughte up of nought."[12] The theme of evil counsel was also employed by the rebels as explanation for the death of Humphrey, and this was later incorporated within the successful follow-up petition to C 49/30/19, presented to the parliament in 1455 and, this time, overseen by York as protector.[13] During the escalating unrest of November 1450, with both the *vox populi* and the reformist York seeking the "trewe lordes," it comes as no surprise that the commons elected Sir William Oldhall, York's chamberlain, as their speaker, before immediately introducing this petition requesting that Gloucester be deemed a true knight.[14] The implications, in Watt's analysis, are that "Gloucester stood for good rule by the princes of the blood and for resistance to the 'traitors' in the interests of the common weal; these claims had now devolved upon York."[15] As Curry rightly cautions, the evidence for York's open condemnation of Somerset for the loss of Normandy is not blatant until 1452, and York's connection with restoring Gloucester's name is not strongly implied until the pushing-through of a very similar petition to the one discussed here in the Yorkist-dominated assembly of 1455.[16] The identification of the scribe, and the information that this affords regarding his patrons, will be drawn on in this paper to reassess the feasibility of York's earlier, silent involvement in both the downfall of Somerset and the rehabilitation of Gloucester.

The identification of the writer of TNA C 49/30/19 as Ricardus Franciscus is supported by a range of paleographical features. The use of a scroll containing a phrase or motto, and wrapped around the ascender or descender of a letter placed on the top or bottom lines of a block of text, is the most characteristic feature of this scribe.[17] In TNA C 49/30/19, the ascender of the **h** at the first mention of Humphrey in the opening line of the petition contains one of the duke's mottos, "moun bien mondain," which also appears in manuscript books owned by the duke.[18] The sheer *extent* of the strapwork, particularly surrounding the initial **h**, is another obvious visual clue, one which has earned Franciscus the reputation as an "innovator on the English book scene, anticipating by as many as ten years the flamboyant styles of writing of Edward IV's reign" (see figure 1).[19] Coincident details in the strapwork may be compared, for example, in Nancy, Archives Départmentales de Meurthe et Moselle, MS. H. 80, Statutes of the Order of the Garter, which has the same diagonal flourishing lines around its ascenders as the ones that appear around the **h** of the opening line of the petition (see figure 4). The Nancy manuscript shares exactly the same heart-shaped extended back on the letter **d** of "dieu" that appears on the **d** of "discret" in TNA C 49/30/19, plus the same shape of the "l" in "glorieuse" that appears on the **b** in "noble" in the TNA manuscript, with its extended ascender which loops back with a very thin returning stroke (see figures 2 and 4).

Aside from the scheme of decoration, the hand of the petition shares each of the most distinctive features of the scribal work of Ricardus Franciscus. To illustrate this, TNA C 49/30/19 will be compared with two known manuscripts by Franciscus, both of which contain his signature, and so contain circumstantial as well as paleographical evidence to attribute them to Franciscus. The first is Nancy, Archives Départmentales de Meurthe et Moselle, MS. H. 80, Statutes of the Order of the Garter, and the second is San Marino, Huntington Library, MS. HM 932, Statutes of the Archdeaconry of London. The TNA petition displays each of the characteristic uppercase letters of the work of Ricardus Franciscus, such as the R in "Remembre" (figure 2, line 1): compare with "Roy" of the Nancy manuscript (figure 5, line 6); the **G** of "Gloucestre" (TNA, figure 3 line 7: compare with "Grey" of the Nancy manuscript, figure 5, line 3), and the **A** of "And" (TNA, figure 3 line 6: compare with the San Marino manuscript, "Assumpcionis" figure 6, line 13). When Franciscus had space, such as in the first line of a new section of the text, he gave his letters extended lead-in strokes, as can be seen in the word "vingt" in the Nancy manuscript (figure 5, line 8).[20] This tendency can also be seen in the TNA petition, giving the page the same distinctive aspect: the word "vnto" on figure 3, line 1, of the TNA manuscript has the same long first stroke, and the same flat bottom. There are many distinctive lower-case letters in the work of Ricardus Franciscus, such as the **y** with a very thin, almost non-existent, descender, as can be seen in "Roy" in the Nancy manuscript (figure 5, line 6). This **y** is shared by the TNA manuscript, such as "Royaumes" (figure 3, line 2). Franciscus has a distinctive initial letter **d** with a looped ascender that curls to the left and an open bottom compartment (see the San Marino manuscript, "diebus," figure 6, line 10), which also appears in the TNA manuscript, for example, in "disposicion" (figure 3, line 1). For a final example, the **g** of Ricardus Franciscus has a top stroke that falls low, leaving two horns at the top of the letter and, like the **y,** it has a very inconspicuous descender (see "magdalene" in the San Marino manuscript, figure 6, line 12). The same-shaped **g** also appears in the TNA manuscript, for example, in "executing" on figure 2, line 2.

It is possible that the linguistic features of the petition TNA C 49/30/19 will reinforce the paleographical evidence that it was written by Ricardus Franciscus. Previous scholarship has presented convincing evidence that Franciscus was French. Lisa Jefferson's comparison of the Nancy text with other copies of the statutes reveal that Franciscus emended, altered or added to the text to "correct grammatical errors, or rephrase a sentence more logically, or add a synonymic doublet word or phrase," concluding that these changes "must have been introduced by someone fully fluent in continental French, not just in Anglo-Norman."[21] To support this, although TNA C 49/30/19 was written in English, the scribe used several French-derived spellings rather than their English alternatives. He spelled memory as "memoire," which the *Middle English Dictionary* reveals was more usually spelled as "memorie" in Middle English.[22] For adversaries, he wrote "adversaires," which was more commonly "adversaries" in Middle English.[23] "Honeur" and "heretiques" were evidently rare in written Middle English, as they are entered in the *MED* as "Old French."[24] Other French-derived spellings had been absorbed into English, and appear frequently in medieval texts in the English language, including "assoille" and "bataille."[25]

The appearance of French, or French-derived words in a petition cannot always be taken as evidence that the writer was of French nationality. There was a period of transition in the 1440s, when English-language common supplications to parliament were beginning to outnumber their French equivalents.[26] Despite this transition, French words continued to appear in petitions written in English.[27] Gwilym Dodd suggested that, in these transitional years, this was a result of clerks switching to French "unthinkingly," or "because they felt that their expression would be better served by 'borrowing' French words."[28] However, the words that Dodd gave as examples were all unusual words, of a specifically legal register. Therefore, there was a need to select a French word that covered a meaning or tone for which there was no appropriate equivalent in English. In contrast, in the case of the more "ordinary" words in TNA C 49/30/19, there is no reason why an English scribe would use the French-derived spellings rather than the more usual English spellings. This would suggest that the writer of this petition was a French scribe writing in English, who unconsciously switched to the spelling system of his native language when he wrote a word that was derived from French.

The linguistic evidence above *supports* the paleographical evidence that the scribe of TNA C 49/30/19 was the Frenchman Ricardus Franciscus. However, for more *solid* support about the identity of the scribe one has to search the petition for linguistic features that were *specific* to Franciscus – perhaps idiosyncrasies, or dialectal features. Richard Hamer has conducted a thorough examination of the linguistic features of written work in the hand of Franciscus.[29] The texts that Hamer studied were all literary, and so were examples of Franciscus's work as a copyist scribe. Hamer has shown that many of the linguistic features of these texts were inherited from their exemplars, as Franciscus copied his exemplars very faithfully.[30] The general accuracy in Franciscus's copying of the spellings of his exemplars made the words that he *did* change particularly striking. Hamer pointed out that the consistency with which Franciscus made certain substitutions means that they must have represented his preferred forms, or dialectal features. He compiled a list of the preferred spellings of Ricardus Franciscus, which is extremely helpful to this study of a petition that was possibly composed by Franciscus.[31]

Finding these spellings in TNA C 49/30/19 reinforces the paleographical evidence that it was written by Ricardus Franciscus. The petition is likely to have been composed in a different way from the literary texts that Franciscus copied. It is unlikely that the scribe copied TNA C 49/30/19 from an exemplar in the way that Franciscus would have copied literary texts: instead it may have been dictated or composed from a rough draft or notes.[32] The general uniformity in the linguistics of petitions makes the latter suggestion more compelling, suggesting that the scribe of TNA C 49/30/19 may have been responsible for the style of the petition.[33] Consequently, this petition could present the preferred spelling systems of the scribe who wrote it. If the preferred spellings of Ricardus Franciscus could be found in TNA C 49/30/19, then this would be strong evidence that it was written by him.

In his literary work, Franciscus consistently used "gh" for the palatal fricative, instead of whatever else he saw in his exemplar: for example he changed "heihe" to "high."[34] In TNA C 49/30/19, the scribe did indeed show preference for the "gh" form in "right," "high," and "flight." The scribe of the petition, like Ricardus Franciscus in his literary manuscripts, did not use Þ (using "th-" instead), and did not use many abbreviations.[35] Hamer noticed that Franciscus used the "wh-" form wherever possible, for example writing "wherfor" instead of "werfor."[36] The writer of the petition also used the "wh-" form, for example in the word "whereupon" (figure 1, line 11). Hamer noted that Franciscus consistently changed "hit" to "it."[37] In the petition, too, the writer used "it" in every instance of the word. Unfortunately, since this petition is a small sample of text compared with a book of hundreds of folios such as Harley MS 4775, it does not contain many of the words that Hamer found Franciscus spelled in a distinctive way (such as "saugh" for saw, "womman" for woman, and "felyship" for fellowship).[38] However, the limited words from Hamer's list that *do* appear in TNA C 49/30/19 support the suggestion that the petition was written by Ricardus Franciscus.

Based on the paleographical analysis above, which is supported by a linguistic comparison between the petition and manuscripts that have already been attributed to Ricardus Franciscus, this document can be added to a body of sixteen manuscripts currently attributed to Franciscus:[39]

Cambridge, St John's College, MS H. 5 (*olim* 208), Christine de Pizan, *The Epistle of Othea*, trans. Stephen Scrope (Fastolf's stepson and a member of his household), in English, c. 1450 to c. 1460, illustrated by William Abell and the Abingdon Missal Master.[40] Dedicated to and probably owned by Humphrey Stafford, who was created duke of Buckingham on September 14, 1444, and killed at the Battle of Northampton on July 10, 1460; potentially commissioned by William Worcester (Fastolf's secretary).[41]

Cambridge, University Library, MS Additional 7870, a French translation of John of Wales' *Breviloquium* corrected by William Worcester in July 1450 (1 to 22v), Jean Courtecuisse's French translation of *Des quatre vertus cardinaulx* (24r to 67v), unidentified French text on the virtues (68r to 71r), c.1450. Fols. 24r to 67v copied by Franciscus; English rubricated initials by an unidentified artist.[42]

London, British Library, MS Harley 2915, Book of Hours, Sarum use, in Latin and French, c. 1440 to c. 1450, illumination in color and semi-grisaille attributed to the Fastolf Master. A prayer composed for John, duke of Bedford (d. 1435) occurs over several folios, leading Reynolds to suggest that it was made for an English aristocrat in his circle: either Richard, duke of York or Edmund or John Beaufort.[43]

London, British Library, MS Harley 4012, Middle English religious miscellany, c. 1460 to c. 1470, no illustration aside from a pen-and-ink drawing of the crucifixion on f. 109r and identified as written by Franciscus.[44] Written for Anne Harling, the niece and ward of Fastolf in the 1430s, and signed by Anne while she was married to her second husband, Sir Robert Wingfield.[45]

London, British Library, MS Harley 4775, Jacobus de Voraigne, *The Golden Legend*, in Middle English, second half of fifteenth-century, decorated with one full border of green-lobed feathering and 2, 3, and 4 line initials throughout by the English border artist of Scott's catalogue number 118.[46]

London, Hospital of St. Bartholomew, Smithfield, Cartulary in two volumes compiled by John Cok in the 1450s and 1460s, parts copied by Franciscus and two historiated initials supplied by William Abell.[47]

London, Worshipful Company of the Tallow Chandlers, Grant of Arms, in French, dated 24 September 1456, signed and sealed by John Smert, Garter King of Arms; portrait of Garter and Company's crest within the initial A by William Abell or the Abingdon Missal Master.[48]

Los Angeles, J. Paul Getty Museum, MS 5, 84 ML. 723 (Sotheby Hours), Book of Hours, Sarum use, in Latin with English rubrics, c. 1440 to c. 1450, illuminated by the Fastolf Master possibly for John de Vere, twelfth earl of Oxford (d. 1462), whose signature occurs on f. 35v.[49]

Nancy, Archives Departmentales de Meurthe et Moselle, MS H. 80, Statutes of the Order of the Garter, in French, dated 1467 and signed "R. Franceys s.R" which may be "scriba/sub Rege," i.e. "written for the king [of arms]."[50] Illuminated initial and green-lobed feathering by the English border artist of Scott's catalogue number 118.[51]

New York, Pierpont Morgan Library and Museum, MS M. 126, John Gower, *Confessio amantis*, in English and Latin, c. 1470, supplied with 106 miniatures by two illustrators from the southern Low Countries and border-work completed by four border artists (the first of whom is the English border artist of Scott's catalogue number 118).[52] Probably made for Queen Elizabeth Woodville, wife of Edward IV.[53]

Oxford, Bodleian Library, MS Ashmole 764, "The first foundation of the office of arms," extracts from "L'arbre de batailles," "Le songe du vergier" and other heraldic texts, in Latin, English, and French, c. 1475, owned by John Smert, Garter king of arms. Three illustrations by Illustrator A of Fitzwilliam Museum 56 and/or the "Three Kings' Master," according to Scott, and border work by Border artist A of Fitzwilliam 56 and the English border artist of catalogue number 118.[54]

Oxford, Bodleian Library, MS Ashmole 789, Writing exercises in English and Latin (ff.1 to 5), c. 1450.

Oxford, Bodleian Library, MS Laud Misc. 570, Christine de Pizan, *L'Epistre d'Othea* and *Livre des quartre vertus*, in French, dated 1450, with ten illuminations by the Fastolf Master, owned by Sir John Fastolf.

Oxford, University College, MS 85, Alain Chartier, *Quadrilogue*, the *Secretum Secretorum, Good Governance of a Prince*, in English, c. 1470, with two illustrations by the "Quadrilogue Master" and borders by the English border artist of Scott's catalogue number 118.[55] Probably owned by Richard Whetehill, controller of Calais from December 1460 and lieutenant of Guînes from 1461 to 1478.[56]

Philadelphia, Rosenbach Museum and Library, MS 439/16 (*olim* Phillipps 4254), John Lydgate, *The Fall of Princes*, in English, c. 1465 to c. 1475, with only the first of seven miniatures by the "Quadrilogue Master," according to Scott, and the border work by the English border artist of Scott's catalogue number 118.[57]

San Marino, Huntington Library, MS HM 932, Statutes of the Archdeaconry of London, in Latin, dated 1447, with two historiated initials by William Abell and signed by "Ricardus Franciscus."

Up to the point of writing this petition, Franciscus had very recently copied, or may have still been copying, Christine de Pizan's *Epistle d'Othea* and the *Livre des quatre vertus*, dated 1450, for Sir John Fastolf (MS. Laud. Misc. 570). It was also probably not long before the petition that he copied Jean Courtecuisse's French translation of *Des quatre vertus cardinaulx* (CUL Add. 7870, ff. 24r to 67v) for Fastolf's amanuensis William Worcester.[58] Worcester's extensive marginal annotations are evident throughout booklet 1 and his colophon on f.22v states that he made these corrections in July 1450; booklet 2, Franciscus's stint, seems to have been conceived as the follow-up to the first booklet since quire signatures that also appear to be in the hand of Worcester show a continuation from booklets one to two.[59] It has also been argued, as noted above, that another copy of the *Epistle d'Othea* (Cambridge, St. John's Coll., MS H 5) translated into English by Fastolf's step-son, was made for Worcester at about the same time as Fastolf's French copy. Further pre-petition work presents itself in the Getty MS. 5 *Hours* which, like Fastolf's Laud. Misc. 570, Franciscus produced in collaboration with the Fastolf Master. Its owner portrait suggests that it was made for John de Vere, twelfth earl of Oxford (d. 1462) who, like Fastolf, was an active campaigner in France. It has been suggested that this manuscript was either made in France in 1441 when de Vere travelled with the duke of York to Normandy, or in 1450 while he was active in Norfolk politics (together with John Mowbray, duke of Norfolk, and Sir John Fastolf) attempting to undermine the local power of the duke of Suffolk's servants.[60] The latter option seems more likely given that the scribe and artist of the Getty *Hours* were already working together for Fastolf in 1450. A final early production presents itself in Harley 2915, a third collaboration between Franciscus and the Fastolf Master, and possibly the first extant example of York's employment of Franciscus.[61]

In the very year leading up to the writing of this petition, therefore, are a potential of four manuscripts made for Fastolf's circle: the *Othea/Livre des Quartre Vertus* for himself, the *Quatre Vertus* and *Othea* in separate volumes for Worcester, and the Getty *Hours* for de Vere. Since it is certain, at least, that Franciscus was copying Fastolf's *Othea/Quartre Vertus* during 1450, the intriguing possibility presents itself that Fastolf may have asked the scribe already in his employment to spare a few hours to draft and then write up a fair copy of a petition for presentation at parliament. Fastolf certainly fits Hans Winter's description as one of the "servants of the noble prince of York."[62] The French Captain was one of the most long-standing members of York's ducal council, receiving a pension of £20 per annum for life in June 1441 to serve as York's councillor.[63] Additional payments were made in May 1445 and in June 1448; and during York's first protectorate, in June 1454, he secured the wardship of Thomas Fastolf for the benefit of his old councillor.[64] Furthermore Fastolf's secretary, William Worcester, is one of the very few identified writers of petitions and would have been very well placed to provide a formulary for Franciscus to follow.[65] Until recently, very little was known about the actual process of drafting a petition (how far its composition was dictated by the clerk or the supplicant) or the extent to which it was a specialized process. Recent research by Dodd, however, suggests that supplications took distinct forms depending on the recipient government department and that "these subtle differences indicate that a certain level of expertise and knowledge was required to make a supplication fit its context, or suit its audience."[66] Since Franciscus's hand is to be found most commonly in manuscripts containing vernacular literary texts and not (as yet) in any other petitions, one would expect that a degree of guidance may have been necessary.

In the context of this particular parliament, it is of considerable interest that two extant documents associated with Fastolf, both desirous of seeing Somerset answer charges relating to the loss of Normandy, demonstrate further overlap in the interests of Fastolf and York.[67] The first is an undated text in French of eight questions to be asked of the duke of Somerset by the council of the king concerning his actions during the surrender of Maine and Anjou.[68] Anne Curry argues that these questions, found among Worcester's material compiled for Fastolf, were written before the total loss of Normandy and before York's return from Ireland shortly before the start of this parliament.[69] The second, Fastolf's "advertiriment" in College of Arms, MS 48, ff. 324r to 325v, which postdates the loss of Normandy, opens with the phrase:

> memorandum, saving your good correction that
> it is right necessarie amonges otheir of my lordes
> articles that there be desired to be made a steward
> of Englond a constable and suche other officers
> lordes of gret worship of good name and fame not
> sclaundered with the vice of covetise for the welfare
> and defence of this reame from the powere of our
> adversaries.[70]

Although this document does not mention Somerset by name, his recent appointment as Constable of England on 11 September 1450 seems to imply him in the very first sentence. The perceived void was to be filled by a self-appointed "lord of good name" when York seized the title of Constable for himself after the battle of St. Albans in 1455.[71] York is noted above in the phrase "my lordes articles," which refers either to the articles that York presented to the king before the November 1450 parliament (where the blame is placed on traitors in general), or to those that York presented against Somerset in 1452. While Watts suggests that the "advertiriment" may have been drawn up as part of an attempt to place Somerset on trial during the November 1450 assembly, Curry argues that the mention of the loss of Guienne (1451) renders it more likely that it refers to the later articles presented by York.[72] This would tie in with Johnson's suggestion that York composed these at Ludlow over the Christmas period of 1451; he adds, however, that they were probably already in the making in November 1450.[73] Furthermore, Johnson's analysis of York's servants reveals that many of the leading men of John, duke of Bedford, attached themselves to York upon his arrival in France in 1436, men who were "heart and soul, committed to the Lancastrian supremacy in France."[74] It has been argued that it was this group, rather than his servants inherited through the duchy and earldom, who exerted the greater influence on York's actions.[75]

Turning to Franciscus's post-petition career, it is not difficult to imagine how a scribe who had been writing for Fastolf and Worcester, both of whom were particularly interested in arms and military affairs, could have found his way to writing for another man with a military background in 1456, the Garter king of arms.[76] Upon Edward of York's coronation as Edward IV in 1461, Franciscus's long association with "the servants of the noble prince of York" could only have meant new advantages, as attested by his copying of Gower's *Confessio Amantis* for the Queen. Fastolf's earlier showcasing of Franciscus's hand to a large government assembly—if, indeed, Fastolf was the agent—was quite possibly a turning point in his career, one that was to help render him "the vogue scribe" of the third-quarter of the fifteenth-century.[77] It may be mere coincidence that on the occasion of York's self-appointment within the Office of the Heralds from 1455 to 1456, we witness Franciscus's earliest extant work for the Garter king of arms, John Smert.[78] Further work for Smert may have followed in 1467 when he copied the Statutes of the Order of the Garter and c. 1475 when he contributed to the collection of heraldic texts in Ashmole 764. Meanwhile, York's son Richard, duke of Gloucester, followed his father in actively seeking the post of Constable which should have, by right, been inherited by the dukes of Buckingham.[79] He filled this role from 1469 to 1483, when upon becoming king, he incorporated the Heralds as the College of Arms.[80]

Where it is frustratingly difficult to reconstruct Franciscus's later patrons, turning to the illuminators with whom he collaborates is instructive. Six of Franciscus's post-1460 manuscripts receive illumination, and every single one of these does so from the English border artist described in Scott's catalogue number 118. This English illuminator worked as part of a small coterie of artists regularly, but not exclusively, employed by the heralds and, later, by Richard III and a number of his close associates.[81] If Franciscus occasionally worked for the king through the office of the Heralds, as Linne Mooney suggests, a number of his other late manuscripts may be placed within the same court circles.[82] The luxurious Gower text in Morgan M. 126, with its scribal inscriptions "vive Le roy Edward IVe" and "vive la belle quod Rychard," was commissioned by Edward's Queen; Harley 4012 may have been ordered by Wingfield once he had been made controller of the King's household after 1471; finally, the armorial device in University College 85 points to Richard Whetehill as its original commissioner, lieutenant of Guînes by the time this manuscript was made.

In summary, the identification of Franciscus as the writer of this petition at a time when he appears to have been heavily engaged in copying literary texts for Fastolf, Worcester, and other close associates, offers an affirmative answer to Curry's important question regarding the extent of York's involvement, in 1450, in both Somerset's downfall and Gloucester's restoration. York's opinion on both these issues only becomes clear in 1452 and 1455 respectively, but the identity of the scribe can pinpoint exactly whom of York's servants and supporters were the likely organizers of the earlier 1450 petition; consequently the strong possibility presents itself that York did indeed delegate this task to the most long-standing among his servants, Sir John Fastolf. If York was rather more active against his adversaries in an earlier period, as suggested by the identity of the scribe and his background, his agency in creating a factionalized government is one that has been long *assumed*, but not proven, by historians.[83] Since the petition is unenrolled, there is no evidence to suggest that this alien scribe necessarily worked in or around Westminster (it would seem odd, after all, to find a Frenchman writing government documents at a time of continuing hostilities with France), it seems that Franciscus was simply in the right place at the right time to pick up a little extra copying from an employer with a particularly French taste in books.

Petitions have only recently been the subject of focussed scholarly work. Initially, attention was given to the content of supplications, to the end of elucidating the political and administrative context of petitioning.[84] Increasingly, political historians have been joined by a lively community of palaeographers, linguistic experts, and literary scholars in analyzing the documentary culture of late medieval England.[85] To date, however, minimal enquiry has been made as to *who* actually wrote these petitions. A notable exception is Linne Mooney's recognition of Chaucer's scribe, Adam Pinkhurst, in one of the earliest Middle English petitions, the famous London Mercers' petition of 1387-1388.[86] Yet again, the nexus between the legal and the literary worlds of composition and copying is revealed in the identification made here of Ricardus Franciscus as the writer of TNA C 49/30/19.

Centre for Medieval Studies, University of York.

Acknowledgements

We would like to thank Anne Curry for bringing this document to our attention and Linne Mooney for confirming our identification of the hand. We are much obliged to Gwilym Dodd and Linne Mooney for their helpful feedback on an earlier draft. All errors are, of course, our own. Our thanks are also due to Mark Ormrod for allowing time to discuss this article during the first meeting of the Andrew W. Mellon Foundation-funded project "The Writing of Petitions in Later Medieval England."

NOTES

1. Kathleen Scott, *Later Gothic Manuscripts 1390–1490*, A Survey of Manuscripts Illuminated in the British Isles 6 (London: Harvey Miller, 1996), volume II, page 318.
2. Martha Rust, *Imaginary Worlds in Medieval Books: Exploring the Manuscript Matrix* (New York; Hampshire: Palgrave Macmillan, 2007), 167. Further studies of Franciscus include Richard Hamer, "Spellings of the Fifteenth-Century Scribe Ricardus Franciscus," in *Five Hundred Years of Words and Sounds: A Festschrift for Eric Dobson*, ed. E. G. Stanley and Douglas Gray (Cambridge: D. S. Brewer, 1983), 63 - 73; Lisa Jefferson, "Two Fifteenth-Century Manuscripts of the Statutes of the Order of the Garter," in *English Manuscript Studies 1100–1700* 5 (1995): 18–35; Martha Driver, "'Me fault faire': French Makers of Manuscripts for English Patrons," in *Language and Culture in Medieval Britain: The French of England, c.1100–c.1500*, ed. Jocelyn Wogan-Browne *et al.* (Woodbridge, Suffolk: York Medieval Press/The Boydell Press, 2009), 420–443; Catherine Nall, "Ricardus Franciscus Writes for William Worcester," *Journal of the Early Book Society* 11 (2008): 207–212.
3. It is important to emphasize that this petition was not entered on the parliament roll itself. Since TNA C 49/30/19 is the original petition which could have been written from anywhere, there is no reason to assume that Franciscus was necessarily working in or around Westminster itself.
4. Both John Watts and Anne Curry refer to Bale's Chronicle in R. Flenley, *Six Town Chronicles* (Oxford: Oxford University Press, 1911), 137, for evidence

that this bill was presented to the 1450 parliament. See, respectively, *Henry VI and the Politics of Kingship* (Cambridge: Cambridge University Press, 1996), 274 n. 53, and *The Parliament Rolls of Medieval England, 1275–1504*, ed. Chris Given-Wilson *et al.* (Leicester: Scholarly Digital Editions and The National Archives, 2005), CD-ROM version (henceforth cited as *PROME*), parliament of 1450, "Introduction."

5. Again, both Watts (*Henry VI*, 274 n. 53) and Curry (in *PROME*, parliament of 1450) suggest that the fiscal issue raised also implies a 1450 dating. The main themes emphasized in the petition are the Duke's royal blood "beyng sone brother and uncle of kings"; it recites a history of his honorable military service, culminating in a description of him "puttyng to flight victoriously" the enemy at the siege of Calais (a pointed contrast, perhaps, with those involved in the very recent loss of Normandy); and, furthermore, it emphasizes the "high drede due obeisance & trewe liegaunce" he "alweyes" accorded Henry VI during the rule of his protectorate and "unto his last end." See *PROME*, parliament of 1450, appendix item 9, for a transcription and translation of TNA C 49/30/19. Curry makes the point here that it is different in content from, and therefore not to be confused with, the later common petition to exonerate Duke Humphrey (TNA C 49/30/18) that was finally agreed in the Yorkist-dominated parliament of 1455.

6. *PROME*, parliament of 1450, Appendix item 11. Emphasis our own.

7. Watts, *Henry VI*, 286. He also refers to this period of brief ascendancy and power as "the Yorkist assault" on royal authority, 290.

8. Gwilym Dodd, "The Rise of English, the Decline of French: Supplications to the English Crown, c. 1420-1450," *Speculum* 86 (2011): 146.

9. As Curry notes in *PROME*, parliament of 1450, "Introduction," the November 1450 parliament had been summoned on the 5th September, a gap of only three months after the close of its predecessor and the second shortest between parliaments during the reign of Henry VI. For further detail on the frequency and length of parliaments during the reign of Henry VI, see also Anne Curry, "'A Game of Two Halves': The Parliaments of Henry VI," *Parliamentary History* 23.1 (2004): 73–102.

10. M. K. Jones, "Somerset, York and the Wars of the Roses," *EHR*, 104 (1989), 287-9. Watts, *Henry VI*, 269-70, 274-8. For a more cautious view see Curry's discussion in *PROME*, parliament of 1450, "Introduction."

11. Benet's Chronicle states that the conciliatory York put Somerset in the tower for his own safety, although, as Curry notes, this chronicler was "a rabid pro-Yorkist" (*PROME*, parliament of 1450, "Introduction"). However, a servant of the war veteran Thomas Lord Scales, a member of York's ducal council, was caught in the attack on Somerset's lodgings (for York's servants see P. A. Johnson, *Duke Richard of York 1411-1460* [Oxford, 1988], 16–19).

Watts, *Henry VI*, 274, sees the attack as "providing York with a pretext to arrest Somerset."

12. British Library, Additional MS. 48031A, fol. 126r-v. For discussion of both bills see Watts, *Henry VI*, 271-274. It is interesting in respect of the borrowed wording that Sir John Fastolf, a member of York's ducal council (see discussion below), sought the articles of Jack Cade and sent his servant, John Payn, to Blackheath in June 1450 to collect them. See Norman Davis ed., *Paston Letters and Papers of the Fifteenth Century*, volume II (Oxford: Oxford University Press, 2004), letter 692, lines 9 to 12. Payn's mission to collect these articles is also discussed in Wendy Scase, *Literature and Complaint in England, 1272-1553*, (Oxford; New York: Oxford University Press, 2007), 188.

13. Cade's complaints, revealing that popular perception in 1450 believed Humphrey's death to have been caused by treason, are discussed by Curry in *PROME*, parliament of 1447, "Introduction." The petition which finally saw his exoneration, TNA C 49/30/18, echoed Cade's rebels in claiming that Humphrey had been "openly named and defamed of treson" "by untrewe and evell disposed plans" (see *PROME*, parliament of 1455, appendix item 12; referenced also in parliament of 1450, appendix item 9).

14. As Curry notes (see *PROME*, parliament of 1450, "Introduction"), Oldhall "epitomised English commitment to France" and had been York's chamberlain from at least 1444. She adds that his presence as a speaker served as "a sharp reminder of past glories and of the possibility that questions might be asked of those deemed responsible for recent failures." See also J. S. Roskell, "Sir William Oldhall, speaker in the parliament of 1450-1," *Nottingham Medieval Studies* 5 (1961): 87–112.

15. Watts, *Henry VI*, 274. A similar view is expressed by Johnson: "In electing Oldhall, the commons were demonstrating their conviction that change was required and that York was the man to achieve it" (*Richard of York*, 87).

16. *PROME*, parliament of 1450, "Introduction." York was Protector of England for the 1455 assembly that saw the restoration of Gloucester's reputation.

17. As Rust comments in *Imaginary Worlds*, 167, if this scribe had remained anonymous then he would surely have been known as the "Scroll-Work Scribe."

18. See Berthold L. Ullman, "Manuscripts of Duke Humphrey of Gloucester," *The English Historical Review* 52. 208 (1937), 670-1, which discusses, in particular, the appearance of the motto in MS. 694 of the Urbinas collection in the Vatican. Until this manuscript was found, there was no manuscript evidence for the following statement by the eighteenth-century antiquarian, John Leyland, that the duke used the motto: "Humfredus multatis scripsit in frontispieces librorum suorum, moun bien mondain" (*Johannis Lelandi*

Antiquarii de Rebus Britannicis Collectanea, volume iii, edited by Thomas Hearne [Oxford, 1715] 58). The rest of the duke's 27 known manuscripts are listed in K. H.Vickers, *Humphrey Duke of Gloucester* (London: A. Constable, 1907), 426ff.

19. Scott, *Later Gothic Manuscripts*, II.319.

20. See Jefferson, "Two Fifteenth-Century Manuscripts," 21.

21. "Two Fifteenth-Century Manuscripts," 23. Hamer also suggests that Ricardus, "seems to have been French, or at least strongly influenced by French scribal models" ("Spellings" 69). See also Carole Meale, "Patrons, Buyers and Owners: Book Production and Social Status," *Book Production and Publishing in Britain 1375–1475*, eds. J. Griffiths and D. Pearsall (Cambridge: Cambridge University Press, 1989), 202.

22. memorī(e) (n.). Frances McSparran ed.,*The Middle English Dictionary*, University of Michigan, 2001, http://quod.lib.umich.edu/m/med/,accessed August 30, 2011.

23. adversārie (n.). *ibid.*

24. honōur (n.) and Old French (h)onor, (h)onur, (h)onneur. Heretīk(e) (n. & adj.) and Old French heretique & hæreticus. *ibid.*

25. asoilen and batail(e): though the *Middle English Dictionary* identifies their origin as Old French, it identifies many occurrences of the words in Middle English texts.

26. This date concerns common petitions: common petitions in English began to outnumber their French equivalent in 1445. The transition occurred almost a decade earlier in the case of private petitions, with English private petitions only outnumbering French language ones in 1437. Responses to petitions in English did not outnumber those in French until 1447. See Dodd, "The Rise of English," 122 and 137.

27. Dodd ("The Rise of English," 127) gave examples, including a petition of 1427 (SC 8/125/6244), in which "marchauntes, possessours, maystres and marryners of þis Rewme of Ingelonde» trading with Guyenne lobbied to have «a *conuement* [knowledgeable] and discrete man" appointed to the office of constable of Bordeaux. The French word *conuement* appears seamlessly within the English sentence.

28. See Dodd, "The Rise of English," 120, for a discussion of the borrowing of French terms by clerks who were writing petitions in English.

29. Hamer, "Spellings," 63–73.

30. For the different scribal attitudes towards copying exemplars, see the work of Angus McIntosh on scribes copying exemplars in dialects other than their own. In such situations, scribes might a) leave language unchanged, b) translate into his own dialect, c) something in between, the scribe copying a mixture of his own forms and the exemplar's. Angus McIntosh, M. L. Samu-

els, Michael Benskin, *A Linguistic Atlas of Late Mediaeval English,* Volume 1 (Aberdeen: Aberdeen University Press, 1986), 15. Franciscus was primarily a type a) scribe.

31. See Hamer, "Spellings," 70–72. Hamer pointed out that his list of the words that Franciscus changed from his exemplar was not exhaustive, since he only studied a sample of Franciscus'ss hand. However, his list gives us an overview of certain preferred spellings of this scribe.

32. For detailed information about the language of petitions in the late fourteenth century, specifically about the conventions of this mode of writing, see Gwilym Dodd, "Writing Wrongs: The Drafting of Supplications to the Crown in Later Fourteenth-Century England," forthcoming in *Medium Aevum.* For more on the drafting of common petitions in the fourteenth century, which were usually written in Anglo-Norman French, see Anthony Musson, *Medieval Law in Context: The Growth of Legal Consciousness from Magna Carta to the Peasants' Revolt* (Manchester: Manchester University Press, 2001), 187-189. Musson also made the distinction between merely drafting petitions, and actually "coming up with and preparing suggestions" (i.e. being responsible for the *content* of the petition), and suggested that the county court had an important part in formulating petitions. Thus, in the case of these common petitions, Musson created the impression of a committee of composers, rather than a single writer. For research into the transition between French and English in the fifteenth-century, see Dodd, "The Rise of English," 117–150.

33. Dodd proposed that "having furnished a clerk with the basic 'facts,' a petitioner may then have left him free to write up the substance of the supplication as he saw fit, placing trust in the clerk's abilities to make the best possible case on the petitioner's behalf." However, though Dodd emphasized the control that the clerk had over the petition, he also cautioned that we should not discount the influence that the supplicant would have had over the "shape and tone" of the petition ("The Rise of English," 120). Dodd wrote this statement about private petitions, but it might be assumed that the same would have been true of common petitions, with the difference that the scribe was under the instruction of a *committee* of petitioners as opposed to an *individual.*

34. British Library, MS Harley 4775, folio 161vb. For several other examples of Franciscus'ss copying of words involving the palative fricative, see Hamer, "Spellings," 71.

35. See Hamer, "Spellings," 70.

36. British Library, MS Harley 4775, 164va. See Hamer, "Spellings" 71.

37. British Library, MS Harley 4775, 23vb. See Hamer, "Spellings" 71.

38. See Hamer, "Spellings" 71.

39. Listed in Driver, "'Me fault faire,'" appendix, and in Catherine Nall, "Ricardus Franciscus," 209-10. Since Jefferson was doubtful about the attribution of some of the thirteen manuscripts that she listed in 1995 ("Two Fifteenth-Century Manuscripts," 22), this grouping deserves thorough reinvestigation. This project is, unfortunately, too big for the scope of a note introducing C 49/30/19 as the work of Franciscus but one doubtful (and easily accessible) example that illustrates this need is B.L. Harley 4012 (see the British Library's Catalogue of Illuminated Manuscripts http://www.bl.uk/catalogues/illuminatedmanuscripts/record.asp?MSID=4496&CollID=8&NStart=4012 for folios 1 and 109.)

40. Johnathan Alexander attributes all of the illustrations to Abell ("William Abell 'lymnour' and 15th Century English Illumination," in *Kunsthistorische Forschungen: Otto Pacht zu seinem 70. Geburtstag*, ed. A. Rosenauer and G. Weber [Salzburg: Residenz Verlag, 1972], 168, item 19) while Scott allocates the color-miniature to Abell and the remaining grisaille-illustrations to the "Abingdon Missal Master" (Scott, *Later Gothic Manuscripts*, II. 264-65).

41. Nall, "Ricardus Franciscus," 209. Linne R. Mooney, "Locating Scribal Activity in Late-Medieval London," in *Design and Distribution of Late Medieval Manuscripts in England*, ed. Margaret Connolly and Linne Mooney (Woodbridge, Suffolk: York Medieval Press/The Boydell Press, 2008), 199.

42. Nall, "Ricardus Franciscus," 207-212.

43. Catherine Reynolds in Richard Marks and Paul Williamson, *Gothic Art for England 1400–1547*, (London: V&A Publications, 2003), 345, and cited by Driver in "'Me fault faire,'" 434. Given that York succeeds Bedford as lieutenant-general of France and inherits most of Bedford's servants (see Johnson, *Duke Richard*, 16-19), he would seem to be a more likely patron than Beaufort. Furthermore, the factional politics that divide York and Somerset, as well as Franciscus's consistent employment by the "Yorkist" circle (as argued below), would also favor York.

44. Identified by Malcolm Parkes in 1977 as reported in E. Wilson, "A Middle English Manuscript at Coughton Court, Warwickshire, and British Library MS. Harley 4012," *Notes & Queries* 24 (July 1977): 299 [295-303].

45. Anne Dutton suggests that this manuscript may have been copied while Wingfield was in exile with Edward IV in 1470 or after their return to England when Edward rewarded Wingfield's loyalty by making him controller of the king's household from 1471 to 1481. A. M. Dutton, "Piety, Politics and Persona: British Library MS Harley 4012 and Anne Harling," in *Prestige, Authority and Power in Late Medieval Manuscripts and Texts*, ed. F. Riddy (Woodbridge, Suffolk: York Medieval Press/The Boydell Press, 2000), 135 (133-46).

46. Scott, *Later Gothic Manuscripts*, II. 319.

47. Scott, "A Mid-Fifteenth-Century Illuminating Shop and Its Customers," *Journal of the Warburg and Courtauld Institutes* 31 (1968): 170, n. 3; Alexander, "William Abell," 170.

48. Attributed to William Abell by Alexander ("William Abell," 167, item 13) and by Driver ("'Me fault faire,'" 429). Scott, however, argues that "the more complex handling of drapery and deeper facial modelling of the Abingdon Master differentiate the two hands" (*Later Gothic Manuscripts*, II. 280. For further detail of the differences between the two limners, see II. 264). Abell's inheritance of Thomas Fysshe's two apprentices in 1450 as well as his eventual tenancy of three shops on Paternoster Row (see C. Paul Christianson, *A Directory of London Stationers and Book Artisans 1300–1500*, [New York: Bibliographical Society of America, 1990], 59–60) suggest that Scott's reservations about the subtle and yet very definite difference in style may be accommodated by the archival indications that Abell's success was aided by a number of talented assistants.

49. Illumination attributed by Alexander, "A Lost Leaf from a Bodleian Book of Hours," *Bodleian Library Record* 8 (1971), 251. Michael K. Jones identifies de Vere as the owner in a private communication to Reynolds, cited in "English Patrons and French Artists in Fifteenth-Century Normandy," in *England and Normandy in the Middle Ages*, ed. David Bates and Anne Curry (London: Hambledon Press, 1994), 308, n. 55.

50. Jefferson, "Two Fifteenth-Century Manuscripts," 19.

51. Identified by Holly James-Maddocks in her forthcoming PhD thesis, entitled "Collaborative Book Production and its Organisation in Fifteenth-Century London: Scribes and Limners from the 1440s to the 1490s," University of York.

52. Scott, *Later Gothic Manuscripts*, II. 322–325.

53. Martha Driver, "Women Readers and Pierpont Morgan Library MS M. 126," in *John Gower: Manuscripts, Readers, Contexts*, ed. Malte Urban (Turnhout: Brepols, 2009), 71–108. See also Martha Driver, "Printing the *Confessio Amantis*: Caxton's Edition in Context," in *Revisioning Gower: New Essays*, ed. R. F. Yeager (Asheville, NC: Pegasus Press, 1998), 269–303 (esp. 282–5, n. 27, 28, 29, 30, 31).

54. Attributed to Illustrator A of Fitzwilliam Museum 56 in Scott, *Later Gothic Manuscripts*, II. 328 and "perhaps" to the "Three Kings' Master" in II. 332, who are both "in some way professionally associated." Scott's divisions of the anonymous illuminators, particularly the miniaturists, surrounding Franciscus in his later career are reassessed at length by James-Maddocks in her PhD thesis. She hopes to shortly publish these findings in a separate article.

55. Scott, *Later Gothic Manuscripts*, II. 318–320.

56. Nall, "Ricardus Franciscus," 210 and 212, n. 18. See also Scott, *Later Gothic Manuscripts*, II. 320.

57. Scott, *Later Gothic Manuscripts,* II. 319 and 321.

58. See Nicholas Orme, "Worcester , William (1415–1480x85)," *Oxford Dictionary of National Biography* (Oxford University Press, 2004; online edn, Oct 2006), http://www.oxforddnb.com/view/article/29967/ , accessed 30 Aug 2011.

59. Nall, "Ricardus Franciscus," 211, n. 1.

60. See Driver, "'Me fault faire,'" 437 (and n. 39 on this page for further reference).

61. We can by no means be certain that it was York rather than Beaufort who patronized this manuscript but see note 43 above for an argument in favor of York.

62. See note 6 above.

63. See Johnson, *Richard of York,* Appendix III "Servants and Annuitants of Duke Richard of York," 231. In 1445, for example, York's ducal council consisted of Ralph Lord Cromwell, Thomas Lord Scales, Sir John Fastolf, Sir Andrew Ogard, Sir William ap Thomas, and Sir William Oldhall, as well as a new receiver-general, John Milewater. See pp. 16–18 for the additions and losses to the circle of ducal servants over the 1430s, 1440s, and 1450s. This ducal council was bound to York by oath; responsibilities included estate administration, contracting debts in the duke's name, acquiring and disposing of property, and control of a ducal seal of arms (see p.18 for references to specific examples).

64. Johnson, *Richard of York,* 148 (n.126) and 231.

65. See James Gairdner, ed., *The Paston Letters* (Gloucester: Alan Sutton Publishing, 1987, repr. of 1904 Library ed.), II, no 59, and see also II, nos. 102, 238. For further references to a handful of other known writers of petitions see Dodd, "Writing Wrongs," 24, n. 96.

66. Dodd, "Writing Wrongs," 17. Dodd argues that "the plaints, bills and petitions to be found at a popular level all adopted basic *ars dictaminis* techniques," i.e. he who could write a formal letter could write a petition, but "petitions for presentation to the crown required skill and training" and a "high[er] level of precision."

67. This is certainly the case by 1452 when York presents his own articles to the council condemning Somerset for misconduct during the loss of Normandy.

68. Joseph Stevenson, *Letters and Papers Illustrative of the Wars of the English in France,* vol. 2, part 2 (London: Longman, 1864), 718-22.

69. *PROME,* parliament of 1450, "Introduction."

70. Transcription by Curry, *PROME,* parliament of 1450, "Introduction." See also Watts, *Henry VI,* 274 n. 57.

71. Johnson, "Richard of York," 159. It is interesting that York takes no other rewards..

72. Watts, *Henry VI*, 274 and n.57. *PROME*, parliament of 1450, "Introduction."

73. Johnson, "Richard of York," 112. The most important of York's articles, according to Johnson, is the Duke's claim that Somerset had kept 72,000 francs given to him to pass on as compensation to those who had lost property in Anjou and Maine, that is, money that should have been given to Oldhall and Fastolf.

74. Including Fastolf and Oldhall. Johnson, "Richard of York" 16.

75. Johnson, "Richard of York" 19.

76. A similar point is made by Nall, "Ricardus Franciscus," 210. William Worcester was the author of the *Boke of Noblesse*, a military treatise he composed for Sir John Fastolf urging the importance of a new campaign in France. For the *Boke*'s rededication to Edward IV and Richard III, see Anne F. Sutton and Livia Visser-Fuchs, *Richard III's Books* (Stroud: Sutton Publishing, 1997), 85–88.

77. As he is termed by Kate Harris in "Patrons, Buyers and Owners: The Evidence for Ownership and the role of Book Owners in Book Production and the Book Trade," in *Book Production and Publishing in Britain 1375-1475*, ed. Jeremy Griffiths and Derek Pearsall (Cambridge: Cambridge University Press, 1989), 178.

78. See note 71 above.

79. Jackson W. Armstrong "The Development of the Office of Arms in England, c.1413–1485," in *The Herald in Late Medieval Europe*, ed. Katie Stevenson (Suffolk: The Boydell Press, 2009), 9–28 (esp. 24).

80. *Ibid*. See also Sutton and Visser-Fuchs, *Richard III's Books*, chapter 4 (esp. 102).

81. The large network of association surrounding this coterie of alien and foreign limners is beyond the scope of this note and is considered in detail in James-Maddocks' forthcoming PhD thesis, University of York. Other scribes who collaborated with this particular combination of illuminators on multiple occasions include the scribe who organized the production of a series of *Genealogical Chronicles* as propaganda for Edward IV, another scribe mass-producing *Nova Statuta*, and the court-poet Pietro Carmeliano.

82. Mooney, "Locating Scribal Activity in Late-Medieval London," 199–200.

83. See, for example, Bertram Wolffe, *Henry VI* (London: Eyre Methuen, 1981), 244, who states "the Commons had the backing of York, and the mantle of Suffolk had descended on Somerset"; Maurice Keen, *England in the Later Middle Ages: A Political History* (London; NY: Routledge, 2003), 349 and 362 where he states that York "could read clearly between the lines of Suffolk's impeachment and Cade's proclamations." See also Watts, *Henry VI*, 274 and 286.

84. From 2003 to 2007, W. Mark Ormrod directed a project to make available the contents of the entire corpus of the National Archives series cf Ancient Petitions (SC 8) via the National Archives' online Catalogue (http://
www.nationalarchives.gov.uk/catalogue/). At the same time the series was
digitized and published (free of charge) through the National Archives'
special facility, Documents Online (http://www.nationalarchives.gov.uk/
documentsonline/). See W. Mark Ormrod, Gwilym Dodd and Anthony
Musson, eds., *Medieval Petitions, Grace and Grievance* (Woodbridge, Suffolk:
York Medieval Press/ The Boydell Press, 2009).
85. Timothy Haskett analyzed the varieties of Middle English dialect used in
fifteenth-century petitions to the chancellor's court (using TNA series C1:
Early Chancery Proceedings) in "Country Lawyers? The Composers of English Chancery Bills," in *The Life of the Law*, ed. P. Birks (London: Hambledon
Press, 1993), 9–23. Gwilym Dodd's analysis of the diplomatic form and use
of "standard" Anglo-Norman French suggests that private petitioning was
closely regulated by the crown, in *Justice and Grace: Private Petitioning and
the English Parliament in the Late Middle Ages* (Oxford: Oxford University
Press, 2007). Previous palaeographical methodologies applied to petitions
revealed that Adam Pinkhurst wrote a petition for the London Mercers
(Linne R. Mooney, "Chaucer's Scribe," *Speculum* 81 [2006]: 97 - 138) and
Thomas Hoccleve, poet and clerk in the privy seal, has also been found to
have written petitions (Helen Killick, "Thomas Hoccleve as Poet and Clerk,"
[PhD diss., University of York, 2011]).
86. Mooney, "Chaucer's Scribe," 97–138. In a chapter in Mooney and Stubbs'
forthcoming book, *Scribes and the City: London Guildhall Clerks and the Dissemination of Middle English Literature 1375-1425* (York: York Medieval Press,
2012), evidence is presented that after 1400 Pinkhurst was working for the
civic secretariat at the Guildhall. A new project, funded by the Andrew W.
Mellon Foundation, "The Writing of Petitions in Later Medieval England,"
led by W. Mark Ormrod in collaboration with Linne Mooney and Gwilym
Dodd is currently underway (until March 2013) to address the key issue of
who actually wrote these petitions. A scribe's background and training will
be analyzed for its effect on the layout, form, and discourse of the petition.

WORKS CITED

Manuscripts

Cambridge, St John's College, MS H. 5 (*olim* 208).
Cambridge, University Library, MS Additional 7870.
London, British Library, MS Additional 48031A.
London, British Library, MS Harley 2915.
London, British Library, MS Harley 4012.

London, British Library, MS Harley 4775.

London, Hospital of St. Bartholomew, Smithfield, Cartulary in two volumes compiled by John Cok.

London, The National Archives at Kew, C 49/ 30/ 18.

London, The National Archives at Kew, C 49/ 30/ 19.

London, Worshipful Company of the Tallow Chandlers, Grant of Arms, 24 September 1456.

Los Angeles, J. Paul Getty Museum, MS 5, 84 ML. 723.

Nancy, Archives Departmentales de Meurthe et Moselle, MS H. 80.

New York, Morgan Library and Museum, MS M. 126.

Oxford, Bodleian Library, MS Ashmole 764.

Oxford, Bodleian Library, MS Ashmole 789.

Oxford, Bodleian Library, MS Laud Misc. 570.

Oxford, University College, MS 85.

Philadelphia, Rosenbach Museum and Library, MS 439/16 (*olim* Phillipps 4254).

San Marino, Huntington Library, MS HM 932.

Primary Sources

Davis, Norman, ed. *Paston Letters and Papers of the Fifteenth Century*, volume 2. Oxford: Oxford University Press, 2004.

Flenley, Ralph. *Six Town Chronicles*. Oxford, Oxford University Press, 1911.

Gairdner, James, ed. *The Paston Letters*, volume 2. Gloucester: Alan Sutton Publishing, 1987.

Given-Wilson, Chris, general ed. *The Parliament Rolls of Medieval England, 1275–1504*, CD-ROM version. Leicester: Scholarly Digital Editions and The National Archives, 2005.

Stevenson, Joseph. *Letters and Papers Illustrative of the Wars of the English in France*, volume 2, part 2. London: Longman, 1864.

Secondary Sources

Alexander, Johnathan. "A Lost leaf from a Bodleian Book of Hours," *Bodleian Library Record* 8 (1971): 248–251.

Alexander, Jonathan. "William Abell 'lymnour' and 15th Century English Illumination." In *Kunsthistorische Forschungen: Otto Pacht zu seinem 70. Geburtstag*, ed. Artur Rosenauer and Gerold Weber. Salzburg: Residenz Verlag, 1972, 166–172.

Armstrong, Jackson W. "The Development of the Office of Arms in England, c.1413–1485." In *The Herald in Late Medieval Europe*, ed. Katie Stevenson. Suffolk: The Boydell Press, 2009, 9–28.

Christianson, C. Paul. *A Directory of London Stationers and Book Artisans 1300–1500*. New York: Bibliographical Society of America, 1990.

Curry, Anne. "'A Game of Two Halves': The Parliaments of Henry VI." *Parliamentary History* 23.1 (2004): 73–102.

Dodd, Gwilym. *Justice and Grace: Private Petitioning and the English Parliament in the Late Middle Ages*. Oxford: Oxford University Press, 2007.

——. "The Rise of English, the Decline of French: Supplications to the English Crown, c. 1420–1450." *Speculum* 86 (2011): 117–150.

——. "Writing Wrongs: The Drafting of Supplications to the Crown in Later Fourteenth-Century England." forthcoming in *Medium Aevum*.

Driver, Martha. "'Me fault faire': French Makers of Manuscripts for English Patrons." In *Language and Culture in Medieval Britain: The French of England, c.1100–c.1500*, ed. Jocelyn Wogan-Browne *et al.* Woodbridge, Suffolk: York Medieval Press/ The Boydell Press, 2009, 420–443.

——. "Printing the *Confessio Amantis*: Caxton's Edition in Context." In *Revisioning Gower: New Essays*, ed. R. F. Yeager. Asheville, NC: Pegasus Press, 1998, 269–303.

——. "Women Readers and Pierpont Morgan Library MS M. 126." In *John Gower: Manuscripts, Readers, Contexts*, ed. Malte Urban. Turnhout: Brepols, 2009, 71–108.

Dutton, A. M. "Piety, Politics and Persona: British Library MS Harley 4012 and Anne Harling." In *Prestige, Authority and Power in Late Medieval Manuscripts and Texts*, ed. F. Riddy. Woodbridge, Suffolk: York Medieval Press/ The Boydell Press, 2000, 133–146.

Hamer, Richard. "Spellings of the Fifteenth-Century Scribe Ricardus Franciscus." In *Five Hundred Years of Words and Sounds: A Festschrift for Eric Dobson*, ed. E. G. Stanley and Douglas Gray. Cambridge: D. S. Brewer, 1983, 63–73.

Harris, Kate. "Patrons, Buyers and Owners: The Evidence for Ownership and the role of Book Owners in Book Production and the Book Trade." In *Book Production and Publishing in Britain 1375–1475*, ed. Jeremy Griffiths and Derek Pearsall. Cambridge: Cambridge University Press, 1989, 163–200.

Haskett, Timothy. "Country Lawyers? The Composers of English Chancery Bills." In *The Life of the Law: Proceedings of the Tenth British Legal History Conference, University of Oxford 1991*, ed. P. Birks. London: Hambledon Press, 1993, 9–23.

James-Maddocks, Holly. "Collaborative Book Production and its Organisation in Fifteenth-Century London." PhD diss., University of York, forthcoming.

Jefferson, Lisa. "Two Fifteenth-Century Manuscripts of the Statutes of the Order of the Garter." *English Manuscript Studies 1100–1700* 5 (1995): 18–35.

Johnson, P. A. *Duke Richard of York 1411-1460*. Oxford: Clarendon Press, 1988.

Jones, M. K. "Somerset, York and the Wars of the Roses." *EHR* 104 (1989): 285–307.

Keen, Maurice. *England in the Later Middle Ages: A Political History*. Second ed. London; New York: Routledge, 2003.

Killick, Helen. "Thomas Hoccleve as Poet and Clerk." PhD diss., University of York, 2011.

Marks, Richard and Paul Williamson. *Gothic Art for England 1400–1547*. London: V&A Publications, 2003.

McIntosh, Angus, M. L. Samuels and Michael Benskin. *A Linguistic Atlas of Late Mediaeval English*, Volume 1. Aberdeen: Aberdeen University Press, 1986.

McSparran, Frances, ed. *The Middle English Dictionary, University of Michigan, 2001*, http://quod.lib.umich.edu/m/med/ accessed August 30, 2011.

Meale, Carole. "Patrons, Buyers and Owners: Book Production and Social Status." In *Book Production and Publishing in Britain 1375–1475*, ed. Jeremy Griffiths and Derek Pearsall. Cambridge: Cambridge University Press, 1989, 201–238.

Mooney, Linne R. "Chaucer's Scribe." *Speculum* 81 (2006): 97–138.

———. "*Locating Scribal Activity in Late-Medieval London.*" In *Design and Distribution of Late Medieval Manuscripts in England,* ed. Margaret Connolly and Linne Mooney. Woodbridge, Suffolk: York Medieval Press/ The Boydell Press, 2008, 183–204.

Mooney, Linne R. and Estelle Stubbs, *Scribes and the City: London Guildhall Clerks and the Dissemination of Middle English Literature 1375-1425.* York: York Medieval Press, 2012.

Musson, Anthony. *Medieval Law in Context: The Growth of Legal Consciousness from Magna Carta to the Peasants' Revolt*. Manchester: Manchester University Press, 2001.

Nall, Catherine. "Ricardus Franciscus Writes for William Worcester." *Journal of the Early Book Society* 11 (2008): 207–212.

Orme, Nicholas. "Worcester, William (1415–1480x85)," *Oxford Dictionary of National Biography*. Oxford University Press, 2004; online edn, Oct 2006. http://www.oxforddnb.com/view/article/29967/, accessed 30 Aug 2011.

Ormrod, W. Mark, Gwilym Dodd and Anthony Musson, eds. *Medieval Petitions, Grace and Grievance*. Woodbridge, Suffolk: York Medieval Press/ The Boydell Press, 2009.

Reynolds, Catherine. "English Patrons and French Artists in Fifteenth-Century Normandy." In *England and Normandy in the Middle Ages*, ed. David Bates and Anne Curry. London: Hambledon Press, 1994, 299–313.

Roskell, J. S. "Sir William Oldhall, speaker in the parliament of 1450-1." *Nottingham Medieval Studies* 5 (1961): 87–112.

Rust, Martha. *Imaginary Worlds in Medieval Books: Exploring the Manuscript Matrix*. New York; Hampshire: Palgrave Macmillan, 2007.

Scase, Wendy. *Literature and Complaint in England, 1272-1553*. Oxford; New York: Oxford University Press, 2007.

Scott, Kathleen. "A Mid-Fifteenth-Century Illuminating Shop and Its Customers," *Journal of the Warburg and Courtauld Institutes* 31 (1968): 170–196.

———. *Later Gothic Manuscripts 1390–1490*, A Survey of Manuscripts Illuminated in the British Isles 6. London: Harvey Miller, 1996.

Sutton, Anne F, and Livia Visser-Fuchs. *Richard III's Books*. Stroud: Sutton Publishing, 1997.

Ullman, Berthold L. "Manuscripts of Duke Humphrey of Gloucester." *The English Historical Review* 52. 208 (1937): 670–672.

Vickers, K. H. *Humphrey Duke of Gloucester*. London: A. Constable, 1907.

Watts, John. *Henry VI and the Politics of Kingship*. Cambridge: Cambridge University Press, 1996.

Wilson, E. "A Middle English Manuscript at Coughton Court, Warwickshire, and British Library MS. Harley 4012." *Notes & Queries* 24 (July 1977): 295–303.

Wolffe, Bertram. *Henry VI*. London: Eyre Methuen, 1981.

Figure 1: Kew, The National Archives (TNA), C 49/30/19; reproduced by permission of The National Archives, Kew, Surrey

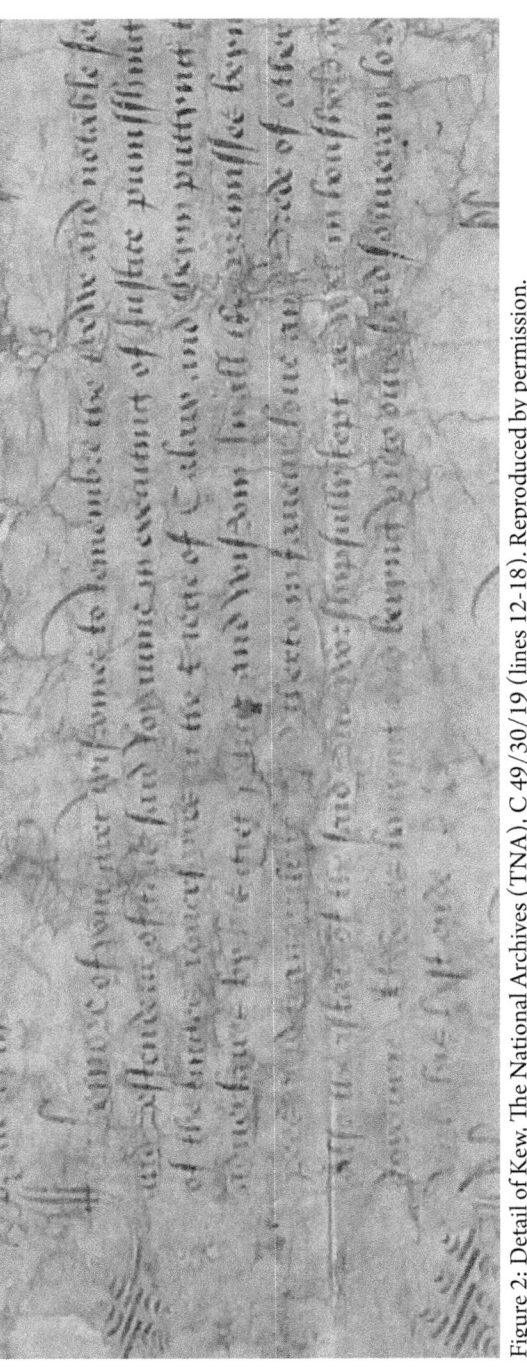

Figure 2: Detail of Kew, The National Archives (TNA), C 49/30/19 (lines 12-18). Reproduced by permission.

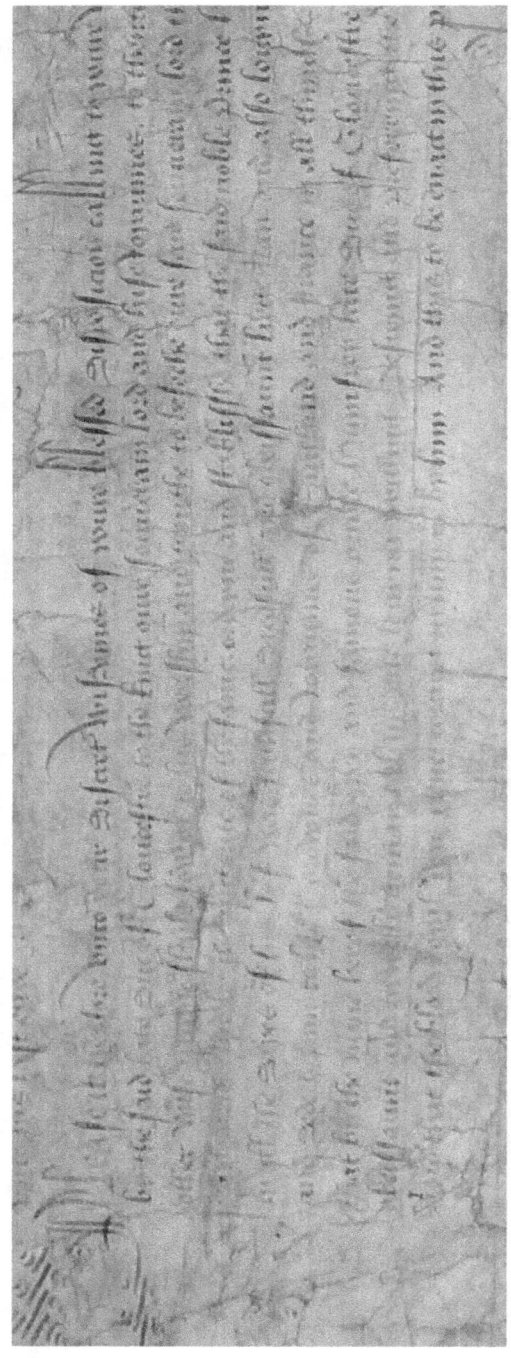

Figure 3: Detail of Kew, The National Archives (TNA), C 49/30/19 (lines 19-27). Reproduced by permission.

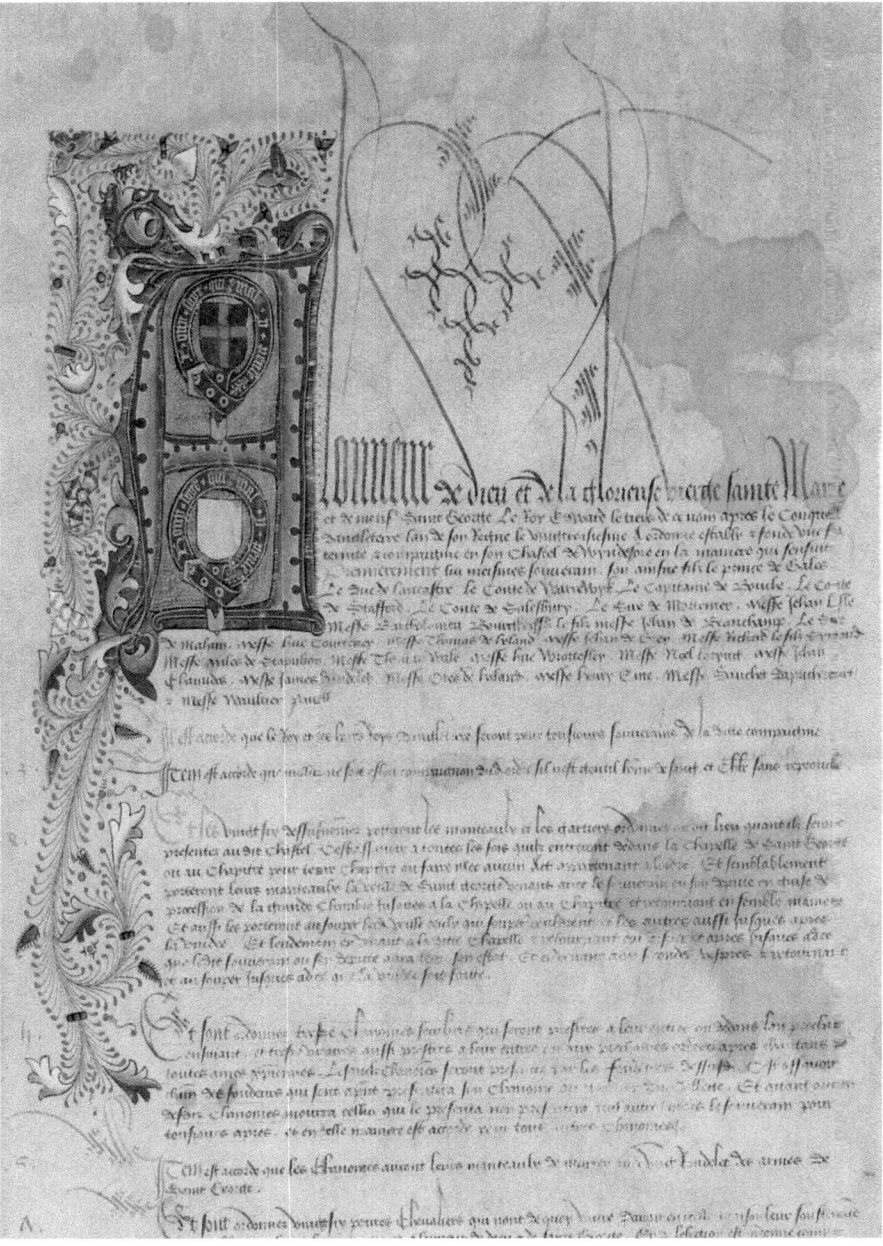

Figure 4: Nancy, Archives Départementales de Meurthe et Moselle, MS. H. 80, Statutes of the Order of the Garter. Membrane 1 (upper half). Reproduced by permission of the Archives Départmentales de Meurthe et Moselle, Nancy.

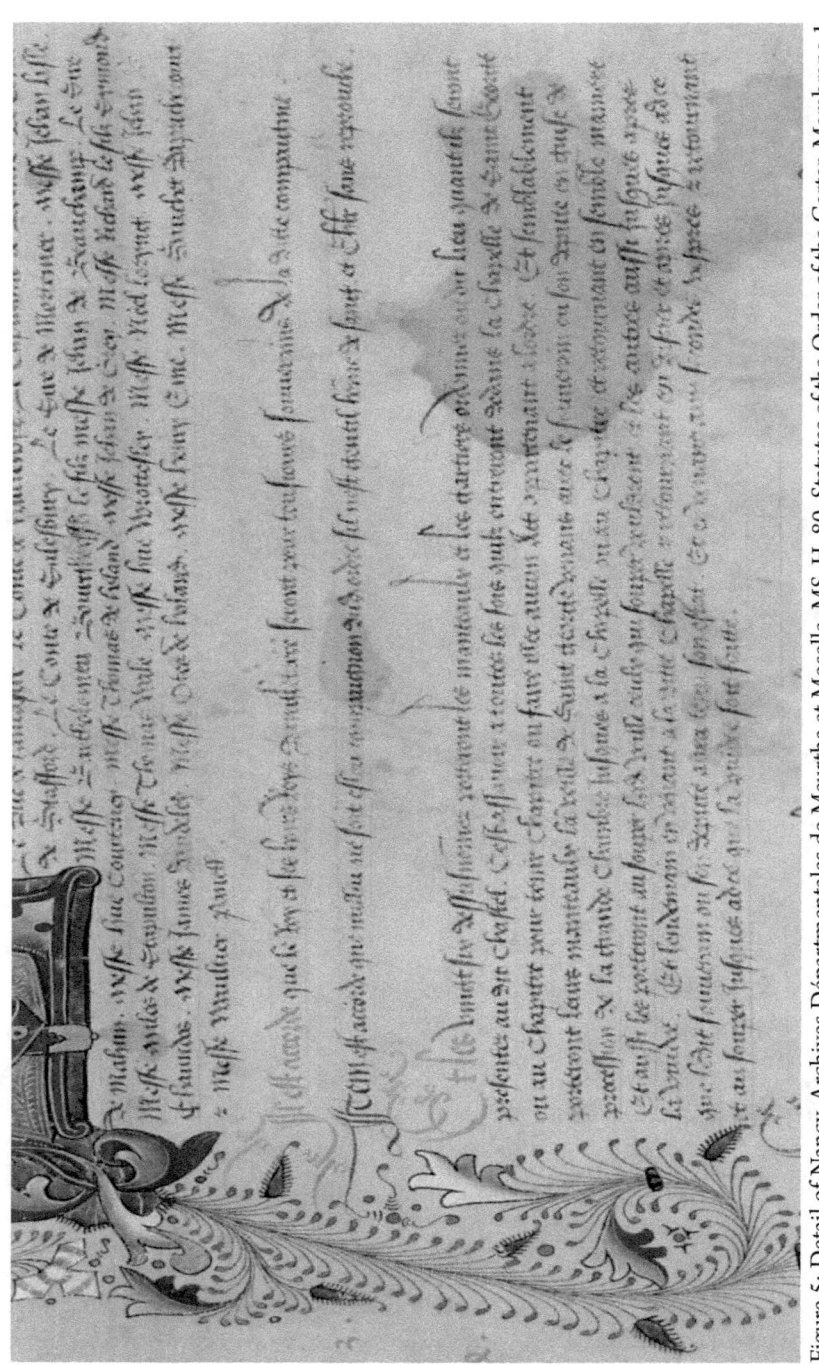

Figure 5: Detail of Nancy, Archives Départmentales de Meurthe et Moselle, MS. H. 80, Statutes of the Order of the Garter. Membrane 1 (lines 6 to 22). Reproduced by permission.

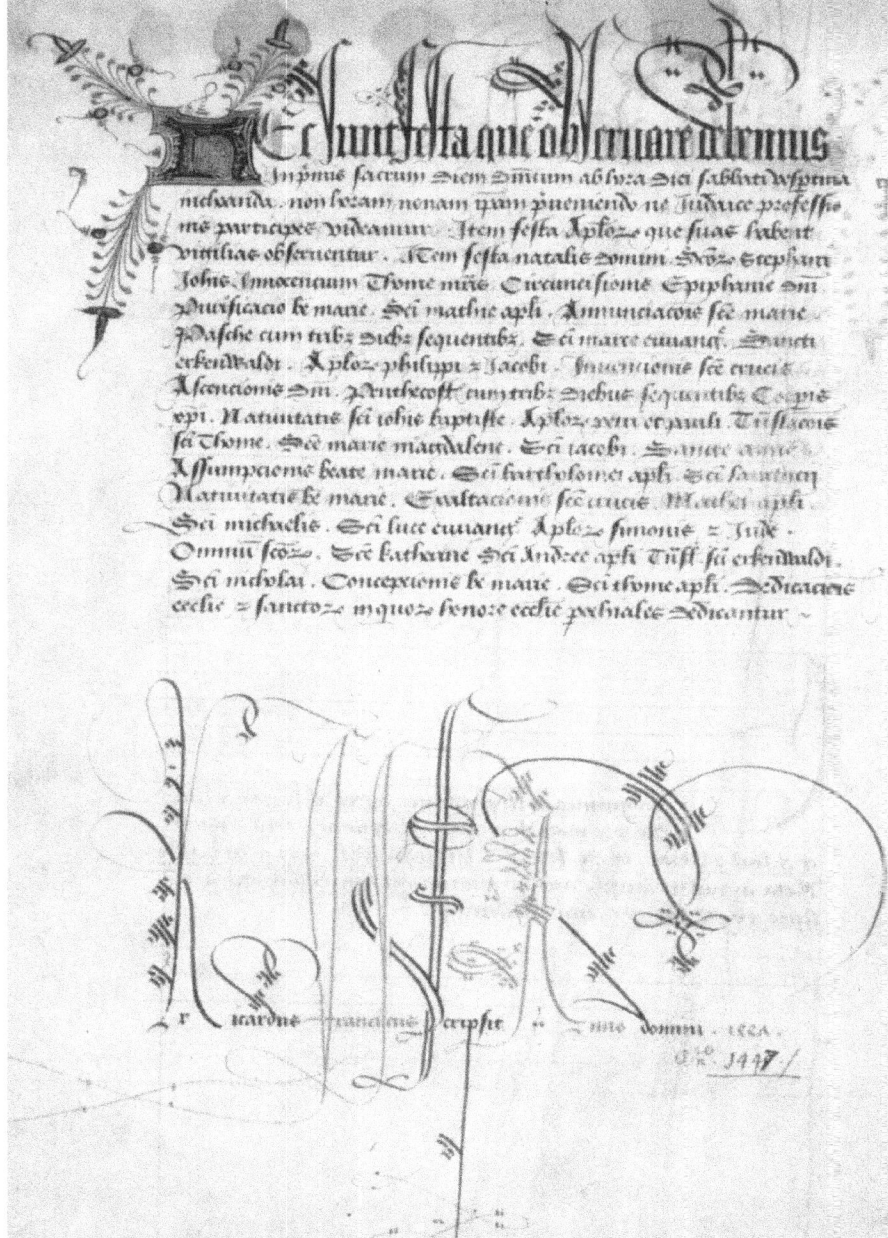

Figure 6: San Marino, Huntington Library, MS. HM 932, Statutes of the Archdeaconry of London, folio 13 verso. This item is reproduced by permission of the Huntington Library, San Marino, California.

Another Manuscript by the Scribe "Cornhyll"

LINNE R. MOONEY AND DANIEL W. MOSSER

When we wrote in *JEBS* 2009 that we would be looking for more examples of manuscripts of major Middle English texts written by the scribe we had identified as "Cornhyll," we hardly expected to find another example so soon as this: New York, Pierpont Morgan Library MS M.875, a copy of John Trevisa's translation of Bartholomeus, *De Proprietatibus Rerum*, is copied by his hand.[1] The handwriting of the scribe here corresponds in every respect to that of the other three manuscripts identified as being written by his hand, which are: Belvoir Castle (Duke of Rutland), John Lydgate, *Fall of Princes*; London, British Library, Harley 1758; and London, Society of Antiquaries 134.

His unlooped **d** has a straight ascender that is often bent low over the bowl of the letter (Fig. 1, line 2, "and"; Fig. 2, 3 lines from bottom, initial of "defyed"; Fig 3, line 2, "feyned"); the base of his lines is not straight but appears to wave slightly above the ruled line (Fig. 1, lines 6 and 7; Fig. 3, line 4); the letters **i** and **y** are often dotted with a slanting hairline sliver (Fig. 1, line 1, "by" and "cerclis"; Fig 3, line 2, "iapes"); the descender of **y** tapers to a hairline with a tight curl to the right at the bottom (Fig. 2, fifth line from bottom, "gleymy"; Fig. 3, line 6, "storye") ; and the anglicana **g** has a lower lobe with squashed appearance and a slight point to the left (Fig. 2, second line from bottom, "gleymy"; Fig. 3, line 7, "song"). All four manuscripts by the scribe also share an atypical form of signatures, consisting of an Arabic number for position in the quire followed by a letter indicating the quire's position in the volume: the typical order in English manuscripts of the fifteenth century is letter followed by number, whether Arabic or Roman.

This newly discovered manuscript also shares the same limner with the others, having the characteristic single stem and leaf extending from the ground to left of a champ initial (Fig. 1, champ initial **S** at line 11; Fig. 2, champ initial **A** at line 11; Fig. 3, champ initial **N** at line 12). Like the other manuscripts by this hand, Morgan M.875 is also decorated to a very high standard, with rose and green initials on illuminated grounds and ¾-borders of rose, blue, green and gold with acanthus leaves at the beginnings of each book, and frequent illuminated 3-line champ initials on rose and blue grounds (see initials of Figures 1 and 2). The scribe writes rubric headings and running titles, and is probably also responsible for the red and blue paraphs. As in the other manuscripts by his hand, the scribe has gone back to carefully proofread his copy, making corrections of individual words through erasure and adding missing lines in the margins keyed to their positions in the text.[2]

Manuscript copies of seven different major Middle English works in four manuscripts can now be attributed to this scribe who signs his name "Cornhyll" at the end of his copy of Chaucer's *Canterbury Tales* in Harley 1758:

> Chaucer's *Canterbury Tales* in London, British
>   Library, Harley 1758
> Lydgate's *Life of Our Lady* in London in Society of
>   Antiquaries 134
> Gower's *Confessio Amantis* in Society of Antiquaries
>   134
> Hoccleve's *Regiment of Princes* in Society of
>   Antiquaries 134
> Walton's translation of Boethius, *Consolation of
>   Philosophy*
>   in Society of Antiquaries 134
> Lydgate's *Fall of Princes* in Belvoir Castle (Duke of
>   Rutland)
> Trevisa's *On the Properties of Things* in Pierpont
>   Morgan M.875

In our 2009 note we argued that this scribe was London-based, in spite of the Western spellings in his *Canterbury Tales* manuscript: those we attributed to his exemplar, since we could find alternative spellings in the other manuscripts.[3] Although the sampling is small (limited to the folios illustrated with this note), those spellings that are regional in the Morgan manuscript are, for the most part, accommodated in the south-west of England. As we have noted previously, the scribe's spelling practices are markedly influenced by the archetypal language of the Lydgate tradition in the Belvoir Castle manuscript, and by the Western exemplars of his *Canterbury Tales* manuscript. Although Trevisa was a Cornishman, his English reflects the locale of his patron, Sir Thomas Berkeley, in south-western Gloucestershire.[4] If Trevisa's Gloucestershire dialect features were reflected in this *Proprietatibus* manuscript, that might account for some of these forms: "I nowȝe" (enough), "douȝter" (daughter), euyl/euel (evil), "nouȝt" (not), and " þey" (though) being the clearest examples. The spelling "orþe" (earth, f. 114rb, last line) is not attested in *LALME*,[5] the *OED*, or the *MED*, but may be related to the "eorth" (linguistic profiles in Shropshire and Warwickshire) and "urþe" (Shropshire) spellings found in the south-west.

The Belvoir Castle *Fall of Princes* had offered the earliest provenance of the three manuscripts at that time attributed to Cornhyll, having been owned by Margaret Neville, wife of Henry Manners, second earl of Rutland and daughter of Ralph Neville, fourth earl of Westmoreland and his wife Catherine, née Stafford. Catherine's inscription at the front of the manuscript written to her daughter Margaret shows that the manuscript was in their hands before 1555 when Catherine died.

The Pierpont Morgan manuscript of Trevisa's *De Proprietatibus Rerum* offers an even earlier ownership: that of the probable first owner, Richard Beauchamp, Bishop of Salisbury (1430-1481; bishop of Salisbury, 1450-81). Beauchamp signed his name at several places in the manuscript: at the end of the table of contents (folios 1-6ra), where he signs "R B Sarr," and at the end, folio 238va, between the explicit and final "Deo Gracias" where he signs "R B Sarr Eps."[6] The manuscript was later owned by the Tollemache family of Helmingham Hall, Suffolk: it may have entered into their ownership in the lifetime of Lionel Tollemache (d. 1669) through his wife Elizabeth, Countess of Dysart, since the arms of Dysart and Tollemache are stamped into the binding of the manuscript; and it was still at their seat of Helmingham Hall in Suffolk in 1869 when it was catalogued for the Historical Manuscripts Commission.[7] Richard Beauchamp may have been the original owner by whom the manuscript was commissioned, or possibly the second: we know that the scribe was active in the 1430s and 1440s, based on his style of handwriting and on the dates of some of the texts he copies: Lydgate's *Life of Our Lady* having been completed c. 1421-2 and Walton's translation of the *Consolation of Philosophy* in c. 1410.[8]

Beauchamp was papally provided to Hereford in 1448; when the Bishop of Salisbury, William Aiscough, was murdered in 1450, Beauchamp was appointed to fill the see, where he remained until his death in 1481. Although he was a supporter of Henry VI, he was kin to the Anne Beauchamp who married Richard Neville, who, through her, became Earl of Warwick, known to historians as "the King-Maker."[9] In the 1450s, Richard Beauchamp was a supporter and advisor of the King and Queen, even though his kinsman

Warwick supported the Yorkist rebels."[10] As a royal supporter who had connections with the rebel side, Beauchamp (owner of our manuscript) was selected to serve as Henry's emissary to the defeated rebels at Worcester, where "Henry offered them their lives, liberty and property, but also to receive them once again as his dear kin and to treat them with the same favour as before."[11] In 1460, apparently having changed sides but still viewed as an intermediary, Beauchamp again served as emissary (this time on behalf of the Yorkists, who had seized London) addressing King Henry.[12] Beauchamp eventually enjoyed King Edward IV's favor as well and was appointed as the first chancellor of the Order of the Garter in 1475.[13]

This manuscript adds another connection of a London-produced manuscript with a west-country owner to the similar connections of the Harley and Society of Antiquaries manuscripts by this scribe; through the Nevilles, it is also connected to the Belvoir Castle *Fall of Princes* manuscript.[14] Since no other manuscript by this scribe can be traced to its original owner, it is possible that others of the four manuscripts were also originally owned by Beauchamp. However, his having signed this Pierpont Morgan manuscript in several places speaks against this, since no similar signatures survive in the other manuscripts. The Harley 1758 manuscript of *The Canterbury Tales* includes on folio 223v a rough signature of "Rychard" written in red crayon in the margin. Manly and Rickert called attention to this name, using it to support their possible identification of the producer of the manuscript as the limner Richard Claidich, who had a shop in the Cornhill district of London between 1428 and 1452,[15] but it could also refer to an owner, "Richard," added either by someone named Richard or by another person in his household. The name occurs beside text in *The Parson's Tale* where the five "spices" (species) of gluttony are described, which might have reminded the bishop Richard Beauchamp himself or a member of his household of his particular weakness to the sin of gluttony.

Given that the scribe and limner collaborated in producing all four manuscripts, the London surname "Cornhyll" in the Harley manuscript and London connections of many of the later owners point to London production. In that case they may simply represent four manuscripts produced by the same scribe and artist working together. (It is also possible that scribe and artist were one man, and equally possible that Manly and Rickert were correct is naming him as Richard Claidich.) The fact that the manuscripts share similar size and layout, level of illumination, and interest in major writings in Middle English suggest that they may have been commissioned by one original owner to form the basis of a library of popular literature written in English, a very grand version of an Everyman's library in the first half of the fifteenth century. Richard Beauchamp himself is a possible candidate for this commissioner with a special interest in literature, but as his birth in

1430 would be quite late for commissioning books produced in the 1420s or 1430s based on the styles of script and illumination, it seems more likely that he was the second owner of only one of them.[16]

University of York and Virginia Tech

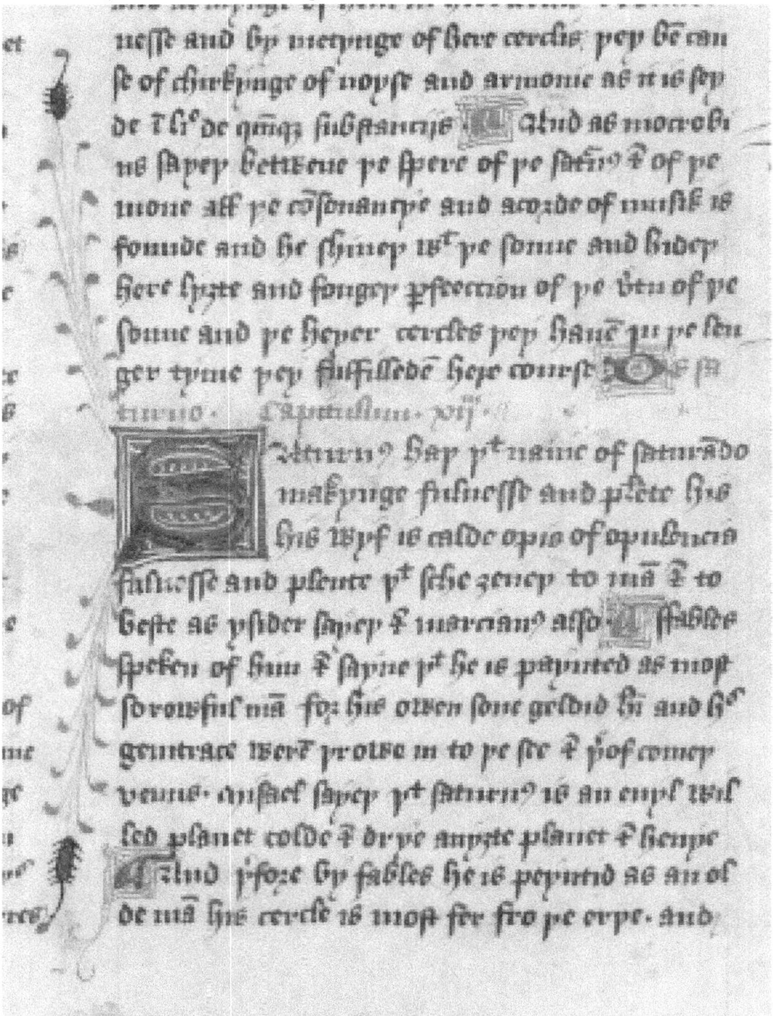

Figure 1. New York, Pierpont Morgan Library MS M.875, folio 114rb, bottom third. Reproduced by kind permission of the Pierpont Morgan Library

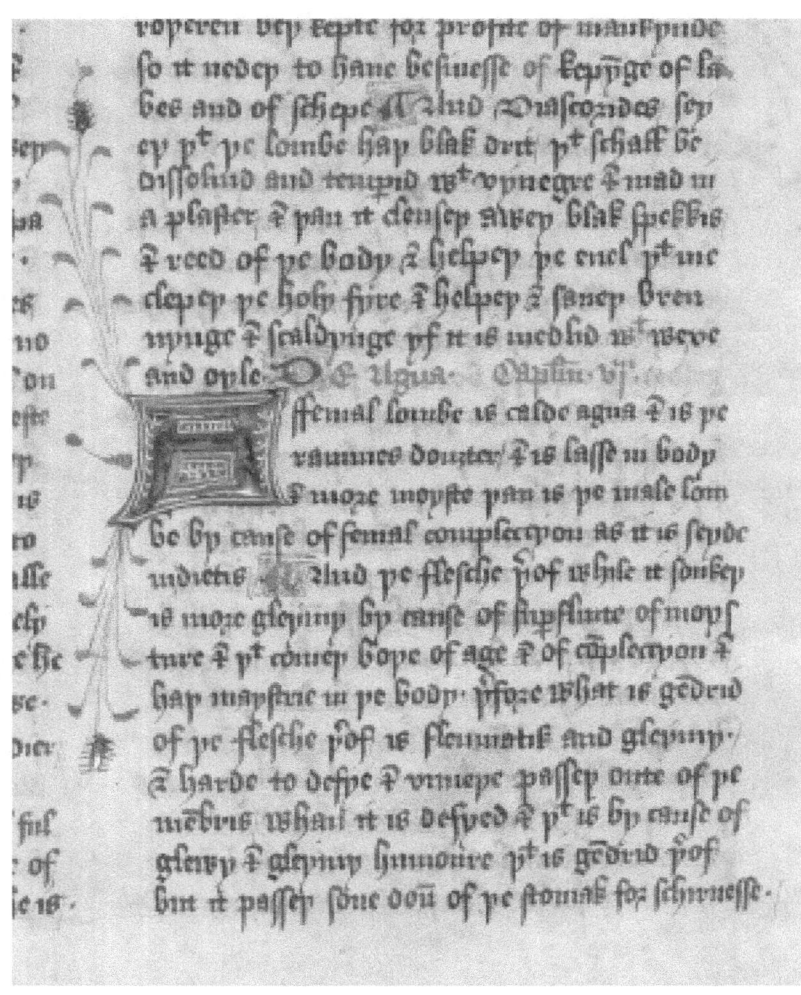

Figure 2. New York, Pierpont Morgan Library, MS M.875, folio 267rb, lower third. Reproduced by kind permission of the Pierpont Morgan Library.

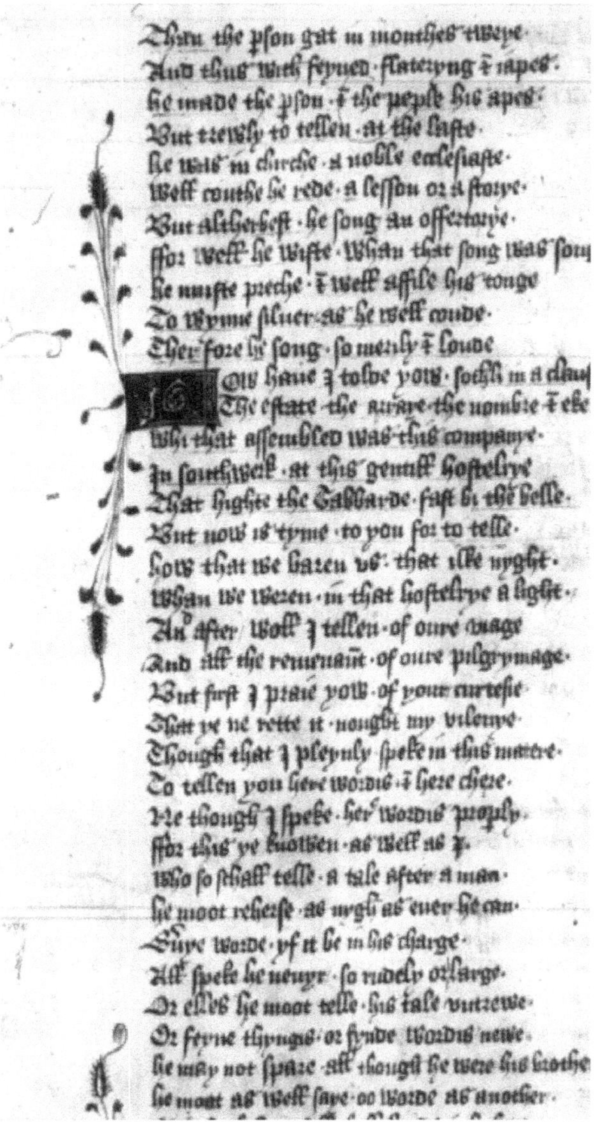

Figure 3. London, British Library, MS Harley 1758, folio 8v

NOTES

1. Mooney first identified his hand in "A New Scribe of Chaucer and Gower," *JEBS* 7 (2004), 131-40. Mooney and Mosser then added the Belvoir Castle (Duke of Rutland) *Fall of Princes* to his manuscripts in "The Belvoir Castle (Duke of Rutland) Manuscript of Lydgate's *Fall of Princes*," *JEBS* 12 (2009), 161-72. We noted that we would be looking for more examples of his hand in the last sentence of this article. The unpublished catalogue of manuscripts in the Pierpont Morgan Library identifies two scribes who "may be distinguished by a variation in pressure, size of the script and precision." This typewritten and annotated catalogue has been published as PDF images in the on-line Corsair catalogue of the manuscripts, http://corsair.morganlibrary.org/cgi-bin/Pwebrecon.cgi?v1=2&ti=1,2&Search%5FArg=trevisa&Search%5FCode=GKEY%5E&CNT=20&PID=B7XSssHndmPghaHmM-v9Ql2WFJ&SEQ=20100830111656&SID=4. Manly and Rickert similarly thought that the Harley MS 1758 was written by two scribes: see John M. Manly and Edith Rickert, *The Text of the Canterbury Tales*, 8 vols. (Chicago: Chicago University Press, 1940), 1.199-200. But closer inspection reveals that both manuscripts were written by a single scribe who could be variable in the size and degree of formality of his hand from one stint to the next: see Mooney's argument in this regard in "A New Scribe of Chaucer and Gower," pp. 131-40. See also the description of the hands in Daniel W. Mosser, "Ha2: London, British Library, Harley MS 1758," *A Digital Catalogue of the Pre-1500 Manuscripts and Incunables of the* Canterbury Tales (Birmingham, UK: Scholarly Digital Editions, 2010), which also argues for a single hand.

2. Manly and Rickert note that the text of *The Canterbury Tales* in Harley 1758 has been carefully corrected, attributing this correction to a supervisor (vol. 1, p. 200), but comparison with the various formal and informal versions of Cornhyll's hand show that most of these are the work of the scribe. Similarly the Lydgate *Fall of Princes* at Belvoir Castle (Duke of Rutland) was carefully proofread and self-corrected by the scribe.

3. Mooney had previously argued for his situation in the west country, based on spellings in both the Harley 1758 MS of *The Canterbury Tales* and the Antiquaries 134 manuscript of Lydgate, Gower, Hoccleve and Walton texts: see "A New Scribe of Chaucer and Gower," p. 135. The earliest identifiable owners of these manuscripts also seemed based in the west country: Harley 1758 being owned in the late sixteenth to seventeenth centuries by Edmund and Edward Foxe, father and son, based near Ludlow but also with London connections, and Antiquaries 134 owned by the baronets Lyttleton of Hagley and Frankley, Worcestershire, and a member of this family noted on a flyleaf that he believed the manuscript had come into their hands from Halesowen Abbey, now at the southern edge of greater Birmingham. Pamela

J. Willetts noted in the catalogue of the Society of Antiquaries manuscripts that the binding was work of a London binder and that notes written into the margins by members of the family indicate that the manuscript was kept in London. See *Catalogue of Manuscripts in the Society of Antiquaries of London* (Cambridge: D. S. Brewer for the Society of Antiquaries, 2000), pp. 60-61.
4. See Jeremy J. Smith, "Studies in the Language of Some Manuscripts of Gower's *Confessio Amantis*," 2 vols. (Diss., University of Glasgow, 1985), 1.197-208. The language of Trevisa is also addressed by Ronald Waldron in "Dialect aspects of Trevisa's translation of the *Polychronicon*," in Felicity Riddy, ed., *Regionalism in Late Mediaeval Manuscripts and Texts: Essays Celebrating the Publication of* A Linguistic Atlas of Late Mediaeval English (Cambridge: D. S. Brewer, 1991), pp. 67-87; esp. Table 4.
5. Angus McIntosh, M. L. Samuels, and Michael Benskin, eds., *A Linguistic Atlas of Late Mediaeval English*, 4 vols. (Aberdeen: Aberdeen Univ. Press, 1986).
6. A hand-written addition to the unpublished catalogue of the Pierpont Morgan Library, now reproduced in PDF images in the on-line Corsair catalogue of the Pierpont Morgan Library (see note 1), indicates that this manuscript was "probably Lord Thomas Berkeley's copy," based on a copy of the dedication at the end of the manuscript, folio 339r: "Endles grase blisse and thanks giue / to our Lordd godd all weldy per thes / translat one that ended / At Barkelet the 6t day of february / Anno Domini 139 1398 the yere of / K Richard the 2d after the conquest / of the 22 / The yeer of my Lordes age Sr Thomas / Lorde of Berkeley that Mad mee make / this seuen and fourty"; but this inscription is added in a hand of the sixteenth century. The catalogue also dates the manuscript to the first decade of the fifteenth century, but both script and decoration are typical of later decades in the fifteenth century.
7. See the on-line Corsair catalogue of manuscripts at the Pierpont Morgan Library (see note 1). According to this catalogue, the MS was examined in 1869 by Arthur J. Horwood (for the Historical Manuscripts Commission) and at another time during the 19th century by Archdeacon R. H. Groome (1810-1889). It was purchased from the Dysart-Tollemache family by Edwin J. Beinecke through A. Robinson and given to the Pierpont Morgan Library in 1955.
8. Ralph A. Klinefelter and Vernon F. Gallagher, eds., *A Critical Edition of John Lydgate's Life of Our Lady*, Duquesne Philological Series 2, gen ed. Joseph A. Lauritus (Pittsburgh, Duquesne University, 1961), p. 7; Walton, John, trans., *Boethius: De Consolatione Philosophiae*, EETS o.s. 170, ed. Mark Science (London: Oxford University Press, 1927; New York: Kraus Reprint, 1971), p. xliii-xliv.

9. When Richard Neville (aged 7) married Anne Beauchamp (aged *c.* 10) in 1436, his sister, Cecily Neville, married her older brother, Henry Beauchamp, whose death resulted in the transfer of Warwick titles from Beauchamps to Nevilles. Cecily and Henry's mother was Isabel Despenser, who had previously been married to Richard Beauchamp, Earl of Worcester (Hicks, *Warwick the Kingmaker,* pp. 26-7). Richard Neville's path to the Beauchamp title was not clear-cut: among the other claimants was Lord Beauchamp of Powicke (Hicks, p. 35). Events in France, the death of Henry and Cecily's daughter, Anne Beauchamp, and Richard Neville's subsequent and fortuitous presence at the House of Lords as earl of Warwick (though he had not attained the age of majority) resulted in the issuance of a letter patent recognizing Richard as Earl, July 23, 1449 (Hicks, pp. 37-9). The appellation 'King-maker' comes from William Shakespeare, *The Third Part of Henry VI,* 2.3.37. Richard Neville was the grandson of Ralph, the Earl of Westmorland, whose first wife was Margaret Stafford. His second wife was John of Gaunt's legitimated bastard daughter (with Catherine Swinford), Joan Beaufort, with whom he had numerous offspring, all of whom were married advantageously: daughter Anne to the Earl of Stafford and Duke of Buckingham; Eleanor to the Earl of Northumberland; Katherine to the Duke of Norfolk; and Cecily to the Duke of York (see Michael Hicks, *Warwick the Kingmaker* [Oxford, UK and Malden, MA: Blackwell, 1998], pp. 13-14, esp. Table 2.3).

10. *Oxford Dictionary of National Biography* (online: http://www.oxforddnb.com/; accessed December 3, 2011): "Clearly Henry VI and the queen regarded him as an intimate supporter. On the other hand, the bishop was a kinsman of Anne Beauchamp, wife of Richard Neville, earl of Warwick, and had known her when they were young. Thus on 10 May 1460 he was the only bishop in the delegation from the crown [Henry VI] to the southern convocation in search of funds. On 19 May he presided there over the trial of the heretic John Brehill. However, as soon as the rebel earls of Warwick, Salisbury, and March entered London in the following month he joined them."

11. Hicks, *Warwick the Kingmaker,* p. 166.

12. Hicks, *Warwick the Kingmaker,* p. 178.

13. *Oxford Dictionary of National Biography* (online: http://www.oxforddnb.com/; accessed December 3, 2011.

14. See our previous notes, JEBS 7 (2004), 135-7 and JEBS 12 (2009), 163-5.

15. Manly and Rickert, *Text of the Canterbury Tales,* 1.203.

16. At his death in 1481, the Bishop left his "*magnum et sumtuosam bibliam meam*" to Edward IV ("*Excellentissimus Principi Edwardo*"). See PROB 11/7, fols. 31r-v, Will of Richard Beauchamp, 8 February 1481. There is also an inscription the South Quire Aisle of St George's Chapel: "Who leyde this booke here The Reverend Fader in god Richard Beauchamp Bisschop of this

Diocyse of Sarysbury and wherfor to this entent that Preestis and ministers of goddis chirche may here haue the occupacion therof seyyng therin theyr divine servyse and for alle othir that lystyn to sey therby ther devocyon askyth he any sp'uall mede yee asmoche as oure lord lyst to reward hym for his good entent praying euery man w'os dute or devocion is eased by thys booke they woll sey for hym this commune Oryson Dne Ihu xpe: knelyng in the presence of this holy Crosse for the wyche the Reverend Fadir in god above seyd hathe grauntid of the treasure of the Chirche to eu'y man xl days of pardun" (http://www.stgeorges-windsor.org/archives/blog/?tag=richard-beauchamp). This suggests another religious volume, possibly a breviary. In February 1473, Edward IV had Beauchamp "appointed master and surveyor of St George's Chapel, Windsor, and became much involved in construccion of the great new chapel" (*DNB*).

Private Reading and the Rolls of the *Symbols of the Passion*

SARAH NOONAN

British Library, Additional MS 22029 is a fifteenth-century parchment roll five inches in width and over four feet in length that contains just one text, a witness of the *Symbols of the Passion*, a lyric also known by its incipit "O Vernicle" (IMEV 2577, Figure 1). It was once quite sumptuous, containing many illuminations and wrapped in brown cloth attached to the roll with red and gold thread. Only shreds of the brown cloth now remain, and several of the opening illuminations have been worn by the rolling and unrolling of the manuscript. The *Symbols of the Passion* survives in twenty witnesses, ten of which are rolls—a truly striking number, since no other Middle English religious prayers or poems have more than one surviving witness in roll form.[1] The poem presents, through a series of twenty-four images and accompanying sections of text, the *arma Christi*—images and symbols of Christ's Passion popular in the later Middle Ages.[2] While the *arma Christi* seem often to have functioned as iconographic focal points for affective meditational practices, in the *Symbols* they are placed in a loosely narrated format. Each of the images and symbols is briefly described and then discussed in terms of what sin (or sins) it might provide protection against.

This essay considers how readers might have interacted with these rolls in both public and private settings and suggests that the prevalent use of the roll format for this text could indicate that a parity existed between how Christ's body and this late-medieval devotional text were read by devout audiences. While it is difficult, if not impossible, to reconstruct with certainty how past readers might have interacted with these rolls, I suggest that the witnesses to the *Symbols*, through their material form and *mise-en-page*, invite readers to consult this poem—a text that is focused on the fragments of Christ's body and the fragmented events of his Passion—in a selective, discontinuous fashion. Just as late-medieval audiences displayed an intense fascination with the ways in which Christ's body could be partitioned, meditating on his specific wounds or the weapons used against him during his Passion, so, too, does it seem possible that the *Symbols* was read by a private reader or an intimate group of readers with a similar interest in the affective power of the part over the whole.

The poem opens with an image depicting the face of Christ imprinted on Veronica's veil (Figure 2). In BL Add. MS 22029, Veronica holds the veil in front of her body, completely covering herself except for her head and hands. Below this opening image, the poem reads:

> The vernacul—I honowre hym [and the]
> þat the made throwe hys pryuy[té];
> The clothe he set ovyr hys face,
> The prynte he lefte ther, of hys grace,
> Hys mowthe, hys nose, hys eyn too,
> Hys berd, hys here he ded also.
> Schyld me, lorde, for þat in myn lyffe
> That I haue synnyd with myn wyttys fyve,
> Namelyche with mowthe of stlawndrynge,
> Of fals othys and bakbytynge
> And makyng boste with tonge alsoo
> Of many synnys that I haue doo:
> Lorde of heuyn, for-zeue it me
> Throwe vertew of the fygure þat I here se.[3]

The poem does not begin with an image or description of the crucified Christ hanging on the cross, one of the most common representations of Christ during the late Middle Ages; nor does it begin with an image of the knife of Christ's circumcision, the chronologically logical point at which to begin this prayer sequence, since it was considered to be the symbolic first moment when Christ's blood was shed for mankind. Instead the poem subverts the narrative order of the events of Christ's life and the Passion as portrayed in the Gospels and forefronts a scene of imprinting, of Christ having transferred the impression of his facial features onto a cloth, thereby highlighting the potential for Christ's body to be transformed, reproduced, and fragmented.[4] It is not a representation of Christ's face that is shown in the opening image and described in the opening stanza, but instead a copy of that face, "the prynte he lefte ther." And this print is decidedly partial, comprised of the compiled fragments of Christ's face: his mouth, his nose, his two eyes, his beard, and his hair. Although difficult to see in Add. MS 22029 due to the wearing of the image, this face floats, disembodied, on Veronica's veil—a representation of a part of Christ's body that is said to protect the penitent not from all sins but rather from a few specific sins committed with the mouth and tongue: slandering, backbiting, and the swearing of false oaths. And although the stanza's final lines ("Lorde of heuyn, for-zeue it me / Throwe vertew of the fygure þat I here se") seem to gesture toward a sense of wholeness, a sense that there is a unified figure to be examined and meditated upon, it is worth keeping in mind that this figure is just a fragment—a representation of a representation of a fragment of Christ's body that protects the reader from the sins committed by pieces of his or her body: his or her mouth and tongue.

As many have commented, the thirteenth century saw an increased interest in bodily integrity and partitioning that continued into the fourteenth and fifteenth centuries; I would like to ask how this cultural and religious engagement with fragmentation could have influenced how this poem, a poem that is itself quite interested in fragmentation, might have been read by late-medieval audiences in its roll form.[5] Modern readers have so far tended to overlook the poem's fragmented textual and visual portrayal of Christ's Passion when considering why so many witnesses of the *Symbols* exist in rolls. One interpretation, still widely accepted, of how late-medieval audiences engaged with the rolls of the *Symbols of the Passion* was proposed by Rossell Hope Robbins in 1939. Robbins suggests that this text was written out in rolls so that it might be displayed within churches, allowing members of a community to view its images and thereby benefit from the indulgences that were often attached to it.[6] He asserts that the "original function of the 'Arma Christi' was congregational" and imagines that "a friar or a parish priest would display such rolls, either holding them up himself, or hanging them from a convenient ledge or niche in the wall, or suspending them from the pulpit."[7] These prominent positions of display would enable members of a congregation to "gain the indulgence by gazing at the roll, and while listening to the priest read the descriptions of the instruments, repeating the *Pater Noster*."[8]

Robbins bases this assumed method of consuming the *Symbols of the Passion* in part on the indulgences attached to some of the witnesses.[9] He focuses his argument on the witness of the *Symbols* found in British Library, Royal MS 17.A.xxvii, attached to which is an indulgence that specifies "Wat man þis armes ouer-se, / For his sinnus sori *and* schereuen be" and "For sy3t of þe uernacul hath graunt / xl dayus to pardon."[10] The emphasis on the benefit of looking at the *arma Christi* in this attached indulgence, an emphasis on looking and seeing that is found elsewhere in the poem as well, leads Robbins to suggest that it was not the recitation of prayers or the reading of the accompanying text that was the intended focus of the poem, but instead the simple viewing of the images, the regarding of the unrolled text put out on display.

In support of Robbins's proposed method of consuming these rolls is the fact that other types of rolls are also thought to have been hung on walls so that they could be viewed in their entirety by groups of people. Linne Mooney, for example, notes that out of sixteen witnesses to "The Kings of England," an anonymous text of propagandistic verse, six occur in rolls; she suggests that two of these rolls show signs of having been nailed up so that the text could be read by passersby.[11] Some genealogical rolls also seem to make the most sense if they are read completely unfurled, allowing for the lines of connection drawn between individuals to be fully followed to their completion, even though at times their length would have rendered actually reading the roll difficult.[12] And a bit further afield, in southern Italy, from the tenth through thirteenth centuries there existed *Exultet* rolls in which the text and illuminated miniatures faced opposite directions, so that the priest could more easily read from the roll while the congregation looked at the images.[13]

Pamela Robinson, however, cautions against assuming that *arma Christi* rolls such as the *Symbols of the Passion* would have been publicly displayed, citing the basic logistical difficulty that "the extant rolls are not nearly large enough for their pictures to be seen at a distance."[14] BL Add. MS 22029 amply illustrates this problem since it is about five inches in width, and so its miniatures are generally less than four inches wide and between one and three inches tall. Other rolls are even narrower, such as Stonyhurst College MS 64, which measures only three inches in width—and seven feet in length. Blairs Mus. 9 (formerly Blairs College MS 13) is similarly proportioned, as are all the other witnesses to the *Symbols* in the roll format that I have examined. If these rolls would have challenged the eyesight of anyone attempting to view their images from even a few feet away, this difficulty does not automatically mean that they would not have been displayed publicly. But it does suggest that the *Symbols* might have been read in alternate ways as well, and it seems probable that the small images on these rolls could have been crafted for a private reader who was able to hold the parchment and regard the images and text from a close distance.

Bodleian Library, MS Add. E.4 further confirms the supposition that the *Symbols* might not have been read while displayed upon a wall or at a distance from the reader, since the poem is paired with a second, unillustrated text, the *Orison of the Passion*. The same scribe writes both texts in a rough *textualis semi-quadrata*, and the shared script of these two works suggests that the *Orison* was not included as an afterthought but was instead originally intended to have followed the *Symbols*. The scribe, however, did not attempt to correct the fact that the final twelve lines of the *Orison* occur on the roll's dorse, apparently because this would not have posed a problem in the reading of the text in this form. If this roll were intended to have been hung up, this format would have made the reading of its text quite inconvenient, since a reader would have had to have had enough access to the roll to flip it over and continue reading on its back to complete the *Orison*.

Also contributing to the likelihood that these rolls were frequently intended for private audiences is the fact that other small rolls have been noted for the imagined ease of their portability. Nicholas Bell, for example, commenting on late-medieval rolls containing musical notation, suggests that music, "such as motets, were often written down on rolls or in unbound *libelli*, two formats which had the advantages of economy and portability, but from the modern perspective the disadvantage of impermanence."[15] Unlike the heavier codex manuscript, rolls—particularly rolls that could fit in the palm of your hand such as those of the *Symbols*—could be easily tucked away in pockets or stored for travel. While the rolls of the *Symbols*, then, might have been hung occasionally for the benefit of a community or congregation, their size and scale strongly hint that they were primarily intended for use by a single reader or a small, intimate group of readers who consulted the *Symbols* at close range and in a private reading environment.

If we assume that the rolls of the *Symbols of the Passion* were most often perused by private readers rather than a larger community of viewers looking at the images from afar, we need to reconsider how this text might have been read by medieval audiences. While the public display of these rolls would privilege the unity of this work, demonstrating how all the *arma Christi* function together as a whole to represent the affective potential of Christ's Passion, the private consumption of these rolls would seem to allow for a more fragmented approach to this work's images and text. As a roll containing this poem was unfurled, a new, self-contained stanza and accompanying illustration would greet the reader (see Figure 3). Each image and corresponding stanza would then offer the reader aid in obtaining forgiveness for a particular sin.

The "I" of the poem, an "I" that is transferrable to each reader and enables him or her to take on the role of the supplicant while reading through the text, begins the poem by requesting that Veronica's veil "Schyld me, lorde, for þat in myn lyffe / That I haue synnyd with myn wyttys fyve, / Namelyche with mowthe of stlawndrynge/ Of fals othys and bakbytynge," but the next stanza quickly shifts the reader's attention to a new symbol and a new sin, depicting the knife of circumcision and inviting the reader to request that the knife "kepe me tylle that I deye" from the "temptacyon of lecherye"[16] The subsequent *arma Christi* continue to provide their own specific forms of protection, with some being more narrow in their focus than others:

the thirty pieces of silver shield the reader "from treson *and* couetyse"; the cloth that covered Christ's eyes protects him or her "from vengawns/ of chyldhode and of ignorawns"; the rods and scourges with which Christ was beaten help to heal sins "of stlowthe and eke of ydylnes"; and the lance that pierced Christ's side helps correct the reader's "stowt pryd also,/ And myn onbuxumnes ther-too."[17] While some readers might have progressed through the text so that they could pray for forgiveness from all the types of sin recounted in the *Symbols*, readers also might conceivably have tailored their reading experience based upon those sins for which they felt they needed the most assistance at a specific moment.

The poem's narrative structure does little to propel the reader through to the poem's end, since only a rough outline of a narrative arc exists in the text. Christ's crucifixion is described as follows (and here I am excerpting the text from five stanzas to draw out only the most narrative sections):

> The nayles throwe fete and handys also, . . .
> The hamyr bothe stern and grete,
> þat droffe þe naylys throw hand and fote, . . .
> The vessel of aysylle and of galle, . . .
> Whan þou thrystyd sore with-alle,
> They gaffe the eysyll with byttyr galle; . . .
> Lord, the spere so scharpe I-grownde,
> þat in thyn herte made a wownde.[18]

These brief narrative markers seem unlikely to have encouraged the reader's continuous engagement. They are repetitive at times (as when one stanza states that the nails went through Christ's hands and feet and then the following stanza repeats the statement that the hammer drove the nails through Christ's hands and feet); and they are additionally divided from each other by prayers for intercession and images of the *arma Christi*. The nails, for example, are separated from the hammer's description by the request, "Lorde, kepe me owt of synne and woo, / That I haue in myn lyffe doo, / With handys handyld or on fote goo," and by the drawn image of a hammer.[19] When facing such a lack of narrative cohesion, it seems quite possible that a reader would have felt little impetus for reading the *Symbols* as a continuous text and could have instead chosen a section of the *arma Christi* to read or meditate upon as he or she deemed necessary.

Although I have focused so far on the witnesses to the *Symbols* that survive in roll form, I would like to turn briefly to the nine witnesses found in codices, since a consideration of how the *Symbols of the Passion* was presented in them can show more clearly how reading this work in its roll form might have invited audiences to engage selectively with its text and images.[20] When occurring in a codex, the *Symbols* is generally grouped with other vernacular or Latin devotional works and is found in modestly sized manuscripts that could be held with ease by the individual reader. The work tends to be written out in a single column and includes illustrations (often illuminated) of the *arma Christi* accompanying virtually every verse of the poem—a *mise-en-page* strongly resembling that employed for those witnesses that occur in rolls. As a group, the codices containing witnesses of the *Symbols* seem, like the rolls, to have been intended for private, devotional use by lay and religious audiences.

All the codices containing the *Symbols* are of moderate size and therefore portable, but one unusually small manuscript, Bodleian Library, MS Douce 1, provides a striking example of how, as with rolls, the materiality of a witness to the *Symbols* could have contributed to the manner in which this work was read. MS Douce 1 is a tiny, mid-fifteenth-century manuscript that measures only 3 inches by 2 3/8 inches.[21] A single scribe wrote out the entirety of the manuscript, which, in addition to the *Symbols of the Passion*, contains short Latin and Middle English devotions and *oratios* centered on Mary, Christ's Passion, and the Holy Name of Christ, and two very brief saints' lives. Due to the miniature size of MS Douce 1, the *Symbols* spans from folio 54v to folio 69v, leaving room for roughly one stanza per page.[22] Illustrations of the *arma Christi* accompany each verse of the *Symbols*, as found in other witnesses, but they are roughly executed, being comprised of uncolored, simply rendered line drawings.

The text in MS Douce 1 is consistently written out in a single column; however, it is striking that the stanzas of the *Symbols* are frequently fragmented by folio divisions and that the illustrations do not always occur on the same folio as the stanza that describes them. This *mise-en-page* visually breaks the poem into pieces, as it is not always possible to read a stanza while simultaneously viewing the accompanying image, thereby weakening the impression—suggested in the roll witnesses of the work—that each stanza and image pairing functioned as a self-contained unit within the larger work. Because the visual unit of the stanza and accompanying illustration is broken apart, I would suggest that MS Douce 1 paradoxically demands that readers continuously engage with the text of the *Symbols*. You have to *turn the page* to read the continuation of the stanza or to pair an image with the text describing it. With a roll, however, the presentation of the text would seem to favor viewing the stanza and accompanying illustration as one of the many self-contained units from which the larger work was constructed. The internal fragmentation, then, of the *Symbols* is more visually apparent in the roll form and contributes, as I suggest above, to the reader's opportunity to select which particular stanzas he or she desired to read in a given moment. Readers of a roll could control how much of the text they could see at a time;

readers of a codex would have had this decision made for them as they flipped through the manuscript's folios.

Much criticism focuses on how rolls might have functioned and signified as communal objects, and some argue that one of the benefits of the roll format is its integrity as a whole document. Anthony Bale comments that "the advantage of the roll format in 'official' settings (guild records, monastic mortuary rolls, armorial registers, alchemical texts, genealogies) is that sheets cannot be removed and so the record's integrity is absolute," and he goes on to assert that "the roll is usually displayed in order to be read, and must be displayed as a whole."[23] But I suggest that in the case of the *Symbols of the Passion*, the form of the roll would have emphasized not the integrity and wholeness of the text but instead the text's ability to be perused effectively and affectively in segments. It would be distinctly more cumbersome to unroll the entirety of a four-foot roll while reading it than it would be to unroll shorter segments as required—and indeed, this is how such rolls are read today by scholars examining them in their respective archives. Of course, consulting a roll in such a manner, unfurling it a section at a time, would not have precluded the reader from reading the poem through to its end. But the continuous consumption of this text should not be assumed and could even be thought of as working against the poem's textual and visual representations of specific fragmented scenes of Christ's Passion and its emphasis on how each scene could work individually to benefit the reader through prayer.

Just as late-medieval audiences, then, displayed an intense fascination with the ways in which Christ's body could be partitioned, meditating on his specific wounds or the weapons used against him during his Passion, so, too, does it seem probable that the roll witnesses of the *Symbols* were read with a similar emphasis on the affective power of the part over the whole. The fact that this text has survived in more rolls by far than any other vernacular devotional text from the fourteenth or fifteenth century seems particularly suggestive of the possibility that the roll form was thought to cater in some way to how readers interacted with this text. When written out on rolls, both the text and its material form appear to encourage readers to move through the *Symbols* by jumping from stanza to stanza, alighting upon those sections most pertinent to their specific devotional needs or goals. While some readers might have progressed through the text so that they could pray for forgiveness for each sin described in the *Symbols*, this text does not appear to demand such a reading, and it seems just as possible that readers could have chosen to engage intensely and affectively with a few sections of the *Symbols* at a time rather than reading the entirety of the text.

Washington University, St Louis, and Lindenwood University

NOTES

1. Rossell Hope Robbins lists only fifteen extant witnesses, of which seven are rolls, in Rossell Hope Robbins, "The 'Arma Christi' Rolls," *The Modern Language Review* 34.3 (July 1939): 415–21, 415. Ann Eljenholm Nichols, however, usefully updates Robbins's list in Ann Eljenholm Nichols, "'C Vernice': Illustrations of an *Arma Christi* Poem," in Marlene Villalobos Hennessy, ed., *Tributes to Kathleen L. Scott: English Medieval Manuscripts: Readers, Makers and Illuminators* (London: Harvey Miller Publishers, 2009), 138. Nichols identifies the following manuscripts as roll versions of this *arma Christi* poem (IMEV 2577): Edinburgh, National Library of Scotland, Blairs Mus. 9 (formerly Blairs College MS 13); Esopus NY, Redemptorist' MS (sine numero); BL Additional MS 22029; BL Additional MS 32006; Beinecke Library, Osborn MS fa.24 (two rolls); Bodleian Library MS Additional E.4; Bodleian Library, MS Bodley Rolls 16; Huntington Library, MS HM 26054; Stonyhurst College, MS 64; NY, PML, Morgan B.54 (atelous).

2. For an overview of late-medieval Passion iconography, see J. H. Marrow, *Passion Iconography and Northern European Art of the Late Middle Ages and Early Renaissance: A Study of the Transformation of Sacred Metaphor into Descriptive Narrative* (Kortrijk, Belgium: Van Ghemmert, 1979). For a discussion of the relationship between the Five Wounds and *arma Christi*, see Eamon Duffy, *The Stripping of the Altars: Traditional Religion in England c. 1400–c. 1580* (New Haven, CT: Yale University Press, 1992), 238–248. For a particularly interesting overview of the use of the *arma Christi* in heraldic images, see Kathryn A. Smith, *Art, Identity and Devotion in Fourteenth-Century England: Three Women and Their Books of Hours* (London: British Library, 2003), 175–177.

3. *Symbols of the Passion*, in Richard Morris, ed., *Legends of the Holy Rood: Symbols of the Passion and Cross-Poems*, EETS o.s. 103 (London: N. Trübner & Co., 1871), ll. 1–14. Ann Eljenholm Nichols is currently preparing a new edition of the "O Vernicle" lyric (IMEV 2577) to be included in the forthcoming volume: Arma Christi: *Objects, Representation, and Devotional Practice in Medieval and Early Modern Europe*, ed. Lisa H. Cooper and Andrea Denny-Brown.

4. Vincent Gillespie comments on the lack of chronological progress in some portrayals of the Passion, rightly pointing out that:

> Metaphorical perceptions of Christ as a book, net, dovecote, stars and so on, operate particularly by removing the image of the laden cross from the linear narrative sequence of the historical events and by subjecting it to intense and continual

> visual and imaginative attention. The suffering
> Christ is abstracted and dismembered to facilitate
> concentrated analysis. The five wounds become
> subjects of separate veneration, the instruments of
> the passion are individually represented, and the
> evolution of iconographic motifs like the Man of
> Sorrows, Christ in Distress and Christ's Last Repose
> represents a shift from a diachronic to a synchronic
> perception of the temporal reality. (122–123)

Vincent Gillespie, "Strange Images of Death: The Passion in Later Medieval English Devotional and Mystical Writing," *Zeit, Tod und Ewigkeit in der Renaissance Literatur* 3 (1987): 111–159.

5. See, e.g., Caroline Walker Bynum, *The Resurrection of the Body in Western Christianity, 200–1336* (New York: Columbia University Press, 1995); Caroline Walker Bynum, *Fragmentation and Redemption: Essays on Gender and the Human Body in Medieval Religion* (New York: Zone Books, 1992); and Miri Rubin, "The Person in the Form: Medieval Challenges to the Bodily 'Order,'" in *Framing Medieval Bodies* (Manchester, UK: Manchester University Press, 1994), 100–122. Caroline Walker Bynum comments that "the years around 1300 saw enthusiastic prying into the body—studying it, severing it, distributing and scattering it"; Bynum, *Resurrection*, 327. And this cultural fascination with the integrity of the body and its potential to be disturbed and fragmented echoes in various ways throughout many religious works of the late Middle Ages. "Artists," Bynum points out, "fragmented the body [as] liturgical and artistic treatment of relics came increasingly to underline the fact that they are body parts ... [and] depictions of the sufferings associated with the Crucifixion—known as the *arma Christi* and the Five Wounds—came in the later Middle Ages to show Christ's body itself in parts"; Bynum, *Fragmentation*, 271. Miri Rubin similarly asserts that "the body in parts, broken, dismembered, fragmented was all too present" in late-medieval culture, as witnessed by representations of Christ's Passion that depicted "a series of wounds or wounded body parts surrounded by wounding instruments; hand, foot, side, sweaty brow"; Rubin, "Person in the Form," 113.

6. Robbins's reading of the display purposes of these rolls continues to carry widespread argumentative weight. In a survey of Middle English lyrics, for example, Julia Boffey comments that "images and short verse texts [pertaining to the *arma Christi*] are occasionally united on manuscript rolls which would have been publicly displayed." See Julia Boffey, "Middle English Lyrics and Manuscripts," in *A Companion to the Middle English Lyric*, ed. Thomas G. Duncan (Cambridge, UK, and Rochester, NY: D. S. Brewer, 2005), 1–18, 3. See also Douglas Gray, *Themes and Images in the Medieval English Religious*

Lyric (London: Routledge, 1972), 51, which states that "it may well be that, as Professor Robbins has suggested, [the 'Arms of the Passion'] were intended to be publicly displayed to stimulate the devotion of the 'lewd' folk (the rubric which is sometimes found at the end grants an indulgence to those who *behold* them)." And Anthony Bale, *The Jew in the Medieval Book* (Cambridge, UK: Cambridge University Press, 2006), 155, states that "the distinctive presentation of the *Arma Christi* in roll rather than codex form has generally been assumed to reflect public or group, rather than private or individual, devotions." Although Bale is careful to attribute this reading to Robbins, he does not actively interrogate this assumption himself except to emphasize that the roll format not only enabled congregational reading but also "is freighted with the *symbolism* of the public roll format [and was] ... designed to partake in a documentary, administrative imaginary"; ibid.

7. Robbins, "Arma Christi Rolls," 419, 419–420.

8. Ibid., 420.

9. See Rossell Hope Robbins, "Private Prayers in Middle English Verse," *Studies in Philology* 36.3 (July 1939): 466–475. In this article, Robbins states:

> the earlier texts of the "Arma Christi" are written on long vellum rolls; and, as I have shown elsewhere, this devotion was originally intended for public exhibition in church before a congregation many of whom would not be able to read. By the beginning of the fifteenth century, however, it evidently had proved so popular that it was taken over for personal meditation, for it is found in two devotional manuals and in one Book of Hours. (469–470)

Robbins's dating of the extant manuscripts of the *Symbols*, however, has come under revision based upon later evaluations; current dating of the rolls and manuscripts suggests there is no divide in dating that would indicate that the rolls were produced at an earlier date than those witnesses included in codices. This revised dating of these manuscripts would seem to suggest that rather than *becoming* a text intended for personal meditations, the *Symbols* always was intended for such use—and that the roll format does not add a congregational element to this text but rather influences how the text was read and understood by its private readers.

10. British Library MS Royal 17.A.xxvii, fol. 80r. This witness is edited in Richard Morris, ed., *Legends of the Holy Rood: Symbols of the Passion and Cross-Poems*, EETS o.s. 46 (London: N. Trübner & Co., 1871), 170–196 at ll. 203–204, 216–217. Nita Scudder Baugh, ed., *A Worcestershire Miscellany: Compiled by John Northwood, c. 1400* (Bryn Mawr, PA: Bryn Mawr College,

1956), 35, suggests, based upon the similarities of format, dialect, and textual inclusions shared with British Library Additional MS 37787, that the 15th-century portion of MS Royal 17.A.xxvii (the manuscript is comprised of two sections, the first dating from the 13th century and the second dating from the 15th century) was written out at Bordesley Abbey in the West Midlands; Add. MS 37787 is also a Bordesley manuscript.

11. Linne Mooney, "Lydgate's 'Kings of England' and Another Verse Chronicle of the Kings," *Viator* 20 (1989): 255–289, 271. Mooney states that "six of the surviving manuscripts . . . are rolls on which the anonymous 'Kings' is the principal, or only, text. Two of these, Bodleian Library Add. E. 7 and Hertford County Record Office, show signs of having been nailed up, just as Calot's poem and pedigree were hung in Notre Dame cathedral for political propaganda in 1425"; ibid., 271.

12. The roll of Bodleian, MS e. Museo 42 (ca. 1467–1469) demonstrates this dilemma; the genealogy of the kings of England contained within it would originally have extended nearly forty feet in length when the roll was completely extended. Pamela Robinson also draws attention to British Library, Cotton Roll xiv.12, which is more than fifty-two feet long, stating that although "such rolls are supposed to have been hung up for display, . . . their length would make it impossible for a reader to see the topmost membranes." She instead suggests that "they were unrolled in sections to be studied privately or used as a teaching aid." See Pamela Robinson, "The Format of Books: Books, Booklets and Rolls," in *The Cambridge History of the Book in Britain, vol. II (1100–1400)*, ed. Nigel Morgan and Rodney M. Thomson (Cambridge, UK: Cambridge University Press, 2008), 41–54, 44.

13. Don C. Skemer, *Binding Words: Textual Amulets in the Middle Ages* (University Park: Pennsylvania State University Press, 2006), 261–262. See also Myrtilla Avery, *The Exultet Rolls of South Italy* (Princeton, NJ: Princeton University Press, 1936); and Guglielmo Cavallo, *Rotoli di exultet dell'Italia meridionale* (Bari, Italy: Adriatica, 1973).

14. Robinson, "Format of Books," 44.

15. See Nicholas Bell, "Music," in *The Cambridge History of the Book in Britain, Vol. II (1100–1400)*, ed. Nigel Morgan and Rodney M. Thomson (Cambridge, UK: Cambridge University Press, 2008), 463–473, 466.

16. *Symbols of the Passion*, ll. 20, 19.

17. Ibid., ll. 31, 55-56, 68, 119–120.

18. Ibid., ll. 97, 101–102, 105, 109–110, 115–116.

19. Ibid., ll. 98–100.

20. The *Symbols of the Passion* survives in the following manuscript codices: Cambridge University Library MS Ii.6.43 (fols. 103r–115v); Harvard University, Houghton Library, MS Typ 193 (fols. 183r–190v); BL Royal MS 17.A.xxvii (fols. 72v–81r); British Library Additional MS 11748 (fols. 144r–

147v); Longleat House MS 30 (fols. 8r–20r); Bodleian Library, MS Douce 1 (fols. 54v–69v); Oxford, Queen's College, MS 207 (fols. 165v–174r); Princeton, Firestone Library, MS Taylor 17 (fols. 2r–8r); Huntington Library, MS HM 142 (fols. 1r–9r). A partial witness also exists in Cambridge, Magdalene College, Pepys MS 2125. Robbins suggests that four codices containing witnesses to the *Symbols* (CUL Ii.6.43, BL Royal 17.A.xxvii, Longleat 30, and Douce 1 (Bodleian 21575)) were produced for readers who "felt the greater need for personal and intimate prayers expressed in the mother tongue" and as such they fall into the category of "manuals of Latin and English devotions and prayers and meditations, in prose and verse"; Robbins, "Private Prayers in Middle English Verse," 466.

21. The manuscript description can be found in *A Summary Catalogue of Western Manuscripts in the Bodleian Library at Oxford* (Oxford: Clarendon Press, 1897), 4:489.

22. The witness of the *Symbols* found in Douce 1 has been edited by John C. Hirsh; for the poem's text and for a description of MS Douce 1, see John C. Hirsh, "Two English Devotional Poems of the Fifteenth Century," *Notes and Queries* n.s. 15.1 (Jan. 1968): 4–11.

23. Anthony Bale, *Jew in the Medieval Book* 154. This statement suggests that a perceived relationship with legal records might have provided the *Symbols of the Passion* with a hint of added authority, subtly linking this religious text with official, legal documents in a fashion similar to the *Charters of Christ*. But Pamela Robinson cautions against too closely associating literary rolls with their legal cousins, stating, "it may be that the roll imbued copies of the statues with a 'quasi-public authority,' since the roll was associated in England with royal record keeping, but that can only have been incidental"; Robinson, "Format of Books," 45.

Figure 1. British Library, Additional 22029 (15th century). By permission of the British Library.

Figure 2. British Library, Additional 22029 (15th century), detail. By permission of the British Library.

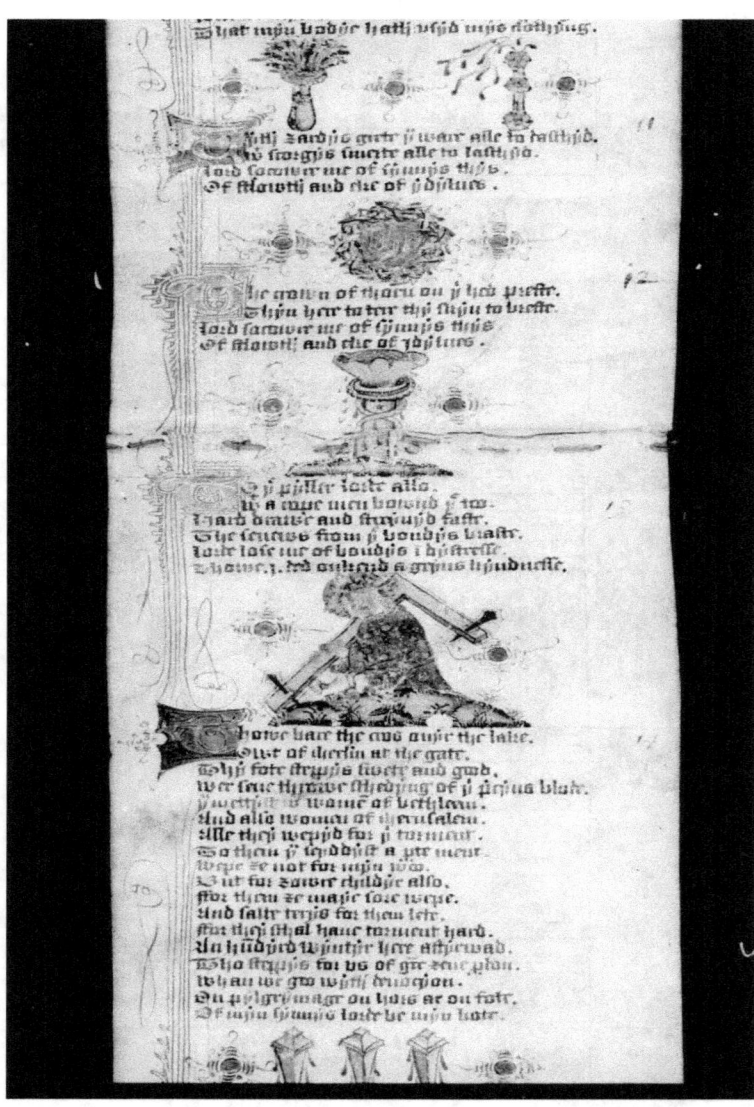

Figure 3: British Library, Additional 22029 (15th century). Here is an example of the alternation between image and text found within the majority of roll witnesses to the *Symbols of the Passion*. It should be noted that Blairs Mus. MS 9, held at the National Library of Scotland, is an outlier to this typical *mise-en-page*; in this witness the images are positioned to the right of the stanzas, making a pictorial border that runs alongside the text. By permission of the British Library.

Notarial Signs and Scribal Training in the Fifteenth Century: The Case of James Yonge and Thomas Baghill

THERESA O'BYRNE

James Yonge (*fl.* 1404–38) was an Anglo-Irish author and legal clerk who is best known for his Hiberno-English translation of the pseudo-Aristotelian *Secreta secretorum*, a mirror for princes which Yonge completed in 1422 under the patronage of James Butler, Fourth Earl of Ormond.[1] During the time Yonge was working on the *Secreta secretorum*, Butler was Lord Lieutenant of Ireland, acting as the deputy of his friend and patron, King Henry V. Yonge, eager to further Butler's political and literary goals, personalized his translation by adding several original interpolations; these highlight many of the cultural and political issues facing Butler and the Anglo-Irish community. Yonge was also the author of a Latin narrative chronicling the journey of Laurence Rathold, a high-ranking retainer of Sigismund I of Hungary, to Saint Patrick's Purgatory in 1411–1412.[2] This narrative, *Memoriale super visitatione domini Laurencii Ratholdi militis et baronis Vngarie factum de Purgatorio Sancti Patricii in Insula Hibernie*—commonly known as the *Memoriale*—imitates many continental examples detailing the visions of pilgrims in the Purgatory, but it is the first of its kind to be written in Ireland. Like his literary counterparts in London, such as Thomas Hoccleve, Yonge's principal career was as a legal clerk, creating and copying documents in the city of Dublin and the surrounding area. Despite the destruction of most of the documents he produced by the Four Courts fire and explosion of 1922, approximately eighty individual deeds in Yonge's hand survive, mostly in parish records. These date from 1404 to 1438 and are largely grants, quit-claims, and deeds of attorney relating to property transfers. Yonge was also a notary public, and a few of the documents which he created in his capacity as a notary also survive.

Notarial instruments are relatively rare in the extant records from Dublin. In a survey of over four hundred individual documents created in Dublin between 1400 and 1475, only sixteen are notarial instruments. These notarized documents seem to have most commonly been created in cases where some impediment or challenge arose in the normal process of a property transfer. The diplomatic evidence issuing from a property transfer in early fifteenth-century Dublin consisted of three documents: a grant of property with a description of the property and the name of the grantor and grantee, a deed of attorney appointing someone to oversee the property transfer, and a quit-claim—often dated several days later than the other two documents—dissolving all interests and rights of the grantor in the property. When they appear, the Dublin notarial instruments often precede the quit-claim in date and reiterate the information given in the initial grant or proclaim that another claimant has no right to or interest in the property. They often record word-for-word an oath made by one of the claimants while touching a Bible. Notarial instruments seek to restore order to legal proceedings that have gone awry and probably helped keep cases out of the courts. Quit-claims dated soon after notarized documents were produced confirm the effectiveness of these documents. The one exception to the use of notarial instruments to help resolve issues with property transfers in early fifteenth-century Dublin relates to the false arrest and detention of John Lytill, a fairly well-to-do Dublin citizen, in early 1406.[3] The dispute surrounding Lytill's arrest by the prominent Dublin citizen and former mayor Robert Burnell appears to have been the result of a debt which Burnell argued that Lytill owed him. The creation of the notarial instrument recording the circumstances of Lytill's false arrest may have allowed Lytill and Burnell time, space, and opportunity to resolve their disagreement while simultaneously providing an official record of events should the case be tried in court.

In his 1412 *Memoriale*, James Yonge identifies himself as a *notarius imperialis*, an imperial notary.[4] Documents preserved among the records of the Parish of St. John corroborate this.[5] Yonge was the notary for John Lytill in the 1406 case cited above, and twice in 1411, he created notarized documents for Simon Doddenale, a Dublin merchant.[6] The other two extant documents notarized by Yonge are among the deeds of the Guild of St. Anne, which was attached to the Church of St. Audoen, located in the western part of Dublin. In 1432, Yonge created a notarized document for Radulph Pembroke, a Dublin merchant.[7] In 1435, he did the same for John Ballybyn and his wife, Johanna, prominent Dublin citizens.[8] All five of these documents are in Yonge's hand, and in keeping with notarial practice, Yonge has placed his personal *signum manuale* in the lower left corner of all the documents.

In his study of the role of the notary in England, C. R. Cheney notes:

> The English notaries' work for private persons
> has left much less trace than those activities in the
> service of the Crown and the Church .... Here
> they could perhaps find more or less permanent
> employment on the same terms (variable and
> uncertain) as other clerical assistants, with the
> extra advantage of being qualified to draw up public
> instruments when required.[9]

The extant documents written by James Yonge indicate that he often straddled
the line between public and private employment in the course of his legal
career; he found work with both the City of Dublin and the Office of the
Irish Exchequer.[10] However, the documents Yonge created in his capacity
as a notary all appear to have been created while he was working for private
individuals. As such, their construction and use provide important new
clues about the private employment of notaries. While Yonge was hired
multiple times by Lytill and Doddenale, he does not seem to have enjoyed
the permanent or semi-permanent private employment posited by Cheney.
Instead, he was hired as need dictated; the income from these contracts
probably supplemented Yonge's income from public duties.

Notarized documents followed strict formulas for their opening lines
in which the date, the location, and the names of the parties were listed.
Each document was authenticated with the notary's *signum manuale*, a line
drawing, which was usually—though not always—in the general shape of
a cross, and a formulaic eschatocol. In this eschatocol, the notary named
himself, asserted his notarial authority, and swore that he had been a witness
to the transaction described in the instrument. The formula began with "*Ego,*"
or "*Et ego,*" and each notary developed his own version of the capital E with
which his eschatocol began as well as his own *signum manuale*. Yonge's *signum
manuale* takes the form of an altar cross on a base. The cross incorporates
simple ribbon interlace and stylized floral embellishment. Yonge places the
abbreviation for Jesus, "IHC," and signs his name in the voids at the base.
In comparison to contemporary practice among the notaries of the York
archiepiscopal records, the E with which Yonge begins his eschatocol is
remarkably plain.[11] While it is larger than his usual capital E, it contains no
extra flourishes and is only about 2.5 times Yonge's standard o-height [fig. 1].

The script Yonge used to create legal documents is a carefully-written,
evenly-spaced Anglicana with consistency in letter forms and a generally
polished appearance. The lettering is comparatively large, and many
individual letters have a high level of brokenness. The spacing between words

and lines is clear. Yonge uses two grades of script, a less formal, workaday Anglicana which is found on most of the legal deeds created by Yonge, and a more calligraphic, formal Anglicana utilized on documents created for high-ranking government officials, such as James Butler or the mayor of Dublin. The hand of the latter group shows an increased care with lettering and spacing. The script becomes more vertical, and the letters are more broken. Calligraphic elements, such as extra flourishes on suspension marks and upper case letters, are also present. Beginning in 1419, documents appear in another hand that seems at first blush to be Yonge's more formal hand. There are, however, some key differences. [figs. 2 and 3] The top chamber of Yonge's **a** is usually round or slightly squared, while the new hand usually closes the top chamber of **a** with an oblique stroke creating a nearly triangular chamber. The second minim on Yonge's **h** usually curves back to the left and trails off parallel to the line of writing. The new scribe puts a hook on **h** which opens to the right. Yonge has several forms of capital **I**, but none of them have a loop which starts and ends in the center of the upright. The new hand has two major forms of **I**: one has a loop in the center of the upright, the other is identical to Yonge's most commonly used form. The **P** which opens standard quit-claims differs between the scribes. Yonge's **P** is made in two strokes, one forming the descender, and a second graceful, looping stroke forming the bowl. The new hand also has a **P** constructed of two strokes; one stroke constructing an I-shaped descender, and the other creating an arc protruding to the left of the letter, then crossing the upright, curving up to form a bowl, and finishing with a straight line back to the right, bisecting the bowl. Yonge uses two slightly different forms of a VB-style **W**. In each, the bottom of the first v—which can be broken or unbroken—is usually higher than that of the second v, and the second ascender is usually only slightly higher than the first. One version tangles the ascenders; the ascenders of the other are often distinct or just touch one another. In both cases, the ascenders are usually closed loops. The new hand employs a **W** in which the ascenders hook to the right and are entangled with one another; the second ascender is usually left open and trails off to the right. The *et* abbreviation in Yonge's hand usually has no descender or a very light one, whereas the *et* of the new scribe has a heavy descender hooking to the right.

The earliest extant example of this Yonge-like hand appears in the St. Anne's Guild papers on a copy of a quit-claim made in 1419. Yonge wrote one quit-claim, and the new scribe made a copy of it.[12] The hand of the Yonge-like scribe is not yet accomplished, with variations in size, spacing and some letter forms. Some hallmark characteristics of the scribe's later hand are present, however, including the beginning **P**, the **I** with the lowered loop, and a nearly triangular upper chamber on many examples of **a**. Yonge and the new scribe also worked together on a land transfer in 1422. The Yonge-like scribe wrote the grant of property and a deed of attorney dated September 19, 1422.[13] The quit-claim for the same transaction is in Yonge's hand and is signed by Yonge in the lower right corner, a rare occurrence in early fifteenth-century Dublin for this type of document.[14] While it is not unheard-of for the documents of a single property transfer to be in different hands, it is extremely uncommon. In most cases, it seems a scribe was employed for the entire transaction, not just for one part of it. Why, then, did the chaplain John Ingoll—for whom Yonge had previously worked—use two different scribes for his property transfer?[15] The similarities between the new hand and Yonge's are striking and suggest that there was a master-apprentice relationship between the scribes, with the apprentice copying the 1419 quit-claim and later writing the grant and deed of attorney in 1422, both under the careful supervision of his master, Yonge.

Three notarized documents confirm this relationship and reveal the identity of the apprentice. In 1431, 1434, and 1436, notarized documents were created by the apprentice; each document has a notarial *signum manuale* in the lower left corner, as per the usual practice.[16] The outline of the cross is identical to James Yonge's, but the name written in the bottom void of the base of the cross is Thomas Baghill. Baghill has appropriated the ribbon interlace of the cross and the slightly scalloped base of Yonge's *signum manuale* He has replaced Yonge's four-lobed leaf with the abbreviation for Jesus, "IHC." Where Yonge's *signum manuale* has the same abbreviation, in the top void of the base of the cross, Baghill has written "xpo"—*Christo*. Yonge's stylized blossoms made of three dots have been replaced by fleur-de-lys designs, echoing the shape and placement of the blossoms, and Baghill has borrowed the restrained, m-shaped flourishes emerging from the points of Yonge's *signum manuale*, but he has placed bold rays on the ends, which sometimes extend into the text of his notarial instruments [fig. 4]. The remarkable similarity between the *signa* of Yonge and Baghill could only have come about through the latter's frequent experience with Yonge's *signum manuale* in his day-to-day activities. The apprentice scribe may have adopted part of his master's notarial mark as a sign of respect or as a matter of course.

The similarity between the crosses was almost certainly not due to a paucity of examples. Yonge and by extension Baghill were familiar with many official documents, and notaries working for the Chancery, Exchequer, and Wardrobe were often called upon to produce notarized copies of documents as an alternative to using the royal seal on such documents.[17] In their official duties, both Yonge and Baghill would have seen documents notarized by scribes from London and elsewhere in England. In 1402, a review of notaries and their credentials in the diocese of London resulted in a list of forty-eight notaries who were allowed to notarize documents. Another thirteen individuals had been working as notaries, but failed to produce their credentials when required.[18] With an approximate population of 50,000, this means a notary for every 900 to 1,000 people. Dublin's far smaller population—estimated at between 5,000 and 6,000 in the early fifteenth century—meant that the city probably only had five to seven notaries working in it at any one time.[19] Besides Yonge and Baghill, at least two other notaries were at work in Dublin between 1400 and 1440, John Jordan, and James Howling. Both used an altar cross template for their *signa manualia*, but Jordan's cross, on a document dating to 1405, has a quatrefoil center with the arms extending from it ending in sharp points. The center of the quatrefoil has a large heart[20] [fig. 5]. James Howling's *signum manuale*, preserved on a 1418 deed, features a cross made up of interlacing which is much more complex than that of the Yonge/Baghill cross, but which is executed with far less precision[21] [fig. 6].

Both Yonge and Baghill probably had many examples from which to draw inspiration when they were creating their own unique and life-long *signa manualia* in *ca.* 1405 and *ca.* 1430, respectively. Yonge and Baghill each created a *signum manuale* that reflected elements then current in English notarial marks. The simple interlace, the stepped base, and the three-lobed stylized blossoms of Yonge's cross can be seen in the *signa manualia* of the 1380s and 1390s preserved in the York Archiepiscopal records.[22] These are also features of the cross of Thomas de Spaldewyk on a 1396 certificate.[23] The interlace and stepped base—as well as long rays similar to Baghill's—are also part of the 1390 notarial cross of John Cossier in the Common Paper of the London Scriveners' Guild.[24] The small m-shaped flourishes like the ones Yonge uses are present on the *signa* of John de Herle, Robert de Esyngwald, and Robert Berall.[25] While long rays were in use on notarial marks as early as the 1360s, most early examples are slender and much lighter than Baghill's. In using these in his *signum manuale, ca.* 1430, Baghill is incorporating a design element that was also current in notarial marks in England. This feature is evident in the notarial marks of Peter de Wynton and Robert de Scurneton in 1423 and 1424, and in the marks of John Chesham in 1417, Walter Culpet in 1423, and John Daunt in 1440.[26] Both Yonge and Baghill use a simple and undecorated **E** to begin their eschatocols.

Authorization to draw up notarial documents came in two forms: imperial and papal. Such permission was granted by deputies of the Holy Roman Emperor for notaries by imperial authority or deputies of the Pope for notaries by apostolic authority. Some notaries held both credentials. Cheney notes that "comparatively few of the English notaries public of [the thirteenth and fourteenth centuries] have left any clue to the date of their appointment by either one or the other authority, while still fewer hint at the order of double appointment." He then lists three cases of notaries who carried the double credential. Most notable among these is that of Richard, son of Henry de Ganyo, a Durham clerk who was credentialed first by imperial authority, and then sometime between 1303 and 1307, he acquired apostolic credentials.[27] While Cheney did not concern himself with notaries of the early fifteenth century, Yonge and Baghill each offer interesting additional evidence concerning double notarial credentials. Yonge describes himself in the eschatocols of the extant notarized documents of 1406 and 1411 as a "*clericus coniugatus Ciuis Dublinii et Dublinii Diocesis publicus auctoritate Imperiali Notarius*" (a married clerk of the City of Dublin and the Diocese of Dublin, and a public notary by imperial authority). He calls himself an imperial notary and a writer or scribe (*scriptor*), rather than a clerk, in his 1412 *Memoriale*. However, in the 1432 and 1435 documents, Yonge refers to himself as a "*clericus coniugatus Ciuis Dublinii publicus auctoritate Apostolica et Imperiali Notarius*" (a married clerk of the City of Dublin and a public notary by apostolic and imperial authority). This indicates that Yonge earned his second credential—and ended his official association with the Diocese of Dublin—sometime between 1411 and 1432. From his earliest extant notarized document, Baghill presents himself as "*clericus Mideii diocesis auctoritate Apostolica et Imperiali Notarius*" (a clerk of the Diocese of Meath and a notary by Apostolic and Imperial authority). Baghill either began his notarial career with both credentials or obtained the second one quite early in his career. The differences between an imperial and papal notary are not well understood, as Cheney attests.[28] However, Cheney does assert that notaries with papal authority were able to create documents for the episcopate and prepare and present documents for the ecclesiastical courts.[29] It was a post reserved for clerks in minor orders, although there is some evidence that the occasional layman was admitted to the ranks of notaries by apostolic authority.[30] In the latter part of his career, Yonge was a clerk tied to the city of Dublin rather than a clerk connected with a diocese; as such, it is possible that he was among these exceptions. Yonge's marital status also suggests that he was a layman. Official papal decrees forbade making anyone who was married a notary, but this rule seems to have become somewhat relaxed by the late fourteenth century. Nonetheless, there are very few known examples of married notaries.[31] Yonge appears to be a rare example of both a married notary and a notary with imperial and apostolic credentials. Both Yonge and Baghill give importance of place to their apostolic credential, evidence further confirming Cheney's argument that the papal credential may have been the more important or prestigious of the two certifications.[32]

Examination of these documents invites questions about Baghill's origins and training. The name "Baghill," as far as I have been able to determine, is unknown in Dublin records before or after Yonge's apprentice worked as a clerk there. Documents in London's Public Record Office indicate that there was a Baghill family living in Yorkshire in the late fourteenth and early fifteenth centuries, and Thomas Baghill or his parents may have come from Yorkshire. This indicates that there may have been ties between Dublin and Yorkshire as well as the ties already established between Dublin and London. Another possibility is that Thomas was from Ballyboghill, an area northwest of Swords in County Dublin, and an area—perhaps not coincidentally—in the Diocese of Meath, of which Baghill was a clerk.

The close relationship of James Yonge and Thomas Baghill implies that notaries and legal scribes did not need to seek training in England. Instead, it appears that there was some provision for on-the-job training of legal clerks in fifteenth-century Dublin. Yonge and Baghill worked side-by-side on the legal documents associated with the 1419 quit-claim and the 1422 property transfer, and Baghill's appropriation of part of his master's *signum manuale* indicates a further close relationship. Scribal training outside of the great population and governmental center of London may have been an *ad hoc* process, approached much like an apprenticeship in any other manual trade. The similarity between Yonge's hand and Baghill's hand in size, spacing, and letter forms suggests that the student may have learned his legal script through close imitation of his master's hand, which was presented to him as an ideal standard for the creation of public documents. While acquiring the technical tools of his trade, the student also gained the necessary legal knowledge and the prescribed formulas for creating an array of documents. With the benefit of Yonge's tutelage, Baghill's career seems to have taken off. His hand appears on notarial and property transfer deeds of the newly-formed St. Anne's Guild throughout the late 1430s. In the 1440s, Baghill's hand dominates the extant deeds of St. Anne's Guild. During this period, Thomas Baghill seems to have been the clerk upon whom the Guild called when properties within the bounds of St. Audoen's Parish changed hands.

To sum up, then, the notarized documents and the strikingly similar hands of James Yonge and Thomas Baghill reveal that the two notaries were likely master and apprentice. The relationship was a close one in which Baghill was encouraged to imitate his master strictly—not only in the legal formulas necessary in creating documents, but also in the size, spacing, and *ductus* of his public hand and in the creation and execution of his personal *signum manuale*. The notarized documents of Yonge and Baghill also provide us with additional evidence regarding the work of late medieval notaries. Comparison of these notarial instruments to English examples suggests that these Dublin public clerks were taking their cues from the work of their English counterparts.

University of Notre Dame, Queen's University Belfast

NOTES

1. Active dates of Yonge expanded by author; T. P. Dolan, "Yonge, James (fl. 1405-1434)," ed. Lawrence Goldman, *Oxford Dictionary of National Biography* (Oxford: Oxford University Press, 2004), http://www.oxforddnb.com/view/article/30224; James Yonge, "*Secreta Secretorum*," in *Three Prose Versions of the "Secreta secretorum,"* ed. Robert Steele, vol. 74, Early English Text Society Extra Series (London: Pub. for the EETS by K. Paul, Trench, Trübner & Co., 1898), 119-248.

2. Hippolyte Delehaye, ed., "Le Pèlerinage de Laurent de Pasztho au Purgatoire de S. Patrice," *Analecta Bollandiana* 27 (1908): 35-60.

3. Trinity College Dublin (TCD) MS 1477, no. 69, 16 March 1406. All dates are adjusted to modern reckoning, with the year beginning on 1 January.

4. Delehaye, "Le Pèlerinage de Laurent de Pasztho au Purgatoire de S. Patrice," 58. All translations mine.

5. TCD MS 1477, several boxes of loose documents dating from *ca.* 1231–1704. Catalogued (with some errors) by John L. Robinson, "On the Ancient Deeds of the Parish of St. John, Dublin, Preserved in the Library of Trinity College," *Proceedings of the Royal Irish Academy; Archaeology, Linguistics, and Literature* 33 C (1916): 175-224.

6. TCD MS 1477, no. 84, 12 November 1411, and 85, 28 November 1411.

7. Royal Irish Academy (RIA) MS 12.S.22–31, fifteen boxes of loose documents dating from the latter half of the thirteenth century to the seventeenth century, document no. 343. These documents are partially catalogued in Henry F. Berry, "History of the Religious Gild of St. Anne, in S. Audoen's Church, Dublin, 1430-1740," *Proceedings of the Royal Irish Academy; Archaeology, Linguistics, and Literature* 25 C (May 1904): 21-106.

8. RIA MS 12.S.22–31, no. 374, 18 January 1435.

9. Christopher Robert Cheney, *Notaries Public in England in the Thirteenth and Fourteenth Centuries* (Oxford: Clarendon, 1972), 64.

10. National Archives of Ireland, RC 8/38, 104. I am grateful to Professor Peter Crooks for drawing my attention to this document.

11. J. S. Purvis, *Notarial Signs from the York Archiepiscopal Records* (London and York: St. Anthony's Press, 1957).

12. RIA MS 12.S.22-31, nos. 330 and 390, respectively, both 28 May 1419.

13. RIA MS 12.S.22–31, nos. 189 and 188, respectively, both 19 September 1422.

14. RIA MS 12.S.22–31, no. 190, 22 September 1422.

15. Yonge worked for Ingoll in 1417. TCD 1477 no. 102, 14 August 1417.

16. RIA MS 12.S.22-31, nos. 253, 27 January 1431, 826, 17 April 1434, and 799, 20 October 1436, respectively.

17. Cheney, *Notaries Public in England in the Thirteenth and Fourteenth Centuries*, 56–57.
18. Ibid., 93–94.
19. Howard B Clarke, *The Four Parts of the City: High Life and Low Life in the Suburbs of Medieval Dublin* (Dublin: Dublin City Public Libraries, 2003), 9.
20. TCD 1477, no. 67, 28 July 1405.
21. National Library of Ireland, D.1549, 5 January 1418.
22. Purvis, *Notarial Signs from the York Archiepiscopal Records*, 34–35.
23. L. C. Hector, *The Handwriting of English Documents* (London: Edward Arnold, 1958), 75.
24. Reproduced in Edwin Freshfield, "Some Notarial Marks in the 'Common Paper' of the Scriveners' Company," *Archaeologia* 54 (1895): 241.
25. Purvis, *Notarial Signs from the York Archiepiscopal Records*, 34–35, 38–39.
26. Ibid., 49–51; Freshfield, "Some Notarial Marks in the 'Common Paper' of the Scriveners' Company," 243–45.
27. Cheney, *Notaries Public in England in the Thirteenth and Fourteenth Centuries*, 85–86.
28. Ibid., 81.
29. Ibid., 44 and passim.
30. Ibid., 87–89.
31. Ibid., 79–81.
32. Ibid., 86–87.

Figure 1. Yonge's *signum manuale* and **E** at beginning of eschatocol. 12 December 1432. Cross is 55 mm. wide x 65 mm. high. RIA MS 12.S.22-31, no. 343. (Author's image appears by permission of the Royal Irish Academy © RIA)

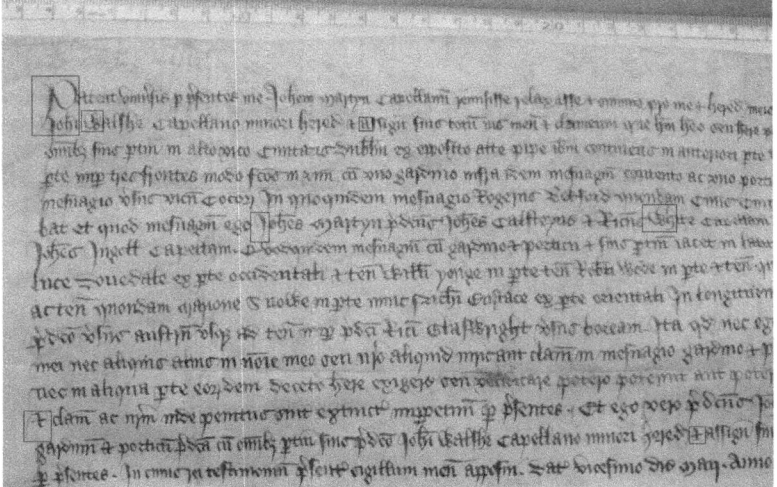

Figure 2. Detail of RIA MS 12.S.22-31, no. 185. 20 May 1432. Yonge's hand. Note a, h, I, initial P, w, and &. (Author's image appears by permission of the Royal Irish Academy © RIA.)

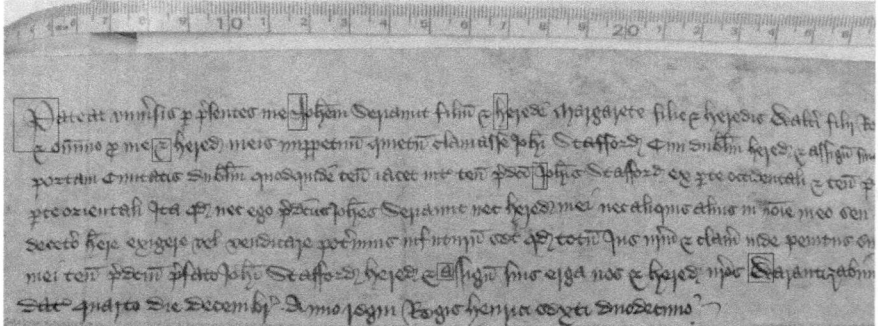

Figure 3. Detail of RIA MS 12.S.22-31, no. 548. 4 December 1433. Baghill's hand. Note a, h, two types of I, initial P, w and &. (Author's image appears by permission of the Royal Irish Academy © RIA.)

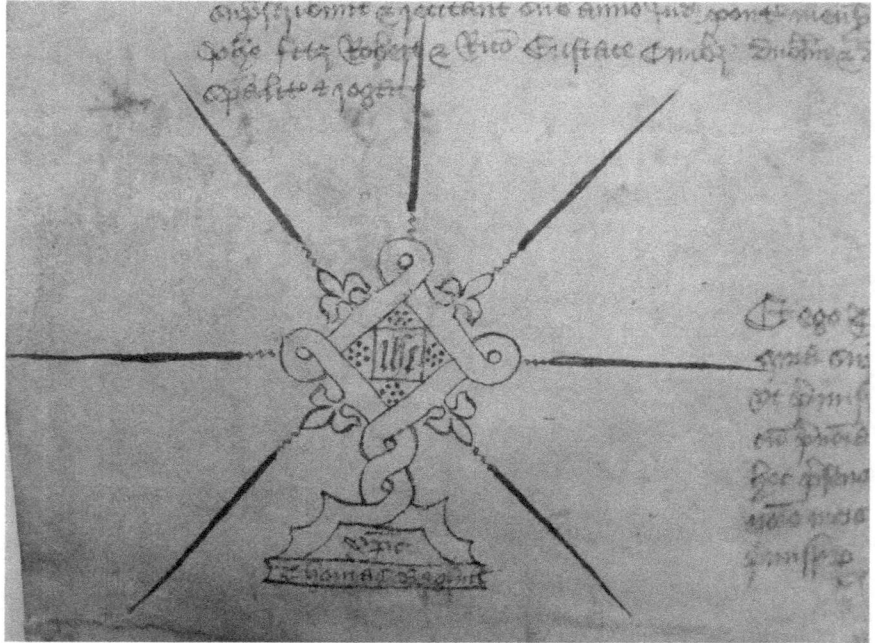

Figure 4. Thomas Baghill's signum manuale and E at beginning of eschatocol. 27 January 1431. Cross is 110 mm. wide x 95 mm. high. RIA MS 12.S.22-31, no. 253. (Author's image appears by permission of the Royal Irish Academy © RIA.)

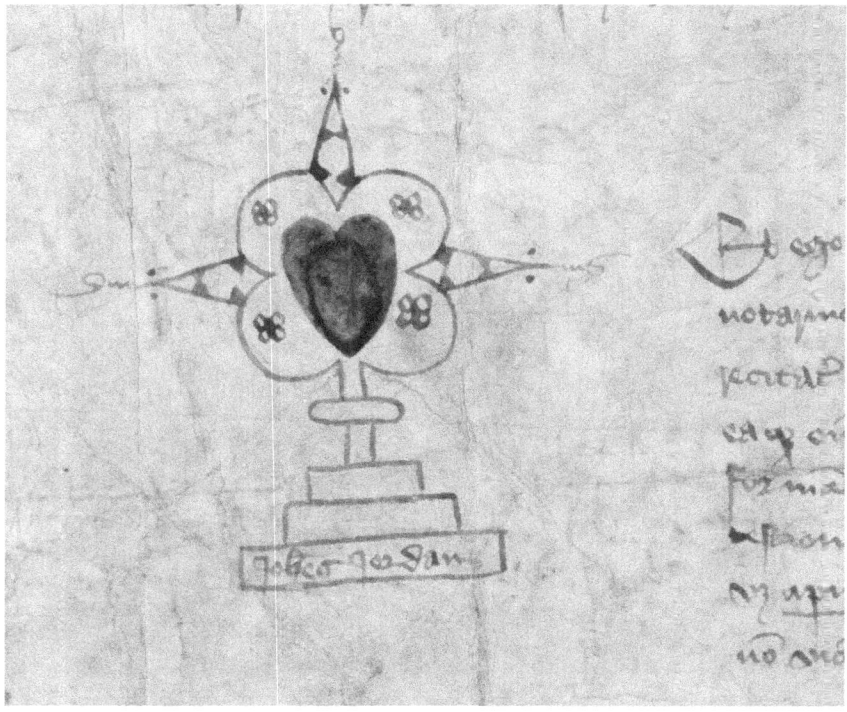

Figure 5. *Signum manuale* and E at beginning of eschatocol of John Jordan. 28 July 1405. Cross is 61 mm. wide x 60 mm. high. Trinity College Dublin MS 1477, no. 67. (By permission of the Board of Trinity College.)

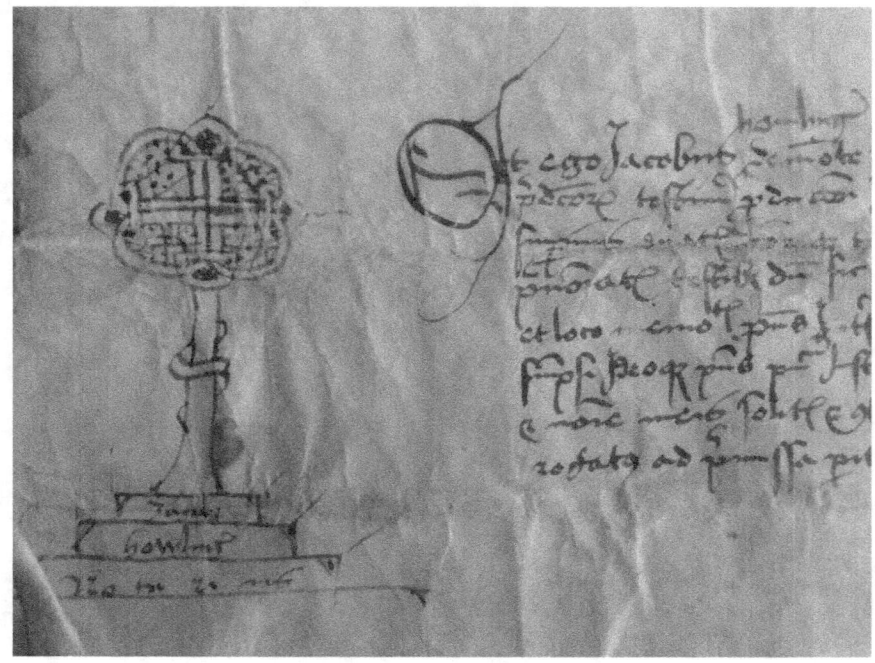

Figure 6. *Signum manuale* and **E** at beginning of eschatocol of James Howling. 5 January 1418. Cross is 57 mm. wide x 64 mm. high. National Library of Ireland D.1549. (Author's image. Deed is the property of the Board of the National Library of Ireland and has been reproduced by permission.)

Longleat House MS 30, T. Werken, and Thomas Betson

DANIEL W. MOSSER

Over seventy years ago, H. C. Schultz observed that Huntington Library MS HM 142 (*olim* "Bement") had a twin "in the library of the Marquis of Bath—Longleat 30. The close relationship between these two manuscripts extends not only to the order of the pieces within the volumes but to certain variants in the texts. Longleat 30 is less elaborately written and decorated and might be by the same scribe who wrote HM 142."[1] That scribe is T. Werken.

In 1950, R. A. B. Mynors identified eighteen Latin and Middle English manuscripts copied wholly or in part by a Dutch scribe who identified himself in several colophons as "T. Werken" and, in more complete fashion, as "Theodericus Nicolai Werken de Abbenbroith," and "theoderici nycolai Werken de Abbenbroeck."[2] The list of manuscripts identified by Mynors as being copied by Werken is included in Table 1 (supplemented by information from Linne R. Mooney's unpublished list of Scribes working in England, 1375-1525).[3]

Many of these volumes were produced for William Gray, who was at Balliol by 1431, graduating about 1434. He was chancellor of Oxford by February 21, 1441, but departed the following year for the Continent, arriving in Cologne in 1442 and relocating to Padua in 1444, where he was awarded a Doctorate of Theology in 1446. On November 18, 1445, he was commissioned the King of England's royal proctor at the Curia and in consequence moved to Rome. He received a series of ecclesiastical positions in England: appointed to the prebendaryship of Barnby, in York (1447) and of Thorp, in Ripon (1448); appointed archdeacon of Richmond (1450); and in 1454, he became Bishop of Ely. During his time at Oxford and abroad, he assembled a large library, the bequest of which constitutes "more than half the surviving library of medieval Balliol."[4] Werken employs scripts of two primary varieties: a gothic textura and a humanist script. As M. B. Parkes notes, he "was an adaptable scribe."[5]

Table 1: R. A. B. Mynors' List of MSS Ascribed to T. Werken

Shelfmark	Contents	Date
Cambridge, University Library Dd.13.2[6]	Works of Cicero, Petrarch, and Poggio	1444
Oxford, Balliol College 66[7]	Franciscus de Mayronis, *Sermonis hiemales*, vol. 1	1444
Oxford, Balliol College 67A[8]	Franciscus de Mayronis, *Sermonis hiemales*, vol. 2	1444
Oxford, Balliol College 80, ff. 107-22[9]	Albertus Magnus, *De sacramento eucharistiae*	[1444]
Oxford, Balliol College 295[10]	*Comentarii* in Ciceronem, Xicho Polentone, etc.	1445
Manchester, Rylands latin 211	*Opuscula humanistica*: Latin translations of Isocrates, Plutarch, and Basil	1445
Oxford, Balliol College 80, ff. 123-55[11]	Bertrandus de Turre, *Sermones quadragesimales*	[c. 1445]
Oxford, Balliol College 238 A[12] and D[13]	Domenicus de Bandino of Arezzo, *Fons memorabilium Universi*	[c. 1445]
Oxford, Balliol College 238B[14]	Domenicus de Bandino of Arezzo, *Fons memorabilium Universi*	1445-8
Oxford, Balliol College 310[15]	Leonardo Bruni, *Epistles*	1445-8
Oxford, Balliol College 287, part II[16]	Dictionary of rare Latin words from Servius's commentary on Virgil by Guarino	1450
Oxford, Balliol College 127[17]	Petrarch, Cicero, Poggio	1450

Shelfmark	Contents	Date
Brussels, Bibl. MS royale 5277	Baldwin of Ford	1453
Oxford, Balliol College 34[18]	Thomas Ringestede (Bishop of Bangor), *Proverbia*	1461
Huntington Library HM 142	Religious Prose & Verse	1467
Cambridge, University Library Ff.3.10	Chrysostom, *Homiliae*	{c. 1477?][19]
Cambridge, Trinity College B.3.21 (100)	Chyrsostom, *Homilae*	[c. 1477?]
Cambridge, Trinity College R.17.4 (990)	Jerome, *Opera*	1477-8
Cambridge, Trinity College R.17.5 (991)	Jerome, *Opera*	1477-8
Canterbury, Cathedral archives lit. e42, ff. 69-74[20]	Supply leaves for 12th century Passionals	n.d.

In 1976, A. C. de la Mare identified a binding fragment owned by Dr. George Salt "containing parts of Book XXIII of Augustine's Contra Faustum."21 De la Mare notes that Mynors suggests possible additions to the list of Werken MSS in his Catalogue of the Manuscripts of Balliol College, Oxford (1963).22 She accepts from this list of additions Balliol MS 15723 but suggests that, while copied by the same hand as Balliol MS 238D, she regards both that MS (assigned to the oeuvre of Werken by Mynors) and his suggested addition Balliol MS 12524 as having been copied not by Werken, but perhaps by Richard Bole, friend of William Gray (for whom Werken produced a number of the MSS in Mynors' list 25). De la Mare also argues for addition to the list "reject leaves for the beginning of a Eutropius found in the bindings of several of Gray's MSS (Balliol MSS 125, fos. 1, 223; 129, fos. 253-4; 229, fo. 171; 279, fos. 1-2)." She also suggests that "[t]hree further MSS (Balliol MSS 135, Guarino, and 237, Festus; London, Lambeth Palace MS 759, Sallust) ... may perhaps be attributed to Werken."26

I came across the coincidence of the compilations in HM 142 and Longleat 30 independently of Schultz while entering data in the *DIMEV*27 for the latter from a microfilm. While it lacks a scribal colophon (as do the various parts of Balliol 80, Balliol 238 A and D, and Trinity College B. 3.21), the handwriting is clearly that of Werken (see further below), and the contents are identical with and in the same sequence as those found in Huntington Library MS HM 142 except for six texts that follow this sequence in HM 142.[28] It is possible that Longleat 30 did once contain these items, as well as a scribal colophon, and those materials were lost.

Table 2: ME Verse Texts in Longleat 30 and HM 142[29]

Marquess of Bath MS 30	Huntington Library HM 142
1. ff. 1-6v *Jesu Lord for Thy holy circumcision* (John Lydgate, 'Kalendar'; **DIMEV 1721-8**)	1. ff. 1-6v *Jesu Lord for Thy holy circumcision* (John Lydgate, 'Kalendar'; **DIMEV 1721-9**)
2. ff. 7-10v *O vernicle I honor him and thee* (*The Arma Christi*; **DIMEV 2577-11**)	2. ff. 7-9 *O vernicle I honor him and thee* (*The Arma Christi*; **DIMEV 2577-18**)
3. ff. 10v-11 *I thank thee lord that thou me wrought* (A prayer of thanksgiving for the Redemption, at the end of the *Arma Christi* [2577]; **DIMEV 1370-5**)	3. ff. 9-10 *I thank thee lord that thou me wrought* (A prayer of thanksgiving for the Redemption, at the end of the *Arma Christi* (2577); **DIMEV 1370-8**)
4. ff. 11-11v *With sharp thorns that beth keen* (*The Wounds of Christ as Remedies against the Deadly Sins*; **DIMEV 4200-8**)	4. f. 10 *With sharp thorns that beth keen* (*The Wounds of Christ as Remedies against the Deadly Sins*; **DIMEV 4200-9**)
5. f. 11v-12 *The arms of crist both god and man* (Indulgence for the *Arma Christi* devotions [1370, 2577, and 4200]; in four MSS only; **DIMEV 3305.8-3**)	5. f. 10v *The arms of crist both god and man* (Indulgence for the Arma Christi devotions [1370, 2577, and 4200]; in four MSS only; **DIMEV 3305.8-5**)
6. ff. 12v-13v *O Jesu Christ of everlasting sweetness* (The Fifteen O's of Christ; **DIMEV 2469-3**)	6. f. 11 *O Jesu Christ of everlasting sweetness* (The Fifteen O's of Christ; **DIMEV 2469-6**)
7. ff. 13v-16 *O Jesu that madest the heavens clear* (The Fifteen O's; **DIMEV 2473-1**)	7. ff. 11v-14 *O Jesu that madest the heavens clear* (The Fifteen O's; **DIMEV 2473-2**)
8. ff. 17-19 *Glorious cross that with the holy blood* (**DIMEV 914-7**)	8. ff. 15-16 *Glorious cross that with the holy blood* (**DIMEV 914-9**)
9. ff. 19-19v *Now Christ Jesu soothfast priest and king* (**DIMEV 2306-1**)	9. ff. 16-16v *Now Christ Jesu soothfast priest and king* (**DIMEV 2306-2**)

Marquess of Bath MS 30	Huntington Library HM 142
10. ff. 19v-20v *Jesu lord that madest me* (Richard de Caistre's hymn; **DIMEV 1727-16**)	10. ff. 16v-17v *Jesu lord that medest me* (Richard de Caistre's hymn; **DIMEV 1727-20**)
11. ff. 21v-22v *Mary mother well thou be* (**DIMEV 2119-41**)	11. f. 19 *Mary mother well thou be* (**DIMEV 2119-48**)
12. ff. 22v-23v *Gaude of virgins the freshest flower* ('Septem gaudia beate Marie'; **DIMEV 896-1**)	12. ff. 19-19v *Gaude of virgins the freshest flower* ('Septem gaudia beate Marie'; **DIMEV 896-2**)
13. ff. 23v-24 *Mary Mother well Thee be* ('An Orisoun to þe fyue Ioyes of vre lady'; **DIMEV 2118-4**)	13. ff. 19v-20 *Mary Mother well Thee be* ('An Orisoun to þe fyue Ioyes of vre lady'; **DIMEV 2118-5**)
14. ff. 24-25 *Our glorious Father that art in heaven* (John Lydgate, paraphrase of the *Pater Noster*; **DIMEV 2711-2**)	14. ff. 20v-21 *Our glorious Father that art in heaven* (John Lydgate, paraphrase of the *Pater Noster*; **DIMEV 2711-3**)
15. ff. 25-26 *Hail glorious Lady and heavenly queen* (John Lydgate, 'Salutacio Angelica'; **DIMEV 1045-2**)	15. ff. 21-22v *Hail glorious Lady and heavenly queen* (John Lydgate, 'Salutacio Angelica'; **DIMEV 1045-3**)
16. ff. 26-46v *Lord in Thine anger up take me not* (Maydestone's version of the Penitential Psalms; **DIMEV 1961-10**)	16. ff. 22v-41v *Lord in Thine anger up take me not* (Maydestone's version of the Penitential Psalms; **DIMEV 1961-14**)
17. ff. 46v-48v *Kyrieleyson have mercy good Lord* (**DIMEV 1831-1**)	17. ff. 41v-44v *Kyrieleyson have mercy good Lord* (**DIMEV 1831-2**)
18. ff. 49-51v *Jesu that hast me dear I-bought*; (**DIMEV 1761-10**)	18. ff. 45-47v *Jesu that hast me dear I-bought* (**DIMEV 1761-11**)
19. ff. 52-53 *Jesu that all this world has wroght* (**DIMEV 1748-2**)	19. ff. 48-49 *Jesu that all this world has wroght*; (**DIMEV 1748-3**)
20. ff. 53-53v *Now now Jesu for Thy circumcision* (**DIMEV 2352-4**)	20. ff. 49-49v *Now now Jesu for Thy circumcision* (**DIMEV 2352-5**)

In addition to the verse materials listed above, both MSS share the prose *Oracio ("Gracias tibi ago ...";* folios 20v-21v in Longleat 30 and folios 17v-18 in HM 142). Following *DIMEV* 2352, in Longleat 30 a second scribe, exploiting space likely left blank by Werken, writes seven lines of an extract from Thomas Betson's "A Ryght Profytable Treatyse Compendiously Drawen Out Of Many and Dyvers Wrytynges Of Holy Men"[30] (see Figure 1), which a third scribe continues, concluding on folio 54v, with "This short prayer folowing taught /oure Lord saint Brigitt Say ye them ofte in the day *Domine Ihesu christe ego cognosco me grauiter peccasse.*"[31] Betson was at Cambridge ca. 1466, rector of Wimbish, Essex from 1466 to 1481, and "a deacon of the Bridgettine abbey of Syon, Middlesex" from 1481.[32] As Betson died in 1516 and the text found wider circulation only in 1500, when printed by de Worde, this is likely a much later addition. The hands are certainly later, the second possibly an attempt to imitate Werken's hand and the third a very accomplished bastard secretary hand. The third scribe writes the concluding prayer in a larger script. The features of this hand are not identical with the facsimile of Betson's hand in Mary Bateson's *Catalogue of the Library of Syon Monastery Isleworth,* a catalogue compiled by Betson.[33] The horned, tailed secretary **g** and the horned secretary **e**, for example, are similar, but the execution and duct of other characters are too dissimilar to suggest a match. Both hands are certainly those of accomplished and practiced writers, however.

The script of the main scribe in Longleat 30 features the more cursive serifs of semiquadrata as compared to the squarer, more calligraphic quadrata feet of the script in HM 142.[34] (In this, it more closely resembles the form of *textura* employed by Werken in Cambridge, University Library, MS Dd.13.2, dated 1444: the earliest of the manuscripts identified as by Werken.[35]) In both manuscripts, one finds the dotted **y** graph with a curved hairline stroke connecting the dot to top of the right-hand fork of the **y**. The **w** graph is comprised of a minim with a serif foot, connected to a B-shaped element by a hairline stroke. In both manuscripts, the base of the minims aligns uniformly and sits slightly above the ruled line. Biting occurs in **de** and **do** combinations. Ascenders are often forked. The **d** graph features an unlooped ascender that slants backward over the lobe at an angle of 45° or more.

In Table 3, note in the first row the similar construction of the **h** in "**Ihu**," with the fine hairline approach stroke on the ascender element, and another fine approach stroke in the formation of the shoulder. Although the script in HM 142 is more calligraphic, the construction of the "**I**" is similar in both MSS, with a pair of nodules projecting on the left side of the body. In the second row of the table, note that both "**y**" graphs are dotted with an accompanying hairline flourish. While the tail elements of this graph differ, the body elements are formed in similar fashion: the script in Longleat 30 is more rounded and that in HM 140 more calligraphic. These characteristic contrasts are also apparent in the examples of "**de**" "biting" in the two MSS, though the "**e**" graphs are both slightly "horned.

Table 3: Comparison of Letter Forms

Longleat MS 30	HM 142
36	37
38	39
40	41
42	43

An indication of Werken's Dutch heritage might be in evidence in the spelling of "God" as "got" at the end of *DIMEV* 1045: "And after oure encynge got bringe us to heuene" (Longleat 30, folio 26; in HM 142 the spelling in the same line is "god" [folio 22v]), and again in Maidestone's version of the Penitential Psalms (*DIMEV* 1961), on folio 30: "But him þat is in got trustynge." With reference to HM 142, Schultz notes that "[o]missions of words and letters from words, and the substitution of incorrect letters, are very frequent."[44] Several examples of these kinds of things are also evidenced in Longleat 30. At line 118 of Lydgate's "Kalendar" (*DIMEV* 1721), Longleat 30 reads "But I pray þe martir seynt Uital" (cf. MacCracken's edition based on Oxford, Bodleian Library MS Rawl. B.408: "But ȝitte y pray þe marter Seynt Vital"[45]), and at line 128 the Longleat scribe writes "a bache" for "a backe" (perhaps motivated by the rhyme word "ache"). In the *Arma Christi* (*DIMEV* 2577), the spelling "bagbiteyng" occurs in place of the expected "bakbiting."[46] At line 62 of the *Arma Christi*, "the" occurs where the third-person plural pronoun "they" is required. In the Longleat text of *Septem gaudia beate Marie* (*DIMEV* 896), the scribe omits an "h" in "thougt." On folio 23v, near the end of that same text, an "r" is omitted: "Nor **neue** fade nor neuer decrese." On folio 31, line 228 of *The Seven Penitential Psalms* (*DIMEV* 1961) reads "As charge of hoge heuynesse" ("hoge" = "huge").[47] Also in the *Psalms*, "trecchery" is construed as "tretherye" (fol. 41, line 726) and "freel" as "vele" (folio 41, line 743) in Longleat 30.[48] At line 908 of the Psalms, where the Wheatley manuscript reads "And alle þat þere ynne are lope" and Ashmole 61 (line 871 in that MS) has "And tho that ben therin istoke," Longleat reads "And hem þat been þe inne I stope."[49] In the following stanza, Longleat has "crouche" for "cross." In *DIMEV* 1831, line 6 in Longleat reads "Kepe vs from harm & all' kynnes vynne"; HM 142 has the same reading except with "winne" as the final word.[50] In *DIMEV* 1761, the first word of line 15 is spelled "Buth"; the Wheatley manuscript has "Bot."[51] While not all of these are evidence of a foreign scribe at work, the tendencies noted by Schultz in HM 142 to omit words and letters is certainly paralleled in these examples from Longleat 30.

In the *Arma Christi* (*DIMEV* 2577), both Longleat 30 and HM 142 have a program of illustration, that in the latter described by Dutschke as "[e]ighteen colored or grisaille illustrations ... f. 7v: Christ beaten with a rod; the hands that abused Christ; Christ blindfolded; the unseamed garment and the dice; a whip and a scourge; the crown of thorns; the pillar and ropes; Christ bearing the cross; f. 8: the three nails; two hammers; vessel; f. 8v: stick with sponge; spear; ladder; tongs, Jew spitting at Christ; f. 9: the cross; empty tomb."[52] Longleat 30 has two miniatures not included in HM 142 (HM 142 is missing a folio at this point). On folio 7, at the opening of *DIMEV* 2577 (the *Arma Christi*) is a one-third page illustration of the Vernicle cloth.[53] Lower down the page is a small illustration of an arm with a knife for the Circumcision. On folio 12v, at the opening of *DIMEV* 2469, is a half-page miniature of the risen Christ in his sepulchre, gesturing at the wound in His side.[54] The sequence in Longleat 30, by a different artist, includes four illustrations on folio 7v (a pelican in its piety, thirty pieces of silver, a lantern, a sword and a stave), four on folio 8 (a rod, hands that abused Christ, Christ blindfolded, the unseamed garment and dice), four on folio 8v (a whip and a scourge, the crown of thorns, the pillar and ropes, a cross), three on folio 9 (the three nails, a hammer, a vessel), four on folio 9v (a stick with a sponge, a spear, a ladder, tongs), and three on folio 10 (Jew spitting at Christ, the cross, empty tomb).[55]

Although Werken was suggested as the scribe of Longleat 30 by Schulz long ago, I hope now we can confidently include this manuscript as part of his output. The handwriting features suggest the Longleat manuscript was copied later than HM 142, and Edden (see note 47 above) asserts that at least one of the texts in Longleat is a copy of the text in HM 142. If so, then the variety of *textura* would not seem to be a temporal variable, as the colophon in HM 142 has the date 1467, some twenty-three years later than the manuscript whose script more closely resembles that in Longleat 30: Cambridge, University Library MS Dd.13.2. HM 142 and Longleat 30 are exceptional in Werken's known output in that they represent collections primarily of English works (Longleat 30—at least in its current binding—is entirely English) and also in that they are the only instance of Werken producing more than one copy of a work. It may be that he made one copy for Gray and a second for Bole, perhaps after Bole returned to England with—apparently—Werken in train.[56] Alternatively, Werken may have undertaken these productions independently for the London market. I have not found another record that identifies the Betson passage added at the end of Longleat 30. Its addition suggests a religious and learned milieu for the manuscript's early provenance, perhaps, given the final surviving text—the Bridgettine prayer—in an Augustinian community.

Virginia Tech

NOTES

1. H. C. Schulz, "Middle English Texts from the 'Bement' Manuscript," *Huntington Library Quarterly* 3 (1940): 443-65, at 443.
2. R. A. B. Mynors, "A Fifteenth-Century Scribe: T. Werken," *Transactions of the Cambridge Bibliographical Society* 1 (1949-53): 97-104.
3. Mynors, "A Fifteenth-Century Scribe," 104, supplemented by Linne R. Mooney's unpublished list of Scribes Working in England, 1375-1525 (from a List Compiled by Jeremy Griffiths, Ian Doyle, and Angus McIntosh, with additions by Ian Doyle, Kathleen Scott, Malcolm Parkes, Richard Beadle, Ralph Hanna, et al.)
4. This account of Gray is compiled from R.A.B Mynors, *Catalogue of the Manuscripts of Balliol College Oxford* (Oxford: Clarendon Press, 1963): xxiv-xlv and from *The Oxford Dictionary of National Biography* (online: http://www.oxforddnb.com/; accessed October 20, 2011).
5. See M. B. Parkes, "Archaizing Hands in English Manuscripts," in *Books*

and Collectors 1200-1700: Essays presented to Andrew Watson (London: The British Library, 1997): 111

6. Mynors, *Catalogue of the Manuscripts of Balliol College Oxford*, 377.

7. Mynors, *Catalogue of the Manuscripts of Balliol College Oxford*, 50-1.

8. Mynors, *Catalogue of the Manuscripts of Balliol College Oxford*, 51-2.

9. Mynors, *Catalogue of the Manuscripts of Balliol College Oxford*, 66.

10. Mynors, *Catalogue of the Manuscripts of Balliol College Oxford*, 313-14.

11. Mynors, *Catalogue of the Manuscripts of Balliol College Oxford*, 66.

12. Mynors, *Catalogue of the Manuscripts of Balliol College Oxford*, 255-6,

13. Mynors, *Catalogue of the Manuscripts of Balliol College Oxford*, p. 258; but see below: A. C. de la Mare suggests this section of the manuscript (Balliol 238D) is not by Werken.

14. Mynors, *Catalogue of the Manuscripts of Balliol College Oxford*, 256-7.

15. Mynors, *Catalogue of the Manuscripts of Balliol College Oxford*, 326-7.

16. Mynors, *Catalogue of the Manuscripts of Balliol College Oxford*, 308.

17. Mynors, *Catalogue of the Manuscripts of Balliol College Oxford*, 105-6,

18. Mynors, *Catalogue of the Manuscripts of Balliol College Oxford*, 24.

19. Originally part of TCC B.3.21, listed below.

20. Parkes, "Archaizing Hands in English Manuscripts," 101-41, l. 8.

21. A. C. de la Mare, "A Fragment of Augustine in the Hand of Theodericus Werken," *Transactions of the Cambridge Bibliographical Society* 6 (1976): 258-90.

22. De la Mare, "A Fragment of Augustine," 287, n. 3. She cites Mynors' (*Catalogue of the Manuscripts of Balliol College Oxford*) listing of "probables" as "Balliol MS 125, Eutropius, etc., probably copied in Cologne between 1442-4 ... and Cambridge, Corpus Christi College MS 76, part ii, Cassian," and as "possible" "Balliol MS 157, Commentaries of Pelagius and Jerome on the Epistles in a 'beginner's' humanistic hand."

23. Mynors, *Catalogue of the Manuscripts of Balliol College Oxford*, 141-2 (Pelagius, Hieronymus, ca. 1447-54, "during [Gray's] sojourn in Italy").

24. Mynors, *Catalogue of the Manuscripts of Balliol College Oxford*, 103-5 (Eutropius, etc., ca. 1442-4, "during [Gray's] sojourn in Cologne").

25. Werken apparently worked as a scribe for Gray, who was accompanied by Bole for much of his European sojourn, but when Bole returned to England—by July 1450—Werken was in his company and producing books for Bole (Mynors, "A Fifteenth-Century Scribe ...," 100-1).

26. De la Mare, "A Fragment of Augustine," 287-8, n. 3. See Mynors, *Catalogue of the Manuscripts of Balliol College Oxford*, 114-17 for Balliol 135 (ca. 1447-54) and 255 for Balliol 237 (ca. 1444-54).

27. Linne R. Mooney, Daniel W. Mosser, and Elizabeth Solopova, with David H. Radcliffe, *The Digital Index of Middle English Verse* (www.dimev.net). I am in the process of renumbering the index, now over 7,000 records as compared

with the original *Index of Middle English Verse*, with 4,287 records. The numbers in Table 2 are thus equivalent to those found in the original *Index* and its *Supplement* (Carleton Fairchild Brown and Rossell Hope Robbins, *The Index of Middle English Verse* [New York: Printed for the Index Society by Columbia University Press, 1943]; Rossell Hope Robbins and John L. Cutler, *Supplement to the Index of Middle English Verse* [Lexington, Kentucky: University of Kentucky Press, 1965]). When the *DIMEV* renumbering is complete, records will display the *DIMEV* number, the number found in the original *Index* or its *Supplement*, and the number found in Julia Boffey and A. S. G. Edwards, *A New Index of Middle English Verse* (London: The British Library, 2005). For example, number 1721 (the first in Table 2) will be *DIMEV* 2863 (both the *IMEV* and *NIMEV* numbers are 1721). Users will be able to search on the basis of any of the three numbering options.
28. The items in HM 142 not found in Longleat 30 are: *Beatus Ieronimus vero hoc modo composuit psalterium sicut angelus domini docuit eum per spiritum sanctum et propter hoc abbreviatum est…* (ff. 49v-54v; prose); Psalms of the Passion (ff. 54v-58; prose); *Incipit letania de beatua virginie maria c beato bernardo edita quicumque eam cotidie devote cataverit ipsa in die obitus sui et apparebit* (ff. 58-59v; prose); Suffrage of Erasmus (ff. 59v-60v; prose, "T. WERKEN" signature and colophon follows, but not in Werken's hand); Suffrage of Gabriel (ff. 59v-60); Lists of the Seven Deadly Sins, etc. (ff. 61-61v); plus several items (see C. W. Dutschke, *Guide to Medieval and Renaissance Manuscripts in the Huntington Library* [San Marino, CA: Huntington Library, 1989], 1.193-4 for the additional texts in HM 142).
29. The contents of this table were complied via MSS searches of the *DIMEV* [http://www.dimev.net] and then editing the results for presentation here. The "Number" information provides *DIMEV* record numbers, followed by a hyphen, followed by a witness number.
30. Begins: "[B]lessed Ihesu criste our lorde god and savyour…" and ends: "and in the worldes during withouten ende. Amen." Printed by Wynkyn de Worde in 1500 (STC 1978).
The text in Longleat 30 can be found in the de Worde edition on sigs. b.3v-b.4v. The extract might have been copied from the de Worde's edition, of which it is virtually a verbatim—though not literatum—version.
31. This Bridgettine prayer also occurs in Huntington Library MS HM 1344 in a series of "Penitential psalms, gradual psalms, and litany…" (Dutschke, *Guide to Medieval and Renaissance Manuscripts*, 2.573-4) and in Lambeth Palace Library MS 3600 (see Alexandra Barratt, "Singing from the Same Hymn Sheet," in Margaret Connolly and Linne R. Mooney, eds. *Design and Distribution of Late Medieval Manuscripts in England* [Woodbridge, Suffolk: York Medieval Press, 2008], 139-60, at 153).
32. *Oxford Dictionary of National Biography*.

33. Mary Bateson, *Catalogue of the Library of Syon Monastery Isleworth* (Cambridge: Cambridge University Press, 1898). See also Plate 22-1 in A. I. Doyle, "A Letter Written by Thomas Betson," in *The Medieval Book and a Modern Collector: Essays in Honour of Toshiyuki Takamiya*, ed. Takami Matsuda, Richard A. Linenthal and John Scahill (Cambridge and Tokyo: D. S. Brewer & Yushodo Press Ltd., 2004), 255-67; at 256. As Doyle notes, Betson's *A ryght profitable treatise...* derives "partly from another, shorter, pamphlet printed by Caxton or Wynkyn in 1491 entitled *Ars moriendi/ that is to saye the craft for to deye for the helthe of mannes sowle*"(265; STC 786).

34. See Dutschke, *Guide to Medieval and Renaissance Manuscripts...*, 1.195: "Written in textura quadrata scripts by 2 main scribes." Parkes notes "details of the script which are characteristic of Werken's hand... are the letter **g, x,** the formation of the **&** ligature, and the practice (unusual among scribes in England) of dividing a word at the end of a line in the middle of a **ct** ligature, but with the linking stroke extended into the margin" ("Archaizing Hands in English Manuscripts," 111), but those comments are with reference to his humanist hand, not the *textura* hand of HM 142 and Longleat 30.

35. See plate VII in Mynors, "A Fifteenth-Century Scribe,"36.

36. See Figure 2, Longleat 30, folio 7v, line 1.

37. See Figure 3, HM 142, folio 22v, 3 up.

38. See Figure 2, Longleat 30, folio 7v, line 3.

39. See Figure 3, HM 142, folio 22v, line 3.

40. See Figure 2, Longleat 30, folio 7v, line 9.

41. See Figure 3, HM 142, folio 22v, line 5.

42. See Figure 2, Longleat 30, folio 7v, line 7.

43. See Figure 3, HM 142, folio 22v, 4 up.

44. "Middle English Texts from the 'Bement' Manuscript," 444.

45. Henry Noble MacCracken, *The Minor Poems of John Lydgate*, Part 1, EETS e.s. 107 (Oxford University Press, 1911, for 1910), 367. This edition uses London, British Library MS Addit. 11748 as its base text.

46. Cf. Richard Morris, *Legends of the Holy Rood: Symbols of the Passion and Cross-Poems*, EETS o.s. 46 (London: Trübner, 1881), 170, l. 10.

47. Cf. Mabel Day, *The Wheatley Manuscript*, EETS e.s. 155 (Oxford University Press, 1921), 29: "As birdeyn of grete heuynesse." Cf. also George Shuffleton, *Ashmole 61: A Compilation of Popular Middle English Verse* (Kalamazoo, MI: Western Michigan University for TEAMS, 2008), line 228: "As charge of grete hevynesse." Valerie Edden states that HM 142 has the reading "*boge heuyness.*" She argues that Longleat (assigned the sigil "Lh" in her discussion) is copied from HM 142 (Hm) and that this is an example of disagreements between the two that the scribe of Lh was able to correct (*Richard Maidstone's Penitential Psalms ed. from Bodl. MS Rawlinson A 389*, Middle English Texts 21 [Heidelberg: Universitätsverlag/Carl Winter, 1990], 36).

48. See Day 1921, 49, 50.

49. See Day 1921, 57; Shuffleton 2008; Longleat 30, folio 45v. If Shuffleton's transcription is accurate, then Ashmole 61 violates the rhyme scheme with its reading. There is no mark of abbreviation that would expand Longleat's "þe inne" to "þere inne."

50. Schulz 1940, 460.

51. See Day 1921, 1.

52. Dutschke, *Guide to Medieval and Renaissance Manuscripts...*, 1.195. Some images of HM 142 are available through the Digital Scriptorium (http://dpg.lib.berkeley.edu/webdb/dsheh/heh_brf?Description=&CallNumber =HM+142; folios 7v-8 include seven of these illustrations.

53. Cf. Plate 492 in Kathleen L. Scott, *Later Gothic Manuscripts 1390-1490* (London: Harvey Miller, 1996), vol. 2 (Longleat MS 30 cited at 1.352).

54. Scott refers to this as "The Man of Sorrows" (1.294), as depicted in her illustrations 399 and 400 in vol. 2 (*Later Gothic Manuscripts*).

55. Almost identical with the sequence in Huntington Library 26054 (a roll; *olim* Tollemache, Helmingham Hall). The sequence in this roll is captured in the series of images available via the Digital Scriptorium (http://dpg.lib.berkeley.edu/webdb/dsheh/heh_brf?Description=&CallNumber =HM+26054).

56. According to Mynors, "[t]hat Werken ... did establish himself in London and in close association with Richard Bole, there is no doubt" ("A Fifteenth-Century Scribe", 101).

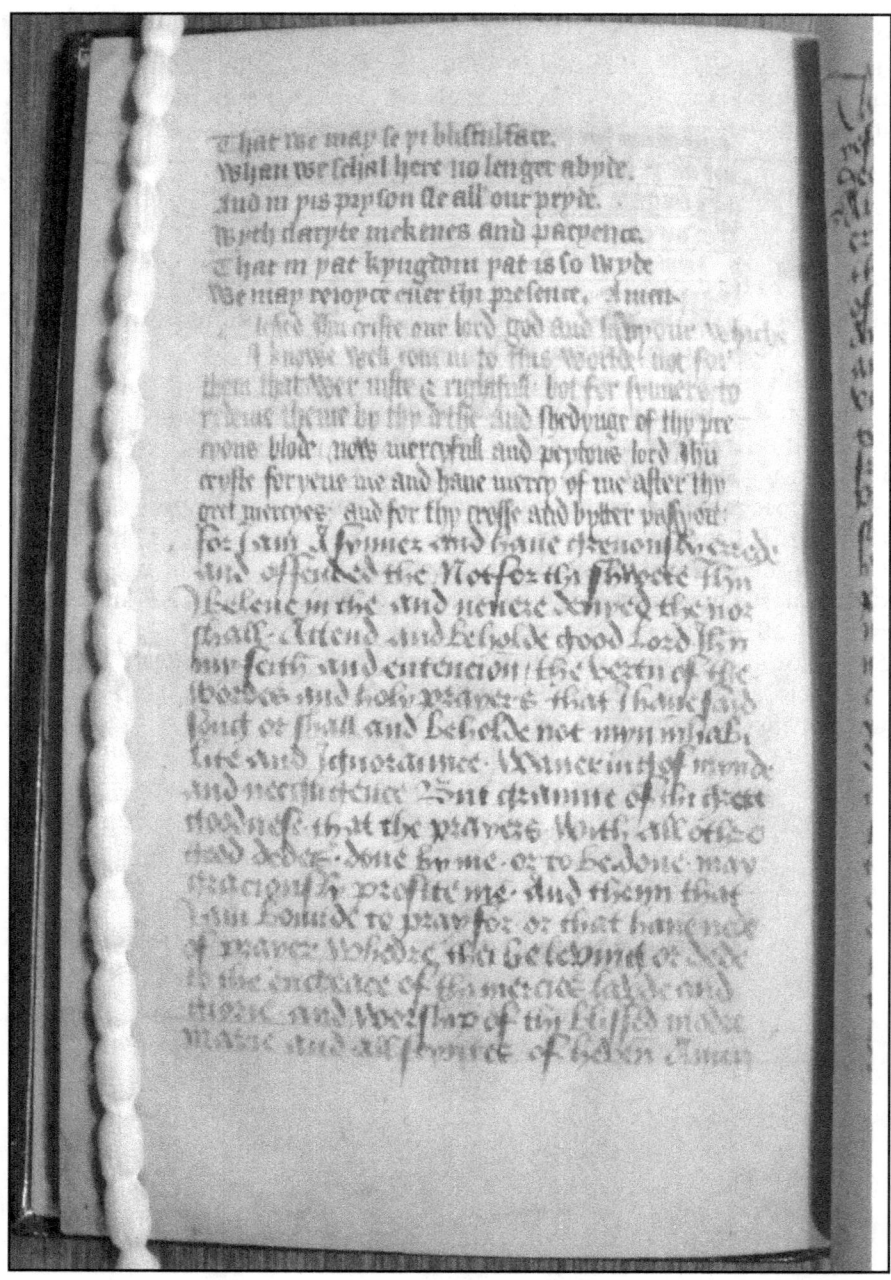

Figure 1: Longleat MS 30, folio 53v. Reproduced by permission of the Marquess of Bath, Longleat House, Warminster, Wiltshire, Great Britain.

Figure 2: Longleat MS 30, folio 12v. Reproduced by permission of the Marquess of Bath, Longleat House, Warminster, Wiltshire, Great Britain.

Figure 3: Huntington Library MS HM 142, folio 22v. This item is reproduced by permission of The Huntington Library, San Marino, California.

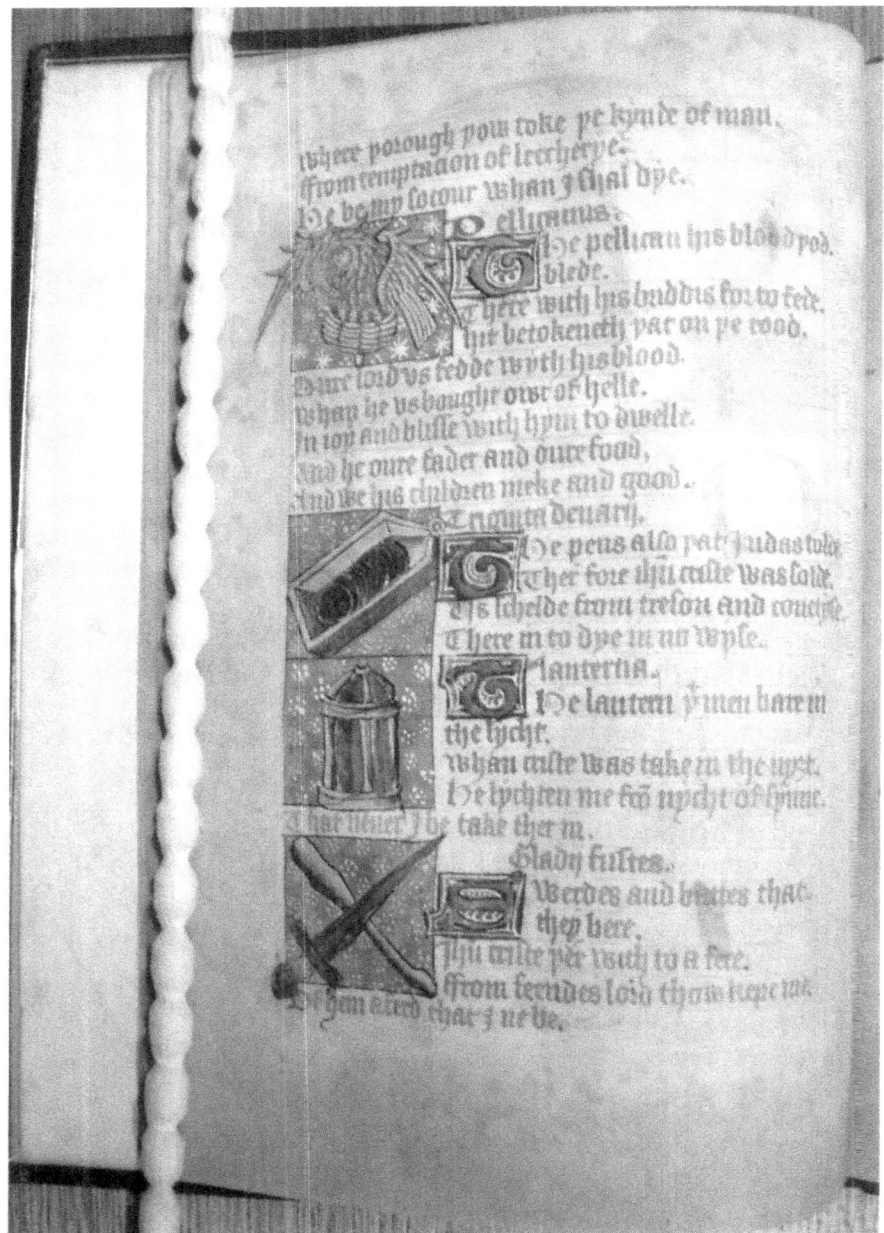

Figure 4: Longleat MS 30, folio 7v. Reproduced by permission of the Marquess of Bath, Longleat House, Warminster, Wiltshire, Great Britain.

Crossing the Text/Image Boundary: The French Adaptations of *Hypnerotomachia Poliphili*

EFTHYMIA PRIKI

Hypnerotomachia Poliphili, published in 1499 by Aldus Manutius in Venice, is not only one of the most famous illustrated printed books of the Italian Renaissance but also, and more importantly, it is considered one of the basic precursors of the emblematic culture that flourished in the sixteenth century. Its 172 woodcuts are not mere additions to enhance the visual aesthetics of the book but rather play a crucial role in understanding the story. This proto-emblematic romance was especially successful in France, where its adaptations and editions present interesting deviations from the Italian edition, especially in the way that text and image interact with each other.

Using the notion of the boundary between text and image, this paper will discuss the ways in which such boundaries are crossed in the 1499 edition of the *Hypnerotomachia Poliphili* and subsequently in the French adaptations of the work, demonstrating that its reception in sixteenth-century France has developed by expansion: the French editions break out of the boundaries of the original work with an iconography that functions as a metalinguistic discourse for the text itself. Furthermore, the intervisual/intertextual game between the original work and its French versions can give us new insights into the history of the *Hypnerotomachia*'s reception.

Hypnerotomachia Poliphili, as the title suggests, narrates the love-quest of Poliphilus which takes place in the dream realm. Poliphilus falls asleep and dreams of traversing several landscapes containing ancient ruins, extraordinary buildings, fantasy creatures and allegorical figures in order to be reunited with his beloved Polia, who in reality, as the epitaph at the end of the book informs us, is dead. The story is divided into two parts: in the first we have Poliphilus narrating his adventures until his final union with Polia in the island of Cytherea, while in the second part Polia takes up the role of the narrator and recounts her own version of their love story, which takes place in a seemingly "real" world. At the end, the couple embraces and kisses, but their affections do not last long, since Polia vanishes and Poliphilus wakes up alone as in the beginning of the romance. The narration is enriched by detailed descriptions of what Poliphilus sees, thinks and experiences and is accompanied by relevant woodcuts.

These woodcuts are mostly representations of many of the buildings, monuments, inscriptions, and other artefacts that Poliphilus describes and of the events he witnesses. Interestingly, there are woodcuts of all the scenes that mark the transitions from one stage of Poliphilus' journey to the other (the dark forest, his second sleep within the dream, the dragon's chase through the portal, the three portals to Queen Telosia's realm, and the boat sailing in the sea).[1] Moreover, the sequence of the woodcuts, especially those which depict narrative scenes, when viewed isolated from the text reveal a progression, signifying Poliphilus's initiatory process in the mysteries of love: from the dark forest to abandoned ruins to the realm of Queen Eleuterylida (Free Will), a pleasant space inhabited by maidens, to the realm of Queen Telosia (Aim), strongly marked by religious rituals (parade, god offerings, wedding and sacrifice, cemetery), to the circular island of Cytherea, where the couple's ultimate union takes place symbolically through the epiphany of Venus. In the second part of the book, we have a new set of woodcuts—all of them depicting narrative scenes, rather than isolated objects— which reveal another sequence of events relating to Polia's conversion to Eros.

Woodcuts and text are interdependent, functioning together to make meaning. The story unfolds through the interaction between textual and visual narration. It is also interesting that in several pages the typed text becomes a visual space as well, by taking different shapes, such as goblets and drinking vessels, creating a "visual-typographical-textual assemblage," a technique that has been termed as "technopaegnia."[2] This technique is intensified in the 1546 Jean Martin edition. The emblematic character of the book is present in both the original Aldine edition and the two French editions discussed in this article. However, this text/image interaction differs in each edition, altering the ways it can be read.

The image in a manuscript or a printed book is a visual space within the textual space. This visual space in the 1499 Aldine edition often appears as a *blank* space to be filled by the recipient's imagination. A good example demonstrating this can be seen on the woodcut depicting the great portal (figure 1). Though this portal is extensively described in the text, its visual representation lacks nearly all of its decorative details, such as the reliefs with the mythological scenes. Instead, the artist has provided the readers with frames delimiting these empty spaces. There is a two-way text/image interaction: the textual space provides the supplement to the visual blank space or the visual blank space provokes the intensification of textual imagination. Thus, the blank space aims to interact with the recipient, giving birth to an imaginative energy.

Though the text provides detailed information of the sights Poliphilus encounters with exact measures, descriptions of their sculptures, colors, materials and so on, the responding images in the woodcuts are plain and at times schematic. The images outline the monuments' layout, while, in some cases, the size of depicted buildings is misleading compared to the actual text. A good example of the latter is the pyramid that Poliphilus finds among ruins after his second sleep. On one hand, the woodcut shows a rather medium-sized stepped pyramid with a rectangular base, while on the tip of the pyramid rests an obelisk as high as the pyramid (figure 2). On the other hand, the text describes a "vast" and "monstrous" stepped pyramid of complex design and encased in "1410 steps or stairs."3 Is this inconsistency deliberate or a mistake? Does it reflect the artist's attempt to adjust the monument to fit the printed page or was it a conscious choice aiming at emphasizing certain parts of the monument (i.e., the obelisk)? Given that we are uncertain of the author's interference with the publication and of the form of the original manuscript—whether it included miniatures or sketches, which might have served as models for the woodcutter—we cannot provide adequate answers to these questions. However, the close interrelationship between text and image in the book leads us to the assumption that the visual choices were indeed deliberate, though their purpose and function are often a puzzle to be solved.

Interestingly, a modern reader of the *Hypnerotomachia Poliphili*, Esteban Alejandro Cruz has ventured to reconcile text and image with digital reconstructions of the monuments and landscapes appearing in the work, not only the ones that have already been visualized in the woodcuts but also those that are only described in the text. His aim is to follow the text as closely as possible, while using the existing images as hints. Through a detailed examination of the measurements and the structure of the building as described in the text, his reconstruction of the pyramid demonstrates the great discordance between the woodcut and the text-based modern reconstruction, which does justice to the scale and magnitude of the "vast" pyramid.[4]

Narrative scenes—either depicting Poliphilus' journey or painted and sculpted scenes which he views on monuments—are represented with more details and sometimes with inscriptions, which allow the reader to identify the events and myths narrated. However, given that the inscriptions are usually in several languages, including Latin, Greek, Arabic and Hebrew, which are not always explained in the text, they contribute to creating a puzzling effect for the reader. The puzzlement is enhanced by the hieroglyphic inscriptions, which basically consist of either symbols resembling Egyptian hieroglyphs (e.g., on the elephant's obelisk— figure 3) or Renaissance hieroglyphs, which are devices created during the Renaissance inspired by the idea of Egyptian hieroglyphs to conceal meaning in an image (figure 4).[5]

In addition, there are woodcuts that function more as allusions to things described in the text rather than as actual representations of what they refer to. For example, the small empty ship sailing in what might be the sea alludes to the couple's journey to the garden island of Cytherea in the company of Cupid, his party and sea creatures.[6] Thus, a single image symbolizes a specific lengthy episode in the story. Without the text, this symbolism cannot be inferred solely from the image. Moreover, the island of Cytherea's topography is shown in a schematic circular inscribed diagram providing a rather perplexing hint of the island's description, for which one needs to turn to the text.[7]

With all of the above examples, I wanted to demonstrate that the text/image boundary in the Italian edition is crossed from the image to the text, with the blank space functioning as a bridge. In other words, to understand the image and fill in the blank spaces, we turn to the text. Consequently, this intensifies the element of *enigma* in the book, which is also evident in its linguistic maze as well as in the cryptic techniques that the anonymous author uses to conceal his identity. The enigmatic aspect of the Italian woodcuts was not wholly transferred to the subsequent French editions, where there seems to have been a reverse tendency to elucidate the text through the woodcuts, which appear in more quantity and are richer in content.

The first French edition was published in 1546 by Jean Martin at the press of Jacques Kerver in Paris and was reprinted twice. The same translation, revised by François Béroalde de Verville, was published at the press of Matthieu Guillemot in Paris, in 1600. The woodcuts and frontispieces in the French editions are not merely imitating the Aldine edition; they rather function as a visual commentary on the work, aiming to fill in the aforementioned blank space. In the Jean Martin 1546 edition, the Italian woodcuts were adapted following the mannerism of the First School of Fontainebleau, an artistic movement originating in the court of the castle of Fontainebleau, where Francis I (1494-1547) commissioned the Italian mannerist painters Rosso and Primatriccio to decorate his gallery.[8] This should come as no surprise, since the Aldine *Hypnerotomachia* had already been circulating in the court of the Valois dynasty since 1509 when Louis XII (1469-1515) returned from Venice having acquired copies of the *Hypnerotomachia Poliphili*.[9] As previous research has shown, the book continued to exercise significant influence during the reigns of Francis I and Henry II (1519-1559) in terms of the architectural and artistic agendas of the two kings.[10]

The differentiation of the images in the Jean Martin edition from the Italian ones is not limited to stylistic adjustments. Another obvious difference is the elaborately decorated frontispiece of the Jean Martin edition (figure 5) with detailed information regarding the book (title, date, publishing house). The Aldine frontispiece (figure 6), on the contrary, has no decorative borders, but only the book's enigmatic title in an upside down pyramid— along with an editorial warning against those who might attempt to imitate the publication— within a blank space.[11]

Furthermore, there are reversed woodcuts,[12] some minor changes in the order of the woodcuts' placement, additions and omissions, while there are a few cases where there have been significant alterations to the way the woodcuts are presented. To be more specific, there are thirteen additional woodcuts which depict either buildings and locations described in the text but are not represented in the Italian woodcuts or additional images of buildings appearing in the Italian woodcuts but depicted here as diagrams revealing the proportional dimensions of a structure (figure 7) or depicted from different viewpoints.[13] Moreover, there are additions to the details of the original images. Instead of being left to the reader's imagination, the blank spaces of monuments, buildings, and objects are covered with decorations, reliefs and sculptures as described in the text (figure 8). Thus, the French 1546 edition attempts to elucidate the original images by adding information from the text. At the same time, two images depicting isolated objects have been omitted.[14] In my opinion, these omissions are not deliberate, since both objects, which are mechanisms placed on top of two buildings, are present elsewhere within the context of their surroundings. Perhaps the French editor was not concerned to emphasize those two mechanisms by presenting them individually and out of their contexts as it happens in the Aldine edition.

Regarding alterations in woodcuts, I will focus on the two most significant: firstly, inscriptions and hieroglyphic sequences are usually accompanied by French translations or additional inscriptions and explanatory text in a way that demonstrates a tendency to make these images as clear as possible to the reader.[15] Secondly, the obelisk in the garden of

Queen Eleuterylida's palace is not depicted as isolated but is incorporated in its context, which is a circular enclosed space surrounded by sculptures of maidens and climbing plants, showing a tendency to visualize a more complete image of the monument by contextualizing it in its surroundings (figure 9).

Overall, the 1546 illustrations are elucidating, using the text to fill in the visual gaps. There is a tendency to explain the text through the images and, thus, to shed light on the visual enigma. This mainly occurs with images depicting buildings and monuments, demonstrating a special interest in architectural and garden designs, which might be connected to the influence *Hypnerotomachia Poliphili* exercised on these disciplines in sixteenth-century France. In this edition, the text/image boundary is crossed from the text to the image, with the image functioning as an authoritative interpretation. In order to understand the text, we now turn to the image to get visual examples of what we are reading.

The 1600 Vervillian edition goes one step further than these earlier editions by attempting to provide an external layer of interpretation, thus stepping out of the boundary of the work itself. This edition is basically a reworking of the 1546 translation, and it includes the same woodcuts with all their differentiations from the Italian edition. Verville's novelty is his new title,[16] frontispiece and his introductory texts, which are intended to present the story as an alchemical allegory. The new frontispiece (figure 10) is filled with alchemical emblems symbolizing the alchemical process, the *Great Work* of the alchemists. Their meaning is explained thoroughly in the introductory essay entitled "Recueil stéganographique contenant l'intelligence du frontispiece de ce livre," which is a story that functions as a mirror romance to the *Hypnerotomachia Poliphili*. Thus, to accomplish his re-interpretation, or rather over-interpretation, of the *Hypnerotomachia*, Verville imposes new visual and textual elements and, in this way, he transposes the text/image boundary outside the "text," creating a new boundary between the "text" and his "paratext"; the latter provides a new commentary on the former.[17] At the same time, the enigmatic aspect re-emerges—but under a new, more targeted, light—through the use of alchemical symbolism in the frontispiece, for which one needs to consult the aforementioned essay, and through the vocabulary used in the new title and in the introductory texts (e.g. *recueil steganographique, riches inventions, voile, ombres du songe*). The enigma aims to provoke the reader to explore the book in order to discover the hidden knowledge therein.

Concerning the text/image boundary in the Vervillian edition, we could say that, on one hand, the frontispiece and introductory essay—Verville's "paratext"—follows the same principle as in the Italian edition where the text is the key to understanding the image, but, on the other hand, the main body of the book is an imitation of the Jean Martin edition following the exact opposite principle whereby the image attempts to elucidate textual elements. However, in the first case, even though the boundary is crossed from the image to the text, there is no blank space for the reader to fill with his or her imagination, but rather the paratextual essay provides us with exact directions of how to cross the boundary and interpret the emblems.

To sum up, in the 1499 Italian edition, there seems to be a tendency to enigmatize through the blankness of the woodcuts and to provoke the reader to use his imaginative energy to complete the visual gaps and solve the "puzzles." On the contrary, in the Jean Martin 1546 edition, there is an attempt to fill in the visual gaps and elucidate the story rather than leaving it up to the reader's imagination. Verville's approach is somewhere in the middle, as we have previously discussed. Influenced by alchemical lore and the art of steganography popular in the second half of the sixteenth century, he decided to dress his edition with an alchemical veil, promising hidden knowledge and mystery. However, the main text is an imitation of the 1546 edition with all of its elucidating woodcuts.

As an endnote, I would like to underline the importance of publishing choices on the work's subsequent reception. Both French editions influenced the way later audiences approached the *Hypnerotomachia Poliphili*. Jean Martin's edition influenced the way the buildings, gardens, and landscapes were imagined and reconstructed by artists, architects and scholars, while Verville's alchemical "paratext" contributed to the *Hypnerotomachia*'s reception as an alchemical allegory, especially by psychologist Carl Gustav Jung who used it as such in his studies, having found many points of convergence between the work and his psychoanalytic theories on the *anima* archetype, the collective unconscious, and the individuation process. More importantly, the fluidity of interpretation relating to the *Hypnerotomachia Poliphili* that allowed the French editors to experiment with the text/image boundaries and that allow every reader to approach it from an infinity of perspectives originates from the choices made in the Italian edition, which enhance the book's enigma.

University of Cyprus

Figure 1. The great portal of the pyramid, Aldine edition (*The Electronic Hypnerotomachia* 1997, 55)

Figure 2. The pyramid, Aldine edition (*The Electronic Hypnerotomachia* 1997, 26)

deua ad intrare nella Elephantina machina exuifcerata.

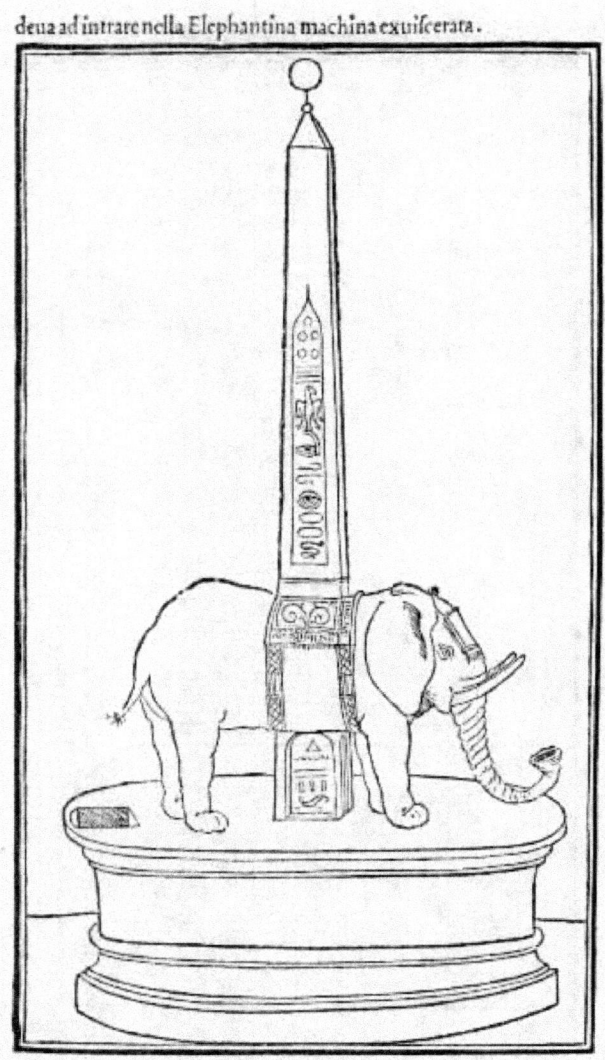

Figure 3. The elephant obelisk with Egyptian-like hieroglyphs on its side, Aldine edition (*The Electronic Hypnerotomachia* 1997, 38)

Figure 4. An example of renaissance hieroglyphs, Aldine edition (*The Electronic Hypnerotomachia* 1997, 41)

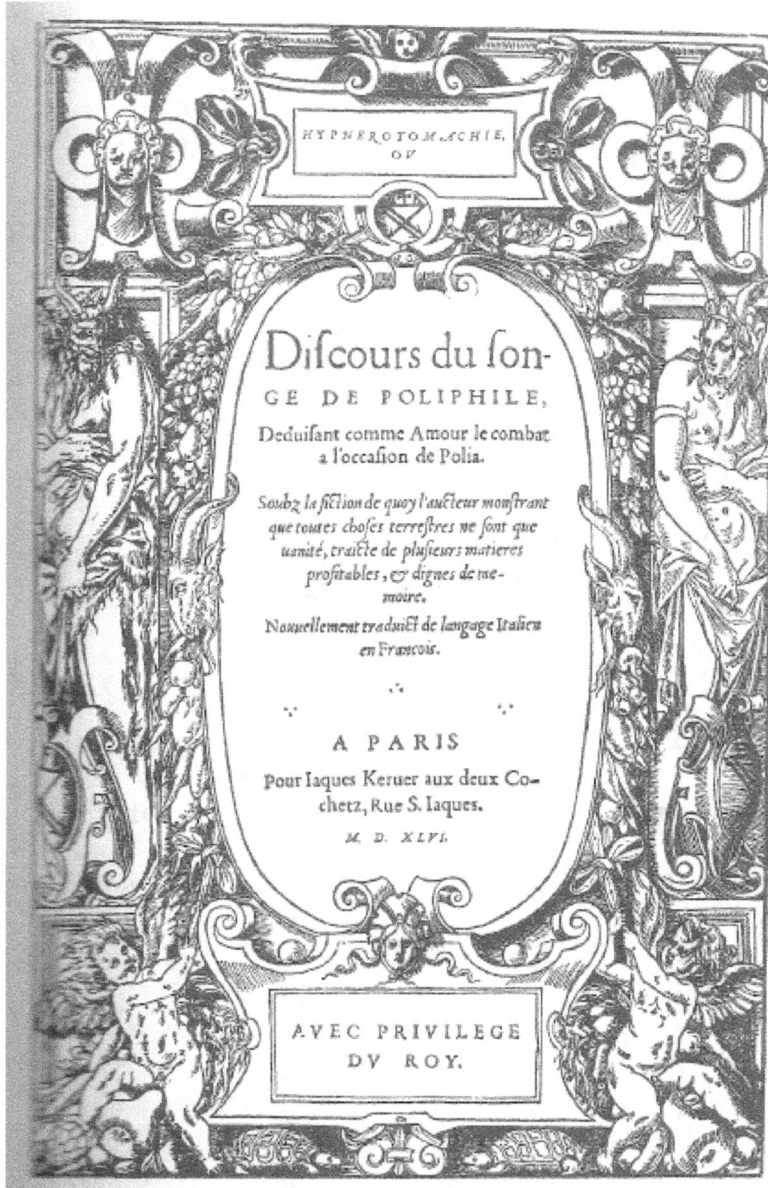

Figure 5. Frontispiece of the 1546 Kerver edition (Polizzi 1994, 1)

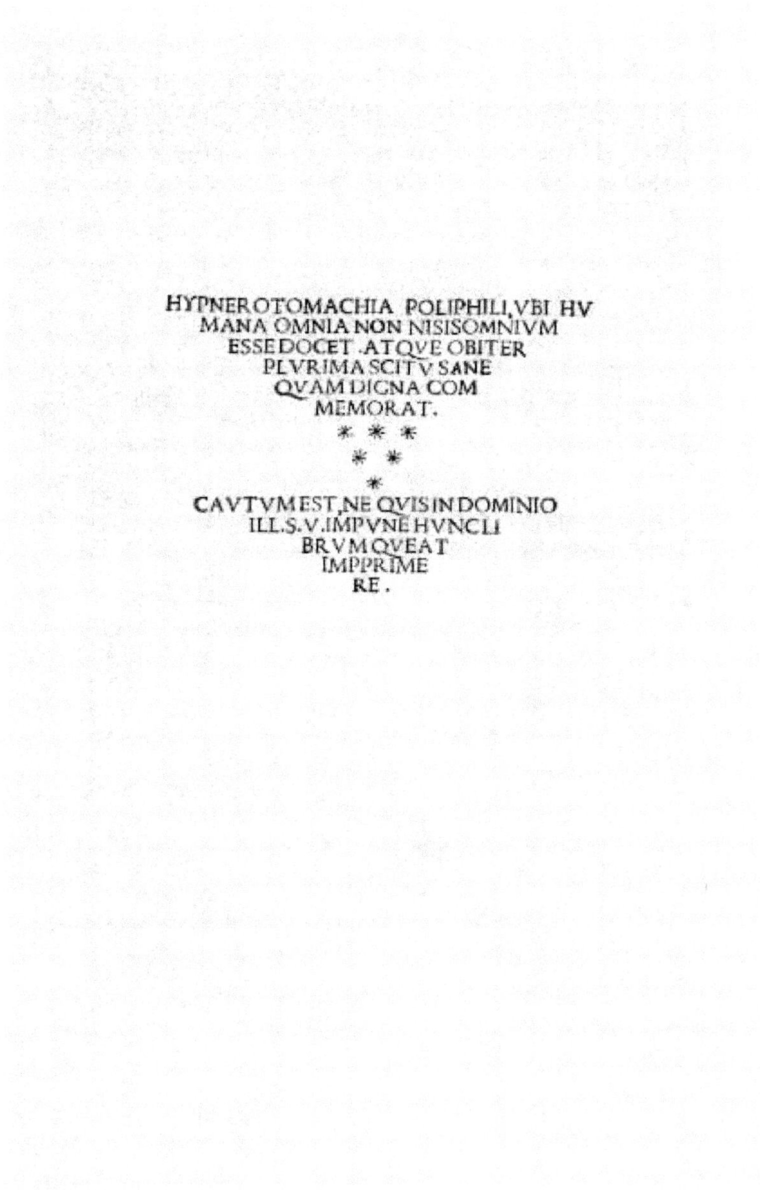

HYPNEROTOMACHIA POLIPHILI, VBI HV
MANA OMNIA NON NISISOMNIVM
ESSE DOCET .ATQVE OBITER
PLVRIMA SCITV SANE
QVAM DIGNA COM
MEMORAT.

* * *

* *

*

CAVTVM EST, NE QVIS IN DOMINIO
ILL.S.V.IMPVNE HVNCLI
BRVMQVEAT
IMPPRIME
RE .

Figure 6. Frontispiece of the 1499 Aldine edition (*The Electronic Hypnerotomachia* 1997, 1)

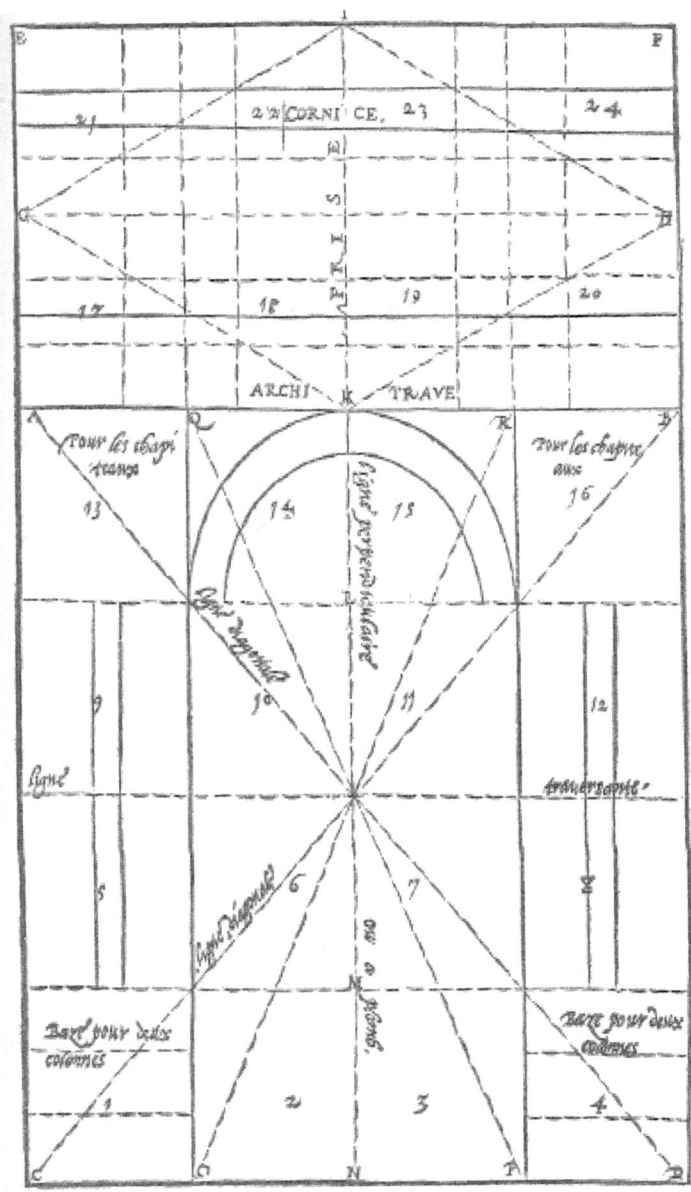

Figure 7. Diagram revealing the proportional dimensions of the portal, 1546 Kerver edition (Polizzi 1994, 47)

Figure 8. The great portal, 1546 Kerver edition (Polizzi 1994, 50)

Figure 9. The contextualized tripartite obelisk, 1546 Kerver edition (Polizzi 1994, 127)

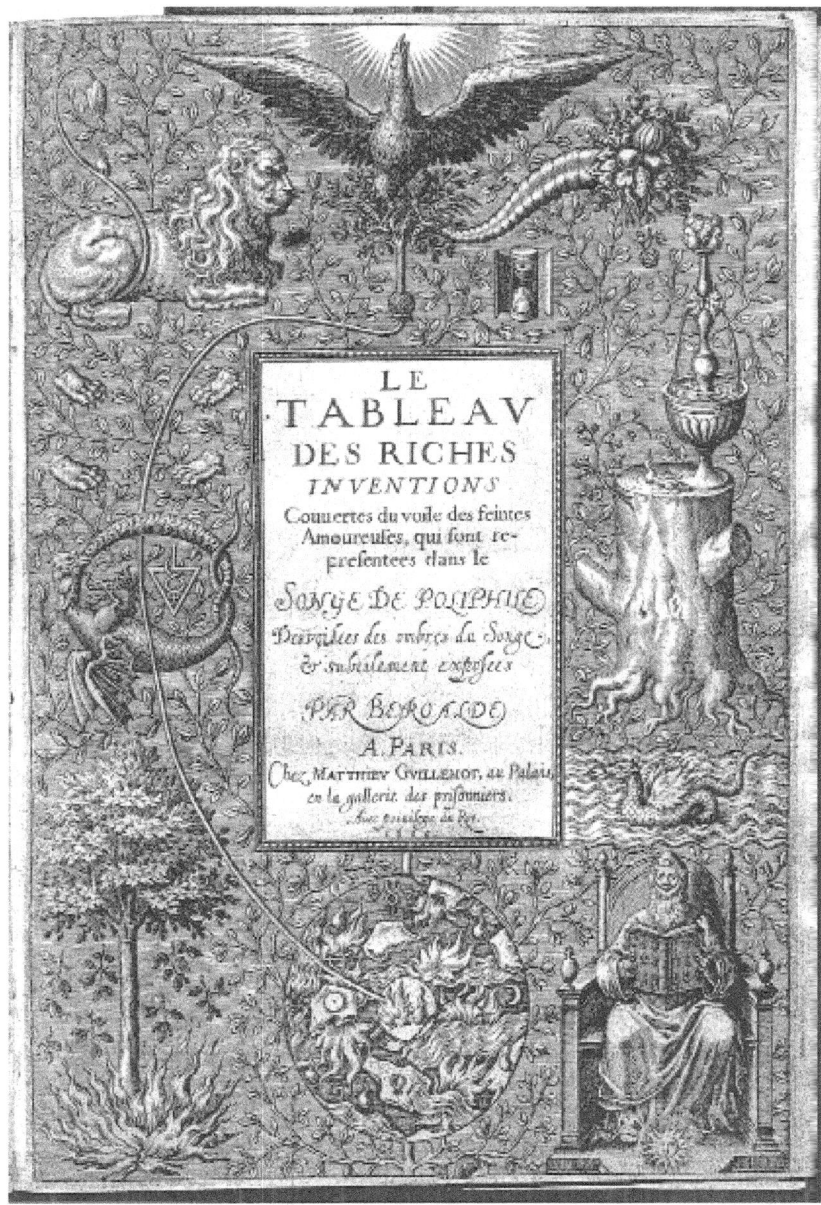

Figure 10. Frontispiece of the 1600 Vervillian edition (S.M.1547, Special Collections, University of Glasgow)

CREDITS

Figures 1-4 and 6 are reproduced with permission from the companion website (http://mitpress.mit.edu/e-books/hp/) for Leon Battista Alberti's *Hypnerotomachia Poliphili: Re-Cognizing the Architectural Body in the Early Italian Renaissance*, by Liane Lefaivre, published by The MIT Press.

Figures 5, 7, 8, 9 are taken from *Le Songe de Poliphile*. Edited by Gilles Polizzi (Paris: Imprimerie Nationale, 1994).

Figure 10 is reproduced from the S.M. 1547, by permission of University of Glasgow Library, Special Collections.

NOTES

This paper was originally presented at the Twelfth Biennial Conference of the Early Book Society in collaboration with the Twelfth York Manuscripts Conference, entitled "Out of Bounds: Mobility, Movement and Use of Manuscripts and Printed Books, 13501550," which took place in York (3-7 July 2011).

1. *Hypnerotomachia Poliphili*. Edited by Marco Ariani and Mino Gabriele, vol. 2. Facsimile (Milano: Adelphi Edizioni, 1998), 14, 20, 62, 135, 291.
2. The term "technopaegnia" is used in reference to the *Hypnerotomachia Poliphili* in the MIT project: http://mitpress.mit.edu/e-books/hp/hyptext1.htm#Technopaegnia.
3. *Hypnerotomachia Poliphili—The Strife for Love in a Dream*. Translated by Joscelyn Godwin (New York and London: Thames & Hudson, 1999), 23-27.
4. Cruz, E.A. *Hypnerotomachia Poliphili —Rediscovering Antiquity through the dreams of Poliphilus* (Canada: Trafford Publishing, 2006), Plate V at 44.
5. Renaissance hieroglyphs have been used extensively in emblem books as well as in printers' marks (e.g. dolphin and anchor, Aldine Press).
6. *Hypnerotomachia Poliphili*. Edited by Marco Ariani and Mino Gabriele, vol. 2. Facsimile (Milano: Adelphi Edizioni, 1998), 291.
7. *Hypnerotomachia Poliphili*. Edited by Marco Ariani and Mino Gabriele, vol. 2. Facsimile (Milano: Adelphi Edizioni, 1998), 311.
8. Blunt, A. "The Hypnerotomachia Poliphili in 17th Century France," *Journal of the Warburg Institute*1 no. 2 (1937): 118. For the work of Rosso and Primatriccio on the gallery of Francis I, see Yvonne Jestaz, *La galerie François 1er du Chateau de Fontainebleau, les dossiers de la SAMCF*, No. 2 (2009).
9. Russell, D. 1995. *Emblematic Structures in Renaissance French Culture* (Toronto: University of Toronto Press, 1995), 89.
10. Hieatt, A.K. & Prescott, A.L. "Contemporizing antiquity: the Hypnerotomachia and its afterlife in France," *Word & Image*, 8.4 (1992): 307.

11. *Hypnerotomachia Poliphili, ubi humana omnia non nisi somnium esse docet. Atque obiter plurima scitu sane quam digna commemorate. Cautum est, ne quis in dominio Ill. S. V. impune hunc librum queat imprimere. Hypnerotomachia Poliphili.* Edited by Marco Ariani and Mino Gabriele vol. 2.Facsimile (Milano: Adelphi Edizioni, 1998): 1.

12. Woodcuts which closely imitate the Italian ones, though adapted in the School of Fontainebleau style, but which are reversed, as if they mirror the original ones.

13. *Le Songe de poliphile.* Edited by Gilles Polizzi (Paris: Imprimerie Nationale, 1994), 47, 81, 84, 121, 124, 126, 196, 276, 277, 288, 290, 291, 292.

14. *Hypnerotomachia Poliphili.* Edited by Marco Ariani and Mino Gabriele, vol. 2. Facsimile (Milano: Adelphi Edizioni, 1998), 81, 211.

15. *Le Songe de Poliphile.* Edited by Gilles Polizzi (Paris: Imprimerie Nationale, 1994), 71, 156, 165, 203, 229–231.

16. Le tableau des riches inventions couvertes du voile des feintes amoureuses, qui sont representées dans le Songe de Poliphile desvoilées des ombres du songe et subtilement exposées par Béroalde (See also figure 10).

17. For the term "paratext" and its functions, see Gérard Genette. *Palimpsests: Literature in the Second Degree* (Lincoln: University of Nebraska Press, 1997): 3, and Gérard Genette. *Paratexts: Thresholds of Interpretation* (Cambridge: Cambridge University Press, 1997).

Descriptive Reviews

GEORGE HARDIN BROWN AND LINDA EHRSAM VOIGTS, EDS.
The Study of Medieval Manuscripts of England: Festschrift in Honor of Richard W. Pfaff.
Arizona Studies in the Middle Ages and the Renaissance 35.
Turnhout, Belgium: Brepols, 2010. ix + 438 pp. 23 B&W illus.

George Hardin Brown and Linda Ehrsam Voigts's Festschrift for Richard W. Pfaff is an impressive collection of sixteen original essays from an extremely diverse group of scholars ranging from seasoned *emeriti* to a post-doctoral fellow. The collection is very much in keeping with Pfaff's liturgical and historical interests, and is split almost evenly into two sections, the first comprising seven essays on liturgical studies, the second comprising nine more broadly historical essays. The Festschrift's end matter contains a bibliography of Pfaff's published works, brief biographies of the contributors, and several indices.

The volume's editors took a very light hand in introducing Pfaff and in preparing the reader for the dynamic breadth of articles contained within the Festschrift (downplaying, for example, the number of Pfaff's articles by half a dozen). Though I would have preferred a more leisurely introduction to such an important scholar as Pfaff, the articles do speak for themselves and to Pfaff through the level of professionalism and intense expertise. Some of the essays address Pfaff directly, for example, Christopher A. Jones in his work on a redaction of a treatise by Amalarius, and Jaroslav Folda in his article on the historiated initials in Yates Thompson MS. 12. In both, the personal gesture of acknowledging the festschrift's honoree is touching. Although the first half of the volume is slightly more thematic than the second, the eclecticism of the more loosely themed "history" section is nevertheless extremely strong.

In the collection as a whole, Elizabeth C. Teviotdale's study of Pembroke College 302 and Joseph Wittig's consideration of the Old English Boethius are standouts among standouts. Weaknesses are very few—one concern was that the quality of images presented in Andrew Hughes's article is problematic, nowhere near the quality of images presented elsewhere in the volume.

The Pfaff bibliography is comprehensive, but I would have liked to have seen the contributor biographies that follow make some sort of connection to the honoree. The volume's final materials, the indices, on the other hand, are troubling. There are three separate indices, one on liturgical feasts, one on manuscripts mentioned in the articles, and one on more general topics. As the editors explain, information is not replicated across the three indices, but they offer no explanation as to why this decision was taken. Adding the more specialized index of feasts to the general index would have done no harm, nor would the inclusion have taken up an inordinate amount of space. The volume lacks a list or index of illustrations and figures, and the index of manuscripts contains no specific references to the illustrations. In addition, the style used in the indices is incorrect in any system of documentation— in particular, I am referring to the use of 'n' to indicate a range of pages. For example, in the general index, "Pilgrimage, 351n52" means that pilgrimage is discussed on pages 351 to 352, whereas immediately below "Piper, A. J., 168n13" refers to footnote 13 which appears on page 168. This would not be a problem if it were a solitary instance, but all three indices contain these errors on a consistent basis.

The Pfaff Festschrift is an excellent addition to any collection of essays on medieval English liturgy and manuscripts, and despite the issues with the indices, the collection is a sound tribute to a great scholar.

Carl James Grindley, The City University of New York

CHRISTOPHER DE HAMEL AND PATRICIA LOVETT, EDS.

The Macclesfield Alphabet Book. BL Additional MS 88887. A Facsimile.
London: The British Library, 2010.
32 (with 14 figures) + 46ff. (facsimile) + 4 (unnumbered).

This book is a delight and offers intriguing mysteries. On the one hand, it is a beautiful facsimile of a unique manuscript, and on the other, the original purpose of the manuscript is difficult to explain. The book is a small manuscript of alphabet designs from the second half of the fifteenth century, but with some sixteenth-century additions. There are only forty-six leaves of parchment, each about 245 mm by 174 mm. It is believed to be the work of a friar, or possibly a Cluniac monk, at Thetford, named Roger Baldry, and until recently its existence was unknown to scholars. It was held in the library formed by the Ninth Earl of Macclesfield at Shirburn Castle in Oxfordshire and was bought by the British Library at Sotheby's in 2009. Alphabet books are rare, so it is an exciting discovery. The work includes fourteen complete alphabets (some with upper and lower case forms, or at least variants) and samples of color decoration. There are glorious foliate letters, and playful, often-bizarre, zoomorphic and anthropomorphic forms. Some of the letters would be difficult to identify if they were not in alphabetical order.

The two introductions, by Christopher de Hamel (7–21) and Patricia Lovett (22–30), consider the manuscript from both a scholarly perspective and that of a modern calligrapher. The original purpose of the manuscript is discussed by de Hamel on pages 16 to 20. He argues that the work could not have been intended for the education of children or even as a practical sample book for calligraphers, because many of the pages contain extravagant penwork linking the letters into a unified page, making them impractical for copying as letters, and some pages show decorative borders independent of text, but these would always be added after the text was written and would be limited by the space left. He argues that the book suggests a more spiritual purpose. Taking the letter forms as symbols of truth, with the alphabet itself a symbol of the codified presentation of the world, it is thus a form of prayer, and one often found in the Christian tradition (e.g., Jesus writing in the sand). This beguiling idea is slightly compromised by the suggestion that it was also produced for a patron, whose mysterious rebus appears at the back of the book. Presumably he would have simply enjoyed its beauty without necessarily seeing any further meaning, but there is no contradiction here: both ideas could be true. Lovett adds a further dimension to this idea when she highlights the evidence that some of the alphabets display the artist's pure love of design: calligraphy is an art form, and sometimes the artists "doodle" for no reasons other than pleasure or experiment.

One is reminded here of a modern parallel from today's computer world. All publishers and printers require ample supplies of useable traditional fonts; but what do the "font packages" give us? Thousands of totally unusable, virtually unreadable, display fonts, but offered with much pride by the manufacturers! To them, the exuberant production is sufficient justification for the exercise, and no doubt it is more enjoyable than the "boring" delivery of practical lettering the customers really want. The modern observation that sometimes the medium appears more important than the message has its medieval antecedents. I am not entirely convinced that the book was not primarily intended to function as a pattern book in a workshop: the practical quibbles about the letters are not necessarily evidence that the book was *consciously* a spiritual exercise. It could have been intended as a sample book displaying to potential customers what the workshop was capable of, a show-off production rather than one intended as a model.

Lovett observes subtle variations in some of the letter forms, allowing her to interpret the way they were created. She praises the quality of the lettering; de Hamel, concentrating on the search for a context, is only slightly less enthusiastic for the caliber of the work. He also sees in the pages evidence for practicalities. Two of the pages show blocks of text without an illuminating letter, seen as samples for how manuscripts were written: text first, decoration afterwards, with each stage recorded in representative examples. He observes that each gathering begins with a principal alphabet, suggesting that originally the book may have been a collection of separate pamphlets, and that the extravagant penwork which on occasion unites the letters into a whole page also makes it impossible to use those individual letters as samples to be copied, because they would be incomplete out of context.

A revelatory observation is that some of the letters are definitely copied from an *earlier* printed original of 1464, though it is not clear in the introduction if just the two illustrated letters are copies, or the whole alphabet. These also suggest the lack of a practical purpose behind the book, because presumably a calligrapher would be unlikely to wish to copy a printed design, helping the case for a spiritual purpose. The compiler wished to record samples of these types of letter to make his survey more complete. But ... perhaps he simply liked the printed letters he copied.

The bulk of the book is the gloriously printed facsimile of the whole manuscript, and my only criticism here is that the modern designer opted to print the pages as bleeds, so the very edges of the original pages are omitted. No doubt no details were lost other than the final few millimeters of page-edge, but I prefer my facsimiles to show everything, even if a modern white border would detract visually.

Shaun Tyas, Independent Publisher

IAN GADD, ED.
The History of the Book in the West: 1455-1700, Volume II.
Burlington, VT: Ashgate, 2010. xlii + 526 pp. 36 B&W illus.

The title of this volume is something of a misnomer. As series editor Alexis Weedon explains in the preface, Gadd's selection of essays for his volume does not detail the history of the book as such, but rather the history of the history of the book. As Gadd explains: "a new kind of interest in the book as an object of study has emerged – one that is more concerned with the book in history, the book as cultural artefact, the book as social phenomenon" (xi). Gadd's premise is a fascinating one and is one of the points that sets this volume apart from its many rivals. Indeed, Gadd has created "a deliberate and considered reflection of how the 'history of the book' has manifested itself" (xi) since the late 1950s. Although no articles older than 1996 are reproduced, the shadow of Lucien Febvre and Henri-Jean Martin's *L'Apparition du Livre* looms large over the introduction.

The volume is divided into four somewhat unequally sized parts: Typography; the Impact of Print; Practice; Selling; and Reading. Gadd has exercised considerable care in his selection of the seventeen essays that appear in his volume. After paying very short shrift to typography —though the two essays chosen to represent such a huge field, works by Blaise Agüera y a Arcas on Gutenburg's type and Nicolas Barker on the Aldine Italic are excellent—Gadd moves on to what would appear to be his major interest, examining competing scholarly opinions about the importance of the book. This approach is at its strongest when Elizabeth L. Eisenstein is balanced against her great critic Anthony T. Grafton. Gadd is also good at recognizing seminal articles. The inclusion of D.F. McKenzie's work on the practice of printing is an excellent idea, but this is also where the limitations of the volume become apparent. Because the articles are reprints, some corners have been cut with regard to typesetting. Most articles, as far as I can tell, are merely photographic reproductions of the original publications. Most of the time, changing font sizes or page layouts is not problematic, but there are times when the exercise of compiling such a volume could have resulted in the originals becoming stronger. For example, the figures accompanying McKenzie's articles are tiny, and extremely detailed. They could have benefitted from being reset. I do not pretend to understand the legalities, but if permission to reprint was forthcoming perhaps more could have been done to make the texts more readable.

I think, also, that reading has not received as much attention as it might well have deserved. Much has happened with regard to the reception of early printed books in the years since 1996, especially with the study of marginalia, but with the exception of Jardine and Grafton's work on Gabriel Harvey this now-burgeoning area seems to be under-represented.

This volume is an excellent resource, however, and what few shortcomings it has are easily excused (it also lacks a table of illustrations). Gadd has done fine scholarly service in this compilation, and his introduction is itself a wonderful entry point to the type of study of book history that is becoming more and more in vogue.

Carl James Grindley, The City University of New York

ALEXANDRA GILLESPIE AND DANIEL WAKELIN, EDS.
The Production of Books in England 1350-1500.
Cambridge: Cambridge University Press, 2011. xix + 375 pp.; 43 figures.

This is a very useful and welcome volume which, in a series of chapters by experts in the field, explores the relevant features of the production of books in England at the end of the Middle Ages. The term "books" was perhaps thought more accessible than "manuscripts," but it is in fact largely manuscripts that are discussed here. Of the thirteen chapters, the first seven deal (mainly) with the physicality of the book, followed by a chapter on its circulation and commercial impact, one on scribes, and another on book production beyond the commercial. Two final chapters look at English books outside England, and the volume ends with an "Afterword." Each chapter provides an overview, balanced by case-studies, with suggestions for future research. There are forty-three illustrations in all, mostly good photographic reproductions in black and white, listed according to chapter at the start of the volume. The volume ends with a very full Bibliography and an Index of Manuscripts, as well as a General Index.

Derek Pearsall was an obvious choice to write the Foreword. The begetter of the York Manuscripts Conferences (although not the only begetter, since the late Elizabeth Salter was his partner in the enterprise) is well placed to compare this volume with the important earlier collection of essays with a similar name (*Book Production and Publishing in Britain 1375-1475*), which came out of the first York conferences and was edited by Pearsall and the late Jeremy Griffiths. As Pearsall says (ruefully, one suspects), "The major difference ... is that in that book the emphasis was on the contents of manuscripts, whether literary or not, and who owned and read them. In this book, the main emphasis is on the methods, circumstances and economy of production." As he again notes, what has happened in the intervening years is that "the 'History of the Book' has taken over." Pearsall himself is someone for whom the text itself is paramount, and not to engage with the text must seem rather like the bad old days of studying Old English grammar but evincing no interest in Anglo-Saxon poetry. He is, however, generous as ever and gracious in his acknowledgement of the precision of scholarship displayed in this volume. It is a different animal; that is all (but for Wendy Scase's response, see the end of this review).

The concise and well-written Introduction by the editors corroborates Pearsall's comments: the volume has been compiled in order to consider books "not in terms of their content, but in terms of contexts and systems for their production and distribution" and aims to introduce "findings, ideas and approaches to manuscript study that have emerged since 1989." It may allude to the familiar themes of readers, libraries and provenances, but its focus is no more the use of books than it is the content of books; instead its focus is the production of books (and so perhaps deserves the 1989 title rather more than that volume deserved it): "how they were made, by whom, and in what locales, using what resources, according to what conventions, in response to what historical circumstances and what technological, economic and political or religious constraints."

Orietta da Rold begins with all the benefits of her prodigious research on "Materials," i.e. ink, parchment and paper, but goes beyond the facts to ask interesting questions about how mere materials can provide insight into book production and reception in general. Daniel Wakelin's "Writing Words" is a rather enigmatic title, but his subject is both simple and illuminating – just how scribes went about writing manuscripts. This is not just the hand, but the process as a whole, and, most interestingly, the scribe's interaction with the process and with the text, well illustrated verbally and pictorially. "Writing" leads naturally to the dialect in which the text was written (although otherwise Simon Horobin's piece stands a little oddly in a chapter focussed on the material book). "Mapping the Words" emphasizes the origin of current historical dialectology (the Linguistic Atlases of Late Mediaeval English and Early Middle English) in dialect geography and provides a historiography of the subject, investigating again (with the benefit of his current research project with Linne Mooney) some of the earlier claims of its scholars (Doyle, Parkes, Samuels, etc.) in relation, for example, to Gower, Chaucer and the London dialect. Stephen Partridge looks next at "Designing the Page," the *mise-en-page* of primarily fifteenth-century manuscripts (indeed almost entirely of *Canterbury Tales* manuscripts) and argues interestingly for the role of, not just scribes, but authors among late medieval "book producers." Martha Driver and Michael Orr continue the visual theme with "Decorating and Illustrating the Page," a relatively sophisticated commercial activity in the period covered by this volume (rather stymied by the introduction of printing). This is an excellent overview illuminated by both authors' extensive researches. Margaret Connolly's "Compiling the Book" moves on to the acquisition of exemplars, the selection and organization of texts to suit audience, and the format and assembly of copies. Interestingly, she also considers the question (a large one which deserves full investigation in some other place) of post-medieval assembly of manuscripts. Alexandra Gillespie next tackles "Bookbinding" in a thorough and informed account which engages with often-neglected late medieval bindings (neglected because plain and unstamped) and their after-life. Examples are numerous and illustrations pertinent and illuminating (if a bit murky).

With the book complete, Erik Kwakkel investigates "Commercial organization and economic innovation": how readers acquired books, and the roles of scribes, illuminators and binders as practitioners and (with stationers) as middle-men in the commercial process. Like Gillespie, he looks at low-cost production, too, investigating "some strategies the patron could employ in order to limit the cost of a book," such as varying the script and writing style (payment to the scribe was the most expensive item in manuscript production), choosing paper rather than parchment (or choosing parchment with imperfections), and either leaving a book unbound or using limp bindings. This is an innovative and interesting chapter. Next, the scribe is the focus of Linne Mooney's chapter on "Vernacular literary manuscripts and their scribes," drawing on her current four-year AHRC-funded research with Simon Horobin, which aims to identify the scribes responsible for copying the manuscripts of the works of Gower, Chaucer, Langland, Trevisa and Hoccleve. Distinguishing between a professional scribe (who might be a scrivener or a royal or civic clerk) and a commercial scribe (such as members of the London Textwriters guild), she considers in particular (but not only) the role of London scribes in copying the texts of the major authors of the late fourteenth century, notably Adam Pinkhurst (identified by Mooney), Thomas Hoccleve and Scribe D, but also lesser known figures like William Ebesham (first uncovered by Ian Doyle), the Petworth scribe, Thomas Usk, and others, some without names or *noms-de-plume*. Here her extensive knowledge of London scribal circles is usefully and interestingly deployed, and this chapter serves as a welcome summary of Mooney's important findings to date. From the commercial aspects of book production, we move to "Book production outside commercial contexts," although Jean-Pascal Pouzet admits that the distinction is "hedged in with a number of difficulties and ambiguities" (not least that "no book was totally immune from commercial logic") which the chapter seeks to resolve. Local patrons and monasteries, particularly the richer and larger, combined commercial and domestic supply of materials; again, their focus may have been limiting cost by, for example, recycling parchment, eschewing binding, borrowing exemplars, second-hand exchanges, and, of course, writing one's own book or (in religious houses) in-house scribal work, where book producers did not have to be paid. This long and carefully argued chapter also includes a discussion on professional and non-professional scribes, building on Linne Mooney's professional and commercial argument, and an intriguing look at the philosophy of otium in a book-production context.

"Censorship" may seem to sit oddly in this context, but Fiona Somerset ably demonstrates its importance in the production and dissemination of manuscripts. She outlines the aftermath of the Blackfriars Council of 1382 and its effect on books, and she discusses the ways in which manuscripts (hard to regulate, as she demonstrates, drawing on Anne Hudson's seminal work and the late Mary Dove's *The First English Bible*) might nevertheless be regulated, as in the cases of John Claydon and Reginald Pecock, and the Carthusian and Birgittine texts, *The Mirror of the Blessed Life of Jesus Christ* and *The Myroure of oure Ladye*, as well as the *Speculum vitae*, but also how those regulations might be thwarted, as (ultimately unsuccessfully) in the 1414 Oldcastle revolt. Finally, John J. Thompson charts new territories in an innovative chapter on English books in Ireland (a better title than his somewhat misleading "Books Beyond England"), considering in particular the impact of the English personnel managing Ireland in the Middle Ages. David Rundle then moves into the age of print to look at "English books and the continent," in particular the role of foreign printers, artists and binders in England, and the circulation of books in and out of Europe (so that "English book," he argues, is rather "a confining name"). Thereafter, Wendy Scase's "Afterword: the book in culture" offers her own viewpoint on the volume's relation to the earlier *Book Production and Publishing*, arguing robustly for the absorption (rather than neglect) of literary studies into the current research and for the intrinsic importance of the new book's focus: "Pursuing a research programme organized around questions to which answers can be right or wrong reflects renewed confidence in empirical research … If we cease to cultivate these scholarly activities, our knowledge and understanding of medieval codices will soon be as limited as our access to Linear A tablets" and, at the end, "we still know very little about the total extant corpus of manuscripts of English provenance that survive from the period 1350-1500 … The present volume offers a steep change in the study of English book production by synthesizing and reflecting on the wealth of research germane to the topic."

Susan Powell, University of Salford

RALPH HANNA AND THORLAC TURVILLE-PETRE, EDS.
The Wollaton Medieval Manuscripts: Texts, Owners and Readers.
University of York in association with Boydell & Brewer:
York Medieval Press, 2010.

This large-format volume is a product of the AHRC-funded research into the Wollaton Library Collection which followed on from the University of Nottingham's Heritage Lottery Fund purchase of ten medieval manuscripts and forty-three early printed books in 2007. These books formed part of the Middleton Collection, a collection sold by the tenth Lord Middleton (together with the Wollaton estate) from 1924 on; the remaining family archive and remnants of the library were transferred to the University from 1947. The collection originated at Wollaton Hall (now Council property near Nottingham) in the time of Francis Willoughby the Builder (1546-1596), but a fire in 1687 led to the transfer of the muniments to their other house, Middleton Hall in Warwickshire. There Francis Willoughby the Naturalist (1635-1672), with his friend, fellow-naturalist and dialect recorder, John Ray, annotated and rudimentarily catalogued them. Almost unknown, the Wollaton Library Collection deserves the thorough and rather splendid format and scholarship provided by the publication of this book.

There are three Parts: Studies, The Catalogue, and Illustrations. The second and third Parts reflect the book's primary *raison d'être* as a catalogue of the collection, as well as its links with the 2010 University of Nottingham exhibition "Saints, Sinners and Storytellers" and its attendant conference. Part I provides seven essays on the collection: "The History of a Family Collection" by the editors, "Sir Thomas Chaworth's Books" (d. 1459, a notable local bibliophile) by Gavin Cole and Thorlac Turville-Petre, "The Wollaton Antiphonal: Kinship and Commemoration" (Nottingham MS 250, made for Chaworth) by Alixe Bovey, "Two French Manuscripts: WLC/LM/6 and

WLC/LM/7" (both thirteenth-century) by Alison Stones, "The Wollaton Hall Gower Manuscript (WLC/LM/8) Considered in the Context of Other Manuscripts of the Confessio Amantis" by Derek Pearsall, "Vice, Virtue and Contemplation: The Willoughbys' Religious Books and Devotional Interests" by Rob Lutton, and "Minding and Mending: Issues in Curating the Medieval Manuscripts" by Dorothy Johnston.

Part II is the catalogue itself, compiled by the editors and divided into "The Wollaton Library Collection" (MSS WLC/LM/1-38), "Associated Manuscripts" (the Antiphonal and MSS Mi LM 2 AND 29), "Additional Medieval Manuscripts in the Middleton Collection," "Dispersed Manuscripts," and "The Willoughby Early Printed Books." "Additional Medieval Manuscripts in the Middleton Collection" deserves a little unpicking in order to demonstrate the various, variable, and serendipitous nature of the material. The section describes ten items of binding materials, a collection of medieval and early modern correspondence, six cartularies with binding materials described separately, four items of separated folios and fragments of rolls the correspondence of Edward Willoughby (c.1520), and "The Lament for Sir John Berkeley" (edited and published by Turville-Petre in *Speculum* in 1982). There are also two separate sections, "Miscellaneous Items" (i.e., even more miscellaneous than the rest) and "Other Nottingham Manuscripts." This is a veritable treasure trove of unconsidered trifles. Also of interest (not that the whole collection is not of interest) are the dispersed manuscripts. When it was inspected in 1911 for an Historical Manuscripts Commission report the collection was still largely intact. The Christie's sale of 1925 was mainly of printed books, although it did include several manuscripts. Although deposited at the University of Nottingham from 1947, parts were then sold at Christie's in 2005, presumably the impetus to the Heritage Lottery Fund award and the AHRC-funded research. Fourteen of the dispersed manuscripts are in University libraries (one in Durham, two in Glasgow, five in the British Library, one in the Wellcome, one in Manchester, three in the United States, and one in Japan). One other manuscript is currently unlocated and another in the hands of an anonymous private collector. Of these, those sold most recently, in 2005, were to Durham (a Vulgate Bible with a fifteenth-century Durham monk's inscription), Yale (pseudo-Augustine and others), and the private collector (a vellum Sarum missal of the mid-fifteenth century). "The Willoughby Early Printed Books" which ends the catalogue is a list of the books dispersed in 1925, largely Latin and of continental provenance, but with some de Worde grammars (sold to the University of Illinois), a Donatus from York (1532), a *Golden Legend* printed by Julian Notary in 1503 (cost £19, recipient McLeish), and various items which might be seen as predictable in an intelligent Englishman's library in the sixteenth century: Erasmus'

Apophthegmes, Thomas Elyot's *Castel of Helth,* Hall's *Chronicle,* Lydgate's *Fall of Princes,* Foxe's *Book of Martyrs,* Castiglione's *The Courtyer,* and so on. All were signed by Thomas Willoughby, first Baron Middleton (1673-1729).

Finally, Part III provides twenty-eight plates, most full-size and in color, displaying the range of materials, types, hands, and decoration. (Here the name of the text, or a short description of its nature, would have been welcome, rather than just the shelf-mark.) Sixteen black-and-white figures show other manuscript pages, together with photographs of the fine Willoughby monuments in Wollaton and Willoughby-on-the-Wolds churches. There are genealogical tables of the Willoughby and Chaworth families, an Index of Manuscripts (both in the Wollaton Collection and elsewhere) and a General Index. All in all, a fascinating and splendid production, and what fun it must have been to work on!

Susan Powell, University of Salford

LOTTE HELLINGA

William Caxton and Early Printing in England.
London: The British Library, 2010. 212 pp. 116 figures.

This new publication by Lotte Hellinga benefits from her outstanding contribution to the publication of BMC XI (reviewed *JEBS* 10, 2007) and will become a standard reference tool for scholars. Not directed at scholars alone, the format of this British Library publication encourages a non-specialist readership as well, and its attractive layout incorporates 116 figures showing title pages, colophons, and other pages from printed books, many in color and most from the British Library collection. (They are distributed throughout the book and are immensely helpful and illuminating to the discussions, perhaps especially those on typefaces. There is a List of Illustrations at the end.) Of the eighteen brief chapters, twelve take the reader through Caxton's life in Bruges, Cologne, and Westminster, interpolate the attempts at printing in Oxford, London, and St. Albans in the 1470s and 1480s, and conclude with Caxton's final years; the remaining six handle Richard Pynson, Wynkyn de Worde, and others of lesser importance. The book is supplied with Further Reading for each theme pursued by Hellinga; these are very useful but (for a scholarly audience at least) do not make up for the lack of an index. For example, a reference to the work of Paul Christianson on p. 150 requires one to look through the themes and alight on Christianson under "The trade in printed books" (p. 198). This is fine for leisurely reading but slightly irritating for academics, although it must be admitted that bibliography by themes is in other ways helpful and elegant.

Hellinga's invaluable experience as part of the BMC XI team enables her to use the recent work of others in that team, such as Paul Needham's important paper research. She raises several interesting questions which neither she nor others have previously addressed, such as: is it right to assume that Caxton's first seven works were all printed in Bruges (40)? Should David

Aubert take center-stage as Caxton's principal associate in his first printing venture (45- 51)? Should the 1490s dissemination of printed devotional texts in English be seen as a quasi-official decision, comparable to Henry VII's decision to print the statutes in English (160)? Did Caxton concentrate on French translations with the prohibitions of Arundel in mind (167)? Many more questions of this sort are raised—and not necessarily answered— in the book, evidence of Hellinga's intense engagement with the period and very conducive to the easy style of the volume. This is an entirely new re-thinking of Caxton and early printing history, firmly replacing Norman Blake and George Painter. It is a pleasure to read and essential for all students and scholars of early print, not to mention the "educated layperson" (who may sadly now be extinct).

Susan Powell, University of Salford

JULIAN M. LUXFORD, ED.
Studies in Carthusian Monasticism in the Late Middle Ages.
Medieval Church Studies 14.
Turnhout: Brepols, 2008. xvi + 367 pp., 45 Figures, 1 Table.

Of all the religious orders, the Carthusians and the Birgittines have provided most material for manuscript and early print scholars over the past thirty-five years, triggered in the 1980s by James Hogg and Michael Sargent for the former and, arguably, Jan Rhodes for the latter. Since then several scholars have focused on the transmission and circulation of texts by both orders, separately and in collaboration. In particular, the 2001 edition of the Syon library catalogue with the appended Carthusian booklists (Vincent Gillespie and Ian Doyle) has encouraged valuable Birgittine scholarship such as *Syon Abbey and its Books* and *Saint Birgitta, Syon and Vadstena* (reviewed *JEBS* 14, 2011).

However, until now there has been no comparable single English-language book collecting the researches of a variety of scholars of the Carthusians. Julian Luxford's edition is therefore very welcome. It brings together a variety of scholars, including Hogg, Sargent and Doyle, although contributions are otherwise by historians and art-historians rather than book-history or literary scholars, explicable by the facts that Luxford himself is an art historian and that the volume had its origins in 2004 IMC sessions organized by the eminent monastic and church historian Joan Greatrex. *JEBS* readers may detect less interest in (perhaps less knowledge of) the contributions of scholars in the field of English literature.

The volume is divided into three parts, Historical Perspectives, Texts and Devotion, Art and Architecture. In his Introduction, Luxford provides a lively personal overview of the historiography of Carthusian scholarship. Due credit is given to Barrie Dobson for his long-term interest in the English

Carthusians, which gave rise to three important Ph.D. theses by his students, Carol Rowntree, Neil Beckett, and Andrew Wines. However, Luxford regrets the lack of English-language material on the Carthusians and of detailed knowledge of the (admittedly small and relatively insignificant) English province. To remedy this (in as far as it is remediable), he introduces a mix of older and younger scholars who focus largely on England (only five of the fourteen chapters are Continental) in the burgeoning fourteenth to early sixteenth centuries of Carthusian growth. Among numerous neglected or under-researched topics (he admits that "availability of evidence will always impose limitations"), Luxford argues that art and architecture have been most overlooked (no fewer than forty-five figures aim to remedy this, although they are generally small, black-and-white, and poorly reproduced— fig. 17 is particularly appalling, even as an impression of a woodcut). The book as a whole is furnished with an Index which includes the manuscripts under their location (New Haven, Oxford, etc.)— a separate index would have been welcome.

James Hogg is well qualified to begin the volume with "Life in an English Charterhouse in the Fifteenth Century: Discipline and Daily Affairs," his research based on the *Chartae* of the Carthusian General Chapter. Of particular interest are the extraordinary happenings at London and Sheen in the early sixteenth century and the 1519 inventory of items taken by Dom Thomas Golwynne from London to Mount Grace in 1519 (copied from E. M. Thompson, with no mention of Ian Doyle's editing of the books in this list). The article is furnished with five appendices (two of them providing an overview of, and extracts from, the *Chartae*). Next, Andrew Wines is the foremost expert on the London charterhouse, and as such he questions received knowledge of "The Founders of the London Charterhouse." Rather than Northburgh and Manny as the founders (see the Survey of London volume reviewed here), he provides convincing evidence for the importance of the first prior, John Luscote, and the merchants and former mayors, William Walworth, John Lovekyn, and Adam Frounceys. City merchants, especially the fishmongers, supported the charterhouse strongly, and their interest was in chantries and prayers for the dead, a Carthusian in his individual cell providing what might today be called a 24/7 post-mortem service. Moving on to the spirituality of the Carthusians, in "'Tribularer si nescirem misericordias tuas': Cardinal Henry Beaufort and his Carthusian Confessor" (with three Appendices), Anselm J. Gribbin considers the case for and against the cardinal's spirituality through the medium of three letters written him *c.* 1446 by his Sheen confessor, probably William Mede, scribe, monk, and vicar of Sheen, who transcribed the letters between 1447 and 1473. His theme, the potent effect of Carthusian spirituality on the state, is also that of Jeremy Catto in "Statesmen and Contemplatives in the Early

Fifteenth Century," who argues that the founders of the seven new English Carthusian houses between 1343 and 1415 were "a group at the cutting edge," prominent in their deployment of Carthusian spiritual works. Finally in Part One, Joan Greatrex writes "Of Monks and Books: The Disciples of Bruno and Benedict in Later Medieval England," and, as befits this Benedictine scholar, she deals with the cross-fertilization of knowledge derived by the reading of Carthusian works by Benedictines, and even by the transfer of Benedictines to charterhouses.

Part Two begins with "Carthusians as Advocates of Women Visionary Reformers" by Dennis D. Martin, who shows the championing by the Carthusians of female visionaries and the use of their visions as an argument for church reform. Indeed, according to a late-fifteenth-century Carthusian, the order was unusual in the proliferation of charismatic visions associated with it. Next, A. I. Doyle considers "A Manuscript of Petrus Dorlandus of Diest's *Viola Animae*," a Durham University Library manuscript (by the Carthusian Peter Dorlant of the Zeelhem charterhouse at Diest in Brabant) which contains six of seven dialogues printed first in Cologne in 1499. Doyle sees the manuscript, copied "collaboratively in batches from a broken-up exemplar" by nine different scribes, as "a pre-published text of the work with an unpublished apologia" (provided as an Appendix) which was written to counter doubts about the orthodoxy of its author, Raymondus de Sabunde. Next follows "Secret Rooms: Private Spaces for Private Prayer in Late-Medieval Burgundy and the Netherlands" by Ezekiel Lotz, who considers the Carthusian "theology of the cell" as applied to the personal life of Geert Groote and Philip the Bold and his family (Philip's daughter-in-law was Margaret of York). Last in Part Two is the fascinating contribution by Michael G. Sargent and Marlene Villalobos Hennessy on "The Latin Verses over the Cell Doors of London Charterhouse." Following the scholarship of Dom Andrew Gray, Sargent and Hennessy investigate the spirituality of these (most likely Carthusian) verses, which survive in four manuscripts and whose predominant theme is the remembrance of death. The chapter is furnished with a critical edition of the verses from John Blacman's autobiographical Latin introduction to his collection of devotional writings in London, British Library, Sloane MS 2515.

Part Three focuses on art and architecture. It opens with Laura D. Gelfand and "A Tale of Two Dukes: Philip the Bold, Giangaleazzo Visconti, and their Carthusian Foundations," the Chartreuse de Champmol near Dijon and the Certosa di Pavia. Luxford himself then writes on "Precept and Practice: The Decoration of English Carthusian Books." Here there is no mention, astonishingly, of Mary Erler's seminal article on pasted-in embellishments, although Luxford tackles the subject himself, as well as internal and "forinsec" (from outside sources) decoration. His conclusions are that approximately a third of extant Carthusian books are decorated in some way (although there is no distinctive iconography or decorative manner) and that devotional woodcuts were particularly popular at the London charterhouse, probably because there were block-makers nearby. Next, Jessica Brantley considers London, British Library, Additional MS 37049, a fascinating but arguably over-discussed manuscript (as Luxford perhaps notes in his Introduction in his comment on the "immense interest" it has aroused lately). In "The Pilgrim in the Cell: Carthusian Readers and Deguileville," she studies the *Pilgrimage of the Soul* "not only as a series of tableaux, but as a series of conversations" with Carthusian readers (who, according to Luxford, seem not to "have read as widely" as other orders— debatable, I should have thought). Next is an item on the architecture of Mount Grace by Glyn Coppack and Jackie Hall, which provides a foretaste of the forthcoming English Heritage Monograph on the 1957-1992 excavations. (For EBS members, the visit to the Yorkshire Carthusian House of Mount Grace during the 2011 conference will remain in the memory for a long time.) The church developed in four stages, the building of 1398 having been much enlarged in the 1420s as a burial place for Thomas Beaufort, uncle of Henry V, and extended again in the 1460s and 1470s as a chantry for Edward IV and his father (the Duke of York) and siblings. Finally, in the 1520s and 1530s the then priors extended it under the patronage of Henry Lord Clifford and his son of the same name and title. Only used by the monks for the divine office, since all other prayer was performed in the individual cells, it had by the time of the Dissolution become an important place for lay burial— perhaps that fact, and its remoteness, explain why it is the best preserved of the ten British charterhouses. The study concludes with a comparison of the architecture of Mount Grace with other Carthusian houses (see the review of *The Charterhouse*, this issue, pp. 392-395) and with other monastic and parish churches local to Mount Grace. Part Three ends with Brendan Cassidy on "The Tombs of the Acciaioli in the Certosa del Galluzzo outside Florence," founded by Niccolò Acciaioli in 1342. From 1174 the Carthusian General Chapter permitted lay burial in church for founders, but pressure was inevitably strong (especially in the plague of 1348 to 1350, during which the London charterhouse was first established), and wider permission tended to be granted. Niccolò's own tomb, an effigial wall-tomb, appears to have been the first in Florence for a lay person.

This volume covers a wide range of spiritual, textual, decorative, and architectural expressions of Carthusian monasticism. As such, it inevitably lacks focus, despite Luxford's valiant introduction, but it is to be welcomed as a volume that raises the Carthusian profile for scholars today by seeking to demonstrate its high medieval profile, even in the small Anglian province.

Susan Powell, University of Salford

SCOT MCKENDRICK, JOHN LOWDEN AND
KATHLEEN DOYLE
Royal Manuscripts: The Genius of Illumination.
London: British Library, 2011.
448 pp., 48 figures (pp. 18-93) +
unnumbered plates for 154 catalogue entries.

This volume has been published to accompany the exhibition "Royal Manuscripts: The Genius of Illumination" which ran at the British Library from November 11, 2011, to March 13, 2012. The volume opens with an Introduction by Scot McKendrick, followed by three essays discussing "The Royal Manuscript as Idea and Object" by John Lowden, "A European Heritage: Books of Continental Origin collected by the English Royal Family from Edward III to Henry VIII," by Scot McKendrick, and "The Old Royal Library: 'A greate many noble manuscripts yet remaining'," by Kathleen Doyle. The catalogue is organized thematically, with manuscripts grouped into sections dealing with "The Christian Monarch," "Edward IV: Founder of the Old Royal Library," "How to be a King: Works of Instruction and Advice," "The World's Knowledge," "Royal Identity," "England and the Continent: Affinity and Appropriation."

The focus of this exhibition of "royal" manuscripts is those books that make up the Old Royal Library, comprising some two thousand volumes, which was given to the nation in 1757 by George II and which now constitutes the Royal manuscripts collection of the British Library. The rationale for the exhibition is more problematic than this straightforward definition suggests; while many of the Royal manuscripts have well-documented royal pedigrees, in other cases their supposed connection with the English royalty remains entirely unknown. Furthermore, other books with demonstrably royal connections are not part of the Royal manuscript collection at all. The

exhibition therefore includes manuscripts from other British Library collections where clear royal provenance is known. Thus we find manuscripts
such as British Library MS Harley 2278, a deluxe copy of Lydgate's *Lives of
Saints Edmund and Fremund*, produced at Bury St. Edmunds and presented
to King Henry VI on the occasion of his Christmas visit to the abbey, despite
the fact that it left the royal collection following Henry's reign. In fact, the
definition of "royal" is still more capacious; it is not restricted to books that
were directly commissioned by, or presented to, members of the royalty,
but includes books mentioned in royal inventories, even if the reference is
centuries after its initial commission. While including such volumes may be
a defensible policy, the further broadening of the category to accommodate
all books containing any kind of supposed connection with royalty suggests
that the defining criterion is unhelpfully broad: "a book may be identified
as royal because it contains a dedicatory inscription, a note of royal ownership, royal heraldic devices or mottos, an image of a contemporary king or
queen, or any one of numerous pointers to a royal aspect to its history" (pp.
19-20). Thus the catalogue includes a book such as the "Ordinances of the
Confraternity of the Immaculate Conception," whose opening miniature
contains a series of royal heraldic images, but which was never intended for
royal presentation. It remained among the brethren in the sixteenth century and was bequeathed to its current owners, Christ Church Oxford, in
the eighteenth century.

Each catalogue entry consists of a full page illustration, often supplemented with further miniatures providing details of particular features of
illumination or decoration. The pictures have been well-chosen and are
beautifully presented, making this volume a sumptuous overview of the visual
grandeur of the illuminated manuscript book. Because the focus is primarily
upon "the Genius of Illumination," the pictures have been selected primarily to showcase this aspect of their production, making them less useful for
paleographers and codicologists interested in the more mundane particulars
of the codex. Each manuscript is accompanied by an account of its history
and provenance; these are mostly informative, although the general audience for whom the volume is intended means that there is an amount of
basic information which is redundant for a scholarly reader. The discussion
of the Psalter of Isabel of York opens with a paragraph explaining the nature
and function of a psalter, even though a number of other psalters precede
this entry in the catalogue. But, despite their introductory nature, and the
necessary compression of these entries, they contain numerous suggestive
cross-references to other manuscripts and a comprehensive bibliography of
secondary sources, and will undoubtedly stimulate much future research.

The British Library is to be congratulated on producing such a beautiful, informative, and modestly priced volume.

Simon Horobin, Magdalen College, Oxford

JAMES H. MARROW, RICHARD A. LINENTHAL, & WILLIAM NOEL, ED.

*The Medieval Book: Glosses from Friends &
Colleagues of Christopher de Hamel*
Houten: Hes and De Graaf Publishers, 2010. xxxi + 467 pp.

This handsome Festschrift for Christopher de Hamel emulates the appearance of the volume of essays published in honor of Toshiyuki Takamiya (*The Medieval Book and a Modern Collector*, reviewed *JEBS* 9, 2006), although from a different publisher. Certainly, the quality of the binding and paper, and the elegance of the typeface and layout make this a precious volume indeed. It is not, however, a formal volume. It exudes fondness, as well as respect, for Christopher de Hamel, not hindered by his stunning photogeneity. The black-and-white photograph of today's cheerful and boyish de Hamel (born in England in 1950 but largely brought up in New Zealand) is required of a Festschrift, but other contributors pop in more—a color photograph at the end of the foreword of a twenty-seven-year-old de Hamel, just as cheerful, outside the Beinecke at Yale, and a black-and-white photograph at the end of the last contribution showing a thirteen-year-old de Hamel, rather serious, inspecting the earliest printed Latin Bible in Dunedin Public Library, Wellington, New Zealand. This is not a common-or-garden variety Festschrift (the subtitle already suggests that), and this review will accordingly differ from other such reviews, in that it too will focus on the charisma of de Hamel as much as the scholarship and knowledge of the contributors who offer a broader range of disciplines and employment than most Festschriften can boast.

As one would expect, friends and colleagues of de Hamel, Donnelley Fellow Librarian of the Parker Library at Corpus Christi College, Cambridge, are many and distinguished. The foreword is followed by a list of the fifty contributors, academics, but also art historians, auction house scholars, and antiquarian booksellers, as well as others throughout the world, who have encountered de Hamel in his sixty years. A brief biography of de Hamel is supplied by a light-hearted Nicolas Barker, followed by a bibliography of his writing compiled by Lynley Herbert (from notes on two books of hours in Dunedin Public Library [1970] to the "Introduction to Art, Academia, and the Trade," edited by Stella Panayotova in 2010). Part 1 is simply labelled "Books" and contains the most articles, twenty in all (each on average eight pages long), beginning with Michael Gullick (publisher of The Red Gull Press) on "A Christ Church scribe of the late-eleventh century" and ending with "Some Deceptive Bookbinding" by Anthony Hobson (former Director of Sotheby's Books and Manuscripts Department, for whom de Hamel worked from 1975 to 2000). In between there are the antiquarian booksellers Richard Linenthal (former director of Quaritch) and Bernard Rosenthal, the Getty and Morgan Library manuscripts curators Thomas Kren and Roger S. Wieck, the Scheide Librarian at Princeton, Paul Needham, as well as the Sotheby's contributor, Timothy Bolton. The "academic" contributors are Ian Doyle ("The Portrait of Laurence of Durham as Scribe"), the art historians Paul Binski, Lucy Sandler, Jonathan Alexander, John Lowden, James H. Marrow, and Jeffrey F. Hamburger, the historians Richard and Mary Rouse and Margaret Manion, the classicist Marvin L. Colker, the palaeographer Michelle Brown, and the musicologist Margaret Bent.

After that tour-de-force, Part 2, on "The Book Trade," contains only five pieces, all quirky and interesting. Lotte Hellinga writes on "Four Book Auctions of the Fifteenth Century," David McKitterick (librarian of Trinity College Cambridge) on "A New Beginning: The Sotheby Bankruptcy of 1836," John Collins (bookseller) on "William Edward Hurcomb, Goldsmith, Gasconader, Auctioneer, and Bankrupt." "Colleagues at Sotheby's" consists of short contributions by ten colleagues, including de Hamel's wife, Mette, whom he met at Sotheby's, and, finally, Sam Fogg (of the medieval art house of that name) writes on "The Provenance of the Bute Psalter."

Refreshed by the change of tone, one moves on to Part 3, "Collectors & Collecting," which deals largely with collectors (in his contribution Nicolas Barker says, "What a collector Christopher would have been, if circumstance had not placed him on the other side of the fence"). Patrick Zutshi (Cambridge University Library) writes on a fourteenth-century archbishop of Riga and Roland Folter (former director of Kraus) on Sir Thomas Phillipps (1792-1872), but the other contributions are much more recent: William P. Stoneman (Houghton Library, Harvard) on Henry Yates Thompson (1839-1928), François Avril (Bibliothèque nationale de France) on Baron Edmond de Rothschild (1845-1934), Stella Panayotova (Fitzwilliam Museum, Cambridge) on Sydney Cockerell (1867-1962), A.S.G. Edwards (De Montfort University) on John Meade Faulkner (1858-1932), Lawrence J. Schoenberg with Lynn Ransom (Schoenberg Database of Manuscripts) on Ernest Cushing Richardson (1860-1939), William Noel (Walters Art Museum) on transatlantic collectors of the illuminator William de Brailes, and Martin Schøyen and Toshiyuki Takamiya on themselves (Schøyen provides a fascinating account of the Crosby-Schøyen codex, and Takamiya a very useful handlist of his Western medieval manuscripts, which delegates at the Exeter EBS conference in 2009 will recall as a most entertaining talk). Less specifically on collectors are the art historian Nigel Morgan on chained books in churches and Robert Weaver (Dulwich College) on collecting fragments. The collector Henri Schiller ends with "The Descriptions Master," a single-page tribute to de Hamel, "Praeceptor Angliae."

What characterizes this volume is that nearly every article is not only scholarly but also engaging. There are frequent anecdotes and a general spirit of bonhomie and warmth which is missing from many Festschriften (not that it is not felt in many, or at least some). Perhaps the dead weight and formality of academia and the lighter weight and joie de vivre of auction houses explains the difference in tone. The volume is enhanced by numerous illustrations (but no list, although photographs are credited); all are beautifully reproduced and mostly in color. There is an index and a separate index of manuscripts. Finally, there is the note: "This book has been typeset in the Emerson typeface designed by Joseph Blumenthal in the 1930s ... Printed on Phoenix Motion Xantur paper by Drukkerij WC den Oude ... Bound Callenbach van Wijk bookbinders ... Design and typography by Jerry Kelly, New York." What a book!

Susan Powell, University of Salford

NORMAN H. REID, ED., WITH MARC BOULAY, RACHEL HART,
ELIZABETH HENDERSON, MOIRA MACKENZIE AND
MAIA SHERIDAN
Treasures of St Andrews University Library
(London: Third Millennium Publishing Ltd., 2010). 160 pp.;
unnumbered plates for 50 items.

This book is a celebration of the history and contents of a great library. Its strategy is to take fifty treasures chosen by scholars who use the library, who write enthusiastic short accounts of those treasures, saying how the library acquired them and why they consider them important. Each treasure is treated to at least one glorious large-scale illustration.

The treasures range from manuscripts (of books, a royal genealogical roll, letters and charters) and printed books to historical photographs held by the library and the university's own medieval seal matrix, of 1414–18; and they range in date from *c.*1189 (the charter of Walter, prior of St Andrews) to 1996, a 35 mm transparency by Scottish photographer Hamish M. Brown. I was impressed to see that Robert Crawford had chosen the library's own receipt books and borrowing registers (1737–1925), and Robin D. A. Evetts chose an architectural drawing of the university library building by Robert Reid, 1827, so the library's own history is included among the treasures.

It seems appropriate to mention only the treasures which fall within the remit of this Society's interests, the early books, but it is a delight to see the later treasures included, and the scholars who chose them write revelatory and affectionate comments.

First, the editor provides a preface, followed by contributions on the history of the library and its Special Collections by Marc Boulay and Elizabeth Henderson. Then come the treasures. In the order in which they appear, of printed books we have the geometrical treatise *Divina Proportione of Luca Pacioli,* 1509; the 1489 edition of Augustine of Hippo's *De Trinitate* and *De Civitate Dei;* a splendid 1478 version of Werner Rolevinck's *Fasciculus Temporum,* a world chronicle, the illustrations showing the extraordinary typesetting in three of the chronicle's pages; the *Quaestiones in quatuor libros Sententiarum* and *Quodlibeta* by John Duns Scotus, printed at Nuremberg in 1481 with hand-coloured illuminated capitals; the earliest known example of St Andrews printing, or any Scottish printing outside Edinburgh, the *Catechisme* produced by John Scot in 1552; the *Cosmographiae universalis* lib VI by Sebastian Münster, 1550, an early printed encyclopedia of breathtaking range, and the earliest such work to present separate maps of the continents; Andrew Melville's copy of George Buchanan's *Rerum Scoticarum Historia* of 1582, not quite the earliest printed history of Scotland, but nearly (the library does own a copy of Hector Boece's *Scotorum Historiae* of 1527 but no-one chose it as a treasure); a 1490 edition of *Sphaera Mundi* by Johannes de Sacro Bosco; the 1607 Venetian edition of Galileo's *Difesa;* a Polyglot Bible of 1514–17, being the first edition of this six-volume work by Cardinal Francisco Jiménez de Cisneros, printed near Madrid; an early printed Book of Hours produced at Paris by Jacques Kerver in 1558, which was purchased by the library in 2007; and the Strasburg 1519 edition of *Das Buch zu Distillieren* by Hieronymus Brunschwig, widely regarded as the first great work on chemistry.

Of manuscript books, we have 'The Original Chronicle' of Andrew Wyntoun, *c.*1550; an illuminated Psalter of *c.*1425–75, introduced by Julian Luxford; the earliest surviving Statutes of St Leonard's College, one of the institutions later absorbed by the university, 1544; a volume of lecture notes on dialectic by John Malcolm, of *c.*1584–6, important for the history of Scottish university teaching; an incomplete manuscript of selected works of Augustine of Hippo of *c.*1190, important as the only manuscript known for certain to have come from the original medieval library of St Andrews Cathedral Priory; a manuscript of the *Timurid Qur'an* from 1441–2, which came to the library as a gift of the East India Company in 1806; and the last treasure in the book, the first minute book of the Faculty of Arts of the University of St Andrews, 1413–1588 and 1615–1728. It contains evidence of the university's attempts to suppress the wearing of weapons, the use of corporal punishment, cock-fighting ... and football, as well as the institution's engagement with the wider world of politics and religious controversy.

The printing quality of the work is magnificent, reproductions being very sharp and with glorious colors which I assume are close to the originals. I was pleased to see that the layout usually included the very edges of the treasures in the photographs, several were presented as double-page spreads, and most of the pictures were printed as large as possible, almost up to the edges of the pages. Particularly impressive was the achievement of one page as a folded extra, so that the manuscript of the Bull of Pope Benedict XIII, which confirmed the foundation of the university in 1413, could be reproduced as large as possible, with an extra photograph concentrating on the attached *bulla*. I must admit, as a publisher, that I am not sure how the printer achieved this miracle, because there are a convenient 160 pages in the book, with no room for waste, and this extra folded page is not an insert but part of the sewn sections.

I have just one quibble. The design of the book, while lavish for the pictures, is mean on the font size, which is tiny and actually difficult to read (the shiny art paper does not help with readability, though it makes a big difference in picture quality). Large margins around the two-column pre-sentation, and generous spacing on the headings, could have been reduced to give the reader a more comfortable delivery of the text, though flicking through the book without reading it, the eye appreciates the elegant layout. The retail price is also a celebration, at only £15.

Shaun Tyas, Independent Publisher

M. B. PARKES
Pages from the Past: Medieval Writing Skills and Manuscript Books
Ed. P. R. Robinson and Rivkah ZimFarnham
Surrey, and Burlington, VT: Ashgate Variorum, 2012, xvi + 382 pp

Malcolm Parkes's *Scribes, Scripts and Readers*, a selection of his shorter publications from 1958 to 1991, is an essential tool within the working libraries not just of palaeographers but of historians and literary scholars as well, and the present volume should quickly find its place on their shelves. The fourteen articles gathered together here, published across the years 1992 to 2007, arranged in four thematic sections, treat aspects of script, punctuation, readership and book supply.

Part I opens with "The Hereford Map: the handwriting and copying of the text" (2006), an account of the entries made in it by a single scribe and of five other items in his hand which are bound into Oxford, Bodleian Library, MS Ashmole 399. There follow three papers written for *Festschrifts*. In "Richard Frampton: a commercial scribe *c.* 1390–*c.* 1420" (2004), for Toshiyuki Takamiya, Parkes, identifying seven manuscripts in one hand, speculates on where Frampton was trained and why he became a freelance copyist of books. "Patterns of scribal activity and revisions of the text in early copies of works by John Gower" (1995), for Ian Doyle, explores early manuscripts of Gower's work in which the hands of two or more scribes are present, with two questions in mind. Do the manuscripts offer evidence for a scriptorium where Gower supervised the preparation and revision of his texts? Or how else might the perceived similarities among them be explained? Parkes points to differing stages of revision and the use of different exemplars by the twenty or more scribes in the six manuscripts examined. He shows that not all could have worked with Gower, and indeed that "no two scribes appear to have worked simultaneously on any one manuscript." In any case, there was no scriptorium at the Priory of St Mary Overeys, and these early manuscripts were most likely made for friends of Gower and admirers of his works. An appendix contains eight plates, each with its own accompanying notes. The piece worthily complements Doyle and Parkes's ground-breaking "The production of copies of the *Canterbury Tales* and the *Confessio Amantis* in the early fifteenth century," written for Neil Ker's *Festschrift* (1978). The scope of "Archaizing hands in English manuscripts" (1997), for Andrew Watson, is huge, covering themes from script imitations and forgeries from the eighth century to the invention of photography. It is an exhilarating read, choc à bloc with valuable insights and nuggets of hard fact about manuscripts, script, scribes, patrons, owners, librarians, booksellers and changing circumstances.

The four papers of Part II reflect the concerns of Parkes's major publication of 1992, *Pause and Effect: An Introduction to the History of Punctuation in the West*. There are no facsimiles for the many passages discussed, which helps to focus attention on the punctuation strategies employed. Good footnotes indicate the availability of reproductions and other analyses where relevant. Three of these papers, given at conferences in Italy, examine the necessity of taking account of punctuation in relation to major approaches to texts that too often fail to notice how they are punctuated. The first, "Latin autograph manuscripts: orthography and punctuation" (1994), makes plain how choices in spelling and abbreviation as well as in punctuation symbols may help in the recognition of a holograph manuscript, yet leaves us with the disconcerting reminder that we should not hope for consistency, even from "accomplished authors." In the second, "Punctuation and the medieval history of texts" (1994), Parkes succinctly demonstrates the importance of recognizing changing fashions in the interpretation of texts not just by scribes but by intervening readers as well, discussing three short passages, from different manuscripts, from Cicero's *De senectute* (x 3), Gregory's *Regula pastoralis* (x 5) and Augustine's *De civitate Dei* (x 6). Thus, the three passages are presented in a variety of garbs, as punctuated in manuscripts that range from the fifth century up into the humanist period – a civilized crash course in the history of punctuation. Parkes, in the third of these papers, "Medieval punctuation and the modern editor" (1999), confronts the unwillingness of editors to engage with the punctuation of the texts they edit. Here his examples, in Italian, French and Latin, come from both prose and poetry. The fourth paper in this section, "Punctuation in copies of Nicholas Love's *Mirror of the Blessed Life of Jesus Christ*" (1997), was delivered at the 1995 Waseda conference centered on Love's writings. In it he shows how, for a group of manuscripts in which there is comparatively speaking little substantive variation, the punctuation can reveal "information about how the text was used and understood by his fifteenth-century readers."

An addendum points out that the Foyle manuscript is now in private hands in North America.

The three papers of part III are on the ways in which Anglo-Saxons read, on different kinds of apparatus developed from the eleventh century onwards to guide readers and on the medieval manuscripts collected by Stephen Batman, an English clergyman of the sixteenth century. "*Rædan, areccan, smeagan*: how the Anglo-Saxons read" (1997) assesses reading in Anglo-Saxon England. At the rudimentary level (*rædan*), mistaken glosses indicate the kinds of difficulties experienced when reading Latin, whether in misdividing words or identifying them incorrectly. Like the Irish and the Welsh, the Anglo-Saxons found construe marks useful, and for help with larger text elements they looked particularly to Bede's *De schematibus et tropis*. Parkes points out that Anglo-Saxon scribes were early in seeking to simplify letter forms and reduce the numbers in use in cursive scripts and that with the lay-out features they developed, drawing on both majuscule and minuscule scripts, they "established the rudiments of the grammar of legibility." After discussing the centrality of reading aloud in learning to read and the role of private reading for reflection, Parkes considers the methods adopted to familiarize readers with the content of what they read (*areccan*). First he describes Latin texts that had both word equivalents in simper Latin and longer explanatory glosses, for example in a *De consolatio Philosophiae* manuscript already in Britain in the ninth century and in an early, fragmentary Servius commentary on the *Aeneid*, Book IV. For biblical texts, patristic teachings were followed, whether by Aldhelm or Bede in the early period or later, in English, by Ælfric, in a thoroughly traditional way. Meditative reading encouraged an active response (*smeagan*), evident in thoughtful translations and in the new vernacular poetry that drew on oral traditions as well as on the literate world of learning. "*Folia librorum quaerere*: medieval experience of the problems of hypertext and the index" (1995) cries out to be transposed to a digital environment. The eight well-chosen plates illustrate the development of critical apparatus from glosses and scholia scattered on the page through the emergence of integrated text and commentary to the increasing sophistication of diagrams, indexes and tables. The magisterial account of "Stephan Batman's manuscripts" (1997), honoring Tadahiro Ikegami, has prompted new identifications, which are given in addenda.

Aspects of supply and loss of book stock are examined in Part IV. Books surviving and, more often, books once in existence but now lost, are identified in Parkes's "'History in books' clothing as evidence for cultural relations between England and the Continent in the seventh and eighth centuries" (2007). The travellers and carriers of books are for the most part English but, as is fitting in a paper written for Éamonn Ó Carragáin's *Festschrift*, Parkes points to the importance of the "synchronizing of Irish and Roman cultures in England" at this time in bringing about "an intellectual *renovatio*," its effects contributing "substantially to the Carolingian renaissance." In "The compilation of the Dominican Lectionary" (2000), Parkes examines the Regensburg copy, now Oxford, Keble College, MS 49. The manuscript, reflecting an early stage of Humbert's compiling activity, includes scholarly annotations that were to disappear from later copies and is therefore an important witness to the development of this *compilatio*. An Addendum draws attention to recent work (2008) on the lectionary by Simon Tugwell. Finally, there is "The Provision of Books," a lengthy and weighty chapter contributed to *The History of the University of Oxford, II: Late Medieval Oxford* (1992). Scrupulously, Parkes notes that the responsibility and some working materials for this essay were inherited from Ker, and he pays tribute also to a galaxy of scholars that includes both editors of the present collection of papers. Parkes surveys all manner of books associated with members of the university from the twelfth century to the opening of a new library in 1488: books as "a portable form of capital"; books as security against cash or other books; individual purchases; books moving in and out of loan chests; books made by students themselves. Book craftsmen are identifiable in Oxford from *c.* 1190. The scripts to be found in these books are discussed, as is the development of various forms of signposting in compilations. It is impossible to summarize the richness of this paper in a short descriptive review. Highlights include the account of the Franciscans and Dominicans and their books and libraries in medieval Oxford – there was a "constant traffic of books brought by friars." And books from Oxford, like their owners, could travel far, fetching up in Italy (Assisi) or Germany (Soest). Cataloguing began seriously with the lists of holdings compiled by the Franciscans of *originalia* in English cathedrals and monasteries, and the houses and colleges founded by monastic orders had growing book collections to keep track of. In effect, Parkes gives us a history of Oxford University and its earliest colleges through books: books assigned to student monks; books reverting to collegiate ownership; books in chains or under key in chests or shelved chaotically; gifts and bequests of books; books made under the *pecia* system. The three Addenda include the URL for David Rundle's invaluable assessment of books owned by or associated with Humfrey, Duke of Gloucester (2010).

The collection is particularly welcome because the original places of publication are widely scattered. As is common to the Ashgate-Variorum series, the original pagination is retained, except that, for one paper published as recently as 2007, it was necessary to reset the materials. In this case the editors have inserted the original page numbers in square brackets within the text. Medievalists generally have cause to thank the editors for their painstaking preparation of the materials in this volume and for equipping it properly with an Index of Manuscripts and a General Index.

Jane Roberts, University of London

PHILIP TEMPLE
The Charterhouse, Survey of London Monograph 18.
Gen. Ed., Andrew Saint.
New Haven and London: Yale University Press for English Heritage, 2010,
317 pp., 158 illustrations.

The Charterhouse is a rather luxurious London retirement home for well-connected bachelors and widowers; it merits the capital in the title of this volume (as if there were only one charterhouse) not just because of the survival of the original almshouse, but also because of the survival of the original school (although Charterhouse School moved to leafy Surrey in 1872). Most Londoners who know the Charterhouse (or Charterhouse School) will know little or nothing of its medieval context, although much has been written on it. The London charterhouse was founded by Walter Manny in 1370/1 around the nucleus of his plague cemetery and chapel, its Carthusian status determined by the bishop of London, Michael Northburgh. It was dissolved in 1538 and bought by Sir Edward North; at his death in 1564, it was bought by Thomas Howard, fourth Duke of Norfolk and became the center of London Catholicism between the 1570s and 1580s. Thomas Sutton bought it in 1611 and founded Sutton's Hospital, an almshouse for eighty old men and a school for forty boys. Both continue to this day, although the "almshouse" caters for fewer old men (but no women) and the school for many more boys (and girls).

Previous scholarship on the London charterhouse (summarized on on pp. 6 to 11 of this volume) has focussed on the medieval and early modern periods, but the present book covers its whole life to the present day. (Its scholarship is even recent enough to refer to Michael Sargent's article in the Luxford volume reviewed in this issue, pp. 373-377, and it acknowledges the invaluable work of Andrew Wines, who also writes in the Luxford volume.)

The Survey of London, under whose aegis the book was written, is part of English Heritage's Research Department and carries out detailed architectural and topographical studies of London parishes. It is as much interested in the twentieth as the fifteenth century, and the book is divided into three chapters on the history of the site (only the first chapter is relevant to our period), followed by six chapters on specific parts of the fabric of Sutton's Hospital then and now (chapters which include the medieval evidence). The remaining chapters deal with buildings in the environs: Rutland House (of which only the lodge survived bombing), Merchant Taylors' School (built on the site of Charterhouse School after its 1872 move), and the medical college of what was St Bartholomew's Hospital (which took over Merchant Taylors' in 1933). The Second World War demolished most of the surviving Merchant Taylors' and Barts' buildings, so that this final chapter deals only with post-World War II buildings.

The focus of the volume is the architecture and archaeology of the buildings of the Charterhouse in their historical context, and of these only the chapterhouse (now the Chapel) survives of the Great Cloister of Sutton's Hospital (i.e., the Carthusian Great Cloister, lined with the monks' individual cells, the chapter-house where they met for business, and the church where they met for divine office). Many timber buildings have inevitably disappeared, and what is left is brick and stone. Much has been discovered since the last World War, which justifies a separate Survey volume arising out of research into the parish of Clerkenwell. The burning-out of Howard House as a result of bombing led to the discovery of Manny's tomb at the foot of the altar steps (1947), and subsequent excavations (published by the Museum of London in 2002) provided the footprints of the church and Little Cloister. Post-war over-restoration by Seely and Paget obscured or removed some original features, and that, as well as the many earlier remodellings, makes the site haphazard and hard to interpret. However, this exemplary scholarly work details all that is and all that it can be known there was, backed up by no fewer than 158 plans and illustrations, many in color. As Appendices are published the extant inventories, the North House (later Howard House) Inventory of 1565 and the Howard House Inventories of 1573, 1583 and 1588.

The architect was Henry Yevele, who built Westminster Abbey for the Benedictines; the charterhouse was mostly complete by c.1420 and underwent a much-needed restoration of the fabric in the 1490s. It was at its peak in the sixteenth century, and Cromwell's agent at the Dissolution (1537) complained that it was too large, the food too good and the almsgiving too generous. The execution of the prior John Houghton in 1531 and the cruel deaths by various means of fifteen other monks who refused to acknowledge Henry VIII's supremacy over the Pope have colored our view of the (undoubted) spirituality of the house – it was also grand and favored by the Establishment. Spirituality and high status were not necessarily incompatible, as the Carthusian martyrdoms showed, and Establishment status meant nothing against the will of the king – in fact, it served to infuriate him more.

Medieval survivals include the chapter-house (now Chapel), the gatehouse, part of the precinct wall, the inner gateway, and "Wash House Court," perhaps originally the site of the lay-brothers' quarters and the guest-house; the house of John Russell, Bishop of Lincoln (d. 1494), can also be identified. There is no evidence of a library (perhaps books were kept in the sacristy strong-room, now the Treasury). The church was decorated inside and out (there was a painted alabaster reredos, and for a gilded and painted statue of St Katherine, see plate 19), and there were four great "tables," i.e., painted inscriptions, in each corner of the Great Cloister alley (for the inscriptions over the cells see Michael Sargent's article in the Luxford volume reviewed in this issue). The well-heeled laity had much to do with the house: in 1500 the former Bishop's lodgings were leased by the mercer Thomas Thwaites, and other buildings were let to layfolk, with possibly more guest accommodation around the Little Cloister (paid for by John Clyderhow, a Chancery clerk). Indeed, "probably, by 1538, the accommodation for guests was considerable." (It is known that Thomas More stayed there for a few years.)

This book is a meticulous piece of scholarship, using, besides archaeological and architectural evidence, the abundant archival evidence, such as the (much-used) conduit plan of c.1442, the 1490 accounts, and the (previously unused) inventories of North/Howard House . It confirms Maurice Chauncy's accounts of the desecration after the Dissolution, as do the 1538 accounts of the keeper, William Dale, and the 1539 inventory and account by the king's commissioners. North turned the church into a dining hall (perhaps a temporary use), and only sixteen years after Prior Batmanson's death in 1531, his body was disinterred by digging into the foundations. The church was used to store the royal tents, and the records of the Master of the Tents, Sir Thomas Cawarden, show that several hundred men were on site in the 1540s, disciplined by day but riotous by night (this has been transferred to a York setting in Sovereign, the third of C.J. Sansom's excellent historical novels on the Dissolution and its aftermath).

All in all, the incarnations of the London charterhouse have been strange and transformative – charterhouse to building site to great house to warehouse to almshouse/school to elite charitable foundation. I am about to make my first visit to attend the 80th birthday of one of its trustees, the distinguished church architect, Donald Buttress, and I look forward immensely to experiencing something of the palimpsest that is the Charterhouse. This volume provides a thorough surrogate experience; its author and the Survey of London are to be congratulated on a scholarly tome which is also an intriguing and fascinating read.

Susan Powell, University of Salford

JOHN SCATTERGOOD

Occasions for Writing: Essays on Medieval and
Renaissance Literature, Politics and Society.
Four Courts: Dublin, 2010. 272 pp. 14 black & white illustrations.

This volume gathers together twelve essays by John Scattergood, Professor Emeritus of Medieval and Renaissance Literature at Trinity College,
Dublin. Seven have already appeared in print, between 2001 and 2008; the
remaining five are new. Those familiar with Professor Scattergood's work
will not be surprised to find here immensely intricate treatments, studded
with detail, of the social, political and literary environments of late medieval
Europe, with an emphasis on England and Ireland.

Most of these essays are described by the author as "occasional" pieces,
both in the sense that they are about texts written in response to external
factors and that they are themselves prompted by such factors. He does
not provide much specific information about what these latter might be, so
the reader can enjoy speculating what it was that might have provided the
stimulus for individual essays.

The collection is divided into two unequal sections. "Movements" treats
broad themes across time and place in the Middle Ages, while "Incidents"
focuses on the more local and specific from the fourteenth to the early sixteenth century. Part I opens with the most ambitious and wide-ranging chapter in the book, previously unpublished: "Redeeming English: Language and
National Identity in the Later Middle Ages." This moves in masterly fashion
from the erasure of English as an "official" language in post-Conquest England to its triumph by the mid-fourteenth century as the national language
of England and also the dominant language of Ireland. "'The Unequal Scales
of Love': Love and Social Class in Andreas Capellanus's *De Amore* and Some
Later Texts" sets off unexpectedly from Ben Jonson but then travels from
twelfth-century Champagne to Margery Paston, via *Le Roman de la Rose,*

Medwall's *Fulgens and Lucres,* and *Aucassin and Nicolette.* "Writing the Clock: the Reconstruction of Time in the Late Middle Ages" examines references to clocks, and time, in Chaucer, Dante, Villon, and the Cely letters, before discussing the invention of the mechanical clock, probably in the late thirteenth century, and its influence on changing concepts of time.

Part II is arranged chronologically, opening with "Elegy for a Dangerous Man: *Piers of Bermingham,*" a contribution to the controversy over this early fourteenth-century Anglo-Irish poem in BL Harley MS 913. The criminal theme continues in "On the Road: Langland and Some Medieval Outlaw Stories," which considers outlaws' equivocal position and their strategies, as evidenced in English and Anglo-Norman texts. "London and Money: Chaucer's *Complaint to his Purse*" considers another controversial poem, setting it beside other texts that attack London as an expensive city where public servants could not rely on being paid (sounds familiar?), and arguing for a precise date in late 1399 when Chaucer wanted out. "Erasing Oldcastle: Some Literary Reactions to the Lollard Rising of 1414" examines yet another transgressive figure and argues that the strange and perplexing post-mortem treatment of the Lollard knight by Lydgate, Hoccleve and others is a response to Oldcastle's refusal to conform to medieval views of the proper role of knights. "*The Libelle of Englyshe Polycye*: the Nation and Its Place" provides a different perspective on the mercantilism so disliked by Chaucer. Scattergood interprets this poem, written sometime after the siege of Calais in 1436 but still popular well into the sixteenth century, as an acute economic analysis of England's place in Europe that sees its power based not on military might but on trade, which in its turn demands a strong navy. Naval power and the French connection figure again in "A Muted Triumph: French Prisoners at Whitby in 1451," which centers on another, neglected, mid-fifteenth century poem. Scattergood explicates at some length this cryptic and internally conflicted text, and explores its position in John Benet's miscellany (Trinity College, Dublin, MS 516), compiled ten or twenty years later.

We move into the early sixteenth century with "'Familiar and Homely': the Intrusion and Articulation of Vice in Skelton's *Magnyfycence*." This examines how the play functions as "a dire warning about the financial consequences, in a royal household, of trusting the wrong people" (214) and anatomizes how the Vices insinuate themselves by means of forgery, identity theft, and sycophantic speech. "Thomas Wyatt's Epistolary Satires and the Consolations of Intertextuality" stays with the court of Henry VIII and looks at three moral satires, written by Wyatt when under home detention in Kent shortly after the execution of Anne Boleyn in 1536, and their multifarious literary influences. The final essay, "John Leland's Itinerary and the Identity of England," links Leland's double view of England, its land owned since time immemorial by old families but also subject to enclosure by "new men," with his descent into psychosis in 1547, a date that coincides with the death of his patron Henry VIII.

Scattergood's usual approach is to take a text, precisely located in time and place, and then explore its wider historical and literary context in great detail. Not every essay in this collection will appeal to every reader, but most people working in the area of late medieval and early modern English texts will find at least one that will engage them. Readers of *JEBS* will also appreciate the author's stress on the manuscript context of many of the texts he addresses. The provision of a useful Index of Manuscripts emphasizes this dimension of the book.

Alexandra Barratt, University of Waikato

About the Authors

Alexandra Barratt is Professor Emeritus at the University of Waikato, New Zealand. She has published widely in the field of women's writing and writing for women in late medieval England, and is currently working on manuscript waste in early printed books held in New Zealand and on medieval manuscripts and their bindings.

Nicole Clifton teaches Middle English literature and language at Northern Illinois University. Her research focuses primarily on Middle English romance and its manuscripts.

Megan L. Cook is the Andrew W. Mellon Foundation Postdoctoral Fellow in English at Bowdoin College.

Martha W. Driver is Distinguished Professor of English and Women's and Gender Studies at Pace University in New York City. A co-founder of the Early Book Society for the study of manuscripts and printing history, she writes about illustration from manuscript to print, book production, and the early history of publishing. In addition to publishing some forty-five articles in these areas, she has edited seventeen journals over fourteen years, including *Film & History: Medieval Period in Film* and the *Journal of the Early Book Society*. Her books about pictures (from manuscript miniatures to woodcuts to film) include *The Image in Print: Book Illustration in Late Medieval England* (British Library Publications and University of Toronto), *An Index of Images in English MSS*, fascicle four, with Michael Orr (Brepols), and *The Medieval Hero on Screen* and *Shakespeare and the Middle Ages*, with Sid Ray (McFarland).

Carl James Grindley is Consortial Associate Professor of General Education at the School of Professional Studies and Associate Professor of English at Eugenio María de Hostos Community College, both of The City University of New York. He is the 2012 recipient of the Cathlamet Poetry Prize for his book *Lora and The Dark Lady* which will be published by Ravenna Press in the spring of 2013. His latest publications in medieval studies are "The Whisper Game," in *Studies in Medieval and Renaissance Teaching*, and "The A-Version Ancestor of BmBoCot," in *The Yearbook of Langland Studies*, both published in 2011.

Joseph J. Gwara is Professor of Spanish at the United States Naval Academy. In 2008, the Bibliographical Society of America awarded him the first annual

Katharine F. Pantzer Senior Fellowship in Bibliography and the British Book Trades.

Simon Horobin is Professor in English Language and Literature and Tutorial Fellow of Magdalen College at the University of Oxford. He is currently editing Osbern Bokenham's translation of the *Legenda Aurea* for the EETS and is also engaged in a collaborative project (with Alex Gillespie, University of Toronto), funded by the Mellon Foundation, which aims to index all the notes made by sixteenth-century scribes in the collection of books owned by Matthew Parker and now in the Parker Library in Cambridge.

Holly James-Maddocks is a final-year PhD student at the Centre for Medieval Studies, University of York. Her thesis, "Collaborative Book Production and its Organisation in Fifteenth Century London," is co-supervised by Linne Mooney and Jeanne Nuechterlein and funded by the AHRC. Holly is a research assistant on the project "The Writing of Petitions in Later Medieval England," co-led by Mark Ormrod and Linne Mooney and funded by the Mellon Foundation, which addresses the key-issue of who actually wrote these documents. She is contributing a fascicle to *An Index of Images in English Manuscripts* (Cambridge II), with Ann E. Nichols (Brepols).

Michael Johnston is an Assistant Professor of English at Purdue University. He is working on a book about the circulation of romance within households of the fifteenth-century English gentry.

Dorothy Kim completed her Ph.D. in English literature at UCLA and is currently an Assistant Professor at Vassar College. She is working on a book, *Medieval Women and English Exoticism*, that reevaluates the early manuscripts of *Ancrene Wisse* and the Katherine Group—Cambridge, Corpus Christi College MS 402 and Oxford, Bodleian Library MS Bodley 34.

Linne R. Mooney is Professor in Medieval English Palaeography at the University of York and an Officer of the Early Book Society. Her research focuses on late medieval English literature and the scribes who copied it. She is PI for a major Arts and Humanities Research Council-funded project to study the scribes who copied works by Geoffrey Chaucer, John Gower, John Trevisa, William Langland and Thomas Hoccleve (working with Simon Horobin and Estelle Stubbs), of which the website is http://www.medievalscribes.com; and also co-author, with Daniel Mosser and Elizabeth Solopova, of the iMEV, a freely accessible web-based version of The Index of Middle English Verse, available in prototype at http://www.cddc.vt.edu/host/imev/index.html. Mooney and Stubbs are writing a book about London scribes of major Middle English literary writings. As the editor of Nota Bene: Brief Notes on Manuscripts and Early Printed Books, she is a regular contributor to *JEBS*.

Daniel W. Mosser is Professor of English and Director of Graduate Studies in English at Virginia Tech. He is co-editor and co-creator of the Thomas L. Gravell Watermark Archive (www.gravell.org), co-editor of *Puzzles in Paper*, author of *A Digital Catalogue of the Pre-1500 Manuscripts and Incunables of the* Canterbury Tales, co-editor and compiler (with Linne R. Mooney and Elizabeth Solopova) of *The Digital Index of Middle English Verse* (www.dimev. net), and the author of articles on Middle English manuscripts, fifteenth-century paper stocks, and Chaucer incunabula.

Sarah Noonan is an Assistant Professor of English at Lindenwood University. She is currently working on a study that considers the relationship between the affective tradition of meditation on Christ's Passion and the reading practices of the laity in fourteenth- and fifteenth-century England.

Theresa O'Byrne is a doctoral candidate at the University of Notre Dame's Medieval Institute. Under the supervision of Kathryn Kerby-Fulton, she is completing a thesis entitled "James Yonge, Scribe, Author, and Bureaucrat, and the Literary World of Late Medieval Dublin." With the support of a Kaneb Pre-Doctoral Fellowship, she recently completed a year of teaching and research at Queen's University, Belfast, under the supervision of John Thompson. Her current research interests include the interaction of literature, culture, and law in late medieval England and Anglo-Ireland and portrayals of Ireland in English and Continental literature.

Susan Powell holds a Chair in Medieval Texts and Culture at the University of Salford, where she teaches the history of the English language, Chaucer, and medieval Arthurian literature. As review editor for *JEBS*, she regularly contributes several reviews to each issue. Her essay "What Caxton did to the *Festial*" appeared in *JEBS* 1 (1997). Her research interests are in manuscripts and early printed books, with particular relation to late medieval and Tudor preaching and devotional texts.

Efthymia Priki is currently a PhD candidate in Byzantine Studies at the University of Cyprus. Her doctoral research deals with dream narratives and initiation processes in medieval, Byzantine and Renaissance literature, focusing on *Livistros and Rhodamne, Roman de la Rose* and *Hypnerotomachia Poliphili*. Her most recent publication is "Elucidating and Enigmatizing: The Reception of the *Hypnerotomachia Poliphili* in the Early Modern Period and in the Twentieth and Twenty-first Centuries," *eSharp 14: Imagination and Innovation* (Winter 2009), pp. 62-90.

Jane Roberts is a Senior Research Fellow at the Institute of English Studies and Emeritus Professor of English Language and Medieval Literature in the University of London. Her publications include *A Guide to Scripts used in English Writings up to 1500* (London: BL Publications, 2005). She is joint author of *A Thesaurus of Old English* with Christian Kay, and she is one of the four editors of the *Historical Thesaurus of the Oxford English Dictionary*.

Yvonne Rode is Reference/Instructional and Archives Librarian at Westchester Community College (NY). Her research interests include the economic aspects of the early book trade. She has published "Sixty-Three Gallons of Books: Shipping Books to England in the Late Middle Ages" in *Manuscripts and Printed Books in Europe, 1350-1550: Packaging, Presentation and Consumption* (edited by Emma Cayley and Sue Powell), University of Exeter Press, 2012.

Martha Dana Rust is Associate Professor of English and Director of the Medieval and Renaissance Center at New York University. She is the author of *Imaginary Worlds in Medieval Books: Exploring the Manuscript Matrix* (Palgrave, 2007).

Robert N. Swanson is Professor of Medieval History at the University of Birmingham, England. He has worked and published extensively on the history of the medieval church from the twelfth to sixteenth centuries, with particular reference to England. His most recent volume is *Indulgences in Late Medieval England: Passports to Paradise?* (Cambridge: Cambridge University Press, 2007).

Deborah Thorpe has recently completed a Ph.D. at the Centre for Medieval Studies, University of York, titled "Writing and Reading in the Circle of Sir John Fastolf." Her research interests include the work of clerks as administrators and textwriters, the production and patronage of manuscripts in East Anglia, and the study of gentry circles, their membership and the interaction within them.

Shaun Tyas is an independent publisher of academic history with a personal interest in the Middle Ages, bibliography and medievalism.

www.ingramcontent.com/pod-product-compliance
Lightning Source LLC
Chambersburg PA
CBHW060307100726
47907CB00002B/317